DISCARD

^{the} **principles**
^{of} **green urbanism**

Transforming the City for Sustainability

Steffen Lehmann

This publication is endorsed by

THE UNIVERSITY OF
NEWCASTLE
AUSTRALIA

United Nations
Educational, Scientific and
Cultural Organization

UNESCO Chair in
Sustainable Urban Development
for Asia and the Pacific

First published by Earthscan in the UK and USA in 2010

Copyright © Steffen Lehmann, 2010

First edition published in the UK in August 2010, launched on the occasion of the exhibition 'Transforming the City for Sustainability: The Principles of Green Urbanism'

All texts and project texts: Steffen Lehmann, UNESCO Chair in Sustainable Urban Development for Asia and the Pacific, and Founding Director of s_Lab Space Laboratory (www.slab.com.au)

Cover design and graphic design: Cida de Aragon, Adelaide

All illustrations are reproduced courtesy of the various copyright owners, the studio participants and the author. This book was printed and bound in China on acid-free 115 gsm paper.

The UNESCO Chair supports the creation of sustainable urban developments worldwide by advancing designs and policies that reflect the concept of Green Urbanism.

ISBN: 978-1-84407-834-9   hardback edition
          978-1-84407-817-2   paperback edition

Earthscan Ltd, UK   Earthscan LLC, USA
Dunstan House, 14a St Cross St,   1616 P Street, NW
London, EC1N 8XA, UK   Washington, DC 20036, USA

For more information on Earthscan publications, see www.earthscan.co.uk or write to: earthinfo@earthscan.co.uk

Earthscan publishes in association with the International Institute for Environment and Development. At Earthscan we strive to minimize our environmental impacts and carbon footprint through reducing waste, recycling and offsetting CO_2 emissions.

A catalogue record for this book is available from the British Library.
Library of Congress Cataloging-in-Publication Data has been applied for.

Pre-publication praise for *The Principles of Green Urbanism*

"Addressing the present day problems of the great industrial cities with ideas which are firmly embedded in the future, this book is a *must read* for all those who want to see a responsible approach to the greening of their urban environment. It addresses one of the great challenges for the urban environment of many of the world's major cities: How do you take an existing urban structure and make it respond to environmental concerns? The content is stimulating and the case studies provide real life examples of a possible way forward. Read it!"

– **Peter Brandon**, *Professor, Salford Think Lab (Manchester)*

"Inspiring! *The Principles of Green Urbanism* is a relevant publication for today's planning problems. Excellent reading for all interested in urban design, and much food for thought."

– **Peter Droege**, *Professor, Chair Renewable Cities Council (Sydney)*

"Highly relevant case studies, based on practical principles for achieving green urbanism. This is an important, highly relevant and very topical book which should be read by decision makers all over the world."

– **Herbert Girardet**, *Professor, World Future Council (London)*

"Steffen Lehmann has a long interest in sustainable cities design and his book provides a critical overview of ecological urbanism concepts, offering a methodology for sustainable design."

– **Ken Yeang**, *PhD, Architect (London/ Kuala Lumpur)*

"This book will become increasingly important as the world recognizes the escalating energy crisis and global warming challenge. It will be a useful resource for many urban design courses."

– **Norbert M. Lechner**, *Emeritus Professor, Auburn University (USA)*

Contents

Chapter 1
Turning Constraints
into Opportunities

Chapter 2
The Principles of Green Urbanism
– Putting it all Together

Dedicated to the people in developing countries suffering the impact of climate change, this book hopes to inspire all urban designers, planners and architects to rethink conventional design practice and to take action to stop climate change.

Globalization and mega-city growth: big feet, small planet

Over the past decade I have tried to make connections between cities and their increasingly global hinterland whilst exploring environmental and social conditions within cities themselves. One conclusion I have reached is that working towards the environmental sustainability of cities can deliver tremendous social and economic benefits. In an urbanizing world we need a fresh approach to looking at cities and novel ways of understanding the impacts of urban living. Unless we change the way we use resources, particularly fossil fuels, we will cause this planet to become uninhabitable. In particular, the seemingly unstoppable growth of large globally connected cities, with their huge appetites for the world's resources, is a development of enormous consequence for the future of humanity, and for all life on Earth.

The job of urban planners, civil engineers and managers is to create spatial structures that satisfy the needs of city people. We want them to provide secure habitats that allow us to move about our cities efficiently, and we want them to provide pleasant spaces for work, for recreation and for meeting people. We want urban environments that are free from pollution and waste accumulation. But we also need to get to grips with the impact of cities beyond their boundaries. Our urban society, with its fossil-fuel powered industrial, farming and transport systems, has unprecedented impacts on the world's ecosystems. The WWF states in its recent *Living Planet Report* that in the last 30 years a third of the natural world has been obliterated. Reversing this collision course between humans and nature is increasingly becoming an, as yet, unaccustomed challenge for city dwellers, architects, civil engineers and urban planners.

Foreword I

Herbert Girardet

This book presents a series of inspiring ideas for urban development, using urban renewal strategies and the conceptual model of Green Urbanism. It is illustrated with remarkable work from design studios which the author of this book has conducted over a period of four years, constantly refining his ideas by using the Australian city of Newcastle as a field of exploration and as a generic case study for all regional cities in the developed world facing a decline in manufacturing industries. Some of the main themes which this book seeks to explore are: Can urbanism ever be green? How can we create cities of physical beauty and social and cultural diversity that are also environmentally and economically sustainable?

In my recent studies, I have drawn on the work by the 19th-century German geographer Johann Heinrich von Thünen. The integration of towns and cities into their hinterland is well described in von Thünen's book 'The Isolated State'. He was the founder of location economics and the first to develop an analytical model of the relationship between markets, farming systems and their location. The medieval town represented his model perfectly. Von Thünen described the inherent logic by which towns were encircled by clearly defined systems of farming and forestry, with four different zones surrounded by an outer zone, each with a different purpose. However, when a major transport route such as a

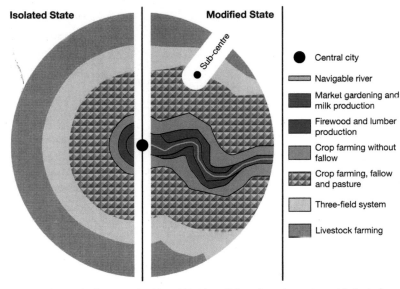

Isolated State   **Modified State**

- Central city
- Navigable river
- Market gardening and milk production
- Firewood and lumber production
- Crop farming without fallow
- Crop farming, fallow and pasture
- Three-field system
- Livestock farming

Fig. 1: City diagram, by the geographer Johann Heinrich von Thünen. He made a major contribution to the understanding of the relationship of urban settlements to their local hinterland. Once significant transport connections are established, their linkages to local farmland and forests tend to be weakened. (Courtesy: H. Girardet; from: *Cities, People, Planet,* 2008)

navigable river, or, today, a motorway, was available, the circles were opened up and replaced by an increasingly linear arrangement. Today global transport systems supply our cities.

Von Thünen's analytical model is still of great relevance today, as the availability of cheap transport systems bringing food and goods from long distances is beginning to be questioned because of their wasteful use of energy, particularly when airplanes fly in food from halfway around the world. In this regard, I find the Eco-City ideas of this publication, which are based on urban farming, productive urban landscapes and the decentralized generation of energy, of great relevance. These ideas are supported with highly relevant case studies, based on practical principles for achieving a new green urbanism. Steffen Lehmann's design studios illustrate well how this new green urbanism will look like. This is an important, highly relevant and very topical book which should be read by decision makers all over the world.

Herbert Girardet
London, October 2009

Professor Herbert Girardet is a recipient of the UN Global-500 Award for outstanding environmental achievements. He is Director of Programmes of the World Future Council, based in London. He is an honorary fellow of The Royal Institute of British Architects and was chairman of the Schumacher Society, UK. He has written 12 books and produced 50 documentaries on many aspects of sustainable development. He has been a consultant to numerous clients, including UN-Habitat, the Greater London Authority, the London Development Agency, the Dongtan Eco-City project, and the cities of Adelaide and Vienna. His most recent book, *A Renewable World – Energy, Ecology, Equality,* was published in September 2009.

Foreword II

Peter Droege

Thinking in the dimension of the city

This book documents ideas for urban renewal and environmental sustainability, using the Australian city of Newcastle as a most suitable case study. It presents the author's conceptual model of *Green Urbanism*; it also presents a series of strategies for the urban regeneration of derelict, post-industrial city centres, and includes documentation of students' speculative work from advanced design studios conducted at the University of Newcastle. By doing so, the book introduces ideas about the future of our cities, with some stunning plans, images and model photographs, accompanied by texts that offer a deeper understanding of the discussed topic.

The text explores ideas and proposals for the revitalization of the typical post-industrial urban landscape, based on strong public space networks, pedestrian-friendly connectivity and a reintegration of urban greenery. The author's discussion offers general insights and strategies that are applicable to other cities seeking ways to reclaim their derelict urban landscapes or are wishing to revitalize abandoned sites to transform them into a contemporary, integrated part of a vibrant and revitalized city centre.

Cities are always in a constant state of transition, and the harbour city of Newcastle is – as many others are – at an important juncture in its evolution. Current thought requires mixed-use urban development to deliver environmental and social outcomes based on holistic ideas of relationships between appropriate densities, typology, transport and public space. The author has worked with his students to devise masterplan proposals that provide a provocative vision of what might be our zero-carbon, fossil-fuel free future: overlapping mixed-use activities, living and working building typologies explored on the urban scale, infrastructure systems for renewable energies, public transport and individual energy-efficient building designs.

The presented visions offer mixed-use solutions that will help to stabilize the global climate and which can regenerate neglected areas of a city, at its core and along its waterfront, by applying different kinds of strategies for both. This has relevance for many similar cities, as much of the introduced strategies are generic and are transferable to any post-industrial condition in the developed world.

Such complex large-scale developments require input from the community into design parameters, and they are a great learning experience for all participants. The crucial task is now: How do you formulate zero-carbon urban design and fossil-fuel free architecture for the 21st century?

The need to build new types of 'renewable cities' poses a huge challenge to classical city planning. This book provides practical answers through the definition of *The Principles of Green Urbanism*, which unfold to the reader as a clear conceptual framework for all involved in urban design, and ensures the proposed strategies are future-proof. What particularly distinguishes this book is its focus on the different contemporary urban contexts one might come across as a professional or a student, and the articulation of a pragmatic set of principles to apply them in the real world. To make this type of urban design and architecture much more common, policy-makers need to use all the tools and legislation at their disposal, including reforming building codes, offering tax incentives, supporting research and mounting public information campaigns.

Steffen has a long history of initiating community outreach projects involving students in design questions relevant to the city. I offer my great appreciation to the author and the team of educators who were involved in the study under Steffen's leadership, and I also applaud the students who took on the challenge so creatively. Education for sustainable development has been adapted by universities all around the world to different degrees, and the new thinking is finally gaining momentum and is being introduced into the various curricula. These studios are a great example for the dynamic relationship that can exist between research, practice and teaching, and how research-based design can drive a teaching initiative.

Steffen Lehmann has given considerable time and continuous energy to tutoring and mentoring architecture students, and to the development of each project with great care and vision. Over the period of four years, the students were given a valuable opportunity for exposure to the realities of challenging briefs and realistic constraints (be it the reduction of energy consumption or the respect for built heritage). The studio process involved an interactive exchange of ideas between the University, the city council, local planning experts, the Port Corporation and consultants from private practice.

The *Principles of Green Urbanism* is a relevant publication for today's urban planning problems. It is inspiring and excellent reading for all interested in urban design and the future of cities. It offers a timely reflection on the relationship between old, energy-hungry, fossil-fuel based city models and the new possibilities of renewable energy technologies. Based on the conviction that design professionals can genuinely make a difference to the lives of ordinary people and the future of our societies, this text book is a helpful tool for all those working in the fields of urban design, urban planning and architecture.

Peter Droege
Sydney/Vaduz, October 2009

Dr. Peter Droege is an urban planner and author who lives and works in Sydney and in Vaduz. He is the Chair of the World Council for Renewable Energy and the initiating director of a Solar-City research development initiative. He has held professorial and advanced positions at MIT, the University of Tokyo and the University of Sydney. He is currently a professor at the Hochschule of Lichtenstein. He is the editor of the book `100% Renewable' (2009).

Preface

Steffen Lehmann

Sustainability... on the urban scale

The ambitious themes of this book, the state and future of our cities and the opportunities to transform entire districts into energy-efficient, close to zero-carbon neighbourhoods, started as a series of lectures which I delivered in the late 1990s at various European schools of architecture and urban design, and papers given at conferences in many parts of the world on the subject of *green urbanism* and *the city as powerstation*. Some of the ideas explored and presented in these forums were still radically new (such as the notion of a *city block as powerstation*), and were intended to stir up debate and controversy beyond the student body. This is exactly what happened. My claim that purely functionality and aesthetic-based solutions were no longer sufficient for the design of our urban environment, and that we generally need to rethink `the city itself', including the criterion for energy use, waste, food and water consumption, was highly provocative to some. In challenging classical city planning, I asked: What if we designed cities for walking and cycling, with human-centred public space networks, on-site energy generation, and compact self-sufficient communities? I claimed that the sprawling suburb had neither an economic, social, nor an environmental future, as it made everything inefficient – from water use to public transport, from energy use to land use. I suggested new organizing principles, energy-efficient urban systems, based on decentralized energy supply and waste recycling patterns, and the radical re-compacting of urban form to allow us to use the district, the town, or the city itself as a powerstation by using the roofs and facades to turn entire districts into productive urban landscapes supported by urban farming.

As usual, things are not as simple as they appear, and at this time I could not be confident that global climate change and urbanization were so closely linked, or even that global warming was a direct result of man-made, anthropogenic interventions in the environment. Today, of course, the scientific evidence is overwhelmingly in favour of this model, and we have reached a much more holistic and robust understanding of the issues surrounding urban ecology, and with widespread concern about the environmental crisis growing, we are now plotting nothing less than a peaceful revolution against old unsustainable methods and practises of urban design.

Climate clock is ticking

Scientists have clearly shown that human activities alter the climate. For instance, the *Urban Heat Island* effect has proved towns and cities are warmer than the surrounding countryside, and there is evidence that weekends tend to be cooler and wetter because of the drop in human activity. Climate change is now understood as a life-shaping force with far reaching impact. The increasing need for a profound restructuring and transformation of the way in which we live, and the way in which we develop, build and operate towns and cities, is widely acknowledged. For instance, a major urban transformation in the way we generate, distribute and supply energy to households is now under consideration on many levels, but its consequences on new urban settlement patterns, future-proof infrastructures, and adaptable building typologies will need to be reassessed.

We have started to connect concepts for sustainable urban development, innovative design processes and strategies with the new realities of finite resources. Thus our singular reliance (in the US, Australia, and in many parts of Asia) on coal and oil as primary resources for energy generation is in need of change. The negative impact of coal-burning on health and the environment has never properly been included in the pricing of the energy generated by coal-fired powerstations. The influential British social thinker Anthony Giddens has put it this way: `An area that becomes dependent upon a few products sold on world markets is very vulnerable to shifts in prices as well as to technological change.' (Giddens, 1999). While black coal will still have a role to play for decades to come, the diversification through an energy-mix, including an increasing amount of carbon-free renewable resources, will be the only sustainable way forward for all nations – be it in the developed or the developing world. Furthermore, global ecological risk is today seen as a shared problem that knows no nation boundaries. With climate change, we face a new type of threat that no civilization in history has had to confront, and with many new uncertainties emerging almost daily, we don't exactly know what the challenges will turn out to be. It is clear that cities will continue to be the place where most energy is consumed and most waste is produced, but cities also provide us with economies of scale that make renewable energy sources viable. It will be in cities where the battle against climate change will be won.

Over the last twenty years, with scientists providing stark evidence of the impact of global warming, the public has become passionate about environmental issues, and governments in all democratic countries have had to accommodate, listen to, and negotiate with, ecological pressure groups. A wide network of environmental organizations, businesses and research institutes have evolved and we have witnessed the empowering of citizens, new models of community participation and a renewed interest in active political discourse and planning. Furthermore, architecture and urban design is now widely seen as an agent for social change and as a means for producing better, healthier communities. I am particularly pleased to see that a vast majority of universities have finally started to redefine their architectural curriculum with a focus on serious research in sustainable design and energy-efficient architecture. While time is running out, it is certain that within the next decade a profound transformation of all our urban settlements will have to occur. Cities will need to be different by 2020.

Shifting focus in the design studio

To this end, with the increasing scientific evidence in the field, I have been able to develop my ideas to include new research on urbanization in the teaching of architectural and urban design studios. Some of the concepts and design outcomes of the more recent studios are presented in this study, in Chapter 3. The reinvention of the design studio is an ongoing process. The studios, which I coordinated as part of Master of Architecture programmes at various universities, dealt with problems of the contemporary city and looked to identify feasible solutions for turning the existing city into a sustainable complex and powerstation. Since most of the building stock already exists, it was necessary that we accepted our main focus be on retro-fitting and upgrading these existing districts.

Post-Oil City: why cities will have to be transformed

This book introduces *The Principles of Green Urbanism* as a conceptual model of how we might be able to tackle the enormous challenge of transforming existing neighbourhoods, districts and cities, and in re-thinking the way we design, build and operate urban settlements. The principles of green urbanism are partly universal, but there is no one single formula that will always work; there are only basic principles, and this book is about identifying those principles and illustrating their application in case studies. To achieve more sustainable cities, urban designers must understand and apply the core principles of green urbanism in a systematic way. The principles can be effective in a wide variety of urban situations, but they always need to be adapted to the specific context, to the site's constraints and opportunities. We need to develop a specific approach for each unique situation, adapting the principles to the particular climatic conditions, site context, availability of technology, social conditions, client's brief, diverse stakeholder organizations, and so on. It is an approach to urban development and urban design that requires a solid understanding of the development's context and its many dimensions, to enable the designer to turn constraints into opportunities and to produce an effective proposal.

Clearly, the design of districts and cities is a very complex exercise. Architecture and urban design has, of course, always had a social (and, therefore, political) dimension. Many towns and cities worldwide are suffering a decline of their centres, and the boarded-up shop fronts of vacant, abandoned buildings in their formerly vibrant 'heart' accelerates that decline. The consequence of decline is the decay of public space, the abandonment of buildings, a run down infrastructure and an increase in unemployment. While studying city centres in different continents (in Europe, Latin America, North America, the Middle East, Asia and Australia), I have found many similarities in a large number of cities in the developed world. There is frequently a need to redefine the city centre's identity and to give it a new role to play. I call this the *post-industrial condition*. It is where we find the shrinking of cities and the lack of investment in them (and, therefore, a high rate of unemployment, run-down buildings, etc) side-by-side with rapid urban growth and boom-precincts. The reason for this is mainly a lack of strategic planning in dealing with demographic changes and economic restructuring. This book discusses this in more detail in Chapter 1 and 2.

The challenge of achieving sustainable urban development is part of the post-industrial condition. The necessity to transform our existing cities into sustainable models affords us a great opportunity to regenerate our post-industrial, and often worn-down, city centres. The imminent decline of the city centre can have adverse implications for entire regions, and requires urgent action. The needs of the urban fabric are largely defined by its (frequently old or obsolete) infrastructure, which will need to undergo a process of renewal. For instance, the public transport system, the energy generation and supply systems, and the infrastructure for urban water treatment, all need to be replaced with a new range of future-proof infrastructures.

To borrow a word from Richard Rogers, there is an 'Urban Renaissance' happening. Cities are engaged in a global-scale competition with each other, mainly about who will lead in the following three areas:

• **To be regarded as an attractive, creative place and a cultural hub**. To be top of the list for quality urban lifestyle means to attract highly-skilled knowledge workers (Vancouver, Melbourne and Barcelona are doing very well in this field, with strong arts, museums and university scenes).

• **To be recognized as a place for secure investment**. To have a framework in place to attract and facilitate global investment capital (Dubai, Shanghai and Singapore have for some time done very well in this field, emerging on the world stage as regional financial business and leisure hubs).

• **To be seen as having a green vision for the future**. To be a leader in green technologies and able to offer an environmentally sound lifestyle, which has a direct link to 'green' jobs growth, innovation and applied research (various German, Danish and Swiss cities have done well in this field, for example, Freiburg, Hannover, Copenhagen and Zurich).

Eco-neighbourhoods, eco-districts, eco-towns, eco-cities

The sustainable district, town or city can be defined as a place where residents work, live and spend their leisure time in compact and well-interconnected communities. Increasingly, people are opting to live close to town and city centres, and this study aims to provide new models of sustainable urban development for inner-city sites, which are often post-industrial brownfield sites, through urban infill and densification models, as well as controlled urban expansion concepts, for instance along reclaimed (formerly industrially used) urban waterfronts.

There are innovative models around for interim use of vacant space which can bring rundown, empty shops and derelict buildings back to life. For example, the sustainability of informal clusters of habitation or occasional usage patterns of a city centre is something that can frequently be seen in many cities around the world. This strategy may be the key to success. In this respect, the Australian city of Newcastle is a good case study. While long-term projects for the redevelopment of the city centre are being developed, many historically important sites in the city are now boarded-up, falling apart or are decaying.

I have co-developed a series of not-for-profit initiatives that tries to solve this dilemma (first in the 1990s in recession-hit Berlin and East German cities, more recently in the declining Australian city centres), that take advantage of the spontaneous and creative possibilities offered by the temporary use of empty buildings to revitalize the downtown area. *Back to the City* and *Renew Newcastle* were two of these initiatives (both established in Newcastle in 2007–08) to find a new identity for the city centre, and short to medium-term uses for buildings which were vacant, disused or awaiting redevelopment. At the start of the *Renew Newcastle* initiative, there were around one hundred such vacant buildings in Newcastle's city centre. The initiatives proposed that interim usage be provided to support some community groups, and by doing so to bring activity back to the otherwise deteriorating centre. These initiatives not only improved the vibrancy of the streetscape but it also restored confidence in the location and helped protect the premises. To succeed with such revitalization initiatives, it is important to define the city centre as a place of potential, rather than decay. The re-use of the unused, empty shop fronts and small-scale laneway structures proved to be ideal for offering low rental spaces for grassroots art galleries, graphic designer and jewellery studios, children's art classes, and spaces for community-based cultural initiatives. These spaces quickly took on the role of *attractors* that brought people back to the area. However, the project was only possible through the good will of property owners who were willing to offer their premises rent free, for temporary use, rather than leaving them empty and at risk.

About the chapters in this book

In all research work, one is never isolated or alone. The text draws on my consultant work for UNESCO and the work with the City of Sydney. In addition, my own explorations and writing have been influenced by the pivotal work of some great academics, who share my passion for cities and urban theory, such as Ulrich Beck, Thomas Sieverts, Christopher Alexander, Richard Sennett, Saskia Sassen, Manuel Castells, Peter Hall, Jan Gehl, Richard Burdett, Herbert Girardet, to name but a few. I am grateful for their influential thoughts and generous discussions. I am also grateful to my colleagues for giving me the opportunity to present my research on over three hundred occasions at leading universities, from Harvard to Oxford, and from Milan, Munich and Melbourne to Berlin, Beijing and Bangkok. You have all been very generous and supportive.

I have found it very beneficial to take one typical post-industrial city as a field of exploration and as a testing ground for new ideas: the harbour city of Newcastle (once the most industrialized city in Australia, now at a crucial point of change in its evolution). With all its contradictions and disconnections, I have found that there is a good case for calling Newcastle 'the archetypical post-industrial city', and this is further outlined in **Chapter 1**. Many of the lessons learnt from this seaport city are of a general and generic character and can easily be transferred to other post-industrial cases.

In **Chapter 2**, the *Principles of Green Urbanism* are laid out as a step-by-step manual that can be adjusted for application in various contexts. These principles have a series of pillars, including: Energy conservation, the use of new technologies (such as combined heat-and-power, or solar cooling); the use of renewable energy sources (such as solar PV, solar thermal, wind on- and offshore, biomass, mini hydro, and geothermal); and the concept of the *City of Short Distances*, all resulting in multiple benefits for both the environment and the economy.

There has been a long tradition in schools of architecture to involve students in real local – even controversial – design projects as part of community outreach. How to re-connect the city centre with the waterfront is always an interesting design problem. In **Chapter 3**, the study presents three such speculative case studies (25 projects) from my design studios in the Master of Architecture programme, and one real case: The award-winning urban design for a large riverfront site. The student projects are of stunning high quality. Case Study 1 introduces ten 'City Campus' projects, which have a focus on densification, infill and strategies for urban renewal. The civic role of public and educational buildings is hereby of particular relevance. Case Study 2 explores an inner-city waterfront development called the 'Port City' project. Four projects look at the expansion along the formerly industrially-used edge of the harbour, where prime sites have become available as heavy industry has retreated, production has closed down, or the industry has moved away from the city centre. Case Study 3 presents eight 'Green Corridor' projects, which have a focus on linear urban consolidation and regeneration: A public space and landscape ribbon running parallel with the integration of a public transport system. Here, the historical city centre and the new waterfront development are 'stitched' together by inspirational design ideas. Case Study 4 presents the urban masterplan for the city of Taree (another town north of Sydney), where principles of sustainable masterplanning of a riverfront site aims to trigger the revitalization of this otherwise less dynamic, rural town.

These case studies give detailed information on how *The Principles of Green Urbanism* can be applied strategically to different sites and contexts. They present a series of models that the urban designer is likely to confront in other cities. It is to be hoped that this book is of help to those readers, and that they give helpful advice for applying the 15 generic core *Principles of Green Urbanism* in various contexts. **Chapter 4** looks at the urbanization of China and India. It forms a conclusion by looking ahead with a long term vision to identify the next steps required, and the research agenda needed, for a *low-to-no-carbon future*, and draws implications for urban design and academic research.

Today, the impact of rapid urbanization processes in cities in the Asia-Pacific and Middle-East regions are a particular concern to many. On the one hand, we face rapidly growing boom cities like Shanghai and Dubai, and on the other hand, there is a growing number of climate refugees from small island states at risk of inundation, or parts of society that are struggling in poverty. As a response, I have established, with support from the United Nations, the *UNESCO Chair in Sustainable Urban Development for Asia and the Pacific*, and I am pleased to note that there is now much more support available for these communities and there is significantly greater research going on in the field. For instance, there is some exploration of such questions as: What could be the new emancipatory solutions for citizens and governments with regard to harmonizing and improving the breathtakingly rapid urbanization processes in Asia? How can we better take into account the particular climatic conditions and the specific social habits of the Asian population when developing large urban projects? And what will be the changing role of the architect and urban designer in this process?

While this study is mainly concerned with holistic approaches to transform existing city districts for sustainability, and with the dying centres of towns and cities in the developed world, it seems that a separate publication (Part II) with the explicit brief of reviewing issues in the Asia-Pacific Region will soon have to follow.

Steffen Lehmann
Sydney/Singapore, September 2009

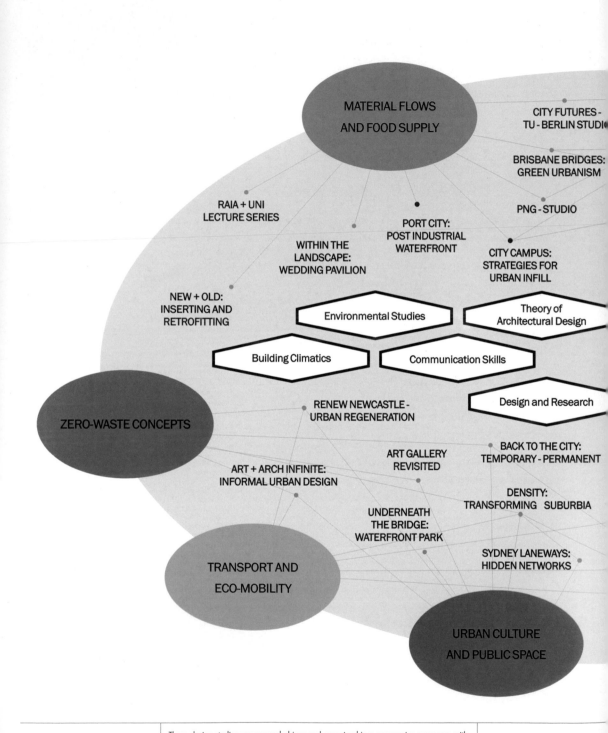

MATERIAL FLOWS
AND FOOD SUPPLY

CITY FUTURES -
TU - BERLIN STUDIO

BRISBANE BRIDGES:
GREEN URBANISM

RAIA + UNI
LECTURE SERIES

PNG - STUDIO

PORT CITY:
POST INDUSTRIAL
WATERFRONT

WITHIN THE
LANDSCAPE:
WEDDING PAVILION

CITY CAMPUS:
STRATEGIES FOR
URBAN INFILL

NEW + OLD:
INSERTING AND
RETROFITTING

Environmental Studies

Theory of
Architectural Design

Building Climatics

Communication Skills

ZERO-WASTE CONCEPTS

RENEW NEWCASTLE -
URBAN REGENERATION

Design and Research

BACK TO THE CITY:
TEMPORARY - PERMANENT

ART GALLERY
REVISITED

ART + ARCH INFINITE:
INFORMAL URBAN DESIGN

DENSITY:
TRANSFORMING   SUBURBIA

UNDERNEATH
THE BRIDGE:
WATERFRONT PARK

SYDNEY LANEWAYS:
HIDDEN NETWORKS

TRANSPORT AND
ECO-MOBILITY

URBAN CULTURE
AND PUBLIC SPACE

These design studios are research-driven and organized in a progressive sequence, with
assignments building-up on each other, increasing in complexity and scale. They include
interdisciplinary, collaborative studios and community outreach. A strong project-based
design studio ethos is complemented by studies in technology, history and theory, and
professional practice. The studio is the place of holistic synthesis. (Diagram 2010)

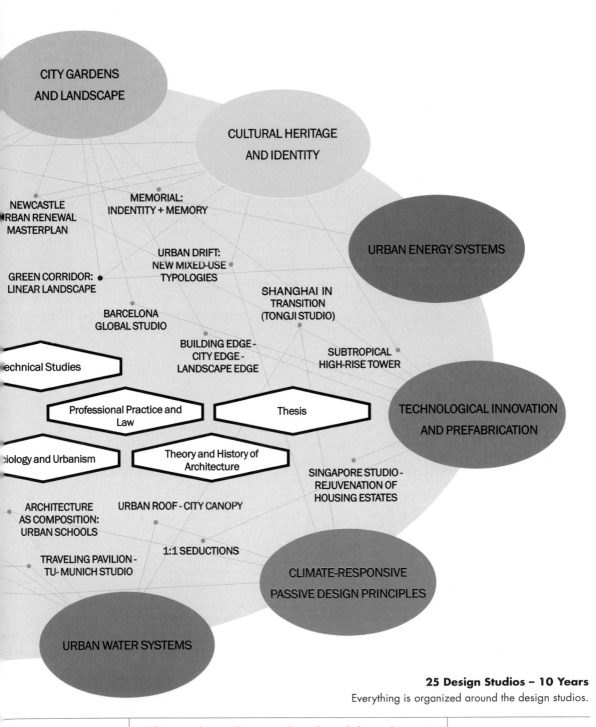

CITY GARDENS
AND LANDSCAPE

CULTURAL HERITAGE
AND IDENTITY

NEWCASTLE
URBAN RENEWAL
MASTERPLAN

MEMORIAL:
INDENTITY + MEMORY

URBAN ENERGY SYSTEMS

URBAN DRIFT:
NEW MIXED-USE
TYPOLOGIES

GREEN CORRIDOR:
LINEAR LANDSCAPE

SHANGHAI IN
TRANSITION
(TONGJI STUDIO)

BARCELONA
GLOBAL STUDIO

Technical Studies

BUILDING EDGE -
CITY EDGE -
LANDSCAPE EDGE

SUBTROPICAL
HIGH-RISE TOWER

Professional Practice and
Law

Thesis

TECHNOLOGICAL INNOVATION

AND PREFABRICATION

Sociology and Urbanism

Theory and History of
Architecture

SINGAPORE STUDIO -
REJUVENATION OF
HOUSING ESTATES

ARCHITECTURE
AS COMPOSITION:
URBAN SCHOOLS

URBAN ROOF - CITY CANOPY

1:1 SEDUCTIONS

TRAVELING PAVILION -
TU- MUNICH STUDIO

CLIMATE-RESPONSIVE

PASSIVE DESIGN PRINCIPLES

URBAN WATER SYSTEMS

25 Design Studios – 10 Years
Everything is organized around the design studios.

Redefining curriculum towards a new agenda in architectural education: Positions in
25 design studios developed by the author over a 10 year period, and their relationship to the curriculum. Integrating the new realities of climate change in the way we
teach architecture and urban design: The *City Campus*, *Port City* and *Green Corridor*
studios are part of a larger strategy to explore 'City Futures and Urban Regeneration'.

Keywords Cities in transition; climate-responsive urbanism; compact communities; carbon-neutral neighbourhoods; case studies: Port City, Green Corridor and City Campus; resilient and adaptive districts.

Introduction: understanding a changing world

`Turning constraints into opportunity' – is a line that is often heard. It's true, a time of crisis is also a time of opportunity. The opportunity most commonly linked to climate change is the creation of `green' jobs in the environmental technologies sector and the likelihood for uptake and large-scale roll-out of innovative renewable energy technologies. But the opportunities and challenges go far beyond technology. We are indeed on the brink of re-inventing how we will create our future urban environment, the creation of new sustainable societies, and we are engaged in nothing less than a peaceful revolution that is changing the way we design, build and operate cities and buildings.

In most countries, cities are now the drivers of the economy and the generator of economic growth. This is also the case in Australia, where almost 89 per cent of the population live in urban areas. The potential for large emission reductions in cities and the built environment exists in all countries. Urban areas, therefore, are the front line for actions

Prologue: Can Urbanism Ever be Green?

to mitigate and adapt to climate change. For instance, the building sector is responsible for approximately 35 per cent of Australia's greenhouse gas emissions (data 2009) and has a significant long-term influence on climate change. Yet this sector has the potential to provide significant immediate emission reductions at zero cost or net savings to our economy, using existing knowledge and technologies holistically.

Architects and urban designers are probably advantaged in their role of providing professional leadership in understanding these new environmental challenges in a rapidly changing world. As professionals, they are trained to envisage possible futures, a profession able (and isn't society expecting them to be?) to imagine how a low-to-no-carbon future might look, and how the urban environment will operate under the `Post-Peak-Oil' conditions. But is it possible for urbanism – with its huge consumption of material and energy, and creation of waste – ever to be truly green?

The aim must be to drive deep, fast, cost-effective greenhouse gas emission cuts in the built environment at the district-wide and neighbourhood scale.

While urbanism is about to reach a 'tipping point' in regard to its carbon emissions and material waste, urbanism will only ever be green, if we base all urban design and planning on holistic and measurable principles to change unsustainable practice: the 15 *Principles of Green Urbanism*, as suggested and laid-out in this publication.

We have all reasons to be optimistic about this. The good message is: yes, we are able to transform and future-proof our post-industrial existing cities through careful strategies of architectural and urban design, and we will have to do it soon, as we are running out of time. The solutions for sustainable urban growth are already available, and they include the use of energy-efficient, zero-carbon urban models, based on renewable energy sources and renewable, more flexible building typologies, combined with new concepts of intensification and densification of the existing districts (more about this in the following chapter).

Where climate change will have most impact

Ensuring energy-efficiency of single buildings alone is not sufficient to solve the complex issues caused by climate change. It needs urban strategies for city districts and methodologies that deal with the social and economic dimensions too.

Urban transformation is already on its way. For instance, the residents of Freiburg (Germany) are generating their own green energy locally and enjoy energy autonomy and car-reduced neighbourhoods; the municipality of Copenhagen (Denmark) started to build the green district Nordhavnen with a highly efficient district heating system; California (USA) is becoming a leader in solar energy use; Malmö (Sweden) is developing carbon neutral residential areas with innovation in waste management; and Singapore has launched a 'Green Masterplan' with the ambition to become a leader in sustainability for the entire Asia-Pacific Region, while London (UK) is setting ambitious greenhouse gas reduction targets for the entire building sector for the next decade. The level of implementation of green urbanism strategies is at different stages in different countries, but more and more cities are joining in the fight against climate change.

As concentrations of human activity, Europe's cities and towns account for 69 per cent of the continent's energy use and thus for most greenhouse gas emissions; and in the US, cities account for around 55 per cent of energy use. But the geographical areas, where climate change will have most impact, are not in Europe or North America. Some of the main threats include:

- rising temperatures
- rising sea levels
- emerging water shortages
- deteriorating food security
- loss of biodiversity
- collapse of energy supply
- growing urban poverty and population growth, and
- overall declining environmental conditions.

The countries and regions most vulnerable to climate change, and at the front lines of global warming, are some of the world's poorest nations. For instance, in Bangladesh, Somalia, and on Small Island States, the population already suffers the consequences of greenhouse gas emissions caused by far away industrialized nations. Sea level rise, loss of drinking water and decreasing food supply, severe flooding, long droughts, prevalence of intense storms, rising soil salinity, and so on – the implications are dire for many millions of people living in the affected, low-lying areas, mainly in Africa and Asia. The consequences of climate change could potentially displace millions of people.

The populations of the world's poorest nations, for instance, Bangladesh, Somalia, and on Small Island States already suffer the consequences of greenhouse gas emissions, caused by industrialized nations from far away and over a long period of time.

Cities are very attractive to migrants, not only because of the jobs they offer but for a wide variety of other reasons, including quality of life, family and friendship networks and good transport connections. High migration rates from rural areas to cities are mostly the result of declining agricultural production, lack of infrastructure and rising unemployment in the countryside. However, with increasing sea level rise, it will be impossible to keep building higher embankments and seawalls forever to keep the sea water out from coastal cities. A series of adaptation and mitigation initiatives needs to be started. Significant financial help from the industrialized nations will be necessary to help the poorer countries and regions to adapt to the growing climate change impact. In this situation, it is clear that the secure future and sustainability of our cities is critical.

Towards a zero-carbon society with low-to-no carbon cities

Many nations have started to introduce legislation and carbon emission trading schemes to help them in their transition towards a low-carbon society. Arguably an ambitious policy of the European Union (EU) is the *Renewable Energy Directive*, which binds all member states to source a minimum of 20 per cent of their energy from renewable sources by 2020, to obtain a minimum of 10 per cent consumption of bio-fuels in transportation, and to reduce carbon emissions by 20 per cent (compared to 1990 levels).

Equally, there has been a new understanding in urban planning. While Europe has rediscovered the historical model of mixed-use, compact city as a paradigm for urban design (with some impressive success in urban renewal in the last two decades), the focus has now shifted towards transformation of low-density settlements in the US, Canada and Australia. What needs to happen with the existing cities in those countries? Too often we still find some of the most inefficient models of sprawling suburbs repeated by planners and architects today. When will these urban planning concepts that continue to foster car-dependency finally be understood as out-dated? One can only wonder how planners in these countries can be so ignorant of the necessity to change, and continue to implement ill-informed, outmoded, `business as usual' planning models.

To exemplify the much quoted `urban transformation' it is helpful to use a real city as a field of exploration in order to arrive at generic principles and insight that has value for all cities in industrialized nations. Our in-depth case study, to show what cold be done, is the Australian city of Newcastle. Newcastle is a typical example of:

- the intensive use of the automobile, where public transport still plays a minor role;
- a city that needs to become more resilient and adaptable to better deal with the uncertainties of climate change
- a city and region closely connected to coal, where around 95 per cent of all energy is generated from fossil-fuel burning powerstations (mostly coal-burning)
- post-industrial conditions, where heavy industry has closed down and moved away
- a fine grain of superb heritage buildings, many of which sit vacant in the decaying city centre
- a university that aspires to play a major role in the future of the city and its urban revitalization and
- a city where some urban development has been started, but is still disconnected from tho rost of tho city due to a lack of an ovorall vioion and tho implomontation of an overall bold urban design that would improve connectivity.

Choosing the case study: the seaport city of Newcastle, New South Wales (Australia)
By making the strategic choice of case study, it was obvious that there would be valuable aspects and advantages in choosing a city on the brink of transformation, and Newcastle appears to be such a city, likely to be on the cusp of great things.

The following chapters introduce this typical post-industrial city as a case study for testing and presenting new urban concepts that deal with climate change. Newcastle is a regional city, with a population of approximately 150,000, located 150 kilometres (around 110 miles) north of Sydney. The city has regional significance as `the Capital of the Hunter Region', an area with a total catchment of approximately 600,000 inhabitants.

Newcastle is one of Australia's oldest cities, founded in 1804. It is New South Wales' second largest city, and has always been in the shadow of Sydney; however, it has served 150 years as the state's industrial capital and `engine room'. For instance, while around 10 per cent of the state's population live in the Hunter Region and in Newcastle, and over 20 per cent of the state's income is generated in this region, it has not received more than 5 per cent of the annual budget over the last decades (expenditure data of NSW State Government's budget in the region; see annual budget figures published on government's web site).

Australia is the world's largest exporter of black coal, and Newcastle is at the centre of this activity, with 91 million tonnes p.a. being exported through the Port of Newcastle (data: Newcastle Port Corporation, 2008). There are attempts to significantly raise this export figure, with the construction of a third coal loader at the port. Once Australia's most industrialized city, Newcastle has already gone through a period of change: Steel production and ship building activities in the city closed-down in the 1990s (with the final closure of the BHP steel plant in 1996); furthermore, as a consequence of the construction of new shopping malls outside town, which have drawn activity from the traditional centre, and much uncoordinated planning, the city's central district has been in permanent decline for the last twenty years. As a consequence, much of Newcastle's historical inner city is disused and vacant. For instance, Hunter Street, once the main street, presents today as a parade of boarded shop fronts and vandalized buildings. Some of these buildings were once considered architectural gems (the 19th-century heritage-listed post office and the state's oldest theatre are now empty and vandalized, and historic pub buildings are in decay or demolished).

After years of neglect, resulting in urban decay, there are finally plans being developed for the city's urban regeneration, for a better infrastructure and a low-carbon future.

Critically, this book is about optimism and hope. The aim of the plans is to rectify the serious problems in the historical city centre, structural problems that clearly cannot be solved easily or without the support and intervention of government. In urban revitalization and the introduction of renewable energy sources, governments have a key role to play. Urban regeneration cannot be left entirely to the private sector to sort out. It is obvious that the city's future hinges to a large degree upon the successful revitalization of the city centre. Once the city centre is again a vibrant, revitalized place, with sustainable design principles embedded, many other positive developments will follow.

Typically, there has been a gradual urban decline. Over the last twenty years, 75 per cent of retail supply has relocated outside the city centre, in large and more easily accessible shopping malls that have been allowed to significantly expand in recent times (e.g. suburban shopping centres in Kotara and Charlestown doubled their size and capacity during 2008-10). These massive suburban shopping malls have dragged other services to the suburbs with them, which has left the historical city centre with a growing number of empty shops plastered with `For Lease' signs. Around 120 vacant buildings were recently counted in the historical downtown area (data: survey 2009, conducted by the University of Newcastle), most of which have been neglected by their owners and left to vandalism, squatting and graffiti. Many of these boarded-up buildings are heritage-listed; however, the owners are unconvinced that sufficient subsidies or incentives are offered to economically justify a renovation or be adaptively re-used. As a consequence, `going to town' to shop has become a tradition long since gone.

This is, of course, not an unusual case. It is easy to list similar cases of dying city centres and suffering regional cities all over the industrialized world. In the US, for instance, Pittsburgh is a former industrial heartland that is now changing its economy to embrace new kinds of jobs and services (as opposed to Detroit – which hasn't managed the transition yet).

We can identify some typical characteristics of these post-industrial urban conditions at the beginning of the 21st century:

- As industry has closed down, prime sites like brownfield sites on waterfront land and inner-city locations (e.g. docklands), have become available for large-scale urban redevelopment. However, the re-use of these frequently polluted brownfield sites requires holistic approaches and huge investment.
- A robust masterplan for renewal is frequently missing for the overall coordinated densification and intensification of the suffering city core. Compacting urban form requires new organizational structures for these districts, with their own new infrastructure. All this requires political leadership to attract investment, and a holistic understanding of the principles of sustainable urbanism.
- There is usually a good fabric of existing buildings associated with the core and the brownfield sites, sometimes heritage-listed warehouses or large industrial structures, flexible and easily adaptable for conversion to new uses.
- The city centre has suffered some population loss. This has particular ramifications for European and US cities, some of which are shrinking. In Australia, as in other countries in recent years, there is some evidence that people are moving back to the historical centres to live closer to work and entertainment; a generation that appreciates a particular lifestyle and the convenience of walking or cycling to work, cinemas, and restaurants. But the issue at stake here is that retail has moved away, unemployment has increased, and boarded-up shop fronts are contributing to the city centre's further decline.

We can identify some typical characteristics of the post-industrial urban condition of cities at the beginning of the 21st century. These conditions are similar in cities in industrialized nations.

There has been a turn-around in the population loss in Newcastle's city centre. Since 1998, around 5,000 people have moved back to live in the downtown area. The City Centre Masterplan (2008, a state government document) predicts that 10,000 new jobs and another 6,500 new residents over the next twenty years for the city, with more 'urban infill' type residential developments likely to be built.

Some further data on the City of Newcastle
Here some background data on the case study:

- Population: 141,752 (census 2006), with an average annual growth of 0.80 per cent. The ten-year period from 1996 to 2006 saw an increase of the Hunter Region's population by 8.6 per cent.
- Age distribution: 27.3 per cent of the population are in the age group of 55 years and older (this is above NSW State average). The group of retirees has the largest annual population growth. The age group of 15 to 24 years old accounts for 13.4 per cent of the population (above NSW State average).

• Employment in the Hunter Region is mostly in retail trade, health care, construction, manufacturing, education and training. The mining sector accounts for 4.5 per cent of employment in the region. In 2008 the unemployment rate was 4.9 per cent. The de-industrialization process and continued diversification of the Hunter Region's economy is ongoing.

• Climate: Newcastle enjoys a mediterranean climate, with around 1,120 mm of annual rainfall (about double the rainfall compared to Adelaide or Brisbane), and approximately double the solar radiation intensity compared to London or Berlin. The average minimum temperature is 4.7 degrees Celsius, while the maximum is 27.5 degrees Celsius.

It is obvious that, with its intensive coal mining and exporting activities, Newcastle and the Hunter Region have a special responsibility in the global fight against climate change. The region's huge coal exports (coal is shipped mainly to China, Japan and Korea), and some prevailing heavy industries, mean that the city has an unusually large carbon footprint. In addition, Hunter Region residents drive around 20 per cent more by car than the Australian average; it is very much an automobile-dependent society, where low population densities make it impossible to run public transport services efficiently.

We are now engaged in nothing less than a peaceful revolution that is changing the way we design, build and operate cities and buildings.

All this makes for an ideal situation, in which knowledge and service-based industries could help to create significant new opportunities in employment and sustainable energy technologies, boosting the economy with `green' jobs.

The large ecological footprint of the Hunter region
A recent survey in the Hunter region has shown that 42 per cent of residents in the region had a second refrigerator, 65 per cent had more than one motor vehicle, 85 per cent had at least one computer at home, and 77 per cent had air-conditioning installed in their homes (HVRF survey, 2009). Only 53 per cent of households had an adult bicycle, and only 11 per cent had a solar hot water system installed.

In Australia, coal is cheap and plentiful. Almost 95 per cent of Australia's power still comes from fossil-fuel powered (mainly coal-fired) powerstations and, unfortunately, it's likely that the country will continue to depend on coal as primary source of energy at least for another decade. The coal of the Hunter region is particularly sought after. It is relatively easy to generate energy with the Hunter's thermal coal (in contrast to Queensland's coal, which is mainly used for steel production). Generating energy from burning coal is the most 'dirty' and inefficient way to produce electricity, creating huge amounts of greenhouse gas emissions.

As part of a global `de-coalification', many nations have issued a ban on the construction of new coal plants, and have moved to increase renewables in the energy mix, compensating for the reduction of energy from coal-burning powerstations.

Identifying principles for sustainable urban development

This book presents, in the following chapter, the 15 *Principles of Green Urbanism*.

'Principles' are different from 'values'. Values represent an internal system which we select to our weighting or preferences. Principles are bigger than values. Principles are more like natural laws, external to our approach or preferences. As urban designers and architects, it is important for us to understand the core principles of sustainable urban development, as, if applied holistically and adjusted to the local context and climatic conditions, they have the potential to guide us towards more sustainable, less energy-intensive design proposals.

15 Principles of Green Urbanism have been identified and are presented.

Many good initiatives are happening worldwide already – and a point of this book is to show that all of this is eminently do-able and achievable, as the technologies are already on the market. However, the presented different Principles of Green Urbanism cannot be approached individually or in an isolated way, as they will not generate the necessary effect. The aim must be to get each of the principles working interactively with the others. If this is done well, the challenge of building cities that are, at the same time green, transit-orientated and pedestrian-friendly, and therefore more resilient to climate change, can be resolved.

What this book is and what it is not

A word about what this book wants to be and what it is not. First of all, this book intends to be a valuable collection of resources for students in architecture and urban design to engage with and to pursue further research. It pulls together many pieces of information that we found to be helpful when working on the design projects illustrated in Chapter 3. This book reveals the ongoing interest in certain types of projects that I have shared over the last four years with my colleagues and students in our 'City Futures' studio. This book is not a scientifically written work. While it presents some quantitative research, we believe that the focus of the design studios and related explorations has to be qualitative, based on careful observations, experiences gained from visiting places and the study of best practice. Scientists, with their necessarily narrow view and evidence-based approach, are limited in their capacity to vision and imagine urban futures, or to take practical action. On the other hand, architects and urban designers are not scientists. They use their own (not always quantifiable) experiences and criteria by applying methods of analysis of context and brief, and they rely heavily on case studies. Members of the urban design discipline will best know how to take advantage of this publication. The chapters are not written as complete texts on the topics, but rather as modules, and are introductions to different specific themes, relying on the reader's own further research.

Most readers will not be familiar with the chosen case study, the seaport city of Newcastle in New South Wales (Australia). Following is a photo series of the current state of Newcastle city centre, to form a basis for a better understanding of the following chapters and design projects.

A diverse and historical city: Newcastle city centre seen from the air, looking south, showing the city centre growing up the Hill. In front: Harbour Plaza, part of the Honeysuckle development. Most traces of the former industrial working harbour are now erased. (Photo: Steffen Lehmann, November 2006)

The city of Newcastle, Australia's second oldest city, founded in 1804, was declared a free settlement in 1822. It is the second largest urban centre in New South Wales, after Sydney. The city centre occupies the north facing slopes of a tall peninsula, overlooking a deep-water harbour. This publication concerns the need for urban consolidation of the post-industrial city centre.

Newcastle city centre by the sea, view from the air, looking towards the Beach Esplanade. There is a compact and walkable city core, which offers great opportunities for urban regeneration and infill. Typical for the post-industrial condition of the city is the lack of appreciation of the waterfront as an asset. The transformation to a tourist destination requires a lengthy urban development process. (Photo: courtesy Suters, May 2004)

The centre shows a tightly-ordered and compact structure. Its basic grid was laid out by surveyor Henry Dangar in 1828, in two by seven blocks. This grid is unique in Australia, situated on the sloping ground of a hillside. In 1857, when the port required a rail link to move coal, this city plan was cut-off from the waterfront. Today, the rail tracks are a barrier to accessing the foreshore, thus hindering the development of the city and isolating the waterfront development from the actual city centre.

City and Port: The prominent grain silos at Newcastle harbour are the largest structure in the city, creating an interesting industrial heritage. The harbour was developed from 1830 on, mainly to support coal mining and the shipping of resources. Today it is one of the world's largest coal-exporting seaports, with over 95 million tonnes p.a. exported (data: 2008). (Photo: Roger Hanley, April 2008)

Harbour development sites are called the `sweet dreams of planners and developers',
but the redevelopment of a working harbour foreshore has its own challenges. While
the continuos pedestrian and cycle paths along the water has become a success,
opportunities to provide better accessibility to the water have been lost, and connections with the city centre are still missing due to the railway line barrier.

New and old, creating a strong sense of place: The Maritime Centre and Museum, an adaptive re-use of the historical wharf building at Honeysuckle urban renewal precinct. The city of Newcastle grew in harmony with the growth of the port, and vice versa. Will the relationship between City and Port need to be reinvented?
(Photo: Roger Hanley, April 2008)

Honeysuckle harbourfront is the redevelopment of 50 hectares derelict land. Today, Newcastle suffers – as many other cities – from a general lack of appreciation and celebration of
its waterfront. The extraordinary natural advantages of these places (just think of the missed
opportunities in Sydney) are not cherished sufficiently, and a change of mind-set is necessary:
public space planning and traffic planning are to be combined to one coherent strategy.

Refocussing Newcastle on the water and its heritage of a great port city: old timber piling of a wharf building, a reminder of the port's golden years. The port activities grew intensively between 1850s (with the beginning of the population boom, caused by the New South Wales `Gold Rush') and the 1890s (slowing down with the economic depression). (Photo: Roger Hanley, April 2008)

New apartment buildings along the public promenade, with private gardens behind
the fence. The linear 'wall-like' development and the continuous standard width of this
monotonous public space has been much critized. How can we make architecture more
specific to its location? (Photo: Roger Hanley, April 2008)

An urban vineyard and new apartment building at Honeysuckle urban renewal precinct, symbolizing a new urban lifestyle. Honeysuckle was initiated in 1992 through the 'Building Better Cities' programme and developed 50 hectares of prime waterfront land, over a twenty year period. (Photo: Roger Hanley, April 2008)

Newcastle's industrial past: The Hydraulic Power Station at Carrington (1877), designed by Colonial architect James Barnet. A real testament to the vision and civic leadership when it was built, and a building of outstanding industrial heritage. The yellow bricks of the symmetrical facade were imported from Holland. Today it is disused and waiting for adaptive re-use ideas. (Photo: Roger Hanley, April 2008)

University House (formerly Nesca House, 1939), designed by Emil Sondersteen in the Art Deco style. In front: Christie Place, a small public garden. This building is the most visible sign of the presence of the University within the city centre.

Newcastle City Hall (1929), with its dominating clock tower terminating the axis of Civic Park. The round building is the City Council's Administration Centre (1977). (Photos: Roger Hanley, April 2008)

Wheeler Place is the most formal town square in Newcastle and forms a forecourt
for the Civic Theatre; looking towards the circular-shaped City Administration Centre
(Romberg and Boyd, with Wilson and Suters, 1977). This stand-alone, round building
is said to have been inspired by 'Torre Velasca' in Milan.
(Photos: Roger Hanley, April 2008)

Wheeler Place acts as town square and forecourt to the foyer of Civic Theatre (Civic Centre Building), which was originally designed in 1929 as a cinema and live theatre by Henry E. White. The theatre was sensitively restored by Suters Snell Architects in 1995 and includes a restaurant and the smaller Playhouse Theatre. In the background is the 36m high *campanile* tower of City Hall.

Newcastle's old buildings `substitute utility for elegance', as a critic once said. The Railway Workshop and Boiler House buildings (from 1874) form an important ensemble from the early days of the development of coal mining and the shipping industry. The heavy railway line was brought to Wharf Road in 1857, with the main purpose of loading the coal onto the ships; a purpose outlived a long time ago. (Both photos: Roger Hanley, April 2008)

Two of the three historical Railway Workshop sheds have been adaptively re-used for the Newcastle Regional Museum, converted in 2010. The gap between the buildings was glazed over as connecting space between the exhibition areas. The museum acts as a cultural hub, complementing other heritage attractions, such as Fort Scratchley, the Convict Lumberyard, and the Maritime Centre.

Newcastle's best modern building is the former Clinical Science Block (also called David Maddison Building, or *New Med 1*, completed 1982) by architect Lawrence Nield. This flexible multi-purpose building, with a dramatically stepped block and a robust concrete frame structure, could have easily been adapted and re-used as a court house or similar. (Photo: Steffen Lehmann, October 2008)

The terraced house (or row house) is a medium-density housing type that originated in England, the Netherlands and France in the 17th century: A row of identical brick houses sharing uniform height and side walls. Newcastle has a fine collection of two and three-storey terraces from the 1890s, now heritage-listed and highly sought after as a form of inner-city living. (Photo: Roger Hanley, April 2008)

The Bank Corner building in Hunter Street, built 1940 in a Classical style. The contemporary re-use of such superb heritage buildings can become the catalyst for an urban renaissance of the city centre. Density has the potential to create a sense of urbanity. (Photo: Roger Hanley, April 2008)

'Since the 1970s retail areas in central business districts declined, as customers shopping by car found the new suburban centres, with their air-conditioning and easy parking, more convenient and attractive.' (Source: 'History of Australian Cities', C. Forster, 1995)

Hunter Street, in the 1970s still a vibrant shopping street and commercial strip, has fallen into decay and many shopfronts are now boarded up. Most of these small-scale commercial row buildings were built around 1900. The photo shows abandoned commercial space in the depressed and vacancy-plagued central business district of Newcastle, challenging the city's notion of itself.

Our revitalization idea, to bring people back to the city centre, is simple: use of derelict and abandoned shopfronts to house community groups, local creative people and artisans, who create and display their wares on-site; building owners allow such interim use of their vacant properties for free. (Photo: Roger Hanley, April 2008)

The impermeable barrier created by old infrastructure (here by the corridor of the heavy railway line, established 1857, to transport coal), cutting off the city centre from the harbour foreshore. For decades, this has made a well-connected public space network and the coordinated urban development of the city centre impossible. (Photo: Steffen Lehmann, October 2007)

This large vacant brick building, the Great Northern Hotel (by Hughes and Moloney, 1938) is located opposite the railway terminus. Its architecture is reminiscent of the Chicago School and could easily be turned into a contemporary loft development. New ideas for sustainable cities need old buildings! (Photo: Roger Hanley, April 2008)

The Newcastle Post Office, designed by Government Architect Walter L. Vernon (1903), built in the magnificent style of a classical Italian sandstone palazzo (Palladian style), with arcades and copper domes. One of the finest buildings in New South Wales, it is disappointing that this jewel is left to rot for years, while no creative idea for its appropriate adaptive re-use seems to be feasible. (Photos: Roger Hanley, April 2008)

Newcastle corners: this charming corner building in Hunter and Bolton Streets, built around 1920, offers a fine grain of architectural detail. It is the adaptive re-use of these kinds of buildings that will help to maintain a well-defined sense of identity and place, and contribute in future to creating a distinctive urban experience. The city's urban regeneration and the adaptive re-use of buildings are good examples of recycling.

Hunter Street today: a tired piece of urban fabric. In the 1960s and 70s, still the vibrant commercial spine of the city centre, the street has been in decline for a long time. Poor strategic planning, the construction of large shopping centres outside the city, and the increasing sub-urbanization of the population has caused the economic decline of the entire city core. (Photo: Roger Hanley, April 2008)

Linear Hunter Street is a typical result of the traffic-dominated city, where shopfronts are lining up along main street. There is a fine grain and rich variety of short building facades; here the city is purposeful and authentic – but today, abandoned and in decline. We can observe a similar decline happening to city centres in developed countries all over the world: the post-industrial condition has an impact on the historical city core.

The street frontages reveal diverse variations of the commercial building type along Hunter Street. These vacant and disused buildings have been left by their owners to decay, contributing to the rapid decline of the city centre core. In 2009, Newcastle had over 120 empty shopfronts in its centre. (Photo: Roger Hanley, April 2008)

Industrial waste and paper recycling, waste minimization: how can we optimize the full life-cycle of products and processes, reorganizing material flows, to approach the state of natural systems, in which there is no waste (what Michael Braungart calls 'to eliminate the concept of waste') – to achieve zero waste to landfill? Image: Carrington's industrial area with waste recycling depot. (Photo: Cida de Aragon, May 2007).

The steel mills had finally closed in 1999, but one heavy industry sector kept going: Mining and shipping coal to Asia, exporting carbon pollution in form of Australia's black coal – a business soon to change in a carbon-constrained economy. One of the three giant coal loaders at Newcastle Port, loading over 100 mill. tons p.a., making it one of the largest coal-exporting ports in the world. (Photo: Cida de Aragon, May 2007)

CHAPTER 1

Turning Constraints Into Opportunities

Introduction

As more and more of the earth submits to urbanization, urban planners are being confronted with a series of design challenges and an urgent need to act on them. Among the most significant environmental challenges of our time is the fossil-fuel dependency of cities and buildings, and their growing demand for energy, land, and water and food security. In this context, avoiding mistakes in urban development at the early stages could lead to more sustainable, polycentric and compact cities that avoid car traffic and which release less greenhouse gas emissions. The first chapter of this book presents research in *Green Urbanism* and introduces models for sustainable urban growth and the intensification of neighbourhoods, to show how cities can transform from fossil-fuel based models to models based on renewable energy sources and densification concepts.

Chapter 1 starts with general observations about the impact of urbanization and climate change, and what is needed globally; it then brings in the concept of *Eco-Cities* and examples of city renewal, before it moves to the specifics of what the design studios propose for the case study, the City of Newcastle. The work from my design studios is presented in great detail in Chapter 3, which illustrates how the studios have addressed the question: how can we best and cohesively integrate all aspects of energy and transport systems, waste and

Cities and the Post-Industrial Condition

water management, passive and active strategies, natural ventilation and so on, into holistic, sustainable urban design, and thus improve the environmental performance of an inner-city district by dramatically reducing CO_2 emissions at the district level. Over the last five years, I have explored with students emergent urban patterns for the regeneration of Newcastle city centre, investigating a step-by-step transformation of it to a more sustainable model. We have also discussed how urbanism is affected by the paradigms of ecology, the need to de-carbonize energy supply, and the need to change modes of transport. Chapters 2 and 3 present the *Principles of Green Urbanism* and three recent examples of the application of such urban design principles: the 'City Campus', 'Green Corridor' and 'Port City' studies.

Whilst the focus of this study is on environmental sustainability, eco-cities and eco-districts must also address social and economic factors if they are to be successful. Sustainability is about more than resource efficiency. Sustainable communities also foster social and economic sustainability.

Re-compacting the city: theorizing sustainability on the urban scale

There is a renewed focus on cities. Historically, environmental movements have focused more on ecological processes and the open landscape, and less on city design. However, it is increasingly being understood that cities play a critical role in shaping the ecological future, that the battle against climate change needs to be won by applying zero-carbon and low-to-no-carbon models to our urban landscapes. This new awareness of the importance of urbanization and its relationship to climate change has brought about a shift in the environmentalist agenda, which now includes issues such as public transport, health, poverty, social exclusion, public space and inner-city landscape. (Pachauri, 2009)

The theme of the 'Future City' is central to the concern of this book, and it argues that urban design is integral to the profession of architecture. With the growth of urbanization, a series of urban design problems and investigations are required to be solved, such as how do we reduce fossil-fuel dependency and ensure the supply of drinking water and food security? The imperative is to avoid mistakes while maintaining standards of living and moving as efficiently as possible towards more sustainable, compact cities with less greenhouse gas emissions, reduced car traffic and shorter supply chains. We clearly need more research that explores different models for sustainability in urban growth and green neighbourhoods, as we move to renewable energy sources. We need to address the questions of how we can best and cohesively integrate all aspects of energy and transport systems, our waste and water management, passive and active strategies for sun shading and natural ventilation, all based on proven knowledge, and it needs to be adapted seamlessly into contemporary urban design to improve the environmental and social performance of our cities. This is the aim: to provide a context for the discourse about emergent urban patterns and the regeneration of city centres, using case studies to accelerate the step-by-step transformation towards more sustainable models for the city. This chapter discusses how urbanism is affected (and can be expected to be even more affected in the future) by the paradigms of ecology and the need to de-carbonize our energy supply and our transport systems.

Let's start with a definition of sustainable development. The term 'sustainability' has become so widely used that it is in danger of meaning nothing. In his study 'Sustainable Architecture: Twelve Things You Can Do To Build Effective Low Cost Houses and Cities', Hotten points out that 'Sustainability and sustainable development are used almost interchangeably.' (Hotten, 2004) Dovers is more careful in his use of these terms and differentiates **sustainability** (an end) from **sustainable development** (a process of achieving that end). (Dovers, 2003) Clearly, sustainability is understood as the (goal of) on-going and long-term maintenance of humans and their ecosystems. To achieve sustainable development outcomes requires many stakeholders to work together. Green architects are immersed within the multi-dimensional process of sustainable development and are key decision-makers, given that, for example, in Australia, approximately three-quarters of capital stock is located in the built environment, making it the most important designed and manufactured element in the human ecosystem. The Australian Bureau of Statistics found that '30 per cent of capital stock is in the form of housing, with a further 45 per cent in non-housing and infrastructure.' (Australian Bureau of Statistics, 1990)

Cities are critical to the shift towards a low-carbon future. More than half the world's populations live and work in cities, which are the major source of waste and greenhouse gas emissions, therefore cities are where we must make the biggest and most urgent changes. (United Nations, 2008) Around the world, forward-looking cities are remaking themselves by investing in sustainable public transport and reducing their greenhouse gas emissions by reducing their car-dependency. This has improved the public realm by creating pedestrian-friendly urban spaces, and thus providing places for people to meet and congregate; giving people cleaner air to breathe; and has made cycling and walking in the city more attractive and safer. Enormous amounts of money are being invested by countries around the world to develop green infrastructure, and to restructure the economy towards a low-carbon future.

We see now the development of innovative urban design approaches based on new urban energy systems, eco-mobility concepts and material recycling.

The emergence of *Sustainable City Theory*

Urban design and the fundamental principles of how to shape our cities has so far barely featured in the greenhouse debate. Much of the debate has circled around ideas about active façade technology or are purely technologically-driven engineering solutions. While innovative engineering solutions are important, alone they will not produce a vibrant city. Cities are extremely complex entities, and major challenges such as food security, excessive fossil-fuel dependency and the growing demand for energy require holistic approaches and whole-of-system thinking to deal with the entire 'urban metabolism'. To achieve this, we need quantitative and qualitative research to come together.

However, this holistic urban dimension (the macro-scale) of cities has frequently been missing in the debate, as sustainability is mostly discussed in relation to `alternative lifestyles' and eco-houses. It appears that there is no clear consensus on the meaning of the term `sustainability' in urban design, or its relationship to urban settlements and the city. This is surprising, since almost half of all energy and materials consumed are used in cities and urban built-up areas (in the US around 48 per cent of all energy is consumed by cities).

The term `sustainability' has multiple meanings – some of which are complementary while others are oppositional and even contradictory. (Kearns, Barnett, Nolan, 2006) In the recent debate about the theory of urban sustainability, the tension between the technical and the social has been an obvious one. If eco-civilization appears to be society's reflection on global industrialization and capitalism, we desire three parameters to be met:

- economic growth
- social development, and
- environmental protection.

As we begin to fully understand the consequences of our dependency on fossil-fuel energy, the automobile, the cost of mobility and ways to integrate sustainable systems into urbanism, we start to suspect that the traditional focus on aesthetics regarding urban composition in the design of cities and neighbourhoods may no longer be sufficient. Cities in the new paradigm need to deliver more outcomes and deal with resources in a very different way. So, how does urban design deal with these new requirements? How should traditional knowledge of urban composition and the aesthetic principles of city-making (as was, for instance, suggested by Camillo Sitte, in his pivotal text in 1889) be expanded to meet the new paradigms of ecology? Indeed, are parts of these new paradigms actually well-known already to urban designers, and is there proven knowledge and established criteria for best practice in city-planning? At Newcastle University I set up design studios to explore such questions as these.

Different schools of thought: from *Green City* to *Green Building*

While London was suburbanized well before the 19th century, German, French and Italian cities were still compact and often surrounded by military walls, with a mix of all ranks of society living closely together. These medieval towns were compact, self-sustaining entities based on local food supply and composting for waste disposal. A major break to this model occurred with industrialization, followed by the introduction of the automobile and the idea of the 'Functional City' in the 1920s. 'Modern cities and their industrial working classes', as Lewis Mumford points out, 'were only made possible through innovations in energy technology and transport.' (Mumford, 1961) With the introduction of the railway and electricity, the 19th-century English city had started to significantly change and become increasingly industrialized (starting in Manchester, Liverpool and London). The new mobility led to sprawling suburbanization (based on cheap fuel) and to dispersed low-density settlements that encroached into the agricultural landscape. This gave rise to an anti-urban approach by designers, formulated as the *Charter of Athens* in 1933 by the CIAM, which quickly became the new widespread orthodoxy of the day, based on separation of functions (zoning), the dissolution of compact urban space and the reduction of densities.

Over the last thirty-five years or so, an international debate on eco-city theory has emerged and has developed as a relevant research field concerning the future of urbanism and the city itself. During that time, a number of architectural schools of thought have been implemented worldwide. One such school is *Technical Utopianism* (a technological idealism that relied on the quick 'techno-fix', as expressed, for instance, in the work of Archigram). Other early writing on green urbanism was available from Ebenezer Howard, whose 1902 book was entitled 'Garden City of Tomorrow', and whose political and social agenda has recently made a comeback. Much later, in 1969, Reyner Banham pioneered the idea that technology, human needs and environmental concerns should be considered an integral part of architecture. Probably no historian before him had so systematically explored the impact of environmental engineering and services on the design of buildings. (Howard, 1902; Banham, 1969) Some other early significant writing on green urbanism has come from Lewis Mumford and Jane Jacobs – although they didn't call it green urbanism. From 'Silent Spring' (by Rachel Carson, 1962), to Victor Olgyay's 'Design with Climate' (1963), to Reyner Banham's 'Architecture of the Well-tempered Environment' (1969), to Ian McHarg's 'Design with Nature' (1969), to the pivotal publications by authors re-connecting urbanism with the climatic condition (such as Koenigsberger, Drew and Fry, or Szokolay, in publications in the 1970s and 80s), to the remarkable 'Brundtland Report' (Brundtland, 1987); the important contributions from Robert and Brenda Vale (`Green Architecture: Design for an Energy-conscious Future', 1991), and the `Solar City Charter' (Herzog et al, 1995/2007), the field of sustainable city theories and climate-responsive urbanism has constantly been expanded. An important contribution came from Guenther Moewes with his book `Weder Huetten noch Palaeste' (1995), which is a programmatic manifesto for designing and constructing longer-lasting buildings. Unfortunately, this relevant book with its revealing insight into the relationship between construction, energy and work, has not been translated into English. Architect Otto Koenigsberger, who emigrated from Berlin to India in 1939 and served there as a government architect until 1951, before he became one of the founders of the *Department of Tropical Architecture* at the Architectural Association School in London, fundamentally transformed architectural thinking and practice with his `Handbook of Tropical Architecture'. He recognized as early as 1950 the limits of resources and energy. Through his experiences in India, Koenigsberger theorized *Tropical Architecture* as a discourse that was climate responsive and energy conscious, and which used local resources, materials and workers in a sustainable way. More recent theories for `Compact Cities' and `Solar Cities' (Vale and Vale, 1991; Burton, 1997; Jenks and Burgess, 2000; Lehmann, 2005) encapsulate the visions based on the belief that urban revitalization and the future of the city can only be achieved through `re-compacting' and using clearly formulated sustainable urban design principles.

In the 21st century we are working in an entirely new context, for which we need new types of cities. As noted by Ulrich Beck, we have arrived in `a new era of uncertainty', where energy, water and food supply are critical. 'We live in a world of increasingly non-calculable uncertainty that we create with the same speed of its technological developments.' (Beck, 2000)

Energy generation plays a major role. We will only be able to tackle climate change if we engage in a renewable energy revolution in order to move from fossil-fuel economies to a renewable energy economy.

Urban theory and its two major changes: overcoming the car-dependent city and climate change

I found that many of the contemporary visions of 'post-oil eco-cities' are directly related to utopian ideas of early Modernism. Following is a short, simplified description of some relevant urban theories (phases) of the last century (rough selection of episodes only):

• The 19th-century city transforming quickly, with the emergence of the Industrial Revolution and the urban working class. Technological development and innovation in the energy, water and transport sectors have been an important influence on the city's shape and transformation. In Berlin in the 1870s, the city was transformed with the construction of James Hobrecht's new sewage system. We can see the same effect in Vienna in the 1890s, through Otto Wagner's new technological concepts (`Stadtbautechnik'), such as innovation in transport, introducing the `Stadtbahn' and new water treatment (`Schleusensystem des Stadtkanals'), which produced a `New Vienna'; urban planning influenced by technology and industrial achievements.

• *Garden City* theory: Ebenezer Howard.
Howard published his concept `Garden Cities of Tomorrow' in 1902, and was involved
in the construction of Letchworth and Welwyn Garden City.

• Functional Zoning: Tony Garnier.
Functional Zoning was the essence of Tony Garnier's `Cite Industrielle' (1917), promoting
the moving of industry out of cities for healthier urban environments.

• *Ville Radieuse* and *Plan Voisin*: Le Corbusier.
Le Corbusier concept of the `Ville Radieuse' (1922/1933) promoted life in housing slabs and
towers situated in parkland with continuous green space. The impact of the automobile as a
major means of transport changed the way cities were laid-out and enabled entirely different,
dispersed city models to emerge (e.g. as a consequence, the emergence of the freeway, the
shopping mall, suburban sprawl). Ludwig Hilbersheimer's model of dispersed slab buildings
for mono-functional housing quarters at the periphery are a good example of this model.

• *Broadacre City*: Frank Lloyd Wright.
Broadacre City (from 1935 on) represents Wright's un-built utopian idea: the longing for
the agricultural life in a decentralized city structure, where every citizen grows food and
is self-sufficient. However, the problem of such a semi-ruralized city is its low density and
that it is not able to accommodate the necessary population. In 1965, Kisho Kurokawa's
concept of `Agricultural City' drew on ideas from Wright's `Broadacre City'.

• Brasilia and Chandigarh: two new capital cities.
Both capital cities, in inner Brazil (urban planning: Lucio Costa) and in North India (urban planning: Le Cor-
busier and others), were designed as car-centric cities. They were built at the end of the 1950s, from scratch.
They symbolize the naive optimism of this time and significant milestones in the modern city debate.

• Critique of the *Functional City* and *Endless Sprawl*: Jacobs, Mumford, Lynch, and Team X.
From 1955 on, the disorderly sprawl and suburbanization of American cities raised great
concern among urban theorists such as Lewis Mumford, Jane Jacobs and Kevin Lynch, giving an early base to mixed-use compact city theory. From 1956 on, a younger generation of
architects formed Team X, criticizing the modernistic zoning theory formulated by CIAM in
1933 in the *Charter of Athens* (with its inhumane principles of abstraction and repetition).

• 1960s groups and individuals.
In 1960, the *Metabolist Group* was formed in Tokyo, and began rethinking urban structure. Around
the same time, Frei Otto started to experiment with light-weight structures and membranes. Various
concepts of urban megastructures were developed by Yona Friedman, Walter Jonas, and by the
Metabolists around Kisho Kurokawa. His writings start to be published with the title: `From Metabo-
lism to Symbiosis'. In 1965, Alexander Mitscherlich raises sharp critique against the degradation of
the built environment through simplistic modern urbanism, in `Die Unwirtlichkeit unserer Staedte'.

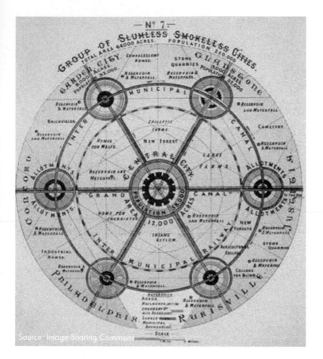

Source: Image Sharing Commons

Utopian ideas for cities' futures

Throughout architectural history, many designers have produced utopian ideas and theories about how to resolve issues of urbanization and questions of urban shape, form 'Garden Cities', to 'Vertical Cities', to 'Cities in the Sky', to 'Agricultural Cities', to 'Walking Cities', and so on. Only a few are introduced in this chapter.

Le Corbusier's 'Ville Contemporaine' expresses a radical idea of city in the way that urban space is predominantly made for cars and shaped by the planning paradigm of 'zoning' of urban functions – as advocated by CIAM's 'Charter of Athens'. Le Corbusier proposed the radical transformation of entire cities. Only twenty years later it became obvious that the separation of functions caused a loss of quality of mixed-use urban life. Le Corbusier's built works immediately faced criticism from many sources, for instance,

Courtesy: Le Corbusier Foundation

Ebenezer Howard's concept of 'The Garden City of Tomorrow' (developed 1902–10) proposed the radial arrangement of circular city clusters. However, the diameter of these proposed circles was 2 km and therefore not walkable. Le Corbusier's Ville Contemporaine and 'Plan Voisin' (1922/1925) was the utopian proposal of a zoned car-dependent city that became the basis for CIAM's Charter of Athens. (Source: LC Foundation)

from Jane Jacobs (`lack of community life'),
Rayner Banham (`failure in environmental
performance') and Jan Gehl (`public space
lacks human scale').

At the beginning of the 21st century, we experience with climate change a fundamental shift concerning the way we design and build communities and how we conceive of urban growth and public space. The aim is to reduce CO_2 emissions while maintaining the high quality of lifestyle. Some of the fundamental questions are:
• How can we enable controlled urban growth and an increase in wealth with considerable reductions in CO_2 emissions?
• How can we overcome the urban-rural disconnect and achieve a better symbiosis between the urban (city) and the hinterland (countryside)?

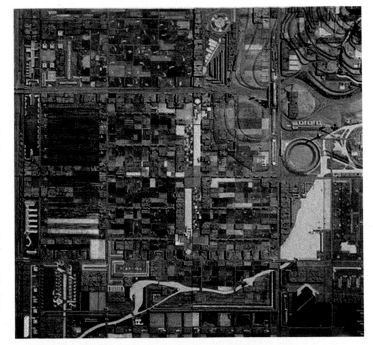

Courtesy: FL Wright Foundation

Frank L. Wright's `Broadacre City' project (from 1935 on) remained a romantic, unbuilt utopia, representing his longing for a self-supporting lifestyle and idea of an agricultural carpet city: A decentralized city structure, where every citizen grows food and lives self-sufficiently. (Source: courtesy F.L. Wright Foundation)

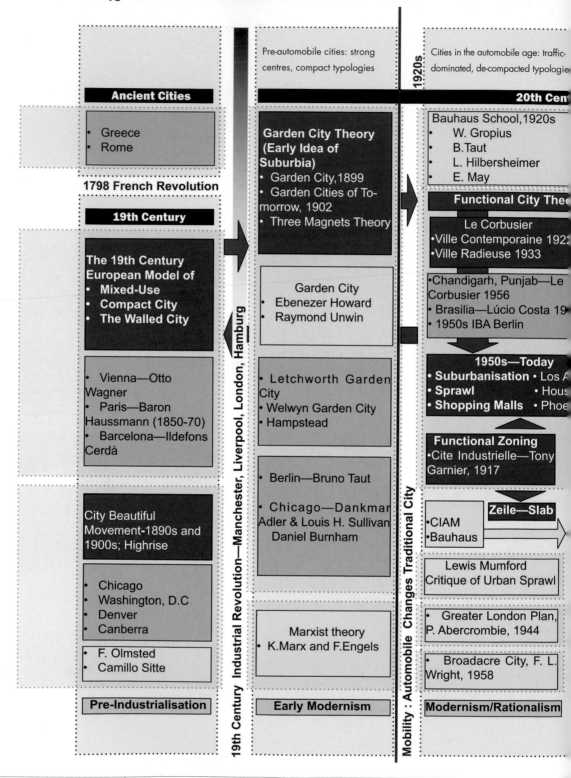

Pre-automobile cities: strong centres, compact typologies

1920s

Cities in the automobile age: traffic-dominated, de-compacted typologie

Ancient Cities

20th Cen

- Greece
- Rome

Garden City Theory (Early Idea of Suburbia)
- Garden City, 1899
- Garden Cities of Tomorrow, 1902
- Three Magnets Theory

Bauhaus School, 1920s
- W. Gropius
- B. Taut
- L. Hilbersheimer
- E. May

1798 French Revolution

Functional City Thee

19th Century

Le Corbusier
- Ville Contemporaine 192
- Ville Radieuse 1933

The 19th Century European Model of
- **Mixed-Use**
- **Compact City**
- **The Walled City**

Garden City
- Ebenezer Howard
- Raymond Unwin

- Chandigarh, Punjab—Le Corbusier 1956
- Brasilia—Lúcio Costa 19
- 1950s IBA Berlin

19th Century Industrial Revolution—Manchester, Liverpool, London, Hamburg

- Vienna—Otto Wagner
- Paris—Baron Haussmann (1850-70)
- Barcelona—Ildefons Cerdà

- Letchworth Garden City
- Welwyn Garden City
- Hampstead

1950s—Today
- **Suburbanisation** • Los A
- **Sprawl** • Hous
- **Shopping Malls** • Phoe

Functional Zoning
- Cite Industrielle—Tony Garnier, 1917

City Beautiful Movement-1890s and 1900s; Highrise

- Berlin—Bruno Taut
- Chicago—Dankmar Adler & Louis H. Sullivan Daniel Burnham

Zeile—Slab
- CIAM
- Bauhaus

Mobility : Automobile Changes Traditional City

- Chicago
- Washington, D.C
- Denver
- Canberra

- F. Olmsted
- Camillo Sitte

Lewis Mumford Critique of Urban Sprawl

Marxist theory
- K. Marx and F. Engels

- Greater London Plan, P. Abercrombie, 1944

- Broadacre City, F. L. Wright, 1958

Pre-Industrialisation

Early Modernism

Modernism/Rationalism

This diagram shows the development of city design over the last centuries: It lists the main tendencies in urban planning and the key protagonists of these tendencies. Two significant breaks are recorded. Firstly, the introduction of the automobile, which has led to the emergence of the *Functional City*. The second is climate change and its consequences. In both cases, fundamentally new models of cities are emerging.

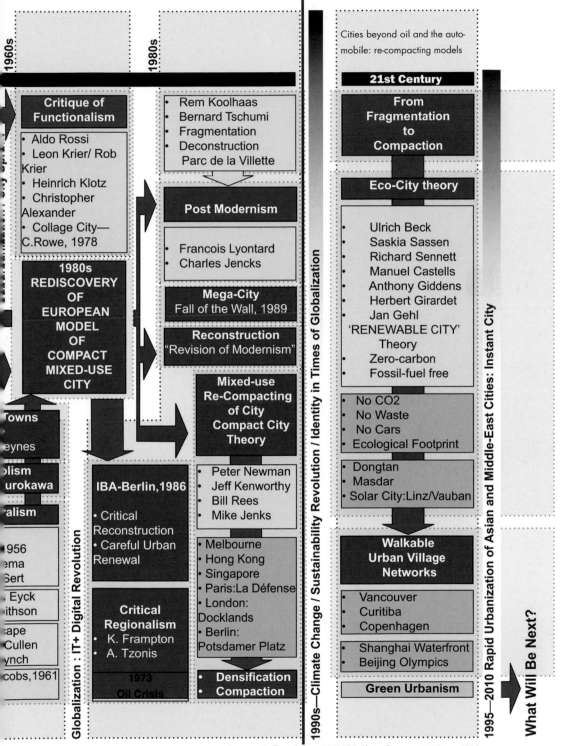

Diagram: Steffen Lehmann, UNESCO Chair. Illustration: W. Dong, 2008

In the 1920s, the introduction of the automobile and zoning leads to *Functional City* theory and the de-compacted, traffic-dominated city. Since the 1970s, the impact of the oil crisis and the gradual understanding of climate change has led to *Sustainable City* theory. The diagram also illustrates that these two fundamental influences have a similar ground-breaking effect on the entire following development of city typologies.

• `Spaceship Earth': Buckminster Fuller; Kenneth Boulding; Ian McHarg; *Club of Rome*.
Around 1965, the multi-talented American futurist Richard Buckminster Fuller introduced the term
`Spaceship Earth'. Working actively as an architect and designer of futuristic transport systems
and inventive structures, he expressed early concerns about sustainability, finite resources and
human survival. Rise of the `green movement' worldwide in the 1970s. `The Economics of the
Coming Spaceship Earth' by Kenneth Boulding (1966) pointed out, that in the past, there was
always some place else to go when things got too difficult and the environment too deteriorated.
McHarg's `Design with Nature' (1969) marked a turning point in the understanding the impact
of urban planning on the environment. Chermayeff and Tzonis define the theory of the `Third
Ecology' (1971). With `Limits of Growth', the Club of Rome argued in 1972 that economic
growth could not continue indefinitely. In the same year, the Stockholm Conference raises environmental concerns, and in 1975 Ernest Callenbach's utopian novel `Ecotopia' is published.

• The rediscovery of the European compact mixed-use city model.
The rediscovery of the `European City' type led to three main tendencies: *Critical Reconstruc-
tion, Post Modernism* and *Compact City* theory, and was formulated by Aldo Rossi, Christopher
Alexander, O. M. Ungers, Heinrich Klotz, Colin Rowe, Leon Krier and numerous others. Rossi
and Krier proclaimed the superiority of the block structure over the CIAM principles of free-
standing buildings in open space, and urban planners worldwide reverted to the urban block
as the best way to regulate the relationship between public and private space. It marks the end
of `Modernism' and its functionally zoned city model. The 1973 *Oil Crisis* had a huge impact
on rethinking cities, which were now understood as energy-hungry, stressed systems, out-of-
balance with nature and ecology. In the 1990s, the cities of Curitiba, Copenhagen and
Barcelona emerged as leaders of change and as models for new thinking about cities. In Berlin
at this time, the notion of `Behutsame Stadterneuerung' (`Careful, Soft Urban Renewal') was introduced. In 1987, the term `Sustainable Development' is introduced with the Brundtland Report.

• Three experimental examples of eco-cities: Auroville, Arcosanti and Curitiba.
These three examples of eco-city planning – Auroville (South India), Arcosanti (Arizona, USA), and
Curitiba (Brazil) – have been widely discussed, but have remained somewhat limited in their results
and been isolated, despite their early achievements. Low-energy infrastructure concepts for all three
cities started in the spirit of 1968 and were enabled through visionary leadership of a few pioneer
personalities, and step-by-step development. Curitiba was an already-existing city that moved in an
ecological direction (probably the most relevant of the three examples), while Auroville and Arcosanti were entirely new, somewhat esoteric urban developments, sometimes described as `ecologi-
cal authoritarianism'. 1992: The UN Rio Earth Conference introduces `Local Agenda 21' (LA21).

• At the end of the 20th century, Tokyo, Sao Paulo, Mexico-City, Mumbai, Calcutta,
Shanghai and Beijing have grown to become endless urban landscapes. They are new
types of mega-cities, which express an impossibility of orderly planning and strategic
regulation. In his 1994 essay, Rem Koolhaas asks `What ever happened to urbanism?'.
In 2000, the term `Climate Change' is getting widely introduced.

• Emerging *Green Urbanism* theory for the 21st century: from fragmentation to compaction. Eco-city theory focuses on adjusting the relationship between city and nature. Sociologists and urban theorists, including Ulrich Beck, Saskia Sassen, Richard Sennett, Jan Gehl, Manuel Castells, Anthony Giddens, Herbert Girardet, Thomas Sieverts, to name just a few, are exploring wider areas such as globalization, urban sustainability, ecology, network systems, information and communication technologies, and other related fields. Federico Butera, Ken Yeang, Richard Burdett, Jaime Lerner and Jeffrey Kenworthy also made some important contributions to the discussion of sustainable urban planning. Solar cities in Linz-Pichling (Austria), Freiburg-Vauban and the Solar District Freiburg-Schlierberg (Germany), Hanover-Kronsberg (Germany), Stockholm Hammarby-Sjöstad (Sweden), the *BedZED Development* in Sutton (South of London, UK), and the green district EVA Lanxmeer in Culemborg (The Netherlands) represent some of the built milestones in sustainable urban development at the beginning of the 21st century. The Swedish city of Vaexjö has been very successful in reducing its CO_2 emissions and will be, by 2015, entirely independent from fossil fuels. The industrial park in Kalundborg (Denmark) is often cited as a model for industrial ecology. The city of Waitakere, in the Western part of the greater Auckland urban region, is New Zealand's first eco-city. In the meantime, 'Sustainability Science' has emerged as a conceptual and theoretical basis for a new planning paradigm. Today, we can recognize two major breaks in the continuous development of cities. The first is connected to the introduction of the automobile, which made possible an entirely different, dispersed city model (the de-compacted 'Functional City'). The second, the full awareness of climate change, is of equal importance and just as far-reaching, raising the possibility of entirely new city models and typologies.

Defining the notions of `Eco-City' and `Sustainable Development'

The concept of 'Eco-City' was first raised by the UN as early as 1971. Richard Register was one of the earliest authors to help coin the term 'eco-city', in his 1987 book *Eco-city Berkeley: Building cities for a healthy future*. Unfortunately, there is still much confusion between the terms 'sustainability' and 'environmentalism'. In the same year, the Norwegian Premier, Mrs Gro H. Brundtland offered, in the pivotal 'Brundtland Report: Our Common Future', a wonderful definition of 'sustainable development', which I believe is still very appropriate:

Sustainable development is development that meets the needs of the present without compromising the ability of future generations to meet their own needs.   **Gro H. Brundtland, 1987**

So, what exactly is the definition of an eco-city? The Wikipedia defines *Eco-City* as follows: 'A sustainable city, or eco-city, is a city designed with consideration of environmental impact, inhabited by people dedicated to the minimization of required inputs of energy, water and food, and waste output of heat, air pollution – CO_2, methane, and water pollution'. It continues: 'A sustainable city can feed itself with minimal reliance on the surrounding countryside, and power itself with renewable sources of energy.' (Wikipedia, 2009) From this definition, it's obvious that the aim is to leave the smallest possible ecological footprint, to produce the lowest amount of pollution as possible, to efficiently use land, to compost and recycle used materials, or to use waste-to-energy technology, so that the city's or district's overall contribution to climate change is minimal. Wikipedia also offers a definition for an *Eco-Compact City*, which points in the same direction: `An *Eco-Compact City* is a city built and developed in balance with the natural environment. It is a city with clear boundaries, with an optimum ratio between density and network of open public spaces, defined by urban mixed-use blocks. The optimum density that characterizes the Eco-Compact City allows the existence of a rich system of small retail, while allowing the creation of an efficient public transit system, allowing its inhabitants to live within a pedestrian-friendly environment that encourages pedestrian movement, the use of public transit, and discourages the intensive use of automobiles.' (Wikipedia, 2009)

In adding to these definitions, I suggest that an *Eco-City*, or *Eco-District*, is a holistic urban design solution that enhances the wellbeing of its citizens, and society as a whole, through integrated urban planning and management that fully harnesses the benefits of ecological systems and renewable energies, and aims for zero-emissions and zero-waste. An Eco-City and Eco-District protects and nurtures its assets for future generations. It is an *ecological civilization*. Industrial civilization has dominated for 200 years. However, it has disregarded nature to the brink of collapse (global warming; climate change). Urban sprawl and environmental pollution have caused severe damage to ecological systems, especially around cities. Socially, industrial civilization has also failed. In an age of global travel and machine-mediated conversations, we have lost much of the real, lasting connections that once sustained communities. Today, *ecological civilization* is seeking a deeper meaning and is again looking to live in harmony with nature. Ecological civilization is the result of a profound reflection on traditional industrial civilization and its effects. The eco-city is the spatial carrier for an ecological, post-industrial civilization.

What will happen with the suburbs? The second life of suburban dreams

The flat, automobile-dominated American, or Australian, suburb is a low-density car-dependent urban area, a result of the age of consumerism, where land use and services are inefficient. The supply of water, energy and public transport can never be efficient in these low-density sprawling districts. As the desire to live in these isolated places diminishes, suburbs will be vacated. This offers us a chance to gradually recycle or eliminate them and even re-naturalize the land as greenfield sites, restoring forests and regenerating the degraded landscape. Vacated suburban houses could be dismantled and recycled, and the space returned to nature. Thus the rolling back of sprawling development enables the planting of new CO_2-absorbing trees.

Sprawl creates high land consumption, energy inefficiency and increased car ownership, but little production of housing.

For thousands of years cities were built for pedestrians, but the automobile changed that and has dictated, and has negatively influenced, urban planning and urban design since the 1920s. Cars dominate cities in rich countries, and they are increasingly swamping poor countries as well. As a result, the new city needs a decisive shift towards centres of car-reduced, mixed-use, high diversity and increased inter-connectedness to realize the required energy-efficiency to make these urban clusters work. Traveling distances in the 'functionally zoned, car-dependent city' (the paradigm for most of the 20th century) are just too great for walking or cycling, and the densities are too low to allow efficient, affordable public transport. Many cities have introduced designated 'urban growth boundaries' to stop the further expansion of the city's urban area, and to limit the decrease of farmland and open spaces around the cities. What is required is a polycentric urban system with an efficient transit-oriented infrastructure, with energy-efficient architecture built around compact centres, designed for pedestrians, cyclists and clean transport. This is the salient characteristic of future eco-districts. It is, therefore, necessary to rethink and re-engineer the way we design and build our cities and how they are operated and how they function as a whole. It is up to urban designers to offer acceptable alternatives in order to get people out of their cars. Californian ecologist Richard Register has pointed out: 'If we compare cities with living eco-systems or organisms, then the organs (infrastructure for transportation, living, working, education, shopping, recreation, manufacturing, etc) are linked together, and they reciprocally complement each other for the benefit of the whole. Shaping the existing city around transit-oriented, compact and vital centres has now been embedded in policies and masterplanning of most European municipalities, as a valid strategy for future urban development. These municipalities encourage building apartments with no car parking provided because residents don't need an automobile. In addition, free public transport in downtown areas is introduced by many cities – from Copenhagen to Stockholm, to Freiburg, to Portland – and more compact communities enjoy popularity.' (Register, 2007)

So, what will happen to the suburbs when it has become unaffordable to life there? We will either see suburban depletion (already, most of these houses have lost real estate value), or the transformation of the suburbs, progressing towards the mixed-use compact city model. Caused by changing demographics, more single housholds and a growing preference for urban lifestyles, the suburban dream of a big house is vanishing. Architects are now remaking the mono-functional suburb, densifying it into mixed-use town centres. In some way, the suburban housing model has created a paradox: the search for living in or close to *Nature* has made *Nature* slowly disappear.

We can break down cities into districts, neighbourhoods and communities.

Density and compactness – two important parameters

Given the complexity of urban planning, and the fact that cities cannot be changed or transformed quickly or easily (it will be a process spanning many years), we need to concentrate first on the components that can be most easily influenced and which will, therefore, deliver positive effects more quickly. For instance, traffic planning can be influenced in a shorter timeframe than, say, the existing building stock, which will require detailed long-term efforts. The impact of traffic planning is closely connected to the city structure and urban layout. That is not to say that maintaining and retrofitting the existing city structure is not also extremely important, compact and walkable districts help to mitigate energy losses of inefficient buildings and reduce CO_2 emissions from traffic. An eco-city, or eco-district, has to have a certain minimum density to deliver the discussed outcomes and to enable easy walking or cycling to key local facilities.

Most literature suggests an average density indicator of no less than 70 to 120 dwellings per hectare in central built-up areas, while even higher densities seem appropriate when analyzing the best European projects (such as Vauban, or Hammarby-Sjöstad). It is vitally important that eco-districts dramatically reduce the need to travel long distances and that sustainable mobility options with regard to public transport are provided. At the same time, there is consensus about re-connecting living with working, making both local options so that you live close to where you work. A suggested target for local employment opportunities is 65 per cent, ideally, though, it would be closer to 80 per cent of employment within walking, cycling or public transport distance. As a rule one could say that one local job or workplace for each household is ideal.

Compactness is equally important as *density*. While there is a danger of over-developing a place (too much density), we can never have too much compactness, that is to say, the optimum relationship between a block's surface (sqm) and its volume (cbm). For the block that makes up the city structure, the ideal is to have less external surface but with a larger volume. A cube would be an ideal shape, if the day-lighting can be resolved; it identifies the optimum geometry for energy-efficiency. The compact blocks of the 19th-century European city (such as we find in Paris, Barcelona or Berlin), with their solid walls (often 500mm thick) and shared circulation, have the most efficient and compact layout. The 1960s urban model of dispersed rows of housing slabs (with much distance between them), forming large mono-functional housing quarters at the periphery, are, energy-wise, the most problematic; these represent the model that has a high car-dependency and a short life expectancy. (Curdes, 1992) Developments need to be pursued as both renewal and densification/infill projects. For instance, pseudo-romantic `eco-villages' which are located 20 or 30 kilometres away from the city centre only offer the possibility of further damage, as they will lead to further sprawl, more transport and loss of green space. Promoting a more intensive land-use with compact models is the first step to climate-proofing the urban development. There is now a need to build more energy-efficient districts as demonstration projects. (The topic of density is further discussed in Chapter 4)

Single inner-city households really consuming more?

Any future implementation of more compact, denser city expansions will need to deal with the issues and challenges that come with higher densities, less distance between buildings, possible loss of green space, social changes and conflicts in inter-neighbourhood relationships as a result of multi-apartment housing. Critiques of increasing density, for example the research work of Dey et al, argue that inner-city, single-person households (with their higher incomes) can have a negative impact on the environment, because they consume significantly more than households in less affluent suburban areas. (Dey et al, 2008). At the same time, the large suburban dwelling is often less insulated and full of energy-consuming appliances and gadgets. Household decisions are influenced by a range of factors, such as the size of physical spaces of dwellings, and issues of social status and cultural values. In Sydney, some 25 per cent of the population lives in multi-unit housing, which has already started to change the social fabric. This proportion is still low in comparison with European cities, but it is predicted to grow to 45 to 50 per cent by 2030. (Newman and Kenworthy, 1989; Burton, 2000) A recent survey in Europe indicated that around 60 per cent of all households in the cities of Zurich, Munich and Frankfurt are now single households (2009). So it raises the question: What kind of housing typologies and concepts are required? Lifestyles within a household can vary considerably. It's impossible to exactly predict how individuals will behave and how much 'sustainable behaviour' will occur. But if we make it easier for residents to act sustainably, for instance by putting the design ideas of this publication into future urban plans, it is more likely that households will perform as expected. With this in mind, future theories of eco-systems should increasingly be applied to entire urban systems, with the aim of strengthening the environmental sustainability and dynamic intensity of urban activities by, for example, ensuring the vitality and quality of public space. A clear advantage of applying such evolutionary approaches in urban design will be that the complexity of urban life and its related processes will be better understood.

Our affluence allows us to accumulate massive amounts of stuff, and we build increasingly larger dwellings to store it.   *Douglas Farr, 2008*

Another challenge is the property ownership model. There is a difference between properties developed for ownership and those for rental, where the chance for environmental sustainable design and technology is much smaller. When renting a property that features power or water saving technology, the owner can not charge more for that dwelling, whereas, an owner builder is more likely to invest in those technologies for the long term savings. We have to develop smarter economic models that support investment in technology, even for rental properties. However, it cannot be ignored that although the anti-sprawl critique, so eloquently raised by Jacobs, Cullen, Mumford and Lynch at the beginning of the 1960s, has led to a negative image of suburbanization, suburban living has remained popular despite its low-density living style causing inefficiencies on many levels: land use, water and energy use, public transport, car dependency, and so on. Currently, the suburban house is a very large house (data 2009: Australians have the largest houses per capita worldwide), consuming huge amounts of energy for cooling in summer. But we must make a change somewhere and inner-city living means, usually, smaller places with less square metres per capita and which consume less energy. [1]

Concepts of urban energy systems: *Energy-Plus-Cities*[+]
In general, the most commonly used energy resources are the following: CO_2-emitting fossil-fuel based resources (oil, gas and coal). Most countries are depending on imports of these resources. Burning coal is the dirtiest form to generate energy, and has huge health impacts which have not much been discussed (or calculated in the price of energy generated from burning coal). Coal resources are estimated to last another 200 years, whereas gas probably another 60 years, and oil has recently peaked and might become already hard to get in less than 10 years (most experts agree, that *Peak Oil* happened in 2008 and was one of the reasons for the *Global Financial Crisis*). This is why we talk about *Peak Oil* and the *Post-Oil City*. Since there is no reliable way to solve the question of disposal of nuclear waste, which might be active up to 100,000 years, we cannot seriously consider nuclear energy as a future-proof solution. This leaves us with five other forms

of energy. Renewable energies do not emit CO_2 and are infinite, which means we can harness these powers from nature without damaging the environment. Wind power, solar power, hydro power, biomass, and geothermal power (hot rocks) are the most commonly used, but their availability depends on the location. Eco-cities and eco-districts will need to be powered by an energy mix, harnessing a major part of renewable energy sources.
Recent research published by the Urban Land Institute and by Arup (ULI, `Growing Cooler', 2007. Arup, `Towards an Ecological Age', 2008) gives comprehensive evidence that there is a direct connection between urban development, urbanization and climate change. Findings point to the principles of sustainable urban growth leading to human settlements that enable their residents to live a healthier quality of life, while using minimal natural resources and supporting maximum biodiversity.

What exactly makes an Eco-District or Eco-City? In Chapter 2, the `Principles of Green Urbanism' are explained in detail to illustrate the holistic nature of the task but as a pointer to how eco-cities can be achieved here are some essential criteria:
• Mixed-use urban consolidation, to ensure that new homes are close to employment, education, shopping, health services, etc., giving the option to walk and to bike (raising mobility concepts such as the *City of Short Distances*, providing good pedestrian linkages, cyclist facilities and safe bike paths), and to use efficient public transport, thus reducing car dependency.
• Urban layouts that allow improved public transport and an increase in pedestrianization to radically reduce car emissions. This requires a very different approach to city planning, where the public domain network and public mass transit are given priority. It is crucial to identify the right mode of low-emission public transport system in each case (e.g. buses, light rail, subway, or other modes). Public mass transit in all major urban corridors must always be given priority, to be faster than private vehicle traffic.
• Residential and office typologies need to be multi-storey, flexible and compact to maximize the land available for green space and gardens, and avoiding sprawl (in Europe, we can recognize already a `renaissance' of the five-storey urban block and town house models).
• Buildings that make the best use of passive design principles and renewable energy sources, such as sun, wind, biogas, geothermal, rainfall (collecting rainwater through green roofs), on-site energy production, and natural cross-ventilation. Applying passive design concepts minimizes the primary energy demands of cities and buildings while maximizing the efficiency of the energy supply (See Fig. 2).
• Power, water and waste systems are decentralized, neighbourhood-based and small-scale (not large and centralized); with urban water management strategies to be integrated.
• Public buildings to be demonstration projects and to become `green icons' that can be replicated. The building should have adaptive facades. The envelope decides about 50 per cent of the energy use, so it needs to be designed depending on orientation, sun angle and climate, e.g. with sun shading angles that can be altered to offset or to optimize solar glare and avoid heat gain.
• Various methods are in place to reduce the need for energy-intensive air-conditioning, such as planting trees, using natural cross-ventilation systems, an increase in water bodies in the city, and green spaces equaling at least 20 to 25 per cent of the city's surface. Every building should have a green roof

or roof garden. These measures counter the `heat island effect' caused by an increase of density and an abundance of asphalt and hard surfaces storing heat, which can make urban areas several degrees warmer than the surrounding rural areas – as much as six degrees Celsius is not uncommon.

• Minimum 50 per cent, up to 100 per cent, of all energy generated from renewable energy sources, such as wind turbines, solar panels, or biogas created from sewage and organic waste. City districts provide economies of scale that make such energy sources viable and can turn all new buildings into zero-net energy buildings.

• Urban designs that emphasize development on land, which has previously been developed

Fig. 1: This diagram by Eco-CityProjects.net illustrates the many different requirements, that a new type of city or district is required to fulfill, to be regarded as successful by its many stakeholders. It is important to balance urban development by clearly defining how the strategies will deliver the priority goals. (Diagram: Courtesy Eco-CityProjects.net, 2008)

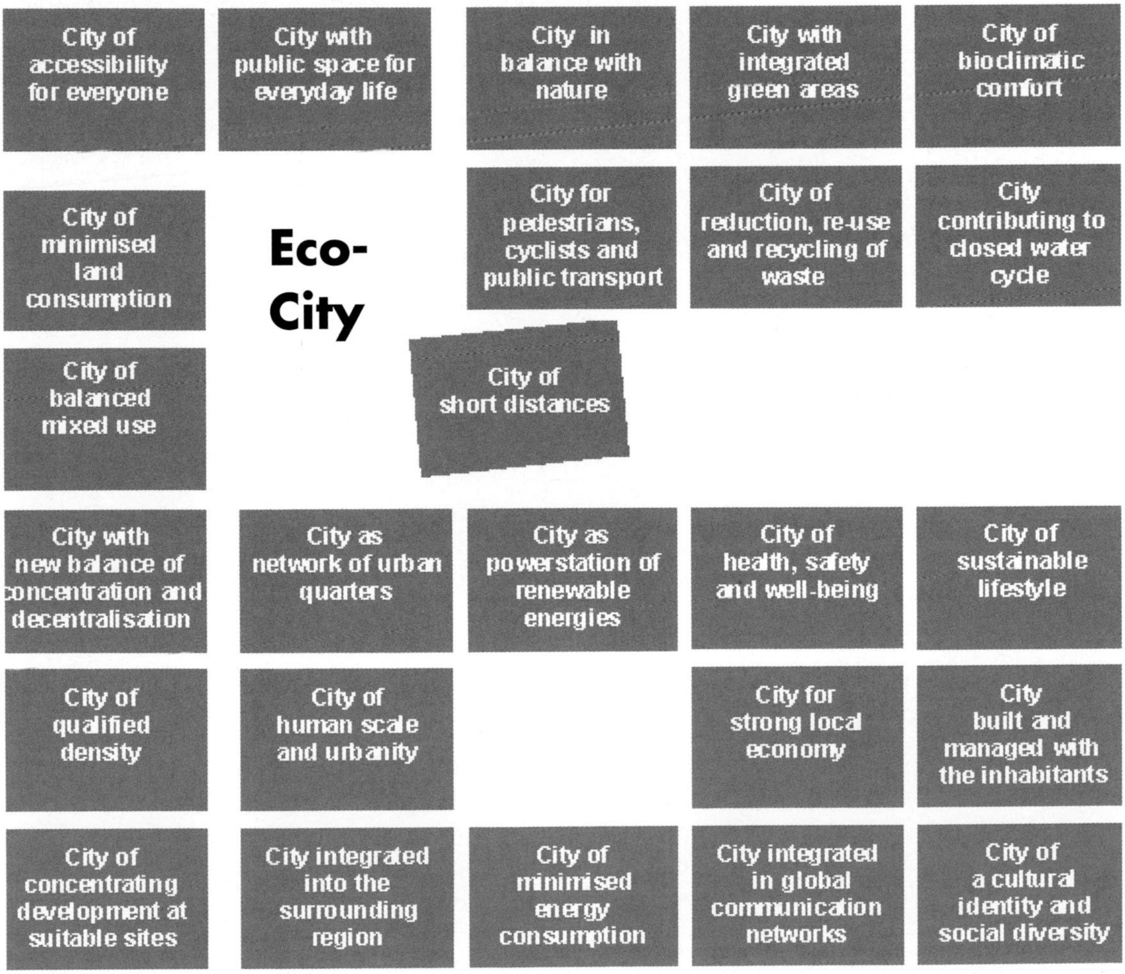

City of accessibility for everyone	City with public space for everyday life	City in balance with nature	City with integrated green areas	City of bioclimatic comfort
City of minimised land consumption	**Eco-City**	City for pedestrians, cyclists and public transport	City of reduction, re-use and recycling of waste	City contributing to closed water cycle
City of balanced mixed use		City of short distances		
City with new balance of concentration and decentralisation	City as network of urban quarters	City as powerstation of renewable energies	City of health, safety and well-being	City of sustainable lifestyle
City of qualified density	City of human scale and urbanity		City for strong local economy	City built and managed with the inhabitants
City of concentrating development at suitable sites	City integrated into the surrounding region	City of minimised energy consumption	City integrated in global communication networks	City of a cultural identity and social diversity

and is of little ecological value (inner-city densification and infill projects; re-use of formerly industrial brownfield sites), integrating existing structures, with a strong emphasis on adaptive reuse and retrofitting.
• Developments where a high proportion of building materials are designed for modular prefabrication, re-use, disassembly and recycling, to minimize the consumption of materials and creation of waste.
• A shift from masterplanning to 'strategic planning', which reflects best practice of compactness, orientation, density vs. overshadowing, and appropriate internal location of cores to optimize concepts of passive design and maximum day-lighting.
• Optimal building density to make public transport viable while avoiding the creation of urban heat islands.
• Decreasing urban sprawl by seeking new ways of allowing people to live closer to their workplaces, and developing new inner-city housing typologies. Since the workplace tends to be in the city centre, one way is to increase density and change the out-dated mentality and behaviour many suburban residents still have towards living in inner-city areas.
• Green space provided that aims to protect and enhance local biodiversity and reduce the urban heat island effect.
• Materials, food and other goods that are sourced from nearby. This will help cut CO_2 emissions caused by transport through shorter supply chains. This includes urban farming using different agricultural systems such as small-scale agricultural plots within the city, thus reducing the distance food has to travel to the plate. The *Cradle-to-Cradle* (C2C) concept has described such a circular economy of materials and closed-loop processes.
• Strict waste management to reduce waste going to landfill and waste during construction; using waste-to-energy strategies, making better use of waste streams; it's better to prevent waste creation in the first place, than to treat or clean-up waste after it has formed.
• The integration of existing buildings (instead of demolition), adaptive reuse and the promotion of cultural heritage (instead of the unproductive 'heritage versus development' debate).
• *Design for Disassembly* (DfD) means that building components are modular and prefabricated, and separate operations are designed to maximize energy, material efficiency and the potential for reuse. This requires that material diversity in multi-component products is minimized to facilitate disassembly and value retention.

Importantly, most of the abovementioned criteria need to be implemented at a very early stage of any development, and some are already detailed within the selection of a site. In the same way, early decisions need to be made about shape and compactness as they have ramifications on the crucial ratio that exists between volume and façade surface. (See: Fig. 3) Only with an optimized ratio can unnecessary heat gain (in summer) or heat loss (in winter) be avoided.

Five basic concepts for sustainable urban development: transforming districts towards low-to-no-carbon urbanism

In regard to compactness of building volume and the importance of retrofitting the existing building stock, Moewes noted in 1995: 'New buildings do never save energy. It is important to understand that the construction of new buildings can never save energy, only the upgrading and retrofitting of existing building stock. Also, the so-called *Energy Saving House* does not save any energy; it just reduces the amount of additionally consumed energy. (...) Compact buildings with larger volume are always more energy-efficient compared to smaller volume buildings. Based on the energy losses in winter and heat gains in summer, the detached family house is the most inefficient form of building; it also consumes too much precious landscape. The 19th-century city block is still an extremely efficient model. (...) The danger of a large cube-like building shape is the issue that it creates deep plans which lead to dark interior areas, dependent on artificial lighting.' (Moewes, 1995; translated by the author)

In addition, we can identify the following 5 essential points for achieving sustainable urban development:
1. The battle against climate change must be fought in cities. Sustainable urban design has the potential to deliver significant positive effects.
2. It is particularly important not to demolish existing buildings, due to their embodied energy and materials. There needs to be a focus on integration, on adaptive reuse and on retrofitting of the existing building stock.
3. A compact urban form with mixed-use programmes and a strong focus on low-impact public transport will deliver the best outcomes. To de-carbonize the energy supply, we need to install small distributed systems in the city, based on renewable energy sources.
4. Stop enlarging the urban footprint and halt sprawl, and protect the precious landscape and agricultural land. Therefore increasing the density of the city and intensifying uses within the existing city boundary.
5. Change includes a whole range of different initiatives that will deliver significant CO_2-emission reductions – it is not one strategy or measure alone.

An attitude of making *place* and *space*

When we revisit the architecture of the masters Louis Kahn or Alvar Aalto, we find that those architects designed buildings based on what they regarded as 'timeless fundamentals', such as the human experience of space, but we also realize a resourcefulness in their use of locally supplied materials. Both masters designed naturally ventilated office buildings (even for the tropics) and incorporated climate-responsive design principles long before the notion of 'sustainable architecture' was introduced.
Seminars accompanying my design studio initiatives at various leading universities illustrated how green principles can creatively support the architect's main design concept (not as a later add-on), and how the basic knowledge of such strategies as night-time cooling, evaporative cooling, solar chimneys, cross-ventilation and thermal mass have existed for centuries, even millennia. Students were introduced to the notion that *sustainability in architecture* is about a fundamental attitude of making place and space, and less about the technological solution for mechanical ventilation or additive mechanical solutions. It was important at the outset of the studio that students recognized that architecture is predominantly about establishing meaning, about the human experience and substance and not about technological machine type sophistication. Therefore a 'green building' is not

always automatically a good work of architecture; to be considered a good work of architecture today, the building has to be energy-effective. (Lehmann, 2005; Scott, 2006) Architecture and urban design have the potential to re-establish our relationship with nature, the climate and the experience of the sun, rain and wind. As Scott notes, such environmentally responsible design is at its best 'when it achieves an outcome in which the environmentally sensible elements are closely linked to the design process and go beyond being additive and become meaningful parts of an architectural whole.' (Scott, 2006) Integration of sustainability within the design process demands that the environmental concept and the urban design concept fully support each other. Re-establishing architecture as a discipline of appropriate ideas requires the identification of environmental strategies that support a unique design idea, which, for instance, reinforces the urban district's, or building's, relationship with the landscape.

Is a better symbiosis between countryside and city possible again?

For hundreds of years, cities were in symbiosis with their rural hinterland: cities provided security, trade markets and religious meaning for the peasantry outside the city. In exchange, the countryside provided a supply of food and materials. With industrialization, this symbiosis has been lost.

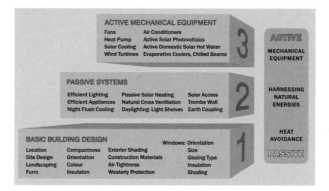

Fig. 2: Diagram of three steps from passive building design to active mechanical equipment. As designers we need to take full advantage of basic, passive building strategies first, before adding any mechanical active equipment. Motto: 'Achieving more with less'. (For a larger version of diagram, see following page 87).

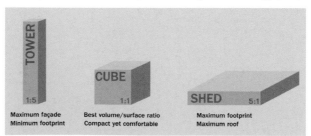

Fig. 3: The search for optimal compactness of buildings ('compact yet comfortable') is relevant, as we want to maximize the passive solar gain without resulting in overheating in summer. Cube-shaped buildings minimize energy loss and heat gain. However, the ideal building shape does not exist; the optimization process depends each time on location, climate and orientation. We don't want a 'city of cubes' either. (Diagrams: S. Lehmann, UNESCO Chair, 2007)

With the end of the 'old' fossil-fuel energy system, urban designers can re-think the relationship between city and countryside as a whole, where the city does not grow at the expense of its rural hinterland. It can be assumed that in ten or fifteen years, the concept of decentralized, distributed energy generation will become standard for newly planned models of green neighbourhoods, where the existing infrastructure of the long-distance grid network will become obsolete and sustainable city districts will be able to act as powerstations for their own demand. In this scenario, consumers become producers. Every citizen in such green districts could generate the energy needed locally and become self-sufficient, and even sell green energy back into the grid (something that has become a reality in Germany due to the government's clever feed-in tariffs for green energy). (See: Fig. 4) The result will be housing districts that generate more energy than they consume. It's expected that the ability to cheaply store this energy as back-up within the community will soon be solved by the development of better battery technology within the next few years. With decentralized systems for energy-generating city districts and zero-waste concepts, the large polluting power plant or landfill rubbish dump in the countryside will become history. The urban settlement can again enter a symbiosis with the surrounding countryside.

The earth's surface consists of two-thirds ocean and one-third land. We have an abundance of salt water; however, the lack of fresh water is a huge global challenge. The land area can be divided into three parts: one dominated by human activity (where the cities are); another by forests (which is steadily shrinking); and the third by desert (which is increasing in size). In other words, we have plenty of deserts that we need to make green again.

In the Asia-Pacific, in the Brazilian Amazon, and in the highly developed countries in Europe, agricultural land and precious natural landscapes are being turned into urban environments. The Annual Report 2009, Statistisches Bundesamt, Wiesbaden documents the growth area of urban settlements and traffic infrastructure in Germany as being the size of 150 soccer fields, or 104 ha. From 2005 to 2008, German cities grew by over 1,500 sq km (by 3.3 per cent). At the same time, agricultural land has shrunk by 0.9 per cent (this is 1,679 sq km). Luckily, the area of sustainably grown forest increased by 0.8 per cent (to 861 sq km). Can denser, more compact cities support 100 per cent of their energy requirements through localized solar and wind energy generation, therefore containing urban growth? While it might not yet be fully technically feasible for every site, there are a couple of demonstration projects that are 100 per cent based on renewable energy, and the local use of solar and wind energy allows the reconnection of energy production with the place of final energy consumption. The possibility for decentralized, on-site energy production through small units close to the point of energy consumption, offers up the chance for an entirely new type of urbanism to emerge. The notion of the city district as powerstation is a reality. (See: Fig. 4)

Urban intensification and densification
In the debate about sustainable urban development, the existing city centre will play an essential role. Triggered by demographic change, increasing petrol costs and the rediscovery of the

GREEN URBANISM

ENERGY and MATERIALS

- Embodied energy
- Material specification
- Supply chain
- Renewable energy solutions
- Energy sources and consumption
- Construction systems
- Prefabrication and recycling
- Energy efficiency
- Resource management

WATER and BIODIVERSITY

- Urban water management
- Water recycling and irrigation
- Urban Farming
- Urban landscape typologies
- Ecosystems' biodiversity maximized
- Grey water recycling
- Storage of urban stormwater
- Climate change impact management
- Waste management

URBAN PLANNING and TRANSPORT

- Urban design
- Social sustainability
- Ecological city theory
- Health and walkability
- Mobility, public Transport
- Infrastructure
- Energy efficient buildings
- Mixed land use
- Housing affordability
- Reducing car dependency
- Subdivisions

Interaction between three main pillars

This diagram illustrates the conceptual model of 'Green Urbanism' (Lehmann, 2006), where a holistic approach and the optimum interaction between the three pillars of: Energy and Materials, Water and Biodiversity, and Urban Planning and Transport improves the environmental, economic and social sustainability of cities. On the scale of the city district, this involves a highly complex interweaving of inter-dependent components.

The three steps from passive to active

ACTIVE MECHANICAL EQUIPMENT

Fans	Air Conditioners
Heat Pump	Active Solar Photovoltaics
Solar Cooling	Active Domestic Solar Hot Water
Wind Turbines	Evaporative Coolers, Chilled Beams

3

PASSIVE SYSTEMS

Efficient Lighting	Passive Solar Heating	Solar Access
Efficient Appliances	Natural Cross Ventilation	Trombe Wall
Night Flush Cooling	Daylighting: Light Shelves	Earth Coupling

2

BASIC BUILDING DESIGN

Windows: Orientation

Location	Compactness	Exterior Shading	Size
Site Design	Orientation	Construction Materials	Glazing Type
Landscaping	Colour	Air Tightness	Insulation
Form	Insulaton	Westerly Protection	Shading

1

ACTIVE

MECHANICAL
EQUIPMENT

HARNESSING
NATURAL
ENERGIES

HEAT
AVOIDANCE

PASSIVE

'Eco-buildings' are now getting increasingly built in many cities and celebrated for setting new benchmarks. But will they deliver sufficient impact in energy savings to be effective in reducing greenhouse gas emissions to stop climate change?

Diagram of the three steps, from basic passive building design principles to active mechanical equipment. Passive design comes first, before adding technical solutions; the aim is 'to achieve more with less'. There is now a need to update the old 'rule of thumb' methods, e.g. for better day-ligthing and more effective use of building mass, and to make scientific progress on these issues. (Lehmann, 2008) Below: Bank building with solar chimneys, Melbourne (BVN).

qualities of living and working in or next to the city centre, the practices of densification and urban infill will put an end to the current expansion of the city's footprint into the periphery. Re-engineering of existing city districts will include retrofitting and the intensification of the districts and quarters adjacent to (or part of) the city centre area. We are already experiencing a trend where city centres in developed countries – regardless of overall population growth or shrinkage – have to cope with an increased demand for all forms of mixed-use intensification. New mixed-use typologies for inner-city densification and the reuse of centrally located brownfield sites is essential in the process of re-urbanizing city centres and the return from the suburbs, or *Zwischenstadt* (the peri-urban), to live in the city. The city core offers short distances, walkability, a high degree of local identity, place-making and opportunities for social interaction.

The design studios explored these tendencies and identified strategies for typical post-industrial city centres, such as Newcastle, NSW. We predict that the intensification of usage will lead to growth and `compactation' towards the core, rather than to further sprawl beyond the edges, with:

- Four- to eight-storey mixed-use blocks (not high-rise, but urban blocks)
- better use of the so far mostly unused roofscape and
- intensification of use on sites of outdated infrastructure (such as former powerstations, port facilities, car parking structures).

In this scenario, the existing public open spaces and parks will gain a new significance, thus they will need to be protected and improved.

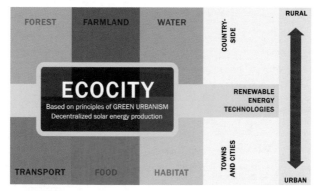

Fig. 4: The entire urban metabolism is based on energy, food supply and waste disposal. In the recent debate, a new symbiosis between countryside and city is emerging: the century-old tension between the rural and urban condition can finally be resolved, where the city stops growing at the expense of its rural hinterland (growth boundary). It is even predicted that new city typologies will emerge out of the better re-connection between the city and the countryside. (Diagram: S. Lehmann, 2006)

Sustainable future transport: a clean mass transit system is essential

The transportation sector accounts for 30 per cent of global end-consumer energy consumption and is responsible for almost 15 per cent of global greenhouse gas emissions. Emissions are growing rapidly, as more and more of the world's inhabitants are able to buy cars and afford air travel, and as an increasing number of goods are being transported. Mobility is going to substantially increase in the future, which means transportation must become more environmentally friendly. In the EU, private cars alone are responsible for 12 per cent of CO_2 emissions. Long-term future planning is essential for transport network corridors. Congestion reduces efficiency and restrains all parts of the economy. Much of the present transport infrastructure is ageing and is constrained by outdated technologies. Fortunately, there are solutions that will reduce both CO_2 emissions and other pollution from this sector. One such solution is the electric vehicle. They are quieter and use only a quarter as much energy as a petrol-driven vehicle. In an electric car, electricity from the battery is converted to kinetic energy with 95 per cent efficiency, whereas combustion engines have an efficiency of only 20 to 30 per cent, with the remainder lost through hot exhaust and the radiator. Driving with an electric motor increases energy efficiency by a factor of 3 to 4 – similar to replacing incandescent light bulbs with energy-saving lamps. The usage of electrical energy will obviously increase due to this usage but if the electricity is generated from renewable sources, electric vehicles have neutral emissions.

If we want a good economy in the long term, we need technologies that are clean and preserve resources. This is an economy which doesn't grow at the cost of our health and the environment.

There are many new approaches to the automobile and its future (reduced) place in the city centre. Reclaiming the city from the dominance of the car means accepting that roads are public spaces, and priority should be given to pedestrians and cyclists. Most cities have no capacity to absorb an increase in cars on their roads and the congestion the present limits cause results in a crying need for the introduction of emissions-free public transportation as soon as possible. High-quality bus services with dedicated bus lanes are an inexpensive alternative to tram and train lines. They do not require the same infrastructure development and the vehicles cost much less than trains. For this reason, many cities have adopted a *Bus Rapid Transport System* for their public transportation. One such example is the Columbian capital Bogota, which built a very popular high-standard bus route in 2000, with four dedicated bus lanes (following Curitiba's model, which is described later in this chapter). Several other cities and countries in Latin America, Asia and Africa have established, or are establishing, similar systems. High-standard bus routes are a natural choice in most city areas. A well developed public transportation network persuades more people to choose a more environmentally-friendly transportation alternative than taking the car.

There is now a strong focus on developing climate-friendly technologies for low-emission buses, using technologies such as hydrogen and bio-fuels. Innovations are in fact changing transit systems on all fronts and in the future it is easy to see high-speed trains replacing short-haul air traffic and new forms of sustainable bio-fuels replacing fossil-fuels in other air traffic. In the longer term, shipping may use hydrogen, producing only steam as exhaust.

Changing industrial manufacturing processes

The need for industrial products is expected to increase substantially in the coming decades, as the world's steadily increasing population attains a higher standard of living. However, industry uses enormous amounts of energy and water; industrial activity causes 40 per cent of the world's CO_2 emissions and 30 per cent of its energy use. Half of the world's electricity generation is needed to run factories. In addition, vast amounts of coal, gas, oil and biomass are burned to produce heat. Industry is exploring better energy management, more efficient pumps, compressors and cooling systems. Even though many companies in the past few decades have made great progress in energy efficiency and in cutting emissions (as well as material consumption and waste creation), the total production volume has increased more rapidly. The result is that industry's total greenhouse gas emissions and energy use has constantly increased. The key to solving the industrial climate challenge is a strong focus on developing more efficient manufacturing processes for cleaner, fully-recyclable products. Frequently, even if the more efficient technology already exists and is profitable, it will not automatically be used, so governments need to encourage companies to use the best available processes and technologies.

Aluminium is, for example, amongst the world's most important materials, for its unique qualities, being light-weight and strong. However, the production of aluminium requires a large amount of electricity. Production of aluminium has doubled in the last 20 years, and it is expected that the world will use three times more aluminium by 2050 as today (e.g. aluminium is necessary to produce lighter cars and air crafts, and much used in construction). Aluminium smelter plants emit CO_2 and require huge amounts of electricity, which in most countries is supplied by coal and gas-fired power stations. The chemical industry is now trying to find 'replacement' materials, a polycarbonate, or a polymer-based, equally light-weight and strong material, that is fully recyclable and can replace aluminium (plastics are already used as alternative to aluminium in the automobile industry).

Recycling and waste management has become a major driver of sustainability and a source for energy generation. In regard to waste, we can learn much from nature's symbiosis. In nature there is no 'waste'; all waste products from one organism are used by others. Factories and their industrial processes need energy, materials and infrastructure to produce useful products, but they also produce large amounts of waste. If we follow nature's example, we may find that what is waste for one company is a useful resource for another.

The selected case study: background to the City of Newcastle

The three recent examples for the application of such sustainable urban design principles in studio teaching were proposals for the Australian city of Newcastle: The 'City Campus', 'Green Corridor' and 'Port City' projects (studios in 2006–09).

These realistic case studies gave a cohort of Year 4 and 5 students a specific focus: to illustrate that it is less environmentally damaging to stimulate growth within the established city centre, than to have it sprawling into formerly un-built greenfield areas. The studio programme did not aim at only a few green buildings, but targeted Newcastle's changing, post-industrial city centre area. A crucial aspect was the shift in scale from the level of individual buildings to the cluster and district level.

The urban development of Newcastle, from its foundation in 1804 to a free settler town, is well documented in Robert Hughes's historical book 'The Fatal Shore', where a compelling account is given of the harsh early years of life in Australia's urban settlements. (Hughes, 1987) Hughes tells the story of Newcastle's settlement and development from a tiny convict outpost to an important port town. The city's more recent urban development is discussed in Clive Forster's publication 'Australian Cities. Continuity and Change' (Forster, 1999). Australian cities are growing today at a rate of around 2.5 per cent per year. Most of the time, the resulting demand for housing is met through the unsustainable development of greenfield sites at the fringes of the cities, further fueling urban sprawl and increasing the city's footprint at the expense of the hinterland.

How is Newcastle changing today? Newcastle is experiencing the same trends as all Australian cities: urban growth due to people gravitating to a coastal lifestyle (the so-called 'sea changers'), which offers the designer the opportunity to do planning corrections while accommodating new residents. This growth has ramifications for the densification of the urban footprint, which also includes suburbia. The ethnic composition of the city is also changing. While the most common non-Australian-born immigrants used to come from the UK and New Zealand, since 2008 the main influx of new migrants has come from China and India. It is expected that the ethnic mix will continue to change over the next 20 years and we will see a vastly more cosmopolitan community, with a critical mass of Asian and second and third generation Mediterranean influences. Gone will be the singular Anglo dominance of the 20th century. It can also be expected that Newcastle will be a part of the changes predicted for other regional and coastal towns, i.e. the decentralization of jobs from Sydney due to a rise in telecommuting; and an increase in the proportion of older people, with particular housing needs, e.g. apartments for 'aging in place'. In addition, inner-city housing will need to stay affordable for a wide range of different groups.

There was much engagement of the studio participants with the actualities of the site, with various stakeholders and real planning processes. The design parameters of these studios were based on the formulation and development of principles for green urbanism and sustainable neighbourhoods, with specific investigations about the future of urban energy and water supply, mobility, mixed-use, emerging housing typologies, and concepts of urban farming.

For over one hundred years, the city of Newcastle was the most industrialized city in Australia, hosting all the (polluting) heavy industries, such as steel manufacturing, aluminum smeltering, coal mining and ship building. The city centre was designed around the one function: to transport and load coal and other goods onto ships in Wharf Road, something that hasn't happened for a long time. Employment in manufacturing, mining and heavy industries in the Hunter Region have, historically, always been high. In 1960 it accounted for over 40 per cent of jobs, today it is 25 per cent. (data: HVRF, 2009). Only coal mining and exporting is still booming. As a result, the identity of the city has changed. This 'new de-industrialized identity' (which is still in the process of evolving) is connected with a growing service sector, creative industries, education and conference tourism. Growing employment sectors are in education, training and health care. (see: data on HVRF website)

For Newcastle city centre, the official modest employment and population predictions are: 10,000 new jobs and 6,500 new residents in the next 20 years. Since 1996, people have started to move back into the city centre, and, over the last ten years, the city centre has witnessed a population increase of around 5,000 residents. Exploring these issues about the transformation of Newcastle offered a good starting point for the studio projects.

The heart of every great region is a vibrant urban core that embodies the spirit of the place and serves as the social, economic and spiritual heart of the community.
In Newcastle, the missing piece in the urban core is the connection between the historical city centre and the revitalized urban waterfront.

Newcastle's changing face: the shift from an industrial to a service society

Previously derelict land and former industrial sites in a prime waterfront location are now ripe for development. The major urban regeneration development (the Honeysuckle development) was started in 1992, with the NSW State Government's 'Building Better Cities' programme, and in 2010 it is almost completed. It has redeveloped 50 hectares of derelict land and buildings along Newcastle Harbour, adjacent to the city centre. The development has introduced a denser form of apartment living and retail. However, it is

| 'Growth Area' | Heritage | Leisure |
| City West | City East | Nobbys |

Fig. 5: The city of Newcastle, once Australia's most industrialized city, is the capital of the Hunter Region, located around 150 kilometers north of Sydney, in the state of New South Wales. The greater population catchments of the Newcastle area are around 600,000 people. The city centre is located on a narrow peninsula between the Pacific Ocean and the port. Through its close proximity to the city centre, the area around the Inner Harbour and Dyke Point (see 'Growth Area') is ideal for a sustainable city expansion along the waterfront, which currently consists of a series of underutilized and derelict spaces. (Aerial photo: Courtesy Suters, 2006)

frequently accused of having sucked-out the vitality of the historical city centre, the now derelict Hunter Mall and the decaying Hunter Street (formerly the main commercial street, located on 'the other side' of a heavy railway corridor). (See: Fig. 5)

Over the last twenty years, most of the retail facilities (72 per cent, by 2008) have moved away to new shopping mall precincts in the suburbs. Despite many attempts to revitalize the entire city centre, the 'Honeysuckle' precinct remains an isolated fragment cut-off from the historical city centre by the railway corridor, and only weakly connected to the existing city through dysfunctional overpass footbridges, which have never worked well. There is now increasing pressure for the introduction of an overall urban vision, the removal of the railway line, and the delivery of a robust framework for future development investments (which otherwise would remain 'dispersed, uncoordinated mosaic projects'). The city of Newcastle has pinned its hopes for the future on real estate development, tourism and the creative industries. The Honeysuckle waterfront has become the site of considerable residential and commercial redevelopment that transforms underutilized areas into a city centre extension by following a familiar model of condos, restaurants, offices and shops.

The irony (or tragedy?) of sustainable development in Newcastle and the Hunter Region is that this city and region is also one of the world's largest coal exporters and it has an extremely large ecological footprint (while the government still pays massive diesel subsidies to the coal mining industries). The coal mining industry is said to be a major air polluter in the region, in contradiction to the tourist development of the area. In general, the social behaviour of Newcastle's population is still fossil-fuel based. For instance, the use of the automobile in the region is around 20 per cent higher than the Australian average (around 90 per cent of all trips are by car). Yet the Hunter Region community receives comparatively little benefit from its coal mining burden and resulting health damages. Some experts say, this is a case of a community's sacrifice for the profit of the NSW State Government. In this regard, Droege noted: 'Australia's domestic coal addiction is staggering but pales in comparison to its exported carbon pollution load. Newcastle exports annually over 100 mill. tones of coal for dirty power generation.' (Droege, 2009) The political reality in 2010 is that Sydney, the state's capital city, does not generate its own power and the Hunter Region has to carry much of the burden for the metropolis; however, Sydney needs the cash flow from Newcastle's coal exports to finance its profligate spending habits. As one can imagine, all this does not greatly assist the Hunter Region's path to sustainability.

Fossil-fuel powered (mainly coal-burning) power stations currently generate 95 per cent of all energy in Australia (data 2008) and – according to the coal lobby – there appears to be no viable alternative to it. The best option is massive solar thermal and off-shore wind-based process energy. This may be viable for heavy industry in future. Office buildings, households and cars are all proximate polluters, and they could run entirely on renewables. Locally, in this debate, there is frequently a lack of distinction between de-industrialization (the Newcastle urban area already has a service based economy) and

Fig. 6: We came, we ruined: the devastation of coal mining. The impact of coal on the landscape and nature is horren-dous, e. g. mercury poisoning, water withdrawal, particle matter in the air, and so on. (Image: coal mine, Image Sharing Commons) There is a large number of carbon-intensive industries that will have to change with the new energy and climate situation. Coal power is only the cheapest option if one looks at first cost, and does not count the expense of the destruction of prime agricultural land, the contaminaton of water supplies, the poisoning of the air, and resulting health costs. There is now fast growing evidence on the increase of deseases and mortality rates caused by coal mining dust.

`de-coalification'. De-coalification means reducing the amount of mining of coal in the Hunter Region and its export through Newcastle Port, as well as de-carbonizing the associated power generation and energy intensive industries (i.e. the aluminum smelters). This is particularly relevant given the city's prominence in academic and mainstream media regarding its claims for livability and leadership in environmentalism.

Designing the *Low-to-No-Energy* and *Low-to-No-Carbon City*

In future, coal will not be an option for energy production due to its high carbon emission per unit of energy (neither is carbon sequestration a safe, sustainable and affordable solu-tion); oil reserves are likely not to last much longer. Nuclear energy faces insurmountable problems, such as the unresolved issue of radioactive waste disposal and other security questions. Renewable energy sources will have to play an increasingly significant role in the energy mix and for urban energy systems.

To achieve a `low energy city', Federico Butera made the following list of actions, pointing out that these combined actions need to be taken to move towards a `renewable built environment':

• Optimize the energy efficiency of the urban structure
• Minimize the energy demand of buildings
• Maximize the efficiency of energy supply
• Maximize the share of clean and renewable energy sources
• Maximize the on-site renewable energy generation
• Minimize primary water consumption and exploit the energy potential of sewage water
• Minimize the volume of disposable waste generated, and use the energy content of wastes
• Minimize the need for transport and optimize transport systems
• Minimize the primary energy consumption of transport systems and mobility; and
• Maximize the share of renewable energy sources in transport. (Butera, 2008)

What does all this mean for the urban regeneration of the city centre? One needs to be mind-ful of the relatively low population density of the Hunter Region and the difficulty in building critical mass for things like cost-effective public transport, viable light rail, or other initiatives. This posits a major difference between the Hunter and the much more intensive development of most of the international examples that are frequently quoted in the literature (Barcelona, Copenhagen, Vancouver, and so on) which have more than triple the population density of Newcastle. The region's population base is only 600,000 people. So as not to set expectations that could not be met, the participants in the design studios were asked to look at case studies and viability models from smaller cities (less than one million), without another similar sized city 60 minutes away. For instance, Vauban District in Freiburg, Germany, was studied.

Exploring different urban models: *City Campus, Green Corridor, Port City*
Large areas of formerly industrially used land – brownfield sites in prime waterfront locations – were used to generate new ideas of compact sustainable urban development and the partial conversion into parkland. The following is a short description of the studio projects *City Campus, Green Corridor* and *Port City*. All were based on a balanced approach to include renewable energy technologies and new types of inner-city green space.

First urban infill and densification; then growth along the waterfront
City Campus – Strategies for Urban Infill aimed to accommodate educational facilities for 3,500 to 5,000 students in the area around centrally located Civic Park. The brief asked for University facilities, including a public library, a flexible performing arts theatre space, buildings to relocate the School of Business and the School of Law, and related research and student services facilities to be partially accommodated into new structures as well as into existing buildings (50 per cent of the brief was to be accommodated in existing buildings through adaptive re-use). The step-by-step relocation of significant parts of the University from its 1960s suburban campus back into the city aimed to increase the University's presence and to revitalize this neglected centre. A new landscape design for Civic Park was part of the project, aiming for a high quality green space, green roofs and increased biodiversity. Students were asked to design the new *City Campus* based on optimized density and include eco-buildings with ideal day-lighting conditions. Each city block had to gain maximum solar exposure for the on-site use of renewable energy generation, combined with good shading devices for western facades.

We found that the urban renewal of the existing city centre can be generated through programmes that carefully develop new densities around transport nodes or along park edges and cultural precincts, thereby improving the quality of urban life for all groups, including disadvantaged residents. 'Sustainable neighbourhood' has been defined as 'a compact community cluster using as little natural resources as possible, with careful consideration for, and improvement of, public space.' (Breheny, 1992; Gauzin-Mueller, 2002) The *City Campus/Green Corridor* projects were to facilitate the revitalization of the city centre along these lines and be instrumental in halting any further decline.
The design proposals were publicly exhibited and discussed, and key recommendations for policy-makers were formulated. (See: Figs 8 and 9)

Port and brownfield developments: urban waterfronts

The rehabilitation and redevelopment of brownfield sites, to find appropriate new uses, is one of the first priorities of environmental and spatial planning based on green urbanism. Most brownfield sites are usually seen as a burden in terms of economic loss and frequently contribute to the degradation of habitat and the deterioration of the quality of life of entire neighbourhoods, thereby creating a whole series of social problems. However, the continuous demand for development land often leads to the reuse of brownfield properties and land that has been abandoned due to heavy industry moving away or closing down. These brownfield sites have deteriorated in a variety of ways and are often contaminated from their industrial past.

The world's most intriguing city centres are the ones located on the water edge, and the most successful waterfront cities are those that are based on developments that celebrate the relationship between the city and the harbour. Large port infrastructures juxtaposed with the cityscape are always an inspiration for any planner and architect. In preparation for this urban design project, similar port redevelopment projects, such as in Hamburg, Rotterdam, Genoa, Vancouver, Copenhagen and Barcelona, were analyzed.

Port City – Reclaiming the Post-Industrial Waterfront was based on strategies for reclaiming the former industrially used waterfront land around Newcastle's inner harbour, a mixed-use urban waterfront development of ten hectares, of which about half had to be dedicated to public parkland. Once the industrial working harbour moved up the Hunter River (in around six to ten years), it was proposed to connect the Dyke Point peninsula with the city centre by a new pedestrian and cycle bridge, so that the now under-utilized land could be turned into a green carbon-neutral city precinct. This mixed-use extension of the city along the waterfront land would be strongly connected to the Honeysuckle precinct by a footbridge. Forging such a strong link between the city centre and the waterfront development, and integrating the existing local community, were both found to be crucial to the success of the Port City.

The aim for the *Port City* was to be a low-emission development, to demonstrate that it is affordable and achievable to make such a major new urban development as carbon-neutral as possible. The brief asked for all energy to be provided by distributed power genera-

21st Century post-industrial City

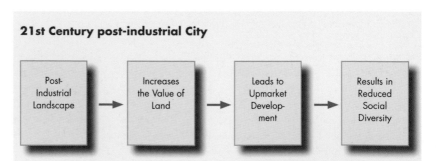

Fig. 7: The city's transformation from the 20th-century industrial to the 21st-century post-industrial condition is not without problems: the increase in land value leads frequently to singular up-market developments, which result in reduced social diversity, gentrification and loss of the vibrant mix that every livable city needs. (Diagram: Steffen Lehmann, 2006)

tion systems from a variety of renewable sources – photovoltaic and windmills (utilizing building roofs and facades), as well as biomass and consideration of geothermal technology. These measures turned the new city district into an `urban powerstation', covering its own energy demands. Students also explored the concept of `energy exchange': the strategic combination of programmes that complement each other (e.g. a supermarket has constant cooling demands and generates waste heat all year round that can be used for heating apartments and a pool).

All sustainability is local.

Students were also asked to test economic realities. There are reliable studies available on the issue of payback on such urban investment and the transformation of the city to sustainable models based on decentralized renewable energy generation. For instance, American scientist Greg Kats is the internationally known author of the most widely referenced study in the US of the costs, benefits and payback times of green buildings and districts. (Kats, G. et al; 2003: `The Costs and Financial Benefits of Green Buildings'; a report to California's Sustainable Building Task Force). (Kats, 2003) This study conclusively demonstrated that sustainable building and the use of renewable energies is a cost-effective investment. Furthermore, according to the economist Sir Nicholas Stern's review (Stern, 2006), delaying the shift to clean energy will cost us more in the long run, and he convincingly pointed out that to weaken or delay the clean energy shift would be poor economic management. The Stern Review is probably the most extensive and reliable piece of work on establishing the costs of global warming. The conclusion is clear: the financial loss caused by not implementing measures would be the equivalent of a 5 to 20 per cent reduction in the gross world product now and for all time. It does, however, require an *Emissions Trading Scheme* (ETS). According to Stern, around 3 per cent of the gross world product must be used annually to ensure that global warming does not exceed 2 degrees Celsius. Peter Head (Arup, 2008), Thomas Luetzkendorf, and Michael Smith and Karlson Hargroves (`Cents and Sustainability', 2010) have also published similar economic studies. All these economic studies were analyzed by the students at the beginning of the studios.

Regenerating the city, dealing with the post-industrial condition

Urban design encapsulates a series of critical and complex dependencies. Questions of scale, ecological footprint, connection to urban public transport, optimized solar orientation, and the maritime heritage of the working harbour were all critical to the project, as were the social integration of the established local community and the need to maintain social diversity. (See: Fig. 7) Optimized building shapes, appropriate orientation, internal layout and the position and size of openings and sun shading were criteria used to enhance natural ventilation and to reduce the need for air-conditioning during the hot summer periods. Students gave special care to the urban layout of the *Port City*, to ensure maximum solar gain in winter (when the sun is low), and avoiding buildings being too close to each other, which would hamper natural lighting and create over-shadowing. One important starting point was to clearly understand the post-industrial city and the changes caused by de-industrialisation. The post-industrial condition is defined by the transition to a society that has a service-based and a knowledge-based economy. It emerged from a manufacturing-based economy, after industrialisation and global capitalism had prevailed for a certain time. Daniel Bell primarily established the idea of the post-industrial society through his work `The Coming of Post-industrial Society'. (Bell, 1973) Most western sociologists maintain that the basis of the post-industrial society began to be formed in the 1960s and that the process has been gaining ground ever since.

In his writing, Bell emphasized the changes to post-industrial society are not merely socially structural and economic, but the values and norms within the post-industrial society have changed as well. He argues that `rationality and efficiency become the paramount values within the post-industrial society.' Eventually, according to Bell, these values caused disconnections between social structures and culture. He notes that `most of today's unique modern problems can be generally attributed to the effects of the post-industrial society. A large number of people may find themselves with no clearly defined role. These problems are particularly pronounced where the free market dominates. They can include economic inequality, or the outsourcing of domestic jobs from, say, Europe or the US to emerging countries, such as China and India; or an emphasis on the arts as a new important economic sector rather than as just a means for personal expression.' (Bell, 1973)

Manuel Castells defines the `post-industrial period' for the US, Japan and parts of Europe as the era 1970 to 1990, characterized by 'a pattern of shifting away from manufacturing jobs', when a new social structure, associated with the rise of the network society emerged. He sees post-industrialism already replaced by an informational society, where the source of productivity lies in the generation of knowledge through information processing. (Castells, 1996) However, the consequences of this transition on urban life and planning remain widely unclear.

Sociologist George Ritzer points out that `this economic transition spurs a restructuring in society as a whole'. (Ritzer, 2007) He goes on to provide a theory based on six changes in social structure associated with the transition to a post-industrial society:
• Within the economy there is a transition from goods production to the provision of services. Production of such goods as steel or textile decline and services such as selling education and offering advice on investments increase. Health, education, research and government services are the most decisive for a post-industrial society. Entire (old) industrial landscapes become obsolete (e.g. the de-industrialisation of cities such as Pittsburgh and Detroit).
• The importance of blue-collar, manual work (e.g. assembly line workers) declines and professional (lawyers) and technical work (computer programmers) come to predominate. Of special importance is the rise of scientists (e.g. specialized engineers, such as environmental engineers). Many mining towns and similar settlements face large-scale unemployment as a result of the increasing importance of both theoretical knowledge and the environment at the expense of manufacturing.
• Instead of practical know-how and empirical knowledge, theoretical knowledge is

increasingly essential in a post-industrial society. Such knowledge is seen as the basic source of innovation. The exponential growth of theoretical and codified knowledge, in all its varieties, is central to the emergence of the post-industrial society.

• A post-industrial society seeks to assess the impacts of the new technologies and, where necessary, to exercise control over them. The goal is a more secure technological world.

• To handle such control and, more generally, the sheer complexity of post-industrial society, new intellectual technologies (e.g. information theory) are developed and implemented.

• A new relationship is forged in the post-industrial society between scientists and the new technologies they create, as well as in systematic technological growth, which lies at the base of post-industrial society. This leads to the need for more universities. In fact, the university is crucial to post-industrial society and, therefore, to the post-industrial city. The university produces the experts who can create, guide and control the new and dramatically changing technologies. Therefore, a city campus is an important catalyst to help to activate urban regeneration processes in derelict city centres. (Ritzer, 2007)

Fig. 8: The *City Campus/Green Corridor Project – Strategies of Urban Infill* studio, proposal (2007; see page 408ff) from the author's studio, by students M. Smith and T. Hulme. Half of the new educational facilities will be accommodated in existing buildings, applying infill and adaptive re-use strategies. Putting carparking around the edges of the city centre allowed the improvement of the central parkland and a strong public space network. Part of the strategy is the revitalization of otherwise obsolete, overlooked urban spaces.

Pierro Cervellati wrote extensively about the characteristics of the post-industrial urban environment in his book `La città postindustriale' (*The Post-industrial City*). He criticized the construction waste and environmental pollution caused by the steady suburbanization process. Typically, the suburbanization process contributed to the abandonment of old city centers, creating large empty areas along the inner-city waterfront (e.g. at former port facilities) or sometimes even within the metropolitan area itself. Cervellati suggested that city planning perspectives orient towards the rebuilding and redevelopment of these derelict urban areas and abandoned buildings, citing the famous case of the Soho district in New York's Manhattan, in which old industrial buildings were transformed into loft apartments and offices. The old warehouses proved to be flexible and adaptable typologies that could easily be turned into great places to work or to live. Importantly, he concluded

Fig. 9: The *Port City – Reclaiming the Post-industrial Waterfront* proposal (2007–08, see page 520ff) from the author's studio, by student B. Campbell. This new city district acts as its own urban powerstation, harnessing solar and wind energy to generate decentralized energy; the harbour water could be utilized for cooling the buildings. The studies aimed to provide new models of sustainable urban development for inner-city sites, often post-industrial brownfield sites, through urban infill and densification models, as well as controlled urban expansion concepts along the reclaimed waterfronts. Living and working on the water edge has always been fascinating, but, what will be the role of the industrial heritage in these new developed districts?

that the post-industrial city does not need further expansion in space and does not need to increase its footprint, but requires instead a step-by-step strategy of redevelopment of the dismissed areas in order to counteract the environmental waste and contamination formerly created by the old industrial era. (Cervellati, 1984)

The participants of the design studios found that the implementation of most of the mentioned urban design rules is made easier if the urban layout of the new district has been properly and carefully configured. Our study took a cohesive approach to demonstrate this. The project study also illustrated how staging of the *Port City* development and the site remediation could be used to drive the design approach and enable a step-by-step transformation. For instance, at the beginning, one could activate the existing Carrington Pump House (heritage-listed, built 1877) as a catalyst and starting point for the entire development. It was envisaged that in the final stage, the *Port City* would offer 2,000 units in a very special inner-city waterfront living and working environment.

From Jefferson's ideal campus to the `Living City Campus'
The history of universities is, to a large extent, identical with the history of continuous growth of their campuses; first as part of the city centre (e.g. like in Oxford or Heidelberg), then, later, outside the city. Today we see the end of the suburban, mono-functional campus. The ideal model is that of a `Science City' as an inner-city quarter, compactly reintegrated into daily urban life, and mixed with facilities for housing, retail, restaurants and sports activities. The design studio `City Campus' presented a variety of proposals for relocating 3,500 to 5,000 students to Newcastle city centre, thus making urban renewal and urban consolidation a reality (see: Chapter 3).

Each studio started with research of historical typologies and models. Precedents of different campus models were plentiful, ranging from Thomas Jefferson's classic `Ideal Campus' for the University of Virginia in Charlottesville (1817), to the more recent, 'structuralist' models such as:
* Walter Gropius: Bauhaus, Dessau (1925–26)
* Ludwig Mies van der Rohe: Illinois Institute of Technology in Chicago, USA (1939–)
* Louis Kahn: The Salk Institute in La Jolla, California USA (1960)
* Louis Kahn: Indian Institute of Management in Ahmedabad, India (1962–74)
* Denys Lasdun: University of East Anglia in Norwich, UK (1965–68)
* James Stirling: Various university masterplans and buildings, for St. Andrews, Cambridge, Leicester, Oxford (1959–65)
* John Wardle: University of South Australia, City Campus (2000–06)
* Fumihiko Maki: Republic Polytechnic Campus, Singapore (2004–08)
* Kees Christiaanse: ETH Science City, Hoenggerberg, Zurich, Switzerland (2006–).

In January 2010, the University of Newcastle announced its `10-Year Plan' to become one of the top three regional universities in Australia, increasing its student numbers by 2020 to 40,000. By then, the university `expects to have moved its business, law and creative arts faculties entirely to a new city campus, and it is anticipated that up to 4,500 students and 500 academic staff will be working and studying at the expanded Newcastle city campus. This will have a positive effect on the city's small business and strengthen the retail sector', it announced. (University of Newcastle, 2010)

Temporary and inexpensive initiatives for urban revitalization: projects with small budget, but big impact
Jaime Lerner, urban planner and mayor of Curitiba, and IPPUC have shown how one can make improvements to life in cities, even if there is no budget, through grassroots strategies and clever management of public space; for instance, the distribution of free bus tickets to the public for helping to clean up the city. His inventive concepts have been described in the book `Urban Acupuncture'.
These concepts were a great influence on my thinking in the late 1990s in recession-hit Germany. At this time, I developed a long interest in creative activities occuring in unconventional spaces and places, i.e. architects and artists working together collaboratively, utilizing vacant urban space and derelict public spaces, as part of a wider urban renewal strategy. I soon realized that, as a result of it, new communities and creative hubs were developed which could play a significant role in urban development. With `Rethinking: Space, Time, Architecture' (Berlin, 2002), I started to formulate tools and strategies for informal urban interventions that would reactivate run-down public space. It has developed as an innovative and inexpensive model for the interim-use of vacant space that has the potential to make an immediate difference to the city.
Today, such `guerilla tactics' have become more common repertoire in cities around the world, where user-communities are empowered to creatively adapt the urban space and create places of unique character. One of such initiative is the *Renew Newcastle* initiative,

which brings empty shops and derelict buildings in Newcastle back to life. It's again a strategy for turning around the decline caused by the post-industrial condition and the construction of large shopping centres outside the city. Traditional city centres in all developed countries are dying. As a consequence, inner-city areas have many vacant premises due to development delays and loss of business to suburban shopping malls. It is critical that municipalities do everything possible to bring much-needed activity back to these ailing city centres to foster growth in the areas.

Bottom–up approaches and grassroots projects in urban design are particularly important to balance top–down development.

In cities in the developed world, large-scale urban development projects frequently have the disadvantage of it taking several years for them to be implemented. During this time not much happens on the sites earmarked for development. They seem to be `frozen in time and decay' until the projects start. In contrast, small-scale interim initiatives can deliver immediate improvement. Small-scale initiatives like artist workshops, small events or interventions in public space, are called *Grassroots Strategies*, and have huge potential. They are characterised by bottom-up approaches and have only a temporary life-span. They are usually subsidized by councils and have the aim of attracting people into the area. Some lessons in such inexpensive but effective initiatives can be learnt from the developing world, where the unforeseen use of the planned city might actually be the key to its success. They can be founded on the sustainability of informal clusters of habitation, or the self-regulation of occasional usage patterns, in many cities around the world, from informal markets in China or Vietnam, to the grassroots initiatives in Bangladesh or India, to social programmes for upgrading *favelas* (slums) in Latin America. All are great models for quick but inexpensive action.

During the time when long-term projects are awaiting development, many sites remain boarded-up for years and are often vandalized. This was one of the reasons for the author's interest in instigating a series of inexpensive, small-scale, not-for-profit initiatives that tried to solve this dilemma, taking advantage of the opportunities offered by the temporary use of empty buildings and spaces downtown.
The advantages of activating the disregarded potential of these urban spaces, and dealing with temporary grassroots projects to support urban renewal, has been discussed in great detail in my book `Back to the City. Strategies for Informal Urban Interventions' (Lehmann, 2009), where I defined the notion of 'informal urban intervention' as a form of spontaneous urban design dealing with urban culture. The topic of collaborative urban interventions is relatively new to the Australian city debate, and was first introduced with my previous book and exhibition project `Absolutely Public', in 2004–05, based on my experiences in Berlin and East-German cities during the 1990s. Since then, the concept has created many spin-off initiatives in local and Australian-wide academic circles (e.g. `CitySwitch', `Fix Our City', etc.), which is a good outcome. In June 2010, the Minister for the Hunter adapted my recommendations for Newcastle's urban revitalization. (Lehmann, 2005; 2010)

The vibrant city needs both top-down as well as bottom-up strategies. It needs large-scale and small-scale initiatives, all at the same time.

Temporary use of abandoned buildings: a success story from East Germany and North England, now replicated in other cities

While greenfield and brownfield sites are familiar categories, so-called `greyfields' are temporarily or permanently abandoned urban spaces, often industrial in their prior use. Concepts for the temporary reuse of abandoned buildings in city centres were developed in the mid 1990s in recession-hit post-unification Berlin and East German cities, like Dresden and Leipzig, as a way of bringing people back to the dying city centres. Since 1993, projects in Liverpool and Manchester by `Urban Splash' and others showed how rundown city blocks can be transformed into thriving new communities, socially and environmentally. The transformation was achieved with a positive vision and the help of local people who lived there and who were empowered to take ownership. In both cases, empty industrial buildings and run-down abandoned structures in the city centre were converted into stunning studio places for creative industries and start-ups, or loft apartments, bringing back life to redundant spaces (and depopulated city centres such as in Eastern Germany and Northern England. See also: www.emptyshopsnetwork.com and www.changing-spaces.org)

New situations do not necessarily have to be 'designed'; they often emerge and develop by themselves out of the potential of authentic urban places and of what already exists.

Today, in the declining Australian city centres, these concepts are reapplied in projects such as *Back to the City* (2007–08) and *Renew Newcastle* (2008), which are initiatives to find short and medium-term uses for run-down public spaces and abandoned buildings. The idea was that community-based groups, cultural grassroots projects and art initiatives were all well placed to use and maintain these buildings and spaces as interim-users, until those buildings and spaces became commercially viable or were redeveloped. The community groups moved in with short-term leases (rent-free) and generated activity in the otherwise vacant buildings and streets. Grassroots community activists can make use of the vacant, abandoned buildings and use them as 'incubators' for their activities or to complement their `guerilla' projects in public space. Planners and architects will need to pay more attention to 'greyfields' and their overlooked role in the urban landscape.

In our case, Newcastle city centre, it was clear it would only take a few more high profile closures of retail anchors and the whole area could easily capsize. To succeed with any revitalisation initiatives, it was thought important to define the city centre as a place of potential rather than of decay. At the starting point of the programmes to invigorate Newcastle city centre, there were around one hundred empty buildings considered useful for immediate interim activities. The re-use of the otherwise unused, empty shop-fronts, small-scale laneways and public spaces proved to be ideal for offering low rent spaces for grassroots art galleries, graphic designers, jeweller studios, children's art classes, and spaces for other community-based cultural initiatives. The projects turned out to be a huge success and the spaces quickly took on the role of `attractors' that brought people back to the otherwise deteriorating centre. *Back to the City* installed 18 collaborative art works (interventions) in public space. *Renew Newcastle* was able to place (in the first twelve months) 36 projects into 24 vacant properties. For both initiatives, maps were published and walking tours to the locations were organized. The initiatives not only improved the streetscape and brought back vibrancy, but it also restored confidence in the location and helped protect the premises.

Of course this initiative was only possible through the trust of the property owners. The important first step was to find property owners of empty buildings and sites who were willing to offer the premises rent-free, for temporary occupation, rather than leaving them vacant and at risk. Every empty building is a liability to the property owner, whereas temporary occupants keep the property clean and secure. This is something that is in the interests of the entire city. [2]

There are many benefits from good urban renewal projects and the rejuvenation of entire districts, making them more mixed-use. The *Back to the City*, and *Renew Newcastle* projects in Newcastle (2008) , the *Laneways By George–Hidden Networks* project in Sydney (2010), and the *Hub-to-Hub* project in Singapore (2011), are all about under-performing public space and real estate, and the disregarded potential of abandoned buildings and spaces in the city centre. Such projects are innovative, low-budget strategies to maintain the vitality and viability of the historical city centre area during a period of redevelopment and post-industrial transformation. They can bring immediate improvement to an urban area as well.

In Newcastle, as in many other cities, the number of shuttered shop-fronts with *closing down*, and *for lease* signs along the high street is alarming. In certain stretches it seems

Fig. 10: The various initiatives: *Back to the City* (2007–08, Newcastle), *Renew Newcastle* (2008, Newcastle), and *Laneways By George–Hidden Networks* (2009, Sydney), rejuvenated the forgotten areas and the dying heart of city centres, attracted people back, and reactivated the small-scale structures that had survived redevelopment trends towards big, bulky retail spaces. Such inexpensive small-scale strategies for urban renewal can have immediate positive effects on the entire centre. It was first during the 1990s recession years in Germany and the UK, that such strategies were developed to keep East German and North English communities intact. Left: Installation `Look-out', part of the *Back to the City* initiative. Right: Run-down Hunter Street in Newcastle, with boarded-up shops and urban decline.

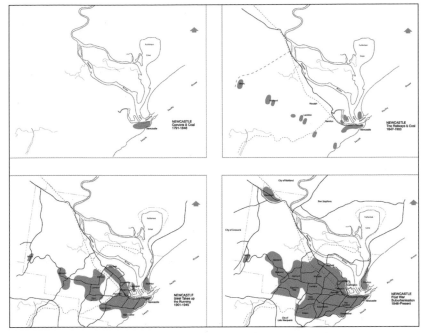

Fig. 11 : Newcastle's stages of growth, from its foundation in 1804 to its city formation, 1945. (Source: Phil O'Neil et al, 'The Making of the Hunter', 2003) Today, little is left of the Coal River penal station. Opened to free settlement in 1822, the town of Newvcastle quickly shed its convict origins and evolved as a Victorian city with a robust mercantile history.

like every second shop has closed for business. It is not only a Newcastle phenomenon, these ghost towns in Australia (and one can quite easily insert here names of towns in Britain, Canada, Germany, France, or the US as well) are an indicator that whole town centres are teetering on the brink of collapse, and much of the discussion concerning the perils of the empty shop-fronts epidemic and the search for potential solutions is simply coming too late.

New housing in existing urban areas: delivering affordable housing through urban consolidation and densification projects.

For too long, local communities have seen the arrival of national brands, frequently mediocre chain stores with unsympathetic facades to the local character, pushing out local, family-owned businesses. On the other hand, bringing back locally owned shops to the community and preserving the strong, resilient culture of family-owned and operated businesses makes a city more interesting and unique for visitors. A good example of this is the Portuguese capital Lisbon. Of all the capitals in the old EU, Lisbon is probably home to the lowest number of multinational retail brands and chain stores. There, the majority of shops lining the boulevards are still local, family-owned enterprises, thus making it a special place with a unique character.

Fig. 12 a, b: Two urban extremes: Left, the city of Houston, Texas (1990). Houston has become the symbol of a car-centric city, where public space has been lost to car parking lots. Right: detail of the 'Nolli Plan' of Rome, by the surveyor and map-maker Giambattista Nolli, 1748 ('La Pianta Grande di Roma'). Rome is the symbol of walkable city, and Nolli's plan shows the city as figure ground plan of built spaces. The public space network is always serving the greater good and has priority in urban design. (Source: Image Sharing Commons)

Fig. 13: The ancient typology of the courtyard house is particularly useful for passive design strategies: the courtyard is a room without a roof, an outdoor patio space, which acts as centre of the house and as 'climate regulator', enabling effective natural cross-ventilation, good day-lighting and circulation, while allowing the winter sun to enter rooms. The courtyard is a common design element in most cities in the Mediterranean, Middle Eastern and tropical regions. In summer, the courtyard can act as extension to the living room, sheltered from the wind and protected from the neighbours' view; rooms can be given large windows without any loss of privacy. Sketch of a central courtyard house by Bernard Rudofsky, from his pivotal book 'Architecture without Architects' (1964). (Sketch: Courtesy Rudofsky, MOMA, 2009)

Right page, Fig. 14: The amount of roadway used by the same passengers travelling by car, by bicycle, or by bus. The photo shows a street in the city of Muenster, Germany, which has a strong focus on public transport and cycling pathes. (Photo: Courtesy Petersen and WI, 2004)

Conclusion: urban consolidation and more compact, medium-density communities

The end of the inefficient suburban sprawl has come. Caused by changing demographics, a decline in family households and a growing preference for urban lifestyle, the suburban dream of the `big house in the green' is vanishing. Architects are now engaged in ways to remake the suburbs, e.g. mono-functional suburbs are getting retrofitted and densified with mixed-use town centres, and boarded-up derelict malls are getting repurposed to offices and apartments. Densifying the existing city with new housing and mixed-use programmes will reduce the energy demand and CO_2 emissions from transport, and achieve a number of other objectives, such as the rejuvenation of entire districts and the intensification of mixed-use neighbourhoods. More good urban renewal demonstration projects are needed, which deliver affordable housing and a well-designed public realm, too.

For this, leadership at the government and municipality level is essential. Government needs to introduce new low-carbon policies and explain these to the community and private sector (the property developers). These policies will facilitate the increase of densities, through urban infill in targeted urban renewal zones, and allow for the redevelopment of vacant and underutilized inner-city sites; this will need to go hand in hand with incentives for the private sector for developing such urban consolidation projects (rather than keep building suburban dwellings).

The most difficult part are probably the policies for deep behavioural change: in the suburban dwellings, as well as in the inner-city townhouses, in general, lifestyles with large ecological footprints are increasing. This is nothing exclusive to inner-city apartment living, it's happening through the entire society. As has frequently been pointed out, higher incomes make the posession of more electrical equipment and more air travel possible, hereby increasing CO_2 emissions per capita. Especially the ever-growing large suburban house is full of stuff that requires more energy to operate, consumes more materials, but is less recyclable. In addition, the suburban dwelling is, most of the time, less well insulated and causes the need for more car travel.

Livability and sustainability: urban regeneration examples

Successfully implemented urban renewal and eco-district projects, in terms of livability and sustainability, demonstrate that holistic approaches deal with all three areas: regenerating the existing city centers; improving and densifying the suburbs; and having a strong focus on the reuse and intensification of brownfield sites. Urban quality and good design make also commercial sense, as the following case studies will demonstrate.

Livability of a city depends to a high degree on the quality of the public space networks. As urban designers, we need to have not only a focus on squares and gardens, but also on what links up with each other: city streets and streetscapes. These are a fundamental part of the public domain of any city, as places to meet, communicate and interact. Decisions regarding the design of streetscapes have to be taken on ecological grounds, concerning their orientation, landscaping, protection from wind, as well as the well-informed choice of materials.

Next step: setting-up an *Eco-City Database* for international best practice

Eco-cities will need to consider significant, tangible and measurable environmental, social and economic gains versus the 'business as usual' case for urban development. They will have to demonstrate greater energy efficiency, better land usage, reduced resource consumption and reduced emissions. All are measurable outcomes.

Best Practice for Eco-Districts and Eco-Cities for a Low-to-No-Carbon Future

Urban design is rapidly changing, and there are now wonderful eco-city initiatives starting worldwide. Some early projects are already fully implemented; for instance, eco-communities such as Freiburg-Vauban and Hanover-Kronsberg in Germany, Gussing in Austria, Samsö Island in Denmark, and Overturnea in Sweden, which have all achieved self-sufficiency by producing renewable energy sources. These new districts and quarters have become significant net exporters of renewable energy, producing even more energy than they consume and feeding the surplus into the grid.

These cities have managed to demonstrate to their inhabitants that it is profitable to invest in renewable energy, and that with decentralized systems, citizens can become independent energy producers. Frequently, the residents themselves have invested in windmills and solar roofs, taking advantage of government subsidies such as the feed-in tariffs in Germany. Citizens in Germany know exactly how much they are going to be paid for the electricity they generate when they become a small-scale solar power producer. The German government has ordered that electricity companies are obliged to pay a set price for environmentally-friendly electricity (solar power prices are set several times higher than the market price), which makes it easier to finance renewable energy projects. As a result, Germany is now responsible for almost half of the world's solar-powered energy production, despite its limited sun radiation.

The government of Sweden has set a national goal of being free from oil by 2020, and Overturnea, a small Swedish town, has achieved this already. Havana in Cuba has successfully dealt with its 50-year embargo and negotiated its early *Peak Oil* experience by becoming virtually self-sufficient in its food supply. Today, Havana is a leading example of local food production through its community gardens and urban farming. Curitiba in Brazil, Copenhagen in Denmark, Hanover in Germany, and Amsterdam in the Netherlands have all demonstrated how to make cities close to independent of the private automobile, by improving public transport and cycling. Malmö in Sweden has built the borough Vastra Hamnen on a former industrial area that contained a large shipyard (2000-2006). This new borough is supplied with energy solely from renewable sources, essentially solar thermal, wind power, water and biogas from waste.

These new solar-powered districts and buildings, with their new type of urban infrastructure, will revolutionize and transform our cities.

Ambitious and large plans for entire new eco-towns are already under way. These large experiments are very important, such as Masdar (UAE) and Wanzhuang (China) and will be a further test-bed for the development of innovative technologies and strategies to learn from for future projects. Masdar is expected to be completed by 2020 and aims to demonstrate to the world that it is possible to live in a sustainable manner in an extreme desert climate, while also increasing the quality of life of the city's inhabitants. The principles laid down for this project include: zero emissions, total recycling of waste, sustainable transportation (cars stay outside the city), extensive use of local materials, locally-produced food, energy generation from sun, wind and waste, and sustainable use of water and energy.

Evaluation of eco-cities

If we want to compare the different initiatives that have worked well, we will need to base eco-city evaluations on scientific evidence and tangible, measurable data. A database for scientific comparison of the different approaches, applied by these leading communities, would be very helpful. The next step is to compare the cities and districts with each other, providing the much needed clarity about the wider application of successful strategies. The 'Ecological Footprint' method developed by Wackernagel and Rees could be a useful way to start establishing such a city ranking based on facts and data, and the surveyed data could be extended. (Wackernagel and Rees, 1996) In addition, we could compare the eco-city models using the *Resource and Energy Analysis Programme* (REAP). This method, developed by the Stockholm Environment Institute, is increasingly being used to arrive at comparative consumption figures based on 'material flow accounting', using comprehensive economic data.

All this would include comparison of the data and facts from each eco-city, such as:
- population density of city
- overall density ratio of city

- total of heating and electricity consumption per capita
- amount of renewable energy generated and consumed
- amount of more electricity produced than is needed
- system of subsidies to calculate real energy price
- amount of water used per capita
- amount of waste recycled, or used for waste-to-energy strategies
- percentage of food produced within a 200 km radius
- percentage of journeys by low-impact public transport
- number of automobile registrations
- amount of sqm of green space per capita
- length of bike paths in city area
- number of trees planted in last 5 years
- number of affordable housing built in last 5 years
- number of green buildings and community facilities in the district
- number and quality of educational programmes to raise awareness, and
- other measurable criteria.

If a meaningful model is to evolve and be useful for a larger roll-out, any eco-city will need to be:

- replicable (a model that is able to be applied to other places)
- practical (meaning: economically viable), and
- scalable (adaptable to projects of different scale).

The resource pressures have been growing because of increased consumption and growing populations. The discovery of how we design, build and operate cities with a very low resource input, an eco-city, has become a matter of survival. Managing limited resources is not so different from managing finances: If you overuse what is available, at some point you have a serious problem.

In a recent interview, Mathis Wackernagel explained why the *Ecological Footprint* (EF) method is of importance: `At the Global Footprint Network, we think like farmers: we want to know how much productive area, or bio-capacity, there is, and how much people use. On average worldwide, we have about two hectares per person. Right now, humanity's Ecological Footprint is *1.4 Earths* – this means it takes the planet over one year and four months to regenerate what humanity consumes in one year. I believe that bio-capacity will become the main currency in the 21st century. We can overuse it like we can overuse financial assets. Currently, we are amassing a big ecological debt, and this debt will weigh heavily on our shoulders. What are the physical manifestations? Forests disappear, fisheries collapse, fresh water becomes scarce, and pollution accumulates in the atmosphere. This has economic consequences. Every day, life is becoming more expensive. All the assets that depend on cheap resources in order to operate, such as inefficient buildings or jets, will decrease tremendously in value. (...) The human footprint is simply too big. If we want to maintain a stable life on the planet, then it would be better to consume no more than Earth can regenerate. Otherwise we inevitably liquidate our ecological assets. If we stay in overshoot, we will further increase our ecological debt, which would severely undermine our economies' ability to operate. Every country has to find out its right balance. Optimal resource consumption depends on the following factors: How much bio-capacity does your country have? And: What is the country's purchasing power compared to the world average? If your purchasing power is below the worldwide average, then it is unlikely you can access more bio-capacity from elsewhere.' (Wackernagel, 2010)

It's like we are living on a large solar collector, the Earth, that transforms solar power into everything we need.
Our planet has a limited surface that has a certain biodiversity, providing us with all the ecological services necessary: water, food, waste sequestration and environmental stability.

Scale comparison of eco-city projects
The question of scale is an important one. To be a relevant model for the future, the eco-city should not be too small. The range of density of eco-cities is between 50 and 150 persons per ha. A comparison of the scale of various eco-cities gives following picture:

Completed
Vauban Freiberg, Germany	38ha	5,000 population (density 130 pers. /ha)
Augustenborg Malmö, Sweden	160ha	8,000 population
Hammarby-Sjöstad Stockholm, Sweden	200ha	10,000 population

Currently under construction
Masdar City, UAE	700ha	50,000 population
Tianjin Eco-City, China	3,000ha	350,000 population
Wanzhuang Eco-City, China	8,000ha	400,000 population

The success stories of culture-led urban regeneration during the 1990s have been widely debated and the author assumes here that the reader will be aware of these cases. Evans and Shaw, among others, have described the new urban mix created in formerly-industrial second-tier cities, such as Bilbao (Spain), Glasgow (Scotland), Dublin (Ireland), Rotterdam (The Netherlands) and Melbourne (Australia), which shows how large transport infrastructure projects (i.e. new railway stations or bridges) and city campus developments have acted as catalysts for urban regeneration, even removing the cities' previously negative image of urban decline. (Evans and Shaw, 2004)

In this context, it becomes obvious that the urban revitalization initiative should always be driven by an urban design vision and architectural perspective, while transport planning needs to fit the form of the city (and not the other way around).

The following are some examples of successful urban regeneration projects:

• Reuse of industrial sites: IBA Emscher Park, Duisburg (Germany)
Caused by the closure of steel mills and coal mines, the Ruhr region went through a major transformation phase. The Internationale Bauausstellung (IBA) Emscher Park introduced the concept of reuse and transformation of the brownfield structures and industrial landscape as a model for sustainable restructuring of the region. The IBA was a 10 year programme by the Land Northrhine-Westfalia between 1989 and 1999, covering an area of 800 sq km. It was designed to initiate restructuring in that part of the post-industrial Ruhr region, the Emscher, which had suffered from the process of structural change, causing economic, environmental and social decline for many decades. One of the exhibition's principle features was that restructuring should take a holistic view rather than simply trying to attract inward investment and jobs. As a result the programme was based around a huge 80 km long, linear landscape park. The unique nature of the exhibition showcased the Ruhrgebiet as an industrial region in the process of transformation. It was not an exhibition in the traditional sense, but was created as a demonstration project to give impetus to new ideas and concepts. The goal: urban development; social, cultural and ecological measures, to be the basis for economic change in an old industrial region. The councils of the 17 local communities of the Emscher region joined the building exhibition upon its formation, including: Duisburg, Oberhausen, Mülheim an der Ruhr, Bottrop, Essen, Gladbeck, Bochum, Gelsenkirchen, Recklinghausen, Herne, Herten, Castrop-Rauxel, Waltrop, Lünen, Dortmund, Kamen and Bergkamen. Some of the leading thinkers behind the IBA were Karl Ganser and Peter Latz.

• Green district in the city: Vauban Solar-City, Freiburg (Germany)
The City of Freiburg is often called the 'European capital of environmentalism'. In the south of Freiburg, on the former area of a French barrack site (size: 38 ha), Vauban, a new *Sustainable Model District* was developed, housing more than 5,000 inhabitants and 600 workplaces (20 per cent of the 2,500 units are public housing). It's a smaller project compared to most of the other eco-city projects, but highly replicable and pragmatic. Together with the Hammarby-Sjöstad district in Stockholm, it is Vauban which has set the most replicable benchmarks. Planning for the district started in 1993, and by 2006, after three development phases, the district was completed and 5,000 people had moved in. The main goal of the project was to implement a green city district in a cooperative, participatory way which met ecological, social, economic and cultural requirements. The city of Freiburg had bought the area from the federal authorities. As owner of the Vauban area, the city was responsible for its planning and development and realized the importance of design thinking in policy. The principle of 'learning while planning', which was adopted by the city, allowed flexibility in reacting to new developments, starting an extended citizen participation that went far beyond the legal requirements, enabling citizens to participate directly in the planning process. The citizen's association 'Forum Vauban' (which has NGO-status) applied to coordinate the participation process and was recognized as the site's legal body by the city of Freiburg in 1995. The major driving force for

the development of Vauban were the ideas, the creativity and the commitment of the future residents, their common desire to create a sustainable, flourishing community (the project was particularly appealing to academics and the middle-class population segment). In the fields of energy, traffic and mobility, building and participation, public spaces and social interaction, new concepts were successfully put into practice.

In the Vauban district:

• The project's structure integrates legal, political, social and economic actors from grass-roots-level up to the city administration.

• all houses are built at least to an improved low energy standard (65 kWh / sqm p.a., calculated similar to the Swiss *Minergie* standard) plus at least 100 units with *Passive House* (15 kWh /sqm p.a.) or *plus energy+* standard (houses which produce more energy than they need, another 100 *plus energy+* houses are planned).

• a highly efficient co-generation plant (combined-heat-power CHP), located within the community, operating on wood-chips is connected to the district's heating grid (the wood-fired community power plant supplies heating).

• solar collectors (about 450 sqm by 2000) and photovoltaics (about 1,200 sqm by 2000) are the common element on the district's roofs; even the street lights are solar-powered.

• an ecological traffic and mobility concept was implemented, with a reduced number of private cars to be parked in the periphery (about 40 per cent of the households are car-free, or agreed to live without owning a car). There is a good public transport system (free bus loops and light rail) and a convenient car sharing system where car sharers get a free annual pass for the tram.

• car-reduced streets and other public spaces act as playgrounds for kids and for places for social interaction (Freiburg has twice as many bicycles as cars).

• joint building projects (about 30 groups of building owners, the Geneva cooperative and a self-organized settlement initiative) are the fertile ground for a stable community, raising ecological awareness.

• there is far-reaching participation and social work organized by 'Forum Vauban', giving a voice to the people's needs, supporting their initiatives, promoting innovative ecological and social concepts, and setting-up a communication and participation structure, including meetings, workshops, a three-monthly district news magazine, publications on special issues and internet-presentations. Social aspects of the development have been carefully planned and include a cooperative food store and a farmers' market initiative.

In addition to this, the Hammarby-Sjöstad district near Stockholm has set new standards for waste management, with a concept that has been winning awards. There is a vacuum-sorted underground waste removal system and residents are given colour-coded biodegradable bags for their waste, and a high proportion of the waste is recycled or composted (over 60 per cent). All this led to substantial waste reduction. Sewage is processed to become gas for fuel cookers, buses and cars in the car pool. The sludge by-product fertilizes a forest that provides wood to heat houses.

• Reborn through good planning strategies: Lyon, Lille and Montpellier (France)
A series of French cities have engaged in urban regeneration with amazing, instructive outcomes. Lyon (France's second largest city) during the 1990s focused on enhancing the public realm in its historic centre and reintegrating disused sites into an extended urban fabric. Today, it is an established regional hub and a prosperous counter-pole to Paris. Lille is a mid-sized city recovering from the loss of its industrial base. The city was struggling after the loss of its heavy industry, and concentrated first of all on re-establishing the economic viability of its urban centre. Montpellier, once a small university town, is now a burgeoning 'technology centre'. Montpellier is of particular interest to Newcastle, as it is one of the regional cities of similar size that has made an impressive transformation and evolution, one which still is ongoing. The recent planning strategies of Montpellier are based on an agenda of concentrated growth (intensification), supported by investment in civic and transport infrastructure. Montpellier, faced with strong growth, began using the transit infrastructure to define patterns of controlled development and interventions that could counteract sprawl. An ambitious regeneration programme brought the whole city centre back to life so that today it has re-emerged as a great regional centre of great popularity, enjoying significant investment.

• Regeneration of urban waterfronts: Seattle (USA) and Vancouver (Canada)
The urban redevelopment of historic industrial waterfronts adjacent to the city centre has been a worldwide phenomenon. While the city's economy once centered on its waterfronts, economic restructuring and industrial decline rendered obsolete many of these places and their ancillary warehouses and rail yards. Some celebrated examples of such redevelopment includes the waterfronts of Barcelona, Amsterdam, Copenhagen, Hamburg, Sydney, Vancouver, Toronto, Seattle, Boston, Chicago (just to name a few). These cities managed to capture the aspirations and imagination of their regions by creating mixed-use waterfront districts that extend the experience of their urban cores to the water's edge. If successful, waterfront redevelopments act as catalysts for wider development, often with positive social, environmental and economic impacts. Both Vancouver and Seattle used their unique opportunity to create great urban waterfronts. Waterfronts were understood as fundamental to Vancouver's and Seattle's history, image and quality of life. Both cities understood that the city's great harbours are too precious to be a traffic artery or a frontage for industrial activity, and turned them into inviting extensions of the city core. Some of the strategies applied as a framework for the renewal of Seattle's and Vancouver's urban waterfronts can be summarized in the following guiding principles: mobility, cultural heritage, economic impact, natural environment, urban ecology, enhancement of the waterfront as a place for people, and the character of civic spaces. Both cities have introduced 'Priority Green Permitting', an accelerated pathway to development approval and financial incentives, assisting innovative projects to become visible models of sustainability. The following issues are interrelated, but they can act as a framework for the renewal of all central waterfronts:
• Connecting the city's unique urban qualities with the waterfront: The waterfront should feel like and function as a seamless extension of the urban fabric. The sloping topography

offers important views and streetscape experiences that unfold toward the water, enhancing connectivity. Distinctive features such as squares and markets should be more directly connected – visually, physically and experientially – to the waterfront. Roadway schemes should be configured to strengthen important relationships.

• Creating a vibrant mixed-use waterfront district with quality public space linking the urban core to the waterfront: The waterfront should become a vibrant urban district with public open spaces that can support informal activities as well as scheduled public events. It should offer access to the water and the experience of water, creating a physical connection to the water that is a central part of the region's heritage.

• Contributing to a citywide mobility plan: Without a highway or railway corridor on the waterfront, tremendous opportunities emerge to develop a thriving urban district that will enrich the entire urban core. To achieve a traffic-free waterfront will require an integrated mobility plan that captures roadway capacity elsewhere, leverages use of transit systems and other non-vehicular transportation, such as bicycles, and integrates the waterfront district into that system.

• Improving the environment: The waterfront plan should integrate with the natural ecology of the shore and protect its ecosystem. It also can support the city's efforts to build a denser urban environment by creating the shared open space that urban density requires. Urban density and compact growth means fewer cars and less pollution.

• Creating a framework for continued development: The waterfront should develop through an open-ended plan that comprehensively establishes the parameters for development and allows for broad-based participation in its continued evolution as an urban place. As a community, we treasure our relationship to water. We aspire to create a great urban waterfront that enriches the social, economic and spiritual heart of the community.

• Model for urban renewal: twin city Newcastle upon Tyne – Gateshead (UK)

Heralded as one of the new creative cities of Northern England, the urban renewal of the twin-city Newcastle–Gateshead is an impressive case. Not long ago, unemployment was high, industry decaying and young people moving away in large numbers to find work in London. A continuous urban renewal-led programme over twenty years was necessary to turn the exodus around and create a positive image. The basic idea is that artistic genius of a younger generation needs affordable studio and loft space to be attracted to a place. High prices of studio space in London became unaffordable, and the re-discovery *zeitgeist* of cheaper northern cities and their previously unfashionable locations started. The regeneration of those cities as cutting-edge cultural and economic centres for the new *Creative Class* evolved (an effect described well by Richard Florida, 2002). Today, the former `Coal Hole of the North' has a vibrant art scene and a growing new economy around IT. A positive city image was created by much published projects, such as the Sage Performing Arts Centre, the Millennium Bridge and the Baltic Arts Centre (the adaptive re-use of a former flour mill, see: Fig. 1, p. 123). In addition, there are few other places that enjoy as much local passion and unbridled enthusiasm as *Geordies* (or *Novocastrians*, as the residents of Newcastle are called) have for their city – and in this regard not too dissimilar to the population of their partner city in Australia. The sense of identity of the population is strongly connected to a sense of belonging to their city. The region is central to who they are and the inhabitants are intensely proud of their heritage. An ambitious regeneration programme has brought the whole city centre back to life. Around 40 per cent of the buildings in the centre are heritage-listed and well preserved, the most impressive of it is the ensemble that forms elegant Grey Street.

Some un-built examples of new eco-city projects, currently in planning or construction phase, include:

• Wanzhuang Eco-City near Beijing (China)

Sustainable development in China has its particular challenges. Every year for the next 20 years it is estimated that up to 10 million people will move from China's countryside to its urban areas. This unprecedented migration will place huge demands on existing cities, and the volume of people is so large that there is no one answer to accommodating them in a sustainable way. The global consulting firm Arup is working on several initiatives with the Chinese Government, private developers and research institutes that will form part of the solution. Wanzhuang Eco-City is one such initiative that will transform a number of existing communities into an eco-city. The site of Wanzhuang Eco-City is in China's Hebei Province, 45 kilometers south-east of Beijing and half way between the nation's capital and the port city of Tianjin. It is close to the city of Langfang, which some have dubbed `China's Silicon Valley' due to its fast developing economy based on computing and technology. The 80 sq km site includes 15 villages with a total population of 100,000. The area has been selected by the Chinese Government for development into a city that will accommodate a population of 400,000 by 2025. The design proposal began with the simple proposition of retaining and enhancing the existing communities through selective renovation and regeneration. Historic buildings and street patterns will be retained as a footprint for the new city and the villages expanded as mixed-use communities which connect through walking, cycling and public transport to create the city. Jobs will be created for residents in a range of different zones. Expansive historic pear orchards, which are a key feature of the region, will also be preserved. The existing villages in the area are culturally diverse and under the Arup scheme will become distinct neighbourhoods with their own local identity. A range of methods for reclaiming and distributing water for drinking and non-drinking (grey water) use have been suggested. In addition, a new public bus or tram network, linking all the villages to Langfang and to a new high-speed rail station, is proposed. Fossil fuel vehicles will be restricted in the city, and a programme of extending the use of cleaner vehicle technologies is being promoted. (See: Appendix)

• Masdar Eco-City, near Abu Dhabi (UAE), currently under construction

This ambitious demonstration project of a planned city 20 km south-east of Abu Dhabi's urban core, launched in 2008 and designed by a team including Foster and Partners et al, will help to realize Abu Dhabi's vision for 2020, which predicts 7 per cent of the total power generation will come from renewable energy sources. It is a government initiative to accommodate 50,000 residents and 60,000 workplaces (a square, approx. 7 sq km in size; total 6 million sqm floor space), is being constructed over seven phases and is due to be completed by

2020. It's planned as an independent `green business park', and its compactness is modeled on Shibam, the thousand years old city in the desert of Yemen. Masdar has equally a compact, self-shading layout with the typical narrow laneways of Arabic towns. This new cty is intended to demonstrate to the world that it is possible to live in a sustainable manner in an extreme desert climate, while increasing the quality of life of the city's inhabitants. The principles laid down for this project include: zero emissions; total recycling of waste; sustainable transportation (cars stay outside the city); extensive use of local materials; locally-produced food; solar energy generation from the sun, wind and waste; and sustainable use of water and energy. It is expected that over 50 per cent of the resident workers will be employed within Masdar Eco-City. Whether it will become a popular place for families to live is still unclear, and it might yet develop as a new kind of business park and innovation centre. In the meantime, the existing Abu Dhabi city is still waiting for retrofitting and public space improvement programmes.

Masdar plans to supply its energy from renewable energy sources. The ambitious plans include the investment of US$20 bn in renewable energy projects in the carbon-free city. Masdar hopes the initiative will earn Abu Dhabi a reputation as the world's main development hub for renewable energy technologies, not wholly reliant on oil profits for its wealth. Research will be conducted at the Masdar Institute of Science and Technology. The technological advancements are significant, such as geothermal power sourced from underground heat that will form an important part of the green city's electricity mix. The biggest source of energy will come from the sun, and a huge solar thermal power plant will be located next to the city.

The city will be skyscraper-free, and photovoltaic (PV) arrays on building rooftops and at a 275 MW solar farm will collect sunlight for power. A desalination plant that will provide fresh water will use solar power as well. The city will also use energy from an innovative hydrogen power plant, utilizing another clean source of energy. To keep energy needs low and the city cool, the masterplan is orienting the city to take full advantage of naturally prevailing sea breezes. A wall encompassing the city and wind towers for buildings will contribute to protecting the population from the harsh desert winds. In addition, buildings will shade the narrow walking lanes, and air will travel through sub-labyrinths (underground ducts) to stay naturally cool. Since the city utilizes a whole range of sustainable technologies, it is expected that energy demand will be reduced by 70 per cent. The developer hopes to save US$2 billion in oil after 25 years. Efforts to conserve water involve plans to recycle at least 80 per cent of the water used. Recycled grey water, such as water from residences and treated waste water, will irrigate the landscape. Through these processes, the city planners hope to reduce water consumption by 60 per cent. (Sources: Masdar; *New York Times; BBC*, all 2009) A zero-waste concept is proposed by composting organic waste (20 per cent) and recycling materials (50 per cent). The organic waste will end up in a compost pile, where bacteria will be added to decompose the material. The remaining 30 per cent waste will be incinerated to generate energy. There will be no cars in Masdar Eco-City; people will never be further than 200 metres from a public transportation point. An electric-powered light rail on elevated tracks will allow easy transport between Masdar Eco-City and Abu Dhabi. To get around the city, people can utilize personal rapid transit pods, (or PRTs); these vehicles will run underground on magnetic tracks, using electricity.

The Masdar City project is now setting new benchmarks for the careful selection of construction materials and processes, in terms of material life-cycle and supply chain analysis. The long-term positive environmental impact that Masdar is pursuing goes beyond the finished city and the outputs of its residents. The Masdar team has developed an approved materials and product directory, including a restricted materials list, a carbon emission table and material guidelines for the construction of the new eco-city. In this way, they are not only creating green buildings, but they are actively driving innovation in the materials and products that are used, helping key suppliers to develop their green product ranges. According to the Masdar product directory, materials and products must meet two of the following four criteria and remain neutral with respect to the others:

• made from salvaged, recycled, or agricultural waste content
• manufactured with resource-efficient, environmentally friendly processes (e.g. conserve water/energy, minimize pollutants and process wastes)
• beneficial to the built environment (e.g. conserve energy, remove indoor pollutants), and
• recyclable at the end of their life. (Masdar, 2010. See: www.masdarcity.ae)

The 'Masdar City Code of Conduct' states: 'We believe the actions of our suppliers are increasingly important factors in our sustainability performance and that they should therefore be viewed as partners in our sustainability aspirations. We take great care in selecting the companies who supply us with products and services, and expect each of them to operate to internationally recognized standards.' (Masdar, 2010. The project involves a large group of architects and engineers, including Foster and Partners, WSP, Transsolar, Systematica, ETA, Ernst & Young, Gustafson Porter, and others). However, the project is not without criticism: Hisham Elkadi argues, 'the project's failure remains in the social and cultural domain, with lack of integral sustainability; it is a gadget-based model. The question, of course, remains whether such efforts should take place at all in such a harsh environment.' (ElKadi, 2010)

A deeper understanding of site and context

From a closer look at these eco-city projects, it is obvious that sustainable design must start from the macro-scale of regional and urban planning (including the planning of new green infrastructure), right through to the design of eco-districts and eco-neighbourhoods leading to new models of urban life, before shifting to architectural design on the building scale. Environmentally-driven urban design and a deeper understanding of site and context have to be the basis of any work, not the exception, grounding our strategies firmly on the optimistic principles of green urbanism. A deep understanding of the site and its wider context (e.g. climate and community) has become even more relevant due to climate change, and this deep understanding has to be one of the key drivers for the urban design process. In this sense, climatic and contextual conditions are form-generating parameters for any project. Since every site has its own unique eco-system, its balance should not be destroyed by the thoughtless construction of buildings and roads. In this regard, Ken Yeang points towards the negative effect of sprawl: 'Urban sprawl irreversibly devastates and fragments eco-systems.' (Yeang, 2009)

As urban planners, we know about contradicting requirements of balancing the need to protect people from winds, but also to take advantage of cooling breezes in summer; or the problem of over-shadowing between buildings and the wish to achieve density and compactness within the district; and in regard to a better understanding of site conditions, contradicting requirements that need to be balanced, with the aim of developing an appropriate urban form, Federico Butera notes:

'Low energy urban design implies that shadow and surface illumination analysis, combined with wind analysis, must be used to optimize the shape, orientation and distances between buildings, in order to obtain maximum solar radiation and wind protection in winter, and minimum solar radiation combined with openness to ventilation in summer. The energy demand of individual buildings can be reduced significantly if this design strategy is adopted. It is not easy to combine these requirements, as they are often contradictory. There are some unmistakable rules, however: Buildings obliged to develop along the north/south axis because of the shape and size of the land, for example, will require more energy both for heating and cooling; or buildings to close to each other will hamper natural lighting, necessitating artificial lighting which increases the internal heat gains: more electricity consumed not only for lighting but also for cooling.' (Butera, 2008)

Feasible energy options and land use: creating an energy roadmap

The earth receives more energy from the sun in just one hour than the world's population uses in a whole year. But, how can we best transform this huge source of energy into useable electricity? Wind power offers huge opportunities too. Theoretically, wind power could supply all of the world's electricity needs. For a country like China, this would mean that it would need to cover around 10 per cent of its land area with wind farms.

The availability of land is crucial, as it defines how much power is consumed by land-area. The question is: how much land area do we consume to supply the energy required? The world's overall population density is about 50 people per sq km. The different countries, of course, vary significantly around the world average. In future, we can expect that renewable energy sources like wind and solar will increasingly compete with agriculture, urbanization and other uses of land. For instance, as their power consumption grows, India and China should expect renewable energy facilities to occupy a significant fraction of their land. Off-shore wind farms here have a clear advantage.

British scientist David MacKay has calculated that the average energy consumption on Earth is 56 kWh a day per person (this equals around the amount of energy that a person currently uses in Mexico and Brazil). However, the average European consumes 120 kWh a day per person. Countries with the highest power consumption in relation to their land area are Bahrain and South Korea (high consumption, but relative little land area). These densely populated, highly industrialized countries consume over 10W per sqm land area. MacKay recommends that 'each country will need to work out its own post-fossil-fuel energy plan', and this plan will largely depend on the individual characteristics of the country: anticipated lifestyle, energy consumption per person, population density, and geographic and climatic conditions (e.g. intensity of sun radiation). (MacKay, 2008)

Brazil, for instance, has managed to generate 80 per cent of its energy through hydro power and bio-fuels. In Middle Europe, the energy use of homes accounts for around 25 per cent of an individual's CO_2 emissions. Eco-districts will need to operate on 100 per cent renewable energy, or as close to 100 per cent as possible. The technical and economic feasibility depends, of course, on the renewable resources available in each location and the cost and availability of the technology. CABE (the UK Government's 'Commission for Architecture and the Built Environment') recommends that 'at least 50 per cent on-site renewable energy generation should be possible and be the minimum standard for any eco-town.' (CABE, 2008) Decentralized energy generation in the districts, with small local units, will play an important role in the future energy mix, where a 'smart grid' will allow direct feed-in of surplus energy.

Ongoing management of the energy supply is also a consideration. The installation of a district-wide *combined heat-and-power* (CHP) co-generation plant might be feasible; this plant captures and uses the waste heat from electricity generation that might otherwise be lost. 'Passivhaus' standards (with extreme high insulation values) and super-efficient appliances should be standard in eco-districts. Visible real-time energy consumption figures should be provided to the residents for the monitoring of each dwelling, to help with behaviour change. The real-time monitoring of power consumption with smart meters (as part of the smart grid) will have a positive effect in private households, since people can check their personal consumption on a daily basis and take measures to reduce costs.

Because the energy topic is so relevant to the 'city of tomorrow', Chapter 2 discusses some technological innovations in the energy sector and how we can de-carbonize the energy supply.

The most sustainable building is the one that already exists. Looking at the life-cycle, green retrofits and adaptive re-use of existing buildings is always better than constructing new buildings.

Transforming the existing building stock

The biggest challenge is, of course, the existing city and the existing building stock. Strategies for upgrading the existing city are likely to be the future field of activity. Unfortunately, it is always harder to achieve higher energy-efficiency through retrofitting existing districts than it is in newly designed districts and neighbourhoods built from scratch (such as is currently happening in China or in the Middle East), where energy-efficiency can be built-in from the ground up. However, making older inefficient districts, older shopping centres and office blocks more energy-efficient can offer the rare advantage of being both economically and environmentally sensible.

Since most parts of the city already exist, it is obvious that a focus is required on the transformation of the existing city or districts to new models based on renewable energy sources and large-scale retro-fitting programmes. We don't have the time to retrofit one building at a time if we want to meet the target of cutting 60 per cent of emissions by 2050. What is needed are city-wide retrofitting programmes that look at the existing city as one whole retrofit project. Governments and municipalities need to be the drivers of this transformation. However, more practical research is needed in the possibility of a city-wide sustainable makeover, from food supply to density, from integration of renewables and clean technology to public mass transit systems, using the ecological footprint analysis to set out a measurable vision of life in sustainable communities of the future.

Bleyl and Schinnerl have extensively researched the potential of energy saving through a concentration of measures on the existing building stock and the advantages of using `energy contracting' as a tool to achieve higher energy efficiency. They note:

`While new building construction rates range between less than one per cent in an average city to over 10 per cent in booming regions, only some new buildings benefit from model energy performance. The majority of saving potential must be realized in the vast and already existing building stock. It is here where a major effort in the urban energy transition process must be made.' (Bleyl and Schinnerl, 2008)

Governments and municipalities are important players in the realization of green urbanism. Local, State and Federal initiatives are major drivers behind the growth of green building, making it happen through their legislation and policies. A good example for this is the recent European Union decision: A new EU-Directive is asking for new buildings to include renewable energy. The energy performance of buildings constructed after 2020 must improve and rely `to a large extent' on renewable energy, according to the deal reached between the EU Parliament and its Council. By the end of 2020, all 27 EU-Member States must ensure that all newly-constructed buildings have a `very high energy performance', under the rules agreed in Brussels in 2009. The energy needs of the buildings must be covered to a very significant extent from renewable energy sources, including energy produced on-site or nearby. The public sector is asked to set an example by owning or renting only this kind of building by the end of 2018, and by promoting the conversion of existing buildings into `nearly-zero' standards.

But not only new buildings are an issue. There are successful 'energy contracting' models available that have been tested by municipalities, to significantly accelerate the retrofitting rate; for instance, the city of Berlin has implemented a model of `Energy Saving Partnerships', which offers a solution for financing the transformation process. It is described in the following paragraphs.

The city of Berlin's innovative model of `Energy Savings Partnerships'

There are also new strategies for municipalities to kick-start the retrofitting and the insulation of their inefficient building stock, for energy-savings beyond high-tech photovoltaic panels and smart grid technology. For instance, Berlin has pioneered such an effective model for improving energy-efficiency in its existing building stock, managing the large-scale retrofit of public and private buildings and introducing changes that guarantee immediate reductions in CO_2 emissions in an average of 25 per cent. In the context of energy-saving contracting, investments for retrofitting can pay for themselves out of contractually-agreed savings within a defined period. How was it done?

The municipality wrote specific requirements into the public retrofit tenders so that winning energy systems companies had to deliver sustainable energy solutions and guarantee energy-efficient outcomes. So far, over 1,400 public buildings in Berlin have been up-graded with these contracts, delivering CO_2 reductions of more than 60,000 tonnes per year. The municipality established an independent organization (the *Berlin Energie-Agentur*, BEA) as the leading energy consultants. BEA is partly owned by the government of Berlin and organizes retrofits for large government and commercial buildings by setting up special contracts (Energy Performance Contracts) between the building owners and Energy Systems Companies (ESCo). When these ESCos apply for the retrofit tenders (usually advertised EU-wide), they agree to make specific energy-efficiencies (these possible increases in efficiencies were calculated at 25 per cent). The ESCos achieve this by install-ing sustainable technologies and systems to reduce energy consumption in the buildings, such as heating control systems, CHP, energy-efficient lighting, self-ballasted lamps, high insulation, energy consumption regulators, etc. These expected savings from the annual energy efficiencies are used to fund the cost of the retrofit measures. Average payback periods are short, only 8 to 12 years. BEA helps the building owners and ESCos to decide how the money will be best paid back to the ESCo. These energy partnerships are highly successful because they don't cost the building owner anything, yet they deliver immediate savings. (All figures supplied by BEA and City of Berlin, 2009) `Across Germany, effi-ciency contracting will cut energy costs by some Euro 800 mill. and reduce CO_2-emissions by 4.5 mill. tones each year', says Michael Geissler, director of BEA (interview 2009).

The municipality's ESCo approach in detail

Energy Savings Partnerships (in some countries called Energy Perfrmance Contracting) have been working successfully for over ten years, but their programme depends on the efficient interaction of all key players. The city of Berlin, through the Senate's Department for Urban Development, initiates the Energy Saving Partnerships between building owners – typically various Berlin district administrations – and ESCos. BEA then acts as the independent proj-ect manager, moderating and managing the process from baseline to contract negotiation. `Building owners agree to establish a tender process for retrofitting their buildings to cut back on energy consumption (bringing together a number of buildings, from 4 to as many as 400, into pools). Then retrofit tenders are issued for these building pools. ESCos that ten-der for the work (large companies, such as Siemens, Honeywell, Eon, or others) use state-of-the-art sustainable technologies and systems to reduce energy consumption in buildings.' (Geissler, 2009) Usually, key measures for Energy Performance Contracting do not include window replacement or full wall insulation, because the payback from the achieved savings would take too long. The winning ESCos must guarantee energy savings using innovative technology, ideas and value for money. The ESCo pays for the retrofit up-front and building owners pay them back over an agreed period (usually 8 to 12 years) in annual installments, which come directly from the energy savings. Once the contract is completed, the building owner realizes the full energy saving. The building owner pays nothing towards the retrofit, but makes guaranteed savings of 25 per cent on their energy bills from day one.

A typical example of a partnership follows, as supplied by BEA. The Energy Saving Partnership between Johnson Controls and the Berlin district of Pankow was entered into in 1998 from a EU-wide tender. The pool consisted of 56 housing estates within the district and a contract volume of around Euro 2 mill. per year for a baseline electricity consumption of around 50,000 MWh per year. The contract started in April 1999 and entered the main performance phase with energy savings becoming active in March 2000. The contract ends in 2013, after a duration of 14 years. CO_2 reductions are 2,500 tonnes per year. Energy Saving Partnerships work well, because they:

- guarantee significant savings by contract
- reduce energy consumption in large building complexes or building pool through investments by the contractor
- refinance the investment through energy savings, and
- allow the building owner to participate in the saved costs.

According to the people involved, the success of the Berlin Energy Saving Partnerships can be attributed to political will, transparent procedures, enforceable standards, and independent experts. Because of its success, the concept has been effectively transferred to other sectors. It has been applied to 15 hospitals throughout Germany and has helped initiate more than 20 projects in Central, Eastern and Western Europe (2009). The programme has transferred well to Bulgaria, Slovenia, Romania and Chile.

Further information on energy contracting and ESCo can be found at the following web sites: www.contracting-offensive.de; www.berliner-e-agentur.de

Fig. 1: The adaptive re-use of a former flour mill building to the centre of contemporary arts 'The Baltic Arts Centre', in Newcastle-upon-Tyne - Gateshead, UK, is part of the twin city's urban regeneration programme of the last 15 years. (Photo: S. Lehmann, 2007)

New jobs in the green economy – drivers of change

In 2009, the European Parliament and the European Council reached an agreement regarding the energy performance of buildings that fixes 2020 as the deadline for all new buildings to be net-zero energy buildings. (EU Directive, 2009) This marks a major breakthrough. Buildings are responsible for around 40 to 45 per cent of the world's energy use, and some of the easiest and most substantial cuts can be activated in the building sector. Energy-efficient urban design is the 'low hanging fruit' that will deliver significant reductions and will nearly always pay for itself.

We need to consider the value that the green economy will bring thousands of new, highly-skilled jobs to the city. It is understood that the role of the government, offering state incentives to facilitate the transformation, will be key. Forward-looking governments around the world now have a green jobs plan and are supporting green industry development rather than leaving it up to the private market to decide what happens. There are great examples for this: In only ten years, over 250,000 new jobs in the environmental technologies sector were created in Germany (between 1989 and 2008), and it is aiming for 500,000 new jobs by 2020. In 2009, US-President Obama invested a US$ 150 billion over ten years with the aim of creating millions of new green jobs. Estimates predict the creation of 5 million new jobs in environmental technologies in the US alone, in the

Drivers of Change: Towards Zero-Carbon Sustainable City Transformation

Fig. 1: A good example of affordable housing and part of a mixed-use, transport-oriented development on a brownfield site, where people live in inner-city apartments close to public transport: the 'Gish' apartment building in San Jose, California (by OJK Architects, 2007). There are 35 units in this complex and a third of them were set aside for disabled residents with special needs and 5 units to support low-income families. The ground floor offers a series of spaces for community services and a convenience store. The building is highly insulated and has a rooftop photovoltaic array for electricity and a solar hot water system. This project has become a model for the State of California for future compact inner-city housing. (Image: courtesy OJK Architects, 2009)

next ten years (*Newsweek*, 2009), many of which will be in re-training trades people, worldwide, the environmental revolution could create over 10 million new 'green' jobs in the next ten years.

In Australia, a recent report by Environment Australia (EA, 2009) claims that the Australian State of Victoria alone could immediately create 26,000 new green jobs, which would revitalize the State's economy and help reduce its carbon footprint. With the right public investment and policy shifts, such high-skilled jobs would be created in five industry sectors: solar hot water technology, wind energy, technologies for energy and water efficiency, waste recycling, and rail manufacturing. In addition, a huge amount of training and education would also be required. A 2008 CSIRO report suggested that in Australia alone 3.2 million existing jobs would need to be transformed, 'greened', and up-skilled over the next ten year period. (CSIRO, 2008)

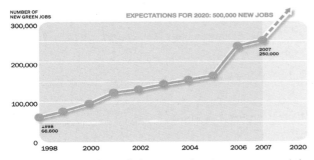

Fig. 2: Diagram showing the growth of new green jobs in Germany over a period of ten years. Having a government that is informed and positive about renewable energy technologies helps. The German government has taken a proactive role in promoting solar and wind power, and offers feed-in tariffs as compulsory higher-priced tariffs for energy generated from renewable sources. As a result, German renewable technology companies are now world leaders.

Replacing the old economy's carbon-intensive jobs and habits

Because green energy is still relatively labour-intensive, it promises many new jobs to replace those tied to the traditional fossil-fuel burning industry. As we replace our dependency on fossil-fuel energy with renewable energy sources, we are replacing the old economy's carbon-intensive jobs. Re-skilling workers employed in construction, manufacturing and services has seen a ten per cent growth per year. But new jobs will also be created for scientists and engineers working on new developments of the next generation PV-cells or energy storage technology; people building wind turbines or solar-powered steam generators; installing solar hot water systems; insulation installers and experts in retro-fitting entire existing office buildings and housing districts; workers upgrading public transit systems, constructing an electrical 'smart grid' that can better integrate renewable energy or affordable plug-in cars. To achieve the required transformation of industry and businesses means that governments in all countries will need to run industry-wide environmental skills audits to help industries get up to speed in the new technologies. New requirements will have to be placed on every business and organization. It is increasingly understood that organizations, like universities or large companies, must play their part in taking on environmental and social responsibilities. These organizations will have to become experts in communicating the changes to their customers and in changing entrenched ways on how to work and manufacture products. Going green poses a challenge, shifting conventional thinking to new ways, for instance, in shifting the way we design, build and operate cities. This shift will be led by organizations supporting innovation, keeping up with technology and setting new standards of carbon neutrality.

But it's not only about the technological transformation of industry and the creation of green jobs, it's also about the transformation of society and securing social justice. The climate change crisis has already triggered huge social transformations in the developed world, as well as in the developing world where the population has also become increasingly concerned about global warming. We see societies worldwide transforming into 'green' societies, moving away from fossil-fuels to renewable energy, and also towards energy-efficiency, energy conservation, and careful restraint in the consumption of energy. In their recent book *Natural Capitalism: Creating the Next Industrial Revolution*, Amory Lovins and Paul Hawken describe how leading-edge companies are now practicing a 'new type of industrialism' that is more efficient in its use of resources and profitable while saving the environment and creating jobs.

Inner-city connectivity and urban renewal: combining *Green TODs* with *Green Urbanism*

The type of urban development we want to see along public transport corridors and at transport nodes are the ones that reduce car dependency and help to transform the city into a commuter-focused city, establishing a highly-urbanized environment focused around a 'green transport-oriented development' (green TOD). (Kenworthy, 2008)

Most experts agree that green TODs are the way forward. It's important to mention that any public transit service, to be viable, needs the minimum of 35 people, and jobs, per ha (this would just enable a viable bus system). This means that a minimum of 10,000 people, and jobs, are required within a 1 km radius of a centre. Higher densities of a green transport-oriented development would obviously make other modes, such as a light railway system, viable. The compact walkable city will work with less car ownership, as we can see in Vauban. This district has only around 130 cars per 1,000 residents, whereas the adjacent city of Freiburg has 400 cars. Singapore offers very good public transport and, at the same time, limits the number of vehicles on the island. Compared to the per-capita income of Singapore, the number of car owners is surprisingly low. Car-sharing models are increasingly gaining popularity. Car-sharing is not a 'poor city's' concept; for instance, Zurich, one of the wealthiest cities worldwide, has the highest car-sharing rate in the world. Bike-sharing models – which are now being introduced – have been extremely successful in Paris, Barcelona, Beijing, Copenhagen, Munich, and many other cities. Most of the time, these models are financed by revenue from property developments, which pay for neighbourhood enhancements, green urbanism strategies and public place-making. Through the work of Jan Gehl, Copenhagen has been successful in reducing its inner-city car parking space by 2 per cent annually, upgrading its public space in an incremental process over two decades.

The combination of *Green TODs* and the principles of *Green Urbanism* is particularly promising, as this reduces the necessity to travel. Green TODs are transit-oriented and include bike and car-sharing. Green Urbanism adds resourceful urban planning which includes community gardens, zero-waste concepts, green architecture, and has energy-self sufficient districts. The city of Vancouver has built around 20 such green TODs in the last decade, which has helped to reduce car travel by 50 per cent.

It's clear that we have to adapt new concepts of mobility, where we anticipate the kind of infrastructure which we will need in 20 years time, instead of designing and building the same `old type' of infrastructure that adds to the problem.

A worldwide celebrated, outstanding example is the land reclamation and urban regeneration case in Seoul (See: Fig. 3): The Cheong Gye Cheon Freeway was turned into a 6 km long public space, a green corridor with river banks. The historically important river had been paved over in 1968, and an elevated highway was stacked above the road. Despite of its historic and cultural significance to Korea, the Cheong Gye Cheon remained covered for over half a century in an underground culvert. Then, miraculously, in 2003, in an act of political will, Seoul mayor Lee Myung-bak began the project of removing 16 lanes of stacked expressway and to restoring the lost stream beneath, and combined it with massive investment in a rapid bus transit system. Two years later, a vibrant park and river had replaced the traffic-choked freeway. Tearing out this inner-city freeway didn't create mass gridlock, as the project's opponents had predicted; traffic actually moves faster and more smoothly today than it did when the freeway was there. In an interview, Seoul's head city planner said that `as soon as we destroyed the freeway, the cars just disappeared and drivers changed their habits. They found a different way of driving or changed their routes.'

Fig. 3 a, b: Before and after: The inner-city freeway Cheong Gye Cheon in Seoul (Korea) has been removed 2003-05, and a naturalized waterway reopened. The images show before and after removal of the freeway. The greening and park lowered the temperatures in the city centre; lower summer temperatures and an improved air quality have been measured.

Coming back to the Newcastle issue: a disconnected city centre

The city of Newcastle has the potential to be a truly great post-industrial, knowledge-based city, and we have arrived at a crucial point in the city's urban development. But it's harder to rebuild and regenerate a city that is in decline. Clearly, a robust long-term strategy for the urban future of the city centre is required. And with forecasts predicting that we will see up to 10,000 more people in Newcastle city centre in the next 20 years (mainly young people moving downtown), our decisions of today will determine the urban development of the city centre for the next few decades. It is important that we avoid further deterioration of our city and, instead, develop its unique characteristics ('The city centre on the waterfront'). It should not be overlooked that smaller cities can sometimes lead urban innovation, so if we are to improve infrastructure, we should also consider new types of infrastructure to build. An opportunity for us to consider options for urban development is afforded by the barrier created by the city's railway line, which hinders inner-city pedestrian connectivity and best practice of urban development. With State Government's interest in regional cities, a remodeling process for the centre and the re-connection with the waterfront is now possible. (See: Fig. 4)

Pedestrian connectivity is a major issue, and no city is able to neglect it. By resolving the connectivity problem in its centre, Newcastle can become a more competitive city and a more attractive one for knowledge workers and for financial investment. For a long time, the Hunter Region has been left behind by the New South Wales State Government's failure to invest sufficiently in regional infrastructure in the area. The NSW State Government has not provided new public transport infrastructure to its regional cities for decades (the high-speed train link proposal between Sydney, Hornsby and Newcastle was stalled in 1998), which is now causing serious social consequences. The state's rail system itself has remained widely unchanged from the original vision developed by engineer John Bradfield in the 1930s and updated in 1956, despite the huge increases in the population. Cities in NSW are now seeing the social consequences of this in the growing divide between those who have access to public transport and those who do not. While the regional city is denied a high-speed train connection to the capital, the situation in Newcastle itself is not great either; the population density is simply much too low for an efficient public transport system such as light railway. *Green TODs* (such as the proposed Wickham Interchange) can only suceed if they have a minimum population density.

The vision for urban revitalization should always come from an urban design and architectural perspective. Transport planning needs to fit the form of the city, not the other way around.

What are the achievable and practical alternatives? Weighing possibilities

An ugly viaduct (such as the freeway along the river in Brisbane) or an equally ugly railway barrier (such as in Newcastle) along the waterfront is always more than just a transportation problem. It's a question of what we want our city to be and how we choose to present ourselves to the world. We must consider what it means to have a strong connection to the waterfront and how that connection can benefit the city core, environmentally, economically and socially. We need to ask ourselves: how can Newcastle create a waterfront befitting the highest ambitions of the city? The decision has significance for the entire city. Eliminating the railway barrier and creating a directly accessible waterfront will redefine the city's relationship to its single greatest asset and resource – the waterfront.

It is also the connectivity inside the city core which is frequently unsatisfying. The challenges we face go far beyond some of the narrow thinking that has characterized the debate on the heavy railway over the years. Transforming the city is based on a clear recognition that remaining with the disconnected `status quo' of the city centre is not an option. The central business district is suffering from serious disconnection. However, by connecting the city centre with the harbour and its waterfront renewal development (Honeysuckle), we would provide a huge catalyst for further transformation that would change and transform the entire centre, with positive flow-on effects generated from it.

Newcastle city centre occupies around 200 ha, while any predicted growth could probably be accommodated on a further 30 ha to 50 ha. This growth cannot be spread too thinly, therefore it needs a clear plan about where higher density can occur and what kind of public domain and public transport system needs to be implemented. More than ever, the coordination of the different parts of the city is important; they cannot be looked at as isolated elements.

The waterfront should feel like and function as a seamless extension of the urban fabric, with strong pedestrian connections.

The `Green Corridor': removing the heavy rail line to remodel waterfront access and increase connectivity

In this context, just offering a couple more crossing points and keeping the rail line would not make much of a difference to the city, and it is only a half-hearted attempt at best in solving the problem. The additional crossing-points would keep the system uncoordinated and further slow it down. It could, in fact, create even more disruptions (making the heavy rail even more unattractive) and would do nothing to unleash the city's full potential. It has become clear that new developments in Hunter Street won't be sustainable until the CBD has a better connectivity to the harbour and to Honeysuckle. The favoured solution should therefore be the removal of the last 2 kilometres of heavy rail, stopping trains at a new transport hub in Wickham, as this is where the necessary land would be available and where we find fewer issues with mine subsidence. This new arrival point to the city requires the design of a new city terminus, a Newcastle Transport Hub, with a public plaza connecting it to the water, where visitors can immediately feel that they have arrived at a seaport city. If Wickham is developed into a green Transit Oriented Development (similar to Parramata or Chatswood in north Sydney), it could become a 'gateway' to the city. The existing Newcastle terminus can easily be adaptively re-used, e.g. as a fish and organic food market, possibly with a conference facility. This idea triggered the brief for the `Green Corridor' studio, and the results of this studio are presented in Chapter 3. This green corridor would become a marvelous landscape spine dedicated to pedestrians and cyclists, as illustrated by the elegant designs presented in Chapter 3.

What should happen, and what form of public transport should then replace heavy rail?

I would like to suggest two prerequisites for taking out the railway line:

1. With a clear focus on the public domain and improvement in connectivity, the open land gained (after removal of the heavy rail) needs to be kept open and used for safe biking, with good landscaping and cycle paths, with only a few areas where new buildings are integrated along the edges, in areas where the corridor widens up. This linear space could be developed into a cultural landscape ribbon walk, with very easy accessibility (a similar long, public strip like this can be found in other great waterfront cities like Copenhagen and Stockholm). This land should remain as high-quality public space in public ownership and become part of the larger network of inter-connected open spaces, accommodating pavilions, gardens, urban farming, and having various other community functions.

2. An efficient bus system needs to be put in place. We cannot afford to find ourselves, later, where we have lost the last two kilometres of heavy rail without having improved the overall public transport system. For small cities that cannot afford light railway, a *Rapid Bus Transit System* (RBTS) with modern hybrid buses using, for instance, electrical and diesel, would be a good solution. This needs to be done in a way that does not add significantly to traveling times and has quick transfer modes between bus and rail and bikes. Also, we need to take into account that having the bus bring you close to where you want to be will gain some travel time, and also reactivate retail along Hunter Street. As long as a high frequency of buses is guaranteed (e.g. operating every 5 to 7 minutes, over 600 buses per day along Hunter Street), the modern RBTS presents a comfortable and affordable solution.

Transport planner Robert Cervero has studied the popularity of the 'TransMilenio' rapid bus transport systems in Curitiba. The Curitiba model has been so successful that it has been replicated in Bogota, Quito, Hangzhou, Jakarta, and many other cities worldwide. His comparison between two Brazilian cities of approximately same size, Curitiba and Brasilia, speaks for itself: (Cervero, 2010)

	Curitiba	**Brasilia**
Population	around 3 mill.	around 3 mill.
Persons p. sq km	3,470	420
VKT (vehicle km traveled) p. capita per year	7,900	16,700
Public Transit trips p. capita per year	355	97

Curitiba's urban strategies and focus on a high-quality bus network dramatically reduced the city's car dependency (another good example would be the Ottawa bus-way system in Canada).

Fig. 4 a, b: The last 2 km of heavy railway line in Newcastle creates an impermeable, fenced-off barrier. The 'Green Corridor' proposals are not about taking away public transport, but about improving it and making it more attractive! It is about replacing an outmoded, 19th-century heavy rail system with a better, more efficient and future-proof system. (Photos: S. Lehmann, 2006)

An efficient bus system as part of the solution

How is it to best get more of the 88 per cent of the Hunter population currently commuting by private car into public transport? Newcastle City Council's target usage for public transport has been set at a modest 30 per cent, but so far little has been done to achieve it. However, there is an option that could resolve this problem.

In more densely populated areas, I usually like to advocate a light railway system or rail-based public transport. However, the situation with the last 2.5 km heavy railway in Newcastle's city centre is different, as it hinders the proper urban development of the city and the population density is far too low to support a light railway system. Extensive economic modeling by Parsons Brinkerhoff has shown that a light railway is not feasible for Newcastle, as it lacks the population density to justify such an investment. Light railway is very expensive and would take resources away from other needs. (See: Reports by Urbis and Parsons Brinkerhoff, Dec. 2008, available online at the HDC website). An alternative solution for the city is a high quality bus-based system, one that can comfortably service all areas, is clean and attractive and makes travelling by bus a positive experience. A fleet of 'green' buses, modern hybrid buses (a mix of express and mini buses can be highly economical) is a particularly good solution for smaller cities – something that all innovative traffic planners worldwide agree on. The Latin-American cities of Curitiba (Brazil) and Bogota (Colombia) have demonstrated how to transform cities with inexpensive, immediate measures by moving residents and workers more quickly, cleanly and efficiently. (See: Figs. 5 and 6)

David Hensher, former Director of the Institute of Transport Studies at the University of Sydney, has extensively explored the many benefits offered to Australian cities by bus-based transit systems, and points to the advantages of a bus rapid transit system. (Hensher, 1999) For Newcastle, a clear investment strategy for buses is most appropriate, together with the promotion of integrated bus travel (and allowing, for instance, free looping buses for under 18 and over 65 years old) connecting Newcastle East with The Junction and back to Wickham Terminal. Bus and rail services need to be able to share the same ticket. Access into buses should be raised at bus stops so commuters can enter at grade, and buses should run frequently. The high frequency of buses needs to be guaranteed. Two types of buses could be in service: longer express buses and smaller buses stopping in a finer grain, making two different loops. Such hybrid buses (low emission vehicles as are in use in Freiburg, Seoul, Singapore and other cities) will become more and more part of the new reality of a low-carbon future, while improving social equity.

Modern bus systems are the most affordable form of public transport. For decision-makers, it is important to understand that public transport does not necessarily need to make a profit; it is part of a public service in any civic society. A democratic city should charge the same bus fare for long or short distances. It is probably fair enough to have short distance commuters subsidizing long distance users who need to reach the suburbs. It is even fairer that car user subsidize public transport (as we can see happening in Singapore and in London, with congestion charging schemes). This is especially useful for financing public transport.

There are some impressive examples of bus systems: The 'TransMilenio' bus systems in Bogota and Curitiba are now moving more passengers per hour and per kilometre than 90 per cent of rail systems, and this is done at only 10 per cent of the cost (and at similar speed). Express buses on roads without traffic lights (on dedicated bus lanes) are faster than non-express light railways. In fact, Rapid Bus Transit Systems can compete with light railway and other systems at a much lower cost, but need modern infrastructure, attractive bus stops and good management. This is why over 83 cities worldwide have introduced an RBTS system in the last 10 years.

Buses have some more advantages; for instance, they do not have to stay on tracks and can minimize time-consuming transfers. Road space should be allocated first to public transport (giving a priority lane over private interests) as private automobiles carry fewer people, take up lots of space and require more infrastructure. Hunter Street is wide enough to run a dedicated bus lane, maybe even one lane in each direction, giving a priority lane to buses in the morning and afternoon peak hours. Putting the new, high-tech bus stops in Hunter Street would generate foot traffic, and bus travellers would further help activate Hunter Street.

An efficient state-of-the-art bus network will convince many car drivers to commute to work by using public transport.

In summary, how to make the bus network attractive:

- Develop a new overall Transport Plan for the city centre, which incorporates pedestrian connectivity, bike paths and public domain connectivity, with a clear pedestrian and cycle priority over private vehicles.
- Integrate a transport fare system (rail to bus transfer, free or discounted), with coordinated timetables.
- Reorganize bus routes (two different loops, with express buses and mini buses).
- Build high-tech bus stops that are fun and useful for older people.
- Initiate IT-based high tech management (Bus Management System with GPS, Smart-Card), coordinated with train schedule, and thus reducing waiting times.

- Create a new operation system for joint revenue management.
- Allocate a dedicated bus lane in Hunter Street and run free high-frequency buses (larger express buses, smaller short distance buses).

With these actions, we make `taking the bus' more popular and acceptable, so people will leave their car in the garage. Buses were for a long time perceived as transport for the poor. It is time to refer to them more elegantly as `Rapid Transit Systems' or `TransExpress' or similar, and not simply as `the old bus'. [3]

Fig. 5 a, b: RBTS: A dedicated bus lane will give public transport priority. Modern bus stops contribute to the better image of 'taking the green bus'.

Fig. 6 a, b: RBTS principles established in Seoul City. These modern hybrid buses offer much more comfort and information to the passengers. Tickets can combine rail, subway, bus and ferry. (Source: Image Sharing Commons)

Unhealthy consumption patterns: reducing car dependency

There is convincing evidence that urban form and quality density (compactness), combined with environmentally-friendly public transport systems, strongly influence energy consumption at the city level. Cities that are more compact, focus better on pedestrians and cyclists, use more clean energy and are less dependent on motorized transport. These cities are not only more energy-efficient but offer a better lifestyle and emit less greenhouse gas emissions.

Thus, a necessary aim is to reduce our dependency on the car. The `car is king' mentality belongs to the last century; it has to stop and must be replaced by a clear commitment to modern and efficient public transport. For instance, Singapore and Seoul have for years invested five times more in public transport than in roads, and by doing so both cities have gradually built some of the world's best, low-impact public transport systems. Cycling is also important, as it provides people with an alternative to cars and public transport for short trips. A recent survey of the city of Newcastle found that 75 per cent of people in the city centre who cycle irregularly would do it more often if there were more dedicated, and safe, cycle routes. For instance, in the last ten years, a series of cycling-friendly initiatives helped to increase the percentage of trips by bike in hilly San Francisco to 2.5 per cent (which is 3 times the rate of Sydney; data: 2009). This was mainly achieved with separate, safe cycle paths and allowing the free transport of bikes on trains.

Obsessed with the private car: the most vehicle-reliant part of Australia
A major issue that needs to be addressed is the Hunter Region's and Newcastle's high car-dependency and increasing reliance on the private motor car, with almost as many vehicles as people, and a failing public transport network. The Road and Transport Authority's (RTA) data for 2005 to 2009 shows a 20 per cent increase in car registrations, and the rise in car registrations is outstripping the region's population growth. Census data shows that more than 90 per cent of workers in the region used a motor vehicle going to work, while the use of public transport decreased by 3.5 per cent from 2001 to 2006, down to only 5 per cent of all trips made by public transport (leading to higher energy consumption and air pollution); the number of private vehicles grew from 370,952 (in 1997) to 516,073 (in 2009). If we retain the rail corridor for non-development uses and offer good cycle ways and landscaping along the green corridor, step by step we will see the building facades facing the new landscaped strip change in order to relate to this new public frontage. A strong public space network that encourages walking and cycling – and makes walking and cycling more safe and pleasant – is the way forward.
Preserving the `green corridor' in public ownership enables the city to use this linear `park connector' for new mobility concepts. In a very short time, the rail corridor could easily be transformed into parkland with pleasant open spaces for cycling and walking integrated with the existing foreshore park. Hunter Street would best serve as the main corridor for green bus services, with a dedicated bus lane and car parking sites on the fringe of the city centre. The historical train station at Watt Street could be adaptively reused and transformed into a modern conference centre.

Here some further urban design matters:
• There is always a multiplicity of complex forces that form a city.
• Urban form affects a city's productivity and resource-intensity.
• Revitalizing the city's dilapidated buildings represents sustainable development.
• Close inter-connections between the different systems are good (e.g. bringing working and living together again, through a city campus and a `town and gown' relationship).
• `Best practice' planning anticipates the infrastructure needs of the future.
• More economic modeling of urban development scenarios is required.
• We need to stop providing new suburban housing without adequate public transport,

which only increases the car dependency further. It makes more sense to focus on inner-city renewal areas, rather than to expand car-dependant outer suburbs without public transport.

So, while we need to continue building infrastructure, we need to think about new kinds of low-carbon infrastructures, and we need to rethink public transport, the role of the car, new types of decentralization for local energy production, the de-carbonization of energy supply, and better water and waste management.

How to finance the line's removal and the remodeling of connectivity?

As long as the railway barrier is not removed and the CBD remains disconnected to the harbour and Honeysuckle, there won't be much revitalization in Hunter Street. It is, of course, the economy which dictates the pace of urban growth. It would seem that Public–Private Partnerships (PPP) is the way forward. If you look at the most successful projects worldwide, it is obvious that PPPs have been the enabling force, requiring excellent public policies and political leadership.

Some of the funding to finance change could come from Rail Corp. Millions of dollars will be saved by removing this part of the railway. According to Rail Corp's own figures (quoted in the local newspaper *The Herald*), they are currently losing around AU$ 4 mill. per year through operating on the last 2.5 kilometres of the inner-city rail line (not including running costs). A report in the newspaper (*The Herald*, 17 April 2009) states that there are 38 full time staff working at Newcastle Station alone. If there are another 5 staff at Civic Station, for a total of 43 staff, this equates to over AUS$3 million p.a. in staff costs alone, not taking into account the cost of maintaining the line and structures and the actual costs of running the trains for the last two kilometers. All these costs would be saved if a new Wickham Station was made the terminus, a green TOD. Rail Corp would obviously save a significant amount of money as a consequence of the removal of the rail line from Wickham on, money that could be reinvested in a better system. TODs are best developed as PPPs.

In addition, a coal levy from mining companies could easily generate significant amounts of investment in our city centre. Now that we have reached the end of the last great coal boom, which is estimated to peak in 2025, it would be highly appropriate to fund local, environmentally-friendly initiatives through the global coal export profits in the city's own harbour.

The heavy railway line's retention cannot be justified by its passenger usage

The actual passenger use of this last 2.5 kilometers of heavy rail is very small. Figures in the recent Rail Corp report show that this last section of the railway gets very little usage, and actually fails to adequately get people from where they are to where they want to go. Given the outcome of a recent residents survey (a HVRF survey, carried out in September 2008, showed that around 70 per cent of the residents support the cutting of the heavy rail) and the real usage frequency, it is unjustifiable to argue for retention of the last two kilometers of heavy rail; this rail section is a throw-back to 19th-century industrial times when ships were loaded in Wharf Road. In effect, we carry 21st-century traffic on infrastructure that was put in place in the 19th century. This is entirely inappropriate for the contemporary

Fig. 7 a, b: The comfort and safety which a Rapid Bus Transit System (RBTS) would deliver including displays to see when the next bus is arriving and high-tech waiting areas. (Courtesy: E. Penalosa)

city where connectivity, easy access and pedestrian linkages are everything. For a service that carries in average of only around 25 to 27 passengers per train, it is ironic that the only real argument against removing the rail is a slightly increased travel time for a few rail users changing to bus services. [4]

Of course passenger numbers are a very important factor in the discussion. Average loadings of passengers on a train are so low that it makes the current heavy rail service questionable on economic and environmental grounds. The choice is between running an outmoded heavy rail system that carries less than 27 passengers per train, or unleashing the potential of a remodelled city centre. The city could significantly be improved in less than five years. To make it happen, we need to propose the best scenario, get the priorities right and identify the three to four catalyst projects that are achievable for bringing the city forward.

The city centre's remodeling for reconnection with the harbour and foreshore
Urban waterfront renewal can only happen when the new developments are strongly connected with the rest of the CBD (see other successfully remodeled post-industrial waterfront cities, such as Boston, Vancouver, Barcelona, Hamburg, Bilbao, Amsterdam and so on). The waterfront provides wonderful possibilities for an `urban stage' to the city.
Today, Newcastle city centre is still disconnected from its major urban waterfront development (from Honeysuckle). The Mall is suffering and shops are closing down in numbers. A more intensive and closer connection between water and the city is crucial and needs to be rejuvenated. This is what we can call `knitting the waterfront project back to the city centre', connecting the historical city to the growth areas along the harbourfront. There is clearly no point in having urban regeneration projects if you cannot get to them. The `City Centre on the Water' is a great, powerful image to aspire to. Successful and sustainable cities have built strong connectivity and have always focused on pedestrian movement and cycling.
Newcastle will have to become less car-oriented. To achieve this, it will need quality public transport: an efficient modern and green bus network. Buses are very much the backbone of public transport in Newcastle. Light rail has only a chance where population densities are sufficient (as proven by numerous cases across the world).

The studio projects were set on the basis, that the railway corridor is kept in public owner-ship and reserved for future smart uses, such as decentralized energy generating (`solar canopy'), water collecting, eco-transport concepts, as carbon-sink, pedestrian and cycling spine, and for urban farming uses.

The construction of a new interchange to terminate heavy rail on the edge of the city centre (at Wickham) would always have to proceed as the first step. The existing heavy railway infrastructure would then need to be removed, as it would be incompatible with the urban design vision and with any light railway that attempted to integrate well into the public domain. As long as the heavy rail is kept, the land will always be considered a heavy rail corridor in an urban area (with all the safety rules for it), and it will be treated as such; Rail Corp will continue to refuse buiding just one extra level crossing in the city, as these are regarded as a high safety risk.

The heavy rail corridor is tearing the city in half, forming a real barrier to sustainable development – creating long, disconnected strips of land. The potential for Newcastle's sound urban develop-ment is still limited by this 19th-century piece of infrastructure.

A far reaching masterplan is needed

Australia is starting to feel the impact of climate change, higher temperatures and ongoing droughts. Newcastle and the Hunter Region are not exempt from this. In conclusion, we will need a far-reaching and comprehensive *Vision 2020 Masterplan for Newcastle* (with a strong focus on the public domain, connectivity and public transport), which nourishes optimism and helps us form the right sort of sustainable framework for Newcastle's urban development. The masterplan would need to offer a staging, so it can be realized step-by-step, as funding becomes available. [5]

Fig. 8 a, b: The linear landscape as public space of high quality: About 2.5 km long (after removal of the heavy rail), needs ideally to be kept open and used for safe biking with good landscaping and cycle paths. Our study recommends a new 'Newcastle' station at Wickham, which will act as 'gateway' to the CBD and maintain heavy rail access to the city (until Wickham). A new public plaza could connect this station with the port. We recommend a string of urban renewal projects and a user-friendly, integrated public transport system, based on buses and cycling. The recommenda-tions of our study are achievable in the next 5 to 10 years. Image left: public space Paris (Photo: S. Lehmann, 2008)

Fig. 9: Curitiba (Brazil): The Rapid Bus Transit System is a great example of how affordable public transport can move a city towards environmental sustainability. The plan is to allocate a dedicated bus lane in Hunter Street and run free high-frequency buses (green hybrid buses: larger express buses, smaller short distance). (Image: Courtesy J. Lerner)

Fig. 10: The new bus route would stop at a series of 8 unique precincts throughout the city, connecting the important precincts and major destinations. Along Hunter Street, these destination stops would be: Administration / cultural hub – retail (redeveloped mall) – health (polyclinic) – education (city campus) – living + working – justice (legal precinct) – leisure (beaches). The *green TOD* at Wickham will need a higher population density in its direct proximity.

Fig. 11 a, b: Dedicated bus lane in Hunter Street, dedicated cycle lanes in the 'green necklace'. (Diagrams: UNESCO Chair, C. Norris and R. Bradley, 2008)

According to the final report of the NSW Government's Urban Task Force (Report, Dec. 2008), the rejuvenation of Newcastle's city centre would provide over 11,000 jobs and bring over AUS$1 billion in economic activity to the city. The document outlines four `catalyst projects' that entail the establishment of an inner-city university campus, a new justice precinct, improved public transport system and the staged delivery of a high-quality public domain. The consultants found: `By pursuing the four catalyst projects, up to 4,700 direct jobs and 7,000 indirect jobs will be created through the construction phase, with approximately 2,400 full- and part-time jobs ensuing.'.. It also would mean an injection of up to 5,000 students into the city as users of the new city campus, which would be built in three stages over a period of 5 to 10 years.

The recent survey showed there is a clear majority in Newcastle that wants the city to progress, who would like to see a better connected city centre, and who would like to have the last bit of heavy rail barrier removed. Clearly, there is work that needs to be done.

Some concluding remarks: prospects for the future

In conclusion, there cannot be one definition of the term `sustainability', as various concepts have expressed a diversity of possible meanings. In the recent debate about the theory of urban sustainability, the tension between the technical and the social has been an obvious one, but so has that between the ecological and the economic. The contributions of the case studies (projects from the design studios) to the discourse can only be a beginning to formulating ongoing explorations, to define a new set of design principles for the city and to arrive at a critical interpretation for future studio teaching.

The first chapter has explored how we might be able to best address in teaching the need for environmental sustainability on the urban scale. The wish to achieve a real difference requires urban designers to re-think the city and urban planning conventions. New compact models for urban growth will be part of long-term strategies for urban renewal and will help to achieve a sustainable, revitalized city centre. Many students were interested in integrating and re-using existing structures, as the most sustainable building is the one that already exists (due to its embodied energy). This approach has the advantage that it keeps the city centre authentic and the public space network vital, while also enabling a careful development of higher densities around transport nodes and cultural and educational facilities. [6]

Today, in many cases, large corporations and department stores have abandoned the city centre, while downtowns are increasingly turned into residential districts and centres of entertainment, education and culture. The *City Campus/Green Corridor* projects propose a denser, mixed-use and revitalized Newcastle city centre, where educational facilities and the university play a major role. On the other hand, the *Port City* project recommends a model for urban expansion – to be applied after having first densified and revitalized the city centre. The main aim of the City of Newcastle should be to connect its dying city centre to the redeveloped harbour by removing the railway barrier, and to keep the rail corridor free for the future, as `green corridor' (the protection can easily be regulated by a legal document and control plan) for future capacity to accommodate light rail. The design of a new Wickham Transport Interchange (the future `Newcastle' station) needs to be part of this masterplan. It is a myth that the last 2 kilometres of this heavy railwayline contribute anything to help the city centre coming back to life.

Our studies have revealed the tremendous potential of a harbour to the city in general and of port-related waterfront sites in particular. The transition from fossil-fuelled urbanism to renewable city planning will be incremental. The timeframe of transforming an existing city district is around 20 years. Sustainability approaches are to be embedded in all new precinct planning guidelines for urban growth areas. Therefore, in conclusion, some of the findings from the urban design studios include:

• Low-density urban form has been for too long a principal contributor to carbon emission, while compact development fosters less driving, more interactivity and ensures that cities remain walkable.

• Retrofitting instead of demolition: It is more sustainable to integrate existing buildings for adaptive reuse.

• We need incremental change in our existing city districts: step-by-step transformations towards more energy-effective districts and neighbourhoods (possibly through street by street retrofits), and retrofitting the urban infrastructure and the improvement of public transport (including the installation of a `smart grid').

• Retrofitting entire business districts requires physical improvement of office buildings, e.g. exchanging the external façade envelopes to improve thermal efficiency and natural ventilation, removing old inefficient technology and increasing the floor area by putting extra floors on top (increasing the land use will pay for the cost of sustainability measurements).

• Demonstration projects are helpful, based on `the power of the good example'; however, there are significant complexities involved in defining a formula for sustainable urban form, and the definition of which urban form is most suitable in any given locality requires a complex optimization process.

• Savings in infrastructure are associated with compactness and urban intensification. Parallel to compacting, there needs to be an emphasis on infrastructure and public transport improvement in under-served suburban areas.

• Making better use of the available potential at local level by generating district-wide renewable energy, utilizing waste heat and cascading energy/water concepts.

• Achieving sustainable, more energy-effective urban form depends on a number of criteria, such as project size, configuration, orientation, density and response to context, and also with integration and re-use of existing structures, mix of use pattern, social condition, and the detailed design solution.

• More emphasis on appropriate compaction, while being sensitive not to increase the urban heat island effect and fully understanding the role of landscape and greenery within the city as carbon sinks.

• Recognizing, overall, that balancing the Hunter Region's projected growth and coal-based industries with environmental considerations is likely to continue to be a major challenge.

We have started to understand sustainable design as a world-shaping force. So many good things have already happened in a short time, and, to conclude Chapter 1, I would like to quote a policy expert. At the *UN Climate Summit COP15* in December 2009 in Copenhagen, the president of the *Bellona Foundation* (Norway), Frederic Hauge pointed out: `The climate crisis is a big, but not insurmountable problem. The greatest challenge is that we have very little time. The leaders of the world are all waiting for someone else to take the first step, and in the meantime we continue to race forward in the wrong direction … It is absolutely vital that the wealthiest countries immediately begin the transition from fossil fuels to renewable energy, and finance the deployment of clean technology in developing countries.' (Hauge, 2009)

Fig. 12 a, b: The light railway tracks of the tram in Barcelona are fully integrated at grade into the landscaping and pedestrians can cross at any point. Right: The comfortable entry and exit of Singapore's green buses add to the high acceptance of the bus network. Standards for energy efficiency, comfort and safety in public transport have significantly gone up in the last years. A growing number of cities have introduced fuel-cell-powered buses. (Photos: S. Lehmann, 2006)

Singapore has achieved an exemplary mobility model, where a relatively high per capita income of Singaporeans is combined with a surprisingly low number of private vehicle ownership. This is possible through high-quality public transport and high vehicle taxes and surcharges, making car ownership undesirable. Transit-oriented development in Singapore is hereby 'empowered' by transportation demand management, which makes public transport a respectale alternative to the car.

THE SUSTAINABLE CITY

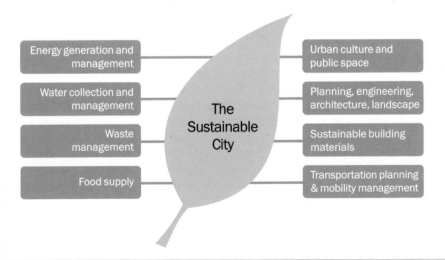

Energy generation and management

Water collection and management

Waste management

Food supply

The Sustainable City

Urban culture and public space

Planning, engineering, architecture, landscape

Sustainable building materials

Transportation planning & mobility management

References

Australian Bureau of Statistics (1990). Australian National Accounts, Capital Stocks 1988-89, ABS, Canberra

Arch+ No 196/197, special issue, Jan. 2010: *Post-Oil City,* Berlin, Germany

Banham, Reyner (1969): *The Architecture of the Well-tempered Environment.* University of Chicago Press, Chicago.

Beck, Ulrich (2000). *Risk Society. Towards a new Modernity.* Sage, London.

Bell, Daniel (1973/1976): *The Coming of Post-Industrial Society. A Venture in Social Forecasting.* Basic Books; Harper Colophon, New York.

Bleyl, Jan and Schinnerl, Daniel (2008). *Energy-Contracting to achieve energy efficiency and renewables using comprehensive refurbishment of buildings as example,* in: Urban Energy Transition, (ed.) Droege, P.; Elsevier, Amsterdam

Breheny, Michael J. (1992). *Sustainable Development and Urban Form.* Pion, London.

Brundtland, Gro H. (1987). *The Brundtland Report. Our Common Future.* UN-Report of the World Commission on Environment and Development. Oslo, Norway; United Nations. Oxford University Press, UK

Burton, Elizabeth (1997/reprint 2000): *The compact city: Just or just compact? A preliminary analysis.* In: Urban Studies, Number 37 (11/ 2000).

Butera, Federico (2008). *Towards the renewable built environment.* In: Urban Energy Transition, (ed.) Droege, P.; Elsevier, Amsterdam

CABE (2008). Report: *What makes an eco-town?* CABE, London (the UK Government's 'Commission for Architecture and the Built Environment'). Report available online.

Callenbach, Ernest (1975). *Ecotopia*; an utopian novel; Bantam Books, New York, USA.

Carson, Rachel (1962). *Silent Spring,* USA.

Chermayeff, S; Tzonis, A. (1971). *Shape of Community: Realization of Human Potential*; Penguin Books, London.

Cervellati, Pierro (1984). *La Città Postindustriale (The Post-industrial City).* Il Mulino, Bologna.

Cervero, Robert (2010). Presentation on public transport at the *World Future Energy Summit 2010* in Abu Dhabi, UAE (20 Jan. 2010).

Curdes, Gerd (1992). *Energiesparende Siedlungsstrukturen*; paper presented at Arbeitskreis Energie, Deutsche Physikalische Gesellschaft (Oct. 1992), Bad Honnef, Germany.

Cullen, Gordon (1964). *The Concise Townscape.* Architectural Press, London.

References for Chapter 1

Dey, Chris et al. (2007). *Consumption Atlas,* developed by ISA at University of Sydney, for the Australian Conservation Foundation; ACF Sydney: www.acfonline.org.au

Dovers, Stephen (2003). *Reflecting on three decades: a synthesis.* In: Dovers, S & Wild River, S (eds), *Managing Australia's Environment* , Federation Press, Sydney.

Droege, Peter (2009). In direct email communication with the author, February 2009.

Elkadi, Hisham (2010). *Advancing Architecture Ecologies*; paper in proceedings CSAAR Sustainable Architecture.

Evans, G.; Shaw, P. (2004). *The Contribution of Culture to Regeneration in the UK: A Review of Evidence,* London.

Florida, Richard (2002). *The Rise of the Creative Class,* Basic Books, New York.

Forster, Clive (1999). *Australian Cities. Continuity and Change,* (2nd ed.), Oxford University Press, UK

Gauzin-Mueller, Dominique, (2002). *Sustainable architecture and urbanism: Concepts, technologies, examples.* Birkhaeuser, Basel.

Girardet, Herbert (2008). *Cities, People, Planet. Urban Development and Climate Change.* (2nd ed.), Wiley, UK.

Hauge, Frederic (2009). In conversation at COP15 UN Climate Summit, Dec. 2009, Copenhagen, Denmark

Head, Peter; et al (2009). *Entering the Ecological Age.* Report by Arup, based on Head's talk for *The Brunel Lecture Series 2008-09,* London. Available online at: www.arup.com

Hensher, D. A. (1999). *A bus-based transit way or light rail? Continuing the saga on choice versus blind commitment*; in: Road and Transport Research, Vol. 8, No. 3, Sep. 1999, Sydney

Herzog, Thomas (ed.) (2007). *The Charter for Solar Energy in Architecture and Urban Planning.* Prestel, Munich.

Hotten, Robert (2004). *Sustainable Architecture: Twelve Things You Can Do To Build Effective Low Cost Houses and Cities,* Seadog Press, Monterey, USA.

Hughes, Robert (1987): *The Fatal Shore*; Australia and UK.

Hunter Valley Research Foundation (HVRF) (2009). *The Hunter Region at a Glance, 2009.* All quoted census data supplied by HVRF; available online at: www.hvrf.com.au

Hunter Development Corporation (2008): *HDC-Report for Newcastle. A report of the NSW Government's Urban Task Force,* with contribution by Parsons Brinckerhoff and Urbis, December 2008. This report was submitted to NSW Government by the Hunter Development Corporation in December 2008, with the inclusion of findings by various consultants (incl. the author's). Available online at: www.hunterdevelopmentcorporation.com.au

Jenks, Mike; and Burgess, Rod (eds) (2000). *Compact Cities. Sustainable Urban Forms for Developing Countries.* Spon Press, UK.

Johnson, Chris (2004). *Greening the City. Landscaping the urban fabric.* Government Architect Publications, Sydney.

Kats, Greg, et al. (2003). *The Costs and Financial Benefits of Green Buildings. Report to California's Sustainable Building Task Force*, Oct. 2003, Sacramento, USA.

Kearns, A., Barnett, G., Nolan, A. (2006). *An Ecological Design Strategy for the Planning and Development of Healthy Urban Habitat.* In: *BDP Environmental Design Guide.* Nov. 2006; The Australian Institute of Architects (AIA), Sydney (available online).

Koenigsberger, Otto (1980). *Manual of tropical housing and building: Climatic design.* Longman, London.

Lehmann, Steffen (ed.) (2005). *Absolutely Public: Crossover Art and Architecture;* Images Publishing, Melbourne.

Lehmann, Steffen, (2006). *Towards a Sustainable City Centre: Integrating Ecologically Sustainable Development (ESD) Principles into Urban Renewal.* In: *Journal of Green Building*, College Publishing, Vol. 1, Number 3 (Summer 2006), pp. 85-104: www.slab.com.au

Lehmann, Steffen (2008). Book chapter18: *Cities in Transition: New Models for Urban Growth and Neighbourhoods;* 409-432. In: *Urban Energy Transition. From Fossil Fuels to Renewable Power;* Elsevier Publisher (ed. P. Droege), Feb. 2008; Oxford UK.

Lehmann, Steffen (2008). *Growth of the post-industrial city: Densification and expansion - Two models for sustainability on the urban scale;* 43-48. In proceedings: *Oxford Conference 2008*, by Oxford Brookes University (July 2008); in: *The Oxford Conference. A Re-Evaluation of Education in Architecture;* WIT Press (Eds. S. Roaf, A. Bairstow); Oxford, UK.

Lehmann, Steffen (ed.) (2009). *Back to the City. Strategies for Informal Urban Interventions.* Hatje Cantz, Stuttgart/Berlin, Germany.

Lehmann, Steffen (2009). *Public Space: Empowering Community, Facilitating Urban Renewal;* 33-58. In proceedings: *Community, Health and the Arts: Vital Arts - Vibrant Communities;* the University of Melbourne (Sep. 2008); published in *UNESCO Observatory* E-Journal, Vol. 1, Issue 4, Aug. 2009; Melbourne, Australia.

Lerner, Jaime (2003). *Acupuntura Urbana,* English translation: *Urban Acupuncture,* Brazil: www.jaimelerner.com

MacKay, David (2008). *Sustainable Energy - Without the Hot Air.* UIT Cambridge, UK; available online at: www.withouthotair.com

Masdar City, Abu Dhabi (2010). Series of brochures published by the Madar City company, especially: *Why is Masdar City sustainable?* See also: www.masdarcity.ae

McHarg, Ian (1969). *Design with Nature;* Natural History Press/Falcon Press, Philadelphia, USA.

Mitscherlich, Alexander (1965). *Die Unwirtlichkeit unserer Staedte. Thesen zur Stadt der Zukunft.* Suhrkamp, Frankfurt.

Moewes, Guenther (1995). *Weder Huetten noch Palaeste. Architektur und Oekologie in der Arbeitsgesellschaft.* Birkhaeuser, Basel.

Mumford, Lewis (1961). *The City in History. Its Origins, its Transformations, its Prospects;* Penguin Books, London, UK

Newman, Peter and Kenworthy, Jeff (1989). *Cities and automobile dependence: An international source book.* Gower, Aldershot.

Newman, Peter (ed.) (2008). *Transitions: Pathways Towards Sustainable Urban Development in Australia.* Springer, Melbourne, Australia.

Pachauri, Rachendra / IPCC (2009). Quote from his speech at the *World Future Energy Summit 2009*, Abu Dhabi, UAE, January 2009.

Pasons Brinckerhoff (2009). Report, March 2009: *Newcastle CBD Integrated Transport: Newcastle.* Available online at the HDC web site: www.hunterdevelopmentcorporation.com.au

Register, Richard (1987). *Eco-city Berkeley: Building cities for a healthy future.* North Atlantic Books, Boston.

Ritzer, George (2007): *The Coming of Post-Industrial Society.* Second Edition. McGraw-Hill, New York.

Rowe, Colin; Koetter, Fred (1978). Collage City. MIT Press, Boston, USA.

Scott, Andrew, (2006). *Design Strategies for Green Practice.* 11-27. In: *Journal of Green Building*, College Publishing, Vol. 1, Number 4 (Fall 2006), Virginia, USA.

Sitte, Camillo (1889; translated in English in 1945). *City Planning According to Artistic Principles.* (German original: *Der Städtebau nach seinen künstlerischen Grundsätzen*). Vienna.

Stern, Sir Nicholas (2007). *The Stern Review: The Economics of Climate Change.* Cambridge University Press (October 2006, published January 2007). Available online at: www.sternreview.org.uk

Szokolay, Steven (2004). *Introduction to Architectural Science.* Architectural Press, Elsevier Science, London, UK.

United Nations (2008). *UN-Habitat's Third World Urban Forum: State of the World's Cities Report 2006/07.* UN Publications, Nairobi; Earthscan, London.

Urban Land Institute, (2007). *Growing Cooler*, study by ULI, USA: www.uli.org

Urban Task Force, Report by R. Rogers et al (1999). *Towards an Urban Renaissance*, London, UK>

Vale, Robert and Brenda (1991). *Green Architecture: Design for an Energy-conscious Future*, London, UK.

Wackernagel, Mathis; Rees, William (1996). *Our Ecological Footprint.* New Society Press, Vancouver BC.

Wackernagel, Mathis (2010). *Mankind is loaded with mounting debt;* interview with Steffen Klatt, in: *Cleantech Switzerland*, Spring 2010, Zurich. www.swisscleantech.ch

Wikipedia, the online encyclopedia; accessed 20th December 2009.

Yeang, Ken (2009). *Eco-Masterplanning.* John Wiley & Sons, London, UK.

Web Sites (Accessed January 2010)

www.enob.info Energy-optimized buildings

www.linz.at/english/life/3199.asp Site on SolarCity Linz-Pichling, Austria

www.oekosiedlungen.de Ecological settlements

www.passiv.at Site of the 'Passivhaus' institute

www.plusenergiehaus.de Site of solar architect Rolf Disch

www.solarsiedlung.de Site of company Solarsiedlung Freiburg

Notes

1. According to the Australian Bureau of Statistics and to CommSec (Report Dec. 2009), Australians have the largest homes worldwide. The Australian house is in average 214 sqm in size; this is in average 7 per cent larger than the average US home, about twice the size of the average European home and three times the size of the average house in the UK. Houses in Australia are now in average double the size compared to 50 years ago; however, the plot size is in average only half the size compared to 50 years ago. The house of today comes with a long series of rooms and garages for three cars are not unusual. Unfortunately, the water and energy consumption has also grown proportionally with the size of the houses.

2. For a long time, Newcastle residents have felt neglected by the State Government's Sydney-centric policies and for not receiving a 'fair share of funding', while the city of Newcastle has fallen into decline. In January 2010, *The Herald* (on 20 Jan. 2010) revealed, that New South Wales State Government has pocketed more than AUS$1.4 billion from Newcastle and Hunter-based authorities in taxes and shareholder dividends over the two years 2007-08, as crucial urban renewal and infrastructure projects continue to go unfunded in the city and region. The majority of money was collected from the region's two coal-burning powerstations (Bayswater and Liddell, both old technology and huge CO_2 emitters); other significant amounts have been collected from energy producers, Newcastle Port Corporation and Hunter Water. This shows how big the business of energy and coal mining is. This figure does not include coal royalties collected by State Government from the region, which adds another AU$1 billion. Despite being home to more than 10 per cent of the state's population and being a key contributor to the state's economy, the city and region only receives less than 4 per cent in funds back from the government in Sydney. This budget is clearly too little, given that the Hunter Region and Newcastle, which contain over 10 per cent of the state's population, generate around 32 per cent of the state's export income and over 20 per cent of the Gross State Product (GSP). Contradicting to NSW State Government's own greenhouse gas emission plans, in March 2010, the construction of another old-technology CO_2-emitting powerstation (2000 MW 'Bayswater B') was approved. Instead of activating large-scale renewables, this will push up the state's GHG emissions by 15 per cent; all to secure cheap baseload power supply for the greater Sydney metropolitan region.

3. New user-friendly public transport systems with less impact on cities, such as bus networks and light railway, have made a comeback as catalysts of urban renewal. In some situations, buses are the better mode of transport, in other more densely populated situations, it's light railway. How do transport experts define *Sustainable Transport Systems*? A

Notes for Chapter 1

sustainable transportation system is one that:
- Allows the basic access needs of individuals and societies to be met safely and in a manner consistent with human and eco-system health, and with social equity within and between generations.
- Is affordable, operates efficiently, offers choice of transport mode, and supports a vibrant economy.
- Limits emissions and waste within the planet's ability to absorb them, minimizes consumption of non-renewable resources, limits consumption of renewable resources to the sustainable yield level, reuses and recycles its components, and minimizes the use of land and the production of noise.

4. Transport planning is just one aspect of urban design and should not be given priority over all other aspects such as good design practice and planning strategy. The masterplan of a successful eco-city needs to contain a diverse range of uses, within a flexible and usable framework, into which a range of passive and active environmental measures have been designed, benefiting from both historical precedence and technological innovation. For instance, social responsibility toward the communities and quality of life are essential parts of the triple bottom line of sustainable development. However, transport planning and identifying the right transport mode for each situation, to achieve sustainable public transport, is important. The City Rail data, supplied by Rail Corp, and published in *The Herald* on 27 Oct. 2008, shows 4,890 entries and exits for stations past Hamilton; or 2,445 each way per day. There passengers are carried on 89 trains, giving an average loading of only 27 passengers per train. On average, 2 passengers get off at Wickham station, 10 at Civic, and 15 at Newcastle. Previous data from *Lower Hunter Transport Working Group*, First Report 2003, show the average loading past Hamilton in 1997 to be 33 and in 2003 to be 29 passengers. That is (data collection: courtesy G. Essex):

Year	Average passengers per train Hamilton-Newcastle:
1997	33
2003	29
2008	27 (this equals moving 20 tonnes per passenger)

According to these figures, there is only an average of 25 to 27 passengers per train that would be affected by shortening the railway line to a new terminus at Wickham. In a recent transport report, G. Glazebrook stated that Suburban Rail needs 10,000 plus passengers in each direction per hour in peak times to be cost-effective. Newcastle Rail (past Wickham) carries 2,445 in each direction over the entire day, and will not be able to achieve cost-effectiveness. (Glazebrook, Report; Sydney, 2009). In the case of the city of Newcastle, it is clear that you can't have a well-connected city and keep the barrier of the heavy railway line. Additional level crossings in urban areas are a high safety risk. While the author generally supports public transport, in this particular case, the last 2.5km of heavy rail has too much negative effect on the Newcastle city center. The brutal rail barrier discourages walking and cycling and should therefore not remain. A 2008 transport report, commissioned by HDC, indicates that Newcastle CBD will be better off with the railway line cut at Wickham, and as a result would have a higher rate of public transport usage. There are around 600 buses per day on Hunter Street, gaining 5,000 extra bus passengers and promoting walking and cycling is preferential to the underutilized ineffective railway. A report by Parsons Brinckerhoff notes that car culture is very strong in Newcastle and the Hunter: Above Australian average, around 82 per cent of all travel to work is done by private car; only 2 per cent of Newcastle LGA residents are using public rail. (Parsons Brinckerhoff, Sydney, 2009) At the beginning of 2010, AECOM Consultants were commissioned by NSW State Government with a further concluding transport study and feasibility study of a Wickham Interchange. Light railway was considered as 'not a viable alternative for Newcastle'. At the moment of writing, this study has not been completed yet, however, first findings indicate: A city bus network, with a city centre loop and bus priority laneways, is a most feasible option; the construction of the Wickham transport interchange is recommendable; the 19th-century Newcastle terminus station could be converted as adaptive reuse to a conference centre. The main problem for efficient public transport in Newcastle is the lack of transport system integration, inadequate resourcing and a piece-meal infrastructure approach. Sadly, in Newcastle operate some of the oldest buses in the State Transit fleet. It appeares that the NSW State Government is not capable of planning for and providing effective and efficient transport services in the Hunter Region, which explains its procrastination about the future of the Newcastle railway line corridor.

5. Australia's weather patterns are changing: According to a recent report by the Bureau of Meteorology, record high temperatures increasingly outnumbered record low temperatures. Bureau scientist Blair Trewin confirmed that record highs had outnumbered record lows by between two and three to one in the past decade. In 2009, Australia experienced three major heat waves, while the last time record lows occurred on that scale was in June 2007. Over the last 40 years, Austrailia's average temperatures have increased by 0.9 degree Celsius. (Report by the Bureau of Meteorology, Canberra, 2010)

6. Planning for the redevelopment of Newcastle working harbour and its brownfield waterfront started around 1991 and was supported by the NSW State Government's 'Building Better Cities' programme. The Honeysuckle Masterplan for the foreshore transformation was approved in 1993, but the development of a Public Domain Strategy took until 2000.

7. The City Campus is a long-term development. On 05 March 2010, the University of Newcastle gave the follow-ing statement: 'Since 2004, the University of Newcastle has grown from 23,000 to 30,000 student enrolments, an increase of around six per cent per annum. The University is projecting further growth of up to 10,000 students over the next 10 to 15 years. The University has developed a strategy to meet growing student demand, which aligns with the vision that the Australian Government has articulated for the higher education sector with increased participation over-all, greater numbers of students from low socio-economic backgrounds and other disadvantaged groups, and regional development. Over the past 20 years, the Hunter Region has undergone major change from its industrial past to a future based on the growth sectors of innovation, personal and business services, and technology. The University is supporting the transition to a new regional economy and building the platform for future growth by exploring innovative ways to teach and learn, and increase the skills of the Hunter community. The University's strategic plan Building Distinction de-scribes our commitment to the region as it grows. The strategic plan advocates increasing our student population, grow-ing our research capability and more closely engaging the community. With government and community support, the University's growth will include expansion into the city. Together with the NSW Government, the University is pleased to call for expressions of interest from private sector partners for the Stage 1 development of the proposed Newcastle City campus. The proposed City Campus: The University's preferred strategy to meet our aspirations in teaching, research and community contribution includes developing a Newcastle City Campus focused on the arts, humanities and social sciences. The City Campus will be developed over a number of stages: School of Business; School of Law; School of Drama, Fine Art and Music; School of Education; School of Humanities and Social Science. The University has joined with the NSW Government to call for expressions of interest from private sector partners for the Stage 1 development, the School of Business, which will comprise 18,000 square metres of space for 2,500 students and 100 staff. Taking 10 to 15 years to complete all stages, the City Campus will consolidate the University's business school, and co-locate its law school with the new justice precinct being considered by the NSW State and Australian governments in the context of the redevelopment of the courts. The completed City Campus will host in excess of 7,000 students and 1,000 staff. Located in more than 60,000 square metres, it will be a prominent, dynamic feature of the city centre bringing people into thriving, contemporary spaces. The City Campus design will encourage engagement and collaboration with the community. It will be more than a collection of buildings in the city.'

Further research

The following pages show a collection of images and diagrams in regard to the topics raised in Chapter 1, to give a wider context and inspire the reader to conduct further research in these fields.

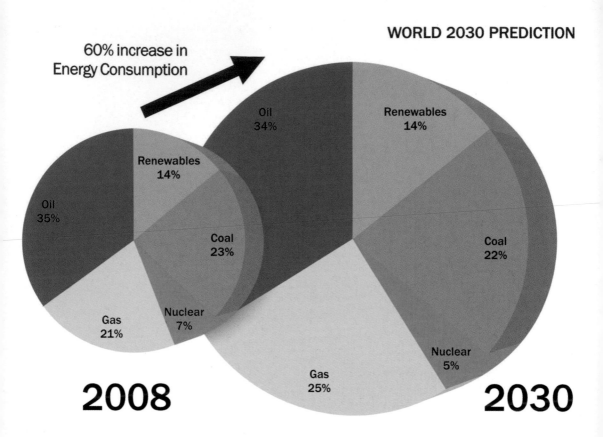

60% increase in Energy Consumption

WORLD 2030 PREDICTION

Oil 34%

Renewables 14%

Renewables 14%

Oil 35%

Coal 23%

Coal 22%

Gas 21%

Nuclear 7%

Nuclear 5%

Gas 25%

2008

2030

Source: UN Department of Economic and Social Affairs, Division for Sustainable Development

Energy and food security for a growing global population

The 'Ecological Carrying Capacity' of the Earth has reached a critical point. Ensuring food supply for a growing population has emerged as a global problem. According to a recent study by the International Food Policy Research Institute (IFPRI, 2009), the number of malnourished people has grown worldwide to 925 million; one of the *Millennium Development Goals* of the UN – to halve worldwide hunger by 2015 – has become unachievable.

Equally, global energy supply has emerged as major challenge: Economic development and population growth in many emerging markets are causing the global demand for energy to increase rapidly. The *International Energy Agency* (IEA, 2007) forcasts that global consumption of energy will rise by over 50 per cent by 2030 if current policies are maintained (what Lord Stern calls 'Continuing business as usual'). China and India alone will be responsible for half the increase. Based on these predicted increases, CO_2 emissions could reach double the 1990 level by 2030, if no action is taken. The following web site gives a good overview of the different commitments by the different nations: The United Framework Convention on Climate Change (UNFCCC) web site: www.unfccc.int/

In his important report on 'The Economy of Climate Change', Lord N. Stern clearly identified that 'doing nothing and continuing business as usual' will be more damaging. We will see a 60 per cent increase in energy consumption over the next 20 years if no action is taken. (Diagram: S. Lehmann, 2008, after: Stern Report, 2007)

GLOBAL ECOLOGICAL FOOTPRINT

The amount of land needed to meet our demand for natural resources and avoid depletion.

1   LIMIT

1.3   CURRENT USAGE

3.8   AUSTRALIA

5.5   USA

Our global footprint is now above 30 per cent of the planet's biological capacity to support life on Earth. (WWF, 2006)

Source: Global Footprint Network

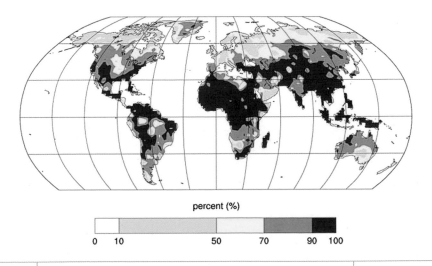

percent (%)

0   10   50   70   90   100

Above: The developed countries, such as the US, Australia, Canada, Japan, UAE and others, are using up a huge amount of finite resources, consuming far above the limits of available resources per capita. Below: The poorer areas in Africa, Asia and Latin America will be the ones hardest hit by global warming, where increases of 4 to 6.5 degrees Celsius by 2100 might occur (red areas on world map). (Map: Courtesy IPCC, 2009)

ANNUAL CO$_2$ EMISSIONS OF HOUSEHOLD

An average 4 person household in Germany produces around 43.5 tonnes of CO$_2$ emissions per year.

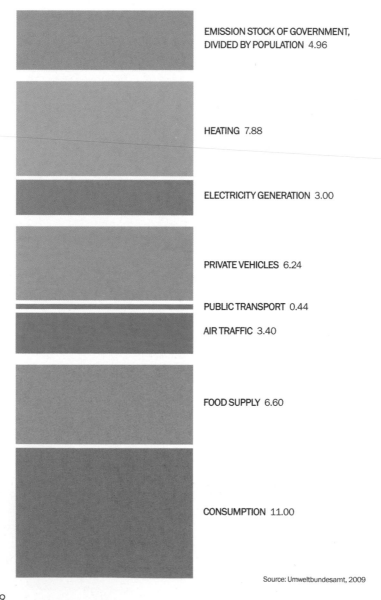

EMISSION STOCK OF GOVERNMENT, DIVIDED BY POPULATION 4.96

HEATING 7.88

ELECTRICITY GENERATION 3.00

PRIVATE VEHICLES 6.24

PUBLIC TRANSPORT 0.44

AIR TRAFFIC 3.40

FOOD SUPPLY 6.60

CONSUMPTION 11.00

Source: Umweltbundesamt, 2009

Diagrams: S. Lehmann, 2009

CO$_2$ emissions of an average German household, per year. Consumption amounts to 25 per cent of all emissions, food and air traffic are significant emitters. While lifestyle and households cause a lot of emissions, a huge amount is caused by the badly insulated building stock and inefficient air-conditioning systems. The goal must be to develop more energy-efficient buildings and systems, while maintaining a high quality lifestyle.

WORLD TOP TEN CO$_2$ EMITTERS, 2009

In 2008, China has overtaken the US as the world's largest CO$_2$ emitter, but per capita, emissions in China are relatively low.

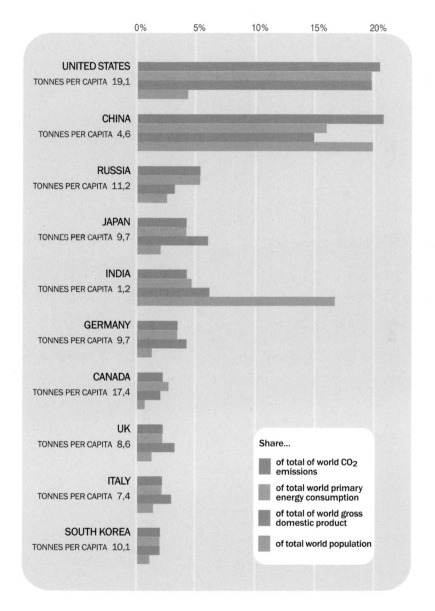

Source: IEA, Germanwatch - Klimaschutzindex 2009

In the meantime, most experts use CO$_2$ emissions per capita in their discussions, not by country; while China and India are large global CO$_2$ emitters, their emissions per capita are still relatively low. Major CO$_2$ emitters per capita are the USA, Australia, Canada, Saudi Arabia, Kuwait, and United Arab Emirates. Not in the graph, but following close-by, are Australia, Saudi Arabia, Mexico, France, Iran and Brazil.

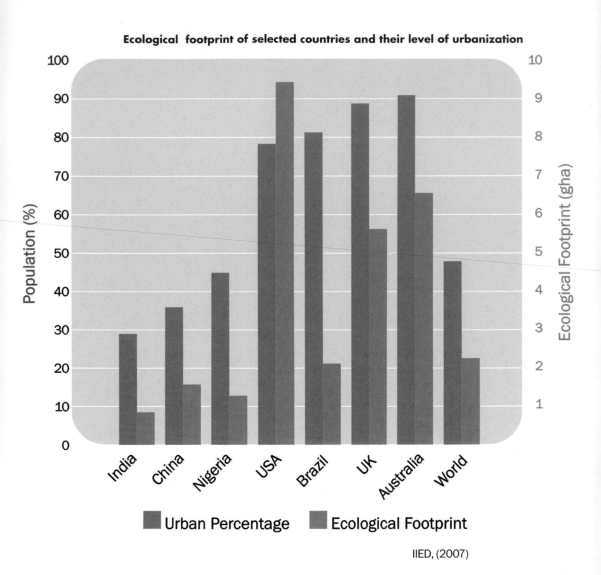

Ecological footprint of selected countries and their level of urbanization

IIED, (2007)

China's urbanization rate

The fast growing urbanization rate of China in per centages (not including Hong Kong and Macau):

1949	10,6% (foundation of P. R. China)	2004	41,8%
1978	17,9% (beginning of opening)	2006	43,9%
2000	36,0%	2008	45,7%
2002	39,1%	2010	50,0% (with population of 1.35 billion)

Comparison of different countries, their urbanization rate and ecological footprint. In the next decade, China's urbanization will surpass 50 per cent, combined with a rapidly growing ecological footprint per capita. The UK, Australia and Japan are some of the most urbanized countries in the world. Brazil is also highly urbanized, but has managed to keep its ecological footprint relatively small. (S.Lehmann, UNESCO Chair, 2008)

Energy consumption: Total primary energy per person

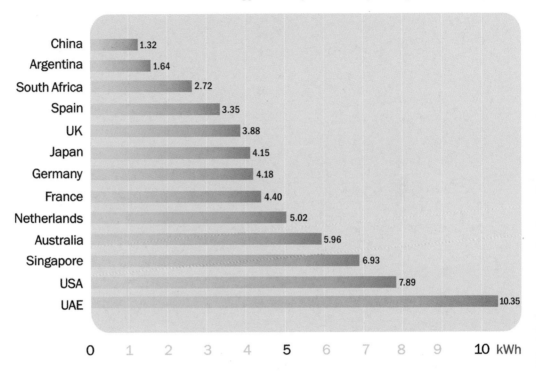

Country	kWh
China	1.32
Argentina	1.64
South Africa	2.72
Spain	3.35
UK	3.88
Japan	4.15
Germany	4.18
France	4.40
Netherlands	5.02
Australia	5.96
Singapore	6.93
USA	7.89
UAE	10.35

After: www.IEA.org International Energy Agency (2009)

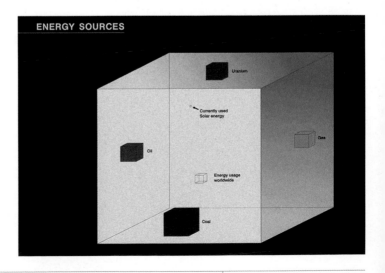

ENERGY SOURCES

In theory, the world's energy consumption could easily be supplied by the sun alone. The infinite, ultimate resource of energy, solar power, remains mostly unused. The energy consumption of different countries varies significantly. David MacKay has calculated that the average energy consumption on Earth is 56 kWh per day per person (as currently in Brazil); however, the average European consumes 120 kWh per day. (Data: 2008)

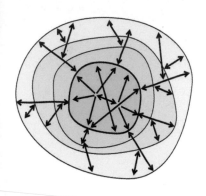 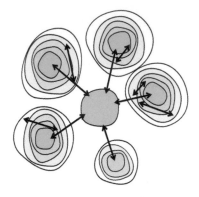 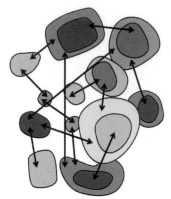

Monocentric city	Polycentric city cluster with "satellite centres"	Network city

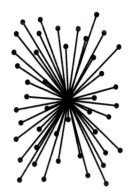 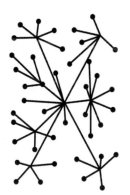  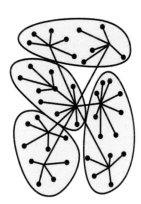

Centralized structure	De-centralized structure	Distributed structure	Hybrid structure

When cities reach a certain size (starting at around 2 mill. population), it is increasingly important that they adapt a poly-central network structure, as the single-cell, monocentric types soon reach their limit of structural growth potential. The development from monocentric to distributed poly-centric network cities recommends 4 or 5 city centres, strongly inter-linked by efficient public transport. (After: P. Rand; C. de Portzamparc)

Correlation between GDP and Primary Energy Demand (1970)

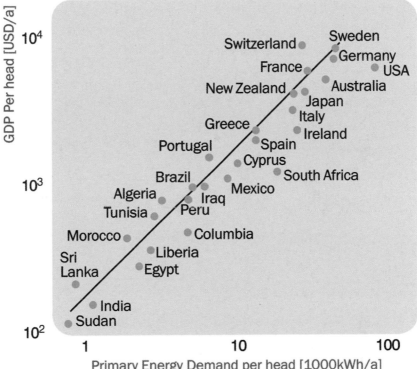

After: Energy Manual (2008)

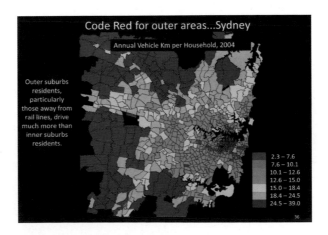

In regard to the Australian suburb, urban planner Rob Adams notes: 'The cost of locating more and more people on city fringes is of serious concern. Many people living in these suburbs suffer real financial difficulties. While the house and land package may initially come with an attractive price, the suburb residents will spend 25 percent of their income for getting to and from work and getting the milk.' (2009). Diagram on Sydney's suburbs, by Peter Rickwood (2006).

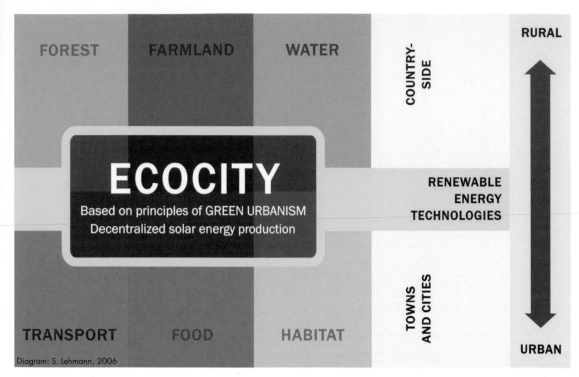

FOREST FARMLAND WATER

ECOCITY
Based on principles of GREEN URBANISM
Decentralized solar energy production

COUNTRY-SIDE

RURAL

RENEWABLE
ENERGY
TECHNOLOGIES

TRANSPORT FOOD HABITAT

TOWNS
AND CITIES

URBAN

Diagram: S. Lehmann, 2006

Masdar Eco-City, UAE:
6 sqkm size, 50.000 residents,
60,000 workplaces.

It is the holistic concept of Eco-City which establishes a better symbiosis and balance between the urban (city) and the rural (coutryside). Below: Aerial view of Masdar Eco-City, currently under construction. Masterplan by Foster + Partners, 2007-09, promoted as: 'No emissions, no waste, no cars!' Such eco-city projects are a testbed for innovative technologies. (3-D image: courtesy Masdar Energy Company, 2009)

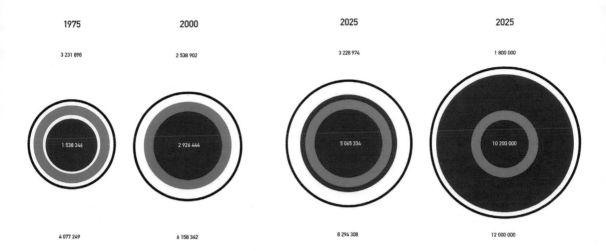

1975	2000	2025	2025
3 231 898	2 538 902	3 228 974	1 800 000
1 538 346	2 926 444	5 065 334	10 200 000
4 077 249	6 158 342	8 294 308	12 000 000

Global population growth

The world population is growing and moving closer together: Around 80 mill. people are added annually to the world population, mainly to cities; by 2050, the global population is predicted to be 9 billion people. It is also estimated that by 2050, 70 per cent of all people will live in cities. In the year 1900, it was only 13 per cent. From 1900 to 2000, the global human population increased fourfold. These population increases and rising standards of living in developing countries will increase the demand for energy. A recent report by *The Outlook for Energy* forecastts that worldwide energy usage will be over 40 per cent higher in 2030 than it was in 2010.

Urban growth is the most rapid in the Asia-Pacific region (around 4 per cent p.a.) and in Africa (up to 5 per cent p.a). For population data, see: www.citypopulation.de

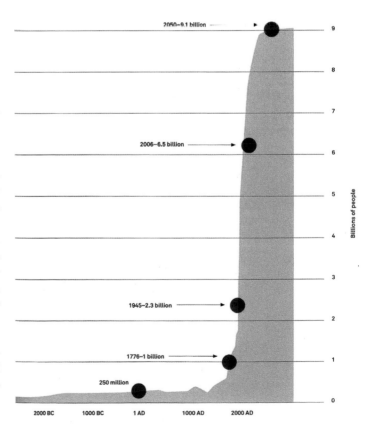

The current crisis is partially caused by explosive population growth, uneven development and competition over finite resources. The world's overall population density is currently about 50 people per square kilometre. Predictions forecast the world population for 2010: 6.5 billion; for 2025: 8.2 billion; for 2050: 9.0 billion people. (Source of diagrams: MVRDV; Al Gore) For data on cities, see also: www.citypopulation.de

Urban population growth

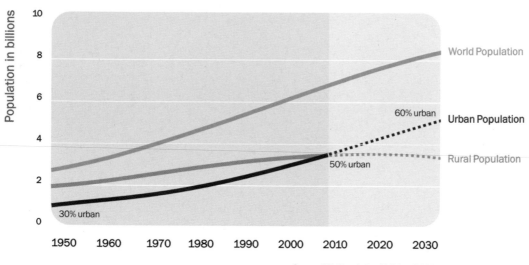

Source: UN, Population Division (2008)

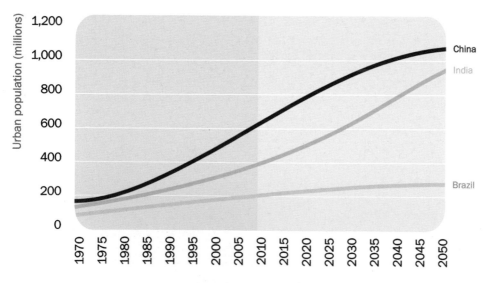

After: WBCSD (2009)

The urban population is growing worldwide, especially in the developing world, where intensive migration from rural areas to cities has occurred over the last decades and is likely to continue. By 2050, China's urbanization will flatten out, whereas India's is still gaining momentum. (Diagrams: S. Lehmann, UNESCO Chair, 2007)

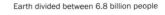

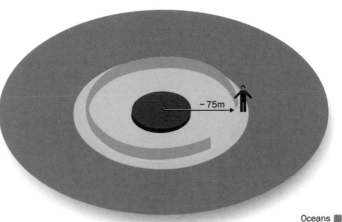

Oceans ◼
Desert and Polar Regions ◻
Tropical Rainforest ◼
Bioproductive area ◻
Transport and Urbanized area ◼

The results of human activity are putting such a strain on the natural functions of Earth that the ability of the planet's ecosystem to sustain future generations can no longer be taken for granted.

Vulnerable coastal cities: With the increase of storm frequency and rising sea levels, the erosion of waterfront land has become an area of major concern, especially for coastal cities (image: Gold Coast). At the same time, we see an increase in droughts, growing difficulty to ensure the supply of drinking water, and water scarcity, which leads to many farmers giving up. (image sources: courtesy ATSE (left); Al Gore (right))

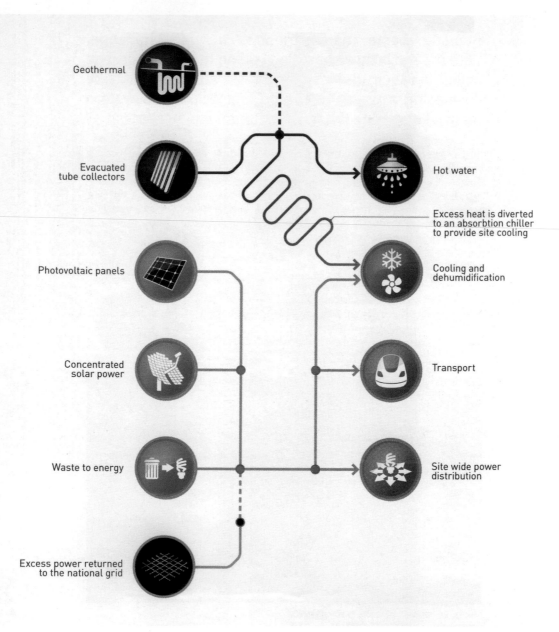

The energy concept of Masdar Eco-City, which aims to be the largest renewable-energy-powered urban development, currently under construction, outside Abu Dhabi (UAE). The diagramme explains the range of energy production and management methods planned at Masdar City, with the aim to provide a high quality of life with the lowest possible carbon footprint. (Image: courtesy Masdar Energy Company, 2010)

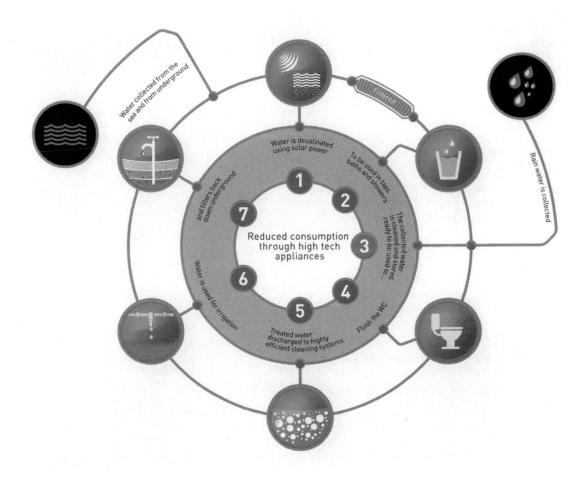

Sustainable energy and water concepts at Masdar City, UAE

Energy: After the efficiency of the city's buildings and demand side systems has been maximized, the most important carbon savings come through electric power generation using renewable energy resources. A conventional city would draw its electricity from a distant CO_2-emitting powerstation fired by fossil or nuclear fuel. At Masdar City, the following techniques are used: Photovoltaic technologies provide the base power load, integrated in roofs and facades; concentrating solar power (CSP) technology for cooling with absorption chillers; evacuated tube collectors (ETC) integrated into buildings to provide hot water; waste-to-energy gasification technology; and geothermal resource for cooling.

Water: A wide range of water-use reduction technologies is introduced, such as: grey and black water recycling, landscaping with low-water-use native plants and seawater greenhouses, hyper-saline water desalination, smart appliances, and high-tech treatment technologies. Here, the goal is to reduce water consumption to 100 litres per capita per day (from the current UAE average of approximately 550 litres per capita per day, the world's largest water consumption).

The sustainable water strategy for Masdar Eco-City, which is currently being built by 2020 in the desert. Water is one of the most precious resources, especially in the Middle East, and the power that is usually required to provide clean, drinkable and usable water is high. This concept has been designed to minimize water waste and to maximize the efficiency of production techniques. (Image: courtesy Masdar, 2010)

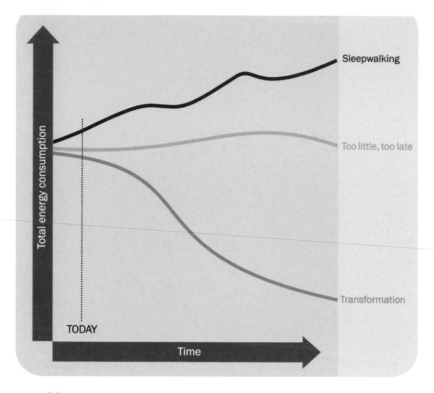

Building energy development: Three possible scenarios   WBCSD (2009)

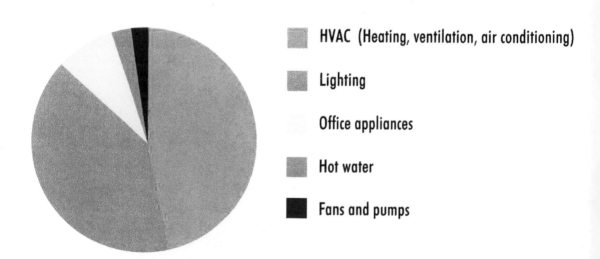

Recognizing that 'business as usual' is not good enough, we need to start transforming our existing cities, and the way we design, build and manage districts and buildings. It is now widely understood that there is an urgent need for action. Below: Diagram shows the typical energy consumption in a large air-conditioned office building in Sydney, mainly for cooling and lighting. (Diagram: Courtesy GBC, 2008)

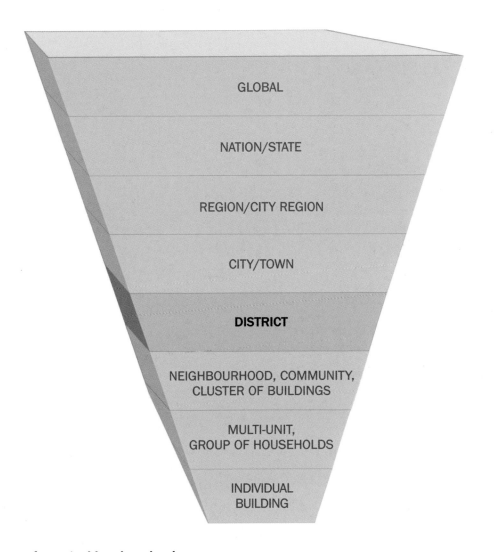

GLOBAL

NATION/STATE

REGION/CITY REGION

CITY/TOWN

DISTRICT

NEIGHBOURHOOD, COMMUNITY, CLUSTER OF BUILDINGS

MULTI-UNIT, GROUP OF HOUSEHOLDS

INDIVIDUAL BUILDING

The layers of sustainable urban development

Sustainable development is a challenging multi-stakeholder process, encompassing multiple dimensions and interdisciplinary knowledge, recognizing a diversity of expertise. *Green Urbanism* is a conceptual model which focuses on strategies for sustainability on the scale of the city district, housing estate and city quarter. It's timely to move beyond the object (single building) dimension, identifying appropriate planning processes for sustainable cities.

Sustainability is now the next definition of quality and we can already see a shift in criteria for good design and construction, for instance by developing new neighbourhoods on what are currently brownfield sites. There are new challenges and responsibilities of architects, urban designers and engineers in the age of sustainability, and thinking on a district-wide scale allows them to roll-out new concepts effectively, including the use of local materials and prefabricated construction elements (e.g. facade systems, integration of services, prefabricated bathroom cells, and so on).

It will be more effective to act on the city-wide / district-wide scale. To take decisive action on the district-scale, or at least on the neighbourhood scale, is required to curb global warming. A single eco-building is less able to create much effect in the reduction of CO_2 emissions; we need to transform the existing districts, by retrofitting entire quarters, street by street. (Diagram: S. Lehmann, 2007)

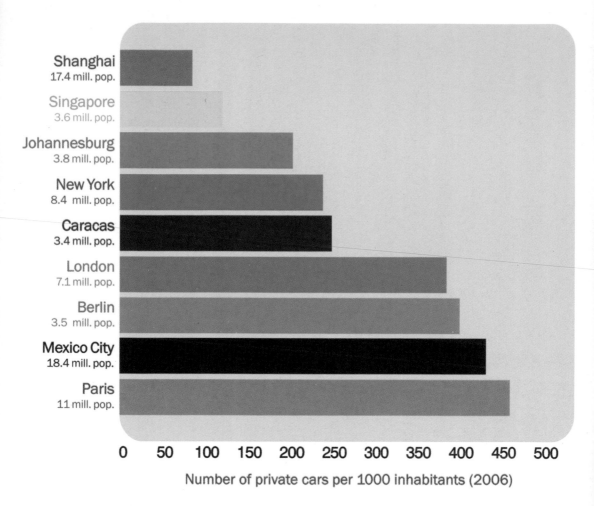

Number of private cars per 1000 inhabitants (2006)

(Populations according: www.citypopulation.de)

The rise of private automobile ownership in China and India

China and India are among the world's fastest growing economies, rapidly urbanizing, with the fastest growth in car ownership. Especially China is rapidly adopting the developed world's unsustainable consumer habits, increasing environmental pollution and damage to human health.

Amazingly, China has now 120 cities with over one million people, and 36 over two million. For instance, Shanghai, with a population estimated at 17.5 million and with 946 buildings over twelve storeys in height (2009) is clearly a global city with rapidly growing automobile ownership. Between 2005 and 2010, China's car ownership had a growth rate of 18 per cent, with the number of cars reaching 84 million by 2010. If the 'Modal Share of Travel' in China eventually mimics the one in the US, by 2030 there will be twice as many cars in China as in the entire world today.

If every Chinese person drove a car then the current known world oil reserves would be exhausted within six months.

Car ownership varies widely from city to city. For instance, Paris and Mexico City have an unhealthy high amount of private automobiles congesting their roads. Singapore simply regulates the amount of registrations by making it very expensive to own a private car. Chinese cities are quickly catching up in the number of car ownership. (Diagram: S. Lehmann, 2006)

Boundary conditions	Energy-optimized building concepts	Evaluation

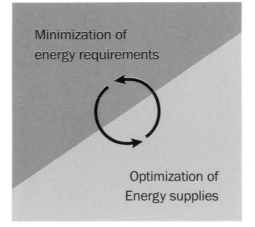

Boundary conditions

Climate

Usage

Legislation

Architectural
Design

Energy-optimized building concepts

Minimization of
energy requirements

Optimization of
Energy supplies

Evaluation

Ecology
(CO_2 pollution)

Economy
(life cycle costs)

Architecture
(quality of design)

Society
(acceptance)

After: Energy Manual (2008)

Courtesy: R. Burdett 2009

Both need to happen: Reducing the energy consumption (demand-side) and, at the same time, improving the energy-effectiveness. In China, we find some of the best initiatives being rolled-out on a huge scale, e.g. the large-scale use of wind power. Wind power could theoretically supply all of China's electricity, although it would need to cover 10 per cent of the country's land with wind farms. By 2012, China will be the world leader in wind power.

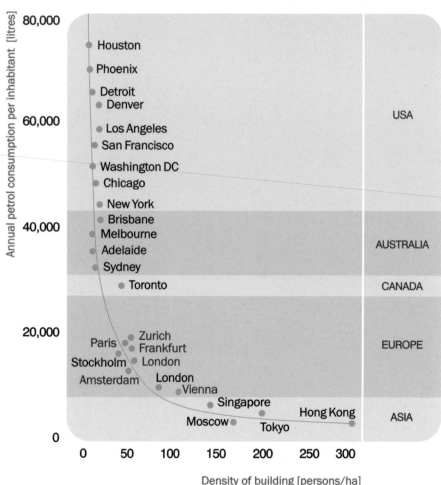

Relationship between Density versus Energy Consumption

Density of building [persons/ha]

After: Newman & Kenworthy

Transport planning and sustainable urban development
Kenworthy and Newman's 1989 study is often refered to in demonstrating a relationship between overall urban density and transport energy use. The researchers used statistical methods to examine the relationship between 'petrol use per person' and 'persons per hectare'. A more recent graph is on the right page. The more compact European and Asian cities demonstrate a better relationship compared to the less dense, more car-dependent and traffic-dominated cities. Increasing densities helps to avoid traffic.

How much energy and petrol does your chosen lifestyle require? Many American and Australian cities with their notorious low density and lack of public transport (such as Houston, Phoenix in the US, or Perth in Australia) will automatically lead to a high consumption of petrol. (Diagram: S. Lehmann, after: P. Newman and J. Kenworthy, 1989)

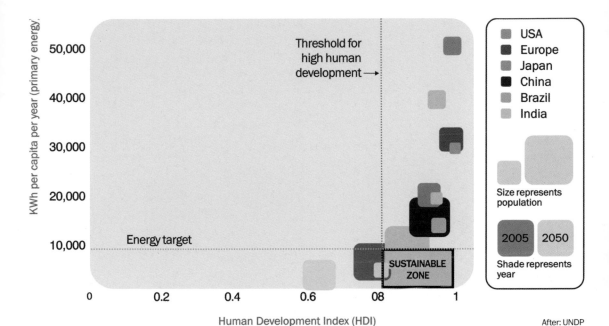

Two important diagrams: The first one shows the relationship between the Human Development Index and the consumption of primary energy. (source: UNDP).
The second diagram illustrates the relationship between urban density and petrol consumption. (Diagram: Courtesy J. Kenworthy, P. Newman). Suburbia is too car-centric; a 3 km distance to buy milk and bread is simply not walkable.

Large-scale suburbanization of the US in the 1930s to 1960s: Low-density suburban sprawl with free-standing houses has led to a model of high land consumption and mono-functional (only residential) areas at the fringe of the city, far away from the workplaces in the city centre. With more people moving back to the city, it's important to redefine mixed-use block models for densification and urban infill.

Aalter

Rom

Vienna

Above: The European City; city blocks with large communal courtyards.
Left: The endless banality of interchangeable suburbs.

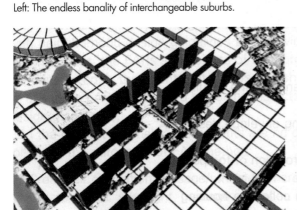

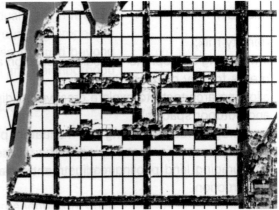

Achieving sustainable urban form: The computer allows us to model the urban futures of cities in China, India, Vietnam, etc.

The 'European City' is a robust model for mixed-use, compact 5 to 8-storey urban blocks, where the groundfloor is not used for living, but for shops, small offices and restaurants, and firewalls and circulation systems are shared. These blocks have frequently a density of 3,000 to 6,000 people per sq km, a good urban density for any city. Rob Krier's scale comparison of public space show clearly the different urban environments.

Source: Courtesy H. D. Lieb

Energy-efficient buildings in Berlin, designed by the author in the 1990s. Prefabrication of large building components (fully insulated elements), constructed entirely off-site in a factory, thereby minimizing material demand and waste on the construction site. Available industrial solutions are now getting re-configured into more efficient construction practice. (Photos: Office buildings at Potsdamer Platz, Hackescher Markt; Eichenallee)

Above: A great example for the successful combination of *new + old*: The adaptive re-use of a 19th-century pumping station building in Berlin to a contemporary dance theatre (architect: Gerhard Spangenberg, 2007).

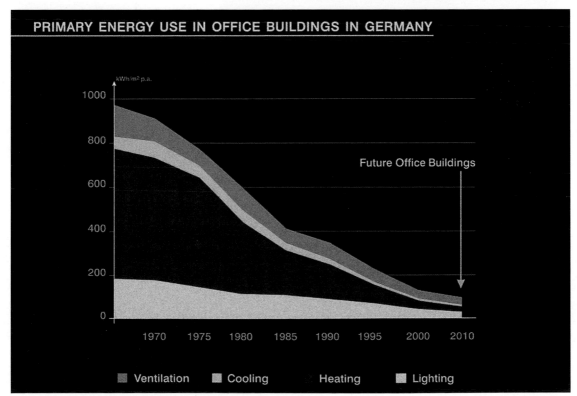

PRIMARY ENERGY USE IN OFFICE BUILDINGS IN GERMANY

kWh/m² p.a.

Future Office Buildings

1970   1975   1980   1985   1990   1995   2000   2010

◼ Ventilation   ◼ Cooling   Heating   ◼ Lighting

The most sustainable building is the one that already exists. Re-using structures, through adaptive reuse, is a highly sustainable practice: Two examples from Berlin. Reducing the primary energy demand: the main amount of energy is consumed by mechanical cooling and artificial lighting. The net-zero energy building and zero emission district are now becoming a reality. (Diagram: S. Lehmann, 2005)

Source: Courtesy ML Corp, London

Source: Courtesy Hamburg Team

The adaptive reuse of inner-city brownfield sites, such as at London Docklands or Hamburg's industrial buildings (images above), is a highly sustainable way to deal with the existing city. It's also a way to keep space affordable. Creative people and fresh ideas require affordable space in old buildings. (Image: courtesy MLCorp London)

Architecture of a pre-air-conditioning era

The adaptive reuse of buildings can deliver many benefits to local communities, especially if the reuse of buildings is part of a wider urban revitalization agenda.

Before the introduction of air-conditioning systems there was a distinctive regional (vernacular) architecture, built with local materials and local knowledge, and shaped by environmental features of the particular place or region.

These two carefully restored Chinese shophouses in Melaka (Malaysia) are a good example for naturally cross-ventilated and day-lit spaces in a tropical climate, and the contemporary adaptive reuse of heritage structures. Passive design principles are very effective in reducing the air-condition dependency, achieving comfort levels without mechanical ventilation. In addition, the use of local materials and the extended life-cycle of buildings are all relevant in increasing the environmental sustainability of cities.

The adaptive reuse and integration of existing buildings (even without particular heritage value) is important for the embodied energy and materials stored in these structures. The most sustainable building is likely to be the one that already exists.

Buildings from a pre-air-condition era are often very energy-effective in the way they achieve high comfort by natural ventilation, even in a tropical climate: renovated Chinese shop houses in Melaka, Malaysia, used by NUS as research centre. Three courtyards ensure good day-lighting and cross-ventilation. (Photos: S. Lehmann, 2009)

INCREASING
ENERGY EFFECTIVENESS OF CITIES

LEGISLATION & POLICY	INCENTIVES & FINANCIAL MECHANISMS	EDUCATION & RESEARCH	TECHNOLOGICAL INNOVATION	SOCIETAL & BEHAVIOURAL
Updating Building Codes	Subsidies and Grants	Education and training	Demonstration projects	Social inclusion
Setting Targets for energy and water reduction	Tax Exemptions	Capacity Building	Prototypes	Equity
Regulations	Incorporating Life-Cycle costing in all financial decision-making	Raising awareness	Redefining Best Practice	Use of energy, water and vehicles
Minimum Standards for appliances	Rebates on PV and Solar Hot Water installation	Publications	R&D in sustainable urban design and architecture	Mixed-use programmes
Restriction on growth of fossil fuel industry	Funding mechanisms	Up-skilling	Upgrading existing building stock	Integrated solutions
Political leadership	An Investment Framework that values Sustainability and Resiliency	Access to Information Networks	Recyclable prefabricated construction systems	Poverty alleviation
Land-use and transportation policy		Appropriate interdisciplinary research	Universal, flexible building typologies	Community awareness Programmes
City-based approach				Reward recycling
				Ageing population

TOP-DOWN AND BOTTOM-UP APPROACHES / ADAPTATION AND MITIGATION

Getting paid for generating renewable energy

Governmental support through legislation, policy, incentives and grants for research is key to many successful developments. For instance, by means of energy input-tariffs (feed-in tariffs for renewable energy), governments can exercise a great deal of influence on the choice of technologies. If entirely left to the private sector, new environmentally friendly technologies usually take too long to be adopted. Germany is one of a few countries that has invested in support of solar energy, and is now responsible for almost half of the world's solar-powered energy production. This has given rise to a thriving solar power and wind turbine industry and has created employment opportunities in the fields of research, manufacturing and installation of renewable energy technologies (250,000 new jobs in ten years). It has also established German industry and universities as world leaders in the field of sustainability expertise.

This diagram points to the many levels of approaches required to achieve energy-effectiveness of city districts; and a transformation of behaviour, in the way we use energy, water, materials, the automobile, etc. It requires both at the same time: top-down as well as bottom-up approaches. (Diagram: S. Lehmann, UNESCO Chair, 2008)

Selecting the right transport modes

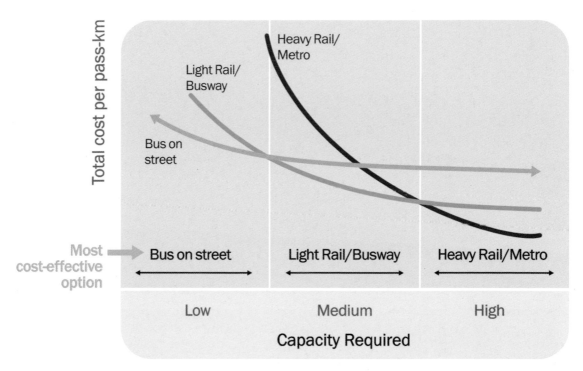

Most cost-effective option →

| Bus on street | Light Rail/Busway | Heavy Rail/Metro |

| Low | Medium | High |

Capacity Required

Light railway supports walkable, mixed-use development, reduces driving and increases health; but it requires a population density above the one of suburbs.

After: G. Glazebrook (2008)

Selecting the right transport mode for a city is essential. For instance, light railway has now been re-introduced in over 400 cities worldwide. However, light railway is expensive and requires a certain population density to be cost-effective. The Brazilian city of Curitiba has achieved major improvement through a bus rapid transit system (BRTS). Images: the tram in European cities, where landscaping continues at grade. (Photo: S. Lehmann)

Cities have their own unique characteristics. The endless grid of Mexico-City; or the divide between poor (living in Favelas, left) and wealthy (living in apartment towers) in Caracas. Right page: Mumbai's most valued and democratic public space is the beach, accessible to all. (Images: courtesy R. Burdett, urban-age.net)

Tokyo is often called 'a city without public space'. Is the underground subway system Tokyo's public space? The small-scale, high quality public spaces, such as pocket parks and more intimate places, inter-connected by a pleasant and safe walking and cycling network system, is the key to a livable city. The streets consist of around 80 per cent of all public space, so there is a good reason to focus on the design of streetscapes first.

Paris

Londres

Berlin

New York

Mexico

Shanghai

Each city is characterized by its own unique grain and structural qualities, which need to be understood and respected, if we want to densify and add to the existing.   Below: Vulnerable coastal cities. Simulation of 5 metres rising sealevel and its impact on the city of Boston, as modeled by engineers from MIT for `Architecture2030.org'. (Image: courtesy Architecture2030) Coastal cities like Mumbai and Shanghai are vulnerable to sea level rise.

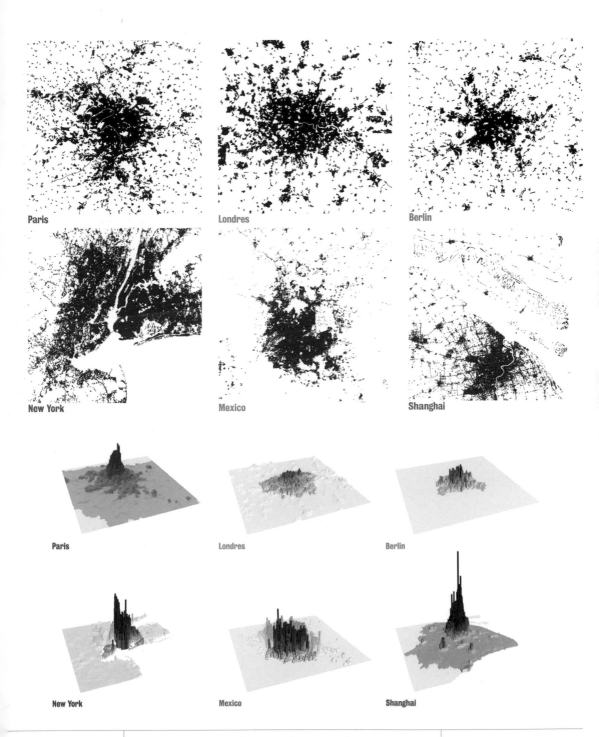

Cities are resource-intensive; they are complex systems under stress.
More research is needed in comparison and best practice of density, compactness,
urban footprint, and its relationship to public space, infrastructure, green space, road
networks and waterways. Below: The density distribution of different cities has here
been visualized and compared. (Source: courtesy R. Burdett, urban-age.net, 2007)

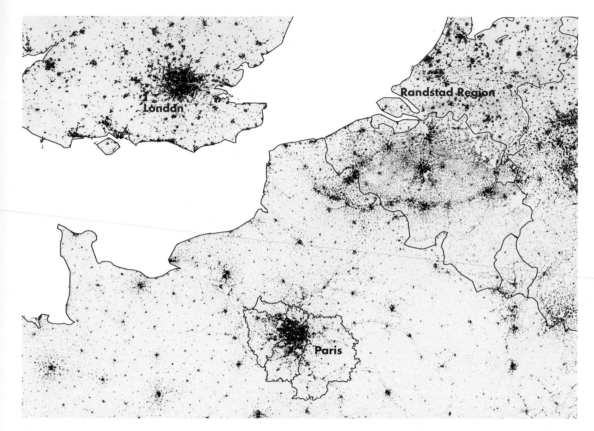

Source: Courtesy City of Stockholm

We can now find a new type of urbanity: the metropolitan region (such as the Randstad Region in the Netherlands, or the Ruhrgebiet Region in Germany), where more people live than in Greater Paris or London. Below: A good European model for best practice of Eco-Cities: The 5-storey Hammarby-Sjostad district in Stockholm, where an old inner-city industrial area has been transformed into a green neighbourhood (2000–2008). www.hammarbysjostad.se

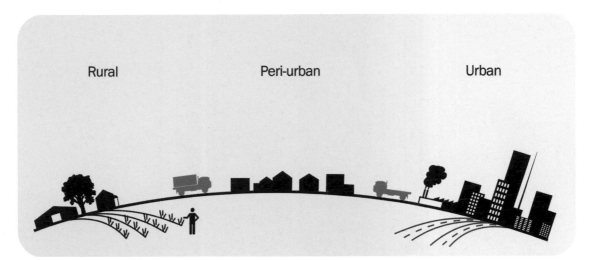

Rural   Peri-urban   Urban

The urban-rural disconnect

For centuries, cities have been entirely dependent on their rural hinterland, growing at the expense of the surrounding landscape. The challenge today is to create a new relationship between the urban (city) and nature, where both can co-exist in symbiosis.

Source: Image Sharing Commons

The tension between the rural, peri-urban and urban remains widely unresolved. For centuries, even millennia, the city has always grown at the cost of the countryside, expanding into agricultural land and vulnerable landscape. There is a long history of seeing the city as something different from the space of the countryside, which is well illustrated in the arts. Here: 'The City seen as place of pleasure and creation'.

Source: Image Sharing Commons

The compact medieval city

Medieval towns worked well on all scales, as they were based on a pedestrian movement network, supplied locally grown food, practised sustainable waste management and were built from locally available materials. Passive design principles were well understood and the knowledge of regional-appropriate building was handed over from generation to generation. As a consequence, craftmanship and vernacular, regional building types blossomed. These towns had continuous urban spaces throughout the city, were walkable, compact in shape and highly mixed-use. The emphasis was on the space between buildings instead of buildings standing in isolation.

How can we best re-apply the lessons from these early urban clusters when designing the eco-district of today?

An illustration of the medieval city of Arles (France) shows the city as a compact mixed-use cluster of buildings, where the optimization of food supply, waste disposal, sharing of facilities (infrastructure) and strategic defence, have all led to a certain model of density and compactness. The 20th-century model of sprawling suburb has ignored this legacy and created a mono-functional, car-dependent and inefficient typology (below: US suburb).

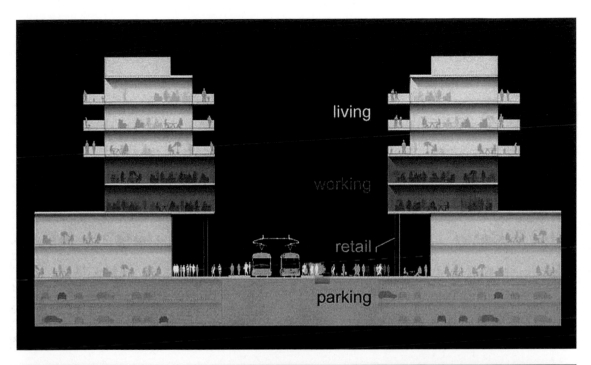

living

working

retail

parking

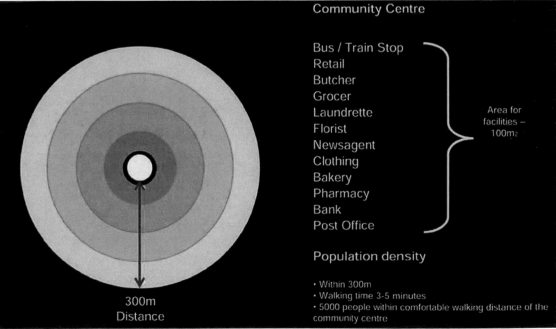

Community Centre

Bus / Train Stop
Retail
Butcher
Grocer
Laundrette
Florist
Newsagent
Clothing
Bakery
Pharmacy
Bank
Post Office

Area for
facilities –
100m2

300m
Distance

Population density

• Within 300m
• Walking time 3-5 minutes
• 5000 people within comfortable walking distance of the
community centre

Above: Mixed-use building typologies, with working, living and leisure in one block
(as layers in each building, not separated next to each other). Mixed-use and compactness are essential characteristics of the sustainable city, where all daily needs are in a
5 minutes walking distance, like in a `compact urban village', based on the concept of
short distances. (Diagrams: Courtesy Foster + Partners, 2008)

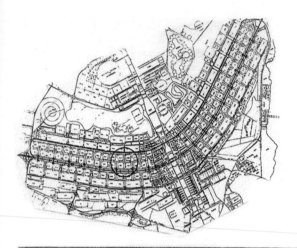

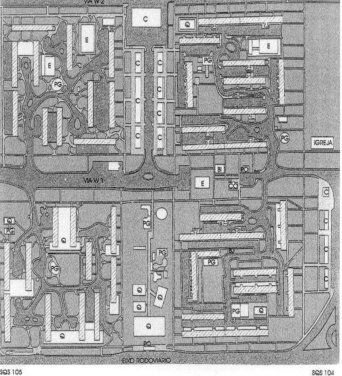

SQS 105

SQS 104

	SUPERFÍCIES AJARDINADAS		
	CAMINHOS DE PEDESTRE		
	SISTEMA VIÁRIO	C	COMÉRCIO
		E	ESCOLA
		BI	BIBLIOTECA
Q	QUADRA POLIESPORTIVA	CO	CORREIO
PG	PLAYGROUND	PO	POLÍCIA

30   90   150

A city designed and built from scratch: Brasilia, the capital of Brazil, designed by architect Lucio Costa (1956–60). In the same way as Chandigarh (the capital city of the Punjab, North India developed around the same time). Brasilia is a highly automobile dependent city, based on CIAM's *Charter of Athens* and zoned in functionally differentiated sectors. The 'Superquadras' are housing blocks on pilotis, arranged around courtyards.

Source: Courtesy S. Behnisch

Source: Courtesy S. Torrance

Architects and urban designers need to stop adding green roofs as an afterthought or to simply meet approval requirements and start integrating them from day one of the design. Most sustainability is not a later add-on, but requires the principles to be a basic ingredient of the first design concept. Images: Guenther Behnisch's research institute in Wageningen (NL, 1998) with a green courtyard. Proposal for a park in Toronto, by S Torrance.

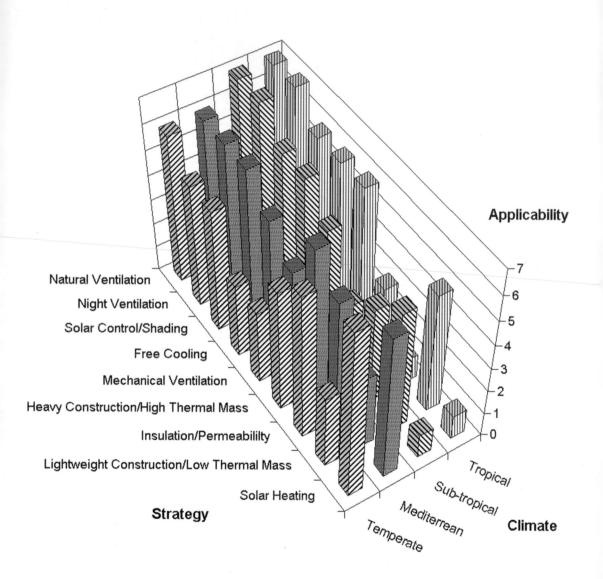

Passive design strategies

For each project, it is important to identify the appropriate passive design strategies according to climatic condition, context and project scale. Applying the suitable passive design strategies (passive design principles) will deliver the quickest pay-back for the sustainability measures.

The most effective form-based urban strategies include: compact, pedestrian-focussed, mixed-use housing communities, with courtyard typologies for effective cross-ventilation and day-lighting, effective shading devices, green roofs, and an interconnceted public space network that maintains its urban wind corridors for maximized cooling through the flow of prevailing summer breezes.

This diagram illustrates the need to identify the appropriate strategies for passive design, depending on the climatic condition of the location and scale of the development. What works in a temperate climate might not work at all in a tropical or sub-tropical one. (Source: UNESCO Chair, Shiel, J. 2008: `Strategies for practical greenhouse gas reductions in the existing building stock'. In: Proceedings ANZAScA 2008, Newcastle)

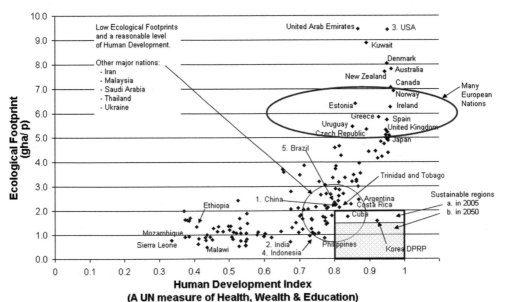

Diagrams: The Ecological Footprint and Human Wellbeing Index, as identified by the UN. (From: UNESCO Chair, Shiel, J., Lehmann, S., Mackee, J., 2009: 'Reducing greenhouse gases in existing tropical cities'. In: Proceedings iNTA-SEGA 2009, Bangkok, Thailand)

Source: Courtesy M. Desai

Passive design principles. Above: Solar chimneys in Ahmedabad, India. Below: Wind catchers of Yadz, Iran.

Source: Image Sharing Commons

Since global warming is caused by the use of energy, the main focus of sustainability must be to reduce the use of carbon based energy. Furthermore, since buildings use almost 50 per cent of all energy, and most of that is for cooling, heating and lighting, all of which are much affected by the sun, solar-responsive passive design of buildings and cities is of the highest priority. (Images: courtesy M. Desai, left; S. Lehmann, G. Murcutt, right)

Above: Verandah at Raffles Hotel, Singapore. Below: Glenn Murcutt house in Northern Territory, Australia.

Therefore we need to redefine and scientifically develop the passive solar design principles, some of them having been around as 'rule-of-thumb' for centuries. These passive design principles include simple (and free) things, such as the orientation of streets and buildings, window size and location, shading devices, colour of surfaces, and so on. Scientifically quantifying the effects of passive design principles is the next step.

These regional buildings are built from locally sourced materials and fully integrated into the surrounding landscape.

Using thermal mass to control heat gain and heat loss: Inside the adobe houses in New Mexico we can find comfortable temperatures during summertime, often 5 degrees Celsius cooler than outside. It's creating its own microclimate ideal for the extreme temperature conditions. Below: The Norwegian earth-covered house has very little heat-loss in winter, due to the earth's isolating quality. (Images: left Flickr Commons; right S. Lehmann)

Source: Courtesy M. Rocha, 2009

Source:Courtesy P. M. da Rocha

In Latin America today, we see a generation of young architects with a good understanding of passive design principles; many delightful examples of architecture designed with the climate in mind. Top: School of Arts with rammed-earth walls, in Oaxaca, Mexico, by Mauricio Rocha (2009). Below: Natural cross-ventilation through the courtyard, in Sao Paulo; subtropical house by Paulo Mendes da Rocha (1978).

Continuous upgrading of public space: Same street, Melbourne 1990...

... and Melbourne 2005. Widening of footpath and removal of car parking spaces, to make walking and cycling more safe and pleasant. (Photos: Rob Adams, City of Melbourne, 2005)

Public space and transport as indicators of good governance

Particularly in rapidly growing cities, the quality of the collective public space and urban transport planning are clear indicators and evidence for the way, how the municipality deals with the rapid growth and the city's management capacity to maintain a balance between growth, sustainability and affordable public transport. Cities in developing countries suffer frequently from under-investment in infrastructure and green space, and are not able to keep pace with the rapid urbanization. Some very positive examples for this balance can be found in Melbourne, Singapore, Barcelona and Copenhagen.

Source: Courtesy City of Sydney

Source: K. Taylor, Adelaide

The constant improvement of the public space network, where a pedestrian-friendly public domain balances urban development, allows us to test higher densities around transport nodes (examples from Melbourne and Adelaide). The aerial photo of Sydney's CBD shows that the city centre is too centralized and monocentric, disconnected from the surrounding flat city sprawl. (Sources: City of Sydney; City of Melbourne)

Are we just consumers, or are we citizens? Singapore experiments with new types of public spaces: Tree-top walk and emerging models of semi-internalised outdoor spaces. The public space of Rio de Janeiro creates the foreground and adds to the delight of the city. It is clear that public space is always more important than a single building. The design of good public space needs to come first, not at the end of a project. (Images: S. Lehmann, 2009)

Interdisciplinarity: The need for thinking in inter-connected ways, rather than in silos, was never greater. Today, all problems of industry are of multi-disciplinary nature, requiring multi-disciplinary teams to resolve them. Interdisciplinary collaboration and co-creation means that the architect or urban designer does not hold the supreme role of deciding from A to Z, but accepts that they are part of an expert team in which everyone contributes; it's more about enabling and transforming than 'inventing'.

	ENERGY SUPPLY			RESOURCE USE			OTHER MARKETS		
SECTORS	Cleaner Conventional Energy	Renewable Energy	Electric Power Infrastructure	Green Building	Cleaner Transportation	Cleaner Industry	Clean Water	Waste Management	Sustainable Forestry and Agriculture
SEGMENTS	Cleaner Coal	Solar Energy	Transmission	Optimized Design	Cleaner Road	Optimized Design	Water Extraction	Waste Collection	Sustainable Forest Management
	Cleaner Oil	Wind Power	Distribution	Sustainable Materials	Cleaner Rail	Sustainable Materials	Water Treatment	Waste Recycling	Sustainable Land Management
	Cleaner Gas	Bioenergy	Energy Storage	Energy Efficiency	Cleaner Air	Efficient Processing	Water Distribution	Energy from Waste Recovery	Sustainable Farming Communities
	Nuclear Power	Hydropower	Demand Management	Water Efficiency	Cleaner Waterway		Water Use	Waste Treatment	Optimized Crops
		Wave Power	Supply Flexibility				Wastewater Treatment	Sustainable Waste Disposal	
		Geothermal Energy							

Interdisciplinary efforts: Sustainability is multi-disciplinary by its nature, it doesn't happen in silos. If we want to achieve truly innovative outcomes, as planners and architects, we need to open-up the disciplinarian boundaries (silos) and adapt holistic approaches based on multidisciplinary working methods. (S. Lehmann, 2007) Energy segments (40) and sectors (9) define the market. (Diagram: Courtesy China Greentech Report, 2009)

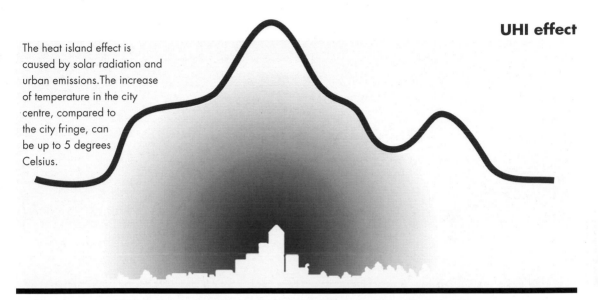

UHI effect

The heat island effect is caused by solar radiation and urban emissions. The increase of temperature in the city centre, compared to the city fringe, can be up to 5 degrees Celsius.

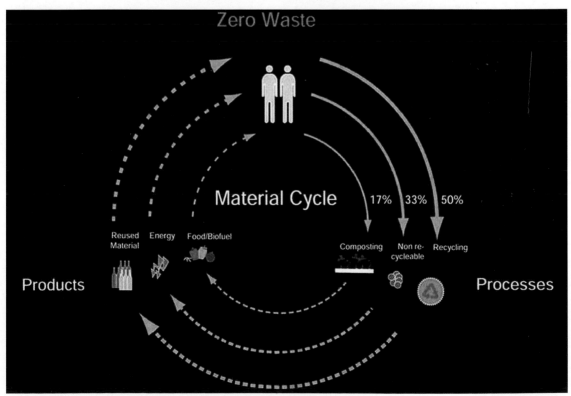

Mitigating the Urban Heat Island effect is essential for highly urbanized areas. Hong Kong, Tokyo and Singapore have adapted new regulations to balance and mitigate the UHI effect, as the new climate will have more hot and extreme weather events. Below: The material cycle of supply and disposal, developed for Masdar Eco-City, where the aim is the 'zero waste city', with a focus on recycling and composting. (Diagram: Courtesy Arup; Foster + Partners, 2008)

With a fuel-efficient car ...   **... you will still cause traffic jams.**

The question is: How to reduce the car dependency of the city residents through urban design?

The walkable and cyclable city

Small bridges and laneways are important elements to improving urban connectivity and offering new opportunities to experience the city. Copenhagen and Amsterdam are the cycling friendliest cities, where over 40 per cent of all trips are made by bike.

Cyclist are reclaiming public space from the automobile: Bike station facility next to Amsterdam railway station. (images: S. Lehmann, 2009). 'Car Cities' have usually weak centres, whereas cities with good public transport ('Transit Cities'), and an urban lay-out that enables pleasant walking and cycling, have strong centres. We want the city to have a strong, walkable city centre, combined with an efficient, low-emission mass transport systems.

Source: Image Sharing Commons

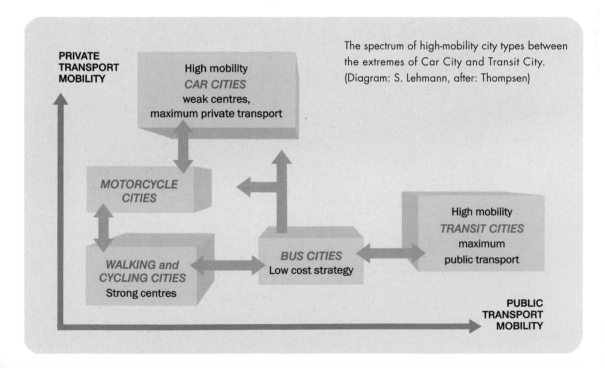

The spectrum of high-mobility city types between the extremes of Car City and Transit City. (Diagram: S. Lehmann, after: Thompsen)

PRIVATE TRANSPORT MOBILITY

High mobility
CAR CITIES
weak centres,
maximum private transport

MOTORCYCLE CITIES

High mobility
TRANSIT CITIES
maximum
public transport

WALKING and CYCLING CITIES
Strong centres

BUS CITIES
Low cost strategy

PUBLIC TRANSPORT MOBILITY

The 'Car is King' mentality, where pedestrians have been banned from the ground plane - as shown in this 1960s planning illustration - was part of the 'Functional, Zoned City' model and triumph of the motorcar, as advocated by CIAM. Such concepts have finally come to an end. Today it is understood that widening roads will only draw in more traffic, and that reliable high-quality public transport is the best solution.

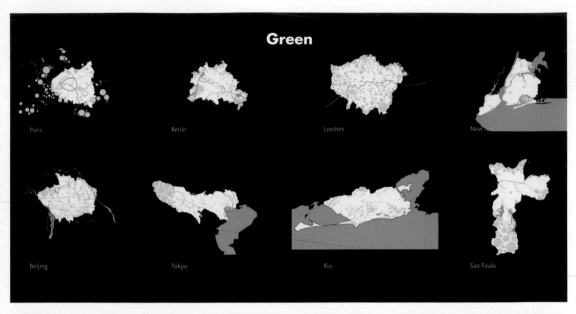

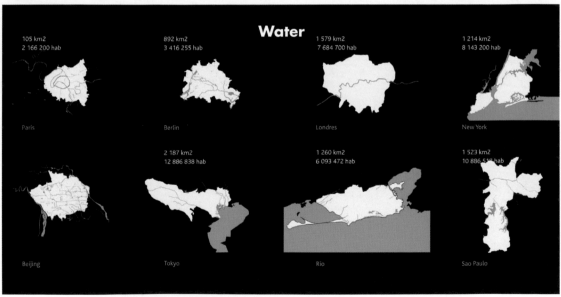

Comparative studies of cities and their infrastructure: Same scale comparison of the cities of Paris, Berlin, London, New York, Beijing, Tokyo, Rio de Janeiro and Sao Paulo. What is the role of green space and parks, waterways, road networks, and the railway system in these various cities? (Diagrams: courtesy C. de Portzamparc, 2008)

Roads

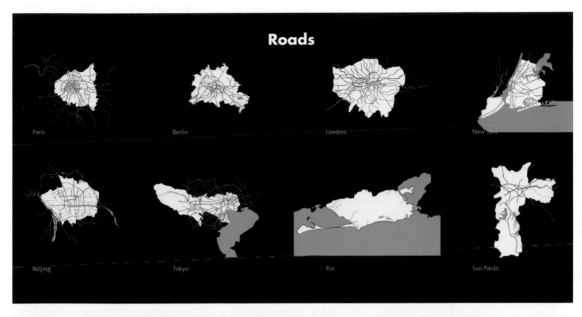

Railway

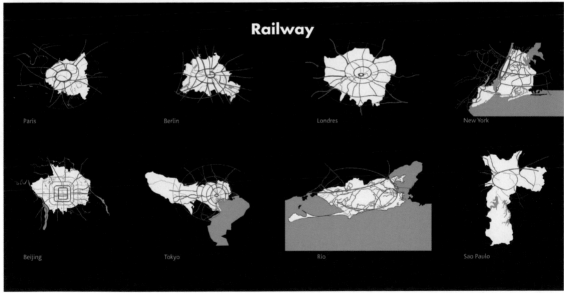

We need more comparative research in qualitative and quantitative aspects of cities, to better understand existing development patterns and identify best practice for sustainable urban growth. A comprehensive, free-accessible database on cities would be helpful to identify international best practice.

Classification of renewables and waste into three groups.

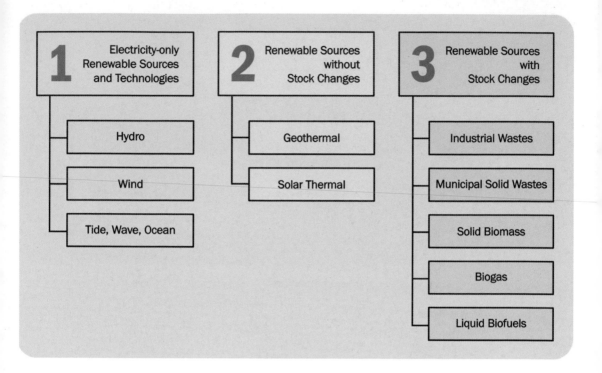

The end of low-density, car-centric suburbia

Virtually every measure of metropolitan density indicates that US and Australian cities are more spread out than those of the rest of the world, especially when compared to more compact European or Asian cities. While the dependence on the car is frequently mentioned, low-density suburbs create a series of other problems. For example:

(1) the public health problems associated with the air pollution caused by sprawl-induced auto traffic; (2) the health consequences of the reduction in walking caused by automobile dependency and lack of public transport (due to low densities, public transit cannot be operated cost-effectively in suburbs); (3) injuries and deaths from increased traffic; (4) the social isolation of residents, caused by the mono-functional structure of the suburb; (5) the wider, alleged intangible costs of automobile dependency, such as driving-induced stress, the isolation of non-drivers; (6) water quality problems associated with suburban developments; (7) the ineffectiveness in land-use, energy distribution and supply, distribution of other services; (8) the additional costs of sewerage and pipes, and so on.

The list goes on, making a strong argument for a more compact, consolidated urban form. Sustainable communities require residential areas to be in proximity of employment (workplaces close-by and home offices), mixed-use walkable districts and a diversity of housing typologies. With climate change, the suburbs represent an increasingly out-dated, unsustainable model of urbanization that we cannot afford to continue. So, a fair question to ask is: What needs to happen with the existing low-density suburbs that already exist?

The different types of renewable energy, waste sources and technologies. Each country will need to develop and work out its own individual 'post-fossil-fuel energy plan' and this plan will largely depend on the country's population density, energy consumption, anticipated lifestyles, and geographical/climatic conditions. (Diagram: S. Lehmann, UNESCO Chair; after: Energie Atlas, 2009)

Source: Courtesy T. Herzog

Source: Image Sharing Commons

Above, left: Solar roof in Singapore. Double-skin facade in Hannover. Below: Our flat, automobile- dominated suburbs of low-density car-dependent urban areas, a result of the age of consumerism, no-places, where land use and services are inefficient: the supply of water, energy and public transport will never be efficient in sprawling districts. As people want to live less and less in these isolated, car-dependent houses, we will gradually need to transform the existing suburbs.

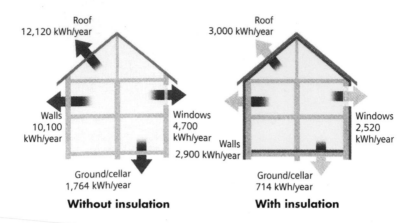

Roof
12,120 kWh/year

Walls
10,100
kWh/year

Windows
4,700
kWh/year

Ground/cellar
1,764 kWh/year

Without insulation

Roof
3,000 kWh/year

Windows
2,520
kWh/year

Walls
2,900 kWh/year

Ground/cellar
714 kWh/year

With insulation

Below: The Graylingwell Zero-Carbon Development uses reclaimed bricks for facades. 40 per cent of all materials are sourced within 40 km from the site. From 2016 on, all new housing in the UK must be 'zero-carbon'.

Source: Courtesy WSP, London

Diagram: There are significant heating (or cooling) losses for a typical home without insulation. By thoroughly renovating and insulating walls and ceilings in existing buildings, and installing double-glazed windows, energy savings (heating) of 56 per cent can be achieved. (image: Courtesy German Energy Agency, DENA) Below: The 36 ha Graylingwell net-zero carbon district with 750 homes, UK. (Image: WSP, 2010)

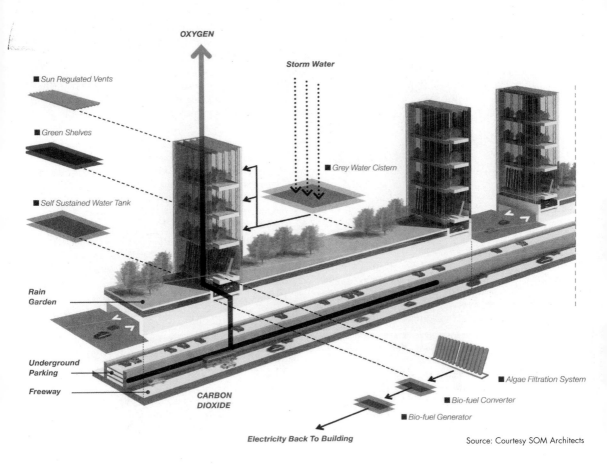

Source: Courtesy SOM Architects

Infrastructural landscape: decentralization requires the construction of new infrastructure

In the 19th and 20th century, large-scale infrastructure, such as powerstations or sewage plants, were seen as undesire-able within urban areas and therefore pushed out of our cities. This has led to huge inefficiencies through large distribu-tion networks, such as the power grid (where power, water, sewage, waste and food all have to be transported long distances). Today, we look again at decentralized systems that reintegrate clean models of 21st-century power generation, water collection, sewage treatment, waste recovery and food production back into our cities, closely integrated into the city districts. This new decentralized infrastructure systems will look differently and are integrated with the communities they serve.

In addition, the city offers unused waste heat and waste water in abundance, which can be activated. For instance, nutrients from manure, biogas from composted organic waste, and waste heat (exergy) from large air-conditioning or underground railway systems – most of the time, we simply discharge these inputs, instead of using them.

The existing *395 Highway* in Washington D.C. will be concealed and covered with a mixed-use development that restores view corridors and creates pedestrian connections across the city. A green roof on top will collect rainwater and a series of 6 `Eco-Chim-neys' will convert exhaust from the highway into oxygen (using bio-filtration systems), before releasing it into the air. (Image: courtesy SOM Architects, 2009)

Source: Courtesy City of Melbourne

Melbourne creates new public waterfront parks that are inter-connected, so that the residents can cycle on a continuous bike path along the river. (Photo: J. Gollings, 2004) In Paris, landscape architect Patrick Blanc has developed a facade greening system for vertical gardens (building by Jean Nouvel). These 'Living Walls' have over 250 species of plants and can rise up to 8 stories high. Not all plants need soil to grow, some can live on synthetic felt on a frame.

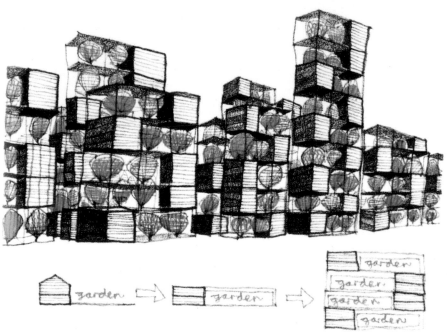

Urban greenery integrated in architecture and public space softens the harshness of the building's edge, here in tropical Singapore. (photo: S. Lehmann, 2009) Below: MVRDV's density concept of vertically stacked gardens (illustration from Chris Johnson's book 'Greening the City'; illustration by Mark Gerada). See also: www. greenroofs.com (Image left page, top: Courtesy City of Melbourne/J. Gollings, 2004)

Source: Image Sharing Commons

The map below shows the land requirements for the world, if energy is supplied from a giant solar field. Concentrated solar power technology converts the sun's powerful rays into useable energy (e.g. steam drives a turbine which generates electricity; the steam can be stored and continue to produce electricity after sunset).

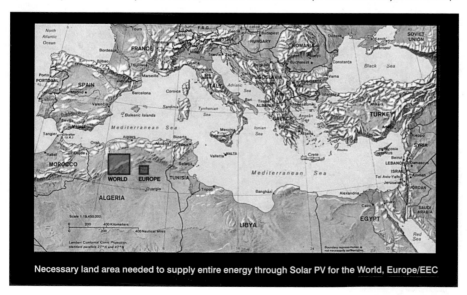

Necessary land area needed to supply entire energy through Solar PV for the World, Europe/EEC

The Earth receives more energy from the sun in just one hour than the entire world population uses in a whole year. But how can we tap into this energy source? How much land do we need to harness this energy? The aerial photo shows the large solar thermal field `Andasol', in Andalusia (Spain). Renewable energy sources will need to provide sufficient energy for an ever increasing world population to maintain today's lifestyles.

Source: Image Sharing Commons

The relatively simple technology of solar hot water systems can be used in a wide range of ways. This is why more and more countries make solar hot water systems mandatory for obtaining development approval; for instance, in Israel, it is normal standard to heat the water using solar energy. The images show the roofscape with solar hot water systems in Tel Aviv, Israel (Images: Flickr Commons Image Gallery)

City structure
insulate buildings
use sunlight
build roof gardens
take advantage of solar gain
build solar heating panels
rely on wind powered ventilation
combine heat and power
introduce geothermal systems
invest in low energy lighting
harvest rain water
segregate grey and black water
go for solar energy
go for wind energy
use ecological building materials
operation
use recyclable building material
introduce traffic calming
widen pavements
increase walkability
implement shared spaces
ensure high design quality
provide outdoor seating
build cycling paths
implement dedicated bus lanes
build tram lines
establish rail as regional backbone
establish radial and orbital rail links
ensure continuous rail systems
focus on higher core accessibility
establish green edges
create regional parks
protected countryside
build green corridors
ensure green fabric
cultivate waterways
establish hierarchy of green space
ensure polycentricity
limit surface coverage of built form
focus on corridor development
establish healthy city-edge condition
design good building -street relationships
concentrate development
build for greater flexibility
ensure mixed use
guarantee workplace/housing balance
deliver high residential density
deliver high workplace density
deliver service density
remove spatial barriers
integrate vertically
integrate horizontally
ensure high permeability
embed opportunities for change
ensure capability to respond to change
focus on retrofitting
emphasize regeneration
ensure overall flexibility
allow for adjustments

Transport
shift from car to public transport
ensure higher occupancy levels for cars
change propulsion for vehicles
introduce car sharing
shift from car to walking
shift from car to cycling
reduce size of private vehicles
reduce car ownership
change load factor for goods movement
introduce city wide cargo management
shift goods from road to rail
reduce commuting distances
reduce distances to services
reduce distances to education
reduce distances for shipping
reduce distances for leisure

CREATE
a balanced and dynamic urban economy

PROMOTE
dense, mixed-use and socially cohesive developments

CREATE
proximity between home, work and open space

DEVELOP
the urban environment to maximize flexibility and long term use

SHIFT
to green mobility by promoting public transport, walking and cycling

INTEGRATE
nature to create a balanced urban ecosystem

ENSURE
resource efficiency by reducing the environmental foot print and waste

MAXIMIZE
local energy production and promote renewable

INTRODUCE
strategic governance to implement metropolitan-wide visions

PROMOTE
a new culture of urban ecology that values sustainable lifestyles

Equity
make public transport affordable
ensure inclusive access to public space
establish public amenities for all
ensure high quality building and urban design
establish just society through redistributive measures
reduce inequality
ensure accessibility for all
sustain local employment
guarantee workplace diversity
forster tolerance
reduce segregation of age groups
ensure education for all
reinforce social networks
reduce crime
reduce risks
create safe environments for children
ensure quality of life for the elderly
guarantee access to housing market
ensure affordability of housing
reduce gated communities
reduce number of homeless
allow recreation for all
ensure public access to river and waterfront
provide resources for public institutions

Consumption
increase share locally produced food
increase share of organic food
reduce meat consumption
introduce re-usable packaging
make use of tap water as drinking water
buy energy efficient equipment
reduce number of baths/showers
buy at a local grocery
buy at local markets
reduce shopping at malls and hypermarkets
shift to renewable energy companies
increase recycling
reduce waste
increase share of locally produced clothing
recycle clothes
decrease share of one=season-clothes
increase repair service of clothes and shoes
avoid overheating of buildings
avoid over cooling of buildings
reduce water consumption
reduce electricity consumption
reduce air travel
reduce motorized trips
reduce driving speeds
combine commuting and recreation
make use of public open space for recreation
establish strong recreational links with nature in city region
buy fair-trade first
make local holidays
engage in non-sonumerist activities

Production
shift national energy mix to renewable
combine heat and power
introduce water to energy schemes
build wind turbines
expand solar energy
decentralize energy production
install district heating
install citywide heating
reduce liquid waste
reduce solid waste
shift to ecotech production
reduce production of damaging products
push creative manufacturing
increase local clothing production
implement urban agriculture
ensure ecological food processing
shift from car to bus and rail production
shift to zero-carbon economy

After: R. Rogers (2008)

Illustrating the many inter-dependencies in achieving sustainable urban development. The principles and strategies differ, based on the location and spatial scale of the urban development, as well as on its cultural and social context. (Diagram after: Richard Rogers, 2008) Achieving social sustainability is often harder than the introduction of technology-driven environmental solutions.

Diagram: S. Lehmann, 2006

20th Century City

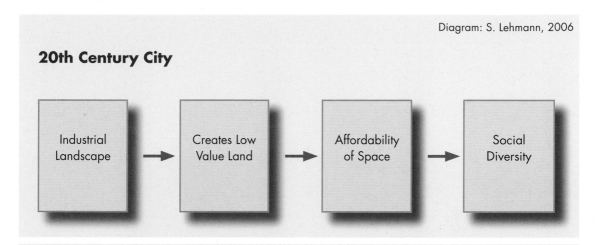

| Industrial Landscape | → | Creates Low Value Land | → | Affordability of Space | → | Social Diversity |

21st Century post-industrial City

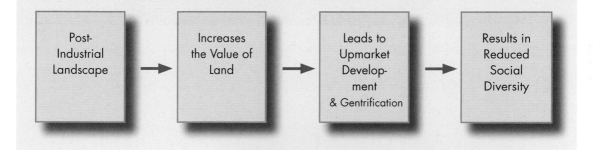

| Post-Industrial Landscape | → | Increases the Value of Land | → | Leads to Upmarket Development & Gentrification | → | Results in Reduced Social Diversity |

Above: The risk of gentrification caused by the post-industrial condition. (S. Lehmann, UNES-CO Chair, 2006) Below: Shopfront of a tired post-industrial city centre before revitalization. Re-using existing buildings and making abandoned, vacant buildings accessible to community groups helps to bring people back to these dying city centres and to create an affordability of space. Artists and creative people need cheap studio space to be able to do their work.

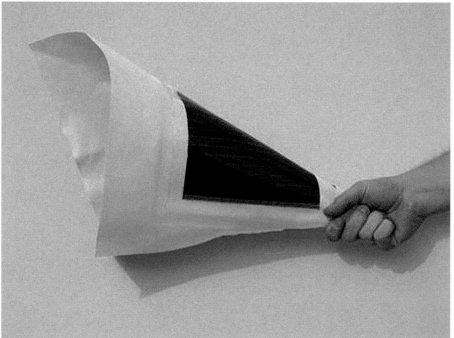

A new generation of thin-film solar photovoltaic (PV) cells, which are flexible and can take on any architectural shape and are therefore easier to integrate into the structure or facade. New thin-film technology utilizes extremely thin material layers in second and third generation PV technology and is frequently applied for building integrated applications. Today, a PV-efficiency of up to 40% is possible. (Images: Courtesy manufacturer)

Solar photovoltaic cells can be integrated in many ways, for instance, creating the roof of a carport. Below: Solar pergola in Barcelona. This large solar canopy at the Port Forum sits on top of a sewage treatment plant; it produces 1.250 kWh / kWp. For efficiency, the solar pergola is tilted at a 35 degree angle. Architects of the solar pergola: Torres and Lapena, 2005. (Image: S. Lehmann, 2006)

CHAPTER 2

The Principles Of Green Urbanism
– Putting It All Together

PRINCIPLE 1
The city based on its climatic conditions and site context

PRINCIPLE 2
The city as a self-sufficient energy producer

PRINCIPLE 3
The zero-waste city as closed loop eco-system

PRINCIPLE 4
The city with closed urban water management and high water quality

PRINCIPLE 5
The city that maximizes landscapes, gardens and biodiversity

PRINCIPLE 6
The city of eco-mobility and an efficient low-impact public transport system

PRINCIPLE 7
City construction using regional materials and prefabricated systems

PRINCIPLE 8
The city with densification and intensification of existing districts

PRINCIPLE 9
The city of deep green building design and solar access

PRINCIPLE 10
The city with special concern for affordable housing and mixed usage

PRINCIPLE 11
The city of local food supply and high food security

PRINCIPLE 12
The city of public health and cultural identity: A safe and healthy city

PRINCIPLE 13
The city of urban governance and sustainable procurement methods

PRINCIPLE 14
The city of education and training in a sustainable urban development

PRINCIPLE 15
Particular sustainability strategies for developing countries

The 15 Core Principles are not independent from each other; they require an integrated approach. The components are cross-cutting in their nature and interrelated with each other. The principles can be effective in a wide variety of urban situations, but they always need to be adapted to the specific context, climatic condition, local opportunities, project scale and site constraints. To create sustainable environments, all systems involved need to be considered simultaneously.

Introduction

After more than three decades of intensive environmental debate – starting in industrial-ized countries in 1973 with the first *Oil Crisis* – there is clearly an increasing demand to explore, assess and critically examine the theories for fossil-fuel free, zero-carbon cities, beyond the scale of the individual building, that is to say, on the urban scale. Only by approaching the issue on a larger city-scale and by re-engineering our urban environ-ments on the neighbourhood and district-wide (city-wide) level, will we have a chance to have a real impact on, and to combat, climate change. In particular, the emergence of a more comprehensive and holistic theoretical model of urban sustainability and eco-city would be of much benefit to many places in the developing world, where there is the most urgency for implementing eco-cities and for making these ideas take root in the collective mind. The Middle East and the Asia-Pacific Region, for instance, are already home to 65 per cent of the world's population; they are the fastest growing regions in the world in terms of increasing economic development, urbanization rate, population growth, energy demands and greenhouse gas emissions. How the leaders and the population of the Middle East and the Asia-Pacific regions respond to the challenge of sustainable urban development will affect the future of the entire world.

The Conceptual Model of Green Urbanism: The 15 Principles

Today, no serious scientific body, university or government research agency around the world is disputing the IPCC's and other major research institutes' core findings: that global average temperature is increasing and that human activity is most likely responsible for it. [1]

However, humankind keeps consuming fossil-fuel energy and other resources – such as water, land, forests, materials, even wildlife – at levels that are not only far beyond what we need, but are far beyond the limits of what the planet can bear. The majority of the world's population are now living and working in urban areas and placing huge demands on energy, resources and infrastructure. According to the United Nations, a very fast process of urbanization is taking place, especially in the developing countries of Africa, the Middle East and Asia, with world population expected to reach 9 billion people in 2050 (this is the medium population forecast used by several bodies, such as by: UN-Habitat, 2008). It has been estimated that 'to accommodate the urban population increase in the next 50 years the equivalent of a new city of 1 million people will have to be built every week.' (Burdett, 2004)

Architecture and urban planning are playing a major role in the challenge of moving towards more sustainable urbanization models. But rather than see our relative wealth in the developed world as an opportunity to build well – designing and constructing longer lasting buildings and cities with enduring infrastructure – we do just the opposite: we keep designing and constructing cities and buildings that are not meant to last more than 20 to 30 years and put in place policies that encourage rapid depreciation, planned obsolescence and minimal expenditures with the lowest bidder.

Thom Fisher notes in regard to the construction sector in the US, the urgency for a paradigm shift: `Rarely has a continent so rich constructed so much of such poor quality in so short a period of time. (...) Human settlement patterns have created such fragmented and polluted natural habitats that biologists now predict that as many as two-thirds of all plant and animal species will be extinct by 2050. Add to that the exponential rise in atmospheric carbon, at levels not seen for the last 400,000 years, and the exponential increase in human population, expected to grow from 2 to 9 billion people from 1950 to 2050, and we begin to see the dimensions of the challenge we face. We stand at a moment in our history when we either choose to inhabit this planet very differently very quickly, or we may find ourselves among the species that we have rendered extinct.' (Fisher, 2010)

Chapter 1 discussed the view that urbanization is widely understood to be a key driver of carbon emissions, resource depletion and environmental degradation. This second chapter introduces the *Principles of Green Urbanism* as a set of strategic parameters, core principles and guidelines to mitigate the harmful impact of urban development on the natural environment, whilst also maximizing design quality and liveability, economic growth, cultural diversity and social prosperity to bring about just and healthy urban developments. This paradigm shift in urban development and energy concepts is essential, as the current situation where 20 per cent of the world's population consumes 80 per cent of the world's resources is unsustainable, unjust and cannot be allowed to continue. However, embedding these principles will require more than merely tweaking a few details of our lifestyle. We must be more reasonable. We must learn to consume less.[2] We must use energy, materials and water more efficiently. We must engage a holistic re-examination of urban design concepts and integrate a *systems thinking* approach in things such as transport, material and waste flow, and water management. In the energy sector, for instance, we need a complete re-examination of how we produce and distribute power in future city districts. This has huge consequences on the design of the city of the future. The core principles presented here explain the components of any eco-city and what can be achieved if urban designers are determined to succeed and are ambitious and willing to act quickly. We need to emphasize the critical role that urban designers, architects, planners and engineers play in solving the issues impacting on our planet. What is at stake is the future of humanity.

In the meantime, the cities of our urbanizing planet have emerged as the incubators and medium for revolutionary change.

After the somewhat limited outcomes of the *UN-Climate Summit COP15* in December 2009 in Copenhagen, there is a growing concern that governments and greenhouse-gas generating corporations are not up to the task posed by climate change. We urgently need vital steps to be made to slow down global warming and climate destabilization. It looks like some municipalities are ahead of other levels of government, and many NGOs and independent organizations have also become active in establishing frameworks to achieve greenhouse gas reductions at the local level. Clearly, the future of our cities depends on us making the shift to a new urban paradigm based on the application of the Principles of Green Urbanism. If we get this right, the city – often thought of as being the most wasteful user of resources – could re-emerge as the solution to, and new model of, sustainability.

How our cities will have to be transformed to a more dense way of living
For centuries, the growth of our cities and transport systems was based on the easy avail-ability of cheap fossil-fuels, land, raw materials and food. This has had a huge impact on the built environment and the physical shape of cities. However, with Peak Oil, the attitude of unsustainable urban growth has changed. More compact cities and growth boundaries are needed to save the remaining landscape and forests from direct human occupation. We are already witnessing a wave of innovations in urban infrastructure, transport, en-ergy and water management systems, as well as new non-polluting production processes adapted by industry. As a consequence, we now need a dramatic rethink and a different approach to the way we plan, design, build and operate cities, one that incorporates the best of these innovations and technological improvements. In this way, new urban models will emerge, where the city establishes a better symbiosis with its eco-system and its sur-rounding hinterland. In regard to the urban–rural relationship, Herbert Girardet notes: 'The dependence of cities on their hinterland and rural surrounding has to be reconsid-ered; cities are entirely dependent on vast inputs from elsewhere. (...) Cities occupy just 2 per cent of the world's land surface, but they consume 75 per cent of its resources. City dwellers profoundly affect rural economies far beyond urban boundaries. The challenge is to create a new relationship between cities and nature.' (Girardet, 2008)

Cities and buildings are resource-intensive and, therefore, have major environmental and social impacts. Buildings and infrastructure have a long lifespan, so that good urban design decisions taken today will have significant ramifications and could, potentially, affect and improve the quality of life for generations to come. As we future-proof and retrofit existing cities and renew much of the infrastructure constructed since World War II (or earlier), we need to think about how we can make the city more resilient. Rather than assuming the continuous availability of infrastructure, Thomas Fisher points out that 'resilient systems have alternative ways of meeting needs: operable windows, day-lit spaces, and multiple forms of cooling, heating and powering what we use. Rather than single-use zoning, single modes of transportation, and monocultures of people and landscapes, resilient communities maximize their diversity: a rich mix of uses, multi-modes of moving people and goods, and as wide a range of native species and socio-economic groups as possible.' (Fisher, 2010)

Urban areas can produce a wide range of environmental problems that arise from the consumption of natural resources and the consequent generation of waste and pollution. The Worldwatch Institute has reported that 'buildings use 40 per cent of all raw materials globally – a staggering 3 billion tonnes each year.' (Worldwatch, 2008) In the USA alone, buildings represent 39 per cent of primary energy use (including fuel input for production) according to the Energy Information Administration. (EIA, 2008) More and more intellectuals, such as Thomas Friedman, are asking if we need to fundamentally change our values and ideas about growth. In 2010, it looks like the whole growth model we have created over the last fifty years is simply unsustainable in terms of economy and ecology. In regard to the need for new values and fundamental changes in the design professions, Sydney-based architect Ken Maher notes: 'Cities fail if they are not civilizing and sustaining in a spiritual sense – if they don't stimulate the senses and provide the platform for enriching emotional experiences. (...) We need to replace the present reality where we seem to live to produce, to consume and to waste. This will require a new view of architecture and urbanism and a new way of designing – what I would term 'deep green design' – with a focus on the ecology of design and an unselfish creative expression. Through making more effective urban spaces, more integrated urban environments, better arrangements of activities and, importantly, new architectural and urban space typologies, we can make a real difference to people's lives and our cities.' (Maher, 2009)

This is a new Industrial Revolution that will probably be more exciting than the steam engine or the motor car.   **Lord Nicholas Stern, 2010**

Green Urbanism is by definition interdisciplinary; it requires the collaboration of landscape architects, engineers, urban planners, ecologists, transport planners, physicists, psychologists, sociologists, economists and other specialists, in addition to architects and urban designers. *Green Urbanism* makes every effort to minimize the use of energy, water and materials at each stage of the city's or district's life-cycle, including the embodied energy in the extraction and transportation of materials, their fabrication, their assembly into the buildings and, ultimately, the ease and value of their recycling when an individual building's life is over. Today, urban and architectural design also has to take into consideration the use of energy in the district's or building's maintenance and changes in its use; not to mention the primary energy use for its lighting, heating and cooling.

Energy, water and food security

This chapter introduces the *15 Principles of Green Urbanism* as a conceptual model and as a framework for how we might be able to tackle the enormous challenge of transforming existing neighbourhoods, districts and communities, and how we can re-think the way we design, build and operate urban settlements. These principles are partly universal, but there is no one single formula that will always work; there are only basic principles, and this book is about identifying those principles and illustrating their application in case studies (which happens in Chapter 3). To achieve more sustainable cities[3], urban designers must understand and apply the core principles of green urbanism in a systematic and adapted way. These principles can be effective in a wide variety of urban situations, but they almost always need to be adapted to the context and the project's scale, to the site's constraints and opportunities. We need to develop a specific approach for each unique site and situation, adapting the principles to the particular climatic conditions, site context, availability of technology, social conditions, project scale, client's brief, diverse stakeholder organizations, and so on. It is an approach to urban design that requires an optimization process and a solid understanding of the development's wider context and its many dimensions before the designer can produce an effective design outcome.

With all this technological progress, we should not lose sight of the fact that a key component in any society's sustainability is more than its carbon footprint.
The future of our societies is not just merely a technical matter of finding more eco-friendly energy solutions, but a question of holistic social sustainability and healthy community.

Social sustainability and a healthy community need to be part of any vision of the future

The future of our societies is not just merely a technical matter of finding more efficient energy and mobility solutions. Inequality and poverty need to be addressed in any sustainable vision of the future. For instance, how do we ensure human working conditions, sufficient means of education, health, affordable housing, domestic comfort and equity in access to jobs and transport?

The design of neighbourhoods and districts has always been a very complex exercise, and the planning of sustainable communities is about empowering its citizens. A community is about 5,000 people in size, and which supports a bus stop. `Citizenship' includes the dependency of one person on another. Urban design has always had a social (and, therefore, political) dimension. As a global society, humans are very well informed and affected by each other, by what is happening in Detroit, Sydney, the Maldives or Darfur. One phenomenon of the developed world is that people are moving back to city centres. However, many post-industrial towns and cities worldwide are suffering a decline in their centres, in which the boarded-up shop fronts of vacant, abandoned buildings in their formerly vibrant 'heart' accelerates this urban decline. The consequence of decline is not only the decay of public space and the abandonment of buildings, but also it is about run-down infrastructure and an increase in unemployment. When studying city centres in different continents, I have found that there are many similarities in the symptoms of decline in a large number of cities in the developed world. The antidote is, frequently, a need to redefine the city centre's identity and in giving the urban core a new role to play. In Chapter 1, I have defined what can be called the 'post-industrial condition': it is where the shrinking of cities and the lack of investment (and, therefore, a high rate of unemployment, run-down buildings, etc.) is found side-by-side with rapid urban growth of certain popular districts or boom-precincts. Both, shrinkage and growth can often be observed side-by-side in the same city. The reason for this is often a lack of strategic planning in dealing with demographic changes and economic restructuring.

'Green neighbourhoods' are districts within communities where regulations, investments and incentives are targeted and design strategies are applied to achieve a larger scale of operations for employing the standards used to create green buildings and cities.

The districts and cities where *the Principles of Green Urbanism* have been applied and integrated in every aspect are urban environments that:
• respond well to their climate, location, orientation and context, optimizing natural assets such as sunlight and wind flow,
• are quiet, clean and effective, with a healthy microclimate,
• have reduced or have no CO_2 emissions, as they are self-sufficient energy producers, powered by renewable energy sources,
• eliminate the concept of waste, as they are based on a circular closed-loop eco-system with significant recycling, remanufacturing and composting,
• have high water quality and which practice sensitive urban water management,
• integrate landscape, gardens and green roofs to maximize biodiversity and mitigate the urban heat island effect,
• take only their fair share of the earth's resources, using principles of urban ecology,
• apply new technologies such as co-generation and solar cooling,
• provide easy accessibility and mobility, are well inter-connected, and provide a low-impact transport system,
• use regional and local materials and apply prefabricated modular construction systems,
• create a vibrant sense of place and authentic cultural identity, where existing districts are densified and make use of urban mixed-use infill projects,
• are generally more compact communities around transport nodes ('green TODs'), with a special concern for affordable housing and mixed-use programmes,
• use deep green passive design strategies and solar architecture concepts for all buildings, with compact massing for reduced heat gain in summer,
• are laid-out and oriented in a way that keeps the buildings cool in summer, but which catches the sun in winter,
• have a local food supply through community gardens and urban farming and which achieve high food security and reduced 'food miles', and
• use multi-disciplinary approach, best practice for urban governance and sustainable procurement methods.

Transition to a predominantly urban world

As the world's population grows, we are accelerating the consumption of limited resources. Many experts see the transition from fossil-fuels to renewable power sources, with the related infrastructure change, being primarily a technological challenge. Nothing seems to be more difficult than overcoming the anachronistic power regime of large utility providers to end the domination of fossil-fuel and to roll-out the available technological solutions in renewable energy. The main hurdles might be institutional and political in attempting to generate policy changes, and in this regard Peter Droege notes: 'Many city leaders correctly perceive this transition not primarily as an engineering or urban planning challenge, but as a social equity, political and economic development task. No technological or logistical barrier hinders a switch away from the present dangerous levels of nuclear and fossil energy reliance. The urban energy transition is a challenge of culture, community and civilization, and of bold institutional, political and policy changes.' (Droege, 2008)

In 1972, the *Club of Rome* formulated, in its study 'Limits of Growth', the negative effect of sprawl and over-consumption of resources. Today, we know that uncontrolled development is a damaging exercise, and that urban growth should occur in existing city areas rather than on greenfield sites. Portland (Oregon, USA) was well ahead of most other cities when, in the early 1980s, it introduced a legally binding 'growth boundary' to stop sprawl and the emptying-out of its downtown area. 'Today, younger people don't desire to live in the endless suburbs anymore, but have started to re-orientate themselves back to the city core, mainly for lifestyle reasons.' (Fishman, 1987) However, as several recent studies of inner-city lifestyles reveal, an increase in consumption can be part of the inner-city renaissance, which often enlarges the ecological footprint of the urban dweller (e.g. research by the University of Vancouver on the effect of higher population density and increase in lifestyle gadgets owned by urban dwellers).

Joel Garreau's seminal book 'The Edge City' describes in detail how large corporations and services started moving out of the city centre (downtown) to new suburban business parks. (Garreau, 1991) 'Edge City' is an American term for a concentration of business, shopping and entertainment outside the traditional urban area, in what had previously been a residential suburb or semi-rural community (also called 'suburban activity centre'). Garreau argues that it has become the standard form of urban growth in the US, representing a new 20th-century urban form different from that of the 19th-century central 'downtown'. *Edge City* occupies a new area that had no urban characteristics 20 or 30 years earlier; it is car-dependent and develops at or near existing freeway intersections and major airports. It is focused on service industries and rarely includes heavy industry.

Today, *Edge Cities* are numerous. There are almost 200 in the United States, compared to 45 downtowns of comparable size, and they are geographically large, because they are built on an automobile scale. An example is Silicon Valley in California. 'Spatially, edge cities primarily consist of mid-rise office towers surrounded by massive surface parking lots and meticulously manicured lawns. Instead of a traditional street grid, their street networks are not pedestrian friendly, hierarchical, consisting of winding parkways (often lacking sidewalks) that feed into arterial roads or freeway ramps,' says Garreau. (Garreau, 1991) He identifies three distinct varieties of *Edge City*:

- Boomers – the most common type, having developed incrementally around a shopping mall or highway interchange.
- Greenfields – having been master-planned as new towns, generally on the suburban fringe.
- Uptowns – historic activity centres built over an older city or satellite city.

The sustainable city of tomorrow will need to be more than an artificial city. The sustainable city of tomorrow will need more than technological solutions (solar, smart grid, etc), efficient public transport, growth boundaries and higher population densities. It will also require an intensified mixed-use programme, a healthy proportion of social housing (affordable, subsidized – most experts agree on a figure of 25 per cent of social housing as minimum to achieve an effective social mix), integration of authentic existing buildings, and innovative methods of social sustainability to overcome the increasing divide between rich and poor, or young and old. (Kostof, 1992; Forster, 1999; Burdett, 2004)

Sustainable urban management and development is one of the most critical issues for the 21st century.   *From the Local Governments' Declaration at the UN Earth Summit, Johannesburg 2002*

So, is a new symbiosis between countryside and city possible?

Managing the urban-rural interface (the `peri-urban', or what Sieverts calls the 'Zwischenstadt') will be a crucial design component for any new urban development. In the past, the medieval town was self-sufficient in regard to all the resources people needed to lead a comfortable life. It was based on a recycling and reusing society. The population lived off the land that surrounded the city, and developed local foods and regional cooking styles. However, with industrialization, we established systems that supplied water and electricity from far-away sources and food supply became global, travelling long distances and adding significantly to CO_2 emissions through its transportation.

In the sustainable city of the future, energy production will be moved from the centralized power station in the hinterland to many small, decentralized places of power generation in the city's districts, connected by a smart community grid. The local use of solar energy, wind energy and biomass will allow a re-connection of energy production with the place of final energy consumption. Through this decentralized, on-site energy production using small, local, building-integrated units (close to the point of energy consumption), the chance for an entirely new type of urbanism emerges, with new settlement typologies and transport structures. In this regard, the green politician Hermann Scheer, who was involved in the development of the German feed-in tariffs in 1999 (as a member of the German parliament, together with Hans-Josef Fell), notes in `Solar City: Reconnecting energy generation and use to the technical and social logic of solar energy': `In the past the production of fossil and/or atomic energy led to a progressive disconnection of the areas of primary energy production from those where the useful energy was consumed, creating a growing need for infrastructure. (…) Exploiting the possibility of sourcing natural primary energy over a wide area in the towns and cities means connecting the areas of active energy use with those of the energy harvest – that is to say with less and in some cases, in the urban centres in particular, with no infrastructure requirement of any kind.' He goes on to further point out: `The use of renewable energies in buildings and in urban planning, and the adaptation of buildings and orientation to the existing natural environment, is a critical element in transforming energy supply at the municipal level. At the same time urban planning – in terms of distances between residential areas, work, recreation and shopping areas – is a key factor in determining transport behaviour and hence energy consumption. There is a need to substantially cut local energy consumption by ensuring that urban planning is oriented to the need to eliminate traffic. (…) Local authorities can use their competences to set the framework for using renewable energies in buildings and urban planning, taking into account bio-climatic conditions. Making the changeover to solar power in building and urban planning represents a historic turning point in building culture and urban development. As a consequence of this development, long-distance transmission networks will in the future become redundant as electricity supply becomes fragmented.' (Scheer, 2006)

The battle for sustainable development is going to be largely won or lost in our cities. It is in the cities of the 21st century where the historic challenge of climate change will need to be resolved. **Klaus Toepfer, 2005**

With the end of the `old' fossil-fuel energy system, urban designers can re-think the relationship between city and countryside as a whole, where the city does not continue to grow at the expense of its rural hinterland. It can be assumed that in ten years the concept of decentralized, distributed energy generation will become a standard for newly planned models of green neighbourhoods and the existing infrastructure of the long-distance grid network will become obsolete, as sustainable city districts will be able to act as 'power stations' for their own demand. (See: Fig. 1) The result will be housing districts that generate more energy than they consume. The ability to cheaply store this energy as back-up within the community will need to be solved by the development of improved battery technology and the roll-out of smart grid technology.

Fig. 1: The compact European block model, as can be found in Berlin, Paris, Athens, Amsterdam, Barcelona and many other cities, has been rediscovered as a very sustainable model: these mixed-use blocks (with retail, offices and restaurants in ground floor, and cross-ventilated apartments in the upper floors) are usually around 4 to 8 storeys in height. Units share circulation and fire walls. The inner courtyards are quiet, so natural ventilation is unproblematic even in the noisy city centre. It is a very robust model for city-making. (Image: Aerial photo of Berlin; source: Image Sharing Commons)

Fig. 2: Satellite image of Australia: As the density reveals, the inhabitation of the Australian continent is concentrated along the eastern, and to some degree along the western coastline, there is a significant urban-rural disconnect. Predictions for population growth in Australia mean that fundamental changes are on the way. Population is predicted to increase to 36 million people in 2050 (up from 21 million in 2010). With climate change and such population increase, Australians will have to make major lifestyle changes, including: increases in housing density especially in low-density suburbs; an end to the reliance on the car; the creation of self-sustaining, compact districts capable of generating their own energy; accommodating population increases in larger regional centres, not just the main cities; transforming metropolitan areas into poly-centric, compact city clusters. (Courtesy: Google Earth, 2009)

Fig. 3: Aerial photo of a typical low-density, car-dependent suburb. The unused roofs indicate that each house has its own fossil-fuel based hot water system. Increasingly, planners are thinking of strategies to transform suburbs. Most mono-functional suburban developments of the last five decades have relied too much upon cheap fossil-fuels and land. In general, a system in which almost all vehicles use one fuel source can never be 'resilient' (in this case oil, which has reached its peak availability). Today, suburbs become residential wastelands: With housing units of roughly the same size and cost, such developments were cost-efficient to build and market, but in the US they have collapsed in value due to foreclosures dragging down the resale price of the houses and made most mortgages negatively valued.

Urban biodiversity: using nature and natural processes as model

Based on concepts of urban metabolism, urban designers are now modelling cities as eco-systems[4], learning about high performance solutions from ecology and nature. Janice Benyus has coined the notion of *Biomimicry*, where lessons from nature are taken to directly inform urban planning decisions. (Benyus, 1997; Head, 2008) Biomimicry uses nature as an inspiration to identify optimum solutions; nature has many lessons to teach us with regard to waste, water use, resourcefulness, structure and the ability to adapt. In `Biomimicry: Innovation inspired by Nature' (1997), Benyus develops the basic thesis that human beings should consciously emulate nature's genius in their designs, emulating natural models in order to design sustainable products, processes and policies that create conditions conducive to life. She promotes the transfer of ideas, designs and strategies from biology and biological patterns to sustainable human systems design. The *Biomimicry* principles as outlined by Benyus, are:

- nature uses only the energy it needs and runs on sunlight (photosynthesis)
- nature fits form to function and recycles everything and doesn't know 'waste'
- nature banks on diversity
- nature demands local expertise, and
- nature taps the power of limits and responds to change.

Hugh Aldersey-Williams explored extensively the relationship between animal structure and buildings (Aldersey-Williams, 2003). Biologists have observed that before eco-systems collapse they often become so inter-connected, productive and efficient that they lose all resiliencies, becoming unable to withstand unexpected outside stresses. Their collapse represents what biologists call an 'adaptive cycle', in which the eco-systems have become more diverse and resilient, but less inter-connected, productive and efficient. Certainly, such observation of principles must be of relevance for all designers of the human eco-system we call the built environment. (Flannery, 2000)

Urban renewal and re-design of the city centre requires support for change

Over the last years, the debate about sustainable cities, with a less car-dependent and more transit-oriented urban form, has gained worldwide momentum. The design projects and ideas presented in this book explore how we are able to address the need for environmental sustainability on the urban scale, with a re-appreciation of the existing city centres. The wish to achieve a real difference requires urban designers to re-think the city centre and its urban planning conventions. New compact models for urban growth will be part of the long-term strategies for urban renewal and will help to achieve a more sustainable, revitalized downtown. In terms of integrating and re-using existing structures, the most sustainable building is the one that already exists (due to its embodied energy). This approach has the advantage that it helps to keep the city centre authentic (by maintaining existing buildings) and the public space network vital, while carefully developing higher densities around transport nodes and cultural and educational facilities. (Beatley, 1997)

The increase of densities, combined with urban regeneration strategies for neglected inner-city areas, are good solutions: It is always less environmentally damaging to stimulate growth within the established city centre, rather than sprawling into new, formerly un-built areas.

Today, in many cases, large corporations and department stores have abandoned the city centre; while downtowns are increasingly turned into up-market residential districts and centres of entertainment, education and culture. Urban renewal involves a series of strategies, such as compaction, densification and intensification. The *City Campus/Green Corridor* projects propose a denser, mixed-use and revitalized city centre, where educational facilities and universities play a major role. On the other hand, the *Port City* project recommends a model for urban expansion – to be applied after having first densified and revitalized the city centre for several years. *City Campus* and *Port City* are catalytic projects of good scale and critical mass, capable of bringing urban improvement quickly. Our study has revealed the tremendous potential of an inner-city harbour to the city precinct in general, and of port-related waterfront sites in particular (see illustration of projects in Chapter 3).

Densification means that we first rebuild and infill the empty quarters of our cities before we further expand the city's footprint into the countryside or build any further suburbs. An important key component of urban regeneration (as discussed in Chapter 1) are the creative industries and creative workforces, which enforces a city's cultural diversity. As pointed out by Richard Florida, the `knowledge-based city' is usually based on a vibrant urban culture and a high-quality university (see the role of the university in places such as Harvard, Oxford, or Heidelberg), as well as on regionally or nationally important museums and galleries. (Florida, 2001)
The `ecological re-design of existing cities' (Girardet, 2008) remains a gigantic task. Sustainability approaches should be embedded in all new precinct planning guidelines for urban growth areas. Preferably, urban development should be supported by a database of best practice of sustainable planning and action at the local level. This means, climate change mitigation and adaptation have to be planned for at a city- and district-wide level, so that optimal solar orientation, biodiversity protection and the roll-out of innovative technologies (including distributed energy generation, stormwater recycling, etc.) are integrated from the beginning. Innovative demonstration projects have now been started in many countries, where, for instance, former sewerage plants are being restored to wetlands and orchards, and where new districts are powered by solar, wind, geothermal, biomass, using co-generation and wood chip options, waste-to-energy CHP technology, and district cooling from near-by river water. Such a database of best practice in sustainable urban development would be very useful, as it would enable everybody to draw on the knowledge and experiences in sustainable urbanism from around the world. UN-Habitat and ICLEI have recently set-up such a database, which is accessible online.

Essential for any urban change is strong urban governance – something that is often forgotten and not talked about enough. City councils need strong management and political support to get their urban visions realized. First of all, municipalities need to make the city a desirable and enjoyable destination, in order to attract new investment, businesses and households. Without a framework for higher job, retail and housing density, no city will be transformed to a more compact community. In regard to this, Gary Pivo, who has written extensively about the densification of Kirkland (a city east of Seattle, which transformed itself to a compact community), gives the following recommendations to city councils: `Regulate growth to balance conservation and development. Land-use controls should be fair and predictable to encourage quality development. (…) A balance must be struck between facilitating growth and insisting that the development be well done.' (Pivo, 1997)

Urban areas are the engines of growth and social change,
and the centres of innovation and creativity.
Urbanization and economic development go hand-in-hand.
The design of cities is about inventing the future.

Barcelona is still seen as one of the best examples of major urban regeneration in Europe, where politicians had a clear vision of the city's future and continuously worked towards it. In the US there are also plenty of great examples for urban renewal; for instance, the revitalization of Fort Worth (Texas). The architect, developer and environmentalist Ed Bass was the driving force behind Fort Worth's downtown revitalization, where he renovated derelict buildings and regenerated the nearly dead city core into a vibrant mixed-use centre. Many of the innovative urban renewal demonstration projects that have now been started are located in Asia; for instance in China, Singapore and Korea. Seoul, the 20 million people mega-city in Korea, is undergoing an impressive urban transformation. Started by Lee Myung Bak (currently president of Korea) and urban planner Kim Ki Ho and others, Seoul is transforming itself towards a more liveable city with green spaces for walking and cycling paths along its re-naturalized rivers. To make Seoul more walkable, the grassroots initiative 'Dosi Yondae' has been founded, and the municipality of Seoul now has a strong focus on green urban design to improve living conditions. The removal of an inner-city freeway and the re-naturalization of the 6 km river bank along the Cheong Gye Cheon waterway is part of this transformation process (see: Chapter 1, p. 127).

Changing urban paradigms: transport planning as example

Manuel Castells has pointed to how a new 'Network Society' has emerged, where global cities have become centres of worldwide networks of capital and information, `where the source of productivity lies in the generation of knowledge through information processing.' (Castells, 1996) Transport systems are the old-type visible network, while data freeways are the invisible ones. The placement of buildings, and how compactly they are grouped, has a fundamental and direct impact on energy consumption and it determines traffic patterns.

A vibrant, livable city depends much on strong pedestrian connectivity and hierarchical coherence of urban space. However, the pressure to accommodate both the automobile and increased population growth led 20th-century urbanists to fail in the design challenge of integrating the competing connective networks, or as Nikos Salingaros puts it: `We have allowed the *car city* to eliminate the *pedestrian city*.' (Salingaros, 2003) During the last century, transport systems were built the way they are because oil and land was plentiful and cheap. This is no longer the case. Most cities complement now their heavy rail system with more flexible light railway and rapid transit bus ways. Transportation is the second largest source of CO_2 emissions in the USA, after electricity generation. Based on the large amount of CO_2 emissions from unsustainable transport practice, the role of public transport is now widely understood to be a very important one. It needs to use low-carbon transport to better connect middle-distance suburbs with job-rich areas and inner-city centres. In the 'East Asian model', for instance in Singapore, Hong Kong, Tokyo and Seoul; clusters of high density districts have been developed along the inner-city metro routes and on top of interchanges (as *green TODs*), and there is a strong commitment by forward-thinking governments to continuously invest in public mass transit systems (investments of over 5 per cent of the GDP is common; for instance, China is currently investing 9 per cent of its GDP in public transport projects such as high-speed trains and subways). These projects are often funded through a combination of a car carbon tax, congestion charges for cars to enter the city centre, tax on fuel, or parking space levies. In these highly populated East Asian cities, some of the world's most efficient low-carbon public transport systems, using metropolitan subways, have been developed. For Australian cities, where public transport has been notoriously under-funded for decades, it seems impossible to reach this high standard of transport. Instead, it will be important to better connect the middle-distance suburbs with the job-rich inner-city business district through new light railway lines and rapid transit bus ways. Constructing subway systems is extremely expensive and time consuming. Larger, poly-centric cities (cities with several centres but without a real or efficient subway system, such as Sydney or Los Angeles) need to find ways to connect their various centres with an efficient, high-speed linkage, such as a monorail, light railway or bus systems.[5] The worst transport mode is still the single-occupancy automobile.

Researchers found that with the aging population phenomenon, the demand for housing near transit-oriented development will increase. The types of households that most likely tend to choose living in TODs are also the types of households that are projected to grow the most over the next 25 years in cities in the developed world: singles, the elderly, couples without children and low-income minority households – all depending on an affordable mass transport system.

By 2020 there will be a variety of different kinds of full-scale eco-city demonstration projects realized, which are the test bed for research, innovation and best practice.

Towards more compact polycentric cities

Innovation and new technology development in the transport sector is rapidly evolving, and the field of transport and traffic planning is a good example of the changing paradigm in urban design, to find an urban form that is generated as response to its climatic conditions and context. There are also many new approaches to the automobile and its future place in the city centre. The aim of reclaiming the city from the dominance of the motorcar, means accepting that roads are public spaces which should accommodate pedestrians and cyclists foremost. Having pedestrians wait at busy intersections for up to four or five minutes for traffic lights to change is not acceptable. It is not surprising that people ignore traffic lights and that there are regular traffic accidents. Municipal authorities need to consider the challenges connected to changing attitudes towards transport. For instance, most cities want to take control of their main arteries that cut through their central business districts, to take out the traffic lights and impose a general speed limit of 20 km/h. This could help to reclaim the public space of the street for pedestrians and give them the right of way. The proposal for so-called 'naked streets' – the term used in some European cities where streetscapes devoid of lights and signs are common – is to discourage driving in the city centre without imposing financial disincentives such as the congestion charge that is levied on motorists entering the centre of London during the day. London introduced, in 2003, the `Congestion Charge', making it expensive to drive into the inner city. The charge reduced traffic in the city centre by around 20 per cent and made walking pleasant again, and it also significantly increased the use of public transport. Such measures are only possible if, at the same time, excellent public transport is available.

Cities can and must become the most environmentally-friendly model for inhabiting our Earth.
The need to re-conceptualize cities and their infrastructural systems, to be compact and polycentric cities, is more important than ever.

The design of the streetscape is crucial. For instance, the street's paving material, its street furniture, its illumination, tree planting, speed limits and general ambience cause most motorists to avoid inner-city `naked streets' as these are seen to be the realm of pedestrians. Many experiments in different cities with `car-reduced' solutions (e.g. Copenhagen has implemented a series of changes in street profiles, gradually reducing the amount of inner-city car parking) show that it is helpful to make the paving for pedestrians the same as for vehicles. It sends a message to the car driver that this space is shared with pedestrians and cyclists. The European experience shows that drivers unconsciously slow down, and do not seem to mind doing so because of the higher quality of their surroundings. The City of Sydney, for instance, has now started to look at how these positive experiences can be transferred to its main arteries through the central business district, and plans have emerged to turn important streets (such as George Street) into pedestrian-friendly zones. It is no coincidence that Jan Gehl from Copenhagen has been an advisor on these plans.
A huge amount of energy goes into transporting goods. For instance, it is estimated that freight transport and logistical activities are responsible for around 11 per cent of all CO_2 emissions in Europe. Only a decisive shift towards the use of local or regional products will help to make a real difference, meaning there needs to be changes in consumer behaviour.

More and more cities want to get away from fossil-fuel dependence and the pollution associated with combustion technology. Adopting renewables will profoundly reduce the environmental impact of urban energy systems, while providing many new local jobs.

Creating truly sustainable, post-fossil fuel cities is perhaps the greatest task of the coming decades. It is also a particular challenge for the architectural and engineering professions that design and built those cities.
Herbert Girardet, 2008

It is now globally understood that public transport must be made more attractive and be complemented by high-frequency light railway and rapid transit bus-ways by for instance, offering a seamless system through integrated fares and ticketing between train, light railway and buses, improving interchanges, displaying real-time passenger information at bus stops, with large-scale expansion of park-and-ride facilities at stations, and offering better facilities for people using bicycles (new bike stations), combined with modern bus stop designs. Dedicated cycle ways are now being introduced everywhere, from China to the US. The City of Sydney has set the goal that in 7 years cycling will make up at least 10 per cent of all transport trips in the city. This is a comparably modest goal; already, today, in Amsterdam and Copenhagen, cycling makes up over 40 per cent of all trips. (See: Fig. 4)

The aim is to have high mobility, but without car traffic.

Upgrading public transport

Good traffic planning is essential for the *Sustainable City of the Future*, and there are plenty of innovative ideas and traffic concepts to reduce our car dependency. Some have become standard in European cities; however, they have not yet been fully embraced by North American or Australian traffic planners. In fact, inflexible traffic planners seem to frequently be the weak link in multi-disciplinary planning teams, hanging on to old ideas and conventions. Just to mention a few of the concepts that could be applied:

• improved computer-regulated coordination of timing between various red lights to avoid unnecessary halts in traffic flow; and improvement of integrated public transport, where rail/bus/tram/subway/ferry timetable schedules are all coordinated with each other.

• step-by-step reduction of inner-city car parking spaces through improvement in parking facilities at the fringe of the historical centre and interchanges, combined with park-and-ride concepts for rail/light railway stations.

• integrated cycle paths that are sufficiently safe and wide (e.g. Melbourne has increased the width of many cycle paths from 1.5 to 2.5 metres), offering bike stations to park and repair bikes (as is common in Netherlands or Japan).

• upgrading of the bus system, because it's the most flexible and affordable way to deliver good public transport (e.g. in Curitiba, Brazil, the modern express buses running in the bus rapid transit system can seat 275 people, transporting over 2.2 million passengers per day) and

• changing attitudes that 'pedestrians are more important than vehicles'. (Curdes, 1992)

Fig. 4: Supporting bike traffic: Cycle-friendly urban planning with bike stations, to promote other means of travel beside cars. (Photo: bike station in Amsterdam, 2008)

The neighbourhood district as a scale of intervention

Since ancient times, *neighbourhoods* have been the basic unit of human settlement (e.g. one neighbourhood forms a village). The neighbourhood district is a settlement unit that has a defined centre and edges, is walkable and mixed-use, and is diverse in terms of building types and people. Most residents will walk a distance of 400 metres (1200 feet), before opting to cycle or drive. A neighbourhood is bounded by major streets and has a population large enough to support a walk-to elementary school. In comparison, the low density of sub-urban sprawl makes it impossible to walk to any destination. All this makes it clear that our design focus should be on the neighbourhood and district scale. Projects are to be located on infill or redevelopment (brownfield) sites, adjacent to existing developed areas and trans-port nodes (avoiding further greenfield sites or masterplanned developments in non-urban areas). *The Principles of Green Urbanism* were developed to further flesh-out these ideas.

The 15 guiding *Principles of Green Urbanism*, for local action and a more integrated approach to urban development

The following is a list of the principles. It must be noted, though, that in order to enable sustainable urban development and to ensure that eco-districts are successful on many levels, all components need to work interactively and cannot be looked at separately. The principles are based on the triple-zero framework (triple-bottom line):

- zero fossil-fuel energy use
- zero waste
- zero emissions (aiming for low-to-no-carbon emissions).

'Zero waste' means that buildings are fully demountable and fully recyclable at the end of their life-cycle, so that the site can return to being a greenfield site after use. Understandably, it requires a holistic approach to put the principles in action and to guide the available know-how to the advantage of the city. The following 15 principles describe the strategies necessary for eco-districts, although they need to be adapted to the location, context and scale of the urban development. It may be difficult at first to achieve some of the principles, but all are impor-tant; they can potentially save money, reach early payback, and improve opportunities for social interaction of residents. The principles offer practical steps on the path to sustainable cities, harmonizing growth and usage of resources. The truly 'carbon-neutral' city has not yet been built, but all projects introduced in this book are important steps towards turning this vision into a reality.

The following principles are practical and holistic, offering and integrated framework, en-compassing all the key aspects needed to establish sustainable development and encour-aging best practice models. The replicability of models is very important. The principles form a sustainability matrix, which will empower the urban designer – to use Richard Buckminster Fuller's words – 'to be able to employ these principles to do more with less.' Much of *Green Urbanism* is common sense urbanism. In the future, *Green Urbanism* has to become the norm for all urban developments.

The sustainability matrix – the *15 Principles of Green Urbanism* – consists of:

PRINCIPLE 1   CLIMATE AND CONTEXT

The city based on its climatic conditions, with appropriate responses to location and site context. What are the unique site constraints, climatic conditions and opportunities?

Every site or place has its own unique individual conditions in regard to orientation, solar radiation, rain, humidity, prevailing wind direction, topography, shading, lighting, noise, air-pollution and so on. The various aspects of this principle include: Climatic conditions, which are seen as the fundamental influence for form-generation in the design of any project; understanding the site and its context, which is essential at the beginning of every sustainable design project; optimizing orientation and compactness to help reduce the city district's heat gain or losses; achieving a city with minimized environmental footprint by working with the existing landscape, topography and resources particular to the site, and the existing micro-climate of the immediate surroundings. Maintaining complexity in the system is always desirable (be it biodiversity, eco-system or neighbourhood layout), and a high degree of complexity is always beneficial for society. Enhancing the opportunities offered by topography and natural setting leads to a city well adapted to the local climate and its eco-system. We can use the buildings' envelope to filter temperature, humidity, light, wind and noise. Due to the different characteristics of every location, each city district has to come up with its own methods and tailored strategies to reach sustainability and to capture the spirit of the place. Each site or city is different and the drivers for re-engineering existing districts will need to understand how to take full advantage of each location's potential, and how to fine-tune the design concept to take advantage of local circumstances. As an aim, all urban development must be in harmony with the specific characteristics, various site factors and advantages of each location and be appropriate to its societal setting and contexts (cultural, historical, social, geographical, economical, environmental and political). In future, all buildings will have climate-adapted envelope technologies, with facades that are fully climate-responsive.

PRINCIPLE 2   RENEWABLE ENERGY FOR ZERO CO_2 EMISSIONS

The city as a self-sufficient on-site energy producer, using decentralized district energy systems. How can energy be generated and supplied emission-free and in the most effective way?

The various aspects of this principle include: Energy supply systems and services, as well as energy efficient use and operation, promoting increased use of renewable power, and perhaps natural gas as a transition fuel in the energy mix, but always moving quickly away from heavy fossil-fuels such as coal and oil; and the transformation of the city district from an energy consumer to an energy producer, with local solutions for renewables and the increasing de-carbonizing of the energy supply. The supply of oil will last shorter than the life-expectancy of most buildings. The local availability of a renewable source of energy is the first selection criteria for deciding on energy generation. In general, a well-balanced combination of energy sources can sensibly secure future supply. A necessary aim is also to have a distributed energy supply through a decentralized system, utilizing local renewable energy sources. This will transform city districts into local powerstations of renewable energy sources, which will include solar PV, solar thermal, wind (on- and off-shore), biomass, geothermal power, mini-hydro energy and other new technologies. Some of the most promising technologies are in building-integrated PV, urban wind turbines, micro CHP and solar cooling. That is to say, there should be on-site electrical generation and energy storage in combination with a smart grid, which integrates local solar and wind generation, utilizing energy-efficiency in all its forms. Solar hot water systems would be compulsory. Co-generation technology utilizes waste heat through CHP combined-heat-and-power plants. Energy-efficiency programmes are not enough. Too often we find that savings from energy-efficiency programmes are absorbed by a rise in energy use. Genuine action on climate change means that coal-fired powerstations cease to operate and are replaced by renewable energy sources. Eco-districts will need to operate on renewable energy sources as close to 100 per cent as possible. As a minimum, at least 50 per cent of on-site renewable energy generation should be the aim of all urban planning, where the energy mix comes from decentralized energy generation and takes into account the resources that are locally available, as well as the cost and the availability of the technology. Optimizing the energy balance can be achieved by using exchange, storage and cascading (exergy) principles. It is, therefore, essential that the fossil-fuel powered energy and transportation systems currently supporting our cities are rapidly turned into systems that are supplied by renewable energy sources. High building insulation, high energy-efficiency standards and the use of smart metering technology is essential, so that if a part of an office building is not in use, the intelligent building management system will shut down lights and ventilation. At home, we can take a series of actions, such as unplugging the television and other electric appliances when on holiday, or producing our own electricity by harnessing renewable energy sources, in order to get off the grid and become self-sufficient.

PRINCIPLE 3   ZERO-WASTE CITY
The zero-waste city as a circular, closed-loop eco-system.
How to avoid the creation of waste in the first place – changing behaviour of consumption?

Sustainable waste management means to turn waste into a resource. All cities should adopt nature's zero-waste management system. Zero-waste urban planning includes reducing, recycling, reusing and composting waste to produce energy. All material flows need to be examined and fully understood, and special attention needs to be given to industrial waste and e-waste treatment. We need to plan for recycling centres, for zero landfill and 'eliminating the concept of waste' and better understanding nutrient flows (Braungart, 2002). Eco-districts are neighbourhoods where we reuse and recycle materials and significantly reduce the volume of solid waste and toxic chemical releases. All construction materials as well as the production of goods (and building components) need to be healthy and fully-recyclable. Waste prevention is always better than the treatment or cleaning-up after waste is formed. Some other systems that need to be put in place are: the remanufacturing of metals, glass, plastics, paper into new products needs to be a routine (without down-grading the product); waste-to-energy strategies are needed for residual waste; and an 'extended producer responsibility' clause is needed for all products. In this context of waste, better management of the nitrogen cycle has emerged as an important topic: to restore the balance to the nitrogen cycle by developing improved fertilization technologies, and technologies in capturing and recycling waste. Controlling the impact of agriculture on the global cycle of nitrogen is a growing challenge for sustainable development. Essentially, we need to become (again) a 'recycling society', where it is common that around 60 to 90 per cent of all waste is recycled and composted.

PRINCIPLE 4   WATER

The city with closed urban water management and a high water quality.
What is the situation in regard to the sustainable supply of potable drinking water?

The various aspects of this principle include, in general, reducing water consumption, finding more efficient uses for water resources, ensuring good water quality and the protection of aquatic habitats. The city can be used as a water catchment area by educating the population in water efficiency, promoting rainwater collection and using wastewater recycling and stormwater harvesting techniques (e.g. solar-powered desalination plants). Stormwater and flood management concepts need to be adopted as part of the urban design, and this includes stormwater run-offs and improved drainage systems and the treatment of wastewater. As part of the eco-district's adequate and affordable health care provisions, it needs to ensure the supply of safe water and sanitation. This includes such things as algae and bio-filtration systems for greywater and improving the quality of our rivers and lakes so that they are fishable and swimmable again. An integrated urban water cycle planning and management system that includes a high-performance infrastructure for sewage recycling (grey and black water recycling), stormwater retention and harvesting the substantial run-off through storage, must be a routine in all design projects. On a household level we need to collect rain water and use it sparingly for washing and install dual-water systems and low-flush toilets. On a food production level we need to investigate the development of crops that need less water and are more drought resistant.

PRINCIPLE 5   LANDSCAPE, GARDENS AND BIODIVERSITY

The city that integrates landscapes, urban gardens and green roofs to maximize biodiversity.
Which strategies can be applied to protect and maximize biodiversity and to re-introduce landscape and garden ideas back in the city, to ensure urban cooling?

A sustainable city takes pride in its many beautiful parks and public gardens. This pride is best formed through a strong focus on local biodiversity, habitat and ecology, wildlife rehabilitation, forest conservation and the protecting of regional characteristics. Ready access to these public parks, gardens and public spaces, with opportunities for leisure and recreation, are essential components of a healthy city. As is arresting the loss of biodiversity by enhancing the natural environment and landscape, and planning the city using ecological principles based on natural cycles (not on energy-intensive technology) as a guide, and increasing urban vegetation. A city that preserves and maximizes its open spaces, natural landscapes and recreational opportunities is a more healthy and resilient city. The sustainable city also needs to introduce inner-city gardens, urban farming/agriculture and green roofs in all its urban design projects (using the city for food supply). It needs to maximize the resilience of the eco-system through urban landscapes that mitigate the 'urban heat island' (UHI) effect, using plants for air-purification and urban cooling. Further, the narrowing of roads, which calms traffic and lowers the UHI effect, allows for more (all-important) tree planting. Preserving green space, gardens and farmland, maintaining a green belt around the city, and planting trees everywhere (including golf courses), as trees absorb CO_2, is an important mission. As is conserving natural resources, respecting natural energy streams and restoring stream and river banks, maximizing species diversity. At home, we need to de-pave the driveway or tear up parking lots. In all urban planning, we need to maintain and protect the existing eco-system that stores carbon (e.g. through a grove or a park), and plan for the creation of new carbon storage sites by increasing the amount of tree planting in all projects. The increase in the percentage of green space as a share of total city land is to be performed in combination with densification activities.

PRINCIPLE 6   SUSTAINABLE TRANSPORT AND GOOD PUBLIC SPACE: COMPACT AND POLY-CENTRIC CITIES

The city of eco-mobility, with a good public space network and an efficient low-impact public transport system for post-fossil-fuel mobility.
How can we get people out of their cars, to walk, cycle, and use public transport?

Good access to basic transport services is crucial, as it helps to reduce automobile dependency, as does reducing the need to travel. We need to see integrated non-motorized transport, such as cycling or walking, and, consequently, bicycle/pedestrian-friendly environments, with safe bicycle ways, free rental bike schemes and pleasant public spaces. It is important to identify the optimal transport mix that offers inter-connections for public transport and the integration of private and public transport systems. Some ideas here include: eco-mobility concepts and smart infrastructure (electric vehicles); integrated transport systems (bus transit, light railway, bike stations); improved public space networks and connectivity, and a focus on transport-oriented development ('green TODs'). It is a fact that more and wider roads result in more car and truck traffic, and CO_2 emissions, and also allows for sprawling development and suburbs that increases electricity-demand and provides less green space. The transport sector is responsible for causing significant greenhouse-gas emissions (over 20 per cent). To combat this effect we need to change our lifestyles by, for example, taking public transport, driving the car less, or car-pooling. Alternatively, we can ride a bike or walk, if the city district has been designed for it. Personal arrangements have the potential to reduce commuting and to boost community spirit. We want a city district which is well-connected for pedestrians, a city with streetscapes that encourage a healthy, active lifestyle and where residents travel less and less by car. `Green TODs' are the future, as these developments can create a range of medium-density housing typologies and provide a variety of transportation choices, achieving a balance of residences and employment.

PRINCIPLE 7   LOCAL AND SUSTAINABLE MATERIALS WITH LESS EMBODIED ENERGY

City construction using regional, local materials with less embodied energy and applying pre-fabricated modular systems.
What kind of materials are locally available and appear in regional, vernacular architecture?

The various aspects of this principle include: advanced materials technologies, using opportunities for shorter supply chains, where all urban designs focus on local materials and technological know-how, such as regional timber in common use. Affordable housing can be achieved through modular prefabrication. Prefabrication has come and gone several times in modern architecture, but this time, with closer collaboration with manufacturers of construction systems and building components in the design phase, the focus will be on sustainability. We need to support innovation and be aware of sustainable production and consumption, the embodied energy of materials and the flow of energy in closing life-cycles. We need to emphasize green manufacturing and an economy of means, such as process-integrated technologies that lead to waste reduction. It is more environmentally friendly to use lightweight structures, enclosures and local materials with less embodied energy, requiring minimal transport. We need improved material and system specifications, supported by research in new materials and technological innovation; reduced material diversity in multi-component products to help facilitate the design for disassembly, value retention, and the possibility of reusing entire building components. Success in this area will increase the long-term durability of buildings, reduce waste and minimize packaging.

PRINCIPLE 8   DENSITY AND RETROFITTING OF EXISTING DISTRICTS

The city with retrofitted districts, urban infill, and densification/intensification strategies for existing neighbourhoods.
What are the opportunities to motivate people to move back to the city, closer to workplaces in the city centre?

The various aspects of this principle include: encouraging the densification of the city centre through mixed-use urban infill, centre regeneration and green TODs; increasing sustainability through density and compactness (compact building design means developing buildings vertically rather than horizontally); promoting business opportunities around green transit-oriented developments; optimizing the relationship between urban planning and transport systems; retrofitting inefficient building stock and systematically reducing the city district's carbon footprint. Consideration will need to be given to better land-use planning to reduce the impact of urban areas on agricultural land and landscape; to increasing urban resilience by transforming city districts into more compact communities and designing flexible typologies for inner-city living and working. Special strategies for large metropolitan areas and fast-growing cities are required. Here, examples of rapid development are being provided by Asian cities. Special strategies are also needed for small and medium-sized towns due to their particular milieu, and creative concepts are needed for the particular vulnerabilities of Small Island States and coastal cities. Public space upgrading through urban renewal programmes will bring people back to the city centre. This will need some strategic thinking about how to use brownfield and greyfield developments and also the adaptive reuse of existing buildings. Remodelling and re-energizing existing city centres to bring about diverse and vibrant communities requires people to move back into downtown areas. This can be achieved through mixed-use urban infill projects, building the 'city above the city' by converting low density districts into higher density communities; and by revitalizing underutilized land for community benefit and affordable housing. In the compact city, every neighbourhood is sustainable and self-sufficient; and uses ESCo principles for self-financing energy efficiency and in all retrofitting programmes.

PRINCIPLE 9   GREEN BUILDINGS AND DISTRICTS, USING PASSIVE DESIGN PRINCIPLES

The city that applies deep green building design strategies and offers solar access for all new buildings.
How can we best apply sustainable design and passive design principles in all their forms and for all buildings?

The various aspects of this principle include: low-energy, zero-emission designs, applying best practice for passive design principles, for all buildings and groups of buildings; dramatically reducing building energy use; introducing compact solar architecture; and renovating and retrofitting the entire building stock. New design typologies need to be developed at low cost, and we need to produce functionally neutral buildings that last longer. We need to apply facade technology with responsive building skins for bio-climatic architecture, to take advantage of cooling breezes and natural cross-ventilation, maximizing cross-ventilation, day-lighting and opportunities for night-flush cooling; we need to focus on the low consumption of resources and materials, including the reuse of building elements; and design for disassembly. Other ideas include: mixed-use concepts for compact housing typologies; adaptive reuse projects that rejuvenate mature estates; solar architecture that optimizes solar gain in winter and sun shading technology for summer, catching the low winter sun and avoiding too much heat gain in summer. It is important to renew the city with energy-efficient green architecture, creating more flexible buildings of long-term value and longevity. Flexibility in plan leads to a longer life for buildings. Technical systems and services have a shorter life-cycle. This means, first of all, applying technical aids sparingly and making the most of all passive means provided by the building fabric and natural conditions. Buildings that generate more energy than they consume, and collect and purify their own water, are totally achievable. We need to acknowledge that the city as a whole is more important than any individual building.

PRINCIPLE 10   LIVABILITY, HEALTHY COMMUNITIES AND MIXED-USE PROGRAMMES

The city with a special concern for affordable housing, mixed-use programmes, and a healthy community.
How does urban design recognize the particular need for affordable housing, to ensure a vibrant mix of society and multi-functional mixed-use programmes?

Land use development patterns are key to sustainability. A mixed-use (and mixed-income) city delivers more social sustainability and social inclusion, and helps to repopulate the city centre. Demographic changes, such as age, are a major issue for urban design. It is advantageous for any project to maximize the diversity of its users. Different sectors in the city can take on different roles over a 24 hours cycle; for example, the CBD is used for more than just office work. In general we want connected, compact communities, for a liveable city, applying mixed-use concepts and strategies for housing affordability, and offering different typologies for different housing needs. To this end we need affordable and liveable housing together with new flexible typologies for inner-city living. These mixed-use neighbourhoods (of housing types, prices and ownership forms) have to avoid gentrification and provide affordable housing with districts inclusive for the poor and the rich, young and old, and workers of all walks of life, and also provide secure tenure (ensuring 'aging in place'). Housing typologies need to deal with demographic changes. We have to understand migration and diversity as both an opportunity and a challenge. Mixed land uses are particularly important as it helps reduce traffic. Masterplans should require all private developments to contain 40 to 50 per cent of public (social) housing, and have it integrated with private housing. Higher densities should centre on green TODs. Essentially, these changes will aim to introduce more sustainable lifestyle choices, with jobs, retail, housing and a city campus being close by with IT and tele-working from home significantly helping to reduce the amount of travel (motto: `Don't commute to compute'). By integrating a diverse range of economic and cultural activities, we avoid mono-functional projects, which generate a higher demand for mobility. Green businesses would be supported through the use of ethical investments to generate funding. The question is: how specific or adaptable should buildings be to their use?

PRINCIPLE 11   LOCAL FOOD AND SHORT SUPPLY CHAINS

The city for local food supply, with high food security and urban agriculture.
Which strategies can be applied to grow food locally in gardens, on roof tops and on small spaces in the city?

The various aspects of this principle include: local food production; regional supply; an emphasis on urban farming and agriculture, including `eat local' and `slow food' initiatives. The sustainable city makes provision for adequate land for food production in the city, a return to the community and to the allotment gardens of past days, where roof gardens become an urban market garden. It is essential that we bridge the urban-rural disconnect and move cities towards models that deal in natural eco-systems and healthy food systems. The people of the eco-city would garden and farm locally, sharing food, creating compost with kitchen scraps and garden clippings and growing `community' vegetables. Buying and consuming locally will be necessary to cut down on petrol-based transport. Such things as re-using paper bags and glass containers, paper recycling and the cost of food processing will need reconsideration. We will need to reduce our consumption of meat and other animal products, especially shipped-in beef, as the meat cycle is very intensive in terms of energy and water consumption and herds create methane and demand great quantities of electricity. Perhaps as much as 50 per cent of our food will need to be organically produced, without the use of fertilizers or pesticides made from oil, and grown in local allotments.

PRINCIPLE 12   CULTURAL HERITAGE, IDENTITY AND SENSE OF PLACE
The city of public health and cultural identity: a safe and healthy city, which is secure and just. How to maintain and enhance a city's or region's identity, unique character and valued urban heritage, avoiding interchangeable design that makes all cities look the same?

All sustainable cities aim for air quality, health and pollution reduction, to foster resilient communities, to have strong public space networks and modern community facilities. This is the nature of sustainable cities. However, each city has its own distinct environment, whether it be by the sea, a river, in a dessert, a mountain; whether its climate is tropical, arid, temperate, etc, each situation is unique. The design of the city will take all these factors into consideration, including materials, history and population desires. The essence of place is the up-swelling of grassroots strategies, the protection of its built heritage and the maintenance of a distinct cultural identity, e.g. by promoting locally owned businesses, supporting creativity and cultural development. New ideas require affordable and flexible studio space in historic buildings and warehouses. Cities will grow according to the details and unique qualities of localities, demographic qualities of the populace and the creativity of the authorities and citizens. The aim of a city is to support the health, the activities and the safety of its residents. It is, therefore, incumbent on city councils to protect the city by developing a masterplan that balances heritage with conservation and development; fostering distinctive places with a strong sense of place, where densities are high enough to support basic public transit and walk-to retail services.

PRINCIPLE 13   URBAN GOVERNANCE, LEADERSHIP AND BEST PRACTICE
The city applying best practice for urban governance and sustainable procurement methods. Which networks and skills can be activated and utilized through engaging the local community and key stakeholders, to ensure sustainable outcomes?

Good urban governance is extremely important if we want to transform existing cities into sustainable compact communities. It has to provide efficient public transport, good public space and affordable housing, high standards of urban management, and without political support change will not happen. City councils need strong management and political support for their urban visions to be realized. They need strong support for a strategic direction in order to manage sustainability through coherent combined management and governance approaches, which include evolutionary and adaptive policies linked to a balanced process of review, and to public authorities overcoming their own unsustainable consumption practices and changing their methods of urban decision-making. A city that leads and designs holistically, that implements change harmoniously, and where decision-making and responsibility is shared with the empowered citizenry, is a city that is on the road to sustainable practices. In balancing community needs with development, public consultation exercises and grassroots participation are essential to ensuring people-sensitive urban design and to encouraging community participation. Citizens need to participate in community actions aimed at governments and big corporations, by writing letters and attending city-council hearings. Empowering and enabling people to be actively involved in shaping their community and urban environment is one of the hallmarks of a democracy. Cities are a collective responsibility. As far as bureaucratic urban governance and best practice is concerned, authorities could consider many of the following: updating building code and regulations; creating a database of best practice and worldwide policies for eco-cities; revising contracts for construction projects and integrated public management; raising public awareness; improving planning participation and policy-making; creating sustainable subdivisions, implementing anti-sprawl land-use and growth boundary policies; legislating for controls in density and supporting high-quality densification; arriving at a political decision to adopt the *Principles of Green Urbanism*, based on an integrated *Action Plan*; measures to finance a low-to-no-carbon pathway; implementing environmental emergency management; introducing a programme of incentives, subsidies and tax exemptions for sustainable projects that foster green jobs; eliminating fossil-fuel subsidies; developing mechanisms for incentives to accelerate renewable energy take-up; implementing integrated land-use planning; having a sustainability assessment and certification of urban development projects. Urban design requires multi-disciplinary approaches, where design and engineering are fully integrated with all other disciplines throughout all phases of each project. This concept must be supported. And new policy frameworks should be created, which accelerate behavioural change, waste reduction and the uptake of renewable energy; which increase cultural diversity and economic opportunity; and activate community purchasing power for green energy and sustainable products, while applying methods of 'environmental budgeting'.

PRINCIPLE 14   EDUCATION, RESEARCH AND KNOWLEDGE
The city with education and training for all in sustainable urban development.
How to best raise awareness and change behaviour?

The various aspects of this principle include: technical training and up-skilling, research, exchange of experiences, knowledge dissemination through research publications about ecological city theory and sustainable design. Primary and secondary teaching programmes need to be developed for students in such subjects as waste recycling, water efficiency and sustainable behaviour. Changes in attitude and personal lifestyles will be necessary. The city is a hub of institutions, such as galleries and libraries and museums, where knowledge can be shared. We must provide sufficient access to educational opportunities and training for the citizenry, thus increasing their chances of finding green jobs. Universities can act as 'think tanks' for the transformation of their cities. We also need to redefine the education of architects, urban designers, planners and landscape architects. Research centres for sustainable urban development policies and best practice in eco-city planning could be founded, where assessment tools to measure environmental performance are developed and local building capacity is studied.

PRINCIPLE 15   STRATEGIES FOR CITIES IN DEVELOPING COUNTRIES

Particular sustainability strategies for cities in developing countries, harmonizing the impacts of rapid urbanization and globalization.

What are the specific strategies and measurements we need to apply for basic low-cost solutions appropriate to cities in the developing world?

Developing and emerging countries have their own needs and require particular strategies, appropriate technology transfers and funding mechanisms. Cities in the developing world cannot have the same strategies and debates as cities in the developed world. Similarly, particular strategies for emerging economies and fast-growing cities are required, as is the problem of informal settlements and urban slums and slum upgrading programmes. Low-cost building and mass housing typologies for rapid urbanization are required in cooperation with poverty reduction programmes. It is essential that we train local people to empower communities, creating new jobs and diversifying job structures, so as not to focus on only one segment of the economy (e.g. tourism). Achieving more sustainable growth for Asian metropolitan cities is a necessity. Combating climate change, which was mainly caused through the emissions by industrialized nations and which is having its worst effect in poorer countries in Africa, Asia and Latin America, with a focus on Small Island States, is a priority.

It is important to note, that a couple of innovative engineering solutions will not deliver a vibrant city. All the technology in the world cannot achieve sustainability and vitality by itself.

The problem of urban design is far more complex.

Designing a city requires holistic approaches, and each time the adaptation of strategies to a unique context: the integration and combination of qualitative and quantitative knowledge.

Our quest to be carbon-neutral: embedding the 15 principles in each development

As urban designers, we cannot afford to undertake projects the way we used to do in the past; 'business as usual' is simply not good enough anymore. While environmental programmes for cities are increasingly driven by masterplanning and design, they are centred on three key elements:

- reducing demand
- increasing the security and efficiency of supply and
- utilizing renewable energy sources.

Cities that have implemented these principles are leading the way

All cities are in a global competition for investment and a highly-skilled workforce. In connection with economic development and population growth, some cities have managed to improve their competitiveness and to progress in terms of human and social development. These cities attract even more investment and well-educated young people from all over the world who want to live and work at these desirable places. Certain cities have positioned themselves as places of environmental leadership, efficient public transport, high quality of education and health services, and places of long life expectancy and good lifestyles (for instance, Zurich, Stockholm, Munich, Oslo, Copenhagen, Barcelona, Vancouver and Singapore are seen as such high achievers). Other indicators, such as affordable housing, opportunities for recreation and leisure, social communities, or political stability, are also increasingly taken into account.

An open, free 'City Database' would be helpful here, where we collect and disseminate examples of best urban design practice and policies from around the world. There are various rankings for international benchmarking available, that list cities based on different indicators. The *Global Competitiveness Index* (GCI) is published annually by the World Economic Forum; and the *Human Development Index* (HDI) rankings are published annually in the UN's Human Development Report, with a particular focus on human well-being beyond economic growth. The HDI rankings provide a composite measure of three criteria of human development: living a long and healthy life, being well educated and enjoying a decent standard of living.

Ranking the quality of living in cities based on their environmental performance

Weak leadership by governments requires strong local governments and municipalities. In fact, many cities are turning sustainability agendas into reality, while their nation in general lags behind. For instance, two initiatives of such newly founded innovative organizations are the cities that have joined together in the Metropolis and the C40 initiatives (see: www.metropolis.org and www.c40cities.org). Metropolis brings together over 100 cities worldwide, and C40 includes forty of the world's largest cities. They collaborate in exchanging information regarding their sustainability agenda, committing them to real CO_2 reduction targets. These municipalities are leading by example. They are willing to reserve a portion of their spending for cutting-edge pilot projects to advance their envi-

ronmental sustainability. A recent study, commissioned by Metropolis and carried out by CISCO, asked the leadership of their member cities to define sustainability and its challenges. The three main challenges identified were:
- encouraging a 'greener' city environment (public transit, recycling)
- making more efficient use of resources (water, land) and
- promoting a more liveable city (urban renewal, anti-sprawl programmes).
  (Metropolis/CISCO, 2009)

Asked about key priorities, the following three issues were named:
- reducing consumption of electricity, overall and in city-owned buildings and facilities
- making their own fleets a carbon-friendly transport fleet
- better governance of urban sustainability initiatives.

Local cities solving global problems

Local governments and city councils are actively driving the push for more sustainable cities and rapid change, marshalling resources to address the problem, orchestrating the input of the private sector and community groups, responding boldly and leading by example in urban innovation initiatives; even in the face of obvious funding challenges. Clearly environmental sustainability is a top priority for cities, acting in partnership with industry, business and community-based organizations.

In this context, one of the most relevant annual surveys is the 'Mercer Quality of Living: Top 50 Cities' ranking, which measures the liveability of cities for its people and expatriates, based on factors such as the quality of the natural environment. It's a comprehensive study that gives a detailed assessment and evaluation of 39 key qualities of living determinants, grouped in the following categories (see: www.mercer.com):
- political and social environment (political stability, crime rate, law enforcement, etc.)
- economic environment (currency exchange regulations, banking services, etc.)
- socio-cultural environment (censorship, limitations on personal freedom, areas for recreation, etc.)
- health and sanitation (medical supplies, and services, sewage, waste disposal, air pollution, etc.)
- natural environment (climate, record of natural disasters, access to forests, lakes, etc.)
- schools and education (standard and availability of international schools, etc.)
- public services and transportation (electricity, quality of water, public transport, traffic congestion, etc.)
- housing (housing quality and affordability, household appliances, maintenance services, etc.), and
- consumer goods (availability of food and daily consumption items, etc.)

The highest ranking cities in the *Mercer Ranking* were all cities that had shown leadership in urban development programmes to implement environmental sustainability and which have a particular concern for good urban governance and sustainability.

According to this ranking, the 20 highest ranking cities are:

1. Zurich, Switzerland
2. Vienna, Austria
3. Geneva, Switzerland
4. Vancouver, Canada
5. Auckland, New Zealand
6. Dusseldorf, Germany
7. Munich, Germany
7. Frankfurt, Germany
9. Bern, Switzerland
10. Sydney, Australia
11. Copenhagen, Denmark
12. Wellington, New Zealand
13. Amsterdam, The Netherlands
14. Brussels, Belgium
15. Toronto, Canada
16. Berlin, Germany
17. Melbourne, Australia
17. Luxembourg, Luxembourg
19. Ottawa, Canada
20. Stockholm, Sweden

These are all cities with a population smaller than 5 million. Obviously it is easier to implement innovative strategies for urban development and place-making in medium-sized cities than it is in very large mega-cities, where introducing any change can take a very long time.

City competitiveness

Cities are trying to improve their competitiveness and respond to new conditions imposed through globalization by implementing large urban projects. What else makes a city a top-ranking city, gaining advantage above others? Cities compete globally with each another, and liveability of cities has been a main differentiator in city rankings for some time. However, the new main differentiator today is sustainability and environmental quality of cities. All the cities listed have enjoyed strong leadership in environmental sustainability and, therefore, offer good case studies for identifying 'international best practice' in the management of urban growth and development. The highest ranked, most progressive cities are the ones that have been able to strategically address their urban issues and to successfully develop their own methods and practices of green urbanism, and who have, over the years, developed a unique approach to urban design.

In 2010, *Forbes* composed a list of 'the smartest cities in the world'. How is 'smart city' defined? Again, being 'smart' refers to having a green sustainability agenda, along with a wider list of other criteria, including: upward mobility, economic progress, good public transport and strong infrastructure. It is the cities' clean air and their commercial prowess that will sustain their success in the decades ahead. Number one in the ranking, Singapore, has reinvented itself as a sustainable global city, becoming an urban model for the entire Asia-Pacific region. The `five smartest cities in the world', each with solid sustainability policies, are, according to the *Forbes Ranking 2010*:

1. Singapore
2. Hong Kong, China
3. Curtiba, Brazil
4. Monterrey, Mexico
5. Amsterdam, The Netherlands.

These ranking are not only a question of environmental sustainability, but also of cultural density: why are certain cities more energetic and diverse, attracting creative people from all over the world? Berlin, Glasgow, Amsterdam and Barcelona have been at the forefront of art-led urban renewal in Europe, with inexpensive studio spaces, experimental and progressive art scenes, and strong grassroots, community and educational programmes including artist-in-residence programmes. These cities enjoy a large student and artist population. New, often ephemeral exhibition spaces and strategies were developed, using informal urbanism to occupy marginal public spaces, with former industrial sites being converted into new type of art spaces. In Sydney, `CarriageWorks' in Redfern is a good example of such an art space, reusing a former railway workshop building. Committed to new forms of interdisciplinary, non-commercial and site-specific artistic work, creative people have started to reuse neglected areas of the city, offering a multi-dimensional process – working (workshop) galleries – while revitalizing public urban space. These projects did not simply produce some creative works in public space, but in addition, developed and debated new forms of interventions and encounters with the public, putting these cities on the forefront as places of such initiatives. Also, Bilbao's radical transformation from declining post-industrial city to a vibrant, rejuvenated metropolis has been widely published and discussed; Bilbao achieved this through systematic urban improvement over a 25 year period, using public-private partnerships effectively.

We can observe significant success by smaller cities in competing with their nation's largest cities (not only in the developed world, but also in China and Brazil). Administration and services are no longer only provided in large cities; production decentralizes away from the larger cities, and smaller cities compete successfully for new investment. Obviously, it's essential for cities to balance development with community needs and the environment. High growth cities which have managed to get this balance right are prospering, as we can see in the cases of very high-ranking cities, such as Zurich, Vancouver, Singapore, Curitiba, Barcelona and Brisbane. (See: Fig. 5) Singapore's focus on increasing liveability has been particularly successful and is fuelled by its strong economic growth.

But how can sustainability best be measured and evaluated?
In order to facilitate the fast and widespread adoption of sustainable principles in urban design, clear benchmarks and agreed methods of evaluation for sustainable development are essential. However, evaluation and measuring of sustainability is still a challenge and

raises questions of definition. Brandon and Lombardi argue that 'the complexity of the problem makes a complete and internationally accepted measure still impossible.' (Brandon and Lombardi, 2005)

For instance, project evaluation needs to take into account:

• What is the project's impact on community?

• How do the locals feel about the project?

• What is the proces how the citizens get engaged?

Commonly available assessment tools, such as LEED, BREEAM, CASBEE, GreenStar, and other evaluation systems are unfortunately still very work- and cost-intensive. Today there are numerous – often conflicting – assessment methods available with different indicators for evaluating sustainable development being advocated. Brandon argues that 'regarding the question of assessing sustainable development in the built environment, it is fundamental to determine whether a community is sustainable in the longer term. However, since there is no common vocabluary or a shared set of values, it is still difficult to build knowledge and enable communication between the stakeholders.' (Brandon and Lombardi, 2005) It is probably impossible to cover every detail and develop a full system for the assessment of sustainable development, as the subject is by far too complex and there cannot be just one solution but many. The following text will further exemplify the complexity of such urban transformation.

Fig. 5: Vancouver's much celebrated mixed-use waterfront: The city council has been increasing densities for a decade, combined with the sensitive regeneration of the urban waterfront, including marshland restoration, high-quality landscaping and public space. The city's development framework included: 'The creation of a vibrant mixed-use waterfront district with quality public space linking the urban core to the waterfront, to develop an urban district with public open spaces that can support informal activities as well as scheduled public events, offering continuous bicycle paths along the water edges, access to the water and the experience of water, creating a physical connection to the water that is a central part of the city's and region's heritage.' (City of Vancouver)
Hamburg, Vancouver, Seattle, Boston, Barcelona, Oslo and many other port cities rediscovered their urban waterfronts and found that the new waterfront neighbourhoods can contribute to a city's overall healthy development. These areas, with their historic warehouses and harbour heritage, offer great potential for high quality urban regeneration. (Photo: courtesy M. Boster, Canada, 2008)

The City as Powerstation and Productive Urban Landscape

Technological innovation in the energy, water and transport sectors has been an important influence on the shape of the city of tomorrow. We can recognize this in the urban transformation of 19th-century Vienna and Berlin where Otto Wagner's new technological concepts (`Stadtbautechnik'), such as the innovation in transport through the `Stadtbahn' (1895) and in water treatment (`Schleusenbauwerke'), triggered a `New Vienna'. There are examples today where city districts go off-grid and become self-sufficient units. Producing energy and food, and collecting and cleaning water in the city districts themselves, means that only little transmission of electricity and transportation of food and water is necessary. Everything is done close to the point of consumption. This concept has many advantages and it gives the city district a new role to play:

- the city district as power station
- the city district as water catchment
- the city district as source of food supply.

In the following part, I describe some current innovations in energy and water infrastructure that are likely to have an impact on the re-design and transformation of city districts.

Transformation: The City as Powerstation and Productive Urban Landscape

Urban Consolidation and City Network

In *A City is not a Tree* (1965), Christopher Alexander argues that the hallmark of designed cities (for instance, like Chandigarh and Brasilia) is that their designers have invariably gravitated to tree-structures, where all sub-units of a similar type roll-up into a single super-unit (from the branches to the trunk), which he believes creates an artificial and ultimately damaging simplification. Alexander contrasts this with the structure of 'organic' cites (for instance, organically grown cities like London and New York), which are organized as semi-lattices, where overlaps and shared functions are the order of the day. Around the same time as Christopher Alexander wrote his critique on urban systems, Jane Jacobs added her voice and the German author Alexander Mitscherlich critiqued the failure of simplistic modern urbanism in his pivotal book *Die Unwirtlichkeit unserer Staedte. Thesen zur Stadt der Zukunft.* (Jacobs, 1961; Alexander, 1965; Mitscherlich, 1965)

Over the last few years, urban renewal strategies have become a major part of any city planning, and the focus of urban revitalization has moved to categories, such as:

- Brownfield and greyfield regeneration projects
- Historical district regeneration with adaptive reuse projects
- Mixed-use urban infill projects for urban consolidation
- City campus and art gallery developments (towards the `knowledge-based city')
- Urban waterfront and port city projects

• Green corridor and public transport infrastructure projects, including green TODs, and
• Eco-district transformation projects, including large-scale retrofitting programmes.

The challenge is not so much about `projects', but about the long-term urban vision, holistic strategic thinking, and changes to behaviour and long-held planning habits and attitudes.

Much research over recent years has identified the suburb as a problematic model that increases urban inefficiencies, whereas urban consolidation and compactness – if done in the right way – can deliver truly sustainable outcomes. For instance, a recent report by the NSW Government Health Commission notes that `urban sprawl was found to have the most devastating effect on health, and can lead to depression, because of the increased social isolation of residents living in suburbs.' (NSW Government Health Commission, Sydney, Feb. 2010) The findings in this report strongly support the position that we need to stop releasing land for new suburbs far way from the city centre and the reach of public transport systems.

In this context, ways to achieve the appropriate compactness and density are widely discussed by urban designers. The question of density and over-shadowing is not new to planning, however it is still of major significance. For instance, density creates a sense of urbanity and can allow office workers to commute on foot to work. In the USA, among the 50 most populous cities, where the largest percentage of commuters walk to work, are also those US cities with the highest urban densities (data: SustainLane, 2009):

Boston	13 per cent
San Francisco	10
Washington	10
New York	9
Philadelphia	8
Sydney, Australia	5

If we look at history, we can discover many great examples of sustainable urban design to learn from, such as the town of Shibam in Yemen, which was first mentioned in the 3rd century AD, as the capital of the Hadramawt Kingdom. The city uses a distinct compact structure to resolve shading issues in the hot and arid climate of Yemen. It has been declared a UNESCO World Heritage Site. The buildings of Shibam are all made out of mud brick, but about 500 of them are tower houses that rise 5 to 11-storeys, with each floor having one or two apartments on it. This high-rise structure was implemented in order to better protect residents from Bedouin attacks. Shibam is often called `the oldest skyscraper city in the world' and is one of the earliest examples of urban planning based on the principle of high-rise construction. The compact town has the tallest mud buildings in the world, some of them over 30 metres high. It is the model that influenced the design of Masdar City, the eco-city currently under construction in UAE. (See: Fig. 1)

The city is not a problem; it is a solution. Every city in the world can significantly be improved within 3 years, and this is not a question of scale or budget.   Jaime Lerner, Mayor of Curitiba, 2007

There are many examples which show that a 'Compact City' model makes public transport, district heating/district cooling systems and water distribution more viable and effective, and the application of decentralized power distribution systems using renewable energy easier. The idea of the 'urban eco-village' describes such compact, clustered, mixed-use neighbourhood modules. As we move to higher densities, planners need to ensure adequate infrastructural capacity.

Source: Image Sharing Commons

Fig. 1: The historical town Shibam in the desert of Yemen has up to 11-stories high mud brick buildings and a very compact lay-out, where the buildings shadow the narrow laneways and each other from the strong desert sun. (Image: Flickr Commons) Shibam is the model for Masdar-City, the zero-emission 'walled city' under construction in the UAE.

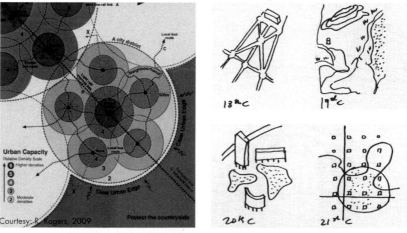

Fig. 2 a, b: Left: Radial clusters of walkable neighbourhoods. (Diagram: Richard Rogers, 2009) Right: Sketch by Bernard Tschumi, showing the development of urban planning over the centuries: 18th-century formal, symmetrical composition of the French park; 19th-century English landscape garden; 20th-century CIAM modernism with towers and slabs in the green parkland; 21st-century asymmetrical composition with activated grid lay-out and strong interconnectedness. (Tschumi, 1984)

Fig. 3: Arata Isozaki's utopian visions 'City in the Sky' and 'City in the Air', developed in 1960-63 (same time as Kisho Kurokawa and the Metabolists developed similar concepts), were ideas of high-rise clusters based on a joint core system (trunks) for plug-in urban housing units, which were prefabricated and arranged like the leaves of a tree. The clusters were systematically interconnected, high above the ground and above the existing city, as a solution for overcrowded Tokyo, while the activities in the existing city below could continue. (Image: courtesy Arata Isozaki & Associates)

Fig. 4: BedZED (Beddington Zero-Energy Development) is a development with around 90 units on a brownfield site in Sutton, Surrey (south of London). 1998-2002. Architects: Bill Dunster, with BioRegional Development Group (Pooran Desai). This is a near-to-zero fossil-fuel energy development, using a wood chip CHP plant. All units have their own small garden and the 3-storey walk-up townhouses are highly insulated, almost achieving the German 'Passivhaus' standard. It is vitally important that eco-districts dramatically reduce the need to travel by car and provide alternative mobility options. The BedZED eco-village includes public transport within less than 10 minutes walk, incentives for bicycle use, as well as reduced car parking and road space. Monitored data of the first eight years occupancy indicate that private car, fossil-fuel kilometres travelled has reduced by 60 per cent as compared to the local average. See also: www. bioregional.com (Photo: Bill Dunster, 2007) [6] In 2009, a zero-emission house was built in the UK by Sheppard Robson Architects, in Watford, called 'The Lighthouse': www.sheppardrobson.com

Not only office workplaces are relevant to ensure short distances between working and living; we also need to reconsider the loation of clean light industries. Reintroducing quiet light industries back into the city will help in getting workplaces closer to the districts where people live, thus cutting-out the need to commute.

What are the immediately available urban design approaches?

It is the operating costs of buildings, not the construction costs that have become increasingly problematic for the urban designer. A sensible trend to combat this problem is to shift away from buildings with intensive technical installations to low-tech passive solutions combined with high insulation and efficient but simple facade technology, including operable windows for natural ventilation (sometimes as mixed-mode systems).

So far, some of the most effective and available urban design approaches identified, include:
- minimizing the consumption of land through more compact development, and densification by containing the footprint
- using existing and renewable urban resources such as brownfield sites, integrating existing underused buildings, structures and sites
- designing urban quarters where walking and cycling is highly attractive, with good landscaping and a diverse mix of uses
- utilizing under-used sites within walking distance of public transport nodes, to reduce reliance on automobiles and to increase pedestrian activity
- developing urban areas where efficient infrastructure systems and public transport are already in place, to further reduce the need for automobiles, as transport-oriented development
- creating a sense of urbanity through increased density and the design of real places, where an urban culture can flourish
- developing sites in a way that the consumption of energy, non-renewable materials and pollution is generally reduced
- better considering the building's placement on the site, orientation and solar issues, with a focus on high quality public space and good landscaping
- designing developments in ways that increase access to affordable housing and transportation choices
- designing spaces with direct access to natural light and air, and an improved orientation to take advantage of passive solar principles, and
- optimizing the orientation and solar exposure to maximise the use of renewable resources in the operation of buildings and districts.

Renewable energy technologies are now mature and reliable, with components built to last for decades, and require minimal maintenance.

Designing with the climate (rather than against it)

It is crucial to get the relationship between building volume and facade surface (the degree of 'compactness') right. Of course, to a large degree, all urban strategies depend on the geographical location and their local climate. In a temperate climate there is a significant advantage in having long west and east facades, using the summer sun to create a cross-ventilation stack effect that draws air from one (cooler) side of the building through to the other (warmer) side. This effect could further be supported by a wind roof, such as a `Venturi spoiler', which uses the prevailing winds to create negative pressure on the facade. A concrete structure provides increased heat storage (thermal mass), while effective solar shading needs to be applied to protect the interior from too much light and heat gain in summer (in combination with the use of high-performance glass). If well designed, the facade allows opening-up in winter to harness the sun's energy for heating. (Daniels, 1998; Szokolay, 2004) On the other hand, in a hot and humid (tropical) climate there are clearly other priorities. Here, it is much more important to ensure the maximum cross-ventilation and to keep massive materials, such as concrete floors or masonry walls, fully shaded to avoid storage of unwanted heat in the building mass. (Koenigsberger, 1973; Drew and Fry, 1979; Szokolay, 2004) In both cases, from the standpoint of energy consumption and the avoidance of heat gain, it is generally seen as an advantage to have compact volumes with a reduced glass facade surface area.

This suggests well laid-out subdivisions, which are ones where living rooms and offices face the right way for passive solar heating and cooling, for the use of solar hot water heaters, for maximum natural day-lighting, and for taking advantage of the local prevailing wind direction to catch cooling breezes. When the building facades are made specific to their orientation, with the intentional placement of closed wall surfaces and small window openings, it will result in substantially lower energy consumption – as well as reducing the dependence on air-conditioning. For office buildings, this means moving away from the air-conditioned sealed building and deep plan layout, to buildings with openable windows and shallow plans (less than 16 metres width) for optimum day-lighting. Those office buildings take full advantage of natural day light for all regularly occupied spaces, which reduces energy consumption and excess heat from artificial lighting. There are demonstrable cost benefits in operating such buildings. (Lehmann, 2005)

The implementation of sustainable design measures frequently implies some additional construction costs, although it is well documented that life-cycle costs are generally reduced. Scientist Greg Kats has extensively researched the costs and benefits of green buildings, and has demonstrated conclusively that sustainable architecture and urban design is a cost-effective investment, with possible payback times of less than a decade. (Kats, 2003) Today, most measures we can take to reduce energy consumption have payback periods of less than ten years.

The `Global Greenhouse Gas Abatement Cost Curve' published by McKinsey & Company in 2007 shows that there is a wide range of measures that can be selected (including measures for urban design and buildings), whereby the majority of these measures are cost-negative and the long-term savings achieved over a 30 year lifecycle outweighs the higher up-front costs. (McKinsey & Company, 2007) With the comprehensive studies of Kats, Stern and McKinsey there is no longer any doubt that green urbanism makes also financial sense.[7]

It is now time for a shift in urban design, based on the principles of green urbanism as a sustainable system approach, to set new standards towards carbon-neutral urban development.

Towards CO2-neutral urban planning through the use of exergy principles

Energy is a major cause of climate change due to the release of CO2 in the combustion of fossil fuels. Some cutting-edge research is currently being carried out at the TU-Delft, where a group of urban planners, architects and energy experts are looking at the better use of waste streams on the neighbourhood and district level. For instance, making use of the waste heat that is normally rejected through cooling towers or is simply blown into the air; or underground railway stations that have a large amount of surplus heat. Their recent study observes that in built-up areas it is important to target the following measures:

1. Applying renewable energy sources: within the foreseeable future there will be no other sources available.

2. Making use of the available energy potential: this is an interpretation of the first measure at local level, but where renewable energy is imported from far away, it is better to make use of locally available opportunities.

3. Making optimal use of waste streams: all buildings and urban areas generate waste streams (waste energy, heat, water, materials, etc.) that could be better harnessed, but rarely are. (Van Den Dobbelsteen, Tillie, Doepel, et al, 2009)

The researchers continue: `In addition to the reduction of consumption and the development of sustainable sources, a waste stream reuse strategy needs to be implemented that makes optimal use of all waste streams – not only for each individual building, but on a city-wide scale, such as a cluster of buildings, where we can strategically combine different systems, energy can be exchanged between different functional programmes, stored or cascaded – based on the different patterns of energy requirements for these different building parts. Also, solar panels and solar collectors, or a heat pump with ground collector systems, can be installed in each individual building; it is even much more economical to set these up at district level.'

Optimizing energy balance: exchange, storage, cascading

From the Dutch study, it's easy to see that waste streams from one chain may be used in a different chain. For example, waste water can be purified and the silt fermented to form bio-gas, which can be reused in the energy chain. Bio-gas fermentation installations can recycle bio-gas from waste water and use combined heat-power systems to generate heat and electricity. Another example is the recycling of heat from ventilated air and waste shower water. There are more typical examples of heat exchange: due to internal heat production, modern offices start cooling as soon as outdoor temperatures exceed 12 degrees Celsius. At these temperatures, homes in the neighbourhood are still required to be heated. This provides the opportunity for heat exchange during spring and autumn. The same applies to the exchange between supermarkets (which require all year long cooling) with homes (frequently with heating requirements).

If a project can be tackled at district level, potential discrepancies in the energy balance at neighbourhood level (for example, excess demand for waste heat or cold) may be solved. At district level it is reasonable to assume that other functions are available, with a totally different demand and, therefore, a different supply pattern. This opens up the opportunity to exchange, to store and to cascade energy and water, especially at the larger amenities such as shopping centres, swimming pools and concert halls, where the energy pattern is so specific that by combining a number of these different amenities it is likely that an energy balance can be established.

The first step is, therefore, the re-engineering of the urban infrastructure. If we apply the new technologies on the district level, we can get maximum efficiencies and cost effectiveness from co-generation plants and distributed energy networks.

Technological innovations for a new energy-mix

In order to solve climate change problems we need to be innovative in activating technological developments in urban planning, establish smart grids and feed-in tariff systems. Most experts agree that we already have the technological knowledge to address the issue of climate change, for instance through zero-emission urban design in combination with new energy infrastructure; however, what seems to be missing is the leadership from government and business. It is still difficult for renewable energy to compete with the largely subsidized fossil-fuel technologies, such as coal, as long as the price of its generation does not include its true costs – the tremendous health costs and the huge damage to the environment caused by CO_2 emissions. However, with the right policies and incentives – such as 'feed-in tariffs' that give a priority to energy from renewable sources – the fast introduction and scale-up of solar and wind power could be accelerated dramatically. (Toepfer, 2005; Scheer, 2007). Jeb Brugmann points out: 'A canny combination of energy efficiency, combined heat and power, wind power, solar energy, fuel cell technology and new storage systems promise a clean and secure urban energy future. The know-how exists to bring urban energy use down by 50 per cent or more without significantly affecting living standards, while creating many new local jobs at the same time.' (Brugmann, 2009) As one of the founders of the *International Council for Local Environmental Initiatives* (ICLEI), Brugmann has been developing 'local action plans' and strategic agendas to implement policies for CO_2 reductions and increased social sustainability for over 600 local governments.

The famous physicist Ernst Ulrich von Weizaecker has recently commented optimistically on the future: 'Our cars, houses and appliances are still wasteful and outdated. But the coming society will be more efficient and more elegant than today's. We experience a paradigm shift toward more energy efficiency and the associated innovations and investments. I see us entering a new epoch of advanced civilization.' (Weizaecker, 2009)

It is a mix of a whole range of different initiatives that will deliver large CO_2 emission reductions; it's not one strategy alone. To de-carbonize the energy supply, we need to install small distributed systems powered by renewable energy sources, installed on the district-level. Efficient resource use in cities depends on the large-scale roll-out of such technologies and the construction of low-to-no-carbon demonstration projects (pilot projects). The following part of this chapter is about these new technological possibilities and their integration at a district-scale, and it clearly shows that one important part of the solution is in the appropriate energy mix. The global climate crisis cannot be solved by micro power plants or distributed solar cell installations alone, these will make an increasingly important contribution to de-carbonizing the energy supply by up to 50 per cent, but, unfortunately, it could be some time before we have entered the `new epoch of advanced civilization', where all city districts have been transformed into autonomous clean power stations. It is still some time away when we will be in a position to entirely stop using big fossil-fuel burning power plants, but it is up to us to accelerate the development towards that time.

Every project needs to start with an `Energy Masterplan' and a `Potential Carbon Sink Masterplan' first, where we identify which renewable energy sources can easily be harvested at the specific location and which carbon sinks need to be maintained and extended.
These layouts will then become the basis for all further urban planning that follows.

RENEWABLE ENERGY

Generating energy on the district scale: de-carbonizing the urban energy supply, developing energy-positive biospheres

Today, 1.6 billion people still live without electricity. Energy is seen as the key to an increased standard of living and it will take some time before renewable energy is available in the amounts needed to compete with fossil fuels. Coal, by contrast, is both cheap and widely available. This is why coal-fired, CO_2-polluting powerstations have been built everywhere. However, almost two-thirds of global greenhouse gas emissions come from the use of fossil-fuel based resources such as coal, oil and gas, and as much as 80 per cent of the world's energy use is still based on fossil-fuels (data: 2010). The price of energy generated from burning coal (the most inefficient and polluting way to produce energy) does not include the true costs. Power producing utilities have not yet been asked to calculate the real cost of this energy, that is the cost of environmental damage and health costs incurred by air pollution. (Ackermann, 1993; Daniels, 2005; Herzog, 2007)

In a sustainable world we must replace fossil-fuel based energy production with renewable energy sources that are inexhaustible, sustainable and do not cause polluting emissions. As long as there is sunshine, wind and water we will be able to harness solar energy, windpower and waterpower. Renewable energy is, therefore, the foundation of any zero-emission city and society. We also need to ensure that economic growth in developing countries is based on renewable energy. We can achieve this by developing new technologies and establishing incentives that make it more profitable for all countries, rich and poor alike, to invest in renewable energy rather than in fossil-fuel based energy.

High consumption countries, such as the United Arab Emirates or Kuwait, are now becoming very cognizant of the fact that their per capita carbon emissions level is about five times that of the world average.

Nuclear power cannot be regarded as an option due to the high risks involved, and nuclear is in fact not without CO_2 emission, as is often claimed. Since the disposal and storage of radioactive waste is totally unresolved, nuclear power remains too much of a security and health risk. For instance, the German government decided that it will not run its 17 existing nuclear powerstations (many from the 1970s) beyond the year 2030. Five nuclear powerstations were switched-off between 2001 and 2010 and the remaining nuclear powerstations will be phased-out in a step-by-step process until 2030. In 2010 in Germany, renewables accounted for 16 per cent of energy delivery. This percentage is constantly growing, and by 2030 it is thought that renewable energy sources will reliably supply 40 per cent of the country's total energy mix (as confirmed by the Minister of Environment Roettgen, February 2010). Nuclear is only seen as 'bridging technology' in the transformation towards renewables and a 2001 law by the German government, which does not allow the construction of any new nuclear powerstations, remains in place.

Replacing fossil-fuel energy sources is technically achievable. The time is right to reconfigure the grid and turn away from fossil fuel and nuclear power to harness the abundant and free sources of renewable power. The aim must be to build districts with distributed renewables and precinct-based renewable co-generation. Managing the district-scale will be the trigger point for entire cities to move towards renewables. The examples of Vauban, Malmo and Woking demonstrate that the construction of energy-autonomous enclaves is already possible and that they represent milestones towards the renewable-driven city.

Today, the portion of renewable energy in national energy mixes still varies widely. For instance in 2010, renewable energy sources accounted for around 28 per cent of Denmark's electricity supply (with 24 per cent of its electricity coming from wind turbines); around 16 per cent in Germany; around 3.5 per cent in Singapore; and only around 1.5 per cent in Australia. Renewable energy needs highly local solutions, and needs to be linked to a 'smart grid' for the import and export of power.

Solar, wind power and the feed-in tariff (FiT)

All experts agree that the development of renewable energy in Europe will continue to increase dramatically towards the year 2020, and it is anticipated that windpower will be responsible for 50 per cent of that growth, as it is already a developed technology. In future, energy will be produced locally and the large electricity grid will only be used as a back-up system. The advantages of exploiting off-shore windpower is that the wind over the ocean is stronger and more stable than it is on land, and the areas available for generation are greater and are not in competition with agricultural land-use.

Solar energy has also seen a great rise in demand. Solar cells are constantly becoming more efficient and affordable, and is a technology that can truly help to solve the climate change crisis. The main reason for the rapid growth of the solar cell industry is that the cells are becoming dramatically cheaper and more efficient. Today, it's not uncommon to get a 25 or 30 year warranty from solar cell manufacturers. In warmer industrialized countries, such as Spain, Portugal, Japan and the south of the US, residents use the most electricity when the sun is shining the strongest, because they want to keep rooms cool by means of air-conditioning. This is the starting point for deploying wafer-based solar cell technology and solar cooling technology on a large scale. New, thin-film, flexible solar cells that can be bent and applied to uneven, curved surfaces, and are, therefore, easier to integrate into facades and canopies of buildings, are now available. New eco-districts can be supplied with energy solely from renewable sources, thus making them truly `zero-emission districts', such as can be seen in the city of Freiburg, Germany.

However, renewable solar and windpower have an obvious disadvantage: energy is created only when the sun shines or the wind blows. It is, therefore, important to be able to store this energy so that it can be used when the overall energy consumption is high or, in the case of solar, at night. The technological challenge is to find an efficient way for storing the energy. At present, batteries are the most widely used form of storage, but they have their limitations in terms of life expectancy and capacity. Another storage option is hydrogen cells, where a fuel cell transforms chemical energy to electrical energy, for instance when hydrogen and oxygen react to produce water and electricity. In addition, a fuel cell is far more efficient than a traditional combustion engine, giving it great potential for zero-emission urban design. If the fuel is carbon-free, such as hydrogen, the `exhaust' will only be water and heat. Hydrogen electricity storage technology is still in the development stage, and further development of storage technology is an important field for researchers to focus on; the development of a couple of new storage technologies can be expected soon.

Every district will be turned from net-energy consumer into energy producer, acting like a mini-power station, where every roof and façade has been activated for power generation.

The German 'FiT' (feed-in tariff system – which has now been replicated in around 50 other countries, and is discussed in detail in Chapter 1) has been the main reason for the quick uptake of renewable energy technologies in Germany, where the skies are often cloudy.[8] With this system, everybody can become an energy producer and feed their surplus energy into the grid, with a 20 year guarantee to be paid above market rates for every Watt that is supplied to the grid (around 4 times the commercial rate). The German system is such that you only get paid if you produce and supply energy, but not for the purchase of the technology. This policy has proved to be very effective and has achieved rapid greenhouse gas abatement combined with the delivery of affordable renewable energy. (Droege, 2009)

Like solar panels, solar thermal collectors exploit the energy of the sun. The difference is that while solar panels generate electricity, solar thermal collectors heat-up water. This warm water can be used in the shower or for heating in the house. In colder climates (e.g. North European countries), heating and hot water consume a lot of energy – over half of all energy used by buildings. Heat pumps can help reduce this consumption by 75 per cent or more. Heat pumps use the same technology as refrigerators, but in the opposite manner. Whereas a refrigerator pulls warm air out of the cabinet, the heat pump pulls warm air into the house. Even though the heat pump uses electricity, it can provide up to three times the energy it needs to continue working. It is possible to extract this heat from air, earth, sea, groundwater and hot bedrock.

Cities and buildings are responsible for 40 per cent of global energy use, and 80 per cent of GHG emissions. Emissions from cities and buildings can immediately be reduced by 50 per cent using today's available knowledge and technology.

Buildings are our biggest opportunity and our biggest failure. While buildings are seen as the `low hanging fruit', meaning CO_2-reductions could easily be activated in the building sector, there are a couple of serious hurdles:

- the real estate and construction sectors have many barriers that prevent arriving at the right environmental answer,
- the sectors are difficult to legislate corrrectly due to complexity of issues and number of players (can we wait for policymakers to get it right?), and
- the building codes are only effective for new build or refurbishment (but most of the building stock in 2020 exists already today and is inefficient)

Rapidly retrofitting (greening) the existing urban centres and their aging building stock, district by district, will be the next big task. New, more efficient technology is significantly smaller in size, only requiring half the space in risers and suspended ceilings, so retrofitting office towers shouldn't be too hard. But what about the energy supply side? There is no question that in Australia the move to de-carbonizing the energy supply over the next twenty years will be a mammoth task. While international permits in an *emission trading scheme* (ETS) will play an important role in Australia's transition to a low carbon future, the country's energy supply is still dominated by fossil fuels (94 per cent), not unsimilar to the US. The current energy mix in Australia is (data: 2010):

44 per cent coal
32 per cent petroleum (oil)
18 per cent natural gas

Most of the CO_2 emissions result from the inefficient process of generating energy by burning coal (or oil). If Australia wants to de-carbonize its energy supply, it needs to continue to phase-out coal and replace it with zero-carbon renewable sources. Recognizing that this requires 'Herculean efforts' from politicians and a much stronger commitment to the development of clean technologies, it is currently impossible to predict how fast the Australian economy can de-carbonize. The lobbying power of, and influence on the government by the large mining corporations is simply too strong for a fast change to be introduced. This, then, will hold back Australia in comparison to worldwide standards. (See: Fig. 5)

Importing and exporting energy through smart grids

A `smart grid' is an intelligent electricity grid that helps to cut consumption, pollutes less and lowers electricity bills. It's a collection of different solutions, essentially a matter of transporting and using electricity in a more intelligent way. An example of it, is the automatic measurement and management of electricity consumption so that the user receives a legitimate oversight of the amount of electricity being used, as well as its cost. It allows the user to adjust electricity consumption through automatic functions ordered from the electricity supplier; for instance in enabling you to use the electricity when it is cheapest as well as choosing electricity from renewable sources. It also allows you to feed-in electricity surplus produced locally. (Knab and Strunz, 2010)

The smart grid will better enable us to address the challenges of integrating renewables, since consumers have the flexibility to switch on or off their electrical devices as they please. The supply side of the grid system must be able to react to these load changes. However, in a system with a high amount of wind and solar power and distributed CHP facilities, accurately predicting generation levels and controllability will be a challenge for the grid operator. According to the *European Wind Energy Association*, integrating wind and solar power into the grid at levels higher than a 20 per cent share requires advanced energy management techniques using a smart grid. The smart grid is explained in detail later in this chapter. For more information on renewables, see also: www.renewables2004.de

We need to profoundly change the way cities utilize resources, reducing our overall demand for energy, water and materials – using the many new technologies now available.
It's widely a question of informing people about the availability of these new technologies.

Despite the described hurdles, technological changes are happening everywhere. For instance, the common street light requires a huge amount of energy, but it can be transformed by using solar-powered LED street lights. This is a very promising technology. The use of efficient LED (light-emitting diodes) lighting technology will reduce global electricity consumption by more than 900 billion kWh per year (estimate by Siemens, 2009), which is twice the annual electricity consumption of France. Based on the current worldwide electricity mix, such a reduction would also lower CO_2 emissions by more than 500 million metric tonnes per year. LED lighting boasts a high level of luminous efficiency and uses up to 80 per cent less electricity than the conventional light bulb. As they last up to 15 times longer, this makes LEDs clearly the light source of the future. The roll-out of solar-powered LED street lighting needs to be part of any retrofitting of city districts. It can deliver savings of up to 7 per cent of a city's total power demand. Payback on such an investment can be reached in less than eight years.

Australia's Coal Exports 2007-08

In 2007-08 Australia produced around 76 million tonnes of brown coal and 325 million tonnes of black coal. Over 75% of all coal is exported. This is around one third of all global coal exports. Almost two thirds of global greenhouse gas emissions come from the use of fossil-fuel based resources, mainly from burning coal.   Source: ABARE, 2008

Fig. 5: Above diagram shows the global supply and export of coal from Australia, its major export earner. Around a third of the Australian coal export goes through the Port of Newcastle. (data: 2009) The Australian government spends huge subsidies to help the coal industry, but still does little about renewable energy technologies. Most politicians seem to be unable to imagine Australia without coal as main export commodity and cannot see past Australia's immense coal and uranium reserves. It appears that the importance of coal has been seriously overstated: people in the Hunter region, Australia's main coal area, have pointed out that it is not 'coal' they are married to but 'jobs'. (HVRF survey, 2009) China and India currently consume 45 per cent of all coal used globally. By 2030, this figure is likely to reach around 80 per cent. (World Energy Outlook, 2007). The future global transport and storage of energy will not be by shipping coal around the world; it will be via hydrogen or methane, by ships that are themselves powered by hydrogen.

COMBINED HEAT-AND-POWER (CHP) PLANT

Moving towards urban-integrated renewable energy systems

Coal-fired powerstations are an extremly inefficient and polluting means to provide electricity, with more than two-thirds of the energy wasted in generation and transmission lines. Technologies called co-generation plants have become very popular in Europe, as they can save energy and help cities become more independent from the large utility companies. For instance, the small city of Woking (in Surrey, UK. A town of 90,000 people) has been at the forefront of decentralized energy in Britain. Its highly efficient energy management system, using a small community grid, has allowed Woking Council to slash energy use by nearly half, reduce city council's CO_2 emissions by 77 per cent since 1990, and reach almost 100 per cent energy autonomy. Woking has, to a large extent, gone off-grid and become energy self-sufficient. Its combined-heat-and-power station (CHP; also referred to as co-generation and tri-generation plants) generates waste heat, which is re-used in winter for heating and all year long as hot water system, and photovoltaic cells on roofs of buildings produce energy locally. Importantly, the Woking case is proving the point that keeping the power generation in direct municipal control is the best way for any municipality to depart from fossil-fuel dependency.

Lynne Blundell recently visited Woking and wrote about the innovative system: 'The generators are connected to users via a private electricity grid owned and operated by Thamesway Energy Ltd – a municipal energy and environmental services company; itself wholly owned by Woking Borough Council. Woking raised capital for energy infrastructure development initially through energy efficiency savings. These savings then allowed the council to invest millions in energy supply innovation and also attracted investment from Danish pension companies – energy systems like Woking's are a common component of investment portfolios for pension and insurance companies across Europe.' (Blundell, 2009) Alan Jones, who set up the Woking power network and who is now heading up London's Climate Change Agency, added to the debate on the benefits of co-generation by pointing out the enormous inefficiency of current power networks. In fact, for every unit of power generated by the network, two units of heat are generated. This heat is then 'thrown away' through big cooling towers. Jones comments: 'In the UK we use 50 per cent of our water resources to throw that heat away; and even more power is then lost in getting it to customers. In the UK, the energy regulator estimates that US$1 billion worth of power is lost each year just in heating up the wires and transformers in the distribution network.' (Jones, 2009) Such losses caused by the large grid network and the resistance in its cables, are avoided with localized distributed energy generation, which uses renewable energy sources and produces power close to the point where it's needed. Alan Jones is now working on the urban energy transition of London, to take the city off the coal-fired power grid and feed London's need for energy through alternative localized power generation.

The City of Sydney is developing plans to take the CBD by 2020 off the grid and to install its own energy supply through a network of tri-generation plants: gas-fired turbines that use the excess heat. These plants will be located at Town Hall and five acquatic centres, providing 70 per cent of the CBD's electricity needs; most of it consumed by the air-conditioning systems of large office buildings. Another example is Freiburg-Vauban, Germany, the eco-district already discussed in Chapter 1. At Vauban, the CHP plant is powered by wood-chips and a small amount of natural gas. The concentrated land use pattern of the 'Compact City' makes district heating and/or district cooling systems even more viable. (Jenks and Burgess, 2000) The power generator is positioned within the community, providing reliably electricity for local consumption. The produced waste heat is captured and reused for the local district heating system, providing space conditioning in winter.

Other municipalities are also achieving significant improvements in the efficiency of their power distribution through combined-heat-and-power plants. Smaller CHP power stations are now commonly used in many European cities. CHP are local powerstations that can be located inside cities and in basements of new office blocks, close to the point of energy consumption, capturing and reusing waste heat and waste energy through district heating systems. Groups and clusters of buildings can share CHP systems. They don't have the high transmission losses and are much more efficient compared to conventional centralized power stations located a long distance away, outside the city. CHP can have the double efficiency, of around 80 per cent, compared with centralized power stations. Energy experts expect that, in future, CHP systems will become the standard and the long-distance electricity grid will only be used as back-up system.

Localized power generation is highly efficient, reduces the built environment energy demand and will become a key strategy for reducing our cities' carbon emissions.

We need to start using the many new technologies available in the energy generation sector. This is especially important for urban planning, where the large roof and facade areas can become sites for localized power generation. Localized energy generation eliminates transmission costs and transmission losses for the local consumer and is, therefore, a promising model for all future eco-districts (in comparison, the thermal efficiency of the centralized, remotely located power stations is only around 35 per cent, with most of the thermal energy lost directly out of the chimney stack and as evaporation through cooling towers).

WASTE

Understanding waste as a resource and part of a closed-cycle urban ecology

The estimated world waste production is around four billion tonnes of waste p.a., of which only 20 per cent is currently recovered or recycled (*World Waste Survey*, Veolia, 2009). Globally, waste management has emerged as a huge challenge, and it's time that a fresh look is given to how best the waste and material streams of cities can be managed. The issue of waste, and the city's ever growing waste production, is of particular significance, if we comprehend the city as a living eco-system with ideally closed-loop management cycles. (See: Figs. 6 and 7)

Waste is nutrients. Waste is precious. We should learn from Nature: Nature doesn't know 'waste'.   **Michael Braungart, 2006**

There are some serious implications around the topic of waste. It is obvious that it is not just waste recycling, but also waste prevention, which has to be given priority. Only about 4 per cent of Australia's e-waste is currently being recycled (Government data, 2008). Most of this highly toxic waste goes into landfill, threatening ground water and soil quality, and an unknown proportion is shipped overseas (legally and illegally), mainly to China. About 37 million computers, 17 million televisions and 56 million mobile phones have been buried in landfill around Australia (report: Total Environment Centre, 2008). This waste contains high levels of mercury and other toxic materials that can be found in most common electronic goods, such as lead, arsenic and bromide. Discharges are a threat to soil and groundwater, and methane gas discharges are a threat in the atmosphere. In the meantime, many large cities are producing an astronomical amount of waste daily and are running out of landfill space. Incineration of waste has gone out of fashion, as it has the disadvantage that it releases poisonous substances, such as dioxins, into the environment, while burning waste with very high embodied energy is not an efficient way of dealing with resources. Environmental groups have successfully prevented the construction of new waste incinerators all around the world. Linear systems have to be replaced with circular systems, taking nature as its model. Much more appropriate is the combination of recycling and composting. Today, recycling 50 to 60 per cent of all waste has become a standard figure for many cities (e.g. the Brazilian model city of Curitiba has been recycling 70 per cent of its waste since 2000). Organic waste is playing an increasingly important role. The small Austrian town of Guessing, for instance, activates the biomass from its agricultural waste and has reached energy autonomy by composting and using the bio-energy to generate power. A recommended split for a city, where no waste goes to landfill, would be:

- Recycling and reusing   min. 50–60 per cent
- Composting of organic waste   20–30 per cent
- Incineration of residual waste   max. 20 per cent

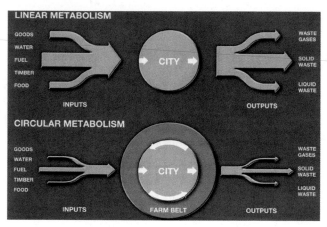

Fig. 6: The flow of natural resources into cities and wastes out of them represents one of the largest challenges to urban sustainability. Circular metabolisms are more sustainable, compared to linear ones. This also has economical advantages. Recycling will continue to be an essential part of responsible materials management, and the greater the shift from a 'river' economy (linear throughput of materials), towards a 'lake' economy (stock of continuously circulating materials), the greater are both the material gains and greenhouse gas reductions. Even so, recycling is only halfway up the waste hierarchy. The greenhouse gains lying in the upper half (waste avoidance and reduction) are, largely, yet to be tapped. The focus of attention needs now to expand from the downstream of the materials cycle, from a post-consumer stage, to include the upstream, pre-consumer stage, and behavioural change. (Diagram: H. Girardet, 1999; Richard Rogers, Anne Power, 2007)

Constantly growing amounts of waste – what can be done?

Waste is also accumulating in the oceans. In recent years, our oceans have devolved into vast garbage dumps. Thousands of tonnes of waste are thrown into the sea each year, endangering humans and wildlife. Since the world's oceans are so massive, few people seem to have a problem with dumping waste into them. But most plastics degrade at a very slow rate, and huge amounts of them are sloshing around in our oceans. Wildlife consumes small pieces, causing many of them to die as the plastics are full of poisons. Some plastic products take up to 200 years to degrade. Every year, around 250 million tonnes of plastic products are produced, and much of this produce ends up in the oceans. The 'Great Pacific Garbage Patch' is half the size of Europe, and in the Atlantic huge amounts of plastic garbage has recently been discovered (report: SEA Organization, 2010); the highest concentration being found close to Caribbean islands, with over 200,000 plastic pieces per sq km. In the North and Baltic seas, although dumping in them has been illegal for over two decades, the amount of waste found in them has still not improved. It is estimated that, each year, 20.000 tonnes of waste finds its way into the North Sea, primarily from ships and the fishing industry. (UN Report, 2010) Experts warn that we've reached a point where it's becoming dangerous for humans to consume seafood. A big problem is the throw-away plastic water bottles made of PET, not only because they significantly contribute to waste creation and CO_2 emissions from transporting drinking water around the globe, but they also release chemicals suspected of being harmful to humans into the water. Together with the largest oil spill in human history, the devastating oil spill in the Gulf of Mexico (2010), it shows how advanced humanity's destruction of entire ecosystems in the oceans has become.

Given these conditions, the international community has been pushing for four decades for massive bureaucratic efforts aimed at clearing the oceans of waste. In 1973, the United Nations sponsored a pact for protecting the oceans from dumping, and in 2001 the European Union established directives that forbid any dumping of maritime waste into the ocean while in port. However, such directives have been ineffective and many experts agree that laws and international efforts aimed at protecting the oceans have failed across the board.

No other sector of industry uses more materials, produces more waste and contributes less to recycling than the construction sector.

With the constant increase of the world's economic activity, there has also been a large increase in solid waste produced per head of population. The waste mix (industrial and urban waste) has become ever more complex, often containing large amounts of toxic chemicals. Obviously, the first aim of a sustainable future is to avoid the creation of waste and to select materials and products based on their embodied energy, life-cycle assessment and supply chain analysis. This needs to be understood holistically. Transportation of input materials, as well as the transportation of the final product to consumers (or to the construction site), is a common contributor to greenhouse gas emissions. The way in which a product uses resources, such as water and electricity, influences its environmental impact, while its durability determines how soon it must enter the waste stream. Care needs to be taken in the original selection of input materials, and the type of assembly influences end-of-life disposal options, such as ease of recyclability, or take-back by the manufacturer. With a huge amount of waste still going to landfill, drastic action is required in urban planning to develop intelligent circular metabolisms for districts, and waste collection and treatment systems that will eliminate the need for landfills.

While the worldwide international average for daily waste generation is about 1 to 1.5 kg per capita, countries like Kuwait and United Arab Emirates top the list, generating an average of over 3 kg of waste per person per day (in comparison, the average Australian resident dumps 1.1 tonnes of solid waste per year; this is also around 3 kg per day). According to the `polluter pays' principle, policies rightly penalize those who generate large amounts of waste. Collecting, sorting and treating waste incurs huge costs, so the focus has to be on avoiding and minimizing waste creation at the first place, in the office, in industry, in households. Waste-wood-to-energy has frequently become an important component of energy concepts for city districts. Waste management and recycling schemes have greatly reduced the volume of waste being `land-filled'. Waste segregation and recycling has also substantial economic benefits and creates new jobs.

Re-using building components and integrating existing buildings (instead of demolition) is a basic principle of any eco-city.

On the way towards a zero-waste economy, manufacturers are increasingly made responsible for the entire life-cycle of their products, including their recycleability, by introducing an 'extended producer responsibility' policy. Luckily, many companies are now doing extraordinary things in the area of recycling and are prolonging the life-cycle of products. For instance, Ohio-based firm Weisenbach Recycled Products, a manufacturer of consumer goods made from recycled materials, holds numerous patents on recycling, awareness and pollution prevention products. It is both a specialty printing firm and an innovative recycler of waste and scrap, repurposing and 'up-cycling' such materials as plastic caps, glass bottles and circuit boards into over 600 promotional items and retail consumer products. According to the company's president, Dan Weisenbach, there has been a changing perception in the business world, where you are more valued if your company is a 'certified green business': 'Even though conservation has been a core principle in our culture since we started, we believe it is important that we take a step to formalize our commitment to sustainable business. The competitive landscape has shifted and it is important for a company to have a history of environmental leadership and integrity. Choosing to voluntarily document all our efforts in an annual sustainability report is a demonstration of this commitment. We have moved past the *bigger is better* era. People want to do business with companies they can relate to and who share their values.' (Weisenbach, 2010)

For centuries, waste was regarded as 'pollution' that had to be collected, hidden and burried. Today, waste is not anymore seen as something to be disposed of, but as a resource to be recycled and reused. It's clear now that we need to close the material cycle loop by transforming waste into material resources. Over the next decades, earth will be increasingly under pressure of population growth, continuing urbanization and shortage of food, water, resources and materials. Waste management and material flows are some of the major challenges concerning sustainable urban development. There is a growing consensus that waste should be regarded as a 'valuable resource and as nutrition.' (McDonough and Braungart, 2002) It has been argued that the concept of 'waste' should be substituted by the concept of 'resource'. McDonough and Braungart point out that the practice of dumping waste into landfill is a sign of a 'failure to design recyclable, sustainable products and processes.' All eco-cities have to embed zero-waste concepts as part of their holistic, circular approach to material flows.

Design for Disassembly means the possibility of reusing entire building components in another future project, possibly 20 or 30 years after construction. It means deliberately enabling 'chains of reuse' in the design. Recycling resources that have already entered the human economy uses much less energy, than does mining and manufacturing virgin materials from scratch. For instance, there is a 95 per cent energy saving when using secondary (recycled) aluminium; 85 per cent for copper; 80 per cent for plastics; 74 per cent for steel; and 64 per cent for paper. (Source: Recycling International, 2008). Through reuse and recycling, the energy embodied in waste products is retained, thereby slowing down the potential for climate change. If burned in incinerators, this embodied energy would be lost forever. It becomes obvious that all future eco-cities will have to integrate existing structures and buildings for adaptive reuse into their masterplanning.

In closed-loop systems, a high proportion of energy and materials will need to be provided from re-used waste, and water from wastewater. We can now move the focus to waste avoidance, behavioural change and waste reduction.

A closed-cycle urban economy will deliver a series of further advantages
- It avoids waste being generated in the first place (and therefore reduces CO_2 emissions).
- It creates closed-loop eco-economies and urban eco-systems with green collar jobs.
- It helps transforming industries towards a better use of resources and non-polluting (non-toxic), cleaner production processes, and
- It delivers economic benefits through more efficient use of resources.

This includes extended responsibilities of producers as well as consumers, such as consumers' participation in recycling schemes. A recent survey showed that 83 per cent of Australians wanted a national ban on non-biodegradable plastic bags, while 79 per cent wanted electronic waste (e-waste) to be legally barred from landfills (survey 2009). Cities will always be a place of waste production, but there are possibilities available that will help make them zero-waste producers, where the waste is either recycled, reused or composted (using organic waste for biomass). The Masdar-City project in the UAE is a good example of such a zero-waste city. The large Japanese city of Yokohama reduced its waste by 39 per cent between 2001 and 2007, despite the city's growth of 165.000 people during this period, by raising public awareness about wasteful consumption and the active participation of citizens and businesses. In Australia, the *Zero-Waste SA* initiative by the South Australian government and the City of Adelaide is highly commendable (See: www.zerowaste.sa.gov.au).

The increase in world flows of scrap, e-waste, recovered plastics and fibres has turned developed countries into a source of material supply for informal trade in emerging countries.

Fig. 7a, b: Left: Developing ways of not wasting waste: Waste recovery facility in Adelaide, South Australia; separating waste from construction sites, where cut-offs are going to recycling instead of landfill.
Right: Waste collection in Pondicherry, India: closing nutrient loops. (Photo: S. Lehmann, 2007)

Fig. 8: Cairo, the capital of Egypt, has grown to over 15 million people and is one of the most densely populated cities in the world (with 32,000 people per sq mile). The economy of `Garbage City' (Manshiyat Naser, the Zabaleen quarter), a slum settlement on the outskirts of Cairo, revolves entirely around the collection and recycling of the city's garbage, mostly through the use of pigs by the city's minority Coptic Christian population. Although the area has streets, shops, and apartments, like any other area of the city, it lacks infrastructure and often has no running water, sewage or electricity. The city's garbage is brought in by the garbage collectors, who then sort through the garbage to retrieve any potentially useful or recyclable items. As a passer-by walks down the road he will see large rooms stacked with garbage; with men, women or children crouching and sorting the garbage into what is usable or what is sellable. Families typically specialize in a particular type of garbage that they sort and sell - one room of children sorting out plastic bottles, while in the next room women separate cans from the rest. Anything that can somehow be reused or recycled is saved. Various recycled paper and glass products are made and sold from the city, while metal is sold by the kilogram to be melted down and reused. Carts pulled by horse or donkey are often stacked 3 metres high with recyclable goods. The circular economic system in `Garbage City' is classified as an informal sector, and people there do not just collect the trash, they live among it. Most families typically have worked for generations in the same area and type of waste specialization, and they continue to make enough money to support themselves. They collect and recycle the garbage which they pick up from apartments and homes in wealthier neighbourhoods. This includes thousands of tonnes of organic waste, which is fed to the pigs. By raising the pigs, the Zabaleen people provide a service to those who eat pork in the predominantly Muslim country, while by eating the perishable rubbish the pigs help to rid neighbourhoods of tonnes of odorous waste that would otherwise accumulate on the streets. Like the famous rubbish dump 'Smokey Mountain' in Manila, Philippines, this could become an official recycling centre? (Photo: Bart Princen, 2009)

To date, little research has been done on measuring the impact of waste treatment systems and waste management changes over the longer term. For instance, the Danish city of Aalborg has proven that better waste management can reduce greenhouse gas (GHG) emissions and that a municipality can produce significant amounts of energy with sustainable waste-to-energy concepts. Two Danish researchers have recently published evidence. Poulsen and Hansen used historical data from the municipality of Aalborg to gain a longer-term overview of how a `joined-up' approach to waste can impact on a city's CO_2 emissions. Their assessment included sewage sludge, food waste, yard waste and other organic waste. In 1970 Aalborg's municipal organic waste management system showed net GHG emissions by methane from landfill accounting for almost 100 per cent of the total. But between 1970 and 2005, the city changed its waste treatment strategy to include yard waste composting, and the city's remaining organic waste was incinerated for combined-heat and-power (CHP) production. Of this, waste incineration contributed 80 per cent to net energy production and GHG turnover, wastewater treatment (including sludge digestion) contributed another 10 per cent, while other waste treatment processes (such as composting, transport, and land application of treated waste) had minor impacts. `Generally, incineration with or without energy production, and biogas production with energy extraction, are the two most important processes for the overall energy balance. This is mainly due to the substitution of fossil fuel-based energy', says Poulsen. The researchers calculated that the energy potential tied up in municipal organic waste in Denmark is equivalent to 5 per cent of the country's total energy consumption, including transport. They also predicted that further improvements by 2020 were possible, by reducing energy consumed by wastewater treatment (for aeration), increasing anaerobic digestion, improving incineration process efficiency and source separating food waste for anaerobic co-digestion. Aalborg's progress shows how far-reaching waste management can be in attaining energy and GHG reduction goals, and should offer encouragement to other cities embarking on greener waste management strategies for the future. (Poulsen and Hansen: *Waste Management & Research*, in: *Science Daily*, 2009). The potential for emission reduction in waste management is very big. It is estimated that within the European Union, municipal waste management reduced GHG emissions from 64 to 28 million tonnes of CO_2 per year between 1990 and 2007, equivalent to a reduction from 130 to 60 kg CO2 each year per capita. With such innovation in waste treatment, the EU municipal waste sector will achieve 18 per cent of the reduction target before 2012, which was set for Europe by the Kyoto agreement.

The waste situation in New South Wales, Australia: a looming crisis?

Australia is the third highest generator of waste per capita in the developed world. In 2006-07, only around 50 per cent of waste collected in the state of New South Wales (NSW) was recycled. Of course, it's always cheaper to simply bury waste than to treat it, with dangerous side effects. For instance, electronic waste is still filling up Australian and US landfills (something not allowed in the EU for 10 years), contaminating soil and groundwater with toxic heavy metals. In the meantime, a waste crisis is looming: the City of Sydney's four landfill sites (Eastern Creek, Belrose, Jacks Gully and Lucas Heights) are reaching their capacity and will be full by 2015, according to a recent independent *Public Review Landfill Capacity and Demand Report* (March 2009). The city's annual 2 million tonnes of waste will then have to be moved 250 km south by rail to Tarago. For a long time, the state government has been inactive and failed to make the recycling shift, lacking recycling policies and investment in recycling technology to cut rubbish going to landfills. Recycling needs to be made cheaper than landfilling, and strong economic incentives are to be provided, along with strategies to get households to dramatically reduce waste creation (for instance, by reducing bin sizes, raising awareness and by introducing the three-bin system to separate organic/garden waste, recycling, and residual waste).

While Sydney's landfill sites are rapidly filling up, and the NSW government has currently no clear plan to address the crisis, Sydney's waste is forecast to keep growing by at least 1.4 per cent a year (due to population increase and increasing consumption). Kerbside recycling collected in NSW increased from 450,000 tonnes in 2000 to 690,000 tonnes in 2007. To make things worse, the NSW government has raised over $260 million in waste levies but returned just 15 per cent ($40 million) of that to local councils for recycling initiatives (data from report, 2009). By contrast, the state government of Victoria gives better support: it raised $43 million in landfill levies and gave it straight back to the agencies responsible for waste management. Despite the smaller levy, Victoria recycled almost 20 per cent more waste than NSW in 2009. The federal government will introduce a *National Waste Policy* in 2011 (aiming for a 66 per cent landfill reduction by 2014) and hopes are high that this will bring about the urgently necessary change.

SCARCITY OF MATERIALS, METALS, RESOURCES

Using less materials

Energy cost is not limited to heating or cooling energy or lighting energy; it is also related to all material flows relevant to buildings. For instance, waste from the production of construction materials and components can be much greater than all other waste streams. To make it easier for architects and planners to specify materials according to their impact (including impacts caused by material extraction, or waste creation from the production process), the information on materials and components needs to be readily available. Different from the *Club of Rome*'s warning in 1972, today, the 'limits of growth' are defined by climate change and the depletion of material resources. We see an increasing challenge through the scarcity of raw materials, especially metals, such as lead, copper and zinc. With natural resources and materials about to run out, we need better resource protection and more effective ways to use them. Several essential metals and resources are already becoming less available; e.g. most platinum, zinc, tantalum, lead, copper, cadmium, wolfram and silicon is concentrated in the hands of three countries, under the control of three large companies. This will soon create major challenges for industries in Europe and the US. Regarding products that use many of these metals in their manufacturing (such as televisions or computers), in a resource-constraint future we will see more:

- recycling-friendly designs, with extended producer responsibility,
- multiple-use devices and expanded product lifecycles,
- long-life products and buildings, with optimized material use,
- products using less packaging,
- a variety of ways to avoid the loss of resources during the product's life-cycle and
- resource recovery through forward thinking reuse, remanufacturing and recycling.

Waste which contains minerals, metals and other nutrients is now understood as precious, and organic waste goes back to the soil. The survival path and rebound effect of materials is understood as extremely critical. Will our landfill sites of today become the 'urban mines' of the future? We can observe the emergence of a new sustainable industrial society, where new industrial systems are introduced that better reuse and recycle waste, and which are based on a new circular flow economy. (Girardet, 2008; Faulstich, 2009) In the meantime, the depletion of several natural deposits in coming closer. In 2008, the *Institut der Deutschen Wirtschaft* estimated the availability and coverage of essential resources and selected metals, as part of a risk assessment for the German industry and the threat caused by scarcity of raw materials (IDW, 2008):

Lead	20 years reserves available, estimated
Zinc	22 years
Tantalum	29 years

Copper	31 years
Cadmium	34 years
Wolfram	39 years
Nickel	44 years

These metals are becoming scarce and consequently more expensive; e.g. copper is much rarer than oil. In addition, it is also important to know what kind products we buy. For instance, 40 per cent of the products in our weekly shopping basket contain palm oil, which if not produced sustainably, can be a cause of deforestation of ecologically precious rainforests. A more conscious use of materials, metals, resources and products is imperative, supported by reuse and recycling.

SOLAR

Advanced solar technologies: solar photovoltaic and solar thermal

Solar energy is by far the most elementary source of life on earth; it is constantly available in abundance, with the potential to replace all fossil-fuel energy resources. Vast panel arrays are the best way to make solar economical. Much of our CO_2 emissions result from the transport of resources, materials and food around the globe. It is not just Middle Eastern oil that generates the energy, Australia and Indonesia supply coal (which is their main export product) across the world. To better address climate change, we will need to develop a whole spectrum of sustainable technologies, not just one, that contribute to a mix in the generation of energy. Legislation is necessary to accelerate this process. Since 2010, for instance, all California based utilities have been required by law to purchase at least 20 per cent of their power from renewable energy producers.

I don't think that any city that is not solar can be sustainable.
Norbert Lechner, 2010

However, which technologies are most efficient depends widely on the context, climate and supporting policies. In areas with much sunshine and strong solar radiation, solar power will have a major role to play. Most of today's commercially available solar PV-cells are made by using silicon, and so are expensive and less competitive with other sources of energy such as wind or biomass. The next generation of solar cells will have to be silicon-free, light, flexible and cheaper, perhaps made from organic (plastic) materials. Such technologies will develop and will make major contributions to decentralized energy generation. Solar cells come in two forms: photovoltaic (solar cell) technology and concentrated solar thermal (mirror; trough technology). The new third generation of solar cells can convert into electricity up to 40 per cent of the solar energy that shines on them, and are thus able to provide the potential for the generation of electricity through district-integrated solar systems, turning each neighbourhood from electricity consumer into electricity provider. With the right government policies and incentives in place, solar power will become more affordable, able to deliver paybacks in shorter times, and will have a significant influence on sustainable urban development. Significant progress has been made in the PV-panel sector. Innovative thin-film photovoltaic technology allows modules to be produced for 70 to 80 cents per Watt, and prices are reducing. The future includes organic photovoltaic polymers that are silicon-free, which will bring the cost of PV-panels down even further. At the same time, new production processes are boosting solar cell efficiency by up to 40 per cent. Even in relatively cloudy and colder cities in Germany and the UK, every roof and facade could be turned into a mini-power station. All flat roofs and car parking structures in the city could, and should, be used for the installation of photovoltaic panels. Utilizing renewable energy sources at the local level, close to the place of energy consumption means that building's facades and roofs have a major role to play. More information on solar energy resources can be found at: www.ises.org

Solar thermal technology works by using trough-shaped mirrors to concentrate the sun's heat into a circulating fluid, which can then be used for raising steam for turbines, both while the sun is shining and in the evening, when it uses stored heat. Thus solar energy can be transported, and energy generated during optimum operating conditions (during afternoon sunshine) is still available at night. Solar hot water systems, along with wind power are the most affordable renewable energy technology around, and it is one that gives the earliest payback. Together, solar photovoltaic, solar thermal and geothermal are able to provide base-load energy generation, but still need political support. Feed-in tariffs that encourage increased commercial investment are one way that authorities could boost renewable energy technologies.[9]

Local distributed energy-generation systems: generating energy on site

Many cities have started to establish a decentralized energy programme (e.g. the City of London, following the example of Woking and Freiburg-Vauban), using design and master-planning to drive the city's strategy for embedding an environmental action plan at the heart of each and every development and to make the city's energy supply more resilient.

Domestic solar hot water systems

Girardet notes 'the take-up of solar hot water systems has been surprisingly slow, given its technological simplicity and fast payback period'. It is truly a 'low-hanging fruit'. Domestic hot water (DHW) heat pumps and solar hot water systems are the easiest and largest contribution private households can make to the use of renewable energy, which can usually deliver payback in less than five years. For instance, in sun-rich Australia only about 8 per cent of all homes have solar hot water systems installed (government data: 2009), and there is still surprisingly little public knowledge about this system. In several other countries these systems have been made compulsory, such as in Israel, Greece and Cyprus, on Hawaii, and by the City of Barcelona.

Renewable energy sources will need to provide sufficient energy for an ever increasing world population, if we want to maintain today's lifestyle.

This must include the phasing-out of risky nuclear power technology and an end to the construction of new coal-fired power stations.

Transforming the city from energy consumer to energy producer

The main influences on energy demand always include the following five factors:

- climate
- urban design
- building envelope
- technical equipment
- user behaviour.

The concept of decentralized energy production is where city districts act as powerstations for themselves, and every citizen can generate energy locally. *Micropower Europe* is one of a growing number of campaign organizations with an interest in promoting the sustainable energy technologies collectively known as 'micro-generation'. Micro-generation, as a logical and beneficial extension to energy-efficiency, offers benefits to citizens, policy-makers and, indeed, to society as a whole through lower carbon emissions, protection from energy price fluctuations and improved awareness. The main technologies of micro-generation are: heat pumps, solar photovoltaic, micro-wind, micro-CHP and biomass. Micro-generation of energy gives citizens a choice of technologies, offering every building owner a financially rewarding power option, while policy-makers can quickly and cost-effectively move towards achieving better energy security, more resilient energy supply and climate change goals.

Australia has a very high sun radiation intensity that is still widely untapped. It has also wind and biomass in abundance. The technologies to harness these infinite powers are already available and on the market. So, what is holding the country back? It is urgently necessary that regulatory barriers are removed as they prevent the uptake of renewable energy, distributed systems and co-generational plants. These barriers are erected and defended by traditional (fossil-fuel burning) energy providers, the coal mining lobby and uninformed regulators, holding back the necessary transition.

The new zero-carbon technologies, which are currently available, will become even more efficient and cost-effective when we start looking beyond the performance of individual buildings to a broader vision of sustainable communities.

Enlarging the scale to eco-precincts, districts and neighbourhoods will unleash the full potential of the green revolution.

Solar cooling systems

It is often mentioned that the potential of solar power is enormous. For instance, the amount of solar energy that hits Australia or the US in one day is about half the world's total annual energy usage. Solar technologies can harness this energy either directly as heat (solar hot water systems) or for conversion into electricity. (See: Fig. 20) Solar cooling is a recently developed technology, using sorption technology, tapping into solar power to cool buildings. Solar cooling uses absorption and adsorption chillers instead of conventional electrically-driven compression refrigeration machines for cooling (the refrigerant sorbent is usually lithium bromide). The cooling can be driven by the waste heat from CHP plants, using a tri-generation system. Currently there are around 400 installations worldwide, with 7 installations in Australia. (Data: SCG, 2010) Solar absorption chillers convert the energy in hot water, from solar collectors, into chilled water (water with around 7 degrees Celsius temperature), which is used for cooling; it's ideal for chilled ceiling elements, thermoactive ceilings, or concrete core activation.

For highly air-condition dependent cities, solar cooling technology is a particularly useful solution to reduce their Urban Heat Island (UHI) effect. The UHI effect creates primarily a night-time problem, when the interior spaces are not cooling down sufficiently over night. This effect is now a reality in many large tropical cities, such as Hong Kong, Bangkok, Jakarta and Singapore. Solar cooling technology would avoid the issue that air-conditioning units blow their hot waste air into the streets, which is getting trapped in the urban environment, adding to the UHI problem. Integration of greenery in the urban environment is essential to mitigate for the Urban Heat Island effect. Planted surfaces have much lower temperatures, heat up less, and improve the micro-climate. Water bodies (urban ponds) have also beneficial effects on the micro-climate, as they help to moderate temperatures in summer through evaporation.

SMART GRID AND ELECTRO VEHICLES – NETWORKING THE CITY AND E-MOBILITY

The new electricity age: smart grids for 21st-century power distribution
Our power grids are facing new challenges. With increasing amounts of renewable energies and distributed generation being introduced, power system control is set to change dramatically. In future, the electricity grids will not only have to integrate large quantities of fluctuating wind and solar power, but also incorporate an increasing number of small, decentralized power producers. However, the problem is that electricity cannot yet be easily stored (due to limits of battery technology) and must be consumed as it is generated, leading to disparities between supply and demand, especially during periods of peak demand. With wind and solar power being variable rather than constant supplies, the generation of electricity will have to become increasingly decentralized – small solar installations on rooftops, biomass plants in communities and mini co-generation plants in all city districts. The previous flow of power from the transmission to the distribution grid, as in conventional systems with one centralized powerstation, will be partially reversed for periods of time. The new infrastructure of tomorrow, that can cope with these changes and intelligently interweave various energy sources, is the `Smart Grid'. This new grid allows buildings and districts to be transformed from mere energy consumers to active participants in the electricity market, where a surplus of self-generated power is fed into the smart grid. The basic idea is to connect numerous distributed and renewable power generating facilities via modern ICT. (See: Fig. 9)

Reliably meeting the growing electricity demand and integrating the increasing share of distributed generation and renewable energy are key challenges in preparing the world's electricity networks for the future. The next generation of electricity networks will need to bring the worlds of IT, communications and energy systems closer together than ever before. The smart grid will have to manage supply and demand of electricity more efficiently, and facilitate the integration of distributed combined heat-and-power plants and accelerate the uptake of renewables. (Knab and Strunz, 2010) Demand side management (DSM) is about making consumption more adaptive. The main objectives of DSM are to reduce critical demand peaks, to shift loads from times of high consumption to times of low consumption and to shift loads from times of low generation to times of high generation. For instance, a solar powerstation and a wind farm can complement one another, as strong winds and bright sunshine do typically not appear simultaneously. Consequently, a well-chosen mix of volatile sources can offset their inherent unreliability to a certain extent. Biogas plants could compensate for the remaining unreliability in the system.

Smart grid refers to a range of innovations in electricity transmission and management that are necessary to make energy systems more efficient and to enable renewable energy to be adopted and integrated on a large scale. Smart grids are a way of improving the capability of local grid networks and facilitating a two-way flow of electricity. Smart grids and smart meters are two-way streets for power, allowing citizens to be the producers of electricity and to feed their surplus power into the grid, and being reimbursed for each kilo watt. Smart grids also allow the better harnessing and integration of renewable energy. For instance, a sunny day can turn a building with solar photovoltaic panels into a robust generator of energy (most places in Australia receive around 2,000 kWh/sqm p.a.). Wind power in particular will benefit from smart grid technology and become more widely used.

New eco-cities present an ideal opportunity to develop and integrate smart grid electricity systems from the ground up. Retrofitting existing districts is more difficult to achieve. From the consumer's point of view, smart grids and smart meters allow electrical appliances to be programmed to operate at times of low electricity use, thus helping to avoid sharp peaks in demand and allowing the more efficient use of electricity throughout a grid. Smart grid technology brings benefits for all stakeholders along the energy conversion chain, such as:
• Environmental advantages through reduction in transmission losses and grid access for large scale, district-wide wind, solar and hydro power plants (bi-directional energy flow and grid integration of decentralized generation).
• Active integration of smart buildings and districts with more reliable network performance and improved monitoring possibilities.

Growth projections by the *Organisation for Economic Co-operation and Development* (OECD) and *International Energy Agency* (IEA) indicate that with the rise in energy demand, a portion of the energy will still have to come from fossil-fuel based resources for the next two decades or so, but a constantly increasing amount of energy will come from renewable energy sources. The pressure to introduce smart grids for the feed-in of renewable energy from decentralized power generators, and also for higher transparency, is now on for large utilities and grid operators. Clearly, though, the conventional (and unsustainable) way most energy is generated, distributed and supplied at this time needs to be fundamentally restructured. A revised and adapted overhaul of conventional, unsustainable approaches will influence future urban form and its infrastructure.

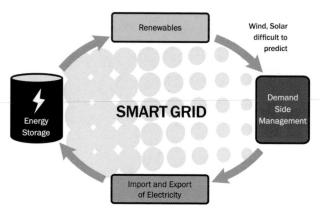

Fig. 9a: Managing the *Smart Grid*, the new grid allows importing and exporting electricity, and the large-scale integration of renewable energy sources. Combining the electricity supply sector with the individual transport system is a key element of future energy supply and transportation scenarios. The diagram above shows how renewable energy sources will be better integrated through a Smart Grid for more efficient management of the demand side, especially with the difficulty in predicting wind intensity and sun radiation. Electrical vehicles offer a balancing capacity, and will be helpful to include their charging modes in the energy mix. With charging stations connected to the Smart Grid, the electric vehicles serve as additional storage system, enabling us to better move energy loads in a more flexible way, dealing efficiently with supply and demand. (Diagram: Steffen Lehmann, 2009)

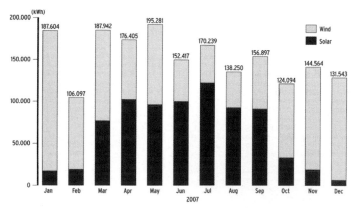

Fig. 9b: Smart Grids are necessary to address the challenges of today's power system, such as the integration of more renewable energies and distributed generation. This diagram illustrates the power generation from solar and wind energy in a virtual powerstation. A solar powerstation and a wind farm can complement one another, as strong winds and bright sunshine typically do not appear simultaneously. The data is taken from an existing virtual power plant operated by E.ON Hanse on the island of Pellworn, Germany. Installed capacity: solar PV-panels: 771 kW Peak; wind: 300 kW. (Diagram: Courtesy Knab/Strunz/E.ON, 2010)

The shift to eco-mobility and public mass transit

It has already been discussed how mobility is an essential part of society, therefore transport has to become less polluting, more efficient, more equitable and less disruptive – both socially and environmentally. The automobile sector is gigantic. In 2000, over 58 million new fossil-fuel burning automobiles were produced worldwide in an industry that employs over 15 million people. Obviously there is a demand for transportation but it is unsustainable to meet this demand by simply expanding the infrastructure of CO_2-emitting transport, e.g. building wider streets, more freeways, more cars. The focus needs to shift to public mass transit systems, electric vehicles and cycling. As mobility increases and accelerates worldwide, urban designers and transport planners are becoming more concerned about issues such as:

- the reliance on non-renewable resources
- inadequate infrastructure and increasing congestion
- inappropriate land use
- increasing health damages through the impact of noise and pollution.

By 2020, it is predicted that, worldwide, over seven million electric vehicles will be on the road (McKinsey study, 2009). Combining the electricity supply sector with an individual transport system will be a key element of future energy supply and transportation developments. The motor industry has slowly (many argue, too slowly) made the switch to electric-powered cars, and there are now two categories: The battery electric vehicle (BEV) and the plug-in hybrid electric vehicle:

- The full-time battery electric vehicles (BEV) are totally reliant for power on the charge stored in their large battery packs (lithium-ion batteries), with the disadvantage of restricted range (around 200 to 300 km), and the time it takes to recharge the batteries.
- The plug-in hybrid (extended range) electric vehicles (PHEVs) use battery packs only for short-range electric-only driving (range around 30 to 50 km), but are also equipped with combustion engines. Since a high proportion of car journeys are only short distance, this is seen as a practical solution by many automobile companies (e.g. BMW, Toyota). PHEVs enable automobile drivers to switch to partial electric driving, without having the limitations concerning the driving range of full-electric cars.

While their widespread use is not expected before 2015, these plug-in full-time electric or hybrid-electric vehicles offer possibilities to achieve several objectives in regard to storage and the Smart Grid, such as:

- Electric vehicles open a gate for reducing CO_2 emissions by means of reducing oil-based fuel consumption in the transport sector and the substitution of electricity from CO_2-free generation capacities such as wind or solar power. Because power generation from these renewable sources fluctuates and is thus difficult to predict, they require additional storage systems as back-ups. Electric vehicles can increase the amount of flexible loads and can be a support as active storage systems in the smart grid, thus securing the power quality of grids and the flexibility of grid operators.

• Electric vehicles can increase the storage capacity by means of decentralized storage systems, without any ecological impact on the landscape or related issues, other than that imposed by the vehicles themselves.
• This new eco-mobility will improve air quality locally and reduce noise, e.g. in city centres, allowing for naturally ventilated city districts.

Urban noise comes mainly from road traffic (80 per cent of all urban noise) and causes higher energy consumption for the air-conditioning of buildings, because windows must be closed, making natural cross-ventilation impossible. With no noise and air pollution, electric vehicles will allow us to re-conceptualize the natural ventilation of city districts and buildings.

There are a couple of much debated e-mobility initiatives. For instance, in 2008, the Israeli government launched the large-scale 'Better Place' initiative, which suggests switching the entire country to electric vehicles. This would be done in partnership with auto-maker Renault-Nissan, and in combination with a reduced tax on electrically powered vehicles. This initiative would make Israel one of the first countries to rid itself of combustion engine cars. Other countries and island states, such as Hawaii, Japan, Singapore and Denmark could follow. More information on this initiative and its clever ownership model can be found at: www.betterplace.com

Technology and design are drivers for any modern economy, and good design is crucial as it helps society to adopt new low-carbon technologies. It's time to look at cities as producers, not just consumers of resources.

Charging stations connected to the smart grid: turning electric vehicles into grid-connected storage units
We are now on the verge of a significant electrification of vehicles. The number of plug-in electric vehicles (PEVs) worldwide could rise to between 12 and 20 million by the year 2020 (estimated total number of cars in use worldwide is around 750 million, 2009) `Fully electric cars could make up 10 per cent of the world vehicle fleet by 2025', estimates Pierre Loing, responsible for product planning and zero emission at Nissan. (Loing, 2010) He points out that this new generation of cars will still initially require government incentives and tax credits in targeted markets to help make the vehicles competitive with conventional vehicles. Governments can show leadership by being the first to replace their own fleet of vehicles with electric vehicles, and by running green buses for public transport. Smaller governments, such as the city state of Singapore, or Israel, or Denmark, are likely to be among the first nations to officially declare the end of the combustion engine car within their borders, followed by car rental agencies and other fleet owners. Therefore, commercial recharge stations will be part of a new urban infrastructure to be built in cities, and the `old' petrol station will disappear.

What is now entering the urban environment is a new charging infrastructure for electric vehicles. Charging stations will need to be available across the country, connected to the electricity grid, turning electric vehicles into mobile energy storage units, with the ability to re-feed energy back into the smart grid. This will make electric vehicles more than environmentally compatible vehicles, they will become an important element of an intelligent energy infrastructure and will contribute to the grid's ability to compensate for fluctuating in-feed from renewable energy sources and distributed generation units. With the seamless integration of e-vehicles into the new smart grid infrastructure (with the various charging solutions combined with information technologies), a self-integrating network emerges that guarantees individual mobility at any time and in a sustainable manner.

Electrical vehicle charging modes will be helpful in boosting renewable energy into the mix. With charging stations connected to the smart grid, we will be able to better move the energy loads in a flexible way, dealing more efficiently with supply and demand. It will therefore be important to set-up electrical grids across borders, internationally (not just locally or regionally). Germany is already aiming to become a leading market for electro-mobility, with the government planning on having one million electric vehicles on German roads by 2020. The German government announced, in 2009, a significant investment in building the necessary urban infrastructure to achieve this.

Combustion engines are inefficient in their energy use. Overall, electric and hybrid electric vehicles are more efficient in the use of energy and will thus help reduce carbon emissions and the cost of travelling. Some of the main hurdles to this at present are the relatively high cost of batteries, the slow innovation cycle in the automobile industry and consumer reluctance to buy cars that can go only a limited distance range before requiring a new charge.

The next generation of cars is closer than we might think. The automobile industry learned from a previous attempt to introduce electric cars in California (in 1970s) that the technology will take some years to succeed in the marketplace. Japanese car manufacturer Toyota, the world's largest car company, showed leadership in 1997 when it introduced a hybrid car, the popular `Prius' model (the world's best selling hybrid car), which is powered by a combination of electricity and petrol. The risk has paid off and Toyota is now the market leader for hybrid cars. The `Prius' achieves 38 km per litre from its fuel, surpassing all other fuel-efficient vehicles and leading to huge CO_2 reductions, and is now sold in 80 countries around the world. Encouraged by this success, Toyota is now looking at incorporating the hybrid technology into all of its vehicles. General-Motors has launched the `Chevrolet Volt', also a hybrid car. The `Tesla Roadster' was the first electric automobile to use lithium-ion battery cells with a range greater than 300 km per charge (it currently takes 4 hours to fully charge the car at 430 volts). Other full-time electric vehicles will follow in 2011, such as the `e-smart' by Mercedes, the `e-Mini' by BMW and an e-car by Nissan; and VW will launch in 2013 the `electro-Golf'.

Batteries will gain more prominence in the future and will be able to meet fluctuating energy production and demand. Battery-powered electric cars will make excellent storage

Global solar boom

The solar industry is a real boom sector: the production of solar PV (photovoltaic) cells worldwide has increased from 200 MW p.a. in 1999, to over 8,000 MW p.a. in 2009. The main producers of PV-cells in 2009 were:

China	2,589 MW p.a.
Germany	1,460 MW p.a.
Japan	1,269 MW p.a.
Taiwan	919 MW p.a.

In Germany, between 1999 and 2008, there were over 53,300 new jobs created in the field of PV-cell technologies.

Newly installed PV capacity, in 2009:

Germany	2,000 MW	USA	340 MW
Japan	400 MW	France	250 MW
Italy	400 MW	South Korea	100 MW
Spain	375 MW	China	80 MW

The mirrored parabolic troughs of the solar thermal powerstation intensify the sun's rays and heat up the oil or molten salt in dark-coloured receiver pipes to 400 to 500 degrees Celcius. This in turn heats water via a heat exchanger, which evaporates into steam that drives a turbine. (Image: 'Andasol 1', Spain. Courtesy Solarmillenium, Linde) Right: PV-installations at a carpark in Arizona and outside Shanghai.

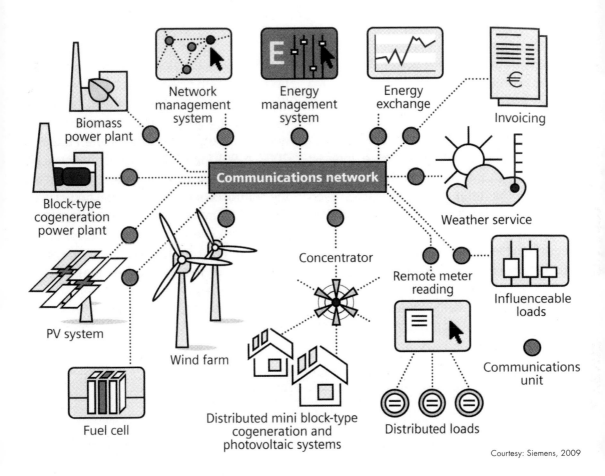

Biomass power plant · Network management system · Energy management system · Energy exchange · Invoicing · Block-type cogeneration power plant · Communications network · Weather service · PV system · Concentrator · Remote meter reading · Influenceable loads · Wind farm · Fuel cell · Distributed mini block-type cogeneration and photovoltaic systems · Distributed loads · Communications unit

Courtesy: Siemens, 2009

Achievable, realistic renewable energy targets for eco-districts

The following energy targets are technical achievable for residential buildings in most locations in temperate climates, such as in Central Europe (for cities with above average sun radiation, these targets could easily be improved):

- Space heating: Superinsulation and improved airtightness, combined with passive heat recovery ventilation, can reduce the need for heating by 80 per cent. The remaining 20 per cent can be achieved from passive solar gain, applying passive design principles.
- Domestic hot water: The annual demand for domestic hot water can be covered by 60 per cent by using solar hot water systems (roof-mounted solar thermal collectors).
- Renewables: 60 to 80 per cent of the annual electric demand can be supplied from building mounted photovoltaic panels. Additional energy could be generated by a community-scale micro wind turbine or a biomass plant.

This diagram above shows the 'virtual power plant', which incorporates a network of multiple small power stations (through advanced IT and Smart Grid as core elements) to form a large, smart power grid. As part of a virtual plant, even small energy producers in the distributed system (producing electricity near where it will be used) can sell their power on the electricity market. (Courtesy: Hassenmueller, Siemens 2010) devices. Cars will be charged during the night when energy is cheap and will feed excess storage back into the grid during the day. In this way electric vehicles will function as mobile power storage units for the smart grid. The focus is now on optimizing the interaction between electric vehicles, the power grid and the technologies needed for storing and bi-directionally transmitting energy derived from renewable sources.

Today's electricity distribution infrastructure is still not up to the task of integrating large quantities of fluctuating wind and solar power, and incorporating the increased number of small, decentralized power producers, but the move towards smart grids has already started. The solution is to develop an intelligent grid that keeps electricity production and distribution in balance. More information on smart grids can be found on the website of the EU's platform for smart grids: www.smartgrids.eu; and on the US National Renewable Energy Laboratory's website: www.nrel.gov

Today's infrastructure is not up to the many new challenges. We need to build a new urban infrastructure, including new smart grids and wastewater treatment plants.

There are also other options for more sustainable transport, such as hydrogen fuel cells and ethanol bio-fuels. Hydrogen can be produced by solar and wind energy, and it can also power fuel cell systems for vehicles and buildings. A growing number of cities have introduced fuel cell-powered buses. Ethanol bio-fuels are also possible, although it is only acceptable as long as its production does not compete for land with the food and agricultural sector, and it has acceptable water consumption. Recently, new biomass formation technology has been developed (based on lignocelluloses biosynthesis) which allows for the production of bio-fuels without competition with food crops.

SOLAR-THERMAL

Solar-thermal powerstations: concentrated solar power (CSP) with power storage

A series of solar-thermal power plants in California's Mojave Desert have demonstrated for over two decades that the technology works reliably, and that a huge amount of electricity can be generated through solar energy. The facilities feed some 350 MW into the grid – enough electricity to power 200,000 households. Solar-thermal power plants will play a decisive role in future energy scenarios. Mirrored parabolic troughs intensify the sun's rays and heat special oil, or molten salt, in dark-coloured absorbent pipes to 400 to 500 degrees Celsius. Like a magnifying glass, the parabolic troughs intensify the sun's rays and concentrate it onto the receiver pipes, where the oil heats up water via a heat exchanger, which evaporates into steam that drives a turbine with an attached generator. Nine such solar thermal powerstations operate in the Mojave Desert in the US. In Europe, a couple of large-scale solar thermal powerstations have been built in Spain ('Andasol 1' in southern Spain, with mirrors covering a surface area of 0.5 sq km, supplying power for 200,000 people in Valencia). In Andalusia, the sun shines for more than 3,000 hours per year. Following the German example, the Spanish government pays a generous 'feed-in tariff' per kWh of renewable energy supplied back into the electricity grid. This guaranteed for the next 25 years.

The lack of storage capacity of most renewable energy sources (to cope with peak demand periods during the 24-hour period) has emerged as a major barrier to their further uptake. However, the *Andasol* plants possess a thermal storage system that allow them to supply green power, even at night. The storage technology is based on a molten salt system for heat transfer. It uses two large tanks, and over the course of the day salt is pumped from the cold to the hot tank, through a heat exchanger train, while in the evening the system is reversed. In this way, it either collects or releases heat for shifts of more than eight hours at a time, allowing for a way to store solar energy for up to eight hours after sunset. This heat storage system is a recent technical breakthrough that allows for continuous electricity generation, avoiding the problem of intermittent grid supply otherwise common to solar and wind energy.

Concentrated photovoltaic (CPV) technology has a high cost reduction potential and is highly reliable. Parabolic troughs are today the most commonly used technology for commercial CSP systems. However, land requirements for these large solar (and windpower) farms are an important issue to consider. We can currently observe moves to dramatically increase the size of concentrated solar power plants, to make them more cost-effective (for instance, the gigantic Desertec project in North Africa). The four main measures to reduce the costs of photovoltaic and CSP, are:
- to optimize production
- to increase volume (scaling-up the CSP plants to 250 MW or more)
- to use less material (e.g. silicon-free PV) and
- to increase efficiency.

Spain, Africa, the Middle East, Australia and parts of Asia and the US are all sunny places receiving high solar radiation. For instance, 90 per cent of the Australian continent absorbs solar radiation of over 1,950 kWh per sq m per year – this is intense solar radiation for over 350 days per year, giving ideal conditions for solar-powered energy generation. With this amount of sun radiation intensity, cities like Sydney, Brisbane, Perth and Adelaide could easily generate over 50 per cent of their entire energy demand from using clean, infinite (and free!) solar energy, thus becoming true 'Solar Cities'. The same is true of Los Angeles, Las Vegas and Phoenix. Researchers estimate that every square kilometre in the Gulf region receives an annual solar power input equivalent to 1.5 million barrels of oil. With billions of square kilometres of desert, the potential for solar power in these regions is truly colossal.

The *Desertec* project is an example of thinking big. It aims for an inter-regional/trans-international 'super grid', based on solar energy, and is considered the largest-ever green energy project. Desertec proposes the export of excess electricity from North Africa to Europe by 2050 on a gigantic scale, mainly using concentrated solar power (Desertec is expected to cover up to 15 to 20 per cent of Europe's energy needs, around 100 GW of installed capacity). A consortium, including 15 of Europe's largest utilities companies and institutions (such as RWE and E.ON), plan to build several large solar thermal power plants and transmission grids to cover 15 per cent of the entire annual European electricity demand. The Desertec power grid could deliver clean solar power from giant CSP solar farms in North Africa (e.g. in Egypt, Algeria, Moroco) and has the potential to generate huge revenue to compensate for drying oilfields and to pay for the transition to renewables. More information can be found at: www.desertec.org

We will make great advances in managing, designing and improving new complex technical systems, such as innovative low-carbon modes of transport, manufacturing, energy and construction systems, and telecommunications.

Research in algae and geo-thermal: turning bio cells into energy wells

Two other areas of research need to be mentioned, both of which are quickly developing and are very promising. Firstly, energy generated from algae. Scientists already know that certain algae, by using photosynthesis, produce oils that can be converted into diesel and other fuels. Algae-based bio-fuels have the environmental advantage that they absorb CO_2 and convert it into oxygen. While today's bio-fuels made from plants like corn and sugarcane are an expanding energy source, they can impact on global food supplies by requiring fertile land and freshwater. Algae-based bio-fuels would not conflict with food supply and agricultural land use. Its potential is large but is still widely untapped. The other technology is geo-thermal, which is already well introduced, and has been for a long time (since ancient Roman times, for space heating and baths). Depending on the geological formation at the site, there are opportunities to tap into heat flows provided by the planet itself, using geo-thermal heat pumps. The earth can precool or preheat the supply air of the ventilation system in an earth pipe. In Europe, there are two large projects that are models for the use of geo-thermal power, used for cooling in summer and heating in winter: Sauerbruch-Hutton's administration building for the German Ministry of the Environment, built in Dessau (2000-05) and Christoph Ingenhoven's UCD Gateway Campus in Dublin, Ireland (2008-13) where geo-thermal energy provides enough power for the entire campus. Further information can be found at: www.geothermal.com

Cities are made up of many unique local urban systems and networks at the district and neighbourhood levels.
These characteristics and systems need to be maintained and made more resilient.

WIND

Wind energy makes particular sense in water-stressed regions

The barriers to de-carbonizing the energy supply by 2050 are mainly political, not technical. Technological innovation in the renewable energy sector is truly impressive. Wind
power, for instance, is the world's fastest growing energy industry (even faster than solar),
especially in off-shore locations in countries with long and windy coastlines (such as Denmark, Sweden, California, China, Australia). Many new wind farm projects are being
built, catching up fast with traditional energies and moving the world forward with clean
energy technology. Wind power is a proven technology that does not consume vast quantities of water for cooling purposes during power production, making it an ideal renewable
energy source in countries with much wind but little water (such as the Middle East, Australia, and parts of the US). The reduction of carbon emissions needs to go hand in hand with
a reduction in water consumption. In fact, producing electricity with wind turbines requires
less water than any other form of energy generation. Water withdrawal for energy production has become a significant problem for water-stressed societies. A coal-burning power
plant requires huge amounts of water for its cooling towers, and coal-fired and oil-based
electricity production consumes 10,000 to 20,000 litres of water per 5 MWh.

Water consumption to generate 5 megawatt hours:

- Wind   5 litres
- Coal   10,000
- Nuclear   12,500
- Oil   20,000
- Bio-fuel 1,000,000   (after: Vestas Wind Systems, 2009)

Wind energy cost factors (*Cost of Electricity*, COE) are lower than solar-generated power
and are expected to be competitive with coal in the next few years (Source: Roland Berger
forecast, 2009). As with solar farms, we see an up-scaling trend in wind farms. New wind
turbines often have a 100 to 120 metre rotor diameter, and very large turbines have an
output of 3.6 MW or more per turbine. However, as discussed earlier in this chapter, the
there is an issue of integrating wind energy into the grid, although smart grids will allow
for the better management of feed-ins of a variety of energy sources.

Global wind power development

It is an exciting time for urban designers to work in the renewable energy technology
market, as a wide range of technologies are rolling out that will lead to new typologies
of eco-cities, based on their new concepts for urban infrastructure, mobility and energy
systems. Urban wind farms are part of these ideas.
The *World Wind Energy Association* (WWEA, forecast 2009) predicts that by 2020 the
total installed capacity of wind turbines will reach an estimated 1,500 GW (GWs) worldwide, accounting for 20 per cent of global electricity consumption. This, may be too optimis-

tic a forecast as it represents a substantial jump in the role of wind energy in the next decade (up from the share of 1.5 per cent in 2010). Though many see this target as hugely ambitious, the *Global Wind Energy Council* (GWEC) forecasts an advanced scenario of almost 1,100 GW of installed capacity by 2020, when at least 10 per cent of the world's electricity consumption will come from wind energy. The *European Wind Energy Association* (EWEA) makes similar predictions. They note that in 2010, around 10 GW of off-shore energy output systems were installed in Europe alone (mainly off the coasts of Denmark, Sweden, the Netherlands, Belgium, Germany, Britain and Ireland), and that will increase to 70 GW by 2020. Over the next 5 years, the largest European wind farms will be built by the UK and Germany (each has over 1,000 off-shore wind turbines approved, but smart grids are still missing). Clearly, wind energy will play an increased role in urban planning of our future cities.

In the last 30 years, the Danish government has pioneered support for off-shore wind farm development and almost 25 per cent of all energy supply in Denmark already comes from wind power. Interestingly, most of this wind power capacity is owned by cooperatives founded by private individuals. It is expected that China will become the world's largest wind power producer by 2012, overtaking the US. China has recently raised its wind energy target for 2020, from 100 GW to 150 GW. The country doubled its installed wind power base in the years between 2006 and 2009. China will not only become a global leader in wind energy, but will also become an important supplier of technical know-how to fast growing emerging Asian economies in Vietnam, Thailand and Indonesia. Another sign of China's renewable energy ambitions is that, under its recent stimulus plan, it has named a new target of 20 GW of solar power by 2020, up from the 1.8 GW installed in 2010. Helping to meet this target will be a generous incentive paid by the Chinese government (around US$3 per Watt, given upfront for solar projects, enough to cover half the capital cost in most cases) and a series of subsidies for other renewables. (Chinese Stimulus Plan, 2009)

MARINE ENERGY

Marine (tidal) energy

Tidal power is, together with solar and wind power, the world's largest untapped renewable energy resource and could well provide clean, reliable electricity on a gigantic scale. In marine energy, we can differentiate three types of power sources located in the oceans:

- tidal power
- wave power
- off-shore windpower.

Tidal power uses *tidal barrages*. The largest tidal barrage operating in the world is located at La Rance, in Brittany, France (built 1966). These barrages require huge investment and can have a serious environmental impact. Technology for extracting power from sea waves is still very much at the development stage, but tides are driven by the earth's gravity and are predictable to a high degree, something which we have not seen with solar and wind energy. Wave power is only efficient in deep water (over 20 metres depth), and wave power plants are relatively hard to build and maintain (costwise). The `Aquamarine Oyster' is a wave power plant currently under test in the UK. The `Pelamis' is a new, promising type of floating off-shore wave device (operating as a marine current turbine), that is currently under test in Portugal and Scotland.

Windpower has already been discussed in the previous chapter. Off-shore wind farms have a series of advantages, such as more continuously strong winds with high speed (far over the minimum of 10 km/h wind speed), no conflict with agricultural land-use, and less opposition from land owners blocking the construction of wind farms; off-shore windfarms are usually built 20 km away from the shoreline. Off-shore wind farms have, therefore, the potential to deliver significant energy at an acceptable cost. A recent study (2009) shows that 23,000 off-shore 5 MW wind turbines would deliver, on average, more energy than all UK households require. The world's largest off-shore wind farm is Horns Rev II, 30 km off the Danish coast, which consists of 91 huge turbines able to supply around 210 MW of electrical power into the network. Denmark is a windy country and enjoys only ten calm days a year; on a windy day, Danish windmills can easily produce up to half of the country's electricity. Denmark already generates over 24 per cent of its energy requirements using wind power and has plans to substantially expand its use in coming years. A number of very large off-shore wind farms are now under construction in Denmark, Sweden, UK and China. While off-shore operations are particularly exposed to high stress situations, off-shore wind power offers the energy independence demanded by the world's largest and fastest-growing economies: China and India.

Energy outlook: with rising global energy demand, more renewable energy is needed in the mix

As was pointed out in the previous chapter, population growth and economic development in many emerging countries is causing the global demand for energy to increase rapidly. China and India alone will be responsible for half the increase in global energy consumption in the next 20 years. Depending on the source, predictions forecast an increase of global energy consumption of between 40 to 60 per cent by 2030, if current policies are maintained (which Lord Stern calls the `business as usual scenario'). (Stern, 2006; International Energy Agency, 2007) This illustrates the need to change policies and to intensify the de-carbonization of the energy supply (a well-balanced energy mix has at least 50 per cent of all energy generated from renewable energy resources).

Looking at the situation realistically from today's viewpoint (2010), it is likely that the necessary shift will not be managed quickly enough. Despite the scientific agreement on its urgency, the change of practice is still dragging on. It is likely that fossil fuels (above all, coal and gas) will continue to be a key source of primary energy for the next two decades, and will be responsible for around 80 per cent of the increase in consumption between 2010 and 2030, with renewable energy sources introduced at a slow pace. Despite renewable energy sources having tripled between 2001 and 2011, the overall global energy demand has risen significantly. For instance, China and India currently consume 45 per cent of all coal used globally. By 2030, this figure is likely to reach around 80 per cent (World Energy Outlook, 2007). Based on these predictions, CO_2 emissions could be double the 1990 level by 2030. This would have catastrophic consequences for the climate. To ensure that greenhouse gas emissions will fall despite these developments 187 countries agreed on the key points of a new climate protection agreement at the World Climate Conference in Bali in December 2007 and they confirmed the limit of a maximum of 2 degrees Celsius for global warming at the UN Climate Summit in Copenhagen in December 2009. This agreement will become legally binding by 2012, when the *Kyoto Protocol* expires. It will require a significant effort from all planners, architects and urban designers to contribute towards this target.

WATER

Living with water shortages
Globally, water quality is declining and the loss of wetlands is further decreasing the ability of ecosystems to filter and decompose wastes. Everyone understands that water is essential to life; a reason why access to clean water has often been declared as a human right. But many are only just now beginning to grasp how essential water is to everything in life, to food, energy, transportation, nature, leisure, identity, culture, social norms, and virtually all the products used on a daily basis. Water is increasingly recognized as a critical sustainable development issue, alongside energy and food security. Since water consumption per person is greater than ever, the efficient use of water and the reuse of waste water in cities has become an increasingly important issue for urban planning. As 97 per cent of all water on Earth is salt water, desalination, if it can be done by using renewable energy and with minimal environmental impact, will soon become a normal process to guarantee a sustainable water supply. Globally, per capita availability of freshwater is steadily decreasing and the trend will inevitably continue as the world's population swells towards 9 billion in 2050 (the most widely accepted prediction of population growth; UN, 2008). Emerging economies are increasing consumption levels as climate change unfolds. With population growth, urbanization and economic development accelerating demand, freshwater is becoming scarcer, and the full value of water is becoming increasingly apparent. In many cities, water has to be piped in from further and further away, and acute water shortages have become the norm. Many regions of the world are reaching a point of 'water stress', where water resources can no longer support the demands of human populations (constantly competing with agriculture and industry for limited supplies). The average water use of Americans is around 600 litres a day; for Australians it is around 500 litres per day (2008). At the same time, nearly 20 per cent of the world's population lacks access to safe drinking water and 40 per cent is without adequate sanitation. Water withdrawals from rivers and lakes has doubled since 1960, according to the UN Millennium Ecosystem Assessment (MEA, 2005) – a four-year, international, scientific appraisal of the conditions and trends in the Earth's ecosystems, completed in 2005.

In the last century, many cities were built at inappropriate locations, despite a lack of adequate local water supplies. With climate change, we will see towns and cities struggling to supply drinking water in the needed quantities. For instance, Barcelona suffered serious water shortages in the summer of 2008; Las Vegas, Phoenix, Tucson and other desert cities need to pipe in water from far away dams; several towns in Australia are running out of water; e.g. Adelaide is now in constant water shortage status, as was Brisbane until the summer deluge in 2010: Australian rural communities, particularly those in the Murray Darling Basin, are under threat form the impact of drought. In South Australia, all households are obliged to install a water tank to capture rainwater, and city golf courses are only allowed to use recycled water; in China, around 400 northern cities face acute water shortages and rising salt levels caused by the overuse of water from the rivers. And the list goes on.

Increases in water efficiency, rainwater harvesting and wastewater recycling are being considered in order to reduce the water dependency of cities. New urban developments aim to be carbon neutral and 'water positive'. Access to freshwater is very much a local issue. If you save water in one part of the world, it does not reduce the issue elsewhere, but if you withdraw water and consume it, it becomes unavailable for your neighbour to use. Industry and agriculture not only need to think about how much water they use, but also how they can improve their practices to reduce water demand. To demonstrate sustainable water management and in looking at what the local freshwater situation is, and what the possible effects on close-by cities will be. Scarcity usually encourages better management of resources. Some assessment tools specify a maximum water consumption of 30 litres per day as sustainable (e.g. GreenStar's Water Calculator).

Urban infrastructure and waste water

There is now an increasing acknowledgement that urban infrastructure and large-scale engineering projects (such as canals, motorway bridges, etc.) are a major shaping force of the built environment. 'Landscape Urbanism', as coined by Charles Waldheim and James Connor, is based on this new understanding of urban topography and landscape, including the new landscapes created by landfill and material consumption. Public urban infrastructure consists of basics, such as water supply and sewerage systems, energy distribution systems and waste disposal, road networks and bridges, public transport and public parkland. Much of this infrastructure has to do with stormwater catchments, black water treatment and the safe supply of drinking water. (Cosgrove, 2000) (See: Figs. 10 and 11)

Most urban areas grow, but are unable to expand their carrying capacity or storage components of stormwater or natural river systems to handle increased flows from flooding and extreme rainfall (both likely to occur more frequently with climate change). Drought and extreme rainfall affect the quality of drinking water supplies and water security in general. The options for adaptation are: to reduce demand (lowest cost adaptation strategy – the community capacity to reduce water demand is often substantial) and/or to increase storage capacity (rainwater tanks, water reuse, or desalination). Desalination and potable

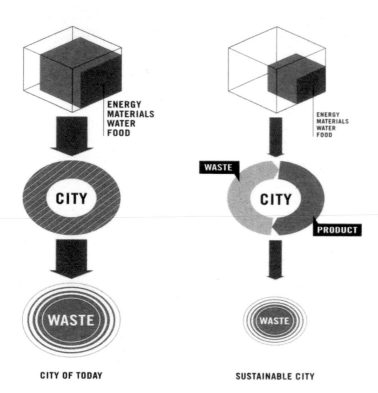

CITY OF TODAY   **SUSTAINABLE CITY**

THE METABOLISM OF CITIES

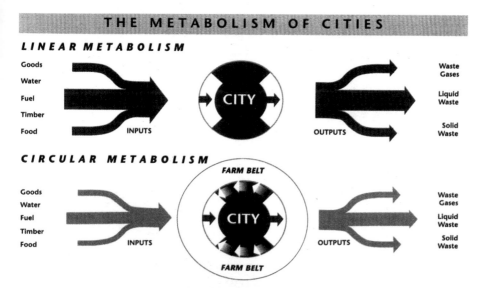

LINEAR METABOLISM

Goods		Waste Gases
Water		
Fuel	CITY	Liquid Waste
Timber		
Food	INPUTS OUTPUTS	Solid Waste

CIRCULAR METABOLISM

Goods	FARM BELT	Waste Gases
Water		
Fuel	CITY	Liquid Waste
Timber		
Food	INPUTS OUTPUTS	Solid Waste
	FARM BELT	

Innovative architects, engineers and planners are now developing new resource use strategies, based on closed loop systems thinking, to achieve a 'circular metabolism'. This means a symbiotic ecosystem, where waste is used as a resource (rather than discarded as a nuisance, disposed off as landfill), stimulating the local economy. (Diagrams: Courtesy Grimshaw Architects, 2010; top. H. Girardet, 1999; below)

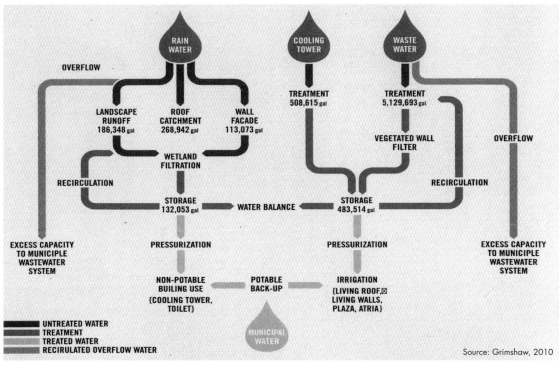

Source: Grimshaw, 2010

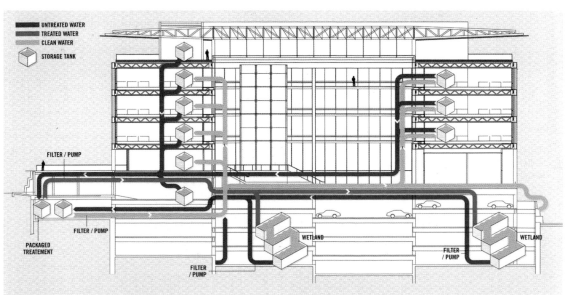

Water systems for the urban environment, based on a holistic approach to water:
Grimshaw Architects' design of the Deacero Headquarters in Monterrey, Mexico.
The project includes a strategy for using plants and landscape as the building's water
filtration system, recycling 100 per cent of the grey and black water to become a net
water producer. (Diagram/Section: Courtesy Grimshaw Architects, 2010)

reuse options require high energy consumption; these are only acceptable if this energy is provided by renewable energy sources.

The emphasis in sewage technology today is on sewage recycling rather than sewage treatment, seeing waste water as a precious resource and nutrient. Girardet points to the issue around current unsustainable practices on the large scale when it comes to water management and the need to put organic matter and nutrients back into farmland. He writes: `If we wish to create a sustainable world we cannot continue flushing nutrients from the farmland that feeds cities and sewage into the sea and polluting coastal waters in the process. (...) Instead of building treatment and disposal systems, we need to construct facilities in which nitrates, potash and phosphates contained in sewage can be extracted and used as fertilizer on farms, orchards and market gardens once again.' (Girardet, 2008)
In fact, much can be done by urban designers to better deal with the water issue. For instance, in 1993-98 all 18 buildings at the Potsdamer Platz development in Berlin were designed with greywater cycle systems, reusing purified wastewater for irrigation of the gardens, feeding it into the urban pond and using it for toilet flushing. No fresh drinking water should be used for any of these functions. In the urban design masterplan for the Australian city of Mildura, it is suggested that a `bio-filtration park' be included, with a series of constructed wetlands as a `nutrient sink' that will filter and clean the greywater to drinking quality and will act as an educational `water park' facility and biodiversity hub, becoming a sustainable eco-system in its own rights (project text, 2008).

The resilient city as *Water Catchment*
The supply of water for urban, agricultural and commercial (industrial) uses needs to be kept in balance. All urban developments built to support a growing community have consequential impacts on the land and water environments. It's now well accepted that the conventional water management approach is highly unsuited to addressing current and future sustainability issues (Butler and Maksimovic, 1999; Wong and Brown, 2009). This critique is based on the view that only sub-optimal outcomes have been achieved from the traditional compartmentalization of water supply, sewage and stormwater services, lacking a holistic approach to the entire water cycle, including issues such as groundwater supply, water quality and flooding.

Wong and Brown argue that: `urban communities are increasingly seeking to ensure resilience to future uncertainties in urban water supplies, yet change seems slow with many cities facing ongoing investment in the conventional approach. This is because transforming cities to more sustainable urban water cities, or to *Water Sensitive Cities*, requires a major overhaul of the *hydro-social contract* that underpins conventional approaches. The *hydro-social contract* is the agreement between communities, government and business on how water should be managed and supplied.' (Wong and Brown, 2009) They continue the argument by defining Water Sensitive Cities as being based on the three key pillars:
• access to a diversity of water sources, underpinned by a diversity of centralized and

decentralized infrastructure,
• provision of eco-system services for the built and natural environment and
• socio-political capital for water sensitive behaviours. (Wong and Brown, 2009)

However, changes in the water system (as with the energy grid) have long lead times and require major investment. In fact, best practice of urban water management is complex, because it requires urban water planning to protect, maintain and enhance the multiple benefits and services of a total urban water cycle. In the past, water managers have often reduced this complexity by focusing on optimizing singular isolated parts of the water cycle (e.g. focusing on supply security). *Water Sensitive Urban Design* (WSUD), as defined by Tony Wong, is based on the integration of the two key fields of 'Integrated urban water cycle planning and management' and urban design. (Wong, 2006) Until today, the *hydro-social contract* that Wong and Brown describe, is based on the promise of providing affordable and unlimited water supply, public health protection through sewage services, and drainage and flood control to support any urban expansion or urban development (which could lead to the over extraction and pollution of water resources). Similar to the energy supply mechanisms in the previous chapter, it becomes clear that with water, this *hydro-social contract* needs to be fundamentally restructured, revised and adapted to

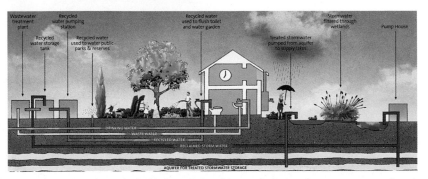

Fig. 10 a, b: Mawson Lakes (north of Adelaide, South Australia), principle diagram of water management and supply system: greywater cycle with treated wastewater requires two taps and a district-wide double piping network (greywater tap clearly separated and identified by purple coloured pipes and fittings). The greywater is pumped from the aquifer storage (Images: Courtesy Delfin Lend Lease, 2007). Adelaide has introduced a water system where reclaimed waste water is 'banked' in underground aquifers (aquifer storage) to be recovered for later use in irrigation.

overhaul the conventional, unsustainable approaches, which will influence the future urban form and infrastructure. Sustainable water management puts clean water back into
the ground rather than flushing it off-site in storm sewers or wastewater pipes. Today it's
increasingly understood that the provision of a second district-wide water supply pipeline
for non-potable water (grey, treated wastewater) is a fundamental basis for preserving
future opportunities for accessing recycled water. Another emerging issue is that of rehabilitation of degraded urban waterways and renewal of the aged water infrastructure. In
Australian urban developments, water sensitive initiatives are progressing rapidly and are
becoming planning standards. They are:

- Treated wastewater is reticulated to households for non-potable use, and after house
  holds have reused the treated wastewater, it can be made available for irrigation of
  gardens and urban agriculture.
- Minimized potable water use for non-potable uses; significant reduction in the volume
  of wastewater discharged into the municipal system.
- Harvested roof water (collected rainwater from roof run-off) is used for toilet flushing,
  laundry and hot water systems.
- Urban stormwater is harnessed, collected and treated, via bio-swales, bio-retention systems and
  constructed wetlands, lakes (detention ponds), and rain gardens, prior to its discharge or reuse.
- Bio-swales (naturalized swales) in lieu of costly storm sewers.
- Natural landscaping using native plants and wetland grasses.
- Permeable paving instead of conventional asphalt for roads, driveways and parking
  lots, designed to naturally cleanse and infiltrate site run-off.
- Generally, understanding wastewater as a valuable resource and nutrient.

For all urban developments, it is increasingly important to use pervious pavement to reduce
stormwater run-off, and to design drought-tolerant, water-efficient landscapes to reduce irrigation needs and potable water consumption. Recent research found that higher-density developments generate less stormwater run-off per household at all scales: with more dense and compact development, run-off rates per household decrease, while denser developments produce
less run-off and less impervious cover than low-density (suburban) developments. (Farr, 2008)
For instance in Singapore, we can see the combination of clever strategies to ensure water security, including: urban stormwater harvesting and retention in ponds fed by swales from roads
and buildings; recycled wastewater schemes; the construction of the Sing Spring Desalination
Plant and the Marina Barrage Waterworks project (converting Marina Bay into a freshwater
reservoir supplied by urbanized catchments). Huge water reservoirs, such as the MacRitchie
Reservoir, have been built to ensure water supply to the ever growing population of Singapore
is secured beyond the water supply contracts it has with neighbouring Malaysia.

Wastewater recycling
A new generation of compact, decentralized sewage treatment plants produces reusable
water by recycling wastewater, using several cleaning stages. After filtering out coarse
material, wastewater flows to a biological reactor, where anaerobic bacteria are added

to digest the organic matter to form biogas, which is then separated and used as an energy carrier. The wastewater then continues to flow to a membrane bio-reactor, where remaining impurities are digested by fine bubbles of air before an ultra-filtration step takes place to remove fine particles. Finally, the treated water flows through an ultraviolet light reactor to eliminate bacteria and viruses, ensuring it is safe for re-use in irrigation, district cooling, car washing, or for household supplies. These new systems consume 50 per cent less energy and produce 65 per cent less sludge compared with traditional sewage treatment systems. The resulting sludge can be treated on site to produce odourless compost.

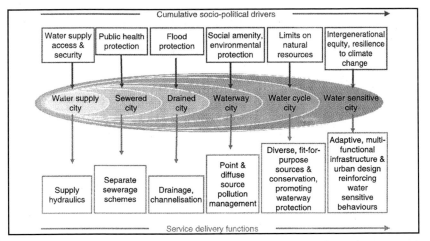

Fig. 11: The urban water management transitions framework (after Brown). This transition framework presents a typology of 6 different states that cities transition through when pursuing change towards more sustainable water management, towards the *Water Sensitive City*. (Brown, 2009) To bring water quality up to drinking-quality standards requires it to go through a series of treatment processes that ensures harmful bacteria and viruses are eliminated.

Fig. 12: Water security and supply is critical to all cities. The fall of Fatehpur Sikri, the famous ghost town in Rajastan, India, close to Agra, is a valid example of the limits to the urban development of new cities. The royal city was constructed by the Mughal emperor Akbar in 1570, and served as the empire's capital from 1571 until 1585, when it was finally abandoned. Fatehpur Sikri had a population of estimated 30,000 people and the city is located on top of a rocky hill. After 15 years, the Mogul finally gave up the new town due to the lack of water supply and irresolvable difficulties in guaranteeing the supply water to all residents. Understanding the site and its natural resources (as well as its limits) at the beginning of each project is essential for any masterplanning.

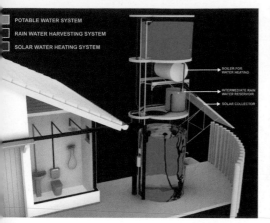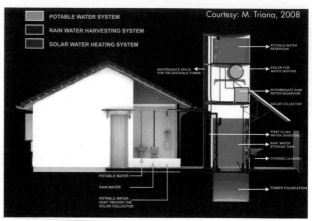

Fig. 13 a/b: An innovative design proposal from Brazil to improve water and electricity use in the suburbs. A high-tech tower – the so-called `Solar water heating and rainwater tower' – which can be placed in any garden or backyard to supply a solar hot water system, rainwater harvesting and potable water filtration. This is an innovative and economical solution to a very common problem related to low-income family housing. Due to the lack of public infrastructure, residents do not always have ready access to drinking water, sewage systems and energy supply. The most serious shortcoming is potable and hot water supply. Basic needs are covered by this tower, which provides a rainwater harvesting system, potable water storage tank and a solar water heating device, all integrated into one structure. The tower itself is composed of prefabricated rings made of ferro-cement. The modular system, adaptable to different needs and local situations, can be incorporated in new houses as well as existing ones, allowing for energy-efficiency and rational water use. Overall this tower can have a substantial impact on the daily living conditions of poor families. Brazil has a housing deficit of 7 million residences and a large proportion of those impacted by the housing shortage are low income families, people deprived of basic water, sewage and energy services. In Brazil, the main residential uses of electricity are for refrigeration, water heating, air conditioning and lighting. Water heating accounts for an average of 24 per cent of energy consumption. (Images: Courtesy Holcim Awards, 2008. Designer: Maria Triana, Brazil) www.holcimawards.org

URBAN FARMING AND GREEN ROOFTOPS

Urban farming: green roofs and productive landscapes instead of global food transport

In 1909, Raymond Unwin advocated in his book `Town Planning in Practice', a limit to the size of developments and the creation of greenbelts around cities, for recreation and local food production. However, in the 20th century, food production has become industrialized and globalized to an extent that fresh produce travels huge distances and wastes a lot of energy. A significant proportion of the food consumed by a city's population could be produced locally within the city, through the cultivation of small-scale, high-intensity urban agriculture, thus cutting out the need for food to be transported around the world. The issue of `food miles' is significant. Several researchers have found that, in the developed world, food typically travels, from field to plate, an average of 3,000 km. Transporting and processing food, therefore, consumes a disproportionate amount of energy. The increase in meat consumption has contributed to this unsustainable phenomenon and has led to deforestation (to gain new farmland to support meat production). In many cases, far more energy has gone into the food than it actually contains.

Local food production needs to be re-integrated into districts and neighbourhoods, for instance through community-based food systems, urban orchards and rooftop gardens. Community gardens, a grouping of garden plots available for small-scale cultivation and urban agriculture, are a great asset in any neighbourhood.

With all these unsustainable behaviours, we have reached the limits of global food supplies and now need to source food locally again. Urban agriculture and cultivation can help to deliver a series of advantages, such as:

- contributing to food security, improving self-sufficiency and economic development of cities,
- establishing reliable local food supply from within the city, for private consumption or for sale in the markets,
- reducing CO_2 emissions from reducing global food transport ('food miles') and the reduced need for cooling,
- supporting poverty reduction by improving nutrition and creating local jobs,
- providing a major income source and food supply to poor neighbourhoods,
- increasing biodiversity in urban community gardens and on green roofs,
- taking pressure off the city's rural hinterland and peri-urban farmland,
- producing organic food, using less water and chemical fertilizers compared to agricultural practice on large farms,
- supporting mitigation for urban heat island effect through an improved micro-climate,
- making efficient use of left-over public spaces, vacant lots and otherwise derelict inner city land,
- providing places for social interaction and community identity, with educational initiatives around gardening and
- improving overall consumption cycles (composting of organic waste, etc.).

For every eco-city masterplan it is essential to set aside sufficient land for urban farming and green space within the city. We can calculate the ratio of public green space to the number of inhabitants.

With simplistic urbanization we have lost the once healthy association with our food and its place of growth. Today, there still seems to be a lack of understanding among planners of the many benefits of urban farming, ignoring the potential to turn cities into productive (instead of consumptive) urban landscapes. Recently, green design solutions have particularly focused on two directions: on the one hand, active power solutions rather than passive design, and on the other hand, a greater emphasis on nature, biodiversity and food supply. The latter ideas are embodied in green roofs, or 'living roofs', which flourish worldwide. Today, most cities have established policies on the principle that removal of potential green area at ground level should be offset by planting the equivalent area at roof level. In many cities, green roofs have become a mandatory requirement for planning approval. While green roofs can help in partially off-setting the footprint of a new building, green roofs deliver various other advantages, such as giving more low energy demand space in the building below, an improved micro-climate, and a productive urban landscape emerging within the city, which can help to grow flowers, but also tomatoes, carrots, cucumbers and lettuce. The typical Australian

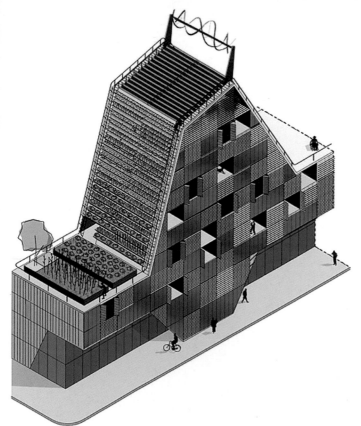

Urban farming

Designing the 'Carrot City': with finite crop-land to feed a growing global population, concepts are now being developed that will build vertical farms. For instance, in Singapore, a city state with over 4.6 million people, 95 per cent of all vegetables consumed are imported. While this is an extreme case, the food transport related to this unsustainable supply chain produces over 28,000 tonnes of CO_2 emissions per year. Singapore's many flat roofs and plentyful sunshine, both largely unused, would be ideal for the introduction of lightweight hydroponic structures on flat roofs, to grow food locally. A recent study at NUS has shown that, for instance, the Tampines Estate in East Singapore (which is a 500 ha housing district with around a 90 ha building footprint) has around 50 ha unused rooftop area, that could immediately be turned into a productive landscape for urban farming without using more land. Rotating hydroponic-farming systems give the plants the precise amount of light and nutrients they need, while vertical stacking enables the use of far less water than conventional farming.

This project for downtown Dallas grows vegetables and generates energy (building-integrated wind turbines and PV solar). Designed by Atelier Data & MOOV (Lisbon) in 2009, the aim was to create a prototype for a sustainable urban community with a focus on the city block. The programme is a mix of residential, commercial and wellness functions, and incorporates parking for 10 car-sharing vehicles. See also: www.urbanrevision.com

Courtesy: R. Rogers, 2008

Courtesy: P. Newman, 2009

The high energy cost of food

Food travels on average from field to plate a distance of 3,000 km. There is also a high energy cost involved in transporting and cooling food. Growing food locally on building roofs would help to reduce this cost, by turning the districts into productive urban landscapes. Small-scale high-intensity urban farming will become (again) an important part of city life. (Top diagram: Courtesy R. Rogers, 2009. Photo: P. Newman).

food basket has travelled in the order of 7,000 km to get to our stores, and up to 65 per cent of Australia's water consumption is food related.[10]   Eco-districts include agricultural fields, from allotment and community gardens, to food boulevards, to urban neighbourhood farms, which reuse nutrients from the urban metabolism, in form of *nutrient recycling*.

All these reasons explain why urban agriculture and gardening is now increasingly seen as an important part of the urban economy and eco-system. In fact, governments in China, Mexico and Cuba have always maintained a high proportion of urban farming and have protected the activity against urbanization. Cuba in particular has become a much admired example of organic urban farming, and orchards with zero-transportation costs – originally triggered by the US trade embargo – today provide employment in Havana for almost 120,000 people. In the 20th century, architect Frank Lloyd Wright and urban planner Kisho Kurokawa took Ebenezer Howard's ideas a step further and developed the idea of the `agricultural city', based on principles of urban agriculture and food self-sufficiency, with allotment and community gardens inside the city. For every eco-city masterplan, it is essential to set aside land for urban farming or the replanting of inner-city orchards within the city structure, planning for CO_2-negative biospheres.

In Singapore, a city state with over 4.5 million people, almost 90 per cent of all vegetables consumed are imported. Alone, the food transport related to this practice produces over 30,000 tonnes of CO_2 emissions per year. Singapore's many flat roofs and plentiful sunshine, both unused for most of the time, would be an ideal starting point for the introduction of lightweight hydroponics structures to grow food locally. In fact, hydroponic (soil-less) vegetable cultivation in greenhouses is now strongly supported by the city state. A recent study on rooftop farming in urban centres at the National University of Singapore (NUS) has shown that in the Singapore Tampines Estate (a 500 ha housing district with around 90 ha building footprint) there are over 50 ha of unused rooftop that could immediately be turned into a productive landscape for intensive urban farming, and various studies are now under way looking at its feasibility. The rooftops of Singapore's public housing estates are particularly suitable to large-scale lightweight food crop cultivation. Lim notes: `with current local vegetable production meeting only 5 per cent of Singapore's present-day needs, the prospect of rooftop farming merits serious consideration. Implemented nationwide, building-integrated agriculture could result in a 700 per cent increase in domestic vegetable production, satisfying domestic demand by 35 per cent. Reducing food imports would decrease Singapore's carbon footprint by 9,052 tones of emissions annually.' (Lim, 2009) Given its super-efficient transport network, Singapore appears to be, in general, a city with an advantageous population density and distribution (density is not as intense as in Hong Kong, not as inefficient as in Los Angeles). The poly-centric city state offers its residents quick access to nature as well as to any of its 3 city centres. The Singaporean Government successfully legislated in 2009 for all new buildings of more than 2,000 sq m, and all government buildings, to meet excellent standards of certification on its assessment tool `Green Mark', using floor allowances as incentives for developers.

Cities are resource-intensive systems. By 2030, we will need to produce 50 per cent more energy and 30 per cent more food on less land, with less water and fewer pesticides, using less material.

Urban gardens: re-integrating greenery and maintaining biodiversity

Currently, there is much research being done into ways of how to better incorporate land-scape as part of urban design, to re-integrate `green-ness' into buildings (especially by architects MVRDV, West 8, Ken Yeang, and by horti-culturalist Patrick Blanc), in other words, solutions on how to achieve a closer symbiosis between the building and nature. Landscape can be understood as the `urban edge, where methods of water management and main-tenance of biodiversity is crucial'. (Johnson, 2000) In recent years, we have seen excit-ing examples of developments of new public landscapes combining with increased urban density, and new recreational landscapes utilizing derelict urban (brownfield) sites. Despite increased densities, the city must still contain small urban gardens for recreationand food supply, in combination with green roofs to collect rainwater for irrigation of those gardens.

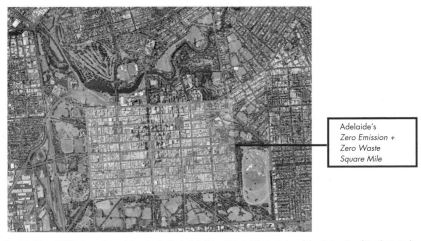

Adelaide's
Zero Emission +
Zero Waste
Square Mile

Fig. 14: Since 2010, the author advises South Australia's `Zero-Waste SA Centre' and the University of South Australia in Adelaide. The vision of a `Solar City Centre: zero-emission/zero-waste Adelaide CBD', with a decarbonization plan, is being developed, with the aim of making Adelaide the first truly sustainable city in Australia. Targeting the central business district, the initiative aims to reduce carbon emissions by 100 per cent by 2030, through retrofitting the existing CBD and densifying it with deep green buildings.

Adelaide CBD has a compact layout, with the wider metropolitan region of Adelaide having around 1.2 million people. Given the city's all year round strong solar radiation of about 210 kWh/ sq m/year (approximately double that of London), a solar-powered central business district would be particularly appropriate and achievable. The vision suggests turning the CBD district into a solar powerstation, using 30 per cent of the green belt that rings the CBD for urban farm-ing; the soil can be kept fertile by composted organic matter from the city centre. Fuel-burning cars would be parked outside the CBD in `solar garages' with access to any part in the city taking no more than five minutes on a free bus loop (electric or hydrogen fuel-cell-powered), or free light railway. The whole urban environment inside the CBD-box would be characterized by good air-quality and minimal noise pollution, thus allowing all buildings to be naturally ventilated. It was estimated that population of the solar district would quickly grow from the current 20,000 to over 30,000 as people moved back into the central district to live in an improved environment and close to their workplaces, cafes and museums. (Aerial photo: courtesy Google Earth, 2010)

Even formerly contaminated sites and rubbish dumps have been successfully re-naturalized and turned into public parkland (e.g. a new park at *Port Forum* in Barcelona; FOA, 2006). In combination with urban parks and farming, the installation of rainwater tanks and the development of more effective recycling water programmes (greywater usage), recycled sewage, and the ability to harvest the stormwater runoff, all need to be part of the overall planning strategy.

Fig. 15: The global demand for food crops is projected to grow by 70 to 85 per cent between 2000 and 2050 (Millennium Ecosystem Assessment, 2005). Intensive small-scale inner-city agriculture (urban farming) can activate unused, disregarded spaces in the city to grow food locally. Former industrial sites and disused lots are being transformed to community gardens. Open space and community gardens are vital for people living in denser apartment developments. (Image: Courtesy HOK, 2009)

It is generally important to ensure the 'hard' appearance of new developments is lessened by soft landscaping, tree planting and vegetation. Innovative ideas of vertical landscaping and the re-creation of ground conditions to roof gardens ('cool roofs' and roof gardens) are now being applied by many designers. 'Green Walls' have recently emerged as another way to integrate greenery back into urban development. One innovative horticulturist is Frenchman Patrick Blanc. (See: www.verticalgardenpatrickblanc.com) Blanc's approach to other modular systems is a creative response to the medium and raises the question of whether it is time to broaden the discussion to look at how horticultural expertise can fit into new models of urban planning and sustainable cities. (Yeang, 2009)

However, Blanc's *Vertical Garden* work has also some critics. For instance, English botanist Mark Cox points out: 'given that Patrick Blanc's systems seem to need considerable maintenance, nutrient feed and large volumes of cycled water, it's fair to question whether this work is installation art, rather than a truly green and sustainable addition to the urban and architectural armoury; it has sometimes even been seen as a 'camouflage' to get planning permission for controversial schemes. Other criticism is that these *green wall* projects are suitable only for temperate climates, or indoors, as unsuitable for cites in cold climates such as Canada or Sweden, or in hot countries such as Australia and the Middle East.' (Cox, 2010) (See: Fig. 16)

The speed of the current loss of ecosystem and biodiversity (disappearing animal and plant species) is at an alarming rate.

Fig. 16: Vertical garden on a fire wall: the green wall at Caixa Forum Museum, Madrid (Spain), by botanist Patrick Blanc. A lush wall garden covers 460 sqm, with 15,000 plants of 250 species (Photo: Image Sharing Commons). Urban concepts that satify the need for inner-city greenery, and incorporate natural ecosystems into urban areas, are increasingly in demand. New York-based architect Emilio Ambasz has developed sensitive concepts, where buildings are completely integrated into the landscape. See: www.emilioambaszandassociates.com

So which eco-districts or neighbourhoods have been setting new bechmarks?

From the many cases worldwide (some mentioned already in Chapter 1), the following built eco-districts stand out for adopting very diffeent approaches in regard to systems integration and leadership by city councils, setting new benchmarks:

• Kronsberg Green District, Hannover (Germany): a large eco-district on greenfield.
• BedZED, Sutton, South London (UK): an urban block as infill on brownfield.
• Ekostaden Augustenborg, Malmö (Sweden): urban regeneration of a neighbourhood in decline.
• Hammarby Sjöstad, Stockholm (Sweden): a new waterfront eco-district on brownfield.
• Neu-Oerlikon, Zurich (Switzerland): a new mixed-use urban quarter.
• Chorlton Park Development, Manchester (UK): once heavily contaminated land on the outskirts of Manchester.
• SolarCity, Linz-Pichling (Austria): a large eco-district on greenfield.
• Borneo Sporenburg, Amsterdam (The Netherlands): a high-density residential island in the former docklands area of Amsterdam.
• GWL District, Amsterdam (The Netherlands): the revitalization of a brownfield site.
• Christie Walk, Adelaide (Australia): an inner-city infill and urban revitalization project.
• Vauban, Freiburg (Germany): an eco-district on a brownfield site, with strong community involvelment.
• Vikki District, Helsinki (Finland): a self-contained green district.
• Dockside Green, Victoria, British Columbia (Canada): a new waterfront eco-district.

Following are the different highlights of three selected projects: Kronsberg, BedZED and Hammarby Sjöstad urban developments, each an important low-to-no-carbon city district.

Kronsberg Green District, Hannover (Germany), 1990 - 2003

Initiated through the EXPO 2000 World Exposition, in the period of just 30 months almost

3,000 homes were built to an exceptionally high ecological standard and above average comfort levels. This large eco-district on a greenfield site (when completed with 6,000 units in total) is the result of a decade-long planning process, driven by the City of Hannover municipality. It's a transit-oriented, mixed-income district which achieved a 75 per cent reduction in CO_2 emissions, compared with conventional developments. This demonstration project of the EXPO 2000 has clearly defined sections for residential and mixed-use usage, creating a `24-hour community'. The reasonable density of over 80 dwellings per hectare is high enough to support a new light railway system with three stations in Kronsberg. These stations are located so that every resident can reach a station in less than 600 metres walking distance. Car usage is discouraged by a reduced number of parking spaces and the main arterial road runs along the edge of the development. Bike paths are provided throughout the district.

The principle aim in developing the new city district was optimised planning and construction for sustainability at all levels. Ecological aims were set within a regulatory framework of compact urban planning concepts, environmentally responsible transport, high quality open space planning, environmentally sound energy supply systems, sparing use of natural resources and raising public awareness. As the City of Hannover owned most of the building plots in the Kronsberg development area, it could exert a strong influence from overall master-planning (to apply the goals of *Agenda 21*), to monitoring and supervision of all construction projects. By 2006 almost 3,300 dwellings had been built, and the final plan foresees a total of 6,000 homes for 15,000 people by 2020. This is a total of 250,000 sqm residential floor space. 90 per cent of all units are multi-storey apartment buildings, 10 per cent (over 300 units) are terraced houses, so-called townhouses). Over 40 different architectural and landscape practices have been involved in the design of the buildings. Every building meets strict green guidelines, called the `Kronsberg Standard': these `Passivhaus' standards[11] ensure high insulation and an energy consumption of max. 15 kWh / sqm p.a. Solar and wind turbines are integrated in the district and there is compulsory connection to the highly efficient a co-generation district heating network. (Moenninghoff, 2005) Other measures include:

- over 60 per cent social (affordable) housing, mostly in 3-storey row houses, with subsidies for developers,
- all buildings with superinsulation and high performance glazing; all houses built to an ultra-low energy consumption standard,
- rainwater collection and water retention ponds; water-sensitive landscaping which allows rainwater to be absorbed slowly into the ground,
- on-site composting facilities and
- high-frequency light railway and buses; only 0.8 parking spaces per dwelling.

The good experience achieved at Kronsberg has led to a resolution by Hannover City Council to extend the standards tested there to the entire city area. These are now implemented in several other projects, and a large scale programme has started to sustainable retrofit the existing housing stock. Numerous instruments and technologies incorporated in the `Kronsberg Standard' can be transferred without much modification to other local authorities, and these have already become common practice in some cities in Germany.

The standards are even transferable and applicable to the situation of many European cities and communities. More information at: www.hannover.de

Fig. 17 a, b: The Kronsberg site plan, which shows medium-density perimeter block layouts, appropriate for the creation of new suburban districts of a residential density of around 80 dwellings per hectare. (Image: courtesy City of Hannover)

BedZED development, Sutton, South London (UK), 1996 - 2002

This relatively small urban infill project (in total 82 units; 20 per cent as affordable, social housing[12]) on a brownfield site, the site of a former sewage works in Hackbridge, in the Borough of Sutton, is an experimental development aiming for carbon-neutrality. *BedZed* sits like an island in the south London suburb of Beddington (*BedZED* stands for Beddington Zero Energy Development). It's a mixed housing/office development that established a number of environmental benchmarks. It can be seen as a useful template for larger urban projects to create carbon neutral eco-communities. The achievement of carbon-neutral status relies heavily on lifestyle factors, and BedZED incorporates several strategies designed to foster a community with a sustainable conscience and green behaviour. (Dunster, 2008) The energy component of BedZED is, what I think, the most compelling aspect of the project, aiming for 100 per cent renewable energy. A combination of passive measures and active technologies are used to achieve carbon neutral status. There are a lot of technological pathways to achieve zero net energy/carbon buildings. What BedZED shows us, is that radically more sustainable buildings are possible, and within reach now, not some indeterminate time in the future. Here is a list of the environmental specifications for the project; the BedZED project highlights include:

> • Living + working units (integrated workspaces) offer residents a chance to minimize the need to travel and eliminate the morning commute (the development incorporates 2,500 sqm office space; in average 80 sqm office per residential unit). The idea is to create both employment and housing on the same compact plan footprint, in one single cross section (which has resulted in deep plans).
> • A compact development with 3-storey living + working townhouses and a reasonable residential density of over 80 to 120 dwellings per hectare.

Other features of BedZED include:

- Car-sharing programme, which uses solar panels to charge a car pool of 40 electric vehicles.
- There is a 0.5 reduced number of car parking spaces on site. Perimeter parking creates a pedestrian-friendly car-free block.
- A series of community and shared facilities are in walking distance, e.g. bike storage and sports facilities.
- Shared garden spaces for local food production. Roof gardens have 300 mm of topsoil and can be planted as gardens or vegetable patches; these are also used for rainwater harvesting for landscape irrigation.
- Air-tight building envelopes with 300 mm insulation: hyper-insulated walls, using masonry (brick and concrete) walls, typical of European residential construction.
- Passive design principles: passive solar heating, with a solar atrium sitting on the south side, using triple glazing with a high solar heat gain character, allowing it to heat up dramatically. Once this atrium has warmed up toward the end of the day, the residents open an inner set of highly insulated triple paned doors to allow the heat into the unit. This solar heating provides the majority of the required heating for the units.
- Construction materials were sourced from within a 50 km radius, and 15 per cent of materials were recycled (recycled steel and bricks; the construction is made of reclaimed steel and precast concrete floor planks).
- The use of 100 per cent on-site generated renewable energy (from 700 sqm building-integrated PV solar, woodchips and biomass); an electric micro-generation sufficient to power both house and car.
- A large district energy system, using a biomass power plant and woodchip-fired CHP system. On-site composting and waste recycling.
- Passive design principles are applied, such as solar heat gain in winter.

Extensive passive use of solar radiation is possible at a glazing fraction of around 40 to 50 per cent for the sun-facing facade. A larger proportion of window area brings to danger of overheating in summer. More information at: www.zedfactory.com

Courtesy: B. Dunster, 2007

Fig. 18 a, b: The BedZED (Beddington Zero Emission Development) project in Sutton, south of London; already completed in 2002, it is still the UK's largest mixed-use, mixed-tenure carbon-neutral development. A prototype development that is a useful template for larger urban developments. It consists of 82 units in 8 buildings, all 3-storey walk-up terrace houses with small private gardens. (Images: courtesy Bill Dunster, ZEDfactory)

Hammarby Sjöstad, Stockholm, and Ekostaden Augustenborg, Malmö (both in Sweden), 2000–ongoing

Hammarby Sjöstad is a new district in the south of Stockholm, based on a masterplan by the City Planning Department. Once completed, this new 200 hectare eco-district will comprise 9,000 apartments, housing a population of 20,000 people, with 200,000 sqm of commercial floor space, attracting a further 10,000 people to work in the area. Approximately half of the total area has been developed to date and it is anticipated that the final scheme will be completed by 2015. The concept for a new district in this location was born in the early 1990s. At that time, the City of Stockholm had developed a plan for development on the north side of the harbour, and this stimulated interest for a more strategic plan for the whole area around Hammarby Lake. Hammarby Sjöstad is built on former industrial brownfield land located on the south side of Hammarby Lake, to the south of the city centre, which has historically formed the natural border to the inner city area of Stockholm. Water is the central focus for the whole development, aiming to transform an old port and industrial area into a modern city district. Impetus was gained for development and infrastructure in the area when plans for Stockholm's bid for the 2004 Olympic Games were being prepared. The core area of Hammarby Sjöstad was envisaged as an Olympic Village, with a strong emphasis on environmental sustainability, which was promoted as one of Stockholm's unique selling points as an Olympic city. Although the bid was unsuccessful, development was already underway and the momentum for change had been established.

Environmental improvements have transformed Augustenborg in Malmö from a neighbourhood in decline to a model of an environmentally adapted urban area. The area is once again seen as an attractive place to live and work. The Augustenborg district was built in the 1950s and was initially considered a highly successful mixture of housing, employment and social facilities. By the 1970s, the 32 hectares neighbourhood was falling into decline. Upgrades to the thermal insulation of the housing estate, with external metal cladding and insulation, were less effective than planned, resulting in damp problems and poor external appearance. Annual flooding from the outdated sewage system led to further problems. The estate suffered a spiral of decline as more people moved out, flats remained unoccupied and the residual population became marginalised with a high level of unemployment. Something had to be done. In the early 1990s the city council set out to improve the area by working with the local housing association and residents. This initial partnership led to the wide-ranging urban regeneration project known as Ekostaden Augustenborg, starting in 1998. The initial focus of the project was on innovative environmental improvements, focusing on water management, resolving the flooding, waste management, and maximizing biodiversity. The project has also introduced a wide range of social concepts, such as a community car pool and an after-school youth club. The estate management company offers employment opportunities to local young adults. The neighbourhood is now once again a thriving place with reduced turnover of tenancies and without long-term vacant properties. More information at: www.hammarbysjostad.se

Fig. 19 a, b: The Hammarby Sjöstad eco-district in the south of Stockholm has reactivated the waterfront. Once completed in 2015, it will consist of 9,000 apartments, housing a population of 20,000 people, with workplaces for 10,000 people. (Photos: Courtesy GlashusEtt, Stockholm,2008)

Residents in these three case study developments produce only about 4 tonnes CO_2 p.a. (instead the typical 12 to 15 tonnes p.a., common for conventional homes in Europe). These cases clearly demonstrate the feasibility of delivering high-quality housing for the lowest possible carbon footprint.

Energy-effciency in the building sector alone could deliver savings of 30 to 35 per cent.   *ASBEC, 2008*

A new planning paradigm that understands the city as social-ecological system

These large-scale demonstration projects contributed strongly to the further development of new standards and benchmarks for eco-districts, but more empirical and quantitative analysis of different patterns of urban densification and transformation is still needed. The cases show that political leadership within city council is essential, as well as a renewed understanding of the potential of urban design to be a way to reshape the city's social-ecological system. Du Plessis notes that 'the idea of the city as a complex system has been around for at least as long as systems thinking. However, the exact nature of social-ecological systems (SESs), or what it is that differentiates SESs from other types of ecological systems, is still open to debate and further research.' (Du Plessis, 2008)

When analysing these three cases (Kronsberg, BedZED, Hammarby Sjöstad), it becomes obvious that the possibility to influence the relationship between transport, density and urban land use is crucial. As discussed in Chapter 1, low density increases car dependency and leads to unsustainable development, where people are forced to constantly commute between the places where they live and where they work or gather. In addition, reducing the need for travel in cities, by creating more compact eco-districts, and applying the whole range of passive design principles are the 'low-hanging fruit' in urban design. Urban planners need to realize that emission reductions have to begin in the re-design of cities, and

Solar thermal collector		Heat transfer	Collector temperature	Application	
Air collector		Air	40-60°C	Air-conditioning only (AHU's)	20°C
Flat plate collector		Water, Water-Glycol	70-90°C	Air-conditioning, slab cooling (Single effect chillers)	15°C
Evacuated tube collector		Water, Water-Glycol	90-120°C	Air-conditioning, slab cooling (Single effect chillers)	0°C
Parabolic trough collector		Thermal oil, Water	120-220°C	Refrigeration, air-conditioning, slab cooling (Double effect chillers)	-20°C

Fig. 20: Using the sun to cool buildings: The next generation of buildings in hot climates will be cooled by solar cooling technology. Different collectors will deliver cooling in different temperature ranges. (Source: P. Kohlenbach, Solem Consulting, 2010) Solar energy is well suited to absorption cooling, because when solar radiation is high, cooling requirements are also high.

that the way we deal with urban growth will have to be reconsidered. New models for retrofitting existing districts are needed. When interviewing experienced planners, one of the reoccurring insights is, that there is no alternative than to move towards a low-carbon future, to become an advocate for the design of social-ecological systems that are part of a low-carbon world, with all new buildings to be carbon-neutral in their energy use by 2020. Eco-districts, such as the cases mentioned before, are clearly the most compelling and effective option for our future and for preventing the irreversible effects of climate change. (Mayer, 2009)

In conclusion, we can say that the *Sustainable City* consists of green districts that are:

• between 3 to 8 storeys high (not less than 3-storey high buildings, no high-rise buildings), made of urban blocks with green roofs and quiet, green courtyards,
• highly mixed-use, with a strong focus on public transport,
• support over 3,000 (up to 6,000) people per sq km, with over 80 dwellings per hectare and a minimum population density of 130 persons per hectare (for US-planners: over 30 dwellings per acre developed land area[13]), located on inner-city brownfield sites,
• have high densities and consist of compact building typologies, in the form of green TODs and eco-districts at transit nodes and along transit corridors,
• have highly-efficient public transport, used for 50 per cent of all trips, which allows a reduction of car ownership in the sustainable city of less than 400 cars per 1,000 residents,
• have walkable distances to avoid car-dependent situations, with over 25 per cent of all trips done by cycling or walking and
• have an energy mix with at least 50 per cent of all energy generated from renewable energy sources.

Courtesy: Cobe, 2010

Courtesy: K. Yeang, 2009

The eco-masterplanning approach, as developed by Ken Yeang, is based on bio-integration for the four infrastructure layers: 'The green eco-infrastructure, the grey engineering infrastructure, the blue water management infrastructure, and the human infrastructure of buildings.' (Yeang, 2009). (Image: Ken Yeang's Zorlu Eco-City Master-plan for Istanbul, Turkey; 2008)

Example for typical unsustainable practice: long supply chain in the construction industry

Stone ordered and cut in Brazil   Stone polished in China   Stone is cladding high-rise in Sydney

shipped to China   **shipped to Australia**

A new generation of eco-districts emerging

Left below: Nordhavnen Green District, Copenhagen (Denmark), currently under construction. During the course of the next 30 years, Nordhavnen (the former commercial harbour area) will become the new sustainable city district of Copenhagen, providing for up to 40,000 residents and the same amount of workplaces. The waterfront and new green belts provide many possibilities for distinctive spaces and an active urban lifestyle. At the same time, mixed ownership and mixed functions will contribute to a diverse city district. The infrastructure is based on the principle of the `5 minute city'. All functions, such as public transport, green spaces, living and working facilities, public institutions and commercial activities, will be located within a short walking and cycling radius. An elevated metro and a `super bike lane' will create a `green loop'. Cobe Architects & Sleth are involved as planners of the Hordholmene Urban Delta, suggesting an energy supply system based on geothermal and wind energy, as well as on energy extracted from sea lettuce. www.nordhavnen.dk (images: courtesy Cobe, 2009)

Below right: Solar District Schlierberg and Vauban Solar City, Freiburg (Germany), both completed.[14] These adjacent districts provide multi-apartment living for 6,000 residents, reusing the brownfield site of a former military base.

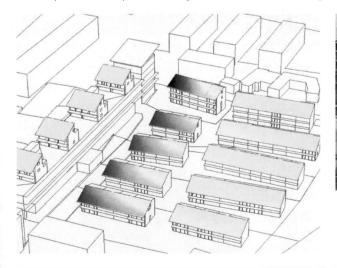

Top: The typical unsustainable supply chain in the construction industry; transporting construction materials, such as natural stone, around the globe. We will soon see a move towards locally-resourced materials. Below: New eco-districts, such as Vauban and Nordhavnen, are acting as a testbed for green innovations. Based on the `One Planet Living' concept, societies in the developed world will need to dramatically reduce their carbon footprint.

The future energy mix: challenges and solutions for a well-balanced combination of energy sources

We have already discussed the innovative technologies that are profoundly changing the urban infrastructure and transforming the way we will design, build and operate cities in the future. In the previous chapter, I reflected on principles of how to best integrate ecologically sustainable development (ESD) into urban design. I pointed out why the most significant environmental challenge of our time is the excessive fossil fuel dependency of cities and their growing demand for energy.

We looked at the fundamental principles of how to shape our cities and how to cohesively integrate energy and transport systems, waste and water management, passive and active design strategies, landscape and urban farming, into a contemporary urban design solution, leading to an improved environmental performance. Research in sustainable urban design recommends an increased harnessing of the energies manifested in existing fabrics – through the adaptive re-use of former industrial (brownfield) sites and the upgrade and extension of existing building structures. It is less environmentally damaging to stimulate growth within the established city centre than it is to sprawl into new, formerly un-built areas. (Lehmann, 2005) Examples for the holistic application of such urban design principles

Pursuing Technological Innovation:
From Smart Grids, to Solar Cooling, to Multi-Storey Timber Construction

are the proposals for the Australian city of Newcastle, presented in Chapter 3: the `Living City Campus', `Port City' and `Green Corridor' projects. The importance of this paradigm shift is particularly pressing for integration of sustainability principles in the urbanization of South East Asian countries and the general need for more sustainable city development in the region, as rapid urban growth of developing cities has, in the past, frequently been poorly managed. This subject will be discussed in Chapter 4. The following part of Chapter 2 will look at the use of prefabrication and timber for highly energy-efficient buildings.

Resistance to lifestyle change and patterns of behaviour

Attitudinal and behavioural changes are hard to introduce. But if people living in the developed world do not make changes to their carbon-intensive lifestyles, their children may face a dark future. Scientists have warned for years that if humanity continues with `business as usual' policies, such as burning large amounts of fossil fuels, global temperatures will rise over 5 to 6 degrees Celsius and trigger catastrophic changes to weather patterns, sea levels and biodiversity, with millions of people being displaced by droughts and rising sea levels.

A major change of our carbon-intensive lifestyles and a shift in attitude of both building designers and users are prerequisites; for instance, to improve a building's energy performance requires most of the time different operation modes and a different building management. However, a recent survey, conducted by the international research organization *YouGov* shows that while overall awareness of climate change was high, people were still resistant to any rise in the cost of living. Almost three-fifths of US residents are reluctant to pay higher prices for electricity and petrol to help combat climate change. (Survey: You-Gov, 2010) In regard to this, Nicholas Stern, who in 2006 authored the most comprehensive report on the economics of climate change, commented: 'The only way we can have a good discussion is if we lay out what the consequences are of carrying on the way we have been carrying on, and to ask people to imagine the lives of their children. The cost of doing nothing is really very high indeed. It is almost too high to express economically.' (Stern, 2010) While UNESCO and many other institutions have launched a series of programmes for environmental education in schools and private households, raising the awareness of students and parents, it seems that behavioural barriers still remain significant.

We will have to be very convincing in terms of best practice examples, and how these new technologies and concepts will really work and can be applied to cities.

Barriers to prefabrication and manufactured housing

Manufactured housing could solve the affordable homes crisis in urban areas and offer new, sustainably assembled housing typologies for inner-city locations, where land prices are high. These prefabricated light-weight structures (e.g. for student housing) would not occupy any new sites, but would make better use of precious inner-city land. However, there is still prejudice against modular, prefabricated housing that needs to be overcome. Citizen opposition is seen as the biggest barrier to manufactured housing developments, where prefabricated housing is wrongly labelled as 'mobile' homes and quickly associated with 'trailer parks' and anti-social behaviour. *Prefabrication* and *Design for Disassembly* (DfD) are major concepts of sustainable design, suggesting modular components that are demountable and easily re-assembled elsewhere. To facilitate the reuse of building components (especially facade systems, structural components or cladding), the connection between the components needs to be mechanical, i.e. bolted rather than welded, so that the joint can be released easily for disassembly. Prefabrication (not like in the 1960s, in Le Corbusier's 'Living Machine') can deliver a mass-produced, precise instrument for compact living, to alleviate the shortage of housing and to introduce a range of affordable housing models. Also it has to be made easier for developers of housing estates to be green, therefore new models of affordable and sustainable housing have to be developed and need to be included in display home centres to raise public awareness.

In all developed countries, the size of homes (sqm per household) has constantly increased between the 1970s and 2000, as has the consumption of land. The increase in the size of building blocks has become a particular problem, and has led to low densities. Bigger and bigger homes are filled with more and more household and entertainment appliances: plasma screens, computer games, billiard rooms, home theatres and built-in bars – because we no longer have those facilities that used to come with life in small towns, when we were able to walk to the shops, parks, cinema, school and library. The concept of the `urban village' can recreate this situation through higher density, bringing amenities back to within walking distance.[15]

Building lightweight is closely connected to the idea of `touching the earth lightly', where structures can be removed when a point has been reached when they are no longer needed, and the site can easily be restored to its original condition.

Concrete and steel have usually a high amount of embodied energy, compared to timber. The widespread use of concrete for construction is an obvious obstacle to designing for assembly or disassembly; concrete buildings are heavy and difficult to dismantle. The Ecosmart Concrete Group has established that `cement production is a major source of greenhouse-gas emissions, accounting for some 8 per cent of $CO2$ discharge globally.' (Ecosmart Concrete, 2008) While the production of cement is energy-intensive and touches on a wide range of sustainability issues – including emissions to air and water, natural resource depletion and employee health and safety – it has also positive characteristics: concrete has the advantage of high durability and longevity. Today, the challenge for the cement industry is how to balance the growing demand for cement with the need to forge a more sustainable industry with clever prefabrication modules. In 1999, the Swiss cement producer Holcim Group initiated the World Business Council for Sustainable Development's member-led `Cement Sustainability Initiative' (CSI), publishing good practice guidelines and procedures to be used by all cement companies at their operating facilities. For more information, see the following sites: www.wbcsd.org, site of the World Business Council for Sustainable Development. www.holcimn.com, site of the Swiss cement company Holcim Group.

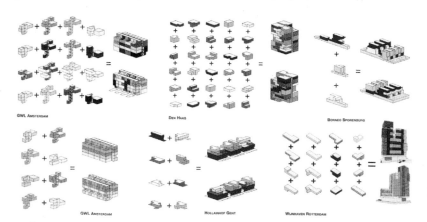

Fig. 1: Typological studies of dwellings: additive affordable housing components, as a kit of prefabricated elements that can be combined in multiple compact ways. Such system thinking, using the advantages of modular prefabrication, can lead to truly sustainable solutions; it also overcomes the problem of high land cost in the city. (Diagram: Courtesy Neutlings Riedijk, 1999)

As pointed out, prefabrication can deliver a series of advantages in achieving a high number of sustainable solutions, by reducing material needs, embodied energy and waste creation. A building that can be dismantled and the elements reused reduces demolition waste at the end of its life. Another advantage of the use of prefabricated modules is the easier integration of building services and technical systems in regard to the building's structure. Building services have a different (shorter) life-cycle as building structures. A modular concept permits the incorporation of services in such a way that these can be easier maintained, modified and exchanged conveniently at any time in the future, without negative impact on the structural system.

The `Solar Decathlon' – an educational initiative to design and build prefabricated, energy-efficient pavilions

Lately, the US Department of Energy has run the `Solar Decathlon', a bi-annual competition between twenty selected university schools of architecture to design and build the most energy-efficient temporary pavilion, to be assembled and exhibited on the National Mall in Washington D.C. This has emerged as a great educational initiative and is a showcase for latest green building designs. Twenty teams of university students compete to design, build and operate the most attractive, effective and energy-efficient solar-powered pavilion, which, when constructed, have their energy consumption measured by a jury. The public is invited to observe the event.

In 2009, the Decathlon was won (for the second time) by a team from TU-Darmstadt, Germany, with the `surPLUShome' project, using a new solution for the integration of photovoltaic cells into the building surface. The team argued that a sustainable development doesn't only take place on the visual design level – there is usually more to it than which meets the eye. The challenge was to integrate functions, design and innovative technologies into one coherent concept, and their pavilion was a good example for such thinking, as it introduced the concept of energy efficiency and sustainability as an integrated, substantial element of everyday life, rather than as a later add-on. To reduce the ecological footprint of the pavilion, the team chose timber as its main material. Wood is a renewable resource that stores carbon, and has a positive life-cycle assessment. To reduce the ecological impact of the building, the team opted for a wooden primary construction, increasing the use of local wood (spruce for construction and ceiling, oak for flooring and frames). As a strong but light material, timber offers high material efficiency and has ideal heat storage properties. The single-room interior provided for maximum space and flexibility. (See: Fig. 2)

This relatively small project included a whole range of cutting-edge technology, which illustrates the amazing technological possibilities for buildings generating significantly more energy than they consume. The project was not only a net-zero user of energy, but generated more power than it used. The pavilion's surface is covered with solar cells – an 11.1 kW photovoltaic (PV) system made of 40 single-crystal silicon panels on the roof, and about 250 thin-film copper indium gallium diselenide (CIGS) panels on the sides that produce an incredible 200 per cent of the energy needed by the house. The pavilion max-imizes PV production and use of the net-metering connection to the electric utility grid on National Mall. The CIGS component is slightly less efficient than silicon-cells, but performs better in cloudy weather. The facade's highly efficient, custom vacuum insulation panels with phase-change material in the drywall, maintains comfortable temperatures (phase-change material in both walls, using paraffin, and in the ceiling, using salt hydrate). Other technologies include: automated louver-covered windows to block unwanted solar heat; a boiler integrated into the heat pump system that allows the system to provide domestic hot water as well as heating and cooling – when passive solar heating isn't enough, the house uses a system that circulates hot water under the floor to produce radiant heat; flat-plate solar collectors on the roof heat the water, which is then used to heat domestic water for the kitchen and bath and to heat the pavilion. In summer, the house uses the solar hot water system to recharge an innovative desiccant dehumidification system that efficiently pulls moisture out of the interior air to maintain humidity and comfort levels. Monitoring systems (smart meters) can track energy use in real time and allows residents to make adjustments that will reduce their energy bills and environmental impact. Such control systems are accessible through the internet and allows residents to monitor power use and turn circuits on and off remotely.

Courtesy: T. Ott, 2009

Fig. 2 a/b: Winning project at the 'Solar Decathlon 2009': the surPLUShome by Team Germany (Technische Univer-sität Darmstadt, coordinated by Manfred Hegger; photos: J. Tetro and T. Ott, 2009). This is the second time in a row that a team from TU-Darmstadt has won this international contest. The 'surPLUShome' is almost entirely covered with photovoltaic panels that managed to generate 19 kW during one day of test runs – more than twice as much as some other contestants. The construction of the facade uses the traditional principle of shingles, which is commonly practiced with slate or wooden plates, using it here with glass PV-modules and acrylic glass. This facade offers effective shading and lighting control systems all in one. In order to generate an energy gaining facade that functions in all orientations, the students used thin-film CIS cells characterized by their ability to function with diffuse solar radiation (thin-film solar shingles, as produced by Dow). For the reduction of the energy demand, the building shell consists of highly insulated and airtight components, Vacuum Insulation Panels (VIP). A vacuum insulation panel (with a width of 50 mm) has the equivalent insulation properties of 250 mm common insulation materials; as a result, the extra 200 mm could be added to the interior space. See also: www.solardecathlon.org

GREEN BUILDINGS

Green buildings, employing passive design principles

The development of green architecture is driven by the depletion of natural resources, increasing urbanization and the need to preserve the balance of nature. Based on their energy consumption, buildings are responsible for 21 per cent of all greenhouse gas emissions. The biggest energy consumers in buildings are technical installations for cooling interiors and lighting. The extensive use of glass surfaces in the facades of buildings (especially in hot, tropical or subtropical climates), and materials that easily store the heat in summer, frequently leads to solar-overheating, which has led to the widespread use of mechanical systems (air-conditioning systems). By careful building design, these systems could be avoided in almost any climate. Instead of the use of air-conditioning systems, substantial improvements of comfort can be achieved by the informed choice of materials appropriate to basic passive energy principles, such as natural ventilation (cross-ventilation, night-flush cooling, mixed-mode systems), summer shading and winter solar heat gain. Solar and wind energy can provide heating, cooling and electric power.

All buildings will have to be energy-efficient by default. The next generation of great buildings will be 100% green.

Most glass curtain wall, high-rise buildings waste a lot of energy, because they collect heat like a greenhouse and then use air-conditioning to cool the interior spaces. Efficient shading devices for the facade can be used as a solution; however, shading systems that allow for daylight and an unobstructed view, but reduce glare and solar heat gain at the same time, are extremely complicated to resolve due to their contradicting parameters.

In hot and arid climates, sun shading is of prime importance, and buildings overshadowing each other are not seen as a disadvantage. For instance, in Abu Dhabi, UAE, 70 per cent of the energy consumed is used to cool buildings. Planned architectural measures are expected to dramatically reduce that figure in Masdar-City. Buildings in this new zero-emission city (currently under construction – see Chapter 1) are built so close together that they provide each other with shade and thus reduce air-conditioning requirements. In addition, all buildings are built on concrete pedestals, which help to maintain cool temperatures by allowing outside air to be brought in to circulate in underground air channels beneath the building slab. The naturally circulated air cools down in the sub-slab labyrinth before the cooler air is allowed to enter the interior spaces from beneath – all without mechanical systems.

Choosing white, non-heat storing materials to cut the solar heat build-up and using green roofs can significantly help mitigate against the urban heat island effect.

Green buildings and passive, climate-sensitive design strategies

There is a good reason, why passive design principles are prefered rather than active systems. 'We need solutions for buildings that can do more with less technology,' argues Gerhard Hausladen. He says: 'The optimization of the building layout and detailing of the facade system are essential for an integrated approach to the design of low-energy consuming cities.' (Hausladen, 2005) Just by optimizing buildings through the application of passive design principles can deliver energy savings of up to 80 per cent. Buildings using passive design principles are usually naturally ventilated (or use mixed-mode systems) and are well lit during the day to minimize active systems of climate control and artificial lighting. Successful buildings of the future will rely on the critical examination of the buildings of the past. (Vale, 1991; Hyde, 2005) There is so much we can learn from such studies, e.g: which passive design principles have been applied and delivered the most energy savings? How has adequate active and passive thermal storage mass been provided? Greg Brooks points out how a site's micro-climate can be modified through careful site planning, leading to 'improved thermal comfort of outdoor spaces, increased capacity for natural ventilation and sun control in buildings, and therefore reduced cooling loads.' (Brooks, 1988; Hyde, 2000)

Traditionally, in cities in Asia and the Middle East, there always existed a large repertoire of climatically adaptive and culturally sensitive urban form, which is found in the traditional use of courtyard typologies and low-rise housing in high-density districts, with narrow, shaded laneways. In addition, there is a variety of passive cooling techniques that can be utilized to develop design solutions for particular climate types, such as shaded spaces with courtyards and atria for effective cross-ventilation, open circulation with breezeways and verandahs, roof ventilation, solar chimneys and similar techniques. The main principles of passive design include:

- Optimal orientation, window size and sun control
- Compact building form
- Building mass modified to increase air flow through site (catching breezes)
- Cross ventilation and day-lighting, with effective external sun-shading (e.g. a louver system for sun control, using vertical shading louvers at the eastern and western facades; these have the advantage of retaining the outside view and are more effective than horizontal louvers)
- Passive solar heating
- Evaporative cooling
- Strategic use of thermal mass (e.g. choice of light-weight or heavy construction materials, with exposed concrete surface)
- Rooftop vegetation, gardens and water surfaces for improved micro-climate,
- Night flush cooling, activating thermal mass (using night purge)
- Sub-slab labyrinths, bringing in outside air through underground, cool air channels beneath the slab
- White facade and roof colouring
- Optimal shading, with wide roof overhangs to shade windows
- Landscaping and westerly facade protection
- High insulation.

These strategies are often combined to make them work together as a system; for instance, by linking high thermal capacity (thermal mass) for heat sink effects with passive solar heating, or with cross ventilation for night-flush cooling (summer cooling). The use of light-weight exterior facade construction elements with low thermal capacity can help to avoid the accumulation, storage and re-radiation of heat. Deep plans beyond a maximum of 15 metres in depth can significantly reduce the effectiveness of day-lighting and natural ven-tilation, leading to greater dependency on air-conditioning systems, thereby negatively impacting on occupant health, comfort, productivity and overall working conditions. Three of the most applicable and widely used passive design strategies include:

- Avoiding large glazing that receives direct sunlight and is unshaded
- Reducing surface-to-volume ratio as much as possible through compact building massing and
- Maximizing daylighting and natural cross-ventilation through slim buildings.

Operational energy is five times that of embodied energy over a forty-year life cycle. From much research, it is obvious that the facade system decides about 50 per cent of the build-ing's energy consumption. The facade system is the interface between interior and exterior. It always plays a special significant role for the room climate and operational costs. The more effectively the building envelope can react to weather changes and user-specific require-ments, the less energy is needed (e.g. most of the time, the facade system decides on lighting, glare, ventilation, shading, solar control, insulation, thermal storage, noise reduction, etc.). In the last decade or so, architects have frequently raised the issue of traditional `rule-of-thumb' for passive design principles, which does not sufficiently quantify the effects. We even find that the application of traditional rules of passive design have not been applied to some new building types at all, particularly in the area of day-lighting, thermal mass, or air-flow in double skin facades. The old rule-of-thumb can actually be wrong. Large glass surfaces of modern buildings facing the sun almost always create climatic problems due to their extreme heat gain. It is increasingly being recognized that a performance-based, quantifiable guidance (with exact performance reporting) for designers is needed.

Good climate design is offering the user maximum comfort for minimum energy. For building services and technology, the motto must be: as much as necessary, as little as possible.   *Gerhard Hausladen, 2005*

Ventilation and air velocity

The era of fully air-conditioned office buildings has passed. The ventilation concept of a building's design significantly influences its operating costs, maintenance and comfort levels. Today, mixed-use systems with a high amount of natural ventilation airchange, or atriums used for better airflow, have become standard repertoire in the planning of office buildings. Avoiding deep rooms (not more than 6 metres) allows for better natural ventila-tion and effective day-lighting. To avoid overheating in summer, any large window area on the west side should be protected with exterior shading devices. Office buildings are now designed with the optimum combination of thermal storage mass and free night-flush ventilation (these office rooms have no suspended ceiling to activate the concrete mass of the slab), which makes mechanical cooling for most time of the year unnecessary. As consequence, operating costs are lower and services take up less space in the building (smaller ducts, units and plant rooms). (Daniels, 2000)

The greener the building, the more attractive it is for tenants

Recent studies show that green buildings earn higher rents and are more sought after by corporate tenants worldwide, thus delivering faster payback to investors and building owners. In a recent study, Eichholtz, Kok and Quigly found that certified green office buildings in the US actually command a premium in rental rates and sales prices over conventional, not-energy-optimized office buildings. In addition, occupancy rates are higher and less volatile than rates in commercial office buildings without a green certificate such as BREEAM, CASBEE, DGNB-Certificate, LEED or GreenStar. It also translates into an improved reputation for the tenant, along with economic profitability and improved employee well-being and productivity: `A green corporate headquarters and the use of green space in general, may signal to stakeholders and customers that a firm has a long-run commitment to a corporate social responsibility policy' (Eichholtz, Kok and Quigly, 2009). A good example for this is the recent lease of the new `Workplace 6' office building at Darling Harbour in Sydney. This GreenStar certified building was fully rented, before completion, to Google for its Australia headquarters, and the tenant was agreeable to a higher rent than market average due to the building's low operating costs, improved resource efficiency and good public image. In future, commercial buildings and office towers not meeting tenant's green criteria will face higher vacancies, lower rentals and value deterioration, while buildings with the appropriate standard will be able to earn more rent and be patronized by high-profile tenants (`sustainable = rentable'). This makes upgrading existing office buildings and turning them into `deep green buildings' clearly a profitable investment that reaches its payback point faster.

Overall, energy-efficiency in buildings is the `low hanging fruit' in emissions reduction, where real results can be achieved relatively easily and quickly. The biggest culprit for energy-efficiency in all building types is the shopping centre. Despite their huge energy consumption through 24/7 mechanical air-conditioning and their excessive need for artificial illumination, there are often no immediate incentives to becoming more energy efficient for their operators, as shopping centres usually buy their energy through fixed bulk contracts that are agreed on for long contracted periods.

In future, green buildings will interact with each other, and the wider urban power infrastructure will form zero-emission clusters of buildings that share urban energy technologies, such as a community smart grid and a CHP plant.
Buildings and districts inter-connected via a smart grid will enjoy a large energy savings potential.

Benefits of sustainable building investment go far beyond cost savings; they deliver multiple advantages when the `product' comes on the market. The first step is always to implement energy efficiency measures in all building design. In Asia and the Middle East it is still common for fully air-conditioned office buildings to consume electricity in the range of 300 to 400 kWh per sqm per year. With the available technology, it would easily be possible to reduce this consumption by over 80 per cent, despite the hot and humid climate in these regions.

Architects and urban designers need to learn to re-focus more on simple methods for reducing energy consumption and carbon emissions, such as applying a more compact shape and an optimized orientation to buildings, using passive design principles (using technology sparingly), as well as better selecting construction systems and materials. Smart buildings, with sophisticated Building Energy Management System (BEMS) and smart metering, support grid stability and allow energy generators to consider other options before adding new generation facilities:
• smart buildings optimize their own energy flow by balancing consumption, storage capacity and decentralized energy generation; and
• smart building clusters are an interactive part of the grid by providing significant generation capacity and demand management potential.

In future, buildings and city districts will produce a surplus of electricity, which will then be fed back into the urban power grid. Therefore, the seamless interaction of smart clusters of buildings with the electrical power grid, through the use of information technology, will enable such buildings to optimize their own energy flow by balancing consumption, storage capacity and decentralized generation. Buildings and districts inter-connected via a smart grid will enjoy large energy savings potential. The amount of energy that can be saved through the intelligent networking of power utilities and consumers, enabled through smart metering, varies from case to case. However, experts generally agree that savings of 25 per cent are realistic, depending on the building type. Shopping malls, for instance, open ten to twelve hours a day but air-conditioned 24/7, have a large savings potential of over 50 per cent. Office buildings, usually unused over the weekend, easily have an energy savings potential of between 20 and 30 per cent.

Reducing air-condition dependency through passive design principles in a tropical climate
Studying the built heritage plays an important role in the shift towards a low-carbon society. It offers a large resource of knowledge about design principles and how architects have operated within the challenges of hot or tropical climates. This knowledge has not been sufficiently discussed and researched. In the light of globalization, it is increasingly understood that the existing, authentic built heritage is a significant contributor to local identity and defines the unique character of any location, helping to achieve social outcomes as well as maintaining the memory of a place. The diversity and rich complexity of tangible and intangible heritage is a constant inspiration that deserves to be maintained and protected.

To conduct research in pre-air-condition built heritage is particularly relevant for the future of the Asia-Pacific Region, where we can find rapid (and often traumatic) urbanization processes combined with too much reliance on outdated models of urban growth and building designs, thus increasing energy demands. This includes an unusually high dependency on mechanical (air-conditioning) systems, thereby creating large CO_2 emissions and high operating costs in both residential and commercial building stock. In current discussions about sustainability and climate change, we can observe a re-appreciation of the built heritage that has been built in harmony with its climatic conditions and geographic locations. The Asia-Pacific region's humid tropical climate poses a particular difficult problem, with temperatures often around 30 degrees Celsius during day-time, around 25 degrees at night, with a high relative humidity of about 90 per cent (e.g. typical for Singapore, Hong Kong, Bangkok, Jakarta, and other large tropical cities, suffering from UHI effect). Such conditions leave little scope for night-flush cooling, and refreshing breezes (air flow) are often lacking. Serious climate engineering strategies are needed, and the de-humidification of the air as part of a cooling process is a preferable option. There are some particularly exciting developments in the innovative area of 'solar cooling'; so far, around 400 installations worldwide already use solar cooling technology. (Data: 2010)

Hong Kong, for instance, has a very high population density and is always praised for its efficient public transport systems. But the city has an extremely high dependency on air-conditioning and is feeling the Urban Heat Island effect; the lack of natural air ventilation in the city has emerged as serious planning issue; most buildings are not even insulated and lack any external sun shading of their facades.

The excessive use of air-conditioning and other 'quick techno-fix solutions', has led to high expectations of indoor living standards and the complacency of architects to solve it 'by simply putting in the air-condition unit'. The ubiquitous use of air-conditioning systems across the Asia-Pacific region consumes a vast amount of energy and has made 20th-century building types, often with deep plans and closed glass facades, fully dependent on the technology. The question of how much the indoor climate should follow the outdoor climate requires new discussion. While the fully air-conditioned building raises a series of health questions, most building codes still require that a maximum of 25 degrees Celsius indoor temperature in offices is not exceeded at any time, even with a 40 degrees Celsius outdoor temperature. Such high requirements are, of course, impossible to achieve without mechanical ventilation.
With the effect of global warming, it is time to update this part of the building code and question the correctness of such high comfort expectations. In addition, the following questions are raised:
- How can energy saving be achieved in the context of expected comfort level (e.g. legislation requiring a maximum 25 degrees Celsius indoor temperature at any time)?
- How to allow as much natural daylight as possible into office spaces, while also reducing solar heat gain (e.g. glazing qualities on the market)?
- How to sustainably cool buildings with large glazing areas, in hot or tropical climates?

Architecture's unfortunate, non-sustainable evolution in the 20th century
While there were many wonderful innovations that transformed architecture and the building sector during the 20th century, there were also some less fortunate development paths. This has been widely discussed in the literature as a critique of functionalism and modernity. From `Silent Spring' (by Rachel Carson, 1962), to Reyner Banham's `Architecture of the Well-tempered Environment' (1969), to Ian McHarg's `Design with Nature' (1969), to the pivotal publications by authors re-connecting urbanism with the climatic condition (such as Koenigsberger, or Drew and Fry, in publications in their in the 1960s and 70s), the field of sustainable city theories and the critique of the lack of climate-responsive architecture, has constantly been expanded. While we explore how renewable energy sources can provide sufficient power for an ever increasing world population to maintain today's lifestyles, we also have to ask how our lifestyles should adapt to the needs of a future low-carbon society, e.g. through behavioural change in the use of energy, water, materials and the automobile. This question is frequently raised by architects Geoffrey Bawa and Glenn Murcutt, both of whom are very experienced in designing for (sub)tropical conditions. Murcutt calls it: `To achieve more with less, and to touch the earth lightly.' (Murcutt, 2009)

Fig. 3: The installation of a typical electrical air-condition system (the ubiquitous fan-coil): small fan-coil systems such as this can be installed during occupancy. The fan-coil blows cold air directly onto the occupants. This ubiquitous use of air-conditioning consumes vast amounts of energy. Instead of phasing these energy-hungry systems out, they are enjoying higher popularity. Of all the major appliances in the home, air-conditioners and refrigerators consume the most energy and cost the most in the monthly electricity bill. Half to two-thirds of the energy consumption of a typical household in Asia or the US goes to operating air-conditioners and refrigerators. Cooling requires, 5 to 8 times the energy of heat the same temperature delta. Mixed-mode systems, which are the combination of natural ventilation with some well-considered active system, could replace the outdated fan-coil technology.

Holistic strategies and integrated approaches: The most successful solutions are now the highly-effective combination of passive design principles with some well considered active systems, for buildings that are built to last longer.

Values and aspirations associated with modernity, combined with everyday expectations of comfort, have evolved in tandem with lifestyle changes. In consequence, some of the misguided and often criticized developments of architecture in the 20th century include:
• Deep plan buildings that disable natural cross-ventilation.
  Correcting development: slim, thin-plan buildings for daylight and cross-ventilation.
• Inflexible, highly specialized typologies.

Correcting development: universal, more adaptable building types.
- Short life-span of buildings as part of our 'throw-away' culture.
  Correcting development: buildings that last longer (60+ years).
- Increased expectations for indoor-comfort, fully depending on mechanical air-conditioning.
  Correcting development: mixed-mode systems, with operable windows and night-flush cooling.
- The automobile-dependent city.
  Correcting development: strong focus on walking, cycling, and efficient public transport.

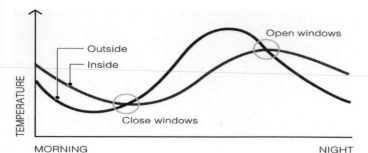

Fig. 4 a, b: This carefully restored 2-storey 'Chinese Shop House' typology in Melaka, Malaysia (used by NUS as TTCL Centre for Architecture and Urban Heritage, 2009) has a series of well-proportioned courtyards, which ensure good day-lighting and natural cross-ventilation within the 200 years old structures. Only a few ceiling fans are operated in extreme heat. (Photo: Lehmann, 2009) Left: Natural cross-ventilation and air velocity can have the effect of reducing the perceived temperature by 2 degree Celsius or more. The temperature difference between night and day can be set to improve thermal comfort through night-flush cooling. (Diagram: courtesy CCAA Sydney, 2007)

Not only is it technological shifts that are required to reduce carbon emissions, but it also requires social, cultural (behavioural) and political ones. (Winter and Widodo, 2009) So, what are the obstacles for re-orienting lifestyles away from electronically chilled climates? It is time to move beyond technical scientific prescriptions of comfort, to consider how social norms have shifted, and to examine the socio-cultural transformations brought about by the introduction of air-conditioning in 20th century architecture. Heritage architecture of the pre-air-conditioning era, ranging from small residential dwellings to large civic structures, offers a 'living laboratory' as a resource for more sustainable living. While these historical buildings frequently display a valid alternative (and there are revival trends visible) – where comfort is achieved with natural cross-ventilation and effective sun-shading for most of the year – the internal loads have become problematical for all architectural design; for example, office equipment (such as copy machines, computers and lighting) produces so much 'hot air' that it requires some form of mechanical ventilation.

A global paradigm shift in urban development and use of resources is essential. Simply put: a situation where 20 per cent of the world's population consumes 80 per cent of the world's resources cannot be allowed to continue.

Behavioural issues regarding the use of water, energy, waste and materials
We need a new set of questions in regard to the social and cultural dimensions of urbanization. It is an inappropriate development that the average size of the Australian home keeps growing and is now the world's largest home (in average 250 sqm in size, with 2.5 garages); it is approximately double the size of the average European home. At the same time, the ever-expanding floor space is located further from the city centre than ever before. We are building bigger houses to store more and more appliances in them. Research has shown, that the building design (applying successful passive design principles), and how the house is used, is paramount to reducing the environmental impact of the home. These considerations are more significant than, for instance, the walling materials used in construction. However, breaking free from passive consumer culture is hard, behaviour changes and lifestyle changes are slow and difficult. It is cultural values about our standards of living that need to change too.

The 20th century not only saw the introduction of mechanical air conditioning systems, but also the specialization of building typologies. This generally led to reduced flexibility and adaptability to changing programmes of usage, or demographic change. To transform society towards a low-carbon future means tackling challenges that extend far beyond the question of sustainable design. The quick 'technical fix' is not going to be sufficient to ensure sustainability over time. The obstacles to re-orienting lifestyles away from electronically-chilled climates are wide, and the reintroduction of traditional passive design principles alone is unlikely to overcome all these barriers. It's seen as necessary to not just engage in a revival of these passive, basic design principles, but also to update the traditional 'rules of thumb' and to place them within a robust scientific framework for a better evidence-based understanding, adjusted to the reality of contemporary construction methods. There is now a need to redefine and update the applicability of these passive 'rule of thumb' strategies.

Studies in energy consumption and ecological footprints have revealed that the most sustainable buildings are the ones that already exist (based on their primary embodied energy and material flow). (Lehmann, 2006) Buildings from the pre-air-conditioning era frequently display a convincing application of passive design principles, such as optimizing orientation, the use of evaporative cooling, strategic use of thermal mass, trompe walls, ingenuitive sun-shading devices for the western facade, solar chimneys, allowance for cross-ventilation and escape of hot air at the highest point in the room, and cross-ventilation adjustable to the changing directions of a breeze through some form of sliding panels (commonly seen in traditional Japanese architecture). Sub-slab labyrinths (underground air channels), activating the thermal mass, have seen a recent comeback in many new projects. We can also find that the use of local materials (combined with employing a local workforce and the locally available technical know-how) has been able to create a regional, vernacular 'style' in architecture. The most common and successful solutions are now the highly-effective combination of passive design principles with some well considered active systems, for buildings that are built to last longer. It's time to start thinking differently about the way we operate and manage buildings and about their total lifecycle impact.

RETROFITTING, RENOVATIONS, ENERGY-EFFICIENT REFURBISHMENTS

Retrofitting existing districts

Climate change requires us to think differently about existing city districts and the existing building stock. The idea of retrofitting and converting city districts into truly sustainable habitats, reconfiguring them into sustainable self-sufficient eco-systems, is particularly important. Most cities have substantial programmes for retrofitting existing commercial and residential buildings and blocks, but there is now a need for a concerted effort to improving them. The existing building stock accounts for the majority of energy use and emissions. By 2020, a 30 per cent reduction target for emissions generated by existing buildings in developed countries is a realistic, achievable goal if we rapidly retro-green our cities by upgrading older districts and quarters to become more energy efficient. Therefore, it will be crucial for governments to use the most effective incentives and policies to deliver desirable outcomes and trigger the up-scaling of renewable energy technology industries. If solar and wind have enough market share, their prices will fall. This is why many experts (including Mark Fulton, Global Head of Climate Change Investment Research at Deutsche Bank, and others) strongly emphasize the role of policy and government incentives for turning concepts of sustainability into practical reality. Policy was the most influential driving force behind the German feed-in tariffs, which allowed for certainty of continuous investment in the solar industry. Shi Zhengrong, Founder and CEO of Suntech Power (China) points out: `The right balanced level of subsidies is essential for the industry of new technologies to develop.' (Zhengrong, 2010) Also the current debate about the *Emission Trading Scheme* (ETS), where carbon emission will be dealt with on a market-driven platform, makes this argument a strong one. The right policy framework is needed to ensure the ETS is funded by the major polluters, who will be required to buy permits.

The ETS is controversial and hotly debated by experts around the world. While it may make funding for the development of renewable energy technologies available, some think of it as a less useful solution. Allan Jones (London Climate Agency), for instance, commented: `This has absolutely nothing to do with emissions trading, this is about getting on and doing it. You cannot tackle climate change by trading; you have to actually do things.' (Jones, 2008)

MULTI-STOREY TIMBER SYSTEMS

Innovation in construction systems: multi-storey residential timber buildings

Advancing construction systems is a way of enhancing the environmental sustainability of buildings. The growing need to increase density in cities and to rethink construction methods for residential buildings has recently led to a series of innovative approaches for multi-storey timber construction systems in Europe. Applied research in new materials and the interdisciplinary collaboration between architects and manufacturers of building com-ponents are driving the innovation and the development of such new structural systems. In addition, the changing role of design teams and `Sustainable Design' appears as an opportunity to bring design, research and application together again.

Beyond the technical aspects of such multi-storey timber construction systems, I suggest we take a closer look at a series of recent case studies of urban timber buildings. The close collaboration between architects and the manufacturers of building components enables the development of prefabricated panel construction systems. Even in what appears to be a simple project there is high complexity in the developed structural system, systemization, detailing of components and realization. I see this as a relevant topic within the context of the current environmental debate and the need to use sustainable materials and systems to ensure housing affordability in environmentally driven projects.

Let's take a closer look at the lessons that can be learnt from the case studies and their use of timber as multi-frame, for multi-level residential buildings. The main objectives of the presented projects are:
• Prototype design of large-scale prefabricated timber elements to improve the construc-tion process and the energy efficiency of building envelopes.
• Modular design for transformation and disassembly: systems not designed for transfor-mation lead to user dissatisfaction, adaptability at high cost, more demolition waste and an increase in the consumption of materials; use of more efficient construction techniques.
• Closing cycles through integrated life cycle design methodologies: Optimization of a frictionless `digital chain' of the entire process, from design, to production, to assembly.

The conclusion suggests that these prefabricated timber systems allow for high-performance construction methods and are adequate for multi-storey residential buildings in urban contexts.

Recent demonstration projects for multi-storey residential buildings using timber construction systems have offered a series of systemic and environmental advantages.

Prefabrication of modular timber wall systems
What will buildings have to be like to achieve the target of CO_2 emissions reduction? What are the new ways in which to build inner-city housing in denser city centres? Build-ing `green' is not something to be bolted on once the design is completed – it needs to be integrated in the conceptual phase from the very beginning. Questions about the kinds of material to be used in regard to the construction system are crucial from the early stage of design. Conventional construction methods frequently result in inefficient structures that rely on the consumption of natural resources; for instance, building with brick and ma-sonry often limits the building's height and leads to heavy, material-intensive construction; using concrete is increasingly regarded as problematical in terms of an ecological foot-

Source: Image Sharing Commons

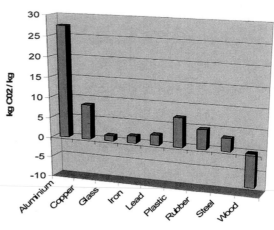

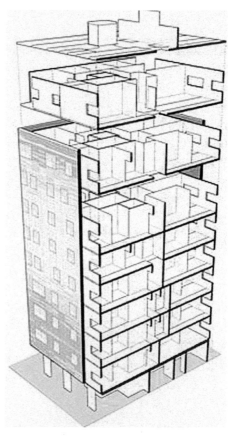

Timber is the only material that can store carbon, and if harvested from a sustainably grown and managed forest, it's a truly recyclable resource and construction material.[16] The graph at the top shows the positive impact of timber, in comparison to other construction materials (source: NSW Dept. of Primary Industries). Since building codes in most EU countries have changed, a 8+1-storey 'timber tower' in London has been completed.

Courtesy: Detail, 2007

A new generation of multi-storey timber buildings

With new technology and changes in building codes, there has been sustainable construction of multi-storey timber high-rise buildings. The apartment building below has a four-storey timber framed construction on top of a concrete base. The pre-fabricated outside-wall elements are highly insulated, with triple-glazing timber-metal windows. A waste-heat recovery system reduces heat loss through ventilation, while, with correct usage by the inhabitants, an effective heat requirement ratio of just 20 kWh/sqm can be achieved.

New cross-laminated GLT timber panels (so-called jumbo multipanels) have revolutionized timber construction: fire-engineered, they can act as load-bearing walls and for fire compartmentation. Below: Switzerland's highest timber building: the 6-storey multi-apartment building in Steinhausen, 2006 (architects: Scheitlin & Syfrig, in collaboration with manufacturer Holzbau Renggli AG). (Image: Courtesy Scheitlin & Syfrig)

print, its embodied energy and its limited possibilities for disassembly; structural steel has advantages in dematerialization, but is expensive and still problematical when it comes to the reuse of structural elements. For a long time, timber buildings have been praised for their affordability and their potential for easy reuse of building elements, and even as a pool of material resources for new constructions. The lightweight characteristic of timber means smaller foundations, as the weight is only around half that of a similar building made of concrete. In addition, timber has regained appreciation since building codes have changed to allow for multi-storey (more than 3) timber construction systems. [17]

If harvested from sustainably grown forests, timber is recognised as a modern material that offers great opportunities for sustainable design. Its many advantages in prefabrication (reduced time and storage space on site, easier site logistics, less construction waste, life-cycle advantages such as recyclable and dismountable buildings, `cradle-to-cradle' material cycle with less embodied energy, less damage to site, etc.) make it an innovative and sustainable way to build. Today, we see a large-scale production of timber components which utilize new structural panel materials and CNC carpentry. The data flow from planning to prefabrication to the assembly on site, benefits from a high levels of automation, systemisation of workflow and frictionless production chains. The forest-based value chain is, therefore, particularly beneficial for small and medium carpenters.

Trees absorb CO_2 and convert it into cellulose and lignin, while releasing oxygen. The use of timber in construction delays the release of CO_2 until the demolition of the building. In addition, wood has an excellent insulation value and presents a sustainable alternative to the commonly used composite thermal insulation systems. Most insulation systems are based on mineral fibre or polystyrene foam. These systems use a high amount of primary energy in production and have high levels of volatile organic compounds, VOCs. It is difficulty to recycle these products. The important criterion for sustainable timber is that it comes from environmentally-responsible forest management practices, in regard to how the timber was planted, managed and harvested. The *Forest Stewardship Council* (FSC) `Certified Timber' certification specifies such qualities for sustainable timber products. Numerous innovations can now be seen in multi-storey timber buildings throughout Europe. Increasing ecological awareness, rising expectations with regard to the health and comfort of home environments and interesting new products from the timber construction industry provide a basis for innovative designs, even in the urban context. (See: Fig. 14) Recent demonstration projects for multi-storey residential buildings using timber construction systems have offered a series of systemic and environmental advantages, such as:
• Prototype design of large-scale prefabricated timber elements, improving the construction process: elements are produced under highly controlled conditions.
• Modular design for transformation and disassembly: Standarization with repeated detailing leads to optimized mass-production of elements.
• Closing cycles through integrated life-cycle design methodologies. waste from production is significantly minimized.

From serial production to digital customization of the sustainable district

The idea of Taylorized serial production of buildings and entire city districts through prefabrication has fascinated many architects, such as Marcel Breuer, Walter Gropius, Konrad Wachsmann, Le Corbusier, Richard Buckminster Fuller, Kisho Kurokawa, Ernst Neufert, Charles Eames, Jean Prouve, Moshe Safdie, Yona Friedmann, Paul Rudolph, Hermann Kaufmann and Richard Horden – just to name a few. Today, with overpopulation, the depletion of resources and materials, and the need for affordable housing, it appears that digital fabrication could allow for mass-production of truly sustainable, low-cost, high-quality solutions, made with the minimum amount of waste and impact on site (since entirely prefabricated off-site). The traditional `Queenslander House' is a good example for this: it is to a large degree prefabricated and lightweight to be easily transported around. The `Micro Compact Home' by Richard Horden (London/Munich) and `System 3' by Oskar Leo Kaufmann and Albert Ruef (Austria) are both completely prefabricated, modular units that could easily form much larger communities, if stacked as clusters. (Bergdoll, 2008) The sequential phases of fabrication, delivery, assembly and disassembly – and this sequence could be optimized using building information modelling (BIM) – enables the designer to consider architecture holistically. Integrated component assembly has been part of the manufacturing revolution in automobile and airplane manufacturing for some time, but seem to have not fully arrived yet in architecture and urban design.

Timber as sustainable material in the urban context

The quality of a building can be measured by its potential to be transformed from a spatial to a material concept without negatively impacting on the environment or economy. If we take a holistic look at energy consumption and the material cycle in the building industry, we find that wood offers many advantages. It has excellent insulation characteristics, it has ideal values of embodied energy, it is relatively easy to recycle and it has insulation qualities that are superior to either metal or concrete. The use of sustainable harvested timber can help to keep the embodied energy content and use of material resources low. It also offers advantages for the use of load-bearing elements, e.g. when a beam penetrates the facade, the resulting cold bridge is much less critical. It is therefore suggested that more buildings could be built in timber to achieve the CO_2 emissions reduction target. For a long time now, timber buildings have been praised for their healthy indoor environments, but the recent `innovative breed' of residential buildings also offers new ways to build for inner-city densities. High-performance timber products, which are now becoming available, offer increased stability, good acoustic insulation and high fire rating (e.g. large-scale, structurally highly stable, cross-laminated panels, such as produced by Lignotrend, Kerto, Renggli – just to name a few). These engineered wood products have a series of advantages:

- Low formaldehyde emission levels.
- Ideal for reducing the amount of material consumption and for easier recycling.
- Designed for disassembly (structural framing, façade systems, entire GLT wall elements, etc.), which further minimizes resources associated with demolition.

Forests in central Europe have been increasing in size every year due to more wood being grown than is used. During its growth phase, wood binds carbon dioxide and retains it for many years (even when the wood has become a building material), thus preventing CO_2 from re-entering the atmosphere.[16]

Depending on how it has been worked and processed, wood can assume manifold characteristics and can positively influence the climate and atmosphere of a building. How we can design with the material, how it can visualize the structural principles and how it is used in the urban environment are exciting challenges for today's architects. All this is accompanied with interesting changes in building codes. New building regulations (e.g. the Building Regulation for Prototypes, a Performance-based Code, 11/2002 in Germany, and similar developments in other countries) will, in the future, allow building timber constructions of up to five storeys or more. Load-bearing components of Building Category 4 (floor of top storey <13m) must be highly resistant to fire, i.e. they must be able to withstand fire for a minimum of 60 minutes (Dehne and Krueger, 2006). As a consequence, building with wood is gaining again in popularity.[18] Therefore, let's evaluate some recent case studies.

Construction systems for assembly and disassembly

Generally, we need to differentiate between wood, timber and lumber. Definitions for use in this paper are:

- Wood: the hard, fibrous, lignified substance lying under the bark of trees. It consists largely of cellulose and lignin. Wood is a natural material and is, therefore, irregular by nature.
- Timber: the wood of trees cut and prepared for use as building material (e.g. beams, posts).
- Lumber: timber cut into marketable boards, planks or other structural members, and which is of standard or specified length.

With these definitions in mind, we can look at an overview of some new ways of using timber in multi-storey residential projects, which has recently developed in a sophisticated manner.

The use of timber in constructio is only 'green' if it is used without the addition of toxic treatment products. Modern approaches to timber construction in Central Europe have undergone innovative changes. Traditional approaches, such as block and half-timbered constructions, or the balloon-frame and platform-frame constructions seen in North America, have given way to today's prefabricated frame, skeleton and solid constructions. The main difference between these systems lies within the hierarchy of the load bearing elements of the building structure as selective or linear elements (Kolb, 2007). These constructions are characterized by the method of assembly of prefabricated structural elements and the structure of the envelope. New procurement methods and ideas for collaboration in project delivery have also emerged, bringing together multidisciplinary teams at all levels. When working with prefabricated timber elements, the designer is required to closely collaborate with the manufacturer of those components to enable real innovation and the development of new prefabricated construction systems. Architecture has, of course, always been the outcome of a manifold of complex understandings and multidisciplinary domains of knowledge and practice. However, we are now witnessing the speedy development of technological possibilities, and a shift to interdisciplinarity appears to be an increasingly necessary condition.

Particular aspects of planning with timber

Generally, building systems consist of similar wall and ceiling elements, though these elements can also be used in combination to form the structure. For example, the applications of solid wood elements in ceilings of frame work structures. Different wall and ceiling elements are produced in various industrial manufacturing processes, during which the performance and, to some extent, the structural properties of load-bearing components are optimized: (See: Fig. 5)

- Wall (vertical structural element)
- Framework: i.e. clad post and beam structure
- Solid wall panels: i.e. stacked board elements, glue-laminated elements
- Solid wall plates: i.e. cross laminated boards, veneer laminated plates.

- Ceiling (horizontal structural element)
- conventional beam structures
- combined timber elements: hollow box girder
- solid ceiling elements: stacked board elements
- solid ceiling panels: cross laminated plates
- combined concrete timber elements.

Industrial, engineered timber elements

Examples of the variety of industrially engineered timber products, made from wood and other materials will be specified on the following pages of the chapter. High-performance composite materials , such as veneer lumber Kerto (layered panels), by Finnforest. Following are some examples of industrially manufactured timber construction elements that offer interesting opportunities for application, as they are widely available in Europe:

- Stacked board elements

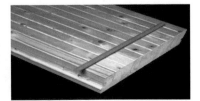

Fig. 5 a: Stacked board element. (Photo: FG Holzbau, TU Munich)

Vertical panels of board are nailed together or conjoined using hardwood pins. The underside of the element is planed smooth and the individual boards can be profiled to enhance the acoustic properties of the interior.

Material: usually spruce, for ceilings, walls
Overall height: up to 240mm
Width of element: up to 2.5m

• Solid cross-laminated timber boards

Fig. 5 b: Assembly of prefabricated floor and wall panels on site. (Photo: FGH)

These consist of at least three layers of pinewood board bonded or pinned together cross-ways, each layer having a thickness of between 15mm to 30mm. Thanks to its resistance, solid wood panelling is dimensionally highly stable and can be manufactured with ready-planed visible surfaces.

Material: usually spruce, for ceilings, walls
Overall height: up to around 280mm
Width of element: up to 4.8m

• Hollow box girder elements

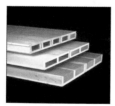

Fig. 5 c: Image of the hollow box girder elements, partly filled with insulation. (Photo: FGH)

Hollow box girder elements consist of several boards (dimension lumber) or chipboard panels (e.g. 3S chipboard) that are bonded, or bonded and screwed together. They are suitable for spanning wide areas. Various manufacturers have developed products with positive acoustic properties. This is achieved by perforating or filling-in the hollow elements. Some companies have developed specific building systems, such as the wall and ceiling panels of the companies Lignatur (see: www.lignatur.ch), or Lignotrend (see: www.lignotrend.de).

• Combined timber-concrete ceilings

The strong bonding capability of wood and concrete is used to optimize the load-bearing properties of ceilings and enhances their structural characteristics in terms of vibration, fire protection (F 90B, 90 minutes fire resistant), noise reduction and room acoustics. The wood and concrete elements are interlocked by means of integrated shear connectors or via appropriate profiling of the wooden layers.

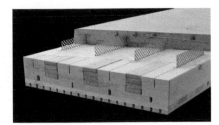

Fig. 5 d: Combined timber-concrete ceiling elements. (Photo: Lignotrend)

The advantage of engineered timber elements, such as GLT, is that every structural member is exactly of the same consistant quality. The application of these industrial elements offers a great variety of possibilities, though some facts regarding the utilization within construction systems should be mentioned:

• Panel or plate

Prefabricated timber frame wall panels are based on grid regularity with several different functional layers. The post and beam structure is the load bearing element for vertical loads, and horizontal loads run into bracing elements, i.e. cladding, with large-sized composite boards (veneer boards, OSB, etc.) or diagonal cladding with sawn boards. Furthermore, thermal insulation and moisture barriers have to be applied within the wall panel. Its advantage lies in its lightweight construction at the expense of a complex application of the described layers, with a rather negative impact on the disposal regarding the ecological life cycle of the building elements. With the possibilities afforded by industrially-fabricated large-scale solid timber elements, new construction systems have been developed in recent years. The plane elements consist of boards (glued, nailed or pinned) and can be used as vertical or horizontal structural elements, which offer an efficient load bearing system. Cross laminated solid timber plates can be formed in two or even three dimensions, and openings can easily be cut into the plates. Due to the advantages of large scale stable plates, their structural efficiency, their reduced number of layers, etc, solid timber plates are very suitable for multiple storey buildings.

• Skeleton construction and pre-fabricated modules

Timber skeleton systems are very efficient wide-spanning structures. The load bearing elements (post and beam) can be differentiated from wall and ceiling elements, thus offering great freedom to design individual space and quality multiple-storey homes or office buildings. Prefabricated space modules consist of structural elements (vertical and horizontal) of the systems mentioned. Size and transportation factors determine the dimension of the module and a high degree of detailing regarding the location and connection of installation, and facing the demands for sound and fire protection is necessary. Industrial-scale, accurate pre-fabrication, coupled with fast and exact assembly, facilitates the various phases of a building project. Intelligent pre-fabricated kits based on smart modularity and easy transportation – such as the `System 3' by Oskar Kaufmann and Albert Ruef, the `Take-away Houses' developed by Gabriel Poole[19], or the prefab container houses by Fender-Katsalides – have enabled the user to choose from a wide variety and combinations of application. Lightweight structural systems in timber have the advantage of their limited weight and consequent reduction in foundation requirements; frequently, load carrying capacities are limited, especially in alteration and extension projects. The pre-fabrication of structural elements offer further cost savings by often eliminating the need for a crane on site and by using skills well known to the building trades.

Increasing longevity: effective protection depends on the detail

Regarding ecological issues and rising energy costs, the challenge lies in the design of energy-efficient buildings, combined with an appropriate climate-responsive concept. Key timber construction strategies are:

- sufficient thermal insulation to reduce energy losses in winter and prevent overheating in summer; and
- high degree of air tightness for the building envelope to prevent construction damage by water condensation.

Designing timber buildings requires a larger amount of careful detailing and precise planning than does other construction methods. Generally, condensation can occur where moist air comes into contact with air or a surface of a lower temperature. Air always contains water vapour in varying quantities, its capacity to do so is related to its temperature – warm air holds more moisture than cold air. When moist air comes into contact with colder air or a colder surface (e.g. a timber element), the air is unable to retain the same amount of moisture and the water is released to form condensation in the element. The moisture from condensed water causes timber to decay, due to wet rot inside the walls. This is hard to detect and may not be noticed until mould growth or the rotting of material actually occurs. Consequently there is a need for a precise, correctly layered and high quality construction envelopes to protect the timber structure from rain and water condensation. Only correct detailing will protect it from humidity and solve the question of surface treatment – to keep maintenance low and to `pre-design' the ageing process and the appearance of the surface. European industries have developed several construction methods to deal with this issue. All of them are based on precise pre-fabrication processes in workshops where wall, ceiling and roof panels are built in transportable dimensions, taking advantage of ideal factory conditions to produce large-scale building modules for manufactured housing. Modern digital fabrication processes thereby allow lightweight structural systems with great variation in form and size. Depending on the function of the building some important demands have to be specified and detailed

in the construction phase documents:
• adequate sound separation in the joints of wall and ceiling
• strategies to reach a sufficient level of fire protection by means of encapsulation or separation of gaps and hollow spaces (e.g. refer to the 'model guideline for technical fire protection requirements for extremely flame-retardant wooden construction components', in the M-HFHHolzR, German building code).

Timber structures in the urban context

Austria's first four-storey timber residential building is regarded as a pioneering project, paving the way for future initiatives in the field of timber construction in urban environments. With recent changes in building codes, Germany and Austria now allow timber buildings up to five and four stories, and in Switzerland up to six stories without major problems (from the formerly three story limit). A 2001 amendment to Vienna's building regulations permitted multi-storey buildings to be constructed from wood; previously wood was mainly used in large quantities for roofing-out trams and for attic constructions. Since the amendment, wood has increasingly been used as a construction material in communal building projects. The first communal developments are finished, while construction of a further seven has already commenced (2008). All in all, 400 multi-family developments are being erected, either entirely from timber or mixed timber/concrete systems. Timber is beginning to establish itself again as a completely 'normal' and sustainable building material in the minds of the city's population. Recent demonstration projects show that sustainable construction using ecological materials with optimum usage of energy can produce results that are both architecturally elaborate and economically efficient. For instance, the new community centre in the town of Ludesch, Austria, completed in 2006 by architect H. Kaufmann, is an example of an innovative and cost-effective ecological building. The project was part of the 'Building Tomorrow' programme sponsored and documented by the Austrian Federal Ministry of Transport, Innovation and Technology. As well as creating a passive building, the objective was to half the specific primary energy consumption, compared with similar and conventionally built, passive buildings, while simultaneously reducing the ecological manufacturing outlay to at least half of that required for non-optimized construction. Dual, and thus comparable, tenders meant that a direct comparison could be made between the 'conventional' and the 'ecologically desirable' construction. The added cost for using ecological building materials was only around 1.9 per cent. The positive experience encouraged all parties involved to take on other challenging projects of this kind.

The following eight case studies are all low impact buildings with a small ecological footprint, using multi-story timber construction systems.

Some selected demonstration projects for multi-storey timber

After having been branded as 'rural, vernacular material' in the last century, some recent European examples of multi-storey, residential timber buildings illustrate the application of timber in urban architecture. All load-bearing components of these cases are in solid timber, built with a high degree of prefabrication. (See: Figs 6-13)

Project 1: Ölzbuendt residential development in Dornbirn (Vorarlberg Region), Austria, 1997 (Architect: Hermann Kaufmann, Schwarzach)

Fig. 6 a: View of the building's western facade, using prefabricated structure and facade elements. (Photo: H. Kaufmann)

This three-storey building is situated on a narrow plot of land within an estate of detached properties and is designed as a passive house. The twelve apartments (six 2-room units, six 3-room units) are compact in design. The combined kitchen, eating and living areas extend throughout the entire depth of the structure. At the southern end of the building is an additional residential and office unit spanning all three storeys. The project's objectives were to minimize construction times to four months by using pre-fabricated wooden units wherever possible, to build as energy-efficiently as possible and to use ecological materials without adding to overall expenses. The architect could rely on a good relationship with the manufacturer of the prefabricated wall systems and a large amount of the final construction details were based on previous successful projects.[20] The insulated shell encapsulates the compact volume of the building: a skeleton construction featuring wooden pillars and suspended, gravel-filled hollow box girder elements. Standard 2.40 m square, pre-fabricated wall elements, insulated with 350 mm thick mineral wool, are mounted in front of the structure to form a friction-free building envelope. Concrete wall-inserts help to make the building rigid and demarcate individual fire zones. The project was designed as a *passive energy house* (to German *Passivhaus* standards). To reach this objective, the architect chose a highly insulated, air-tight shell as timber frame construction with narrow posts, free of thermal bridges, minimizing heat loss. More info at: www.woodworks.org

Fig. 6 b, c: Details of the highly insulated wall panel system using prefabricated elements (2.4x2.4m), developed by the architect in close collaboration with the industry. Advantage: rapid, low-impact construction. (Photos: H. Kaufmann)

The individually controllable, decentralized ventilation system manages the flow of fresh air while doubling as a heating system. Fresh air enters the building via a geothermal heat exchanger, and waste heat from the kitchens, bathrooms and WCs is recycled via a plate-type heat exchanger. A central solar system supports the production of hot water. The balconies on the west side of the building and the open walkway with the stair-well on the eastern side are light steel constructions. The character of the facade is defined by the serrated weather-boarding in larch, which underscores the block-like appearance of the construction. Changes in colour and texture of the permanent untreated wooden cladding were taken into account in the planning process.[21]

Project 2: Senior housing complex in Neuenbuerg (Stuttgart), Germany, 1996 (Architects: Mahler-Guenster-Fuchs, Stuttgart)

Fig. 7: View of the four residential buildings facing the river. (Photo: C. Richters)

This serviced housing complex for the elderly consists of thirty units in four identical buildings along the banks of the River Enz. The four storey structure is a mixed concrete/timber structure (a 'wood-concrete hybrid'). The main structure is a reinforced concrete core (staircase walls) and concrete skeleton clad with timber, and is extended with a timber post and beam structure as balconies on both sides. However, the architects are confident they could have built the project entirely as a timber structure, and want to try this approach with another client. The long balconies run the entire length of the building and act as a shading device, especially on the long western facade where they offer protection from the strong afternoon sun. The large sliding elements add a delightful taste of irregularity to the elevations. A series of enhanced fire safety measures were realized, including a 90 minute fire resistance level construction for all primary structural elements of the balconies, which are also access and escape routes. The surface of the Douglas timber is untreated, unpainted and requires no maintenance. The roof is clad with plates of polycarbonate, which is translucent and allows daylight to penetrate. Underneath this layer are solar collectors. The whole project is a good example of a simple and affordable construction method with a strong tradition in vernacular buildings, as well as in German Modernism. It implies not only straight-forward structural solutions in an unsentimental way, but also considers daily functions and usability. To achieve the high quality in detailing, the architects spent a significant time on site guiding the construction phase.

Project 3: Svartlamoen multi-apartment building in Trondheim (Norway), 2004-2005 (Architects: Brendeland & Kristoffersen, Trondheim)

Fig. 8 a, b: View of the five-storey residential building in Trondheim. (Photo: J. Musch)

One of the most remarkable, and probably tallest, timber buildings in Europe can be found in Trondheim: a low-cost housing project. When a competition held in 2002 demanded that timber be used as the main construction material, the architects responded with a convincing concept that was also cost-effective: two buildings with an overall area of 1030 sqm, and open external steel staircases. The ground floor of the main five-storey building, which measures 6 m x 22 m, contains rooms that can be commercially used. On the four upper floors, units of 120 sqm in size can be used by groups of up to six people. Compact individual rooms lead to attractive community rooms with large windows facing the sun. The auxiliary building turns the ensemble into a protected courtyard with six individual apartments and a generous patio area. The entire construction was made out of of 144 mm solid cross-laminated timber boards developed and produced by the Austrian company Santner, and clad with Norwegian larch. The untreated timber surfaces of the load-bearing elements are visible inside in all rooms.

Ecological and flame-retardant aspects played a crucial role in the choice of the glue-laminated timber (GLT) elements. After being granted a special waver, the architects were able to create a timber building five storeys high instead of the maximum three storeys usually permitted in Norway. With the solid GLT elements defined as firewalls, each floor could be treated as an independent fire zone. The load-bearing panels, which were supplied with ready-textured surfaces, are integrated into the facade and thus give rise to a freely-definable floor layout without any obstruction from columns. The separating walls made from 96mm thick GLT panels are not part of the structural system. The sandwich structure of the outside wall consists of a 200 mm thick layer of mineral wool surrounded by gypsum fibreboards and clad in untreated larch. The weight of the building is less than half that of a similar building made from concrete, which simplified the construction of the foundations. The use of pre-fabricated elements reduced the construction time significantly (from June 2004 to completion in April 2005). Through the efficient assembly of the timber elements, four workers managed to erect the main structure in just ten working days.

Project 4: Spoettelgasse residential development in Vienna (Austria), 2005
(Architect: Hubert Riess, Graz)

Fig. 9 a: The building seen from the courtyard. (Photo: H. Riess)

The building is Vienna's first four and five-storey timber residential construction and has received awards for its bold design and innovative use of timber. It is regarded as a pioneering project, opening the way for future initiatives in the field of wooden construction in an urban environment. This pilot project with 150 units was implemented in the wake of a 2001 amendment to Vienna's building regulations. The new laws permitted buildings of four storeys with outer walls of wooden construction, provided that the ground floor was of concrete construction. Fire protection requirements played a central role in the building's planning and, in close collaboration with the authorities, criteria were laid down to ensure such requirements were met. The judges of the competition wrote the following about the project: 'This, the first four-storey timber residential property (in glue-laminated timber) on a solid timber base in Vienna, is particularly impressive on account of its bold and pioneering design. It was thanks to the work and dedication of the planning team that both the building developer and the city authorities were ultimately convinced of the feasibility of a project to build a multi-storey timber home within the framework of the current legal provisions. We would also like to emphasize the interdisciplinary approach adopted in project development and the largely structural application of timber.' (See also: *proHolz Austria*, www.wienwood.at)

Fig. 9 b: Image of on-site assembly of prefabricated board ceiling elements. (Photo: KLH Austria) Prefabrication can turn the construction process into a high-tech manufacturing process, reducing the time and weight by 50 per cent.

Project 5: Muehlweg residential development in Vienna (Austria), 2006
(Architects: Hermann & Johannes Kaufmann, with Riess & Untertrifaller, Schwarzach,
Vorarlberg Region)

Fig. 10: View from the courtyard, facing the buildings. (Photo: B. Klomfar)

In December 2003, the `Urban Renewal Fund' of Vienna invited tenders from developers
for a construction project focusing on `wood and hybrid wood/concrete constructions'.
One hundred public housing units were to be built with an emphasis on the ecological
and economic benefits of timber and mixed constructions. The winners were Riess & Untertrifaller in collaboration with the construction cooperative Kaufmann (both, architects
and manufacturers in one), using a design and construct process. The new development
is one of the pioneering projects in the field of multi-storey timber constructions. Within the
site, each project developed its own urban character. A terraced house and an L-shaped
building surround an internal courtyard, offering outdoor space for communal use. The
four-storey buildings offer two different plans. The north/south-oriented terraced concept,
with its maisonettes, has a two-storey timber construction on the second floor erected on
top of a podium of reinforced concrete. The timber ceiling between the ground and first
floors is inserted. Contrasting with the above are the three storey superstructures made
from pre-fabricated GLT elements built on top of the concrete basement of the east-west-
oriented units. The entire four storeys of the building are clad in larch. The obligatory fire
protection belts lend the building a horizontal layering.

The many floor-to-ceiling French windows provide an eye-catching contrast to the naturally
ageing wooden facade. The project was built to an impressive tight schedule: ground breaking was in August 2005. Off-site pre-fabrication of elements and the resulting optimized
construction process (driven by the architect) meant that the apartments were ready for occupation by October 2006. The project was a success because planners and public authorities
succeeded in working closely together on a consistent basis. In an interview, Kaufmann explains `the necessity of an early dialogue with the consenting authorities in order to develop
solutions for the fire engineering, and to share specific knowledge on timber construction
on a competent and open basis.' (...) `When working with prefabricated timber systems, it
requires the architect's close collaboration with the manufacturer to enable genuine innovation.' (H. Kaufmann, in journal *Zuschnitt*, no.20, 2005; p. 20, www.zuschnitt.at)

Project 6: **Holzhausen multi-family home in Steinhausen** (Switzerland), 2006
(Architects: Scheitlin-Syfrig & Partner, Luzern)

Fig. 11: View of the six-storey building in Steinhausen. (Photo: Renggli AG, Switzerland)

This residential project is a model for learning about ecological construction and modes
of living; an educational showpiece. A new fire protection standard in Switzerland, introduced in January 2005, permits the construction of timber buildings of up to six storeys
with a 60-minute fire-resistance capability. The multi-unit complex in Steinhausen, designed
by architects Scheitlin-Syfrig & Partner (in collaboration with manufacturer Holzbau Renggli AG), is Switzerland's first six-storey timber building, with a four-storey timber framed
construction (TFC) on top of a concrete base. The project replaced an existing two-storey
building and makes more intensive use of the 1600 sqm site area. Each storey accommodates two spacious apartments, 145 sqm or 165 sqm in area, with the main rooms
and large balconies oriented to the south and west. Cedar wood, anthracite coloured
windows, fibre cement cladding (produced by Eternit) and corrugated sheet panels on the
balconies characterize the building's appearance. The basement and ground floors are
solid masonry constructions.

Highly insulated, pre-fabricated outside-wall elements made from wood form the thermal
skin on the ground floor. From the first floor onwards only the central core, consisting of
the staircase and the lift, are made from reinforced concrete; while the walls are a frame
construction and the ceilings are acoustically decoupled, beamed constructions. The timber-metal windows feature triple-glazing with a very good u-value. The comfort ventilation
system, with waste-heat recovery, reduces heat loss through ventilation, while, with correct
usage by the inhabitants, an effective heat requirement ratio of just 20 kilowatt hours /
square metre can be achieved. A heat pump, with a geothermal probe, supports both
the heating and the domestic warm water systems. Fine-tuning of individual measures
meant that the development was able to surpass the criteria laid down by the stringent
'Swiss Minergy' standard. The highest quality of timber buildings today can be found
in particular regions with a long tradition of carpentry, such as in the Swiss canton of
Graubuenden, in the Austrian provinces of Vorarlberg and Steiermark, and in the southern German state of Bavaria.

Project 7: The tallest wooden housing block `Timber Tower`, London Hackney
(UK), 2007–09 (Architects: Waugh & Thistleton, London; developer: Telford Homes)

Fig. 12 a, b: The nine-storey (eight + one) timber building in London's East End, Murray Grove, Hackney. This is currently the tallest wood-frame housing block worldwide. (Photos: Waugh Thistleton, London)

This experimental project, a nine-storey residential tower called `Stadthaus` (with 30 units) in an urban context, is a model for the innovative use of new fire-engineered, load-bearing wall panels and structural timber. Built of cross-laminated `Jumbo Plywood Panels` (entirely prefabricated and manufactured by company KLH Massivholz in Dornbirn, Austria), the entire structure is constructed of prefabricated, cross-laminated timber (CLT) panels, including the load bearing walls, floor slabs and even the stair and lift cores.

The building consists of 19 private apartments, 10 social housing units and a resident's office. The upper eight stories are made from CLT panels, the ground floor is made from cast concrete with short pile foundation, made possible by the reduced building weight. According to architect Andrew Waugh, the timber structure will save 125 tonnes of CO_2 emissions compared to a concrete structure of similar size (emitted over 21 years estimated operation). If calculating the emissions avoided by not using steel or concrete, and taking into account the fact that wood stores CO_2, the savings are even equivalent to about 300 tonnes of CO_2. The prefabricated panels are up to 9 metres in length, with cut-outs for windows and doors. As they arrive on site, they are immediately craned into position. The exterior cladding is made up of 5,000 Eternit panels which are up to 70 per cent made of recycled waste timber. The building has a quarter of the weight of a comparable concrete building and in consequence, the entire structure was erected by four carpenters in only 10 weeks. The entire building process was fast and reduced construction time from a standard 72 weeks to only 49 weeks in total. The Stadthaus uses a platform configuration, with each floor set on the walls below and joints secured with simple `off-the-shelf` screws and angle plates. Meeting the requirements for fire protection was relatively straightforward: timber is self-protecting in the sense that it will char on the outside, preventing heat build-up at the centre and allowing it to retain its strength during a fire for longer periods than steel or even concrete. As such, the CLT panels were designed to resist fire by calculating charring rates. More info at: www.waughthistleton.com

Project 8: Wooden housing block `e3' in Berlin Mitte (Germany), 2007–09
(Architects: Kaden & Klingbeil, Berlin)

Fig. 13 a, b: The `e3' residential timber building in Berlin Prenzlauer Berg, a 7-storey timber structure. (Images: Courtesy K & K Architects, 2009)

This is a seven-storey wood-frame housing project in Esmarchstrasse, Berlin Prenzlauer Berg, using the same technology as the previous project in London. The CLT panels are cross-laminated, which means that loads can be transferred in one direction (e.g. for supports or girders) or on all sides, creating unique design opportunities. CLT panels have three or five layers and a fire resistance of 30 minutes. Combined with a layer of drywall; this achieves fire resistance ratings of 60 and 90 minutes. An external staircase tower allows for short escape routes, which helped with the approval. Supplied by Austrian manufacturer KLH Massivholz (Dornbirn), the CLT panels are made from industrial dried spruce boards stacked together at right angles and glued over their entire surface, much like jumbo plywood. Prefabricated at the factory, the panels arrive at the construction site in sizes of approximately 16 x 3 metres. Wall panels were pre-cut for windows and doors. Larger apartments are located on the lower floors and the smaller on the upper floors; allowing for the structural walls to be easier placed to minimize the load on each individual wooden beam. The external wall construction includes 80mm insulation, an air gap and rain screen cladding to reduce noise from outside. This cladding is also made from timber: a combination of wood pulp and cement tile.

All of the timber used in the production of CLT panels comes from forests that are certified as being sustainably managed (in Austria, more trees grow in managed forests than are taken out); the CLT panel is a very appropriate material for low-cost, high-density housing, and it saves CO_2 emissions. The construction of this timber building was around 15 per cent cheaper compared with an identical structure in concrete, caused by faster construction and smaller foundations; the reduced building weight allowed the foundations to be reduced by 70 per cent. Taller wood structures are achievable and efficient: according to the engineers, an all-timber structure is feasible up to 25 stories. More info at: www.infoholz.de

Lessons learnt from these case studies

The presented case study projects all have in common:

• the initial designs and subsequent commissions were the outcome of architectural design competitions, which is a way to raise quality in architecture;

• the sophisticated timber wall systems for energy-efficiency were especially developed for the projects; and

• that during the procurement of these projects, productive team integration was achieved by the leadership of the architect, leading a collaborative approach with the system manufacturer.

Timber, if harvested from a sustainably grown and managed forest (e.g. a forest where carbon stocks are being maintained, with strict forest management), is a sustainable construction material, more so than steel. In the past, the argument was that timber was limited in height, and this is where steel and concrete came in as prefered construction materials. With recent technical developments and changes in legislation, timber can be considered for multi-story buildings; even beyond 10-storey structures. A series of recent research studies have pointed to the many advantages of building timber, in addition to its carbon storage capacity; for instance, a 2009 study by the New Zealand Ministry of Agriculture and Forestry found, that using timber in large-scale commercial buildings could significantly reduce the environmental impact of such developments. The study used LCA-methods and looked at both the life-cycle energy use as well as CO_2 emissions of a six storey timber structure, compared with a similar building constructed of concrete or steel.

The conditions under which architecture is practiced (and the effects that these have on built outcomes) have seen significant changes over the last decade. However, when interviewing the teams of the presented case studies, the importance of upholding the leading role of the architect during the entire project procurement was repeatedly mentioned as an important criterion for the success of the project. The architect is still seen as the discipline member most appropriate to imagine, visualize and coordinate a project to completion (rather than handing it over to a project manager who has often been only marginally involved in producing the drawings and is not trained to synthesize complex input). This appears to be particularly important for the development and implementation of innovative fire-engineered solutions, on which the successful completion of these timber projects heavily depends. It is also clear from the comments of the architects that in each case a close collaboration with the manufacturer of the timber components was essential and helped make innovation possible.

Forging closer relationships between architects and component manufacturers

In the presented case studies, the architect has been identified as the leader of innovation and the construction procurement process – which indicates that the architectural profession can still be a reliable manager of time and budget. As Driver points out, 'the strength of an architect's vision for sustainable construction at the start of a project can only navigate the processes that lead to the project's completion without compromise if the architect is allowed a central and continuous role throughout. We have seen that this is possible on developer-led 'design and construct' projects through an emphasis on long-term relationships and through providing a wide platform of knowledge and expertise.' (Driver, 2007)

Fig. 14 a, b: Left: Prefabricated timber container 'System 3', exhibited at the 'Home Delivery' exhibition at the MOMA in New York, 2008; architects: Oskar Leo Kaufmann and Albert Ruef, KFN Systems (Austria). Right: Prefabricated apartment building, close to Bern, Switzerland, 2008; architects: Halle 58, Bern. (Photo: Courtesy Halle 58)

Architects are talented in synthesizing problems, prepared to take and manage risks, and have been professionally trained to coordinate complex tasks under tight constraints. They frequently demonstrate a cohesive understanding of the building process and are, therefore, likely to be leaders of technological change, which can give them a higher degree of design control. It appears that the architectural profession is able to guide the full consultant team and other disciplines involved. Kaufmann points out: 'Adapting *lose-fit* design strategies is necessary to provide for the required flexibility when developing new solutions and construction methods with industry, extending project-based knowledge.' (Kaufmann, 2007)

Time is obviously well invested in long-term relationships between architects and manufacturers to develop new methods, not only for a single projects but also for generally new and better ways to build (despite the obstacles that a project-organized sector brings along). Over the last twenty years or so, there have been some great examples of collaborative, risk taking architects, continuously innovating in the timber industry: Swiss architects Burkhalter & Sumi and Peter Zumthor; German architects Thomas Herzog and Otto Steidle; Norwegian architect Sverre Fehn; as well as some contemporary Japanese architects (Katsuhiro Ishii, Shigeru Ban), have been forerunners in the rediscovery of timber as a contemporary and sustainable construction material. They have combined it with both a vernacular, regional approach to design, and with innovative application. These practices have succeeded over the years in building-up substantial expertise in timber constructions, driving today's innovation in this field through their competitive advantage. The experience of builders and architects in the last twenty years is now preparing the way for innovative approaches in building as well as in research activities. For instance, the dynamic, giant roof structure by Herzog and Natterer for the EXPO 2000 in Hannover ('the world's largest GLT timber roof'; Natterer, 2002) is an elegant sculpture and an impressive demonstration of the structural possibilities for timber shells. With the height restrictions on residential timber buildings being lifted, new methods of fabrication are been developed. The aim is to fully mobilize the capacities of new manufacturing methods towards a more effective use of the unique characteristics of the material. As a result, new lightweight and high-performance components are being developed, minimizing waste on the construction site through prefabrication.[22] It is highly likely that the future will put even more requirements on the architect and engineer to use green materials in prefabricated timber systems, and apply components that facilitate reuse and recycling.

Keeping the architectural qualities and the design vocabluary in the foreground, with prefabrication we can increase the durability of buildings, while using materials and resources more sparingly.

Barriers for innovation in the timber construction industry

The construction sector is still far behind the development and innovation of other industry sectors (such as the automotive or IT sectors). But the energy technology and recycling sectors, for instance, have very much developed and are closely connected with and impacting on the building sector. This has implications on the way in which we design, build and operate cities and buildings.

The precondition for innovation in the building sector, which is a rigid project-organized sector, deserves a closer look. As noted by Nelson, 'the interplay between projects, project teams and firms (companies/manufacturers) is intrinsic to the innovation system of the construction industry.' (Nelson, 1993) However, Nelson explains, 'multiple layers of communication exist in the building process, and the involved parties function under different technological regimes.' This means that innovation and technological change (e.g. a shift towards more sustainable building systems) are highly affected by the sector in which they take place. (Malerba, 2004) Obviously, there is a main difference between the various players, which are the multidisciplinary planning team, the building component manufacturer (supplier), and project-based contractor: that is, that in the project-based construction industry, 'innovation occurs within projects, whereas in functionally organized manufacturers R&D departments exist.' (Malerba, 2004) It can also be observed that in individual projects, such as the presented case studies, the collaborative coupling between architect and manufacturer is usually 'tight', whereas in the permanent network (e.g. between manufacturer and contractor) it is 'loose'.

The supply industry of building components (in our case, the manufacturer of prefabricated timber wall systems) is expected to innovate in order to encourage CO_2 emission reductions, while contractors are urged to later-purchase the new technology by means of energy policy that is imposed on new construction. This fact makes the building components manufacturer potentially a good partner for any architect striving for innovation. However, reality shows that trustful and long-term relationships between the involved parties – which is widely seen as a necessity for learning processes and innovation – are rare and difficult to realize in one-off project-based industries. Much of the success depends on the personal relationship between architect and manufacturer.

Vorarlberg, the second smallest Austrian province, has emerged as a leading region with a tradition of building craft and sustainable timber construction. A number of pioneering architects have established a strong technical, functional and economical vocabluary, while retaining the unique regional style. One of these leading architects is Hermann Kaufmann, who is now working on a 20-storey timber high-rise building, which is pushing the boundaries of load-bearing timber structures even further. He noted as main barrier to innovation: `The availability of relevant expertise is thought to be crucial for the success of innovative projects, but project-based companies appear to select their employees on the basis of availability instead of expertise.' (Kaufmann, 2009). In general, this condition makes it hard for architects in a continuous search for innovation (`how can we improve this?') along a circular routine of processes. `Practice-led research' means that architectural practices need to build-up their internal knowledge-base and experience, and the capacity to properly store and re-apply this knowledge, with the aim of constantly developing it. On the other hand, once the architectural practice has gained such innovative expertise, it can more easily engage in a meaningful collaboration with the relevant manufacturers, which would otherwise continue producing standardized components.

Timber's place as construction material in the 21st-century city
In regard to sustainable development, Tzonis has noted: `The long-term negative impact of the application of techniques and materials of construction on material resource consumption and environmental physical quality is now a prime concern in architecture. The task of inquiry is just beginning.' (Tzonis, 2006)

The environmental dimension has certainly enriched architectural thinking, shifting the attention to a search for long-term sustainable developments. It is very likely that multi-storey timber-framed constructions will make an important contribution to the future residential market, facing the challenges of sustainable architecture. Such innovative developments will change the perception of timber as a `low status' material (the notion of `living in a timber box'). With all its sustainable qualities and various advantages, the author suggests that wood is a contemporary construction material of the 21st century. Numerous multi-storey commercial and residential buildings throughout Europe demonstrate the manifold possibilities and exploitability of timber and its technologies. While it is true that biogenic construction materials are not cheaper than their conventional counterparts, the challenge is to use existing resources responsibly in order to create comfortable, intelligent and environmentally compatible buildings.[23]

Larger projects in timber construction require specialized consultants to avoid common mistakes in detailing and surface treatment. Often it can be observed that there is a decline in the client's commitment to building sustainable from the start to the end of a project. Therefore, clear objectives are necessary in the planning process. Timber is tailor-made for the task of inner-city residential projects, as the presented housing developments have shown. Wood structures are predestined to pursue this new course to become show-piece projects for sustained building solutions.

The presented multi-storey examples have their own individual appearance, defined through the materials used in their construction. They look elegant and architecturally attractive. They are not only examples of aesthetic refinement, they also demonstrate that timber allows for an energy-efficient, sustainable architecture that can be adapted to provide the community with healthier buildings and a more sustainable building regime for our cities. We can conclude:

- multi-storey timber construction will make an important contribution to the future residential market;
- architects and system manufacturers are key players in the process of creating sustainable buildings in timber, for affordable inner-city housing.

Food and waste have to be considered as main drivers for cities and architectural design. Both call for innovation and invention.
Sir Nicholas Grimshaw, 2010

Conclusion: change can happen, and fast

In his book `Hot, Flat, and Crowded. Why we need a Green Revolution – And how it can renew America', Thomas Friedman argues: `No wonder the WWF's *Living Planet Report* 2008 concludes that we are already operating 25 per cent above the planet's biological capacity to support life. And that is before we add another billion people by the early 2020s.' (Friedman, 2008) The situation has become urgent, because the way of life we have got used to over the last decade cannot continue this way without catastrophic consequences. Significant change is necessary. Friedman notes: `The green revolution is not about the whales anymore. And it is not about `our children's children,' a generation so distant it is really hard to get energized about it. This is about us. This is about the world we and our children will inhabit for the rest of our lives and whether we can find a way to create wealth – because everyone wants to live better – without creating toxic assets in the financial world or the natural world that overwhelm us.'

The increased use of prefabrication and timber in construction can be a helpful strategy to reduce GHG emissions and deliver affordable housing in compact developments, overcoming the main problem for inner-city housing: the high land cost. This chapter looked at the amazing technological possibilities available and the need for accelerating the transition to green urbanism based on renewable energy sources and a circular urban metabolism. The use of prefabriction and modular timber construction systems could be such a pathway, in combination with on-site renewable energy generation. History shows that significant change can be achieved in a short time, in, say, five to eight years. The positive message is that if there is a desire and an urgency to make the change, it can and will happen quickly. In order that the shift to 'renewable cities' takes place as quickly as possible, it is vitally important to build more pilot demonstration projects, based on the principles of green urbanism, using all technologies available. This will engender public confidence and dispel critics. It will also show that a combined mix of renewable energy options can deliver firm and reliable power and a better urban life – compared to the current fossil-fuel systems – without the CO_2 emissions.

Thinking about long-term scenarios is relevant to decision making, to accelerate our action for sustainable urban development and to go for radical approaches, if we want to avoid the high costs of non-action or delay.

In this context, urban design offers the greatest opportunities for CO_2 reductions. It is the lowest of the low hanging fruit.

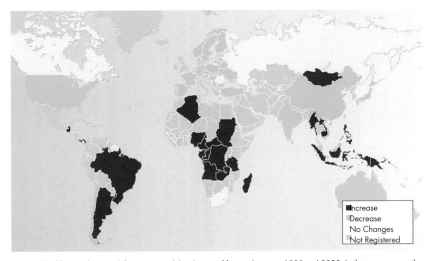

Increase
Decrease
No Changes
Not Registered

Fig. 15: World map, showing deforestation and the change of forests, between 1990 and 2005. In the green areas, the amount of available timber is increasing and sustainable harvesting of timber is possible. In the red areas, a destructive consumption level of timber resources and deforestation has been reached. (Source: spiegel.de, 2008)

Acknowledgement:
Regarding the research on timber construction systems, I acknowledge the discussions and collaboration with Frank Lattke for his significant contributions, 2008.

References

Ackermann, Kurt (1993). *Stadttechnik. Semiar Schriften-Sammlung*. Universitaet Stuttgart, Germany.
Aldersey-Williams, Hugh (2003): *Zoomorphic. New Animal Architecture*; Lawrence King Publishing, London, UK.
Alexander, Christopher (1965). *A City is not a Tree. Parts I & II*. Essays first published in: *Architectural Forum*, Vol. 122, No 1, April 1965, pp 58-62 (Part I); and Vol 122, No 2, May 1965, pp 58-62 (Part II). New York.
Alexander, Christopher (2003). *The Nature of Order*. Centre for Environmental Structure, Berkeley, USA.
Alexander, Christopher; with Ishikawa, S. and Silverstein, M. (1977). *A Pattern Language*. Oxford University Press, New York.
Australian Bureau of Statistics (1990). *Australian National Accounts, Capital Stocks 1988-89*, ABS, Canberra
Banham, Reyner (1969). *The Architecture of the Well-tempered Environment*. University of Chicago Press, USA.
Beatley, T.; Manning, K. (1997). *The Ecology of Place: Planning for Environment, Economy, and Community*. Island Press, Washington DC.
Benyus, Janine (1997). *Biomimicry: Innovation Inspired by Nature*. Jetson Green, Illinois and New Jersey, USA. www.janinebenyus.com
Bergdoll, Barry; Christensen, Peter (2008). *Home Delivery. Fabricating the Modern Dwelling*. Catalogue, MOMA New York.
Blundell, Lynne (2009). *UK town bypasses electricity grid and slashes power use*; in: *The Fifth Estate* Online News, (22 Aug. 2009), Sydney.
Brandon, Peter; Lombardi, Patrizia (2005). *Evaluating Sustainable Development in the Built Environment*. Blackwell Publishing, Oxford, UK.
Breheny, Michael J. (1992): *Sustainable Development and Urban Form*. Pion, London, UK.
Brooks, G. (1988). *Site Planning: Environment, Process and Development*. Prentice Hall, New Jersey, USA.
Brown, Rebekah, Wong, Tony, Keath, N. (2009). *Urban Water Management in Cities: Historical, current and future Regimes*. In: *Water Science Technology*, Vol. 5, No. 59, p.847-855, Melbourne, Australia.
Brugmann, Jeb (2009). *Welcome to the Urban Revolution. How Cities are Changing the World*. ICLEI; Bloomsbury Press, London, UK
Brundtland, Gro H. (1987). *The Brundtland Report. Our Common Future*. UN-Report of the World Commission on Environment and Development. Oslo, Norway; United Nations. Oxford University Press, UK
Burdett, Richard (ed.) (2004). *Density and Urban Neighbourhoods in London*. Enterprise LSE Cities, London, UK.

References for Chapter 2

Burton, Elizabeth (1997 / reprint 2000). *The compact city: Just or just compact? A preliminary analysis*. In: *Urban Studies*, Number 37 (11/ 2000).
Butler, D. and Maksimovic, C. (1999). *Urban Water Management – Challenges for the Third Millennium*. In: *Progressive Environmental Science*, Vol. 3, No. 1, p. 213-235, London, UK.
CABE (2008). Report: *What makes an eco-town?* CABE, London (the UK Government's 'Commission for Architecture and the Built Environment'). Report available online.
Castells, Manuel (1996). *The Rise of the Network Society*. Blackwell, Oxford, UK.
Cox, Mark (2010). In direct email conversation with the author. London, UK.
Cervero, Robert (2010). *Transportation Policies and Planning for Sustainable Development*. Presentation Jan. 2010 at the *World Future Energy Summit*, Abu Dhabi, UAE.
Cosgrove, W.J.; Rijsberman, F.R. (2000). *World Water Vision: Making Water Everybody's Business*. Earthscan, London, UK.
Curdes, Gerd (1992). *Energiesparende Siedlungsstrukturen*; paper presented at Arbeitskreis Energie, Deutsche Physikalische Gesellschaft (Oct. 1992), Bad Honnef, Germany.
Curdes, Gerhard (1993). *Stadtstruktur und Stadtgestaltung*. Kohlhammer, Stuttgart, Germany.
Cullen, Gordon (1961/1964). *The Concise Townscape*. Architectural Press, London, UK.
Daniels, Klaus (1995). *Technologie des oekologischen Bauens*. Birkhaeuser, Basel/Berlin, Germany.
Daniels, Klaus (2000). *Low-Tech, Light-Tech, High-Tech. Building in the Information Age*. Birkhaeuser, Basel/Berlin, Germany.
Dey, Chris et al. (2007) *Consumption Atlas*, developed by ISA at University of Sydney, for the Australian Conservation Foundation; ACF Sydney: www.acfonline.org.au
Dehne, M. and Krueger, U. (2006). *Fire Protection in Multi-storey Timber Construction*; in: *Detail* 10/2006, pp. 1142-1144; Munich, Germany.
Dovers, Stephen (2003). *Reflecting on three decades: a synthesis*; in: Dovers, S. & Wild River, S. (eds.) (2003). *Managing Australia's Environment*, Federation Press, Sydney.
Driver, Kevin (2007). *Developing the role of Inclusion*; in: *Architecture Australia*, July 2007, Melbourne, Australia.
Droege, Peter (2009). In direct email communication with the author, February 2009.
Droege, Peter (ed.) (2008). *Urban Energy Transition. An Introduction*; in: *Urban Energy Transition. From Fossil-Fuels to Renewable Power*. Elsevier, 2003, Amsterdam.
Droege, Peter (ed.) (2009). *100% Renewable. Energy Autonomy in Action*. Earthscan, London, UK.
Du Plessis, Chrisna (2008). *A Conceptual Framework for Understanding Social-Ecological Systems*. In: Burns, M.;

Weaver, A. (eds) (2008) *Exploring Sustainability Science*. Sun Press, Stellenbosch, South Africa.

Dunphy, R.T.; Fisher, K. (1994). *Transportation, congestion, and density: New insights*. Urban Land Institute, Washington DC.

Dunster, Bill; Simmons, Craig (2008). *The ZEDbook. Solutions for a Shrinking World*. Taylor & Francis, Oxon, UK.

Ecosmart Concrete (2008). Info at web site: www.ecosmart.ca/enviro-cement.cfm

Eichholtz, Kok and Quigly (2009). *Doing well by doing good? Green Office Buildings*. Study at the University of California Energy Institute, Los Angeles, USA.

Fisher, Thomas (2010). *A Fracture-Critical Future*; in: *ACSA News*, Feb. 2010, p.2-3, ACSA, Washington DC, USA.

Fishman, Robert (1987). *Bourgeois Utopia. The Rise and Fall of Suburbia*. Basic Books, New York, USA.

Flannery, Tim (2005). *The Weather Makers. How Man is changing the Climate*. Atlantic Monthly Press, Sydney, Australia.

Florida, Richard (2002). *The Rise of the Creative Class*. Basic Books, New York, USA.

Forster, Clive (1999; 2nd edition). *Australian Cities. Continuity and Change*. Oxford University Press, UK

Friedman, Thomas L. (2008; updated edition 2009). *Hot, Flat, and Crowded. Why we need a Green Revolution – and how it can renew America*. Picador, New York, USA.

Garreau, Joel (1991). *The Edge City. Life on the New Frontier*. Anchor Books/Doubleday, Random House, New York.

Gauzin-Mueller, Dominique, (2002). *Sustainable architecture and urbanism: Concepts, technologies, examples*. Birkhaeuser, Basel/Berlin, Germany.

Gehl, Jan (1971). *Life between Buildings. Using Public Space*. The Danish Architecture Press, Copenhagen, Denmark.

Girardet, Herbert (2008, 2nd ed.). *Cities, People, Planet. Urban Development and Climate Change*. Wiley, London, UK.

Gore, Al (ed.) (2006). *An inconvenient Truth. The Planetary Emergency of Global Warming and what we can do about it*. Rodale/Bloomsbury, USA. www.climatecrisis.net

Green Building Council of Australia (2008). Report: *Valuing Green*. GBCA Sydney, Australia: www.gbca.com.au

Grimshaw Architects (2009). *Blue, Issue 1: Water, Energy and Waste;* Grimshaw, London/Melbourne.

Hall, Peter; Pfeiffer, Ulrich (2000). *Urban Future 21. A Global Agenda for 21st Century Cities*. London, UK.

Hausladen, Gerhard; de Saldanha, M.; Liedl, P.; Sager, C. (2005). *ClimaDesign: Lösungen für Gebäude*. Callwey Publisher, Stuttgart/ Birkhaeuser, Basel/Berlin (english version), Germany.

Head, Peter (2009). *Entering the Ecological Age*. Report by Arup, based on Head's talk for *The Brunel Lecture Series* 2008, London. Available online at: www.arup.com

Hegger, Manfred; Fuchs, M.; Stark, T.; Zeumer, M. (2007). *Energy Manual - Energie Atlas. Sustainable Architecture*. Birkhäuser Verlag, Basel/Berlin (Edition Detail, english version), Germany.

Herzog, Thomas (ed.) (2007). *The Charter for Solar Energy in Architecture and Urban Planning*. Prestel, Munich.

Holcim Awards for Sustainable Construction: Since 2006 organized by the Holcim Group, CH. See: www.holcimfoundation.org

Howard, Ebenezer (1898; reprint 1989). *Tomorrow, A Peaceful Path to Real Reform*. (1902 re-issued as: *Garden Cities of Tomorrow*), ATC Books, Builth Wells/Faber and Faber, London, UK.

Humpert, Klaus (1997). *Einfuehrung in den Stadtebau*. Kohlhammer, Stuttgart, Germany.

Hyde, Richard (2000). *Climate Responsive Design: A Study of Buildings in Moderate and Hot Humid Climates*. E. & F.N. Spon, London, UK.

IPCC Report (2001; 2008). *Climate Change: Synthesis Report - Summary for Policymakers*. Geneva, CH; available online: www.ipcc.ch

Jacobs, Jane (1961). *The Death and Life of Great American Cities*. Random House, New York, USA.

Jenks, Mike; and Burgess, Rod (eds.) (2000). *Compact Cities. Sustainable Urban Forms for Developing Countries*. Spon Press, London, UK.

Johnson, Chris; Hu, Richard (2008). *Connecting Cities: China*. Research publication for the *9th World Congress of Metropolis*, Sydney. Metropolis Pubblication, Barcelona

Kats, Greg, et al. (2003). *The Costs and Financial Benefits of Green Buildings*. Report to California's Sustainable Building Task Force, Oct. Los Angeles/Sacramento, 2003, USA.

Kaufmann, Herrmann (2009). *Wood Works. Oeko-rationale Baukunst - Architecture Durable*. Springer-Verlag, Berlin, Germany.

Kearns, A., Barnett, G., Nolan, A. (2006). *An Ecological Design Strategy for the Planning and Development of Healthy Urban Habitat*. BDP Environmental Design Guide, Nov. 2006; The Australian Institute of Architects, Sydney (available online).

Koenigsberger, Otto H.; Ingersoll, T.G.; et al (1979/1980). *Manual of tropical housing and building: Part I. Climatic design*. Longman, London, UK.

Kostof, Spiro (1992). *The City Assembled. The Elements of Urban Form through History;* Thames & Hudson, London, UK.

Knab, S.; Strunz, K. (2010). *The Smart Grid;* in: *TU-Berlin International*, No. 65, issue Jan. 2010, Berlin, Germany.

Kolb, Josef (2007). *Holzbau mit System*. Birkhäuser, Basel/Berlin, Germany.

Krier, Rob (1979). *Urban Space*. Rizzoli International, New York, USA.

Le Corbusier (1948). *Concerning Town Planning*. Yale University Press, New Haven, USA.

Lehmann, Steffen (2006). *Towards a Sustainable City Centre: Integrating Ecologically Sustainable Development (ESD) Principles into Urban Renewal*. In: *Journal of Green Building*, Vol. 1, Number 3 (Summer 2006), pp. 85-104. College Publishing, USA: www.slab.com.au

Lehmann, Steffen (ed.) (2005). *Absolutely Public: Crossover Art and Architecture;* Images Publishing, Melbourne.

Lehmann, Steffen (2008). *Book Chapter 18: Cities in Transition: New Models for Urban Growth and Neighbourhoods;* pp. 409-432; in: *Urban Energy Transition. From Fossil Fuels to Renewable Power;* Elsevier Publisher (Ed. P. Droege), 2008; Oxford, UK.

Lehmann, Steffen (2008). *Growth of the post-industrial city: Densification and expansion - Two models for sustainability on the urban scale*; pp. 43-48; published in proceedings: *Oxford Conference 2008*, by Oxford Brookes University (July 2008); in: *The Oxford Conference. A Re-Evaluation of Education in Architecture*; WIT Press (eds. S. Roaf, A. Bairstow); Oxford, UK.

Lehmann, Steffen (ed.) (2009). *Back to the City. Strategies for Informal Urban Interventions*. Hatje Cantz, Stuttgart/Berlin, Germany.

Lehmann, Steffen (2009). *Public Space: Empowering Community, Facilitating Urban Renewal*; pp. 33-58; published in proceedings: *Community, Health and the Arts: Vital Arts - Vibrant Communities*, by the University of Melbourne (Sep. 2008); in: *UNESCO Observatory* e-Journal, Vol. 1, Issue 4, Aug. 2009; Melbourne, Australia.

Lieb, R. D. (2001). *Double-skin Facades*. Birkhaeuser; Boston, Basel, Berlin, Germany.

Lim, Y. Astee; Kishnani, Nirmal (2009). *Building-integrated Agriculture: Utilising Rooftops for Sustainable Food Crop Cultivation in Singapore*; in: proceedings iNTA-SEGA 2009 Conference (Dec. 2009), Bangkok, Thailand.

Lynch, Kevin (1981). *Good City Form*. MIT Press, Cambridge, USA.

Maher, Ken (2009). A.S. Hook Address given by K. Maher on 27 October 2009 in Sydney; in: *Architecture Australia*, Vol. 99, No 1, Jan./Feb/ 2010, pp. 51-53, Melbourne, Australia.

MacKay, David (2008). *Sustainable Energy - Without the Hot Air*. UIT Cambridge, UK; available online at: www.withouthotair.com

Malerba, F. (2004). *Sectoral Systems of Innovation: Concepts, Issues and Analysis of Six Major Sectors in Europe*. Cambridge University Press, Cambridge, UK.

Mayer, Amelie-Theres (2009). *Nachhaltige Quartiersentwicklung im Fokus flexibler Strukturen*. Vdf-Hochschulverlag, ETH Zürich, Switzerland.

McHarg, Ian (1969). *Design with Nature*, London, UK.

Metropolis: the organization consisting of over 120 member cities: commissioned Survey by CISCO, 2009: *The Urban Innovation for Sustainability*, survey presents top priorities of municipal leaders around the world and their efforts to create more sustainable cities (available online: www.metropolis.org).

McKinsey & Company (2007; Version II, 2009). Report: *Pathways to a Low-Carbon Economy*; available online: www.lowcarboneconomy.com

McDonough, William; Braungart, Michael (2002). *Cradle to Cradle: Remaking the Way we Make Things*. North Point Press, New York, USA.

Mitscherlich, Alexander (1965). *Die Unwirtlichkeit unserer Staedte. Thesen zur Stadt der Zukunft*. Suhrkamp, Frankfurt, Germany.

Natterer, Julius, et al (1994). *Holzbau Atlas Zwei*. Institut fuer Internationale Architektur-Dokumentation; Munich, Germany.

Nelson, R. (ed.), (1993). National Systems of Innovation. A comparative Analysis. Oxford University Press, Oxford, UK.

Newman, Peter and Jennings, Isabella (2008). *Cities as sustainable ecosystems: Principles and practices*. Island Press, Washington DC, USA.

Newman, Peter and Kenworthy, Jeff (1989). *Cities and automobile dependence: An international sourcebook*. Gower Press, Aldershot.

Newman, Peter (ed.) (2008). *Transitions: Pathways Towards Sustainable Urban Development in Australia*. Springer, Melbourne, Australia.

OECD (2003). Report: *Environmentally Sustainable Buildings. Challenges and Policies*. OECD, Paris.

Owens, S. (1986). *Energy, Planning and Urban Form*. Pion Press, London, UK.

Pachauri, Rachendra / IPCC (2009). Quote from his speech at the World Future Energy Summit, Abu Dhabi, UAE, January 2009.

Pivo, Gary (1997). *How do you implement less auto-dependent urban form?* Report for the Washington State Transport Commission, May 1997; Seattle, Washington, USA (report available online).

Poulsen, Tjalfe and Hansen, Jens Aage (2009). Paper in: *Waste Management & Research*, 2009; in: *ScienceDaily*, 10 Dec. 2009, UK.

Power, Anne; Rogers, Richard (2000). *Cities for a small country*. Faber & Faber, London, UK.

Register, Richard (2002). *Ecocities. Building Cities in Balance with Nature*. Berkeley Hill Books, Berkeley, USA.

Register, Richard (1987). *Eco-city Berkeley: Building cities for a healthy future*. North Atlantic Books, Boston.

Renggli AG (2005). *MFH in Steinhausen: Switzerland's first six-storey timber building*. Project documentation of Renggli AG), Sursee, Switzerland.

Salingaros, Nikos A. (2003). *Connecting the Fractal City*. Keynote speech to 5th Biennal of Town Planners in Europe, April 2003; available online. Barcelona, Spain.

Sassen, Saskia (2000). *Cities in a World Economy*. Pine Forge Press, California, USA.

Scott, Andrew, (2006). *Design Strategies for Green Practice*. In: *Journal of Green Building*, College Publishing, Vol. 1, Number 4 (Fall 2006) pp. 11-27, USA.

Scheer, Hermann (2002); (original in German, 1999). *The Solar Economy. Renewable Energy for a Sustainable Global Future*. Earthscan Publications, London, UK.

Scheer, Hermann (2006). *Energy Autonomy. The Economic, Social and Technological Case for Renewable Energy*. Earthscan, London, UK.

Sennett, Richard (2003). *The Fall of Public Man*. Penguin Books, London, UK.

Sinclair, Cameron/Architecture for Humanity (ed.) (2006). *Design like you give a damn. Architectural responses to humanitarian crises*. Thames & Hudson, London. www.architectureforhumanity.org

Sitte, Camillo (1889; translated in English in 1945). *City Planning According to Artistic Principles*. (German original: *Der Städtebau nach seinen künstlerischen Grundsätzen*). Vienna. English version, 1965, Random House, New York.

Stern, Sir Nicholas (2007). *The Stern Review: The Economics of Climate Change.* Cambridge University Press (October 2006, published January 2007); available online: www.sternreview.org.uk
Stern, Sir Nicholas (2010). In private conversation with the author at the *World Future Energy Summit,* Jan. 2010, Abu Dhabi.
Sudjic, D. (1992). *The 100 mile City. San Diego.* Harcourt Brace Publisher, Los Angeles, USA.
Treberspurg, Martin; and Stadt Linz (eds.) (2008). *SolarCity Linz-Pichling. Nachhaltige Stadtentwicklung / Sustainable Urban Development.* Springer-Verlag, Berlin, Germany.
Tzonis, Alexander (2006). *Rethinking Design Methodology for Sustainable Social Quality*; in: Ban, J.-H. and Ong, B.-L. (eds.): *Tropical Sustainable Architecture,* Princeton Architectural Press, USA.
UN-Habitat/United Nations (2010). UN-Habitat's *Fifth World Urban Forum*: State of the World's Cities Report 2010/11. UN Publications, Nairobi; Earthscan, London, UK. In parts available online: www.un.org
UN-Habitat (1996). *An Urbanizing World. Global Report on Human Settlements.* Oxford University Press, Oxford, UK.
Urban Land Institute (2007). *Growing Cooler,* study by ULI, Washington DC, USA; available online: www.uli.org
Urban Task Force, London (1999; report). *Towards an Urban Renaissance.* E&FN Spon Press, London, UK.
Von Weizaecker, Ernst Ulrich (2009). Interview: *Why increased efficiency will lead to a more advanced civilization.* In: *Pictures of the Future,* Spring 2009, p. 37. Munich, Germany.
Vale, Robert and Brenda (1991). *Green Architecture: Design for an Energy-conscious Future,* London, UK.
Vale, Robert and Brenda (2000). *The Autonomous House;* Thames & Hudson, London, UK.
Wackernagel, Mathis; Rees, William (1996). *Our Ecological Footprint.* New Society Press, Philadelphia, USA.
WEC (World Energy Council) (2004). *Energy Efficiency: A Worldwide Review.* WEC, London, UK.
Wikipedia, the online encyclopedia; accessed 20th December 2009.
Wong, Tony (ed.) (2006). *Australian Runoff Quality: A Guide to Water Sensitive Urban Design*; p. 1-8. In: *Engineers Australia;* Canberra, Australia.
Worldwatch Institute: The independent institute promotes *Vision for a Sustainable World,* analyzing interdisciplinary environmental data from around the world, how to build a sustainable society. See: www.worldwatch.org
Whyte, William H. (1980). *The Social Life of Small Urban Spaces.* Conservation Foundation, Washington DC, USA.
Yeang, Ken (2009). *Eco-Masterplanning.* John Wiley & Sons, London, UK.
Zhengrong, Shi (2010). The founder and CEO of *Suntech Power* (China), in conversation with the author (20 Jan. 2010).

Web Sites and Online Sources (Accessed January 2010)

Timber architects:

Baumschlager Eberle, Vorarlberg Region, Austria	www.baumschlager-eberle.com
Brendeland Kristoffersen, Trondheim, Norway	www.bkark.no
Herrmann Kaufmann,Schwarzach, Austria	www.kaufmann.archbuero.com ; www.holz.ar.tum.de
Company KLH GmbH, Dornbirn, Austria	www.jkarch.at and www.klhuk.com
Thomas Herzog + Partner, Munich, Germany	www.herzog-und-partner.de
Mahler Guenster Fuchs, Stuttgart, Germany	www.mgf-architekten.de
Halle 58 Architects, Bern, Switzerland	www.halle58.ch
Hubert Riess Architekt, Graz, Austria	www.archinform.net
Scheitlin-Syfrig + Partner, Luzern, Switzerland	www.scheitlin-syfrig.ch
Kaden + Klingbeil, Berlin, Germany	www.kaden-klingbeil.de
Timber structures	www.woodworks.org
Business Council for Sustainable Energy, Australia	www.bcse.org.au
Centre for Cities (UK)	www.centreforcities.org
Potsdam Climate Institute	www.pik-potsdam.de
Eurocities	www.eurocities.org
International Union of Architects (UIA)	www.uia-architects.org
Solar Consulting Engineers	www.transsolar.com
Senatsverwaltung fuer Stadtentwicklung, Berlin	www.stadtentwicklung.berlin.de
Site of City Research	www.experimentcity.net
Mega-City Research site	www.future-megacities.de
Barcelona Public Space site	www.publicspace.org
German Government Sustainable Building site	www.solarbau.de
German Energy Efficiency site	www.oekozentrum-nrw.de
German Green Building site	www.dgnb.de

Notes

1 Even with an immediate cut in all CO_2 emissions, it's likely that the earth's climate will continue to increase over 1 degree Celsius. In regard to the fourth and most recent IPCC assessment report (Assessment Report AR4, 2009) from the Intergovernmental Panel on Climate Change (the IPCC is an independent UN body, consisting of 2,500 scientists worldwide): in scientific findings there can be different views. It has been criticized, for having a few figures in the report that are incorrect; the report is a massive compilation of over 3,000 pages of scientific evidence. The mistakes were corrected in 2010, such as the following two points: a. While it is correct that glaciers' ice shield is melting, this doesn't occur as fast as was claimed in the original report. Glaciers in the Himalaya will not yet have fully disappeared by 2035. b. There is currently no evidence to support the claim that global warming could cut rain-fed Northern African crop production by up to 50 per

up to 50 per cent by 2020. This figure was seen as exaggerated and was corrected. The next IPCC Report is due to be published in 2013. Let's not forget: it's likely there is always a small number of faults, when thousands of pages of scientific evidence are compiled; it doesn't devalue the IPCC's important work as a whole. See at: www.ipcc.ch

2 The Australian Conservation Foundation (ACF) documents greenhouse gas emissions (and therefore energy use), comparing the emissions of suburbs with inner-city developments. While this neglects the huge amount of emissions caused by commuting daily by car to workplaces in the central business districts, it looks at the direct energy use of these different living scenarios. Due to less affluence and differences in available income, few residents in the outer suburban areas have energy-intensive lifestyles compared to inner-city apartment living, ACF findings show. For instance, in inner Sydney, there are 37 tonnes of greenhouse gas emissions per capita per year; in inner-west Burwood (a middle-distance suburb) it is 'only' 22 tonnes; in outer-west Parramatta 20 tonnes, and on the fringe at Campbelltown 16.7 tonnes of emissions per year. Similarly in Melbourne, Central Port Phillip (inner-city apartment living) has 27 tonnes per capita, inner Darebin has 23 tonnes, and outer Melton suburb has 18 tones. The reason behind such differences in CO_2 emissions (and direct energy consumption per head) are various, but include increased energy spent on clothes drying and heating, and lifts and lighting in inner-city apartment blocks.

3 A definition of 'sustainable' is derived from the Latin verb 'sustinere', which describes relations that can be maintained for a very long time, or indefinitely (Judes, 1996). The idea of 'sustainable urban development' originated at the 1992 UCED Conference and Earth Summit in Rio de Janeiro. It is based on the concept of balanced environmental planning instruments and methods, of which a great variety of visions for urban development has been created. However, 15 years after Rio, there is still no global mandatory commitment to a cap on carbon emissions.

4 Maintaining and maximizing biodiversity is crucial, also in the urban context. The more species living in an ecosystem, the heathier and more productive it is. There are currently around 8 million unique species of life on the planet, if not far more. A 2008 study by the International Union for Conservation of Nature (IUCN) found that:
- nearly 1 in 4 mammals worldwide was at risk for extinction
- overfishing and acidification of the oceans are threatening marine species
- with deforestation and urbanization the earth is getting irreversible biologically impoverished, and
- global warming could drive a million species to extinction by 2050.

5 Having lived for 3 years in Tokyo myself, I can confirm that the Japanese capital city is a public transportation

Notes for Chapter 2

paradise, where you truly can go anywhere without a car. Tokyo uses only a third of the energy used by Los Angeles, because it has a much higher population density, better mixed-usage in its districts, and an efficient low-impact public transport system that is affordable.

6 Bill Dunster's BedZED development in Surrey was the start of the *One Planet Living* concept by BioRegional, which is based on the idea of local self-sufficiency and equity in the use of available resources and food.

7 Refer to: Kats, Greg, et al (Oct. 2003): The Costs and Financial Benefits of Green Buildings; a report to California's Sustainable Building Task Force. American scientist Greg Kats of Capital E is the nationally known author of the most widely referenced study of the costs and benefits of green buildings. This study has demonstrated conclusively that sustainable building and the use of renewable energies is a cost-effective investment. Other studies on the cost of green buildings have recently been provided by Jerry Yudelson (US) and Romilly Madew (Australia).

8 In Germany, the feed-in tariff (FiT) system was pioneered by the Green Party and it guarantees a set price for 20 years; the introduction of the feed-in tariff has already led to a 100 million tonnes reduction in CO_2 emissions (according to a recent report by the German Federal Government). Following the German example, the Spanish government pays also a 'feed-in tariff' (almost 27 Euro-cents per kWh of renewable energy supplied back into the electricity grid, guaranteed for the next 25 years, but with the global financial crisis the payback amount per kW has been drastically reduced). The feed-in scheme encourages ordinary German households to become energy producers. The EEG act (Erneuerbare Energien Gesetz) allows any citizen to feed unlimited electricity into the national grid. Government-run utilities buy this energy at a determined price, under a 20-year contract. Recent law requires all new German homes to meet 10 per cent of their heating requirements with renewable energy. In Germany, between 1996 and 2007, the share of electricity generated from renewable energy sources increased from 4.2 to 15 per cent, a development triggered by the FiT. The goal of the German Ministry for the Environment is 30 per cent of the electricity from renewable energy sources by 2020.

Wastewater recycling rates are equally important. Water recycling rates by the 12 major water utilities in different Australian states vary widely: for instance, Hunter Water (Newcastle) lags behind most other utilities, only recycling 8 per cent of water; SA Water (Adelaide) recycles 31 per cent. Recycling has a much lower impact on the environment.

9 New technological developments in solar electricity gradually brings down prices of PV-modules. In Australia, some of the most promising new solar innovations are the thin-film technologies (such as *Sliver* cells, developed at the ANU), and the crystalline silicon on glass (CGS) cells (developed at the UNSW).

10 Urban farming data according to N. McGowan: 'Food-Oriented Design for Thought', in: *Urban Design Forum*, Issue No. 89, March 2010, p.2

11 The German 'Passivhaus' standard has a verified 15 kWh /sq m per annum energy use, which it achieves with high insulation values, high-performance windows (double, often triple-glazing), elimination of thermal bridges between interior/exterior and building parts, and use of a heat recovery ventilation system combined with high air-tightness. Site of the German Passivhaus standard: www.passiv.de

12 The affordability of housing varies widely around the world. Recently, the US consultancy *Demographia* released a report (the 6th Annual International Housing Affordability Survey 2009, released February 2010) with data of 272 urban areas around the English-speaking world (USA, Canada, NZ, Australia, UK, etc.), comparing their housing affordability. According to their findings, Vancouver is the least affordable city; Australia has 11 of the world's 25 least affordable cities or urban areas for housing, including Sydney, the Gold Coast and the Sunshine Coast as the three of the four least affordable places. Other places with similar restraints and lack of affordable housing include cities in California, Florida, Honolulu and London. Report available online at: www.demographia.com

13 One hectare is 2.47 acres. One hectare is 10,000 sqm, or 107,000 sq feet. One acre is 4,050 sqm.

14 The European energy sector has gone through a number of significant structural changes within the past ten years. Until the mid of the 1990s, the power market was still characterized by regional state-owned monopolies; but with the 1996 liberalization of the EU energy sector, competition was introduced and the focus shifted towards a more sustainable power system. In 2008, the EU adopted the European Climate and Energy package to transform Europe into a low-carbon economy and increase energy security, with legally binding targets for emissions: by 2020, greenhouse gas emissions will be cut by 20 per cent, the share of renewable energies will be increased to 20 per cent, and energy-efficiency will be improved by 20 per cent.

15 Affordability is of prime importance when discussing housing. Numerous recent studies have shown that energy-optimized buildings can achieve a payback of their sustainability measures in less than 10 years (e.g. Kats, G. et al: The Costs and Financial Benefits of Green Building, 2003). Long-term savings in energy consumption, operation and maintenance (life-cycle costs) are more important than slightly higher construction costs at the time of the building's erection.

16 Carbon dioxide can be safely sequestered through the natural process of forests that lock carbon up in trees and soils. However, a study reported in New Forests (2006) concluded that: 'An area covered with a plantation managed for maximum volume yield will normally contain substantially less carbon than the same area of unmanaged forest'. Hereby, native forests seem to be the best way to capture carbon. A similar study in Oregon found that 'a 450-year–old natural forest stored 2.2 to 2.3 times more carbon than a 60-year-old Douglas fir plantation on a comparable site'. Unfortunately, we cannot plant enough trees in time and not all soils are suitable. The World Rainforest Movement calculated: to compensate for the carbon we are currently releasing into the atmosphere every year would require planting four times the area of the US with trees.

17 Similar changes in building codes have been made in the UK (1991 England and Wales Building Regulations) and in Australia (1996 BCA), enabling multi-residential timber framed construction (MRTFC) beyond their historical height limitations into medium-rise structures, higher than four storeys.

18 The increasing popularity is also visible in education: there is a new interest in urban timber buildings, with several universities now offering postgraduate programmes (for instance, at TU Munich, TU Vienna, TU Dresden, TU Innsbruck, ETH Lausanne, Helsinki University, etc). See information at: www.forum-holzbau.com and www.infoholz.de

19 Refer to: www.gabrielpoole.com.au of GEPDC Architects (Australia). The idea is to provide affordable and high-quality homes, so-called 'take away houses', which are factory built and developed in close collaboration with a manufacturer; see also: www.gatewaymanufacture.com . The ideas are based on modular timber houses developed by Richard Buckminster Fuller and Konrad Wachsmann in the 1950s.

20 In private conversation with Hermann Kaufmann (Chair for Timber Architecture, TU Munich; November 2009), which further outlined the innovative capacities of using timber-based elements for multi-storey inner-city apartment buildings and for improving the energy efficiency of the building envelope.

21 For further project documentation: see www.energytech.at - the platform for innovative energy technologies.

22 There are several research institutes dedicated to innovative construction with timber. Some examples: since 2002, the Austrian architect Hermann Kaufmann has held the Chair for Timber Architecture at the Technical University of Munich and Michael Flach from the University Innsbruck has developed significant teaching and research efforts, in collaboration with Hans Hartl, the Chair for Timber Constructions at the Technical University of Vienna.

23 Engineered wood products, such as the weather resistant Laminated Veneer Lumber (LVL) 'Kerto' from Finland (www.Finnforest.co.uk), are good examples of this development.

Further research

The following pages show a collection of images and diagrams in regard to the topics raised in Chapter 2, to give a wider context and inspire the reader to conduct further research in these fields.

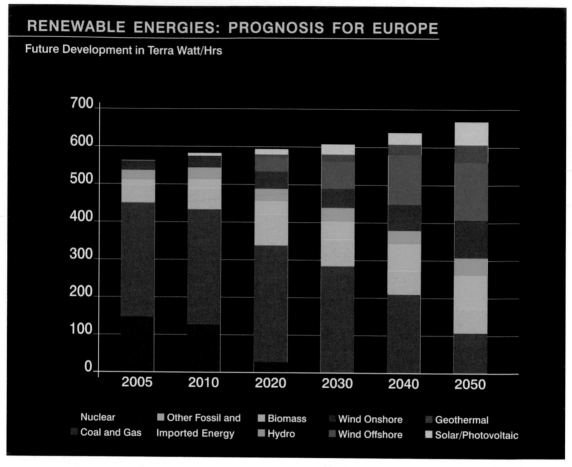

RENEWABLE ENERGIES: PROGNOSIS FOR EUROPE

Future Development in Terra Watt/Hrs

Legend:

Nuclear	Other Fossil and	Biomass	Wind Onshore	Geothermal
Coal and Gas	Imported Energy	Hydro	Wind Offshore	Solar/Photovoltaic

Courtesy: CGS, 2008

Renewable energy sources are a revolution. Wind power (especially off-shore), geo-thermal energy (heat from the earth), solar and biomass energy offer great potential and will play a major role in the zoning-out of fossil-fuel based resources, such as coal, oil and gas. However, without public subsidies for research and governmental support, many technological solution would not have been developed.

Renewable energy technologies: creation of new green jobs in Germany

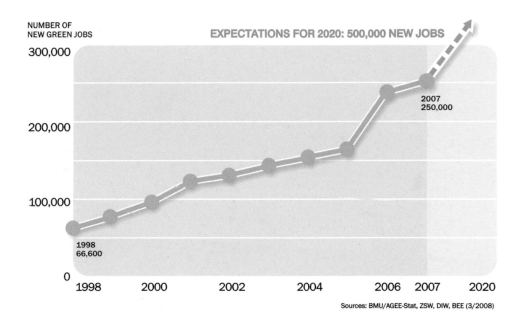

Sources: BMU/AGEE-Stat, ZSW, DIW, BEE (3/2008)

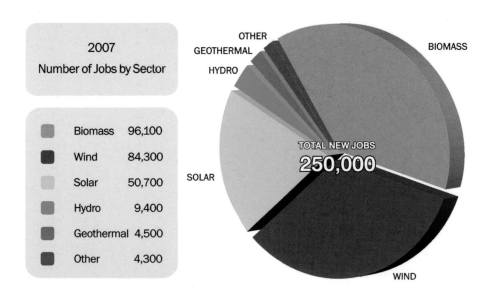

Plenty of new `green jobs' are created in the environmental technology sector. Germany, for instance, has created over 250,000 new positions in only ten years. This requires political leadership and thinking further ahead than the next opinion poll and election. Many of the new technological solutions will become profitable as soon as restrictions are placed on the use of fossil fuels. (Diagrams: S. Lehmann, UNESCO Chair)

WORLD 2030 PREDICTION

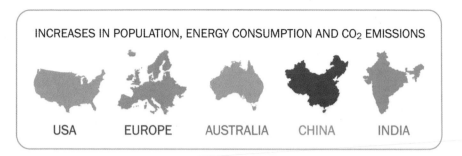

INCREASES IN POPULATION, ENERGY CONSUMPTION AND CO_2 EMISSIONS

USA   EUROPE   AUSTRALIA   CHINA   INDIA

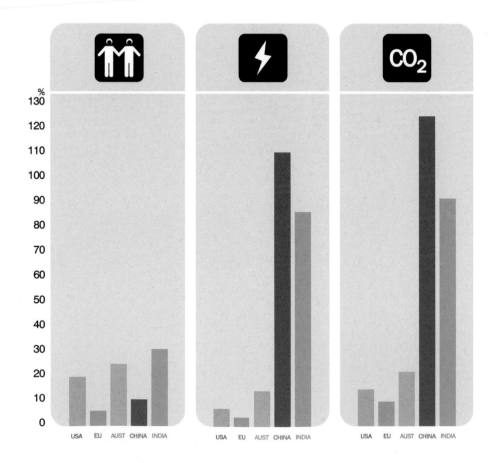

Source: US Energy Information Administration

Predictions for 2030: Population increases are most significant in India. However, the rise of energy consumption and CO_2 emission will most increase in China. On the other hand, Europe will see very little growth in population and energy production, compared to the emerging nations. (Diagram: S. Lehmann, UNESCO Chair; after: EIA)

Courtesy: Arup, 200

Too ambitious to be realized? Arup's project 'Dongtan Eco-City' (2006-08), which was planned as a new city for 500,000 residents outside Shanghai, was stalled in 2008 and will not be built. However, other large-scale eco-cities are going ahead and will be implemented in China, and in other rapid urbanising nations. Large bodies of water were part of Dongtan's urban water management strategies. (Images: Courtesy Arup, 2007)

Courtesy: T. Ito, 1993

Eco-Cities will look different. Green ribbons of a continuous infrastructural landscape will offer recreational escape between compact quarters, where biodiversity, trees as carbon sinks, and community gardens play an important role: landscape and gardens are essential components within these new type of eco-cities. (Image: Courtesy Toyo Ito; proposal for Shanghai, 1993)

The City as Living Ecosystem

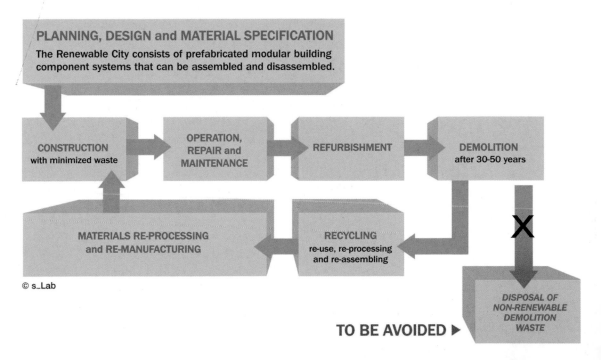

PLANNING, DESIGN and MATERIAL SPECIFICATION
The Renewable City consists of prefabricated modular building component systems that can be assembled and disassembled.

CONSTRUCTION
with minimized waste

OPERATION, REPAIR and MAINTENANCE

REFURBISHMENT

DEMOLITION
after 30-50 years

MATERIALS RE-PROCESSING and RE-MANUFACTURING

RECYCLING
re-use, re-processing and re-assembling

© s_Lab

X

DISPOSAL OF NON-RENEWABLE DEMOLITION WASTE

TO BE AVOIDED ▶

Courtesy: GMP, 2002

Above diagram: understanding the city as an eco-system, based on circular closed loop planning, not linear. (Diagram: UNESCO Chair, Lehmann, 2008) Below: large water bodies create a better microclimate and can be used to cool buildings. Urban development proposal for a new campus in China. (Image: Courtesy GMP; proposal for Songjiang University of Visual Arts and Design, Shanghai, 2002)

Source: Image Sharing Commons

A new suburb at the fringe of Mexico City: The cookie-cutter approach lacks diversity and creates too much car-dependency. Below: good urban infill projects, such as here in Melbourne's St. Kilda, offer a variety of plans for different lifestyles and bring people back to live in the city centre, close to their workplaces. Modular prefabrication, as once promoted by Le Corbusier (right), has still much potential for affordability.

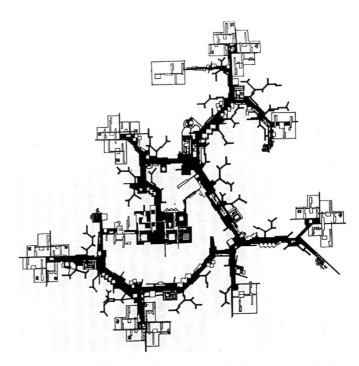

Courtesy: P. Davidson, 2009

Top right: a public space network diagram by Candilis-Josic-Woods (1963); their work was much influenced by the structure of North African cities. Barcelona's Cerda grid is made up of blocks of 140x140 metres length (aerial photo, top left) delivers the much enjoyed urban density of the Catalan city. Below: Melbourne's Federation Square is not a flat public space, but offers an interesting change of levels.

Courtesy: City of Melbourne 2008

Public space makes the plan

Public space is always more important than the individual building: it structures the city and creates the foreground to architecture. Citizens, you are the city!

Liveability: most life in cities happens between buildings

In his book `Life Between Buildings. Using Public Space', Jan Gehl points out the shortcomings of functionalistic city planning, and argues that `the more time people spend outdoors, the more frequently they meet and talk.' Gehl proved a direct link between the high quality of public space and the number of outdoor activities and meaningful interaction between people. Humanistic planning principles are important in times, when cities are undergoing great changes in the process of growth. `Let's increase the number of urban spaces which are pleasant for walking and inviting activities', he points out. `The battle for urban quality is often won, or lost, at the small scale. When buildings are narrow, the street length is shortened, the walking distances are reduced and street life is enhanced.' (Gehl, 2010)

Courtesy: City of Barcelona 2007

Upgrading public space is a continuously ongoing process. The City of Barcelona (siteplan below) is a great example of 25 years of ongoing urban renewal initiatives, creating a high-quality walkable and livable environment, taking advantage of the waterfront. The cities of Melbourne and Sydney (top) are now concentrating on improving their car-dominated streetscapes, as this includes 80 per cent of all public space. (images: courtesy city administrations)

Electro vehicles and a clean urban environment

One of the great advantages of the electro vehicle is that the urban environment will be free of noise and air pollution. This will allow urban designers to re-design the city with districts and buildings based (again) on natural ventilation: even on the most busy street, we will be able to open the windows and cross-ventilate office buildings and residences naturally, thereby reducing the dependency on air-conditioning. Of course, it will be crucial that the electricity is generated with renewable energy sources, not from coal-burning powerstations. In addition, we'll need:

- Behavioural change (consumer behaviour)
- Systems measuring the consumption
- Governmental policies and incentives.

A new urban post-oil infrastructure is already emerging, where walking and cycling is made more pleasant, the entire public transport infrastructure is upgraded with well-designed stations (Image: tram station in Munich, 2009), intelligent transport systems, and electro vehicles that can plug-in for rapid charging of their batteries. Top: Light-weight bike models are easily folded and carried on the tram or bus. (Photos: S. Lehmann, 2009)

Source: Image Sharing Commons

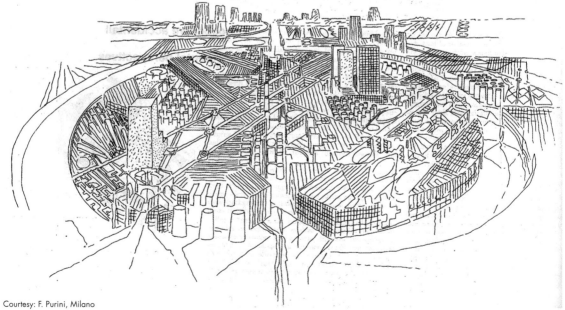

Courtesy: F. Purini, Milano

Why do certain public space work so well and others don't? Above: St. Mark's Square in Venice, Italy, with its fine proportions, high quality materials, framed by interesting buildings that share the same materials and collonnades. Below: Franco Purini's sketch 'Ideal City' (1974) draws on ideas of the Renaissance, when architects like Scamozzi tried to define the ideal city form. (Image: Courtesy F. Purini)

Using passive design principles

Above: `Ramada House' by Judith Chafee (1974), Tucson, USA. A large shade structure in timber covers the entire house, like a table, protecting it from the strong Arizona sun. Such a shade structure, open on all four sides to catch breezes, is called `Ramada'. (Photo: S. Lehmann, 2010)

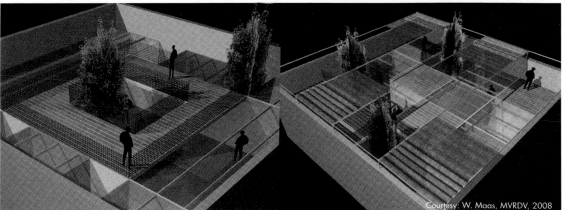

Courtesy: W. Maas, MVRDV, 2008

Above, right: SANAA's slim, narrow housing slab in Gifu (Japan) is ideal for effective natural cross-ventilation, for living in the hot and humid Japanese summer. (image: courtesy SAANA, 2001) Below: MVRDV are constantly searching for new housing typologies that integrate green in contemporary ways: courtyard and atrium types, roof gardens. (image: Courtesy MVRDV, 2003)

Courtesy: W. Mitchell, MIT,, 2008

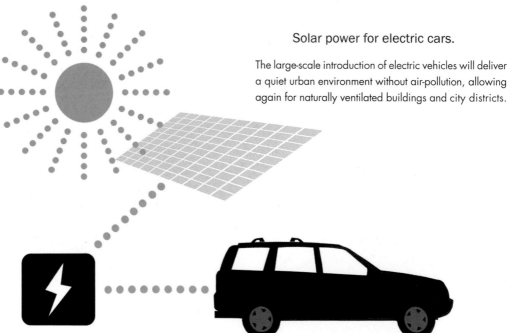

Solar power for electric cars.

The large-scale introduction of electric vehicles will deliver a quiet urban environment without air-pollution, allowing again for naturally ventilated buildings and city districts.

New designs for electric vehicles and eco-mobility concepts are getting developed everywhere around the world, with improved range and quick recharging times. (Top image: Courtesy Media Lab, MIT, 2005) But it's not just the electric car that will bring clean transportation: There are plug-in hybrids, biofuels, hydrogen, algae fuels, and other new clean technologies that will revolutionize the entire transportation sector.

Upskilling through training and access to information networks.

10 m² of solar cells can cover the
electricity needs of one household

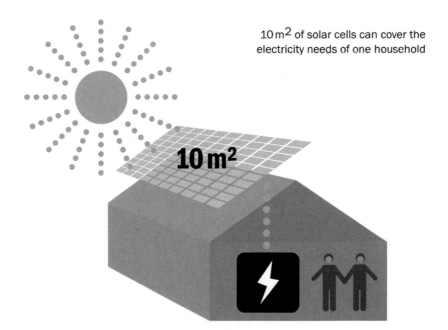

After: BIG (2008)

The size of a 10 sqm solar field can power one standard household, emission-free and silently. The use of small-scale wafer-based solar cells – or solar panels – has rapidely grown since the cells are becoming dramatically cheaper and better. Over the past ten years (2000–2010), costs for solar cells have fallen by almost 10 per cent a year because the technology has developed and the volume has increased.

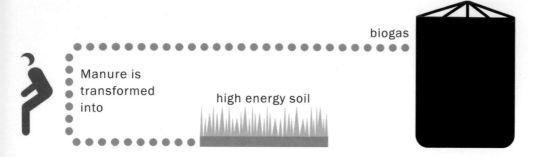

biogas

Manure is transformed into

high energy soil

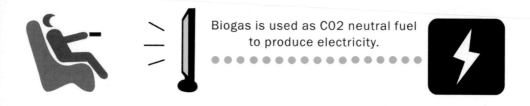

Biogas is used as CO2 neutral fuel to produce electricity.

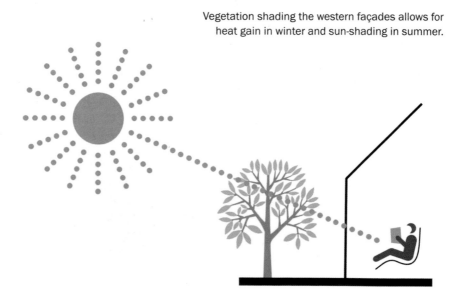

Vegetation shading the western façades allows for heat gain in winter and sun-shading in summer.

Biomass, such as plants, trees and algae, grow by absorbing the sun's energy and CO_2 from the atmosphere through photosynthesis. Biogas produced through composting of manure and organic waste from plants and food, can be used to generate energy. Waste equals nutrients; biogas from wet organic waste and food waste is relatively simple to produce. The next step is to better quantify the effect of passive design principles, to give designers a clearer guidance.

5000 windmills can fuel all cars in Sydney.
When parked, hydrogen cars supply water and electricity

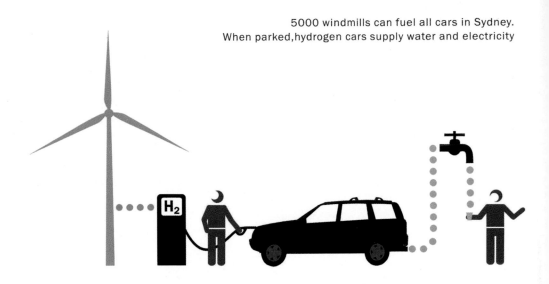

Rainwater collected from roof
and façades may cover 75%
of household water needs.

A hydrogen fuel cell transforms chemical energy to electrical energy; for instance,
when hydrogen and oxygen react to produce water and electricity. A fuel cell is far
more efficient than a traditional combustion engine, and environmentally friendly: the
only 'exhaust' is water and heat. Below: rainwater collection and harvesting is a way to
save precious drinking water. (Diagrams: S. Lehmann, UNESCO Chair, 2008)

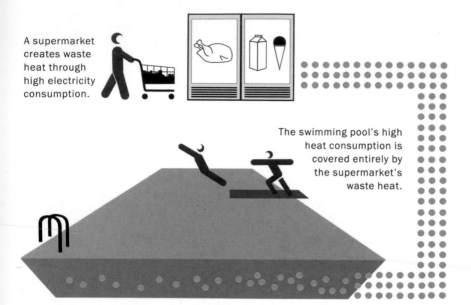

A supermarket creates waste heat through high electricity consumption.

The swimming pool's high heat consumption is covered entirely by the supermarket's waste heat.

Courtesy: L. Blundell, 2009

Substituting coal-fired powerstations

Results of recent studies clearly show that existing renewable energy sources available in Australia (as a mix of solar, wind and biomass) are cost-effective and capable of substituting for coal-fired powerstations. (Studies by Diesendorf, and others, 2007)

The combination of energy efficiency, renewable energy, and natural gas (as an interim bridging fuel; natural gas is the least polluting of the fossil fuels, and is used in both co-generation CHP plants and in combined-cycle powerstations), may be less expensive than continuing to build and operate coal-fired plants, even without considering the environmental and health costs of burning coal. See: Diesendorf, M. (2007). *Paths to a Low-Carbon Future. Reducing Australia's Greenhouse Gas Emissions by 30 per cent by 2020*; a report to the NSW government, July 2007. Available online: www.sustainabilitycentre.com.au

Energy exchange between building programmes: based on Exergy principles, we can now plan and assemble the various parts of a large building in a way to re-use the waste heat and waste water, and achieve a better overall energy balance. Below: the CHP co-generaton plant in the town of Woking (UK); the entire town went off-grid in 2008 and became self-sufficient, based on its improved energy management.

Grey water recycling through bio filtration

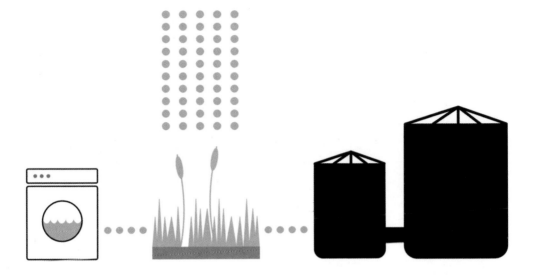

Day lighting/lighting control

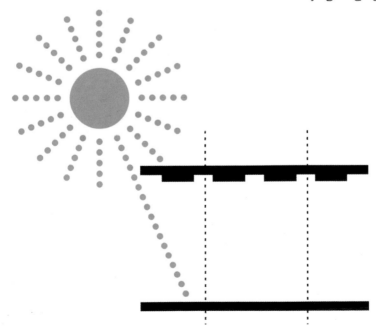

Grey water recycling through the natural process of bio-filtration is part of sensitive urban water management. Below: buildings are responsible for approximately 40 per cent of the world's energy use, and some of the easiest and most substantial emission cuts can be found in the building sector. For instance, through a focus on energy efficiency and by avoiding unnecessary overheating of buildings in summer.

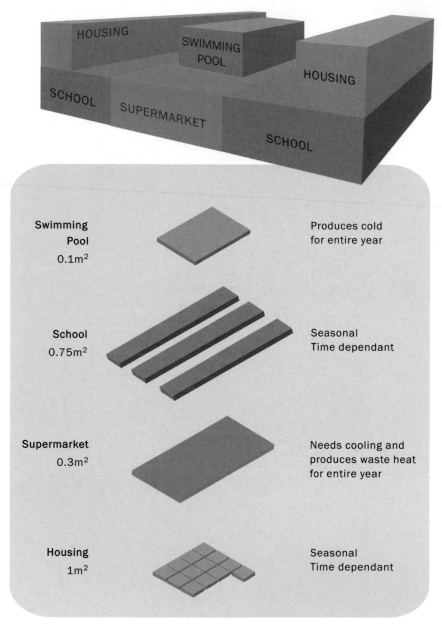

Energy exchange - strategic combination of programmes reusing waste heat and water.

Swimming Pool 0.1m²		Produces cold for entire year
School 0.75m²		Seasonal Time dependant
Supermarket 0.3m²		Needs cooling and produces waste heat for entire year
Housing 1m²		Seasonal Time dependant

After: Dobbelsteen (2009)

Energy exchange, based on exergy principles, helps to use the otherwise wasted energy, heat and waste water: different parts in a district are strategically combined, according to their electricty consumption and waste heat production, to balance them against each other, so that the overall energy and water consumption is reduced. In addition, local energy production, heat pumps and smart grids will systematically improve the energy balance.

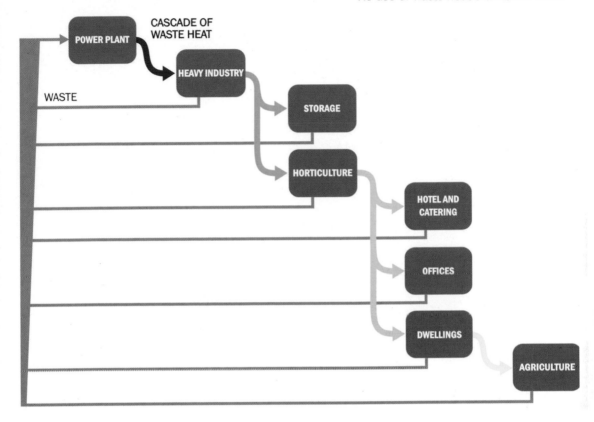

Re-use of waste heat and waste water

After: Dobbelsteen (2009)

Solar electricity driven cooling system

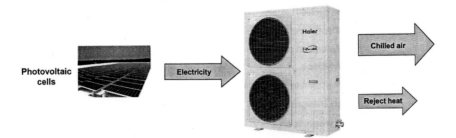

Courtesy: P. Kohlenbach, 2008

Cascading principle: we can recover waste heat and waste water using heat pumps, heat recovery systems and grey water cycles. Below: solar cooling technology, with absorption chillers, using absorption technology to produce chilled water or air for cooling, is another relatively new technology which will revolutionize buildings. Currently, there are around 400 solar cooling systems worldwide in use. (Data: 2010)

Courtesy: Atelier 5, Zurich

Swiss firm Atelier 5 designed, as early as in 1957–1961, the mid-density housing estate Halen (Siedlung Halen), close to Bern, as a new concept for compact carpet planning typology. In total 81 multifamily units are built as 3-storey terrace houses, in two standardized types of 4 and 5 m width, in `beton brut' concrete. Each unit has roof terraces and small front gardens; the centre of the estate is kept car-free.

Courtesy: E. Penolosa

Reclaiming public space with the bike: free bike rental schemes, such as in Paris, have been introduced by over 50 cities worldwide. Bike stations for secure parking and safe bike paths, separate from traffic and sufficiently wide, are part of a new bike infrastructure and an urban cycle scheme. (Images: S. Lehmann; E. Penolosa)

Retrofitting and adaptive re-use of existing buildings

Existing industrial buildings, like warehouses or former factories, are often very flexible in plan, which allows for a longer life of buildings. Retrofitting means: bringing old buildings back to life with an entirely new function, without destroying the integrity of the original building and its character. The most sustainable building is the one that already exists, and which can be integrated into an urban renewal masterplan.

The adaptive reuse of existing buildings: former factory buildings as a cultural centre, with a contemporary extension (architect Lina Bo Bardi, 1977-86): SESC Pompeia Cultural and Sports Centre, Sao Paulo. Below: on 'Borneo Sporenburg' island in Amsterdam, a new waterfront community enjoys 4 and 6 storey housing types that allow direct access to the canal (masterplan by West 8, and others). (Photos: S. Lehmann, 2009)

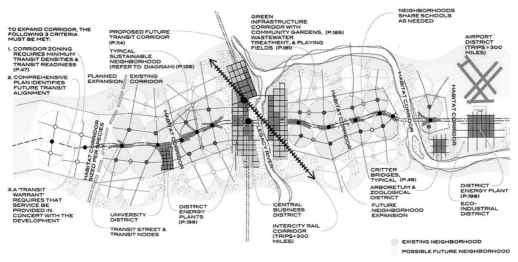

Courtesy: J. Lerner, Curitiba

CORRIDOR DENSITY: NECESSARY TO FREE PEOPLE FROM AUTOMOBILE DEPENDENCE. MIN 7 DWELLING UNITS PER ACRE (DU/A) TO SUPPORT BASIC BUS SERVICE HIGHER PREFERRED FOR BETTER SERVICE & MODE (15 DU/A TROLLEY) 22 DU/A LIGHT RAIL (P. 111)

CORRIDOR LAND USE MIX: TO ACHIEVE A 1:1 JOB - HOUSING BALANCE

NOTE: THIS DIAGRAM IS SIMPLIFIED. DEPENDING ON TRANSIT AVAILABLE, OTHER CONFIGURATIONS OF THIS DIAGRAM ARE EQUALLY VIABLE.

DIAGRAM ON PAGE 113.

TO EXPAND CORRIDOR, THE FOLLOWING 3 CRITERIA MUST BE MET:

1. CORRIDOR ZONING REQUIRES MINIMUM TRANSIT DENSITIES & TRANSIT READINESS (P.47)

2. COMPREHENSIVE PLAN IDENTIFIES FUTURE TRANSIT ALIGNMENT

3. A 'TRANSIT WARRANT' REQUIRES THAT SERVICE BE PROVIDED IN CONCERT WITH THE DEVELOPMENT

PROPOSED FUTURE TRANSIT CORRIDOR (P.114)

TYPICAL SUSTAINABLE NEIGHBORHOOD (REFER TO DIAGRAM) (P.126)

PLANNED EXPANSION

EXISTING CORRIDOR

HABITAT CORRIDOR SIZED PER SPECIES

UNIVERSITY DISTRICT

TRANSIT STREET & TRANSIT NODES

DISTRICT ENERGY PLANTS (P.199)

GREEN INFRASTRUCTURE CORRIDOR WITH COMMUNITY GARDENS, (P.185) WASTEWATER TREATMENT, & PLAYING FIELDS (P.181)

LEGACY RIVER

HABITAT CORRIDOR

CENTRAL BUSINESS DISTRICT

INTERCITY RAIL CORRIDOR (TRIPS<300 MILES)

NEIGHBORHOODS SHARE SCHOOLS AS NEEDED

HABITAT CORRIDOR

HABITAT CORRIDOR

CRITTER BRIDGES, TYPICAL (P.49)

ARBORETUM & ZOOLOGICAL DISTRICT

FUTURE NEIGHBORHOOD EXPANSION

AIRPORT DISTRICT (TRIPS >300 MILES)

DISTRICT ENERGY PLANT (P.199)

ECO-INDUSTRIAL DISTRICT

○ EXISTING NEIGHBORHOOD
○ POSSIBLE FUTURE NEIGHBORHOOD

Courtesy: D. Farr, 2008
©FARR ASSOCIATES

The inexpensive *Bus Rapid Transit System* (BRTS) in Curitiba, Brazil, now replicated in Bogota: futristic bus stops and modern express buses raised the image of the bus, while offering an affordable solution to Curitiba's traffic congestion. 80 per cent of the bus passengers own a car, but prefer to take the public BRTS to work. Below: the `suatainable corridor' concept by Douglas Farr proposes a density that supports walking and bus services. (Source: Courtesy D. Farr)

Courtesy: ATSE, 2009

Distributed solar power generation

`With the feed-in tariff for solar power, energy generation and distribution is entirely changing. Instead of just a few external suppliers in the form of large, monopolized energy companies, countless people become self-sufficient and there are many local or regional energy suppliers. This radically changes the ownership structure for energy plants.' (H. Scheer, 2007)

Courtesy: Hannover Messe

Transmitting energy over long distances through the large grid leads to significant energy loss (up to 40 per cent of the energy is lost). Smaller, decentralized systems with wind and solar energy, producing electricity locally, close to the point of consumption, have many advantages. Left: concentrated solar power with moveable mirrors. Below: Building-integrated PV, which works at the same time as sun shading device, at the Hanover Congress Centre.

Solar districts as powerstations, generating more energy than they need

Roofs and building facades offer large surfaces, which are most of the time exposed to the sun, with multiple opportunities for passive energy gain and active generation; e.g. systems, such as PV-modules and solar heat collectors can be integrated. The Solar District Schlierberg in Freiburg (Germany), adjacent to Vauban Solar City and the historical city centre, consists of 59 *Plus-Energy+* terrace houses (3-storey); 9 of these houses are on top of an office building, the so-called *Solar-Schiff*. The houses are a new generation of net-zero-energy solar buildings, occupied by 200 residents and developed by architect Rolf Disch (1999–2006); they need very little energy due to their compact shape and high insulation (U-value is 0.28 W/sqm K); the required energy is easily generated by the 49 sqm size PV solar on the roof. (Image: courtesy btga, Wuppertal)

Courtesy: R. Disch, 2009

Vauban Solar City, a green district in Freiburg (Germany), built on an inner-city former military base. The *Plus-Energy-Houses* generate more energy than their occupants need, which allows them to feed energy into the grid. As a minimum, we should aim for at least 50 per cent on-site renewable energy generation for any urban development. Below: The 'Solar Schiff', by architect Rolf Disch, et al (2003).

Courtesy: RPBW, 2009

Living roofs and roof gardens

Green roofs collect rainwater and create opportunities for active gardening, vegetable cultivation and social gathering. Roof and facade can solve 90 per cent of the environmental problems.

Roof plan of Vauban Solar District, Freiburg

Produces about 5 W per sqm of land area (power density).

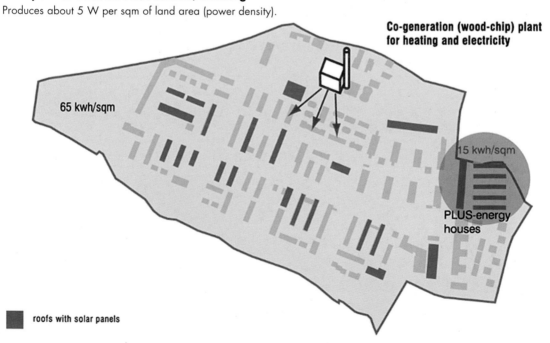

Co-generation (wood-chip) plant for heating and electricity

65 kwh/sqm

15 kwh/sqm

PLUS-energy houses

roofs with solar panels

A large green roof: the 'Living Roof' of the Californian Academy of Science, in San Francisco (by Renzo Piano Building Workshop, 2006) is publicly accessible and a main feature of the building's exhibition. Below: the roof plan of Solar City Vauban (Freiburg, Germany) shows how the new quarter acts as a powerstation, generating its own energy locally, on-site. (Diagram: Courtesy Schroepfer, Hee, Werthmann; 2006)

Source: Image Sharing Commons

Green roofs and intensive small-scale gardening in the city: providing fresh local food

Green roofs often have the problem that they provide for too limited biodiversity, while the necessary soil adds to structural loads, and - if water-intensive plants are selected - the greenery increases the need for much more irrigation and water consumption. However, today there is a lot of knowledge available about how to do green roofs sustainably.

Local food production: urban farming in Havana, Cuba, has been widely acclaimed as a success story, since these community gardens, urban market gardens and fields create jobs, provide locally grown food on a very short supply chain, without the need for CO_2 emitting transportation, which keeps the food supply affordable. Furthermore, the gardens mitigate the urban heat island effect. With over 50 years of US trade embargo, it was also out of necessity that the people of Cuba have started urban farming and community gardens in the city centre of Havana. Everything about food, from its production to transportation to purchase, has an environmental impact. In a carbon-constrained future, it makes no sense to ship chicken and fish from the US to Asia for packaging and then back to US supermarkets, burning energy along the way. A new food-labeling system in Sweden estimates the carbon impact of menu items. Motto: `Don't eat anything that took more energy to ship than to grow.' Right image: Hydroponic farms are growing vegetables in trays, ensuring even light levels to each plant.

Instead of formal city parks: urban farming in Havana's city centre, Cuba. Hydroponic systems for urban farming are a way for vertical farming to grow food all year round (like salad and vegetables that don't need soil), on top of existing flat roofs, using the city districts for food supply. These light-weight agricultural acitivities on top of the existing city, will become (again) a normal part of city life, procducing also biomass, and helping to restore the environmental balance.

Courtesy: Detail, Munich, 2008

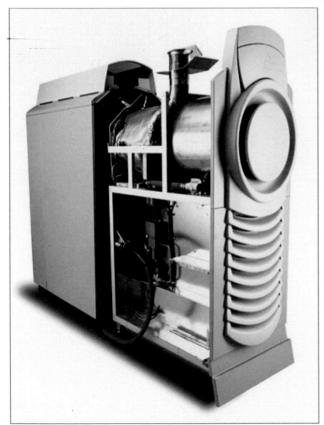

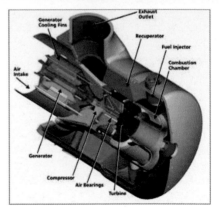

Co-generation and tri-generation: energy recycling

Co-generation (also called Combined Heat-and-Power, CHP) is the use of a heat engine or a powerstation to simultaneously generate both electricity and useful heat. Tri-generation is the use of waste heat from an electrical generator to produce hot water and chilled water (via absorption chillers).

Top left: replacing conventional street lighting with LED street lighting, if solar powered, can reduce the electricity use of a city by 15 per cent; in addition, LED light lasts longer. Right: reinforcement of the slab, with tubes for pumping chilled water to activate the thermal mass of the concrete slab. Below: a co-generation (or even tri-generation) power plant in the building's basement utilizes the otherwise wasted excess heat. (Images: manufacturers)

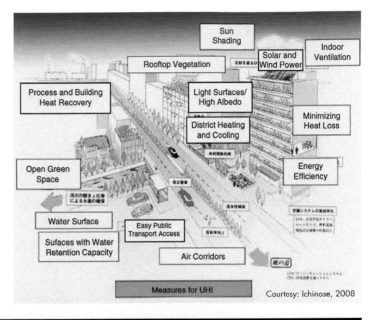

Courtesy: Ichinose, 2008

Top diagram: there are numerous measurements for mitigating the Urban Heat Island (UHI) effect, which becomes important when densifying a city district, such as roof, facade, material and colour selection and ventilation corridors (Source: Ichinose, Japan). Below: the comparison of a building's running costs, between a conventional building and an energy-optimized building, calculated over 30 years, can be as much as 40 per cent.

In India, we can observe dramatic changes from an almost medival structure of craftsmanship to the industrialized age, bringing along with it the availability of all kinds of new materials and environmental degradation. Above: IIT campus by Louis Kahn, built in the 1960s in locally produced brick. Right: a naturally cross-ventilated university building at CEPT in Ahmedabad. (Photos: S. Lehmann, 2007)

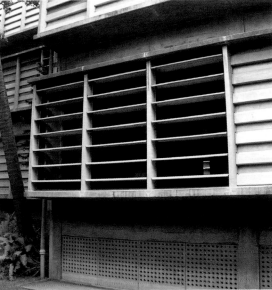

Courtesy: Troppo, 2008

Top: Golconde Guest House, a dormitory in Pondicherry, India (1948, by A. Raymond). One of the earliest modern buildings in India, it shows a good understanding of designing for a hot and humid climate. Below: for the passive design principles, such as a shaded verandah and out-door room, engineers will better quantify the effects, to give clearer guidance to the designers. (Image: Courtesy Glenn Murcutt and Troppo, Bowali Visitor Centre, 1992)

The *Mt. Cenis Continuing Education Academy* building in Herne, Germany (architects: F.-H. Jourda; stage 2 with M. Hegger, HHS, 1999–2005), is part of a new generation of buildings which produce the energy they require to operate. Total energy requirements of this building are 32 kWh/sqm p.a. It contains the various building parts like houses inside a large overall envelope, creating a protected public atrium space.

Courtesy: M. Hegger, 2007

The structure of the large envelope (incorporating the academy, town hall and hotel) is used for collecting passive and active solar energy; its roof and facade is clad with 3,500 PV-cells (BIPV). The timber structure is 100 per cent recyclable. The huge interior atrium space is neither heated nor air-conditioned; it's an intermediate zone, creating its own protected microclimate, like a traditional glass house. (Photos: courtesy M. Hegger, 2007)

Singapore is a leader in the integration of greenery in urban planning. The city state's motto is `A Tropical City in a Garden'. Singapore's first `zero-emission building' was opened in 2009; it is a government initiative: a retro-fit and demonstration project, illustrating integration of PV, green roofs, solar roofs, light shelves, and many other ideas; closely monitored, it delivers valuable data. (Images: S. Lehmann, 2009)

Courtesy: IBA Emscher Park

Courtesy: HOK, 2009

Embodied energy

Long distance transportation of materials uses energy and contributes to CO_2 emissions. One of the most important environmental factors often overlooked, when designing and specifying materials for construction, is the amount of energy required to create and transport building materials. Some building materials can be sourced locally and have much less embodied energy than others, and we need to utilize these materials wherever possible.

Adaptive re-use of industrial buildings

Above: the adaptive re-use of the former industrially-used landscape, often combined with treatment of a contaminated site, is a major area of activity for urban designers in developed countries. After steel manufacturing, coal mining and other carbon-intensive industries have closed down, it's important to find ways for the integration and reuse of the industrial heritage; as a way to sustain and maintain the history and identity of the region. Remember: the most sustainable building is the one that already exists. (Emscher Park, landscape project by Peter Latz and others, 1991–2000. Images: courtesy P. Latz)

Below: bamboo is a fast-growing grass (in fact, it's the fastest growing plant in the world), which has recently been rediscovered by contemporary architects, such as Shigeru Ban, as an ecological construction material and for its fantastic characteristics: a sustainable construction material of high strength, flexibility and stiffness, which is much more affordable than steel. Image of a bamboo structure in Thailand.

Top: IBA Emscher Park, the industrial landscape park at Duisburg Nord, in the Ruhr (Germany); reusing the post-industrial landscape of former steel production and coal mining plants. Top right: hydroponic farming is making use of empty disused sheds that were originally built for the US car industry, but are now not required by the shrinking automobile manufacturers. (image: courtesy HOK, 2009).

Courtesy: R. Horden, 2010

Courtesy: MOMA, 2008

Lightweight and local materials for compact and prefabricated design solutions

Above: the Smart car, Richard Horden's 'Micro Compact House M-CH', and Oskar Kaufmann and Albert Ruef's 'System 3': all examples for a growing awareness, that large-scale and material/energy intensive is not necessarily the most appropriate in the 21st century. This era is about reduced consumption, sustainable methods and the discovery of qualities in the small scale. Lightweight means less embodied energy, saving material and transport energy, and producing minimal waste. Right page: ETFE foil was used as facade material for the Beijing 'Water Cube'; by PTW (2007). This fully recycleable material needs low energy for its production. It can be used as a cladding or roofing system, supported by a cable net system. ETFE are pneumatic cushions made of a polymer (ethyl tetra fluoro ethylene), which are kept inflated to ensure structural stability and good insulation properties.

Double-skin facades are a practical solution, when the site faces a noisy road – allowing for natural ventilation without admitting too much noise. Otherwise, double-skin facades do not reduce energy consumption *per se*, as they lead to higher maintenance and investment costs. However, if applied correctly, they can have a series of advantages for natural ventilation and sun shading of high-rise towers.

Lightweight + compact + prefabricated = sustainable. We will see cleaner, healthier and fully-recycleable materials that improve indoor air quality and are locally produced. Left: 'System 3' by Oskar Kaufmann & Albert Ruef is a prototype for a modular kit system made of large formate, cross-laminated timber construction elements which are digitally fabricated, thus radically reducing construction waste: www.klh.at

Above: the student dormitory Oskar-von-Miller Forum in Munich (designed by Thomas Herzog & Partner, 2007–09) is a new generation of energy-efficient, urban infill buildings that utilize a whole series of technologically-driven strategies: building-integrated PV, solar cooling absorption chillers on the roof, green roofs, activated thermal mass, and double-skin facade system with moveable shading devices in the cavity. (Images: S. Lehmann, 2009)

CHAPTER 3

The Case Studies

PORT CITY

GREEN CORRIDOR

CITY CAMPU

This aerial photo shows the location of the 3 main projects of exploration, using the city of Newcastle as case study: City Campus, Port City and Green Corridor. (Aerial photo: M. Woodward; Google Earth, 2009)

City Campus and urban renewal

The transformation of university campuses into 'living champions of sustainability' offers a particular opportunity to test and demonstrate emerging new technologies and urban design strategies. Designing a new campus can set a benchmark for how we develop academic buildings and define, what the future of teaching and research will be.

The following is a short description of the studio objectives, the assignment and the brief, for students in the Master of Architecture programme. It represents the starting point from which they developed their design proposals for the *City Campus*, based on the principles of green urbanism.

'Gown and Town': Why a *City Campus*?

In Australia over the last ten years, universities have been commissioning innovative architecture and enabling architects to realize their ideas of how teaching and learning might occur in the 21st century and how a campus might be integrated into the existing city fabric. It has ushered in a period of expansion, where old university buildings are being upgraded, new facilities designed, and younger universities are looking for a more progressive image.

A campus itself can be like a small city. Alternatively, it can be integrated into the urban

Case Study 1
City Campus – Densification, Urban Infill and Urban Renewal

fabric and be used to revitalize the city centre. The 1960s campus model as a greenfield development outside the city clearly has its limitations, and is regarded as less appropriate for the improvement of relationships between 'gown and town'. In addition, every dollar spent on the City Campus benefis the town three-fold in terms of student accommodation, food, entertainment and cultural activities.

Over the last three years (2006-08), the NSW State Government has developed the 'Six Cities Strategy', which includes Newcastle, and which has important implications for the relationship between the University and the City (see 'City Centre Plan', adopted by Newcastle City Council in October 2007: www.planning.nsw.gov.au/newcastle).

Clearly, as the second largest employer in the Hunter Region and being one of only a small number of Australian universities outside a capital city, the University is conscious of the critical role it plays in supporting the local community through its intellectual, academic and research activities, and also as a generator of economic, social and cultural benefits. In future, the University wishes to more actively contribute to the city and to increase its community engagement, consistent with its Institutional Strategic Plan 2007-2011 (see: www.newcastle.edu.au/strategicplanning/).

There is a growing recognition of the local dimension in the relationship between city, industry and university, in terms of the translation of science, arts and research into applied innovations that benefit local industry through closer interaction between knowledge creators and users. The City Campus of a research-intensive university could act as a key component for urban regeneration and facilitate the emergence of a 'creative city', linking cultural facilities, research institutes and public space. Thus it is assumed, for example, that the physical organization of facilities in clusters around Civic Square, say, with a strong cultural interface, would help to ensure that high value research activities deliver a real benefit to the city. Good examples of this are university towns such as Oxford, Cambridge and Heidelberg.

With a new 'City Campus', education will play a much greater role in the future life of the city centre (the notion of a 'Learning City').

The University of Newcastle, a research-intensive university, was established in 1965, and today is a regional university with a student population of about 30,300 (data: Jan. 2009). Two-thirds of those students are based at Callaghan Campus. The Faculty of Education and Arts is the largest Faculty, with more than 7,500 students enrolled. Female students outnumber males on campus; there are 17,000 women, compared with 13,300 male students. The annual growth of student numbers is currently around 10 per cent. This figure includes some 4,000 (or 13.3 per cent) international students from more than 80 countries, a figure that will grow over the next decade. Studies have shown that international students are used to more intensive uses of campus facilities, including evening sessions (especially in the library and computer labs). A 2004 study found that over 14 per cent (approximately 4,200 students, and growing) lived at inner-city post codes. Many students and academics prefer a city-based university, and prefer to live close to, or in, the urban centre, which can offer a city experience without the high living costs, such as in Sydney or Melbourne.

Urban renewal

Urban renewal of an existing city centre can be generated through programmes that carefully develop new densities around transport nodes and along park edges and cultural precincts, thereby improving the quality of urban life for all groups, including poor and disadvantaged residents.

The aim of the City Campus project is to carefully use design strategies for urban infill and regeneration of the neglected downtown area. Students are asked to look beyond the boundaries of the available sites, to the ecological footprint of the city centre. The design of such an inner-city campus needs to be creatively derived from a rigorous analysis and understanding of the site and the brief. A new landscape design for the central park (Civic Park), which aims for a high quality green space, green roofs and increased biodiversity within a sustainable neighbourhood of eco-buildings, is part of the design exercise. 'Sustainable neighbourhood' is defined as 'a compact community cluster using as little natural resources as possible, with careful consideration and improvement of public space.'

The urban renewal process in Newcastle has entered a crucial phase. The priority is now to continue the transformation process of its stagnating city centre into a vibrant place to live, work and explore. This includes the protection and conversion of Newcastle's heritage buildings and their adaptive re-use. There is a need for a high-quality 'Public Space Program', for the creation of good urban places, to lift the benchmark of public space and to strengthen the city core.

Urban renewal is the process of regenerating areas of cities that have become abandoned or are in a state of decay. Urban renewal involves the upgrading of existing areas of the city, or their selective demolition. It includes the integration of the old and the new (so-called 'piece-by-piece urban design') and the identification of new uses for existing buildings. It plays a major role in the economic, social and cultural development of the city. A vibrant city precinct will foster collaboration between academia and the city, attract investment and inducements for creative people to move to Newcastle. It is time to recognize the context of the bigger issues that Newcastle is facing, for example, how we will live more densely and compactly, and how we can move around the city more conveniently, without emitting greenhouse gases. A greater connection with what is undeniably the city's best asset, the waterfront (in all its forms: harbour, river, beach), right on the fringe of the downtown area is desirable. We need to understand the waterfront as open space, and its unrealized potential in terms of the experiences people might have along it. Of all the design fields, urban design has the greatest impact on cities. It draws together the overlapping concerns of city planning, landscape architecture, civil engineering, architecture and other disciplines.

The brief for the City Campus
The brief suggests relocating the identified functional parts of the University from its 1960s suburban campus back to the city centre. Both formal and informal learning spaces are necessary for different kinds of interaction and ways of teaching and learning. The masterplan needs to cater for specialist places, such as particular purpose-built research spaces (around 20 per cent of the brief) for small-scale operations, as well as general teaching and learning environments. The aim is the integration of the various following Schools and Faculties into the community fabric.

The components of the City Campus brief
- School of Business (Stage 1): 6,000 sqm for teaching.
- School of Law with law library (in close proximity to Court House) (Stage 1 or 2): 4,000 sqm for teaching.
- Public Library (combined joint Uni+City library facility): 'the core' 7,000 sqm.
- Drama and Performing Arts Theatre, close proximity to the Conservatorium, seating 500: a flexible space 20x30m, total: 2,000 sqm.
- Faculty of Arts and Education: 15,000 sqm.
- Offices for Administration (growing with stages)
- Offices for Academic Staff (administration and academic: total around 1,000

academic staff, 14,000 sqm).
- Specific offices for research (Research centres, including the `Incubator', growing with stages) total: 10,000 sqm, in identifiable building parts.
- Other support facilities (which become necessary when you insert a community of 7,000 students and 1,000 staff): 2,000 sqm.
- Related educational and non-educational facilities, e.g. artist-in-residence housing. Total for City Campus brief: around 60,000 sqm.

The Project

Students are asked to start with an assessment of possible sites for the development or relocation of facilities, and the expansion of key mixed-activities in the city centre. The studio will explore those hypothetical thoughts, will develop strategic ideas on options and explore design opportunities for further potential sites within walking distance to each other, the aim of which is to strengthening the pedestrian experience. It will also examine the capacity of the ideas and their 'best fit' opportunities in regard to the strategic directions for the City of Newcastle itself, and for the NSW State Government.

It is assumed that this study will include:
- Nurturing a service and knowledge-based economy for the city and the region;
- Raising the level of professional debate and input regarding the future of the rail corridor and the city centre of Newcastle;
- Achieving a high level of investigation and visioning of the future;
- Enhancing the already existing strong links between the University and the city;
- Fostering direct community engagement for an outward-looking institution;
- Strengthening public space connectivity;
- Continuing to focus on appropriate mixed-use developments, public transport and public domain issues, within clear masterplan visions;
- Improving access to the harbour edge and the integration of the Honeysuckle development into the city centre.

It is therefore expected that the participants in the studio will:
- Develop visionary recommendations for future strategic planning of such a campus precinct, with buildings of architectural distinction;
- Explore models of connectivity to existing facilities and levels of engagement with the surrounding community, through spatial organisation for increased interaction;
- Develop various 'Campus Plan' design proposals based on the notion of a sustainable 'Green City Campus' with the university as a catalyst for precinct revitalization (one of the nodes along the Green Corridor);
- Make a statement about the University in the heart of the city while also being part of a revitalized heart; and
- Design a mixed-use City Campus precinct that includes student accommodation (min. 500 units) within walking distance of the educational facilities.

The project combines a series of different typologies, such as theatre, library, office and exhibition buildings, student housing, educational facilities, retail, etc. Urban design and architecture is understood as an assembly of formally related parts whose relationship with each other is not arbitrary. To develop the compositional skills, the studio introduces strategies to:

(i) interpret works of other urban designers as compositions,

(ii) analyze precedents, and

(iii) develop students' own compositional skills.

The most successful masterplans will aim to positively affect neighboring sites as well. Urban infill and the adaptive re-use of existing structures is a chance to repair the essential relationship between buildings and public space, transforming a run-down area into a thriving mixed-use precinct.

The architectural historian Colin Rowe wrote a pivotal publication `Collage City' (1978) about the collection and collision of disparate elements that create a stimulating city. In a similar way, by using the principle of collage, the campus infill can stitch the centre together and be responsive to the existing street plan. Prime importance has to be given to the campus circulation, therefore the basic organization of the campus needs to be understood.

A Jeffersonian University Village has been a popular model for centuries. The Jeffersonian planning concept, first developed for the University of Virginia, is based on the notion of an 'academical village' and usually consists of a central and open common green space (still with human scale), with all building entrances facing this green space. The concept provides a robust framework for growth and the capacity to order long-term growth and change, while 'stage one' of the campus development is able to create an identity and sense of place for the new campus. Most of the new masterplanned greenfield campuses follow this idea of the village around a tree-lined lawn (rectangle). The centerpiece ('nucleus') of the village is always the university library, a hub of student activity placed on a linear spine (axis). The planning principles are:

• pedestrian access – everything is in walking distance;
• integration of community facilities (e.g. cafes, art galleries, sports facilities, etc);
• environmental and waste management that minimizes the ecological footprint;
• individual buildings with a distinctive architectural flair.

`Green Campus' initiatives

Sustainable Strategy, to enhance the city's and buildings' passive performance:

One of the most difficult challenges confronting architectural students who wish to incorporate sustainable principles of design, lies in understanding what the most appropriate tools to use are, and how and when to efficiently and effectively integrate them into the design process.

A sustainable city helps to accelerate the uptake of renewable technologies. The Newcastle City Centre will need to consist of a series of energy-efficient buildings to minimize the environmental footprint and to reduce greenhouse-gas emissions. These will need to be combined with concepts that aim to reduce maintenance and operational costs. Students will need to exemplify the way solar and wind energy can best be harnessed, and also how to ensure good day lighting and well-lit internal spaces, to reduce artificial lighting loads, as these are a significant portion of the energy consumption of buildings because of the power they consume and the cooling load they generate.

Large organizations, like universities, with the power to act indepen-dently should take matters into their own hands and begin to reduce greenhouse-gas emissions now.   *Yale President R. Levin, 2007*

Steps to enhance passive performance
1. Optimize shape and orientation (massing, volume, compactness).
2. Use passive solar strategies, site strategies, water saving strategies.
3. Utilize high flexibility and adaptability of structure, leading to buildings that are more useful over time.
4. Consider lighting and day lighting strategies; clarify window configuration, fenes-tration (identify best ratio of wall to window opening for each façade orientation).
5. Envelope design with a focus on prefabrication, assembly and disassembly (recy-cling), including insulation and shading devices (allowing winter sun penetration; blocking the western sun in the afternoon).
6. Consider ventilation systems, including natural ventilation strategies (all offices and classrooms require operable windows for natural ventilation; mixed-mode systems).
7. Clarify energy-efficient heating and cooling systems, activating the building's thermal mass; utilize solar cooling technology.
8. Use renewable energy sources (e.g. PV for generating electricity locally; the notion of 'Solar City': explore a mix of diversified energy sources, such as solar, wind, bio-mass) for decentralised energy generation with small units, at the scale of the district.
9. Select materials for low embodied energy (using local and recyclable materials).
10. Introduce ideas for landscaping (hard and soft) to reduce site impact; make use of rooftops; rainwater collection.
11. Consider parking and public transport requirements: due to its central location, it can be expected that in future 75 per cent of all students and residents arrive without using a private automobile.

The University of Newcastle aims to be a leader in environmentally sustainable campus planning. The University's current energy consumption is 35 per cent lower than the Aus-tralian university sector average (University of Newcastle data: April 2009). A new City Campus will need to deal with both mitigation and adaptation strategies in urban devel-opment. The research on climate change has two main points of emphasis: environmental protection, the mitigation of further changes in the climate due to human influences; and protection from the effects of climate change and the adaptation to the consequences of climate change. Mitigation includes the development of new technologies which use fewer resources and produce fewer emissions. Adaptation encompasses measures for reducing the vulnerability of natural and human systems to the adverse effects of climate change.

Media release on the *City Campus*

'The University's proposal to expand the presence in the city centre is a real one. The Hunter Development Corporation submitted in December 2008 its Newcastle City Centre Renewal Report to the NSW Government, which features a prominent role for the University. The University is currently investigating the feasibility of developing a Newcastle City Centre campus focused on the arts, humanities and social sciences; and redeveloping our Callaghan campus to sharpen its focus on health, engineering, science and technology. Preliminary discussions with key stakeholders have been conducted, including talks with federal and state Members of Parliament and local council representatives, and the feedback has been very positive. The University Council has established a reference group with broad representation across the city; it is a project in its early stages, that is expected to take 10 to 15 years to realize.' (Statement issued by the University on 05 July 2009)

Visions

The visions of 'City Campus', 'Green Corridor' and 'Port City' (the regeneration of the Newcastle port land) present probably the city's most significant planning opportunity for decades, and they have the potential to make the urban renewal of Newcastle a reality, while realizing the strategic aspirations of a contemporary university.

The design proposals of the studio were publicly exhibited and discussed at the end of the design studio, and key recommendations for practitioners and policy makers were formulated.

Some literature of the recommended studio reading includes

Alexander, Christopher, and H. Neis, A. Anninou (1987): *A New Theory of Urban Design*. Oxford University Press, London and New York
Alexander, Christopher (1979): *The Timeless Way of Buildings*, Berkeley, California
Benevolo, Leonardo (1980): *The History of the City*; MIT Press, Cambridge
Bentley, Ian (1999): *Urban Transformations: Power, People and Urban Design*, Routledge, London
Berge, Bjorn (2nd edition, 2009): *The Ecology of Building Materials*, Architectural Press/Elsevier, London
Dober, Richard (1963): *Campus Planning*. Reinhold Publishing, New York
Ellsworth, Ralph (1960): *Planning the College and University Library Building*, Pruett Press, Colorado
Gandelsonas, Mario (1991): *The Urban Text*, MIT Press, Cambridge
Gehl, Jan (2003): *New City Space*, Danish Architecture Press, Copenhagen
Gosling, David; and Maitland, Barry (1984): *Concepts of Urban Design*; Academy Edition, London
Kurokawa, Kisho (1992): *From Metabolism to Symbiosis*; Academy Edition Press, London
Leacroft, R. and L. (1984): *Theatre and Playhouse*, Methuen Press, London
Lynch, Kevin (1981): *Good City Form*, MIT Press, Cambridge
Lynch, Kevin (1960): *The Image of the City*, MIT Press, Cambridge
Marshall, Richard (2001): *Waterfronts in Post-Industrial Cities*; Spon Press, London
Rossi, Aldo (1966): *L'Architettura della Citta*, Marsilio Editori, Padua (1982 English edition: *The Architecture of the City*)
Rowe, Colin and Koetter, Fred (1978): *Collage City*, MIT Press, Cambridge
Schmertz, Mildred (ed.) (1972): *Campus Planning and Design*, McGraw-Hill / Architectural Record, New York
Tschumi, Bernard (1994): *The Manhattan Transcripts*, London, Academy Editions
Ungers, Oswald Matthias (1997): *City Islands. The City within the City*; in: *The Dialectic City*; Birkhaeuser, Germany

Research on precedents: buildings for educational purposes

The following campus examples will be analyzed in the studio:
- Walter Gropius: Bauhaus, Dessau (1925-26)
- Johannes Duiker, Open-Air School, Amsterdam, 1929-30)
- Alvar Aalto: Finish Institute of Technology, Otaniemi (1955-64)
- Hans Scharoun: Geschwister-Scholl-Gymnasium, Luenen (1956-62)
- Peter and Alison Smithson: Secondary Modern School, Hunstanton (1949-54)
- Louis Kahn: Richards Medical Research Building, Philadelphia (1957-64);
  Phillips Exeter Library, Exeter (1967-72);
  Indian Institute of Management, Ahmedabad (1968-70)
- Le Corbusier: Visual-Arts-Center, Harvard Campus (1961-62)
- Vilanova Artigas: FAU-USP Faculty Building, Sao Paulo (1961-65)
- Universidad Central de Venezuela, Caracas, by Carlos Villanueva (1944-73)
- Kresge College, university of California in Santa Cruz, USA, by Moore & Turnbull (1966-74)
- Mario Botta: Secondary School, Morbio Inferiore (1972-77)
- James Stirling: Leicester University Engineering Building, Leicester (1959-63);
  History Faculty Building, Cambridge (1964);
  Buildings on the campuses of Oxford and St. Andrews;
  Research Centre WZB, Berlin (1979-87)
  Cornell Centre for Performing Arts, Ithaca (USA, 1983-88)
  Municipal Library project, Latina (Italy, 1983)
  Music and Theatre Academy, Stuttgart (1987-95)
  Singapore Temasek Polytechnic Campus (1991 95)

A series of other important educational buildings by architects Kevin Roche & John Dinkeloo, SOM, Gunnar Birkerts, Paul Rudolph, John Andrews, Giancarlo de Carlo, Candilis Josic Woods, OM Ungers, Max Bill.

More recent examples include:
- Alvaro Siza: Oporto School of Architecture Buildings, Porto (1987-96)
- Peter Wilson: New City Library, Muenster (1987-93)
- Arno Lederer: Salem College, Ueberlingen, Germany (1998-2000)
- Toyo Ito: Mediatheque Sendai, Japan (1995-2000)
- Ortner & Ortner: University Library in Dresden (1998-2002)
- Rem Koolhaas OMA: Seattle Central library, USA (2005)

A series of recent campus extensions includes the work by architects: Raphael Moneo, Steven Holl, Arata Isozaki, Fumihiko Maki, Wiel Arets, Herzog & de Meuron, Rem Koolhaas (on campuses such as: Harvard, MIT, University of Minnesota, Yale, etc.)

The following Australian universities' City Campuses have been analyzed

- RMIT Swanston Street Campus, Melbourne, by various architects (1990s)
- University of Notre Dame in Fremantle, Perth (WA)
- University of South Australia, Adelaide (SA)
- University of Ballarat, Camp Street Campus, Ballarat (VIC)
- University of Tasmania, City Campus Launceston (TAS)

Recent Australian examples of educational buildings include:
- Lyons: The John Curtin School of Bio-medical Research at ANU, Canberra
- Hassell: Various university facilities, Sydney/Melbourne/Brisbane
- Daryl Jackson: Various university facilities, Sydney/Melbourne/Brisbane
- FJMT Richard Francis Jones: Auckland Uni School of Business; Law Faculty Building, University of Sydney
- Donovan Hill: Various university facilities, Brisbane
- John Wardle wth. Hassell: Kaurna Building at the University of South Australia, City Campus, Adelaide
- Bligh Voller Nield wth. John Mainwaring: University of the Sunshine Coast Library, Queensland
- Bligh Voller Nield: University of the Sunshine Coast Faculty of Arts Building, Queensland
- UNSW, Sydney: Building L5 and Sir Webster Building, New South Wales
- Design Inc: Bio21 Building at the University of Melbourne, Victoria
- Woods Bagot: UWA Business School; City Campus of University of Notre Dame, Fremantle, Western Australia
- University of Ballarat Camp Street Campus, Victoria
- University of Tasmania, School of Fine Arts, Hobart, Tasmania

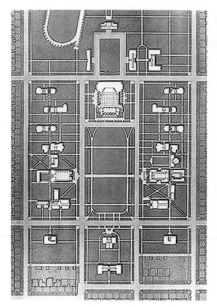

Fig. 01: Site plan of the Pomona College campus (1905), following Jefferson's classical plan with a central quarangle.
Fig. 02: Informal learning spaces at TU Munich.
Fig. 03: Aerial photo of an Oxford University college.

Fig. 04: Aerial photo of Civic Park and City Hall, Newcastle, 1973. (Archive Newcastle Library)
Fig. 05: James Stirling and James Gowan, 1959. Leicester University Engineering Building, a classic.

Fig. 06: Campus of the Indian Institute of Management (IIM), Ahmedabad, India (1968-70). (Photo: S. Lehmann, 2008)

The Campus – a Miniature City

Teaching fuses theory with practice, constantly evolving through changes in teaching and learning methodologies. The city campus is like a miniature city, consisting of a series of urban buildings, which provide flexibility for such future changes. The next-generation places of learning and new research facilities are best designed to foster and facilitate research cross-fertilization through spaces for structured and informal social encounters between academics, students and the broader community.

Fig. 07: John Wardle Architects with Hassell, UniSA City West Campus, Adelaide, 2001-05.

Fig. 08: City campus for Bocconi University Faculty of Business, Milan; Grafton Architects, 2008. Examples of figures 05 to 08 illustrate well, how much the image of the entire university can gain through the construction of outstanding facilities.

408

INTEGRATING CAMPUS WITH COMMUNITY

This masterplan proposal looks at creating an identifiable, compact city campus within the civic precinct. Civic Park is to be merged with the city block containing City Hall, the Civic Theatre and the Council Administrative Centre, creating one large, car-reduced city block that is identifiable as the urban centre. A large promenade running south from the town square, Wheeler Place, links the two blocks, drawing people through the site. This creates a strong pedestrian link between Civic and the cultural precinct of Darby Street. Multiple courtyards and thoroughfares are strategically located throughout the block to encourage public interaction. These outdoor spaces have strong connections to their surrounding buildings – existing and new – with the size and shape of these structures helping to define their use. The proposed university and public buildings are located around these outdoor spaces, providing users with desirable outlooks and breakout spaces. The buildings focus on creating a unified urban language for the entire precinct, with attention to architectural detail and the choice of materials. The masterplan defines the optimal building density, on the scale of the district. A higher density in the centre creates a sense of urbanity and community, and integrates the campus within the city. The use of local renewable energy sources (every kind of solar application; biomass; geothermal) ensures a minimized ecological footprint of the new campus.

CITY CAMPUS

1

1 Timothy Hulme,
   Michael Smith:
   Masterplan
   perspective

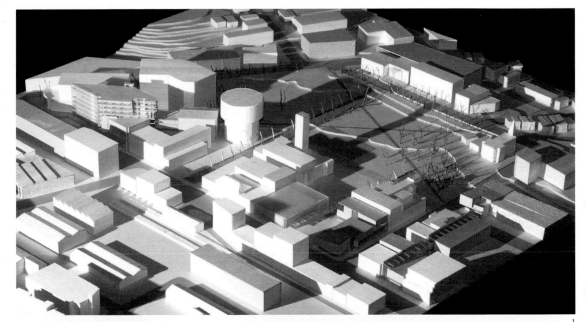

| | | 1 Timothy Hulme,
Michael Smith:
Masterplan model | 2 Timothy Hulme,
Michael Smith:
Civic Park link,
night perspective | |

1

1   Michael Smith:
    Joint City and Univer-
    sity Library, Cnr
    Burwood and Hunter
    Streets, day perspective

2

1

2

3

| 1 Michael Smith: Joint City and University Library, Cnr Burwood and Hunter Streets, model | 2 Michael Smith: Joint City and University Library, Cnr Burwood and Hunter Streets, entry | 3 Michael Smith: Joint City and University Library, Cnr Burwood and Hunter Streets, entry |

1

2

1   Michael Smith:
    Joint City and Univer-
    sity Library. Detail section
    with double facade,
    naturally ventilated

2   Michael Smith:
    Joint City and
    University Library,
    Hunter Street
    elevation

1

1   Michael Smith:
    Research Centre
    'Incubator' on TPI
    House site,
    entry perspective

1   Michael Smith:
    King Street,
    entry perspective

2   Michael Smith:
    Auckland Street,
    perspective from
    the park

1

2

| 1 | Timothy Hulme:
Drama Theatre and
town square,
Hunter Street.
Night perspective | 2 | Timothy Hulme:
School of Business,
Auckland Street.
Perspective |

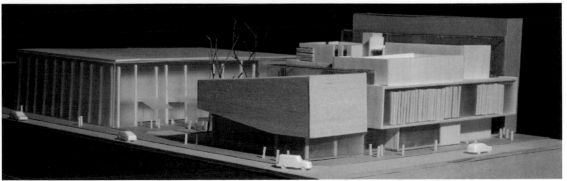

1   Timothy Hulme:
    Interior foyer, School
    of Business,
    perspective

2   Timothy Hulme:
    Auckland Street,
    perspective

3   Timothy Hulme:
    Drama Theatre and
    School of Law. Model

PERMEABLE URBAN TOPOGRAPHY

This masterplan proposal for the City Campus is based on an articulated topography that creates focus locations within the open public space system through the manipulation of hard and soft spaces. The revitalization of the park is paramount to the design intent. The park works to embody the University's inner-city campus with a unifying identity. It extends and cross-pollinates the surrounding urban fabric, offers informal learning spaces, and has a strong focus on walking and cycling. The concept of articulated topography means: Buildings sit in the landscape, responding to the built features of the park and the subtle detail of the existing heritage buildings within the precinct. The new performing arts theatre building acts as a gateway to Civic Park from Hunter Street, folding up and out of the topography as a significant civic gesture. The new library and council administration building on Burwood Wedge utilizes the park axis to develop an extruded Northern façade, allowing maximum light penetration to the integrated spaces serving both library and council. Employing environmentally sustainable design principles, the School of Architecture and the Faculty of Business and Law buildings are derived from their educational typologies. Whilst form still follows function, the function has become more complex. ESD-principles are a part of this evolution, affecting the user experience, creating tailored micro-climates to augment humanistic well-being and healthy workplaces for an outward-looking institution.

CITY CAMPUS

1

1   Elizabeth Brown,
    Joshua Rhodes:
    Masterplan
    model

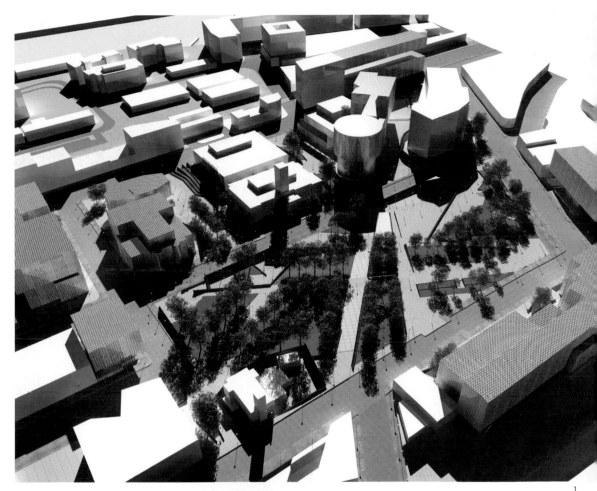

1

2

First things First, The Park...
Stage 1. Business & Law + Council & Library +Carpark +
   Student services
Stage 2. Drama Theatre + Student Accommodation +
   Fine Arts + Student health
Stage 3. School of Architecture

Carpark

Council & Library

School of Architecl

Student services

Business & Law

Drama Theatre

Student health

Faculty Exhibition spaces

Reinterpretation of existing
Vietnam War Memorial

School of Fine Ar

3

1 Elizabeth Brown, Joshua Rhodes: Masterplan Perspective	2 Elizabeth Brown, Joshua Rhodes: Civic Park Perspective	3 Elizabeth Brown, Joshua Rhodes: Masterplan, Staging diagramme

1   Joshua Rhodes:
    Joint City and Uni
    Library Cnr Burwood
    and Hunter Streets
    Perspective

1

2

2 Joshua Rhodes:
Joint Council/Library
Burwood Street
Perspective

1

2

| 1 | Joshua Rhodes: Joint Council/Library Cnr Burwood and Hunter Streets Perspective | 2 | Joshua Rhodes: Joint Council/Library Cnr Burwood and Hunter Streets Sectional perspective | | |

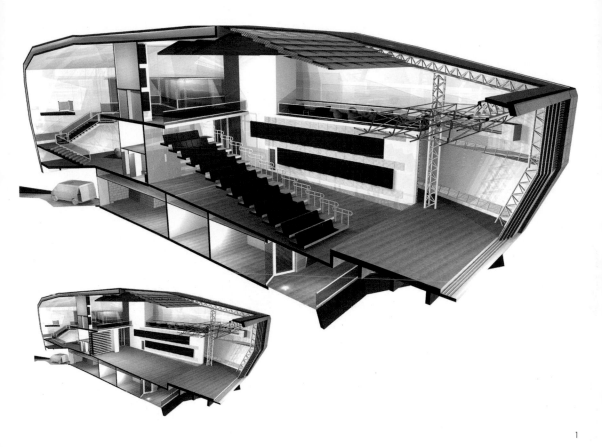

1

2

3

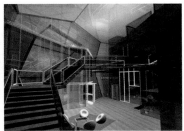

4

1 Joshua Rhodes:
   Drama Theatre
   Hunter Street
   Sectional perspec-
   tives

2 Joshua Rhodes:
   Drama Theatre
   Hunter Street
   Internal perspective
   of foyer

3, 4 Joshua Rhodes:
   Drama Theatre
   Hunter Street
   Internal perspectives

1

2

1   Joshua Rhodes:
    Drama Theatre
    Cnr Auckland and
    Hunter Streets
    Perspective

1

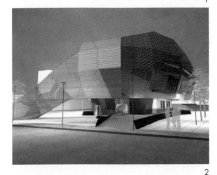

2

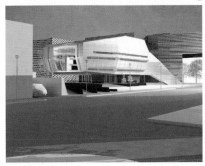

3

4

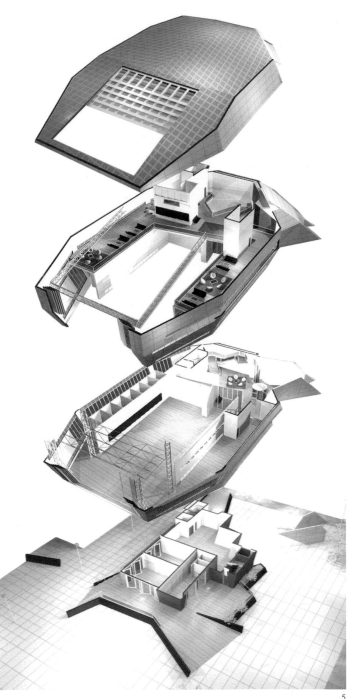

5

1- 4 Joshua Rhodes:
Drama Theatre
Auckland Street
Perspectives

5   Joshua Rhodes:
Drama Theatre
Cnr Auckland and
Hunter Streets
Exploded axonometric

1   Elizabeth Brown:
    School of Business
    and Law, Cnr King
    and Auckland Streets.
    Perspective

2   Elizabeth Brown:
    School of Business
    and Law.
    Sectional perspective

1

2

1   Elizabeth Brown:
     School of Architec-
     ture. Darby Street
     Perspective

2   Elizabeth Brown:
     School of Business
     and Law. Model

URBAN INFILL + LANDSCAPE URBANISM + LOCAL RENEWABLES

Each element of this city campus masterplan is used to support an environmentally sustainable system of 'open exchange' to improve resilience and adaptation. Buildings and landscape coexist, becoming both stage and media, places and edges that promote symbiosis and the exchange of knowledge. The new buildings provide a variety of interaction types, depending upon the individual site constraints, building functions and user groups. Some buildings focus on internal exchange patterns whilst others centre on external exchange. The approach to the park provides a green rejuvenation of the existing urban context, through the use of irregular eucalyptus tree plantations (urban forest) and collections of native grasses. Each site incorporates the new irregular landscape, through its integration in, around and, in some cases, on top of the buildings. This gives the precinct a recognizable association. The masterplan creates a family of buildings where each element embodies a unique approach and character, creating an ongoing dialogue between sites within the precinct. The building design has a focus on energy-efficient technologies, the local generation of renewable energy with building-integrated solar PV, the use of green roofs to collect rainwater, and the provision of effective sun-shading and natural cross-ventilation through long, narrow building slabs.

1

CITY CAMPUS

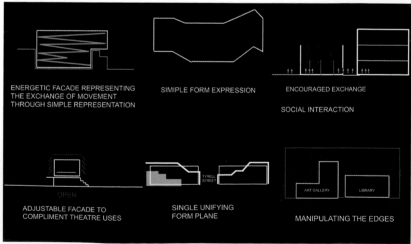

ENERGETIC FACADE REPRESENTING
THE EXCHANGE OF MOVEMENT
THROUGH SIMPLE REPRESENTATION

SIMPLE FORM EXPRESSION

ENCOURAGED EXCHANGE

SOCIAL INTERACTION

OPEN

ADJUSTABLE FACADE TO
COMPLIMENT THEATRE USES

TYRELL
STREET

SINGLE UNIFYING
FORM PLANE

ART GALLERY   LIBRARY

MANIPULATING THE EDGES

2

1   City campus library:
    precedent by Bolles-
    Wilson, City Library
    in Muenster, 1992,
    with skylight

2   Nicholas Cini and
    Katherine Daunt:
    Diagrammatic
    analysis

1

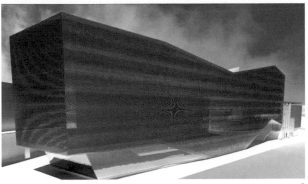

2

3

1 Nicholas Cini and
   Katherine Daunt:
   Masterplan with
   urban forest concept

2 Nicholas Cini and
   Katherine Daunt:
   Joint Council/Library
   Hunter Street
   Perspective

3 Nicholas Cini and
   Katherine Daunt:
   School of Law
   Auckland Street
   Perspective

1 Katherine Daunt:
School of Business,
Hunter Street
Perspective

1

2

3

1 Katherine Daunt:
   School of Business,
   Aurkland Street
   perspective

2 Katherine Daunt:
   School of Business
   Internal crossbridges
   perspective

3 Katherine Daunt:
   School of Business
   Hunter Street
   Model

1	Katherine Daunt: School of Business Hunter Street Entry perspective	2	Katherine Daunt: School of Business Christie Place Perspective

1

2

1   Nicholas Cini:
    School of Fine Arts,
    Laman Street:
    Integrating the
    NRAG and Library

2   Nicholas Cini:
    School of Fine Arts,
    Laman Street
    Perspective

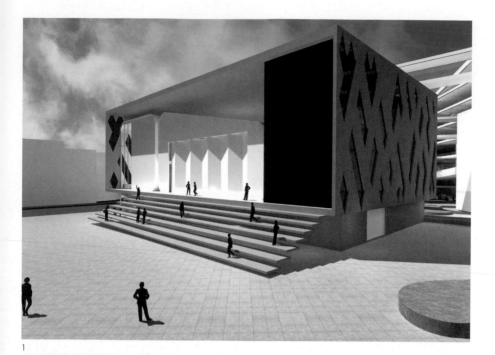

1

2

| 1 | Katherine Daunt: Drama Theatre Wheeler Place Perspective | 2 | Katherine Daunt: Drama Theatre Burwood Wedge Perspective | | |

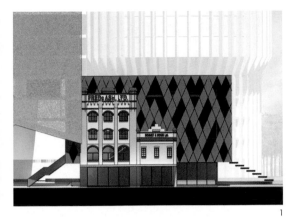

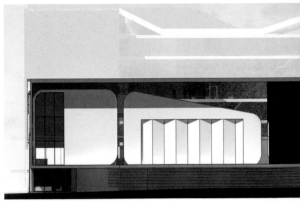

1

2

3

1 Katherine Daunt:	2 Katherine Daunt:	3 Katherine Daunt:
Drama Theatre	Drama Theatre	Drama Theatre
Hunter Street	Wheeler Place	Hunter Street
Elevation	Elevation (closed)	Perspective

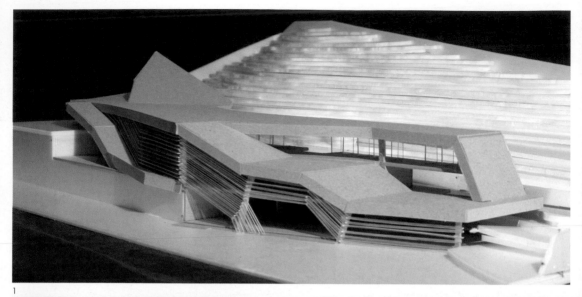

1

2

| 1 Nicholas Cini: School of Architecture, Darby Street, Model | 2 Nicholas Cini: School of Architecture, Darby Street, Perspective | | |

1

1   Nicholas Cini:
School of Architec-
ture, Darby Street,
Perspective, showing
western sun shading

1

2

3

4

1 Nicholas Cini: School of Fine Arts, Laman Street Perspective	2 Nicholas Cini: School of Architecture, Darby Street Perspective	3, 4 Nicholas Cini: School of Architecture, Darby Street Perspective

1

1   Nicholas Cini:
    School of Architec-
    ture, Darby Street
    Perspective

THE EMBEDDED LINEAR CAMPUS

The expansion of the University into the city centre injects a stimulus of over 3,000 students into the dying city. The effect of this is more than the provision of lecture theatres and classrooms. Cafes, bookshops, computer labs, bars and other hubs, such as 'Pinkies', will progressively occupy the inner city. Rather than focussing on the sites around City Hall – already an established urban centre – western Hunter Street provides substantial opportunities for a linear concept of urban regeneration. An early site selection process noted as many as sixty vacant sites and buildings immediately available along Hunter Street. The design for the city campus was influenced by Koolhaas' unbuilt Parc de la Villette, where the park was deconstructed into four layers, dividing the site into articulated 'strips': Scattered 'Confetti' holding minor functions such as kiosks, and large existing buildings which hold the major functions. Following this approach, this City Campus sees each site along Hunter Street as the 'strips' capable of holding isolated and independent functions. The main street itself provides the axial boulevard with pre-existing public transport services – including free buses and a parallel green corridor for cycling. This enables sites along the main street to be connected, within a ten-minute journey. The vacant or 'for lease' sites along the street are seen as the 'confetti', providing random University incisions. Finally, larger buildings have been designed to accommodate specific faculty needs. Utilizing the vacant sites allows a passive integration of the University into the fabric of the city, embedding this linear campus into the urban context.

CITY CAMPUS

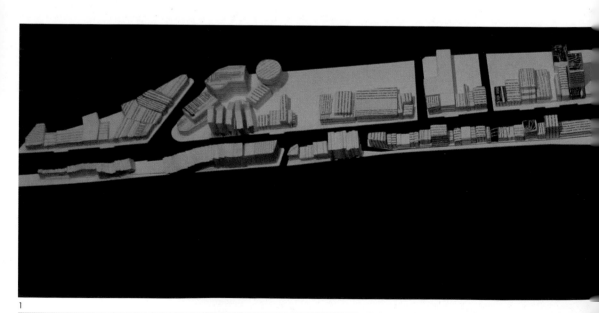

1

1   Dean Cotter,
    James Craft:
    Masterplan model of
    the linear campus
    concept

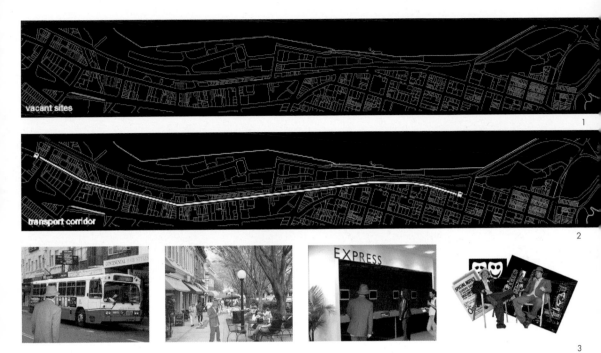

vacant sites

1

transport corridor

2

EXPRESS

3

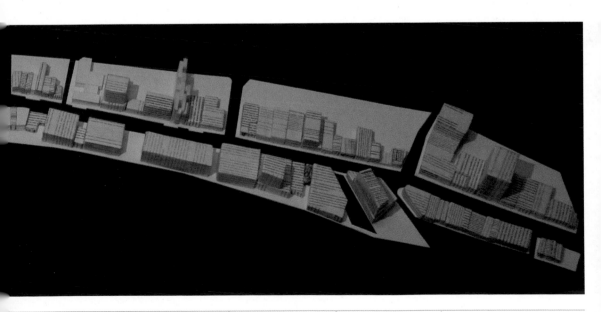

| 1 | Dean Cotter, James Craft: Vacant sites Analysis diagramme | 2 | Dean Cotter, James Craft: Transport corridor diagramme | 3 | Dean Cotter, James Craft: Masterplan, Various perspectives |

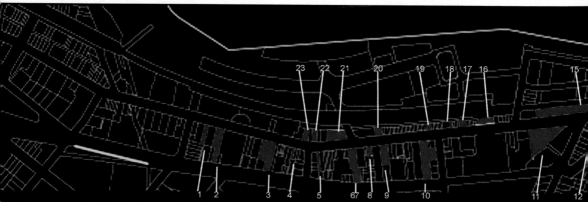

ite selection

Academic offices. 2. Fine arts, arts offices and car parking. 3. architecture. 4. computer lab. 5. computer lab. 6. Academic offices. 7. administration. 8.
2. Computer lab. 13. Auditorium. 14. Academic offices. 15. Library. 16. Drama theatre. 17. Research centers. 18. Exhibition space. 19. Lecture theatres. 20.

2

1 James Craft:	2 Dean Cotter,
Library	James Craft:
Hunter Street	Site selection
Perspective	analysis diagramme

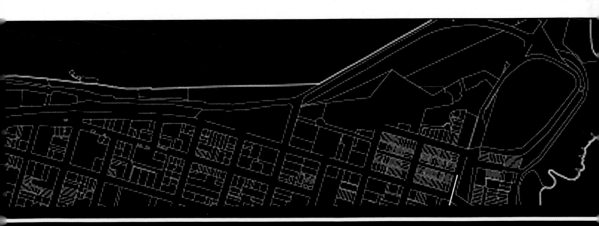

munity room. .9. classrooms. 10. Student services and car parking 11. Business and law, council administration offices. park de la villet
Fine arts. 22. Class rooms. 23. Lecture theatres.

1 James Craft:
   Library
   Hunter Street
   Perspective

1

2

1	James Craft:	2	James Craft:
	School of Fine Arts		School of Fine Arts
	Hunter Street		Hunter Street
	Entry perspective		Perspective

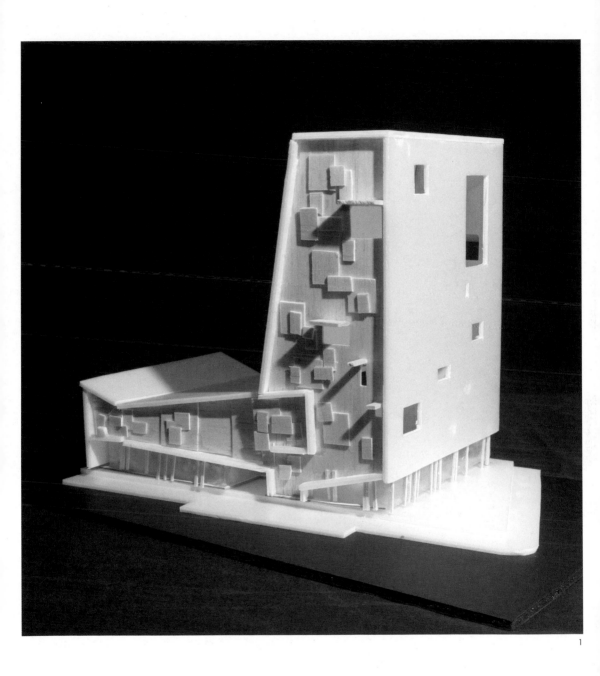

1

1   James Craft:
    School of Fine Arts
    Hunter Street
    Model

1

2

1 Dean Cotter:	2 Dean Cotter:		
School of Architec-ture building, Hunter Street Perspective	Drama Theatre Hunter Street, Perspective montage		

1   Dean Cotter:
     Drama Theatre
     Hunter Street,
     Night perspective

2   Dean Cotter:
     School of Architec-
     ture. Hunter Street,
     Perspective

3   Dean Cotter:
     School of Architec-
     ture. Hunter Street,
     Entry perspective

SPACES, SKINS AND SURFACES

The urban strategy of programmatic diversity, pedestrian-friendly, informal urban spaces and compositional layering is used throughout the proposal and adopted to the requirements and opportunities around the Civic precinct site. Parallel strips (running from east to west) divide the site. Each strip becomes an independent car-reduced zone, which relates to its location across the site. Within this layout, roads, building types and a major pedestrian spine are integrated into the urban framework. The park is also divided into three zones, to create an active zone, a buffer zone and a quiet zone. Major paths are then placed on the site running from north to south. Objects, called 'activators', are located in public spaces around the site, creating a sense of place and scale, providing different functions and continuity throughout the city, with solar systems installed. The 'activators' generate their own energy locally. The aim is for the city campus to power itself with renewable sources of energy. A final layer of found objects is located in the composition of the park. This includes the existing sandstone terracing, the fountain in the park, and the historical train line, originally running diagonal across the park.

CITY CAMPUS

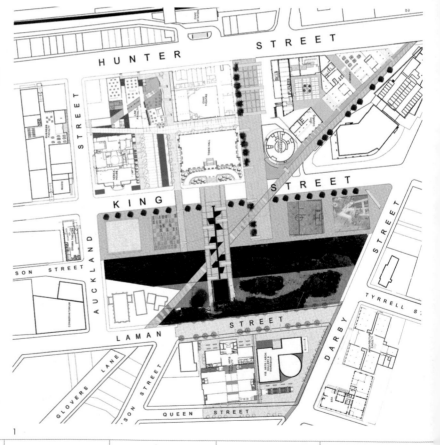

1

1   Gabriel McLean,
    Bronwyn Nymeyer:
    Masterplan
    Site plan

1

2

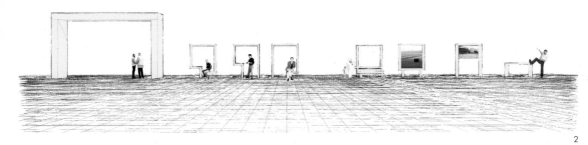

3

4

1 Gabriel McLean,
   Bronwyn Nymeyer:
   Masterplan
   Analysis diagrammes

2 Gabriel McLean,
   Bronwyn Nymeyer:
   Activators
   Perspective

3 Gabriel McLean:
   Joint Council/Library
   Burwood Street
   Elevation

4 Bronwyn Nymeyer:
   School of Law
   Hunter Street
   Elevation

1

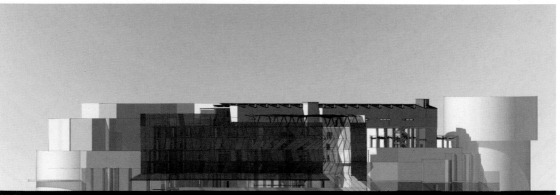

2

1 Gabriel McLean:	2 Gabriel McLean:
Joint Council/Library	Joint Council/Library
Cnr Burwood and	Wheeler Place
Hunter Streets	Elevation
Perspective	

1

1   Gabriel McLean:
    Joint Council/Library
    Hunter Street
    Perspective

1

2

3

| 1 | Bronwyn Nymeyer: Drama Theatre Cnr King and Auckland Streets, Perspective | 2 | Bronwyn Nymeyer: Drama Theatre King Street, Elevation | 3 | Bronwyn Nymeyer: School of Law Hunter Street, Perspective |

1

2

3

1 Bronwyn Nymeyer:
   Drama Theatre
   Cnr King and
   Auckland Streets
   Night perspective

2 Bronwyn Nymeyer:
   School of Law
   Christie Place
   Perspective

3 Bronwyn Nymeyer:
   School of Law
   Christie Place
   Night perspective

NETWORK AND CONNECTIVITY: THE PUBLIC SPACE NETWORK

This masterplan focuses on the creation of a pedestrian connection across the harbour to Dyke Point peninsula and the future 'Port City', by extending Darby Street with an open green space and elevated footbridge. The masterplan is inspired by an initial topographical study of the larger context of the city, in particular the winding form of the Hunter River. A conceptual approach was derived by thinking about the movement of water. Water does not move in straight lines but snakes a path, responding to topography and geological formation. Similarly, the arrangement of the University programme in this scheme creates a path that winds around information centres and cafes, past lecture theatres and galleries, pulling the passer-by into the life of the campus. The most important first step in the rejuvenation of the city centre is to densify, compact and increase population. Buildings will use every kind of practical solar application, including solar thermal for cooling and 'solar sunrooms' (wintergardens). It is proposed that the existing circular council building be given over entirely to student accommodation. This will provide a hive for 24-hour-hub of activities right in the city heart, making it a far more comfortable space to inhabit and pass through after dark. Commercial activity will be stimulated by the sudden injection of thousands of people into a precinct that is currently underutilized. This revitalized urban network will have increased pedestrian connectivity between the harbour and Darby Street by removing the heavy railway barrier.

CITY CAMPUS

1

1   Evan Howard and
    Tafara Mbara:
    Masterplan site
    model

1

2

3

1   Evan Howard and
    Tafara Mbara:
    Masterplan context
    map

2   Evan Howard:
    Internal perspective

3   Evan Howard:
    External perspective

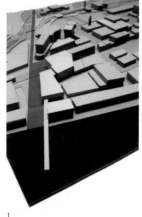

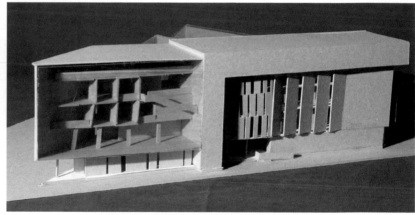

1

2

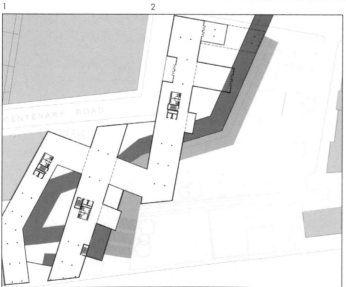

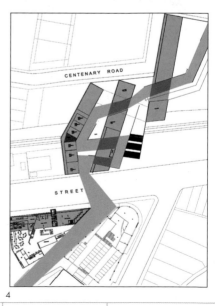

3

4

| 1 Evan Howard: Joint Council/Library Cnr Burwood and Hunter Streets Model | 2 Evan Howard and Tafara Mbara: Masterplan site model | 3 Evan Howard and Tafara Mbara: Masterplan site diagram | 4 Evan Howard and Tafara Mbara: Masterplan site diagram |

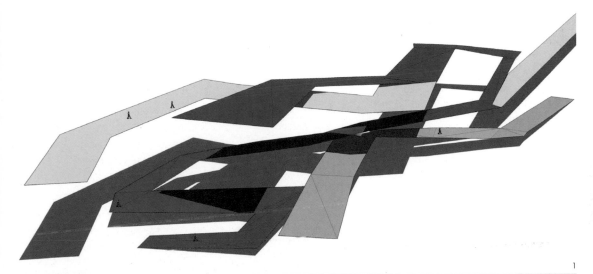

1   Evan Howard:
    Masterplan site
    diagram

2   Evan Howard and
    Tafara Mbara:
    Masterplan site
    photo diagram

DIAGRAM, SITE AND OBJECT: FAST-TRACKING THE CITY'S TRANSFORMATION

The proposal is to celebrate the city centre's diversity by creating a rich slice of public, compact and pedestrian-accessible urban space from the lower-end of Darby Street to the harbour. The proposal works with the north-south axis created by the Library, Civic Park, City Hall, the Civic Theatre and Civic train station, creating a link from the cultural precinct to the developing harbour foreshore. The masterplan ties into the existing railway workshop sheds at Honeysuckle, which can be used by the University for teaching, exhibitions and cultural events. The heavy train line is turned into an underground subway from Wickham to Newcastle, allowing pedestrians (and traffic) across the existing railway corridor and unlocking new visual corridors from the city centre to the harbour. The new landmark Business and Law Faculty tower sits above the platform concourse of the new Civic Station gateway complex. The Burwood Wedge site is reactivated as the eastern edge of the campus with a new 24-hour library. Christie Place garden is regenerated, leading onto an open ground floor gallery and public space for the New School of Fine Arts, which sits adjacent to the existing Civic Theatre. A double glazed playhouse floats above, marking the western edge of the city campus. Adaptive re-use of the historic library creates the new administration centre for city council, overlooking the park and City Hall.

CITY CAMPUS

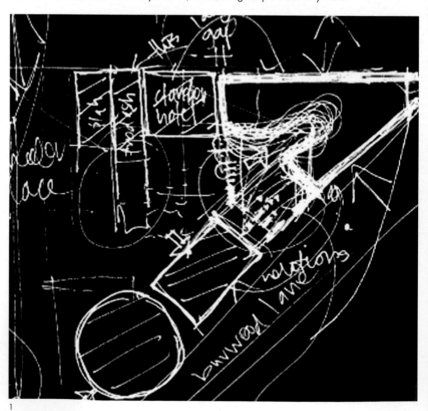

1

1 Sarah Donnelly,
   Lachlan Craggs:
   Burwood Wedge
   Site plan, sketch
   diagram

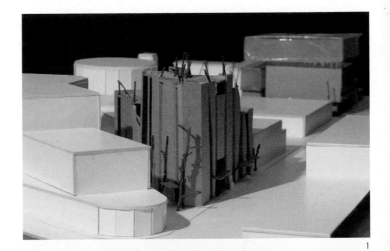

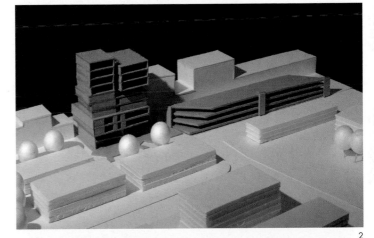

1   Sarah Donnelly:
    Library
    Hunter Street,
    Model

2   Lachlan Craggs:
    School of Business
    and Law Faculty in a
    tower, Civic Station,
    Hunter Street Model

3   Sarah Donnelly:
    School of Fine Arts
    and Playhouse,
    Hunter Street
    Model

1

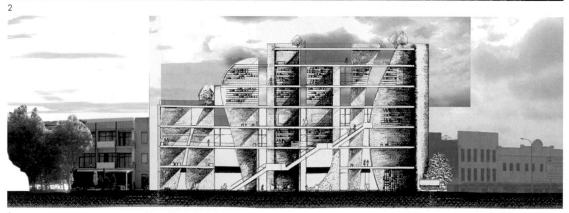

2

3

| 1 Sarah Donnelly: City + Uni Library Burwood Street, Hand rendered elevation | 2 Sarah Donnelly: Library Hunter Street, Hand rendered elevation | 3 Sarah Donnelly: Library Burwood Street, Hand rendered section | |

1

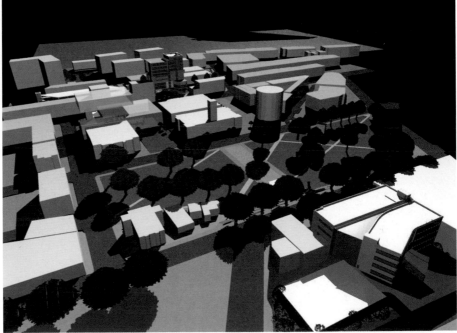

2

1 Lachlan Craggs:
   School of Business
   and Law Faculty Tower,
   Civic Station, Hunter
   Street Perspective

2 Lachlan Craggs:
   Civic Park
   Aerial perspective

THE KNOWLEDGE-BASED CITY

How to realize the strategic aspirations of a contemporary university? While there are a number of precious cultural items already present throughout the city centre, they are fragmented and do not communicate with each other. To create a unifying 'wholeness' across the site; heavy rail is replaced by a 'green' light rail system to increase connectivity, while the boundaries of the existing cultural buildings are 'blurred' to fit into the new urban topography, which has been generated by stitching the interstitial spaces together, creating a manipulated ground plane. To enable harmony between the old and the proposed new programmes, this masterplan suggests sub-dividing the programmatic requirements into four categories: Public, semi-public, semi-private and private. These categories are organized along the three major strips of the masterplan according to the themes: Art Strip, Green Strip, and Public Hub. Artistic activities and informal public spaces are located in the Art Strip; research, library functions and gardens are located in the Green Strip; and public activities and student services are located within the Public Hub. The masterplan exemplifies the urban transformation that is currently taking place, from industrial centre to a more compact, inter-connected 'knowledge-based city'. Street corners are occupied by a new breed of memorable 'green' buildings.

CITY CAMPUS

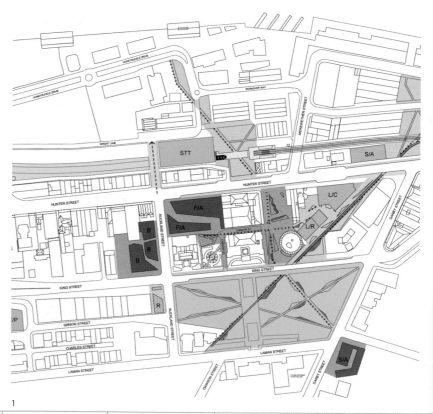

1

1 Andrew Cavill,
  Andrew Dowe:
  Masterplan

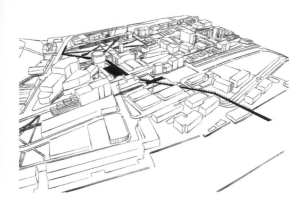

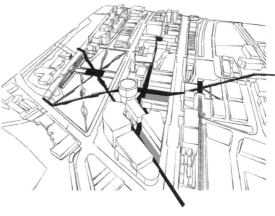

1

2

3

1	Andrew Cavill,	2	Andrew Cavill,	3	Andrew Cavill,
	Andrew Dowe:		Andrew Dowe:		Andrew Dowe:
	Axis diagram		Axis diagram		Masterplan
					perspective

1

2

3

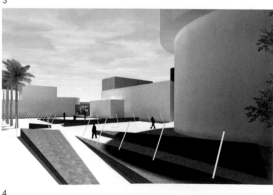

4

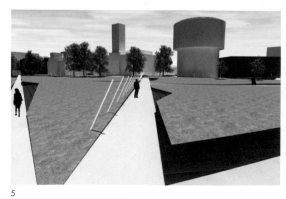

5

1-5 Andrew Cavill,
     Andrew Dowe:
     The new landscape
     design for Civic
     Park

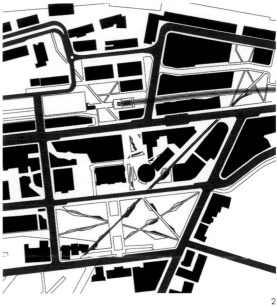

1

2

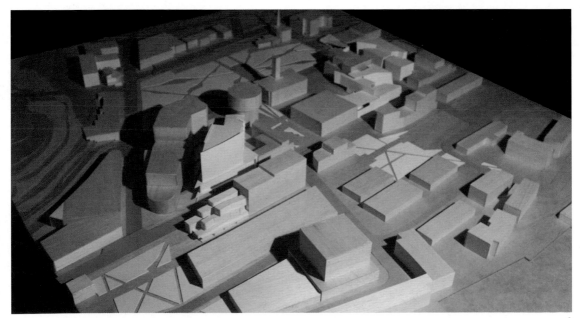

3

1   Andrew Cavill,
    Andrew Dowe:
    Diagram of
    transport systems

2   Andrew Cavill,
    Andrew Dowe:
    Diagram of streets

3   Andrew Cavill,
    Andrew Dowe:
    City Campus model

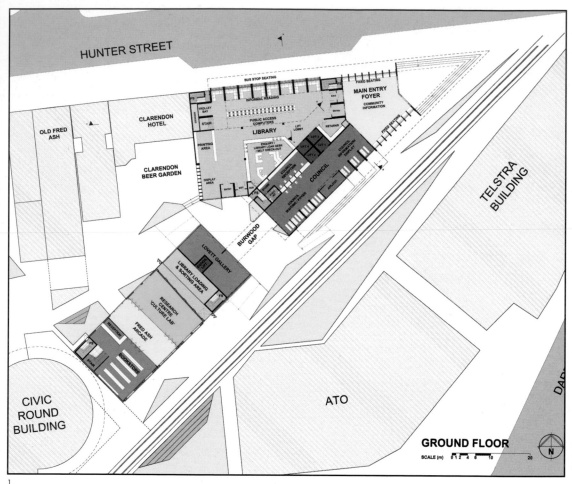

GROUND FLOOR

SCALE (m) 0 1 2 4   6   10   20

N

1

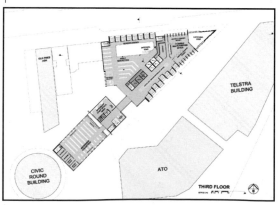

THIRD FLOOR

2

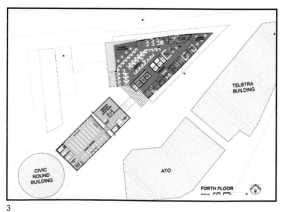

FORTH FLOOR

3

1 Andrew Cavill: Library Ground floor plan	2 Andrew Cavill: Library Third floor plan	3 Andrew Cavill: Library Fourth floor plan

1

2

3

| 1 Andrew Cavill: Clarendon perspective | 2 Andrew Cavill: Corner perspective | 3 Andrew Cavill: Council entry perspective |

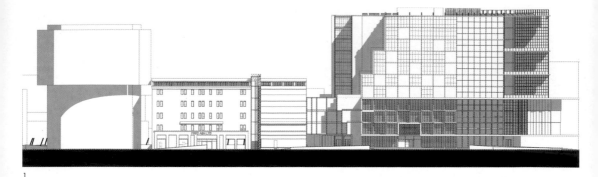

1

2

| 1 | Andrew Cavill: Library, Burwood Street elevation | 2 | Andrew Cavill: Uni + City Library, Hunter Street perspective |

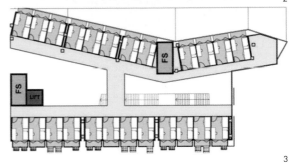

| 1 Andrew Dowe: Student accommodation, Hunter / Darby Streets, perspective | 2 Andrew Dowe: Student accommodation, Light rail perspective | 3 Andrew Dowe: Student accommodation, Third floor plan | 4 Andrew Dowe Student Accommodation Perspective Render from green corridor |

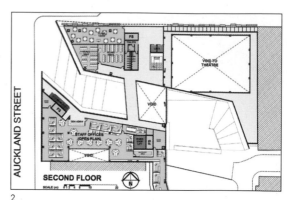

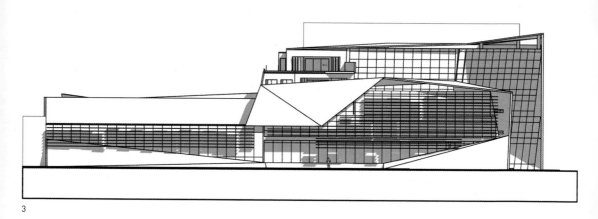

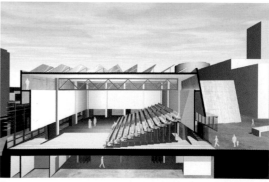

| 1 | Andrew Dowe: School of Fine Arts and Performing Arts Theatre. Ground floor plan | 2 | Andrew Dowe: School of Fine Arts and Performing Arts Theatre. Second floor plan | 3 | Andrew Dowe: School of Fine Arts and Performing Arts Theatre, Hunter Street elevation | 4-5 | Andrew Dowe: School of Fine Arts and Performing Arts Theatre, Sectional perspectives |

1

2

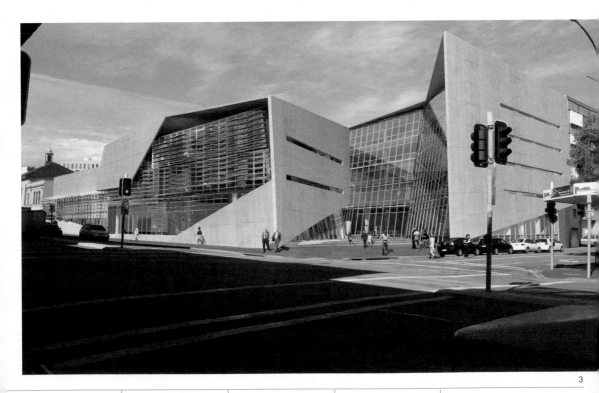

3

| 1 Andrew Dowe: School of Fine Arts and Performing Arts Theatre, Photomontage | 2 Andrew Dowe: School of Fine Arts and Performing Arts Theatre, Overall perspective | 3 Andrew Dowe: School of Fine Arts and Performing Arts Theatre, Photomontage |

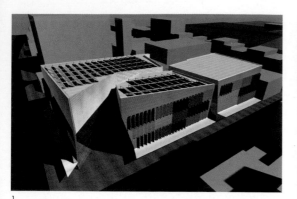

1

2

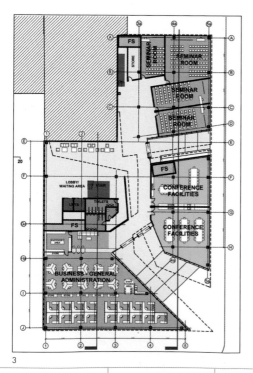

3

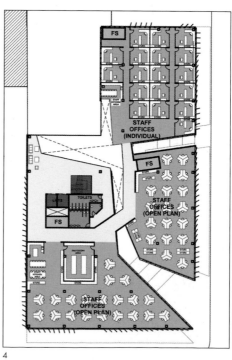

4

1 Andrew Dowe:	2 Anrew Dowe:	3 Andrew Dowe:	4 Andrew Dowe:
Business Centre	Business Centre	Business Centre	Business Centre
Perspective	Street photomontage	Ground floor plan	Third floor plan

1

2

3

1 Andrew Dowe:
   Business Centre
   Sectional perspectives

2 Andrew Dowe:
   Business Centre
   Sectional perspectives

3 Andrew Dowe:
   School of Business,
   Photomontage
   Auckland Street

1

2

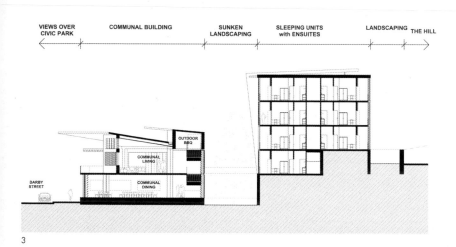

VIEWS OVER CIVIC PARK — COMMUNAL BUILDING — SUNKEN LANDSCAPING — SLEEPING UNITS with ENSUITES — LANDSCAPING — THE HILL

3

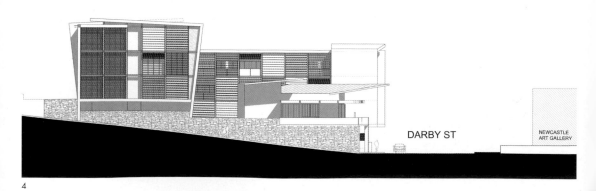

4

1 Andrew Cavill: Student accommodation, Darby Street Photomontage	2 Andrew Cavill: Student accommodation, Second floor plan	3 Andrew Cavill: Student accommodation, Long section	4 Andrew Cavill: Student accommodation, Street elevation

1

2

1	Andrew Cavill: Student accommodation, Photomontage Darby Street	2	Andrew Cavill: Student housing overlooking the park, Second floor plan

CONNECTION AND INTEGRATION: POST-INDUSTRIAL IDENTITY

The new library is a long beam, a 'superstructure of knowledge', while Civic Park is turned into a productive urban landscape where ideas of inner-city farming, agriculture and gardens are tested. Locally grown vegetables and fruits will be harvested from the gardens and green roofs, supplying the local restaurant scene. This reduces the distance food has to travel from field to fork. Two main ideas drive the masterplan concept:

- the densification of the existing city, and
- the integration of the new city campus into the existing city fabric.

New compact buildings are based on sustainable design principles, where most spaces can be operated without air-conditioning, using effective natural cross-ventilation. Sensitive lighting systems and the maximum use of day-lighting will ensure these buildings will only use a quarter of the energy required by conventional buildings. With the aim to de-carbonize the energy supply, the entire quarter will need to be transformed with decentralized, distributed energy generation systems to fully harvest renewable energy sources, such as wind, solar and bio-mass. The city campus generates all its energy from on-site renewables, collects and recycles rainwater and waste, and prioritizes pedestrian access. Most of the energy needed will be produced at the place of consumption, and will come from renewable sources. The result will be a campus with an 80 per cent reduction in greenhouse gas emissions.

CITY CAMPUS

1

1   Romi McPherson and
    Lachlan Seegers:
    City sketch and
    concept

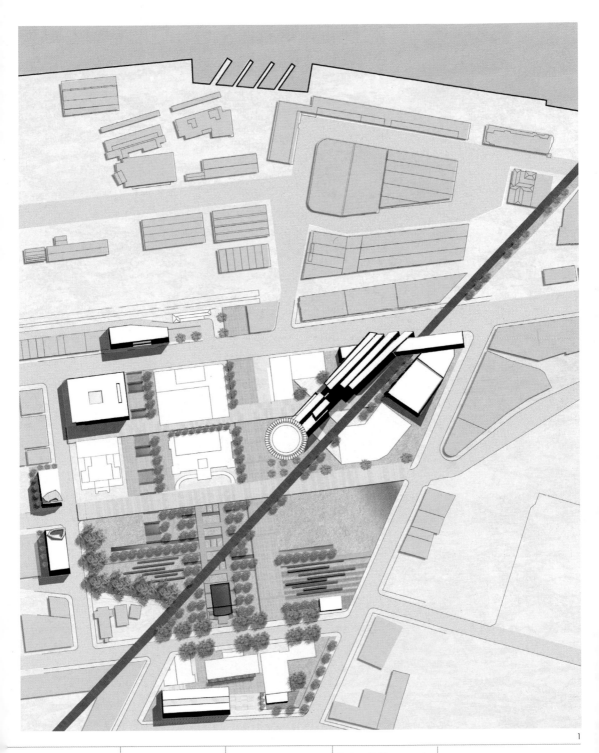

1 Romi McPherson and
   Lachlan Seegers:
   Masterplan

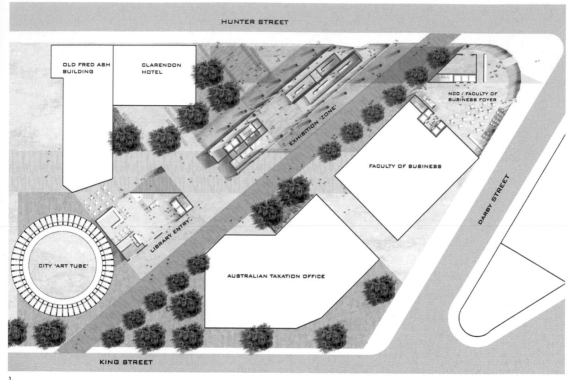

HUNTER STREET

OLD FRED ASH BUILDING

CLARENDON HOTEL

EXHIBITION 'ZONE'

NCC / FACULTY OF BUSINESS FOYER

FACULTY OF BUSINESS

DARBY STREET

LIBRARY ENTRY

CITY 'ART TUBE'

AUSTRALIAN TAXATION OFFICE

KING STREET

1

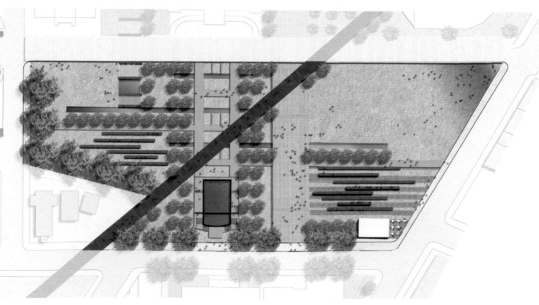

2

| 1 | Romi McPherson and Lachlan Seegers: Ground floor plan | 2 | Romi McPherson and Lachlan Seegers: Park concept plan for water recycling (filtration fields) | | |

1

2

3

1   Romi McPherson and
    Lachlan Seegers:
    Masterplan model

2   Romi McPherson and
    Lachlan Seegers:
    Masterplan model

3   Romi McPherson and
    Lachlan Seegers:
    Masterplan model

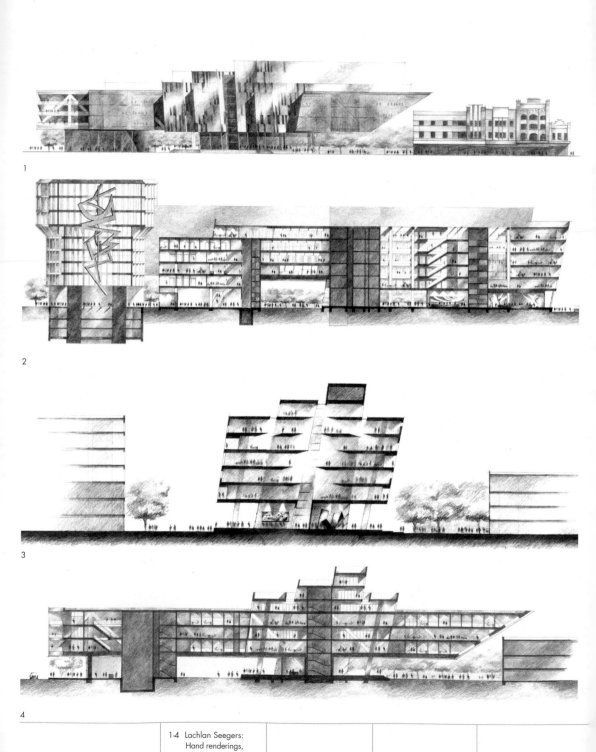

1

2

3

4

1-4 Lachlan Seegers:
Hand renderings,
Sections and
elevations

1

2

| | | 1 Lachlan Seegers: Hand sketch of library | 2 Lachlan Seegers: Hand sketch of library | |

1   Romi McPherson
    Perspective, School
    of Fine Arts and
    Education, Queen
    Street site

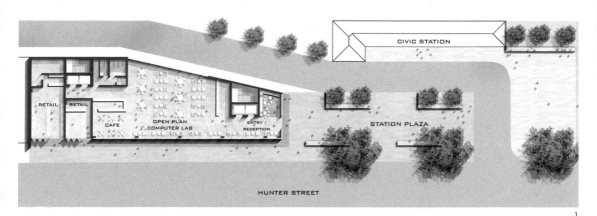

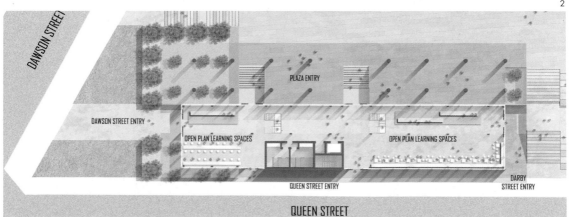

1   Romi McPherson:
    School of Business,
    Civic Station site,
    Floor plan

2   Romi McPherson:
    School of Fine Arts
    and Education,
    Floor plan

3   Romi McPherson:
    Ground Floor plan,
    Entry from Queen
    Street

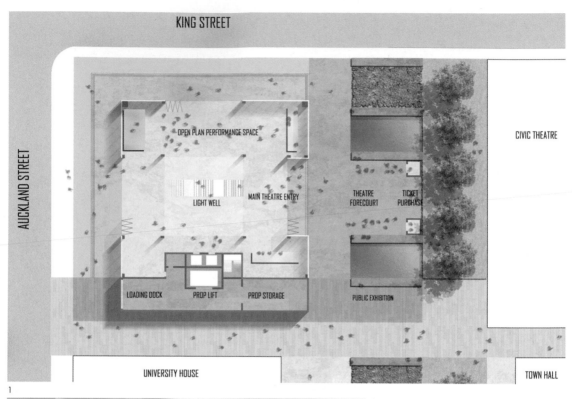

KING STREET

AUCKLAND STREET

OPEN PLAN PERFORMANCE SPACE

LIGHT WELL   MAIN THEATRE ENTRY

CIVIC THEATRE

THEATRE
FORECOURT

TICKET
PURCHASE

LOADING DOCK   PROP LIFT   PROP STORAGE

PUBLIC EXHIBITION

UNIVERSITY HOUSE

TOWN HALL

1

2

3

1 Romi McPherson: Performing Arts Theatre, Faculty of Arts and Education, Ground Floor	2-3 Romi McPherson: Elevation and Section, Performing Arts Theatre

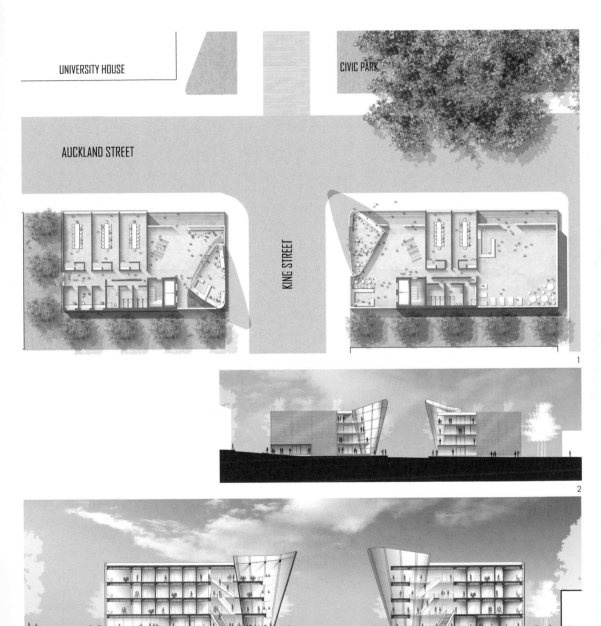

UNIVERSITY HOUSE

CIVIC PARK

AUCKLAND STREET

KING STREET

1

2

3

| 1 Romi McPherson: School of Law and School of Business, with Research Centres 'Incubators' | 2 Romi McPherson: School of Law and School of Business, Elevation | 3 Romi McPherson: Section through Research Centres |

A GREEN LIBRARY, EARTH-COVERED

The park serves as an entry point to the library and as a backdrop for students using the reading bays, while the library itself becomes an extension of public space. The building develops its own poetic proposition, with a unique feeling and ambience, thus creating a memorable *heart* for the new 'Learning City District'. Amenities are conveniently integrated: The Library and Information Common (the library's information technology hub, with free wireless connection in the park) is located in the central parkland, in the middle of the campus quarter, serving as an easily accessible information point. The library design utilizes sustainable building principles, such as natural cross-ventilation and effective sun shading, combined with a green roof to off-set the buildings' footprint in the park. The building's roof has an interesting section allows filtered light to penetrate from above, while precious books and documents are well protected from the harsh Australian sunlight. The main library space is passively cooled, as it benefits from almost zero heat gain even in extreme summer weather. There will be a high occupant comfort level, as well as a highly controlled material selection, using only local construction materials with low embodied energy and short supply chains. Landscape ideas and pedestrian movement have priority. While the landscaped roof garden harvests rain water, this roof garden also creates a gathering place for the community, where the role of the monument and public art within the urban fabric can be further explored.

CITY CAMPUS

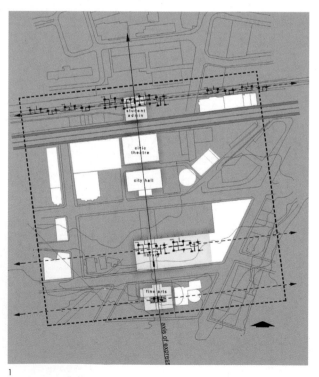

1

1 Sarah Jozefiak:
Library
Masterplan

1

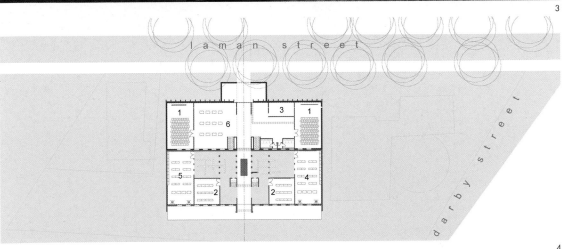

2

3

4

| 1 Sarah Jozefiak: Long site section | 2 Sarah Jozefiak: Library seen from Civic Park, Photo montage | 3 Sarah Jozefiak: Photomontage, reuse of the railway line corridor: Public space strategy | 4 Sarah Jozefiak: Library plan of entry level | |

1

1   Sarah Jozefiak:
    Library, green roof.
    Perspective, looking
    down axis towards
    City Hall

1

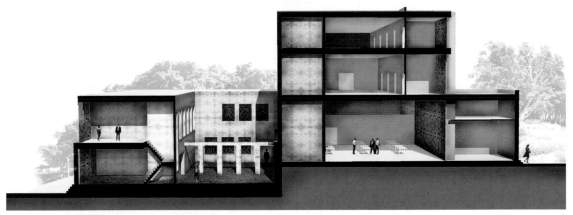

2

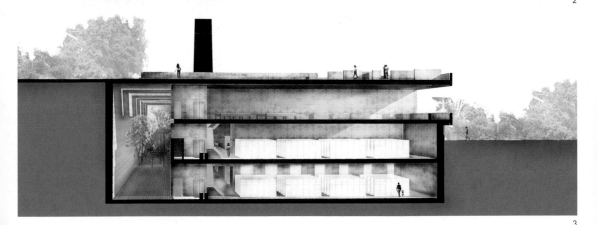

3

| 1 Sarah Jozefiak: School of Fine Arts, Photomontage, entry from Queen Street | 2 Sarah Jozefiak: Section, School of Fine Arts, incorporating existing Library | 3 Sarah Jozefiak: Library, Section and Photomontage, Civic Park |

A CITY OF PARKS AND PUBLIC OPEN SPACES

In this project, the surrounding context is allowed to communicate and suggest the urban proposition of the masterplan. This is used as a way to maintain and strengthen the unique character of a place. The city campus needs to be a precinct of planned complexity, a mixed-use district that fosters activities throughout the area. Reliable public transport with a Bus Rapid Transport System (BRTS) will keep other places within easy reach of each other. The network of public spaces offers jogging paths and cycleways. The masterplan suggests a future 'Learning City' which integrates University facilities with urban living, culture and administration; a masterplan that can be realized step-by-step (in 3 stages), in a flexible way. The University environment will add to the cultural and intellectual value of the city centre, support innovation (research activities in the 'Incubator'), offer employment opportunities and provide nearby businesses with opportunities for collaborative research. New buildings will utilize climate-responsive, passive design strategies with natural ventilation and activated structural mass, to reduce the need for air-conditioning. Geothermal deep heat technology will be explored as a possible renewable energy source.

CITY CAMPUS

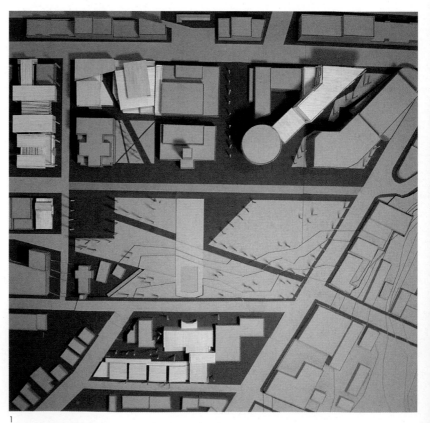

1

1 Kine Husas,
Benjamin Yeo:
Masterplan model,
showing urban infill

1

1   Kine Husas,
    Benjamin Yeo:
    City Campus
    masterplan

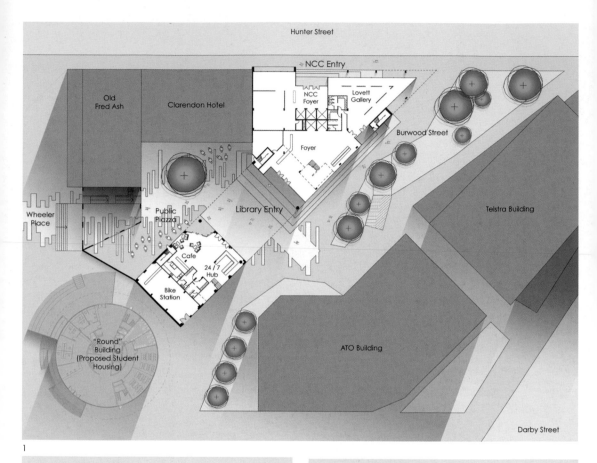

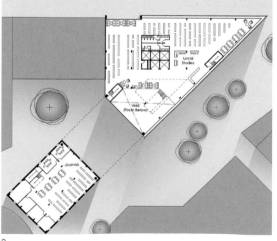

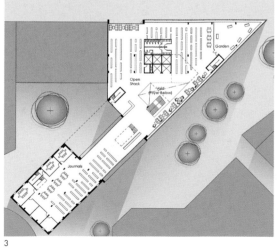

1   Kine Husas:
Library + Council
Administration
Centre, Ground
Floor plan

2   Kine Husas:
Library, Third Floor
plan

3   Kine Husas:
Library, Fifth Floor
plan

A House must be like a small City, and a City like a large House.

Aldo van Eyck, 1960

If you design a House, think of the City.

Luigi Snozzi, 1970

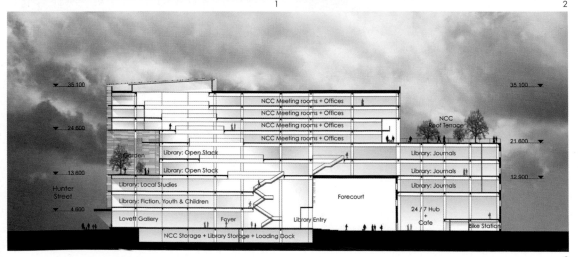

1	Kine Husas: City + University Library, corner Hunter Street	2	Kine Husas: City + University Library, entry court	3	Kine Husas: Long section through Library and Council Administration Centre

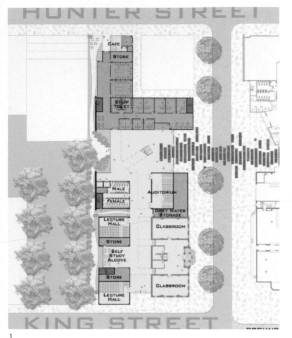

1

2

3

1-2 Benjamin Yeo: School of Business, Auckland Street, plans	3 Benjamin Yeo: School of Business, Auckland Street, photomontage, from King Street	

1   Benjamin Yeo:
     School of Business,
     Photomontage,
     Hunter Street entry

2   Benjamin Yeo:
     School of Business,
     Photomontage,
     Hunter Street entry

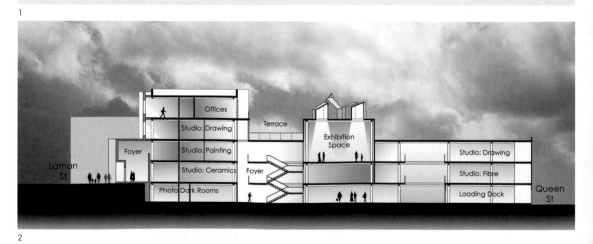

Laman Street

Dawson
Street

Church

Newcastle
Regional
Art Gallery

Storage

Photo Dark Room

Workshop

Photo Dark Room

Courtyard

Courtyard

Studio:
Printmaking

Studio:
Painting

Courtyard

Laundry

Loading
Dock

Common
Area

Admin

Queen Street

1

Laman
St

Offices

Studio: Drawing

Terrace

Exhibition
Space

Studio: Drawing

Foyer

Studio: Painting

Studio: Fibre

Studio: Ceramics

Foyer

Photo Dark Rooms

Loading Dock

Queen
St

2

1	Kine Husas: Student housing along Queen Street, Floor plan	2	Kine Husas: School of Fine Arts, incorporating existing Library, long section		

1

2

3

1 Kine Husas:	2 Kine Husas:	3 Kine Husas:
Student housing	Student housing	Student housing
along Queen Street,	Queen Street,	Queen Street,
Perspective garden	Perspective	Perspective

PERFORMING ARTS THEATRE

In addition to students' City Campus design work in the Master (MArch) programme, an assignment for 3rd year undergraduate students deals with the design of a public building on a prominent inner-city site, within one of the developed masterplans. The building's design is based on a realistic brief, in this case for a new performing arts theatre and public space. The brief asks for a flexible theatre space (a super-flexible box space, 20 x 30 m in size; 7 m clear height; seating 500 persons) that could be used for lectures, classical theatre performances, dance and contemporary pieces. It is essential to design a facility that could be easily adapted to the many different needs of the School of Drama, Fine Art and Music. Questions of typology, civic form, the role of public buildings and public space, and opportunities for architectural articulation were explored. Green roofs for rainwater collection, public arcades and day-lit foyers are all part of the vocabluary. The site utilizes the neighbourhood of the adjacent Civic Theatre, where delivery to the workshops could be shared.

CITY CAMPUS Performing Arts Theatre

1

1   Matt Healy:
Theatre,
Sectional perspective

1

2

3

| 1 | Adam Bennett: Performing Arts Theatre, Internal perspective, foyer | 2 | Adam Bennett: Theatre, Site Plan showing concept of pedestrian permeability | 3 | Neil Brown: Theatre entry from Christie Place, Night perspective |

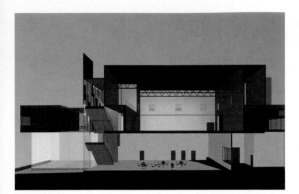

1

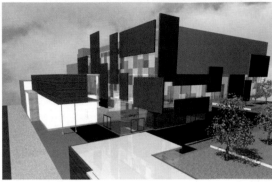

2

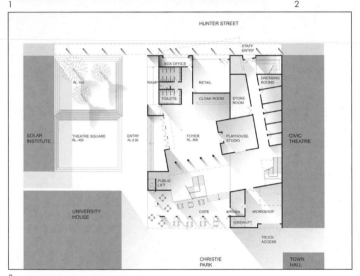

3

4

| 1 Timothy Griffith: Theatre Sectional perspective | 2 Timothy Griffith: Theatre, Perspective Hunter Street | 3 Kine Husas: Performing Arts Theatre, Groundfloor plan | 4 Kine Husas: Theatre, Perspective montage from Hunter Street |

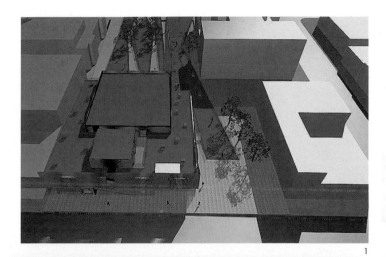

1 George Mather:
   Theatre,
   Hunter Street
   Perspective

2 George Mather:
   Theatre, seen from
   Christie Place,
   Perspective roof
   access

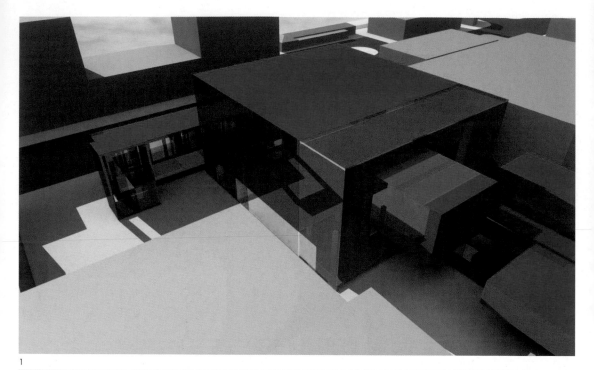

1

2

1   Onai Najibullah:
    Theatre,
    Aerial perspective

2   Onai Najibullah:
    Theatre,
    Hunter Street
    Perspective

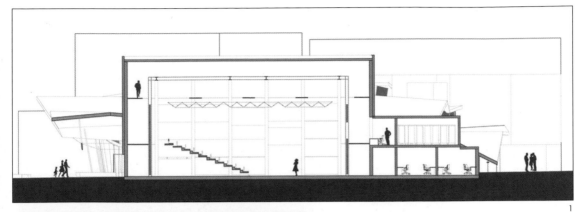

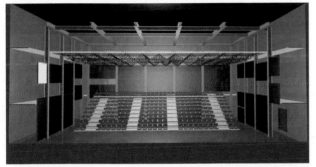

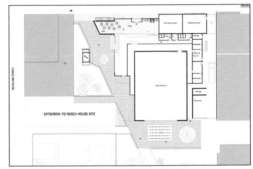

| 1 Sean Pettet: Theatre, Section from Hunter Street to Christie Place | 2 Sean Pettet: Theatre, Sectional perspective | 3 Mathew Woodward: Theatre, Groundfloor plan | 4 Mathew Woodward: Theatre, Hunter Street Night perspective |

The Case Studies

Port City Vision
The following text is a short description of the studio objectives, assignment and brief, which was the starting point for the students in the Master of Architecture programme to develop design proposals, based on the principles of green urbanism, with the aim to design a new neighbourhood and ecosystem on what is currently a brownfield site.

Urban Waterfront: Expanding the city along the water edge
Successful waterfront cities are based on developments that celebrate the relationship between the city centre and the harbour. So, how can we achieve an integrated approach in waterfront regeneration in Newcastle?

'Port City – reclaiming the post-industrial waterfront' is a special urban and architectural design project for students in their final year, where a cohort of ten students in four groups devise masterplans for Newcastle's inner harbour area. Its aim is to explore the potential for staged urban development of the ten hectare site at Dyke Point. Approximately half the site is to be dedicated to public parkland and the other half is to be developed as a sustainable extension of the city centre along the waterfront. By 2016, the industrial port use of this area will have moved further up the Hunter River and the land will become available to be used for a new inner-city precinct, connected to the Honeysuckle Boardwalk

Case Study 2
Port City – Expanding the Urban Waterfront

by a pedestrian and cycle bridge. Forging a strong link between the city centre and the waterfront development, and integrating the existing Carrington community are crucial to the success of the Port City. Questions of density, scale, compact land use, ecological footprint, alternatives in urban public transport, renewable energy generation, and the maritime heritage of the working harbour are all critical to this design exercise.

The Port City project is based on an overall strategy for reclaiming post-industrial waterfront land. It is a mixed-use urban waterfront development of ten hectares of prime waterfront land, of which about half is to be dedicated to public parkland. Once the industrial working harbour has moved up the Hunter River, Dyke Point could be connected with the centre by a new pedestrian and cycle bridge, so that the now underutilized land is turned into a sustainable city precinct.

Port City is aimed to be a 90 per cent emission–free development, where all energy is provided by distributed power from a variety of sources – photovoltaic, wind, biomass and consideration of geothermal – to demonstrate that it is affordable and achievable (already today) to make all major new urban developments carbon-free and based on renewable energy sources. Questions of density, scale, urban public transport (a looping light railway 'super connector' is suggested), optimized solar orientation, and the maritime heritage of the existing working harbour are all critical to the design, as well as the integration of the established Carrington community. The staging of the Port City development is used to drive the design approach, and will activate the existing Carrington Pump House as a catalyst and starting point.

Analysis of international examples of other Waterfront Cities

Part of the initial task is the analysis of successful waterfront projects in the following cities: Amsterdam, Rotterdam, Hamburg, Barcelona, Genova, Newcastle upon Tyne/Gateshead, Oslo, Malmo, Bordeaux, Singapore, Vancouver, Seattle, Sydney, Melbourne, and Cairns. The analysis of these precedents will help to identify international best practice of waterfront cities. Lessons learnt during this phase will show that these new waterfront neighbourhoods make a significant contribution to the city's overall developmental idea.

Fig. 01: Wharf Road in 1875; today, the site is occupied by the Honeysuckle Boardwalk precinct.
(Photo: Courtesy Archive Newcastle City Council)

Background

A port is always in the domain of engineering and large transport infrastructure; and to transform an industrial area (like a former port landscape) into a human environment (like a residential area with cultural facilities and good public spaces) involves a huge transformation and regeneration process. Clear staging processes of such a development is crucial.

The project asks for a masterplan for the waterfront area around Dyke Point, and students are asked to write their own mixed-use brief, and to then select a focus area within their own masterplan to develop a more detailed architectural design proposition for the waterfront site. The masterplanning is organized as group work, whereby the Newcastle Port Corporation will act as the client, assisting in the development of a real Port City brief, and will supply site plan material.

Fig. 02: Historical photo of Wharf Road and the industrially used heavy railway, around 1910. Historically, the railway line was not meant to transport people or serve any other purpose than the fast loading of coal onto ships.

Fig. 03: Aerial photo of the Boardwalk and Inner Harbour area, showing the closeness of Dyke Point peninsula to the Honeysuckle precinct. The land of Dyke Point is man-made, reclaimed land. (Photo: S. Lehmann, 2006)

The Brief

The student teams will identify their own briefs and focus areas. Principles for inner-city urban neighbourhoods that the group can agree on and understand to be their own are needed. In this process, students are asked to consider and incorporate the following aspects:

- The Port City should offer around 1,500 to 2,000 units for waterfront living and working, to ensure the Port City will be (in its final stage) a new living quarter with a critical mass, with a population of over 5,000 people.
- A variety of dwelling types should be integrated into each urban block (developing a variety of architectural typologies, not one-size-fits-all approach).
- The Port City should include a well-integrated centralized commercial area, with higher densities nearest to community facilities and transport nodes.
- Higher density mixed-use will mainly occur facing green corridors and along open spaces.
- A network of shared bicycle/pedestrian pathways safely separated from road ways, with a public bicycle station, creating a clear hierarchy of public spaces.
- Strong landscaping themes with attractive outdoor spaces and public parkland is to be included to maximize biodiversity.

Sustainable outcomes delivered through strategic masterplanning

The waterfront should feel like and function as a seamless extension of the existing urban fabric. The students are asked to formulate proposals to develop the 10ha site in a manner that cohesively incorporates sustainability throughout all stages of development: from master planning to architectural design, to suggestions regarding construction and operation of the Port City. Therefore, each team will define a sustainability framework for their masterplan that sets out a vision for the site and a set of objectives to guide the urban development decision making. The students are asked to decide on their sustainability vision, aspirations and key objectives; they are also asked to decide how to measure the sustainability performance and to look at the economic viability and proposed ownership structure of their proposals. For instance, considering models for community ownership of utilities and grid-connected, semi-decentralized power supply systems to facilitate the introduction of locally distributed (decentralized) energy generation.

The historical Carrington Hydraulic Pump House, built 1877, designed by the government architect, James Barnet. is still a major landmark of the port landscape. The adaptive re-use of this heritage-listed Pump House could act as starting point triggering the development of the Port City precinct.

The design proposals were publicly exhibited and discussed at the end of the design studio, and key recommendations for practitioners and policy makers were formulated.

Fig. 04: Sydney Walsh Bay inner-city waterfront housing, reusing existing finger wharves. Until 1970, Sydney used to have 27 finger wharves, however, only six are left today. (Photo: S. Lehmann, 2007)

The recommended studio reading includes

General Literature on Urban Design, Methodologies and Typologies:

Hall, Peter; Pfeiffer, Ulrich (2000): *Urban Future 21. A Global Agenda for Twenty-First Century Cities.* London
Legates, Richard T; Stout, Frederic (eds) (1999): *The City Reader.* London, New York.
Kostof, Spiro (1991): *The City Shaped. Urban Patterns and Meaning through History.* London.
Kostof, Spiro (1992): *The City Assembled. The Elements of Urban Form through History.* London.
Marshall, Richard (2001): *Waterfronts in Post-Industrial Cities*; Spon Press, London.
Mumford, Lewis (1963): *History of the City / Die Stadt. Geschichte und Ausblick.* Koeln, Berlin.
United Nations Center for Human Settlements (Habitat) (2003): *The Challenge of Slums - Global Report on Human Settlements 2003.* Nairobi.
UN-Habitat (ed.) (2004): *The State of the World's Cities 2004/2005.* Annual Report, Nairobi

Reading on City Culture, Urban Spaces, Urban Patterns:

Appadurai, A. (1997): *Modernity at Large. Cultural Dimensions of Globalization.* London et.al.
Alsayyad, Nezar (ed.) (2001): *Hybrid Urbanism. On the Identity Discourse and the Built Environment.* Westport.
Bacon, Edmund (1978, revised edition): *Design of Cities.* London.
Krier, Rob (2003): *Town Spaces.* Birkhaeuser Publishers, Basel.
Lootsma, Bart (2000): *Superdutch.* London.
Maki, Fumihiko (1994): *The City and Inner Space. In: Wolfgang Boehm (1994): Das Bauwerk und die Stadt,* Vienna.
Rapoport, Amos (1977): *Human Aspects of Urban Form. Towards a Man-Environment Approach to Urban Form and Design.* Oxford et al.
Rykwert, Joseph (1976): *The Idea of a Town. The Anthropology of Urban Form in Rome, Italy and the Ancient World.* Princeton.

Reading on Global City and Urbanism:

Castells, Manuel (1989): *The Informational City. Information Technology, Economic Restructuring and the Urban-Regional Process.* Oxford.
Clark, David (1996): *Urban World - Global City.* London/New York.
Lo, Fu-Chen; Yeung, Yue-Man (eds.)(1998): *Globalization and the World of Large Cities.* New York.
Oencue, Ayse; Weyland, Petra (1997): *Space, Culture and Power. New Identities in Globalizing Cities.* London.
Rowe, Colin; Koetter, Fred (1978 / 1997): *Collage City.* (Original edition Cambridge Mass. 1978) Basel et al.
Sassen, Saskia (1991): *The global city: New York, London, Tokyo.* Princeton University Press, Princeton
Sassen, Saskia (1998): *Globalization and its discontents. Essays on the New Mobility of People and Money.* New Press, New York
Sieverts, Thomas (1997): *Zwischenstadt. Zwischen Ort und Welt, Raum und Zeit, Stadt und Land.* Bauwelt Fundamente 118. Braunschweig.

Reading on Sustainable City:

Breheny, Michael J. (1992): *Sustainable Development and Urban Form.* Pion.
Brundtland, Gro H. (1987): *The Brundtland Report. Our Common Future.* Report of the World Commission on Environment and Development. Oslo, Norway / United Nations.
Gauzin-Mueller, Dominique (2002): *Sustainable architecture and urbanism: Concepts, technologies, examples.* Birkhaeuser, Basel
Girardet, Herbert (2008): *Cities, People, Planet. Urban Development and Climate Change.* Wiley, UK
Herzog, Thomas (ed.) (2007): *The Charter for Solar Energy in Architecture and Urban Planning.* Prestel, Munich
Jenks, Mike; and Burgess, Rod (eds) (2000): *Compact Cities. Sustainable Urban Forms for Developing Countries.* Spon Press, UK
Kats, Greg, et al. (2003): *The Costs and Financial Benefits of Green Buildings.* Report to California's Sustainable Building Task Force, Oct. 2003.
Newman, Peter and Kenworthy, J. (1989): *Cities and automobile dependence: An international source book.* Gower, Aldershot.
Scott, Andrew, (2006): *Design Strategies for Green Practice.* In: *Journal of Green Building,* College Publishing, Vol. 1, Number 4 (Fall 2006) pp. 11-27
Stern, Sir Nicholas (2007): *The Stern Review: The Economics of Climate Change.* Cambridge University Press (October 2006, published January 2007): www.sternreview.org.uk

General Studio Reading on Cities and Urban Design:

Abrahamse, J.E., et al (2006): *Eastern Harbour District Amsterdam. Urbanism and Architecture*, NAi Publishers, Rotterdam.

Cumberlidge, C. and Musgrave, L. (2007): *Design and Landscape for People*, Thames and Hudson, London.

Conrads, Ulrich (1964; 1970): *Programs and Manifestos on 20th-Century Architecture*, The MIT Press, Cambridge.

Curtis, William J. (1982): *Modern Architecture since 1900*, London.

Fonatti, Franco (1982): *Elementare Gestaltungsprinzipien in der Architektur*, Akademie der bildenden Kuenste, Wien.

Frampton, Kenneth (1983): *Towards a Critical Regionalism. Six points for an Architecture of Resistance,* in: Foster, Hal (ed.) (1983): *The Anti-Aesthetic*, New York.

Frampton, Kenneth (1995): *Studies in Tectonic Culture. The Poetics of Construction in 19th and 20th Century Architecture*; Cambridge: MIT Press.

Geuze, Adriaan and West8 (1995): *Landschapsarchitectuur*, Catalogue SRM Foundation, Rotterdam.

Giddens, Anthony (1999): *Runaway World*; London.

Giedion, Sigfried (1941): *Space, Time and Architecture*, Cambridge: Harvard University Press.

Johnson, Paul-Alan (1994): *The Theory of Architecture*. New York, Reinhold.

Kienast, Dieter (2002): *Kienast Vogt: Parks and Cemetries*, Basel.

Lehmann, Steffen (ed.) (2005): *Absolutely Public. Crossover: Art and Architecture*, Images Publishing, Melbourne.

Lehmann, Steffen (ed.) (2009): *Back to the City. Strategies for Informal Urban Design*, Hatje Cantz, Stuttgart/Berlin.

Lyall, Sutherland (1991): *Designing the new Landscape*, T&H, London.

Norberg-Schulz, Christian (1980): *Genius Loci: Towards a Phenomenology of Architecture*. New York: Rizzoli.

Ockman, Joan (1993): *Architecture Culture 1943-1968. A Documentary Anthology*, New York.

Rudofsky, Bernard (1964): *Architecture without Architects;* New York: MOMA.

Tzonis, Alexander, and Lefaivre, Liane (2003): *Critical Regionalism. Architecture and Identity in a Globalized World;* Munich: Prestel Verlag.

Weston, Richard (2004): *Plans, Sections and Elevations: Key Buildings of the 20th Century*, London.

Fig. 05 a, b: 'HafenCity' in Hamburg, one of Europe's largest urban renewal projects, to be built over a 25 year period, 1995-2020. Left: The historical Kaispeicher building is adaptively re-used as basis for a new Philharmonic Hall by Herzog & De Meuron. (Photos: Courtesy by H. Bruns-Berentelg, HafenCity Authority, Hamburg)

Fig. 06 a, b: Part of the 'Learning from other Cities' phase: The urban development of former industrially-used islands in Amsterdam's port, transformed into a residential precinct for over 25,000 people. Photo above: the site in 1985; below: the site after the transformation, in 2005 (Photo: Courtesy by masterplanner West 8)

Fig. 07: Row of canal housing with direct water access, 5.5 metres wide, showing a diversity of facade designs and architectural languages; several different practices were involved. (Photo: S. Lehmann, 2009)

Borneo Sporenburg, a residential district on an island in Amsterdam (completed 2004), offers a variety of housing types and distinctive apartment blocks along the waterfront. Of the 17,000 new housing units in the docklands, those in Borneo Sporenburg are the most innovative, with a vision of urban living as part of the city's phased urban regeneration plan. Architecturally distinctive buildings create significant landmarks within the harbour landscape. The variety of dwelling types ranges from 4-storey terrace houses with patios to apartment blocks. Borneo Sporenburg reversed the social trend towards a dense urban core inhabited only by childless couples or singles, with extremes of high and low income, while the suburban fringe is occupied by middle-class families. This development demonstrates that family housing is not incompatible with dense urban inner-city areas.

Fig. 08 a, b: The winning masterplan project for East Darling Harbour, now called Barangaroo Development, by Thalis and Berkemeier, 2006. (Images: Courtesy P. Berkemeier, 2006)

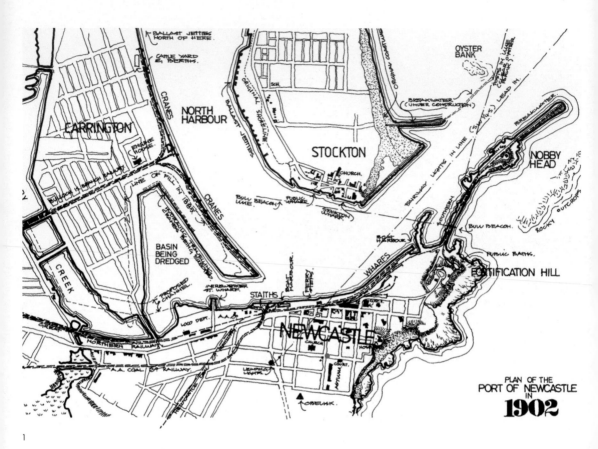

PLAN OF THE
PORT OF NEWCASTLE
IN
1902

1

Diagrams, showing the
historical development
of Newcastle port over
the years (1902 and
1984), reclaimed and
manmade land.
(Figure ground images:
B. Jordan)

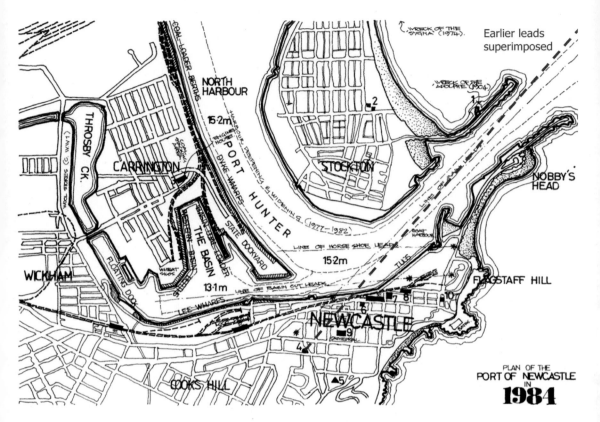

Panorama photo 'Newcastle from the Dyke', by M. Vaniman, 1904 (courtesy: State Library of NSW; Dixson Library). American adventurer Melvin Vaniman (1866-1912) arrived in Australia in 1903 and photographed various cities. His distinctive photographic panoramas were always taken from high above ground or from a balloon.

PORT CITY

1

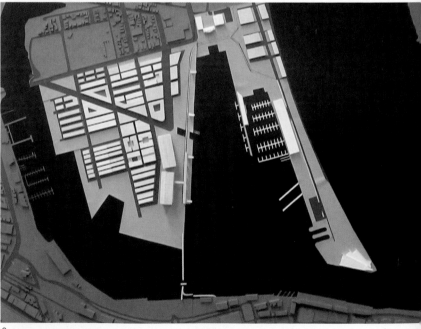

2

1 **Masterplan I**	2 **Masterplan II**		
Bede Campbell	Judith Bujack, Walid El Chiekh, Joyce Lim		

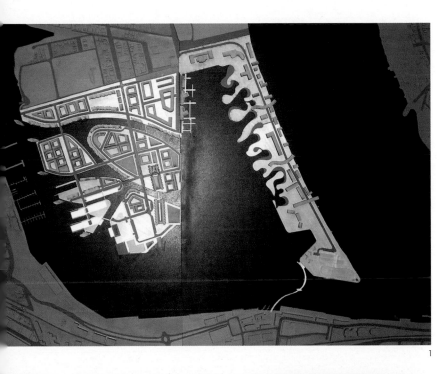

1

2

1 **Masterplan III**
Robert Mann,
Cassie Stronach

2 **Masterplan IV**
Ruby Pauwels,
Patrick Maitland,
Cherry Williamson,
Michael Whitley

A SUSTAINABLE FUTURE FOR NEWCASTLE'S WATERFRONT

It is envisaged that by 2015 the industrial usage located on the Inner Harbour waterfront will have retreated and moved further up the Hunter River, thus releasing prime waterfront sites for sustainable urban development of a new inner-city eco-district: Port City. The aim of this project is to explore the potential for staged urban development of the fifteen hectare site at Dyke Point, and to study the material and waste flow on the urban scale. Approximately half the site is dedicated to public parkland, and the other half is to be developed as a sustainable extension of the city centre along the waterfront.

By 2015, the industrial port use of this area will have moved away and the land will become available to be used as a new inner-city green-district, closely connected with downtown via a new pedestrian and cycle bridge. Questions of density, scale, ecological footprint, urban public transport, renewable energy generation, and the maritime heritage of the working harbour were all considered during the design process. This proposal questions the feasibility of the city's 2008 Draft LEP planning proposal, which earmarks Wickham as having height limits of new buildings up to 90 metres on some lots. Instead of moving the city centre further west towards Wickham, this masterplan looks at creating an extension of the current city centre along the waterfront, via a pedestrian bridge over to Dyke Point. The high density of the proposal allows for a large portion of this land to be given back as open space and public parkland.

PORT CITY

MASTERPLAN I

1

1 Bede Campbell:
Perspective of pedestrian bridge from
Newcastle foreshore
to Dyke Point

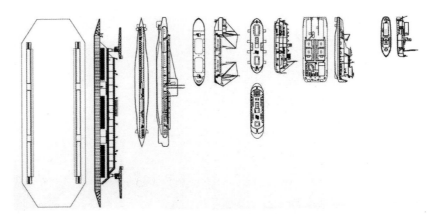

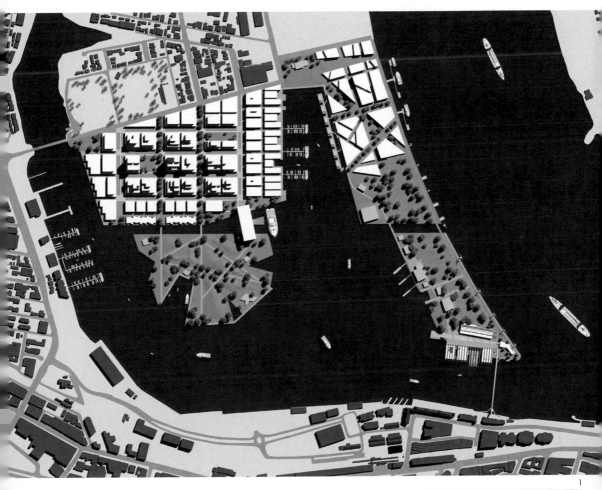

1 Bede Campbell:
Masterplan,
figure ground plan

1

1 Bede Campbell:
View of Masterplan
from Wickham

2 Bede Campbell:
Dyke Point with energy
generation from wind
turbines, taking advan-
tage of coastal winds.

Port City will explore the
potential of urban wind
turbines, harnessing the
constant windspeed of
over 10 metres p. sec.

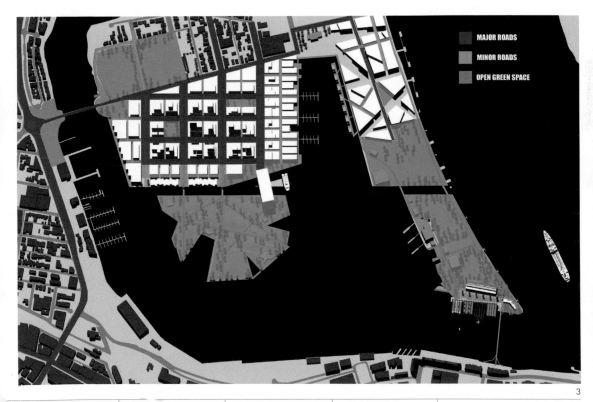

MAJOR ROADS

MINOR ROADS

OPEN GREEN SPACE

1 Bede Campbell:
Site Concept of city
expansion along
waterfront

2 Bede Campbell:
Site connections

3 Bede Campbell:
Site strategy,
land uses and street
pattern

1

1 Bede Campbell:
   View of Port City from
   Newcastle, with the new
   pedestrian bridge (swing
   bridge) in the foreground

1

1 Bede Campbell:
View of Port City
Masterplan,
looking towards
Newcastle

NCMI - NEWCASTLE CENTRE FOR THE MOVING IMAGE AT PORT CITY

The initial idea for this project within the Port City masterplan came from visiting the *Australian Centre for the Moving Image* (ACMI) at Federation Square in Melbourne. ACMI has a television station component integrated within the building, which is currently occupied by *SBS Television*. The idea was to include a television station and studio in the project, and to design a new facility for *NBN Television*, which is currently hidden away in a residential area within Newcastle. NBN's mission statement says:

> 'NBN Television is committed to providing and achieving Australia's most successful combination of local and national programming and broadcasting, whilst retaining prominent regional presence and identity within Newcastle.'

This design project is an opportunity to give NBN a highly visible presence and identity on one of Newcastle's most prominent sites, Dyke Point. The large media screens will encourage activities along the foreshore, aiming to re-vitalize the entire area. The exo-skeletal design of the building's structure reflects the portal frames of the former State Dockyard sheds on site, which are to be integrated and re-used as a film production facility, as well as for multi-level carparking. The existing administration building will also be kept, refurbished and integrated as a Multi Media Library.

PORT CITY

1

1 Bede Campbell:
Aerial view of the
NCMI, part of the
sustainable Port City

1 Bede Campbell: Sectional perspective through NCMI cinemas

2 Bede Campbell: Section through NBN Studios

3 Bede Campbell: Section through NBN Offices

4-5 Bede Campbell: Perspectives of NBN Offices; Night view from pedestrian bridge

1

1 Bede Campbell:
External screen
gallery with plaza
and large-scale
structure

1

1 Bede Campbell: Cinema entry to the Centre for the Moving Image

PORT CARRINGTON URBAN WATERFRONT

The redevelopment of the Carrington peninsular and Dyke Point offers the opportunity of integrating a new urban development within the existing fabric and reconnecting the water edges. This will give the harbour back to the residents of the city. The industrial history of Carrington, with its many social layers, has been retained with some of the historic and industrial features integrated for modern uses, combining the working port that Newcastle was built on with the modern lifestyle that is emerging as the city grows. The masterplan has incorporated public transport with light rail and ferry terminals within the project. An 'urban village' culture is encouraged, with pedestrian and cycle ways linking the commercial centre, cultural hubs and the foreshore. The development has an underpinning of sustainability, affordable housing, and water collection and retention on site. Energy is produced within the precinct, on-site, by solar panels on roofs and wind turbines along the parkland of Dyke Point.

The peninsular parklands deliver not only open space for the public, but also a water filtration and retention system. The landscaping provides layers of different native species that collect and absorb run-off, and removes contaminants to prevent them entering the harbour and waterways. This also provides a habitat for the community to enjoy in the heart of the city.

PORT CITY

MASTERPLAN II

1

1 Judith Bujack, Walid El Chiekh, Joyce Lim: View looking through suburban area of the masterplan

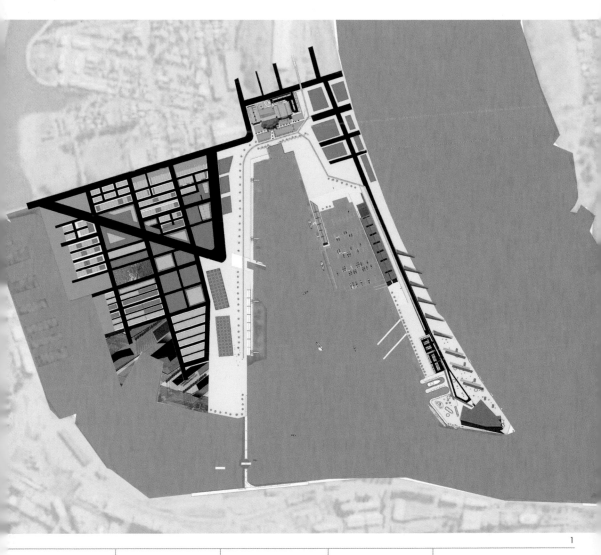

1 Judith Bujack, Walid
El Chiekh, Joyce Lim:
Masterplan of Port
City

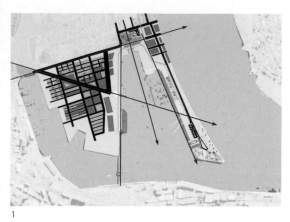

1

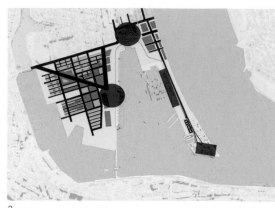

2

3

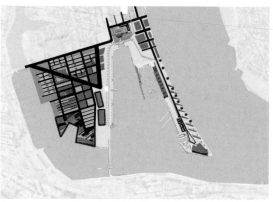

4

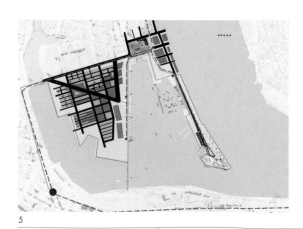

5

■ **Residential**

■ **Mixed Use**

■ **Commercial**

1 Axis and views	3 Green bus and ferry routes	5 Light rail loop and pedestrian / cycle access
2 Cultural activity nodes	4 Energy supply and resources	

1

2

1 Judith Bujack, Walid
  El Chiekh, Joyce Lim:
  Aerial view looking
  north east of lower
  Carrington

2 View from the
  historic Pump House,
  looking north
  towards Newcastle

1

2

1 Judith Bujack, Walid
El Chiekh, Joyce Lim:
Aerial view of
Port City masterplan

2 Judith Bujack, Walid
El Chiekh, Joyce Lim:
View of the grain
silos with proposed
ferry wharf

1 Judith Bujack, Walid
El Chiekh, Joyce Lim:
Proposed cruise
terminal at re-used
grain silos

32.55 SOUTH – NEWCASTLE YACHT COMPLEX AND MARINA

This project within Port City Masterplan II is designed to provide professional facilities to host international regattas, and to promote Newcastle as a premium nautical destination for all types of vessels. The complex provides a sheltered marina in the heart of a working seaport that relates back to the heritage that shaped Newcastle into what it is today.

The complex incorporates facilities from the the 'first-interest' point in sailing – a Sailing School. It then develops, with the Cruising Yacht Club and the building of maintenance facilities. The public areas open the foreshore to the community by providing commercial leases with facilities such as a restaurant and bar. The site provides spectacular views of the harbour and head-lands, enabling spectators to watch the start and finish of both club and international regattas from an elevated viewing gallery. These new buildings consist of modular prefabricated elements, for assembly and dis-assembly on site.

PORT CITY

1

2

1 Judith Bujack:
   View looking east,
   towards pavilion,
   from new marina

2 Judith Bujack:
   Perspective looking
   south from the
   historic Pump House

1 Judith Bujack:
External perspective
of public promenade
beside the Cruising
Yacht Club

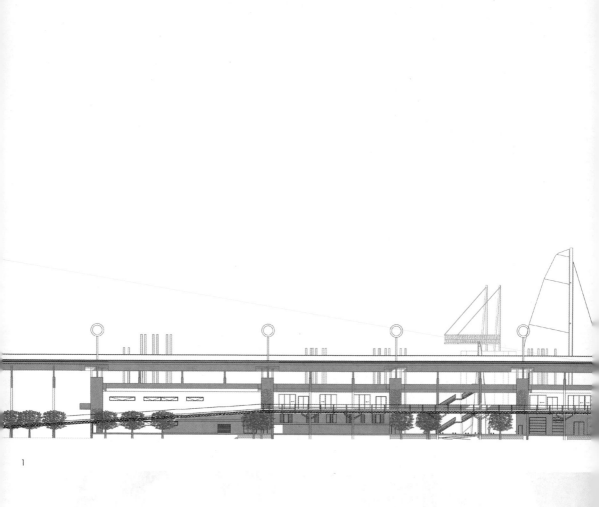

1

1 Judith Bujack:
Line drawing long
east elevation of
the yacht club

2 Judith Bujack:
East elevation of the
yacht club complex,
with graffiti silos
behind

1 Judith Bujack:
  Perspective looking
  south towards
  proposed marina

1

MULTI-CULTURAL COMMUNITY CENTRE - CARRINGTON

Most Australian towns are rich in diverse multicultural communities. This project provides a community centre that offers informal social space, where participation through the use of a multi-media library and a flexible theatre space will act as a cultural platform to the local and greater Newcastle community.

Local history and social sustainability plays a big part in the design of any cultural centre. Placing the two new buildings, the library and theatre, side by side with the Hydraulic Power Station (built 1877), will maximize visibility and will emphasize its importance. After its adaptive re-use, the Power Station will provide locals and tourists with a permanent exhibition of the city's history and will act as the Port City information centre. Both library and theatre will use steel, glass, timber and concrete in order to portray the new Newcastle, while the Power Station will be renovated with local sandstone, in coherence with its' great past.

PORT CITY

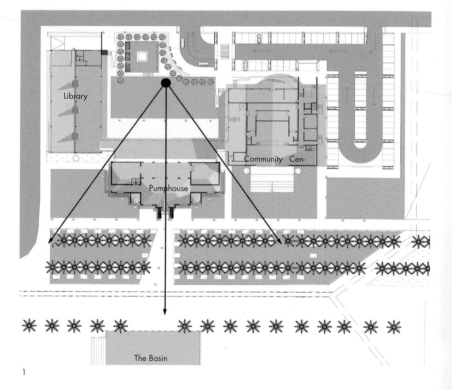

1

2

| 1 Walid El Chiekh: Groundfloor plan | 2 North Elevation, Community Centre, Pump House, courtyard, and library | | |

1

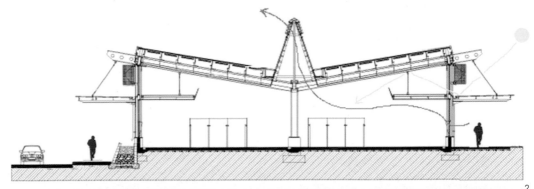

2

3

| 1 Internal perspective, Carrington Library | 2 Section showing light and ventilation | 3 Night perspective | |

NEW LANDFORMS: THE 'CURE' DEVELOPMENT AND ART GALLERY

This proposal has been developed from the chameleon-like history of the changing land-form of what is today known as Carrington. Originally, the Inner Harbour was composed of small islands and sandbanks, which formed and shifted by natural forces (as depicted by the historical painter Richard Browne). However, continual human intervention and land reclamation has transformed Carrington into the utilitarian shape it has today. The industrial use of this land has been a barrier between the harbour, the people of Carrington and the city beyond. It is envisaged to reconnect Carrington to Newcastle Harbour, as well as connecting the new urban 'hub' to Honeysuckle, via a new pedestrian and cycle bridge.

The concept recalls the past landforms of Newcastle's waterfront and restores the intimate connection of the city to its harbour on a human scale. It continues Young Street and the urban character of the Carrington neighbourhood through to the harbour, as a mix between residential and commercial components that can exist side-by-side, and at the same time maintains some of the light industry and craft-making facilities. The proposed urban density is around 80 to 100 persons per hectare to ensure vibrancy of public spaces and feasibility of green, decentralized infrastructure.

PORT CITY

MASTERPLAN III

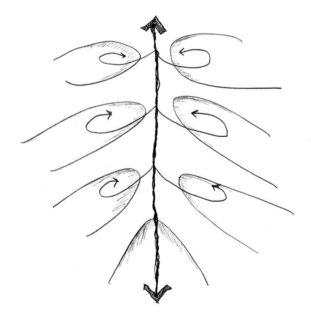

1

1 Robert Mann, Cassandra Stronach: Masterplan diagramme

Responding to the rising coastlines, this project forms a new urban/coastal landscape.

1

1 Robert Mann,
Cassandra Stronach:
Port City Master-
plan with the CURE
and NRAG locations

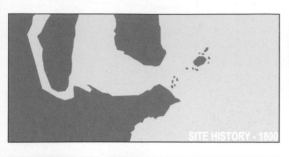

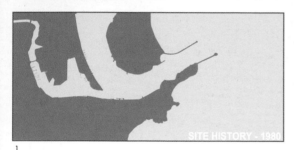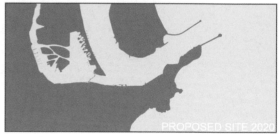

1

"Here we have geological specimens from every part of the world. The whole expanse of ground has been built up of ballast from the ships that come to our harbour. In one place we tread upon a layer of London flint, next a collection of stones from the shores of the sunny Mediterranean. These are succeeded by a rocky mound from Scandinavian coasts and these in turn give place to blue stone from Melbourne, green trap from New Zealand, limestone from Singapore and even the sun burnt bricks and glazed uncouth carvings from a dismantled village in far off China."

- Newcastle Morning Herald and Miners Advocate, (NMH) 7 November 1877

2

1 Diagrams of
  changing shoreline
  of Newcastle
  Habour, reclaimed
  and man-made

2 Quote from: *The
  Newcastle Morning
  Herald,* 7 Nov. 1877

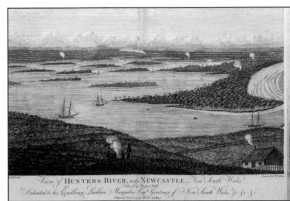

1

"*You can see from my map what a fearsome passage one has*
"*Vous verrez par ma carte quell affreux passage il faut*
to traverse in order to reach this beautiful river. The roaring
franchir pour arriver dans cette belle rivière. Les mugissements
of the waves, crashing one upon the other and breaking with
des vagues qui, se jetant les unes sur les autres et se brisant avec
a terrible noise on the steep rocks of the island, and raging
un éclat épouvantable sur les rochers escarpés de l'isle,
as they roll onto the sands of the opposite shore, would make the
et roulant avec impétuosité les sables du rivage opposé feroient
most intrepid sailor tremble. "
trembler le marin le plus intrépide. "

F. Barrallier, French Surveyor describes the
Hunter River, on an expedition to Newcastle.
24 June 1801.

2

		1 Historical paintings of Newcastle Harbour	2 French survey of Newcastle Harbour, dated 24 June 1804	

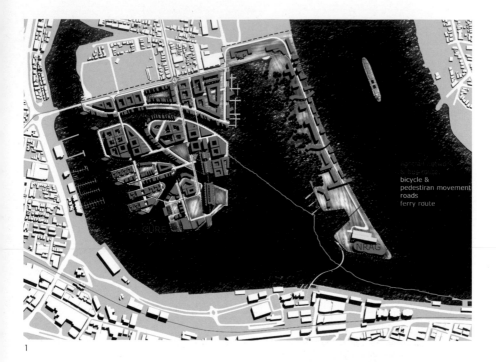

bicycle &
pedestiran movement
roads
ferry route

1

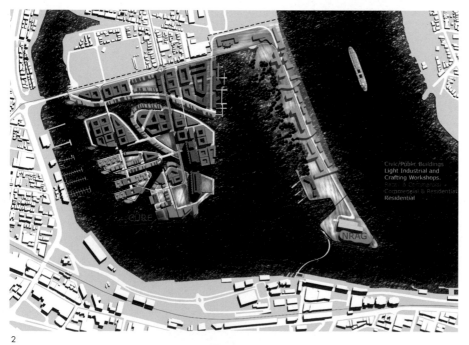

Civic/Public Buildings
Light Industrial and
Crafting Workshops.
Retail & Commercial
Commercial & Residential
Residential

2

1 Robert Mann,
Cassandra Stronach:
Diagram:
Methods of
circulation

2 Robert Mann,
Cassandra Stronach:
Precincts within
the Port City
Masterplan

1

1 Robert Mann, Cassandra
Stronach: Perspective
across pedestrian and
light rail bridge: A new
mobility concept

1

1 Robert Mann,
   Cassandra Stronach:
   Wetlands, the harbour
   landscape is restored to
   a more natural state

1

1 Robert Mann,
Cassandra Stronach:
Perspective of hous-
ing along masterplan
shoreline

CURE – CARRINGTON'S URBAN RESIDENTIAL ENVIRONMENT

CURE Harbour Living represents a major portion of this Port City proposal. It has been designed to respond to the need for accelerated urban development, reducing the sprawl of suburbia and refocusing on city-centred life. The scale and density of CURE targets a void in the residential market and is meant to supplement particular housing needs, such as harbour access living, ranging from compact and affordable studio apartments with water access, through to boutique luxurious tower suites, not currently present in the city's context. Compact mixed-use design with medium-to-high density will ensure the necessary environmental performance of this new district.

This development will provide public space including residential and recreational areas for the community, with direct access to the deep-sea harbour and other lifestyle facilities within the Port City, as well as close proximity to the city centre for people to live, work and play. The residential portion of CURE uses three housing typologies: High-rise apartments, studios, and 3 to 4-storey walk-up canal houses, each with numerous variations in form and size, to satisfy the diverse housing expectations of our time. Practical environmental design principles, along with quality detailing, provide housing fit for one of the great inner-city working harbours.

PORT CITY

1

1 Robert Mann:
Perspective of 3 to 4-
storey row housing
with direct water
access

1

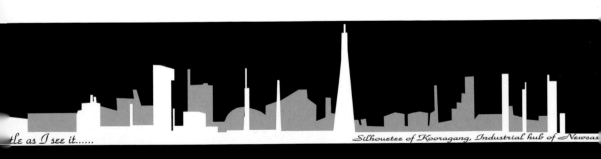

2

1 Robert Mann:
 Site Plan of new Port
 City district

2 Proposed skyline
 of Newcastle and
 Kooragang Island

Tower Detail
Scale 1 : 25

Southern Facade
Level R 18

1

2

1 Robert Mann:
  Facade detail of
  apartment tower

2 Perspective from
  the Boardwalk,
  towards the CURE
  development

1 Robert Mann:
Interior perspective
with view out to
Newcastle city over
the harbour

A REGION ART GALLERY ON DYKE POINT

This project explores the possibility of relocating *Newcastle Region Art Gallery* to Dyke Point, a prominent site on the harbour landscape. The original competition brief (from 2005) was adapted, with the assistance of the former gallery director. It is intended that the design represents not only the 5,000 art works strong (and rapidly growing) collection of the gallery, but also the process of making art and the particular art culture of the city. This is done through the addition of a Community Arts Centre (CAC), a large open and publicly accessible storage area, with study facilities, and an extensive art and sculpture park for installations and experimental landscaping, which provides the public with a range of experiences and interaction.

The gallery design is a composition of dichotomous built forms, offering two distinct environments: One, the existing utilitarian sheds (relics from the city's ship building past) have been adapted for re-use as the gallery's back of house and the CAC. The other is a modern free-form building in which the art is displayed. The façade is clad in glass etched with a pixelated pattern of well-respected local artist, John Olsen's painting 'Life Burst' of 1964 (in the gallery's collection). The site has spectacular views which the public deserve to enjoy, hence the circulation space, which loosely encapsulates the private and contemplative galleries within. Much natural light penetrates this 'breathing space' corridor and filters through to the galleries.

PORT CITY

1

1 Cassandra Stronach:
External perspective
from proposed
pedestrian bridge

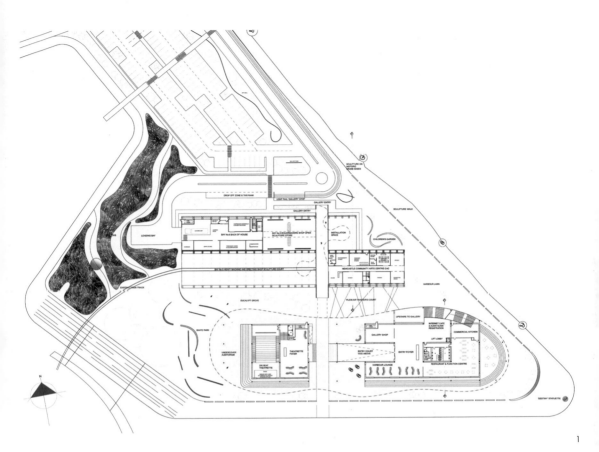

1

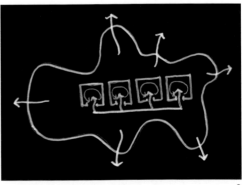

2   3

| 1 Cassandra Stronach: Ground plan | 2 Location Plan | 3 Building diagram |

1

1 Cassandra Stronach:
  Internal perspective,
  facade detail with
  printed glass panels

1

1 Cassandra Stronach:
Facade detail, with
the city skyline
in the background

1

2

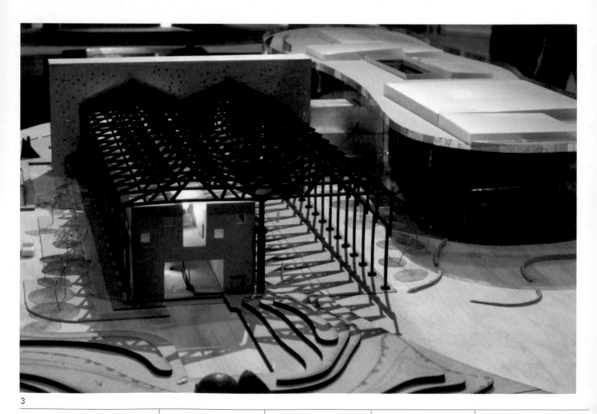

3

1 Cassandra Stronach: Internal perspective of circulation area, reusing the existing structure

2 Photograph of model with facade detail

3 Photograph of model: Re-using the existing steel structure as a resource

1

HARBOUR LIFE – A HOLISTIC SUSTAINABLE DISTRICT

The vision for Harbour Life is to create an integrated revitalization plan that incorporates innovative sustainable design systems to re-energize Carrington waterfront. The people of Harbour Life will be part of a holistic sustainable living, working, playing environment that fosters essential health and wellbeing, protects the environment, and stimulates the senses within one unique waterside community.

PORT CITY

MASTERPLAN IV

1

2

| Patrick Maitland, Ruby Pauwels, Cherry Williamson, Michael Whitley | 1 Patrick Maitalnd: View looking north through university campus | 2 Michael Whitley: View looking north over residential area |

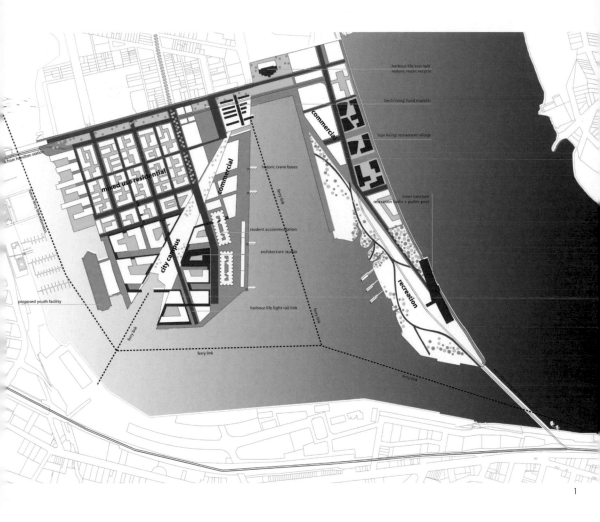

harbour life 'eco hub'
reduce, reuse, recycle

fresh living 'food markets'

'ripe living' retirement village

inner sanctum
relaxation baths + public pool

commercial

historic crane bases

mixed use residential

student accommodation

ferry link

commercial

architecture studio

city campus

recreation

proposed youth facility

harbour life light rail link

ferry link

ferry link

ferry link

from hamilton station

future tram link extension

ferry link

1

1 Patrick Maitland,
Ruby Pauwels,
Cherry   William-
son, Michael Whit-
ley: Masterplan

WATER AND WASTE MANAGEMENT

The aim of the proposed strategy is to maximize opportunities for the conservation of drinking water to achieve reduced consumption of fresh water per capita. Similarly, the masterplan will employ waste management techniques for the reduction of consumer bi-products and organic waste through grey water, black water, and a residential/commercial recycling station.

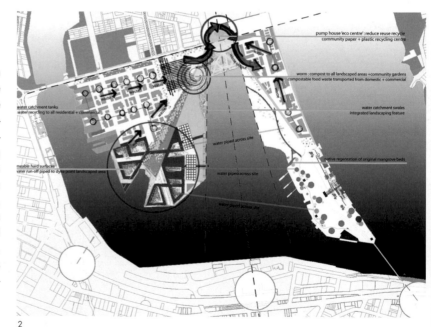

1

HUMAN COMMUNITIES AND CULTURE

To develop a vision which protects the history of the site, recognizes its place within a multi-cultural society and responds to the social needs of an emerging community. The masterplan provides the inhabitants with access to the waterfront, attractive open spaces, a variety of commercial and residential opportunities, balanced by having areas for both stimulation and relaxation of the mind.

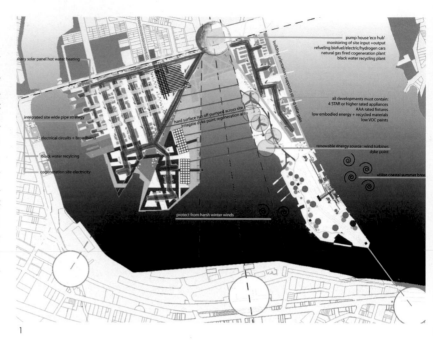

2

1 Maitland, Pauwels, Williamson, Whitley: Water and waste diagram

2 Human communities and culture diagram

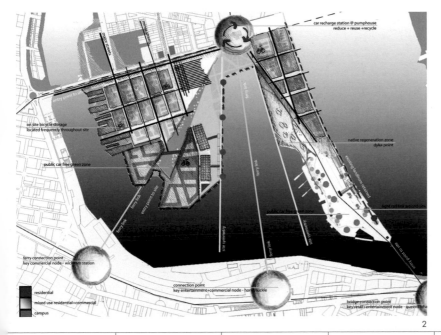

LAND USE AND TRANS-PORTATION

To develop a fully integrated transportation strategy that maximizes alternative transportation options to include walking, cycling, ferry and a light rail system. The objective is to provide strong links to the city centre, decrease air pollution, and enhance community vibrancy. The masterplan incorporates multiple housing typologies, the lay-out of streets, major and minor axes, and allotment gardens to encourage strong community interaction.

ENERGY AND SUSTAINABLE BUILDINGS

Urban growth and rapid urban development offers opportunities for fast and radical transformation of communities and city districts. All buildings in the masterplan will be built to the highest energy-efficiency standards and will use building-integrated photovoltaic panels (BIPV) and small wind turbines, for decentralized local energy generation, harnessing solar and wind power.

		1 Land use and transportation diagram	2 Energy, sustainable building and innovation diagram	

1

1 Cherry Williamson:
View over market
roof toward the
historic Pump House

1

1 Ruby Pauwels:
  View across park
  land towards public
  swimming pavilion

INNER-SANCTUM BATH HOUSE: THE SPA AND WELLNESS CENTRE

The proposed inner-sanctum bath house, spa and Harbour Life Swimming Centre is an invigorating building complex, located along the reclaimed harbour edge, which forms part of the overall *Harbour Life* masterplan for the Carrington brownfield site. The key objective is to create a design that implements advanced environmentally sustainable development (ESD) technologies, provides a unique public swimming pool experience and soul-soothing health retreat, targeting both overseas tourists and local residents. The complex's design has evolved around a need to re-introduce the ancient act of bathing into society, and to provide opportunities to improve the aging community's wellbeing through restorative therapies and daily activity.

The conceptual development of the building is rooted in the geographical history of the site and is complimented by five key themes: Circulation and journey, water and its recycling process, light, materiality, and provision of external views that create interaction with the harbour surrounding the site. The floating roof above the garden walls creates a hovering volume that filters the daylight onto the exercising, swimming bodies. The large roof is ideal for the integration of solar PV-panels.

PORT CITY

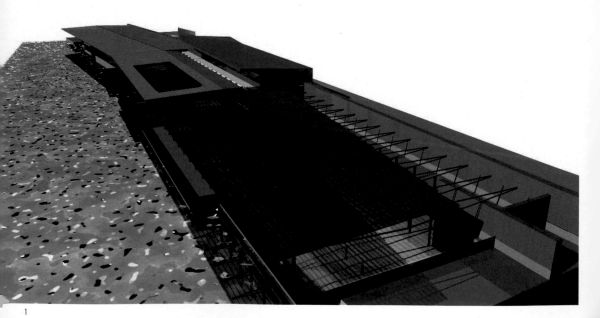

1

1 Ruby Pauwels:
Aerial perspective
of harbour side
outdoor swimming
pool

Inner Sanctum Well
Harbour Life Swimming

1

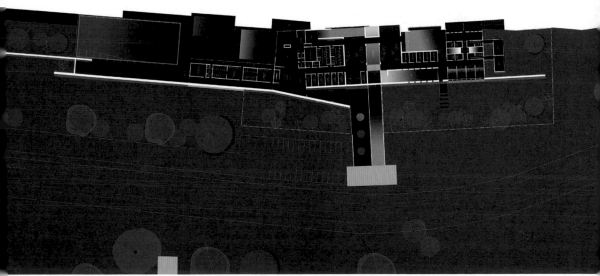

2

1 Entrance foyer of the
  Inner Sanctum
  Bathhouse, Spa
  and Wellness Centre

2 Ruby Pauwels:
  Groundfloor Plan.
  The bath house is
  located on the
  harbour edge

1

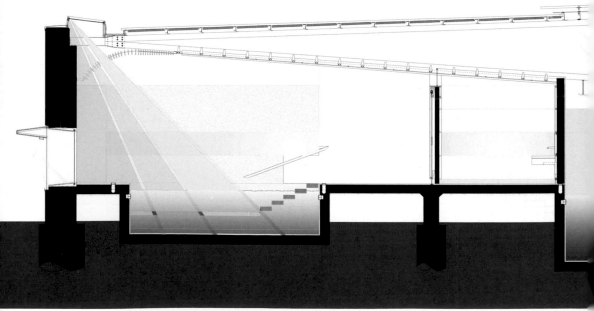

2

	1 Ruby Pauwels:
	    Internal perspective
		2 Long section through
		    pools to deck,
		    protruding over
		    the harbour		

1

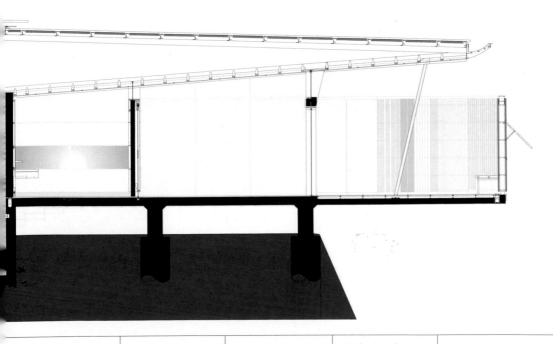

1 Ruby Pauwels:
External perspective
of deck overlooking
the harbour

1

2

3

| 1 Ruby Pauwels: Internal perspective of smaller pool area | 2 Ruby Pauwels: Entry to baths | 3 Covered pool, looking over harbour |

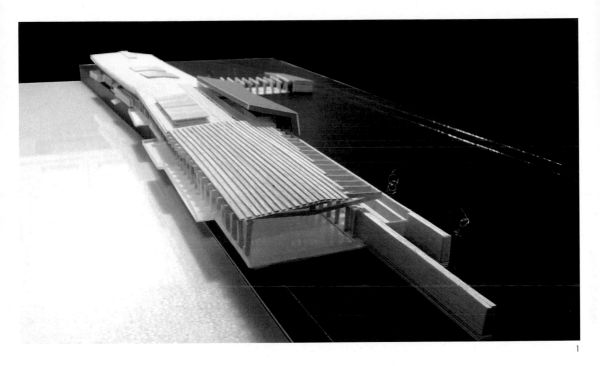

1

2

1 Ruby Pauwels:
  Photograph of
  model

2 Photograph of
  model

FRESH LIVING HARBOUR MARKET

Port City has a particular focus on closing resource flow loops for food, water, energy and waste. Food security and the flow of supply and disposal (e.g. waste-to-energy strategies) are considered as essential elements of any sustainable urban development.

The *Fresh Living Harbour Market* project is suggested as a long-term investment initiative by a highly-specialized property development company, and forms part of the larger urban development scheme Harbour Life for the area of post-industrial land on Newcastle's Inner Harbour.

The harbour market design explores concepts of the traditional marketplace and innovative retail typologies to create an interactive and contextually responsive market complex for this new precinct, offering organic local food produce. Important parameters for the design are the urban pattern of the existing context, transportation links, demonstrative landscaping with urban farming, and the public water front boardwalk. The complex integrates local fresh produce and seafood speciality retail outlets, fine dining and cafe facilities, lettable office spaces and an interactive cooking school, all underneath one large-scale roof structure. This complex roof is made of glue-laminated timber and steel elements.

PORT CITY

fruit / vegetable

bread / pastry

retail / cookware

butcher / deli

seafood

RETAIL THEMES

1

1 Cherry Williamson:
Context plan

1 Cherry Williamson:
Detailed section
through roof and
market structures

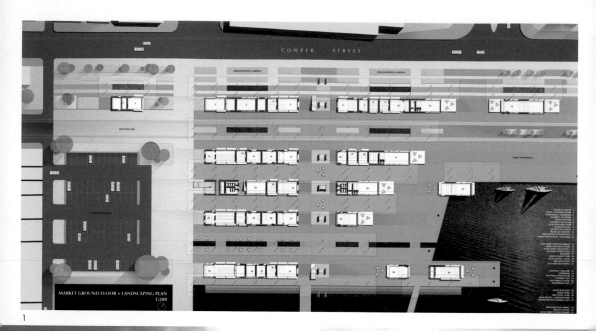

MARKET GROUND FLOOR + LANDSCAPING PLAN
1:200

1

2

3

1 Cherry Williamson:
  Groundfloor plan,
  showing relationship
  to harbour front and
  delivery area

2 Short section

3 Longitudinal section

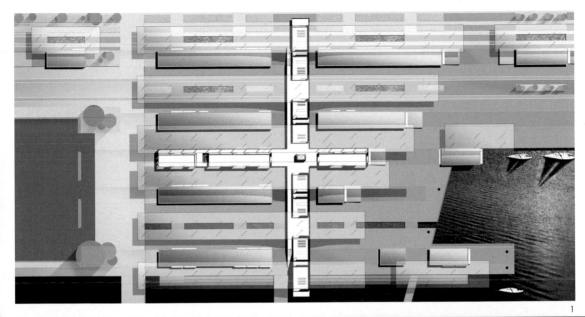

1

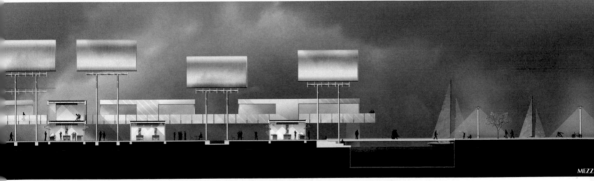

1 Cherry Williamson:
Mezzanine floorplan

RIPE – A LIVING RETIREMENT RESORT

Most countries in the developed world are facing an aging population. This proposal is the city's first luxury living resort for those over 55 years of age, integrated into the new masterplanned *Port City* environment on the Carrington peninsula. The project includes a mix of units: 108 aged care beds, 30 assisted (serviced) living units, 120 small one bedroom and study apartments, and 100 two bedroom and study apartments. All apartments have harbour or ocean views and are set amongst landscaped gardens and community facilities, providing an aging-in-place environment.

Community facilities include various activity spaces, such as a workshop, internet lounge, theatrette, library, quiet lounge, gymnasium, an outdoor swimming pool, tennis courts, and a public restaurant and bar. Retail space incorporated into the project provides shopping for daily goods, as well as services to the residents and neighbouring community. Prefabrication of modular housing units and construction elements (including floor-high concrete prefab elements stacked on-top of each other) is seen as a significant component to achieve an environmentally sustainable project. During summer, the cooler seawater is used for cooling the apartments.

PORT CITY

1

1 Michael Whitley: Perspective, showing framed and screened facades, for optimal sun-shading

Closed community

Semi-open community

Open community

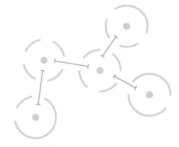
Integrated communities

1

2

3

1 Closed community,
semi-open commu-
nity, open community
& integrated com-
munity structure
diagrams

2 Michael Whitley:
View from the
harbour

3 Site plan showing
the eight building
parts

1

1 Michael Whitley:
External perspective,
independent living
apartments and
public restaurant.

High quality inner-city
living on the waterfront
will attract more people
back from the suburbs.

1 Western view of
  independent
  apartment building

2 View of eastern
  facade of
  development

1

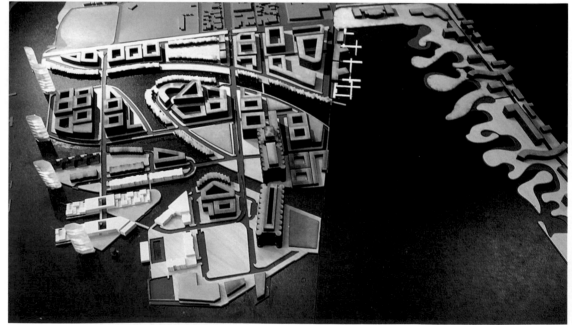

2

1 Robert Mann: Exhibition of Port City masterplan with model of apartment tower

2 Cassandra Stronach, Robert Mann: Masterplan model for Port City. (Photos: S. Lehmann)

1

2

3

| 1 Public exhibition of Port City masterplan proposals, November 2007 | 2 Bede Campbell: Masterplan model for Port City | 3 Patrick Maitland, Ruby Pauwels, Cherry Williamson, Michael Whitley: Masterplan model |

The Case Studies

Exploring options for a *Green Corridor*: improving urban connectivity

The following text is a short description of the studio objectives, assignment and brief, which was the starting point for the students in the Master of Architecture programme to develop design proposals, based on the principles of green urbanism. The linear urban regeneration along the corridor is to be based on new strategic ideas of density and productive inner-city landscapes.

`Vision 2020' – an *Urban Action Plan* to improve connectivity

The transformation process of Newcastle CBD must be bold in order to embrace the necessary changes to revitalize the city. The current lack of connectivity between the city's various elements has been described as unacceptable by several planning experts. Having isolated parts in a city limits the growth and development of the CBD. Therefore we need to ask questions like: How can we connect the declining city centre with the Honeysuckle development and a revitalized harbour front?

Currently, less than 3,000 passengers per day use the existing railway line to Newcastle station, mostly for travel to work during peak hours. In total, the line is served by around 80 trains per day. It creates a railway barrier, thus detracting from the potential economic

Case Study 3
The Green Corridor – Urban Connectivity and Linear Landscape

benefits of Honeysuckle. The railway line does not serve the city centre well.
Growth: The City Centre Master Plan (Department of Planning, 2008) predicts that there will be 6,500 new residents in the CBD by 2020. The particular issues of a CBD on an elongated peninsula are acknowledged. There is a need to make it a destination. Newcastle city centre is divided into three sub-centre areas:

- The City East is an area of heritage and has a particular beach lifestyle, with limited possibilities for new development.
- Civic is an area with some growth potential, especially for the City Campus, culture and administration (mainly 6 to 8 storey, max 36m height). The Honeysuckle development will be completed by 2013. In this area, there is potential to create higher density and compactness.
- The City West is the area with the largest growth potential, around Wickham station, with some sites able to build up to 60 to 70 m high.

Background: masterplanning the *Green Corridor*

This assignment aims to explore design proposals regarding opportunities for improving the connectivity between the historical city centre and the new waterfront development area (Honeysuckle). Once the heavy railway is stopped at a new transport interchange hub (a modern station) at Wickham, many opportunities for better urban development and stronger connectivity between the harbour and city emerge. The studio will reveal the urban design potential of opportunities that emerge out of this. A series of important nodes along the `Green Corridor' exist, which can be developed in various ways, including opportunities for the developments of a new retail precinct, court house, city campus and other facilities.

Fig. 01 a, b: Swing gates were used for crossings, as seen in the photo left, dated 1906. A tram used to go down Hunter Street, but was taken out in 1960. (Photos: Courtesy Historical Archive, Newcastle Region Library)

The brief asks, therefore, for masterplans that will facilitate inner-city revitalization and improve urban connectivity, and which will answer questions about the advantages of low and medium-rise, dense urban elements and the importance of strong connectivity in public space networks.

When activating connectivity, architecture, infrastructure and landscape can come together to define a space of intensified urban life. We start by testing the need to provide improved access and connectivity between the foreshore and the city. The urban future of Newcastle city centre has gained public attention with the proposal to redevelop the entire Hunter Mall precinct, which could inject new life into the dying centre and potentially encourage a renaissance of the city and its precincts. However, the railway line between Wickham and Newcastle stations is seen as a limit to such a development and one that obstructs urban revitalization, which has already started with the Honeysuckle harbourside development. This formerly industrial waterfront precinct has been reborn with a mix of new developments encompassing residential, retail and commercial programmes.

Today, the area along Hunter Street and Wharf Road is a mix of bland facades, boarded-up shop-fronts, individual developments, heritage-listed landmarks, and vacant sites used for parking cars. The old city centre's and Hunter Street West's inability to capitalize on the Honeysuckle revitalization is clearly linked to the rail line barrier and the limited permeability that it allows. The masterplan needs to ensure that the city centre can again be an area of cultural, educational and public facilities, giving a strong 'heart' to the city. The area around Civic Square historically forms the city centre, and the University of Newcastle is already a stakeholder there, with the Conservatorium of Music, University House, and Northumberland House (in Auckland Street).

The task is, therefore, to explore ideas and opportunities to enhance connectivity between the city and the harbour edge, to develop an urban vision for the `Green Corridor' (formerly the heavy railway corridor), and to expand the University's presence in the city centre, with a new City Campus as one of these nodes (`Education Node'). The terminus complex itself offers great opportunities for adaptive re-use.

Fig. 02 a, b: The physical barrier created by the corridor of the heavy railway line, bisecting the city centre. The site: A 2.5 km long and around 20 m wide stripe, the Green Corridor (once the heavy railway is terminated at Wickham). (Photos: S. Lehmann, 2009)

There are already initiatives that are centred on the Civic precinct, including the redevelopment of a site behind University House (formerly Civic Arcade); the need for a joint City+Uni Library (7,000 sqm), possibly in connection with the Graduate School of Business and School of Law; a new Drama and Performing Arts Theatre (2,000 sqm), in walking distance to the Conservatorium. There is also the need for two new Court Houses (Federal and State), each with 10 court rooms (each 12,000 sqm), creating a new legal precinct, possibly in combination with the School of Law building (4,000 sqm). Furthermore, a new Cruise Passenger Ship Terminal has been suggested along the harbour edge.

Therefore, one of the main objectives is to improve access to the harbour edge and to integrate Honeysuckle development into the city centre. To connect the Honeysuckle precinct more strongly to the CBD's urban spaces and community, it is expected that the new facilities open-up spatially to the city, and partially take on a bold, memorable architectural language.

In preparing the designs, the studio participants will be required to engage in `virtual' discussion with a range of organizations and individuals, including the City of Newcastle, and to model the options under various scenarios, in stages.

How do you stage your Rail Corridor Masterplan?
Strategic masterplanning includes the identification of objectives and strategies and the development of a framework for decision making that will inform the following:

- Sustainable urban planning principles
- Replacement of heavy rail with an alternative public transport system
- Strong linkages between the various elements
- Identification of project priorities and timelines
- Formulation of a delivery strategy to enable completion in five years (probably in 2 to 3 stages)
- Development of a 'Structure plan', from which appropriate briefs can be devised for the masterplanning of the former Rail Corridor
- Utilization of components of the University learning landscape (campus zones, facilities, services, spaces, circulation, networks, way finding and access)
- Development of appropriate briefs and built forms within an overall conceptual vision (your masterplan).

Particular key nodal points for further development along the green corridor, for urban interventions and architectural projects, are:
- Wickham Interchange Transport Hub
- Cottage Creek / Health (Policlinic)
- Worth Place (Public space and affordable urban housing)
- Civic: Arts, culture, administration hub with City Campus
- Carrington Footbridge / Dyke Point (future access to Port City)
- Civic Station / Merewether Street: Legal precinct
- Darby Street (to be continued to the harbour edge)
- Adjacent Hunter Mall: Large and small-scale retail
- Newcastle Terminus (adaptive re-use of station complex).

The studio is divided into three parts
The design studio emphasizes design process over product. It is organized in three steps:
- First, an investigation into the contextual language of the city centre (understanding the 'pattern language' of typical Newcastle urban/architectural elements and their scale) and the needs of the residents in regard to the public domain (questionnaire survey).
- The second part focuses on urban design strategies that will lead to a specific 'Rail Corridor Masterplan', with intensive siting strategies for a series of buildings, and the creation of a vision for the renewed Newcastle.
- The final part of the studio focuses on a series of selected sites from which the student chooses to develop two more detailed, fully developed (individual) architectural responses, within his/her own proposed masterplan.

Site selection
Size, future expansion, visibility and planning constraints are all major criteria for the site selection. The available sites are restricted in size and building heights. The plan needs to identify ways of making efficient use of those sites by developing functional links and keeping areas open for public space. The proposal should aim for a dense, compact, urban city

centre, and be aware of the need for compact planning and tight organization. It is suggested that the 'Green Corridor' remains in public ownership, as a reserve for the future. It has a total size of around 6ha, and a length of 2.5 km.

Strong, easy connectivity (permeability) for pedestrians and cyclists is very important, as we can see in many other cities such as Copenhagen, Barcelona and Melbourne that linear parkland with soft and hard landscaping, and cycle lanes, improve biking. Along the 2.5 km long green corridor, the width varies, for instance at Worth Place, where it widens. There are some opportunities here to build new structures in and along the corridor, e.g. pavilions for cafes. Darby Street can be continued towards the harbour to create a square or pocket park at the intersection with the corridor.

Catalytic projects, supporting `higher order' functions of the city centre
The city centre renewal can be driven by the following 6 main catalytic projects:

• Justice Centre: two new Court Houses
The Legal Precinct: Two new Court Houses will be built (Federal Government and NSW State Government), each with 10 court rooms, each around 12,000 sqm. The legal precinct is currently at Bolton Street. The preferred sites for the Federal Government are: the Civic Arcade site in Auckland Street/Hunter Street; or at Honeysuckle. How can the new School of Law best connect with the Legal Precinct?

• Education and Research: the City Campus
The University: Planning a new City Campus, an educational precinct. Staging is very important: There are 3 stages, and the total space requirements amount to 60,000 sqm (e.g. 4 x 15,000 sqm packages). Of this: 60 per cent teaching; 40 per cent research and other. The city campus could be in 4 separate buildings, all in walking distance to University House and the Conservatorium, possibly on sites along Hunter Street, Burwood Wedge and Honeysuckle. The move will happen in five to ten years.

Stage 1 and 2 are: School of Business (6,000 sqm for teaching) and School of Law (4,000 sqm for teaching + Law Library). Stage 3 is likely to be the Arts and Education Faculty. The University wants this new 'Arts, Humanity, Social Sciences' City Campus to be integrated in the urban fabric, and be concentrated, not dispersed. Total: 7,500 students and 1,000 staff. The research buildings need to be identifiable units. This will trigger a demand for student housing around the campus and in the CBD. There are also plans to combine the new City Campus with a major Conference and Convention Centre, which could hold up to 1,500 delegates. A Conference Centre in combination with a 3 or 4 star hotel (200 rooms).

• Culture: Art Gallery, Regional Museum and Performing Arts Theatre
The new cultural precinct around Civic Park includes the NRAG Art Gallery extension along Darby Street (3,500 sqm), and the new City+Uni Library (7,000 sqm). The new Regional Museum was recently relocated to the railway sheds at Honeysuckle.

• Retail Space and Urban Living

The private development of a new shopping centre along Hunter Mall: 60,000 sqm over three city blocks mixed-use, with 100 apartments and some commercial facilities on top. It has been decided to open the Hunter Mall for slow traffic.

• Leisure Facilities and Cruise Terminal

Newcastle Port Corporation suggested building a new Cruise Terminal for 300 m long cruise ships, as a tourist attraction. Where is the best place for it? A preferred location is opposite Customs House, in the vicinity of Queens Wharf. This could involve the adaptive re-use of Newcastle Station. However, there are commercial issues: A Cruise Terminal may not be viable, as it depends on an unpredictable international market.

• Transport Hub and Commercial Centre, Railway Station and Office Tower

Wickham Transport Hub (a new station as 'Gateway' to the CBD) will be a modern, efficient interchange railway station, where all passengers can quickly change from trains to waiting 'green' buses (and vice versa). This new transit hub connects buses, bikes, and water taxi with the arriving heavy railway. Next to the railway station will be a new office building, 60 m in height, a small tower. The rail terminal needs to have a significant public plaza in front of its main entry, which opens directly to the harbour and gives a magnificent view down towards Nobby's Lighthouse. The arrival at a new Harbour Plaza will convey the feeling of 'arrival' in the city. The location of the station would preferably be in the flood-free zone east of Stewart Avenue (located where the current Wickham Station is); it is assumed that the traffic of Stewart Avenue will be redirected via the Gordon Avenue bypass. The new station will have 4 platforms: for two trains from Sydney/Central Coast, 250 m in length, and for two trains from Maitland, with a 100 m length. A new bus terminal will be next to the station, possibly on the car park behind the 'Store'.

In conclusion, the *Green Corridor* is a linear park, a well-connected walking landscape, which includes agricultural fields, urban forests and food boulevards, reusing the nutrients from the urban metabolism (nutrient recycling).

The design proposals were publicly exhibited and discussed at the end of the design studio, and key recommendations for practitioners and policy makers were formulated.

The recommended studio reading includes

Benyus, Janine (1997): *Biomimicry. Innovation inspired by Nature*, New Jersey Clark, R. and Pause, M. (2005): *Precedents in Architecture*. John Wiley, New Jersey

Boyd, Robin (1960): *The Australian Ugliness*. Cheshire, Melbourne

Borden, I; Kerr, J; Rendell, J.; Pivaro, A. (eds) (2001): *The Unknown City: Contesting Architecture and Social Space*, MIT Press, Cambridge

Brotchie, JR, et al (eds) (1995): *Cities in Competition: Productive and Sustainable Cities for the 21st Century*. Longman, Melbourne

Broadbent, G (1990): *Emerging Concepts in Urban Space Design*, Spon, London

Bull, Catherine (2002): *New Conversations with an Old Landscape*. Images Publishing, Melbourne

Campbell, S.; Fainstein, S. (eds) (2003): *Readings in Planning Theory*, Blackwell, Oxford

Carmona, M.; Heath, T.; Oc, T.; Tiesdell, S. (2003): *Public Places – Urban Spaces: The Dimensions of Urban Design*, Architectural Press, Oxford

Clark, R. and Pause, M. (2005): *Precedents in Architecture*. John Wiley, New Jersey

Coupland, A. (ed.) (1997): *Reclaiming the City: Mixed use development*, Spon, London

Cullen, Gordon (1961): *Townscape*, The Architectural Press, London

Cuthbert, Alexander (2003): *Designing Cities: Critical Readings in Urban Design*, Blackwell, Oxford

Cuthbert, Alexander (2005): *Design of Cities, Urban Design and Spatial Political Economy*. Blackwell Publishers, London

Dovey, Kim (1999): *Framing Places: Mediating Power in Built Form*, Routledge, London

Ellin, N. (1996): *Postmodern Urbanism*, Princeton Architectural Press, New York

Evans, G. (2001): *Cultural Planning: An Urban Renaissance?*, Routledge, London

Fagan, RH; Webber, M. (1994): *Global Restructuring: The Australian Experience*. Oxford Uni Press, Melbourne

Fincher, R; Jacobs, J. (eds) (1998): *Cities of Difference*, Guildford, New York

Florida, Richard (2002): *The Rise of the Creative Class*, Basic Books, New York

Forster, C. (2004): *Australian Cities: Continuity and Change*, OUP, Melbourne

Frampton, Kenneth (1995): *Studies in Tectonic Culture. The Poetics of Construction in 19th and 20th Century Architecture*; MIT Press, Cambridge

Gehl, Jan (2003): *New City Space;* Danish Architecture Press, Copenhagen

Gehl, Jan (2010, 6th edition): *Life between Buildings. Using Public Space;* Danish Architecture Press, Copenhagen

Glazebrook, Garry (2009): Discussion paper *A Thirty Year Public Transport Plan for Sydney*, available at: http://www.dab.uts.edu.au/research/

Gospodini, Aspa (ed.) (2005): *Urban landscape transformations*, in: *International Journal of Sustainable Development and Planning*, London

Hall, Peter (1996): *Cities of Tomorrow: An intellectual history of urban planning and design in the 20th century*, Blackwell, Oxford

Head, Peter (2008): *Entering an Ecological Age*, Arup, London (report available online at: www.arup.com)

Hensher, D. A. (1999): *A Bus-based Transitway or Light Rail?*, in: *Road & Transport Research*, Vol. 8, No. 3, September 1999, Sydney

Jacobs, Jane (1961): *The Death and Life of Great American Cities*, New York: Random House

Kostof, Spiro (1992): *The City Assembled. The Elements of Urban Form through History*, Thames & Hudson, London

Krier, Rob (2003): *Town Spaces*, Birkhaeuser, Berlin

Lang, Jon (2005): *Urban Design: A Typology of Procedures and Products*, Architectural Press, Oxford

Mackay, David (2008): *Sustainable Energy - Without the Hot Air*, UIT Cambridge, UK (available online at: www.withouthotair.com)

Moore, J.; Ostwald, M. (eds) (1997): *Hidden Newcastle. Urban Memories and Architectural Imaginaries;* Gadfly Media, Sydney

New South Wales Government (2007): *SEPP 65 – Design Quality of Residential Flat Development and Residential Flat Design Code*, available at http://www.planning.new.gov.au/

Ratcliffe, J, Stubbs, M; Shepherd, M. (2002): *Urban Planning and Real Estate Development*, E&FN Spon, London

Rowe, Colin; Koetter, Fred (1978): *Collage City*, MIT Press, Cambridge

Stemshorn, M. (2001): *Dream City. On the Future of Urban Space*, Hatje Cantz, Stuttgart

Urban Design Advisory Service (2000): *Mixed-Use Urban Centres: Guidelines for mixed-use development*, Sydney: NSW Dept. of Urban Affairs and Planning, Sydney

Fig. 03: New forms of inner-city, emission-free, decentralized generation of energy, by using wind power and solar energy.

Fig. 04: The 'Highline Park' in Lower Manhattan, New York City, 2008. By establishing a linear public park on top of a disused former railway viaduct, and connecting two areas in the city, the Meatpacking District was turned into a fashionable neighbourhood (Image: Architects Diller Scofidio Renfro): www.thehighline.org

Fig. 05: New forms of inner-city, emission-free transport. Proposal by Nicholas Foulcher (year 3), 2008. A series of 'bike-canoe-towers' are placed along the waterfront, where travelers can secure their bike and change transit mode to continue their travel by canoe.

Fig. 06: Diagram of dedicated bus lane in Hunter Street, and parallel cycleways in the new linear landscape, with crossing Darby Street.

STITCHING TOGETHER: THE PUBLIC ROLE OF THE GREEN CORRIDOR

Mixed-use urban consolidation is a way to ensure that new homes are close to employment, education, shopping, health services and public transport. *Green Urbanism* means applying best practice of urban design, compactness, optimal orientation, density and passive design principles. The bike-oriented city helps to reduce car dependency. In this masterplan proposal, the green corridor takes on the important civic role of stitching the historical (but decaying) city centre back together with the new waterfront development along the harbour edge. With the removal of the heavy railway barrier, multiple design opportunities have opened-up for connecting the city with the harbour, and for improving pedestrian connectivity through a pleasant public space network.

The *Linear Park* acts as backbone, capable of connecting the series of existing urban and green spaces that are currently separated. This urban plan is developed through the principle of repetition, continuity and a restriction of the typological diversity. Pedestrian access network and cycle routes are generously and clearly defined, to encourage walking and cycling, and for improving pedestrian mobility within the city core. Various hard and soft public-realm spaces are interwoven in the masterplan, enhancing views to the harbour. The theme of `eco+media' is also expressed in `energy islands' along the green corridor.

THE GREEN CORRIDOR

1

1 George Mather:
Masterplan;
Stitching strategy

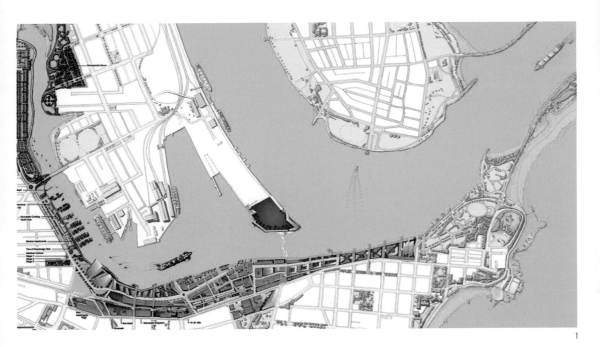

1

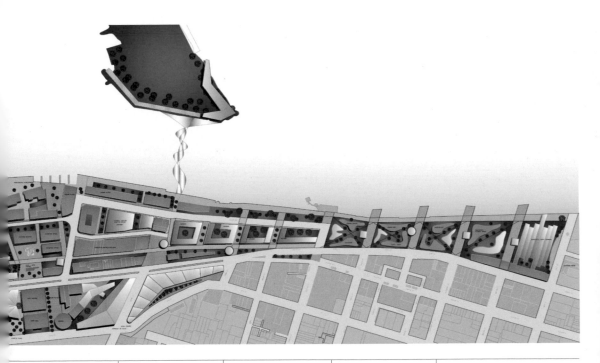

1 George Mather:
Overall city centre
plan

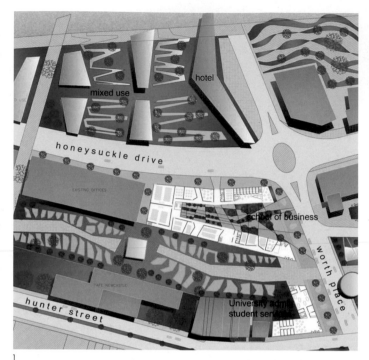

hotel

mixed use

honeysuckle drive

EXISTING OFFICES

school of business

worth place

hunter street

TAFE NEWCASTLE

University admin
student services

1

2

3

| 1 George Mather: School of Business site plan | 2 Locally generated wind energy | 3 George Mather: School of Business and Green Corridor perspective |

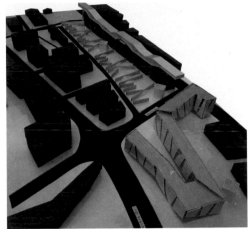

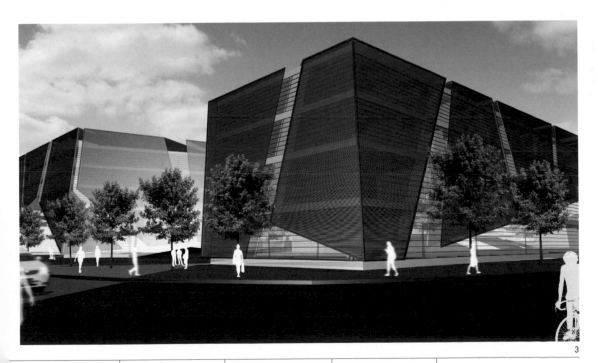

1 George Mather:
School of Business,
Honeysuckle Drive
perspective

2 George Mather:
Model

3 George Mather:
School of Business
perspective

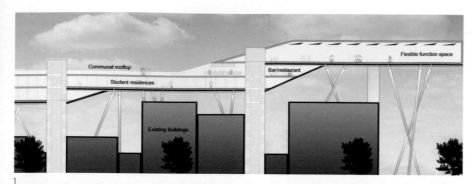

1

2

3

1 George Mather: 'Units in the Sky' section	2 George Mather: Student housing model	3 George Mather: Hunter Street photomontage

1 George Mather:
Student housing,
Green Corridor
perspective

2 George Mather:
Student housing
photomontage,
looking north

CONNECTIVITY: A MASTERPLAN FOR PEDESTRIANS AND CYCLISTS

Refocussing Newcastle on the water and the port.

Instead of self-referential form-making, this masterplan proposes that all new buildings follow a clear hierarchy of public spaces, like 'pearls on a thread'; or like a human spine. This spine connects the linear CBD to the harbour by visually illuminated paths, integrating vegetation strategies, trees, umbrellas and paving. Careful retrofitting of the existing city and an emphasis on public transport are part of the strategy.

Urban farming with micro community gardens are a sustainable way for growing fresh organic food in the heart of the city. The well-known resourceful concept of allotment gardens is applied. Jobs are created, as local people run these community gardens, creating a green city centre beyond oil. The linear ecological connectivity of the continuous 'Green Corridor' is essential, while the physical impact from cutting across the corridor by roads and pathways is kept to a minimum. Buildings are designed to optimize natural ventilation and day-lighting, therefore reducing the need for mechanical equipment and cooling. Solar collectors and micro wind turbines are used in buildings to harness renewable energy. Focus areas within the masterplan are the library and the new railway station. Modern, low-emission buses are scheduled to meet arriving trains and pick-up passengers next to the platform, ensuring that travel times are shorter.

THE GREEN CORRIDOR

1

1 Peter Golema:
  Masterplan

1

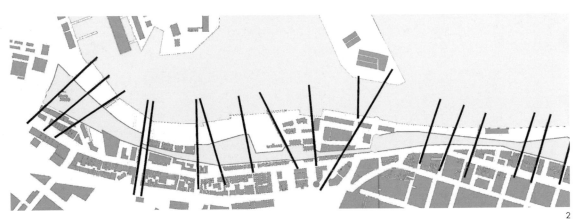

2

1 Peter Golema:
Human Spine -
Urban Spine,
concept diagrammes

2 Peter Golema:
Connectivity
diagramme

1

2

1 Peter Golema:
  Library,
  Burwood Lane
  perpective

2 Peter Golema:
  Library,
  Aerial view
  Hunter Street

1 Peter Golema:
Digital Library,
Hunter Street
perspective

2 Peter Golema:
Library perspective

1

2

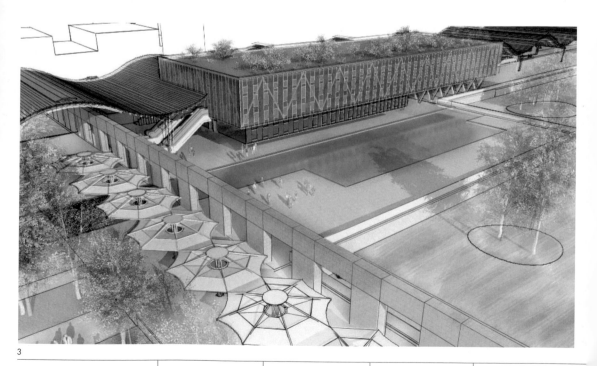

3

1 Peter Golema:	2 Peter Golema:	3 Peter Golema:
Newcastle Station	Station and bus	Station and
perspective	network,	conference centre
	with umbrellas	perspective

1

2

3

1 Peter Golema:
  Station and Green
  Corridor perspective

2 Peter Golema:
  Green Corridor
  perspective

3 Peter Golema:
  Green Corridor
  perspective

FUTURE WATERWAYS CITY: CONSTRUCTED ECOLOGIES

This masterplan combines a big urban idea of a new water system with appropriate architectural solutions. An `aqua-corridor' (new canal) leads to a constructed wetland ecosystem that cleans and filters polluted run-off water and sewage, and increases the rainfall capture. Retention ponds, water collection systems, and bio-filtration swales form part of this urban water management system, where grey water reservoirs link back to the tidal harbour and aid the survival of the city. To reduce the urban heat island effect (UHI) and to increase biodiversity within the city, the open green space and waterways provide the essential balance for a higher density sustainable district.

The city engages with the new water edges with small-scale elements, regaining an intensive water connection. Foot bridges set up a new system for pedestrians and bikes. A special focus is given to the new `gateway to the CBD', the railway station, with a large, dynamic roof. The roof is clad with solar panels and generates all energy needed to operate and illuminate the terminus. This is the first zero-carbon railway station. For the new station, a seamless system is proposed through integrated fares and ticketing between trains and buses, improved interchanges, real-time passenger information and large-scale expansion park-and-ride facilities for bikes (with bike stations along the green corridor), as well as car parking next to the new station (for park-and-ride mode).

THE GREEN CORRIDOR

1

1 Robin Palmer:
  Masterplan of
  'Waterway City'

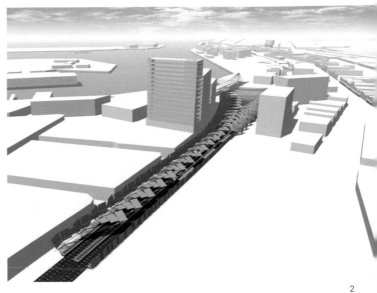

| | | 1 Waterway City precedent | 2 Robin Palmer: Zero-carbon station as gateway to the city centre | |

1

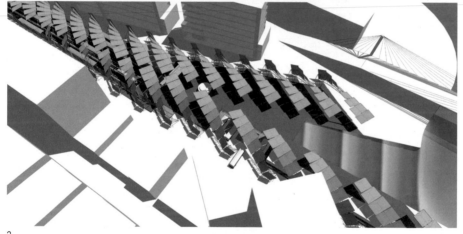

2

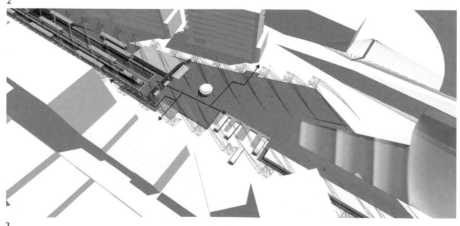

3

1 Robin Palmer:
Newcastle Station
site plan

2 Robin Palmer:
Solar roof
perspective

3 Robin Palmer:
Station circulation
showing rail-bus
interchange

1

2

3

1 Robin Palmer:
Station platform
perspective

2 Robin Palmer:
Station perspective

3 Robin Palmer:
Model of station
interior

1 Robin Palmer:	2 Robin Palmer:
Station roof	Station and corridor
photomontage	canal photomontage

1

2

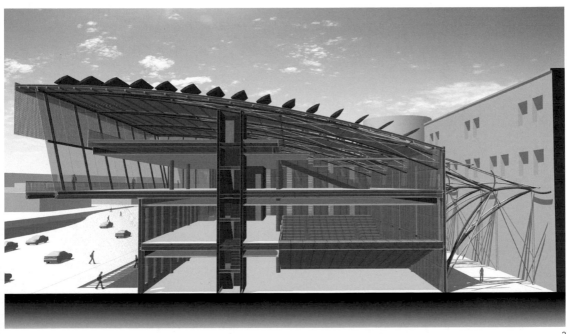

3

1 & 2 Robin Palmer:
School of Law,
connection to
University House,
perspectives

3 Robin Palmer:
School of Law
section

GREEN CITY CENTRE BEYOND OIL: THE LIVEABLE + HEALTHY CITY = WATER URBANISM

This masterplan develops a visionary methodology for growth and change, including the management of urban water. It increases the connectivity between neighbourhoods and aims to establish strong links through efficient urban stormwater management principles. Stormwater is captured and filtered for re-use and irrigation throughout the district, whilst establishing pedestrian linkages and allowing biodiversity back into the city centre. The water-based landscape introduces constructed wetlands into the urban context. The area around the new station is surrounded by medium-density housing and commercial facilities (transport-oriented development). The cutting of the railway line at Wickham unleashes the full potential of Newcastle's urban development and enables the city centre to be re-connected with the beautiful water edge of the working harbour. The harbour offers a magnificent resource for everybody to use, always interesting to observe.

For too long the barrier of the heavy railway line has held the city back in truly engaging with best practice of urban development, reflecting appropriately the status as the State's second largest city. The city has lived with this barrier for a long time, constrained by a transport decisions made in the 19th century. This masterplan dwells on the urban wetland connecting to the harbour in various locations, and maximizes the connection with our most magnificent natural resource, the sea port.

THE GREEN CORRIDOR

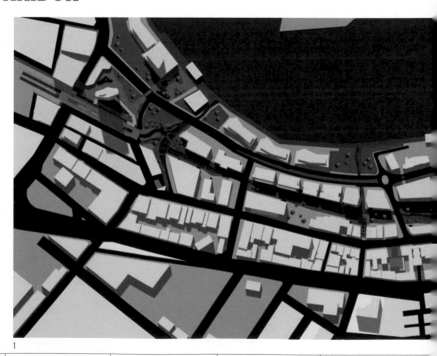

1

1 Matthew Wood-
ward: Masterplan

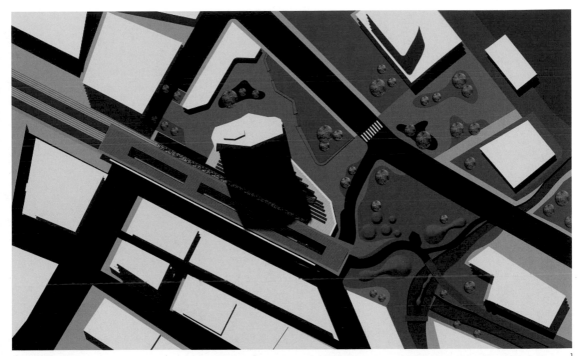

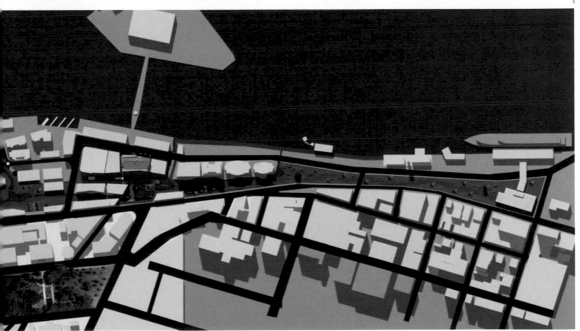

1 Matthew Woodward: Newcastle station site plan

Water urbanism

In this proposal, the *Green Corridor* is a well-connected linear walking landscape, which includes agricultural fields, an urban forest and water retention ponds. The urban rainwater recovery system uses rainwater collection (including rainwater from the green roofs of the buildings) in storage tanks, a network of ponds and greywater re-use for irrigation. Water is kept clean by bio-mechanical purification. *Water urbanism* creates a pleasant microclimate and inner-city landscape.

At the same time, to turn Wickham Interchange in a *green TOD*, it requires appropriate population densities and some high-rise to succeed. This proposal suggests to combine the new *gateway* to the CBD with a *park connector*.

1

1 Matthew Wood-
ward: Urban
wetland
perspective

1 Matthew Wood-
ward: Station
perspective

2 Matthew Wood-
ward: Station aerial
perspective

3 Matthew Wood-
ward: Station interior
platform perspective

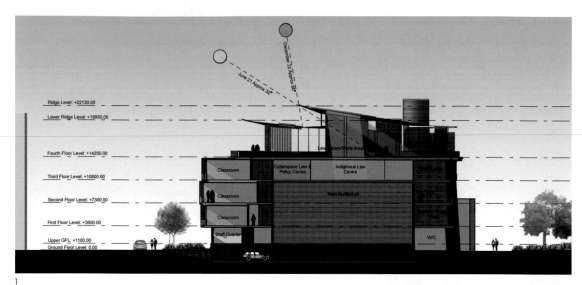

1

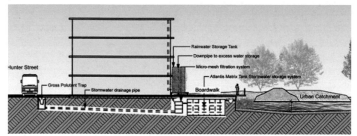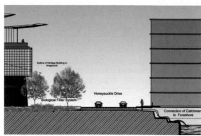

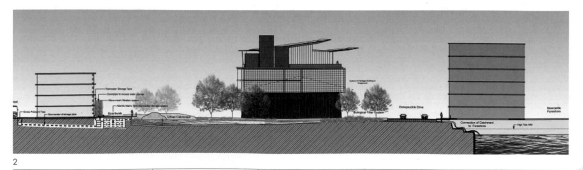

2

1 Matthew Wood-
ward: School of Law,
section

2 Matthew Wood-
ward: Water
management
strategies, capture
and storage

1

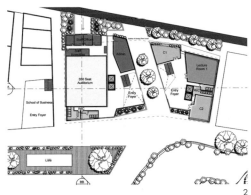

2

3

1 Matthew Wood-
ward: School of Law,
Darby Street
perspective

2 Matthew Wood-
ward: School of Law,
ground floor plan

3 Matthew Wood-
ward: School of Law,
Green Corridor,
perspective

URBAN BUSHLAND (URBAN JUNGLE)

The next 30 years will be spent fighting the impact of rising global temperatures. The 'Urban Bush – Urban Jungle' concept acts as a carbon storage and maximizes biodiversity in the city centre. Greywater cycles, rainwater harvesting and bio-filtration in urban wetlands are main strategies for urban water management. Newcastle is a town with a low population density, an abundance of public space and noticeably derelict zones. The 'Urban Bush' is a scheme focusing on unused space being given back to nature and, in doing so, creating interesting spaces which have a positive impact on the city's culture and aesthetic.

The new railway station at Wickham, public harbour plaza and office tower generate an interesting composition. Overall, it's a thought-provoking and innovative masterplan proposal, transforming the former railway line into an integrated part of an urban bushland, with bike paths. It includes a strong concept of public connectivity, with natural vegetation slowly taking over the existing, heavily mechanical city. It uses the 'Urban Bush' to reduce existing pollution and to minimize harmful CO_2 emissions. Other environmental advantages include:

Micro-climate regulation, air quality management, biodiversity conservation, soil water management, carbon storage, and reduction of the urban heat island effect. The Urban Bush is a concept hinged on the re-naturalization of urban spaces and the co-habitation with various animal species. It creates a new forest as carbon sink and CO_2 absorber.

THE GREEN CORRIDOR

1

1 Jonathan James:
Masterplan of
'Urban Bush'

1 'Green Wall'
  concept of
  Patrick Blanc,
  Paris

2 Jonathan James:
  Green corridor and
  residential pods
  perspective

1

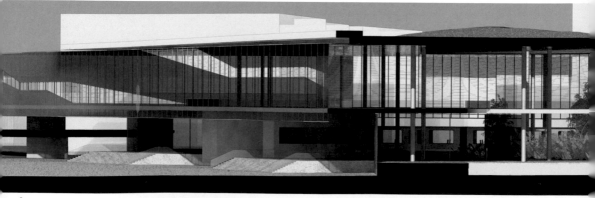

2

1 Jonathan James:
 Newcastle Station
 perspective

2 Jonathan James:
 Newcastle Station
 section; publicly
 accessible
 'Living Roof'

1

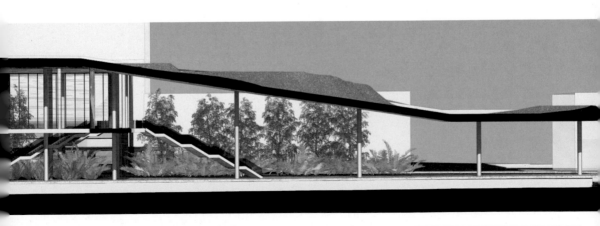

1 Jonathan James:
   Newcastle Station
   interior perspective,
   arrival platform with
   bushland

1

2

1 Jonathan James:
  Library perspective,
  cnr Burwood Lane
  and Hunter Street

2 Jonathan James:
  Library perspective

1 Jonathan James:
Courtyard on library
roof perspective

2 Jonathan James:
Library with public
courtyards on roof
perspective

URBAN GREEN COMMUNITY AND TRANSIT-ORIENTED DEVELOPMENT

Newcastle City Centre has become a city of two different halves, divided by the long linear heavy rail line. With the removal of the line from Wickham Station eastward, it is important to consider the progression of the urban development of Newcastle in stages. The following masterplan takes a City West, City Centre and City East approach, identifying clusters of activities and the fusion of precincts along the linear CBD peninsula. City West will see the new transport interchange at Wickham leading straight onto other modes of public transport, including bicycles for hire for commuting across the city centre, and incorporating bus-bike transit systems.

The mix of uses re-introduced into the city centre will make for a self-sustaining society where people come to live, learn, work and play. Finally, City West incorporates adaptive re-use of Newcastle Station as an organic food market where local produce from the urban agriculture can be purchased by the public. This proposal activates and re-introduces life into all areas of the city, leading to a sustainable society and the future growth for the city of Newcastle. A new library is inserted as flexible, zero-carbon building. The existing railway station is adaptively re-used as organic food market. Generator for the urban form is a well-balanced massing derived from solar geometry: Density and solar access have always to be negotiated, to avoid overshadowing due to over-development.

THE GREEN CORRIDOR

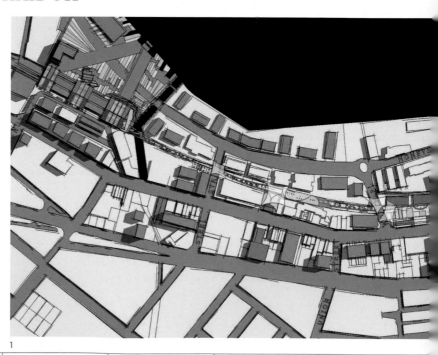

1

1 Toni Butterworth:
Masterplan

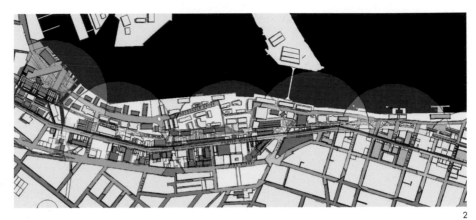

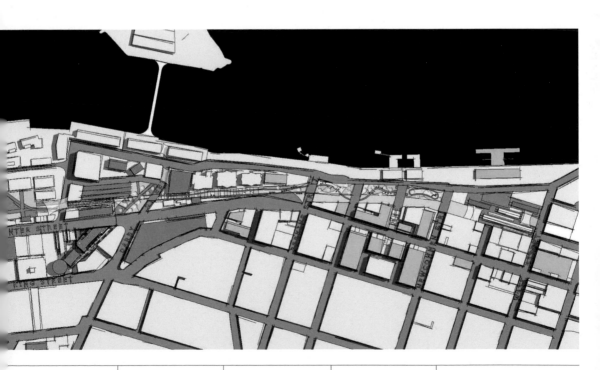

1 Free rental-bike
  concept, Paris

2 Toni Butterworth:
  Transport diagramme

JURY/JUDGES

CIVIL COURTROOM

PUBLIC FOYER

CRIMINAL

JUDGE

PUBLIC

SHERIFF'S OFFICES

PUBLIC FOYER

CIVIL COURTROOM

CRIMINAL

JUDGE

TYPIST'S OFFICES

PETTY SESSIONS OFFICES

COURT OFFICES

SECURE FOYER

OFFICES PUBLIC ENTRY

SECURE BASEMENT

1

2

1 Toni Butterworth:
Court House section

2 Toni Butterworth:
Court House
perspective

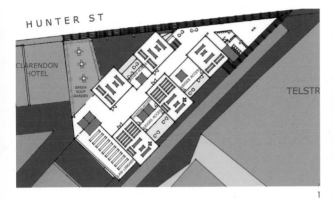

1 Toni Butterworth: Typical Court House plan with 5 courtrooms per floor

2 Toni Butterworth: Court House, cnr Burwood Lane and Hunter Street

3 Toni Butterworth; Court House Hunter Street perspective

1 Toni Butterworth: Newcastle City Station, photomontage	2 Toni Butterworth: Newcastle City Station with office tower		

1 Toni Butterworth:
Green Corridor,
linear parkland

INCREASING CONNECTIVITY – BRINGING THE CITY TO THE WATER EDGE

Urban change is inevitable. The heavy rail line currently divides the city into two long and disconnected strips of land. By removing this barrier, one opens up over 15 locations for easy pedestrian access between Wickham and Newcastle Station. The new masterplan sets out a clear direction on how the city can realize its full potential and best serve the people of Newcastle and the Hunter Region. Applying the principles of Green Urbanism will allow for catalyst projects to transform the city into a vibrant centre. The relocation of parts of the University to a City Campus (60,000 sqm) and the new Justice facilities (25,000 sqm), the revitalization of retail, a new transport interchange and the removal of the last 2.5 kilometres of heavy rail are all key parts in this proposal for a contemporary, future-oriented central district.

Much of the plan is driven by the urban water and water cycle concept. The use of solar canopies shows the harnessing of natural resources for local energy production in the city, using solar power to provide illumination at night. It is through sustainable solutions in the upgrade of the city centre that Newcastle will prosper. By applying Green Urbanism principles we can ensure a sustainable future for the post-industrial city.

THE GREEN CORRIDOR

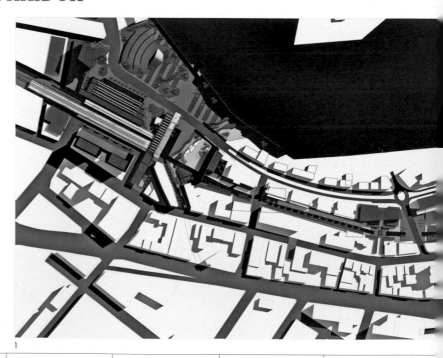

1

1 Benjamin White:
Masterplan with
'Solar Corridor'

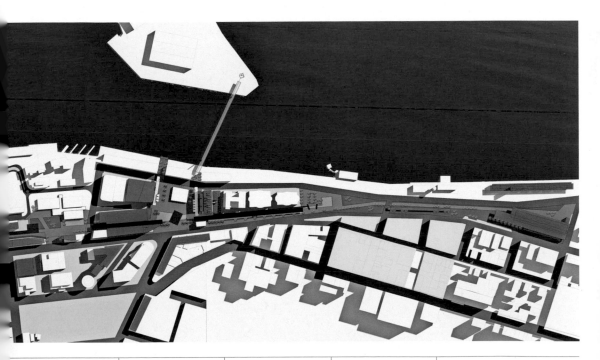

| | 1 Solar Roof by Torres and Lapena, Barcelona | 2 High Line park, New York City | 3 Benjamin White: Cottage Creek perspective | |

1

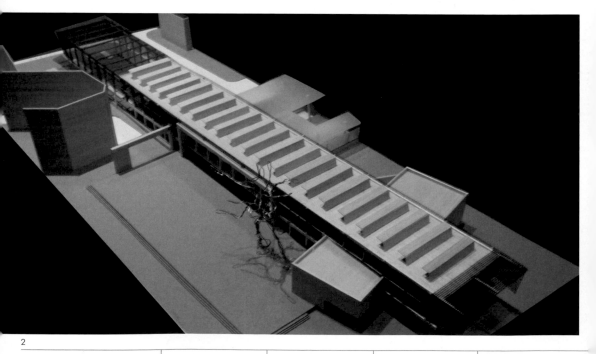

2

| 1 Benjamin White: Newcastle Station elevations | 2 Benjamin White: Newcastle 'Gateway' Station model | | |

1

2

1 Benjamin White:
  Outdoor auditorium

2 Benjamin White:
  Newcastle Station
  entry perspective

1

2

1 Benjamin White:
  Station perspective,
  View from public
  harbour plaza

2 Benjamin White:
  Solar canopy
  generating energy
  for illumination

1 Benjamin White:
Court House,
perspective

2 Benjamin White:
View from solar
corridor towards
new Court House

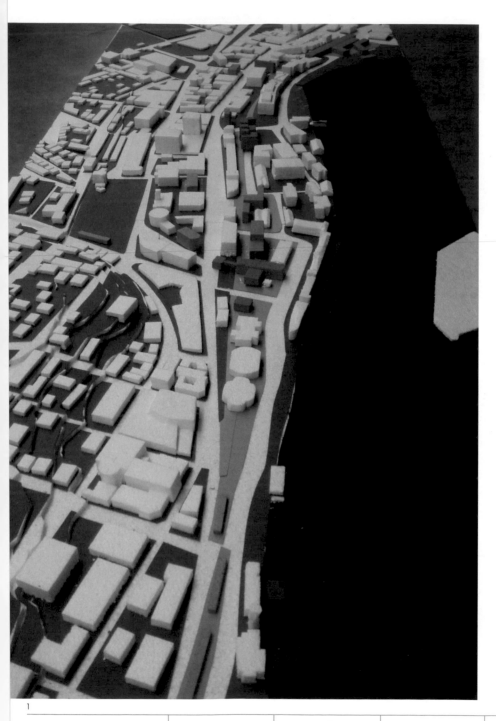

1

1 Claire Sibert:
Masterplan
model of CBD

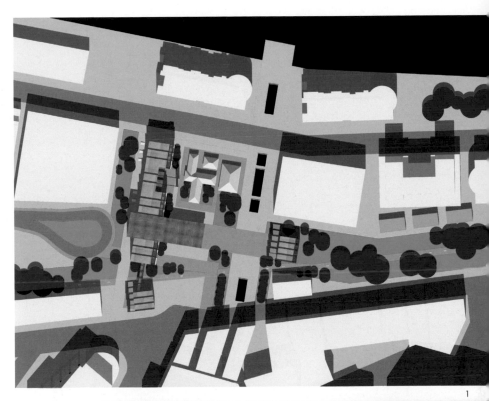

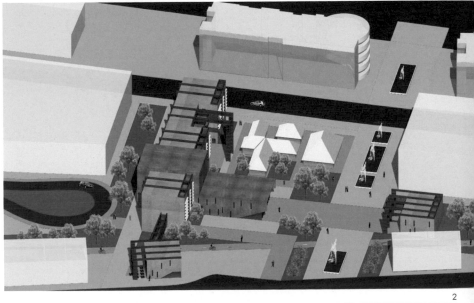

1 Claire Sibert:
Library
Site plan

2 Claire Sibert:
Library and public
space, isometric
view

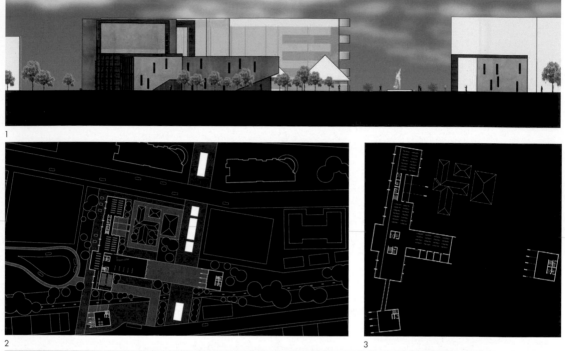

1

2

3

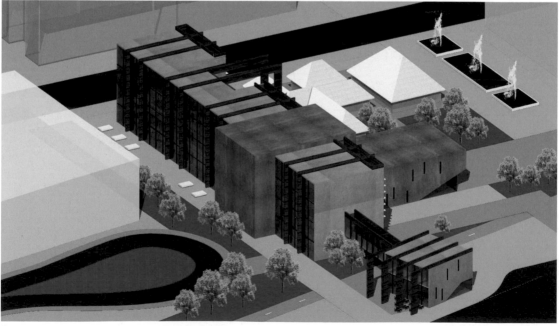

4

| 1 Claire Sibert: Library elevation | 2 Claire Sibert: Library, site plan diagramme | 3 Claire Sibert: Library First floor plan | 4 Claire Sibert: Library perspective |

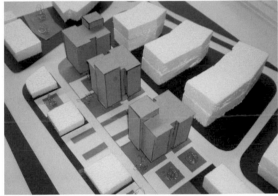

1 Claire Sibert: Student housing elevation; '3 villas'

2 Moveable louvers suggested for shading of western facade

3 Claire Sibert: Student housing model

2 Claire Sibert: '3 villas' perspective

FULL CYCLE: LIVING AND PLAYING THE OUTDOORS

1

2

THE GREEN CORRIDOR

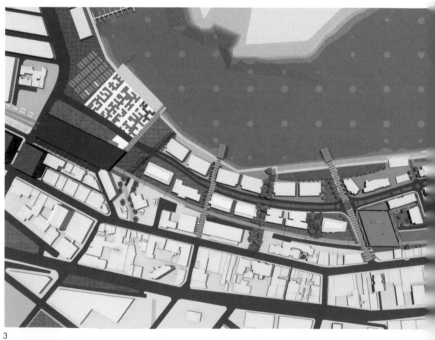

3

| 1 Lee Bateman: Green Corridor, with reminiscence of previous heavy railway infrastructure | 2 Lee Bateman: Linear Green Corridor as city spine | 3 Lee Bateman: Masterplan with fingerwharves |

1

2

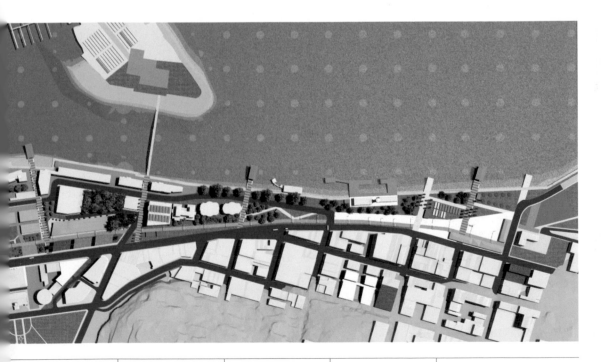

| | | 1 Lee Bateman: Solar canopy over fingerwharf | 2 Lee Bateman: Student housing with community gardens | |

THE GREEN WATERFRONT CITY

1

THE GREEN CORRIDOR

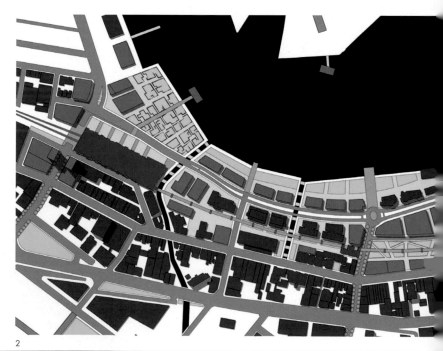

2

| 1 Sarah Maguire: Green Corridor and pavilion | 2 Sarah Maguire: Masterplan | | |

1

2

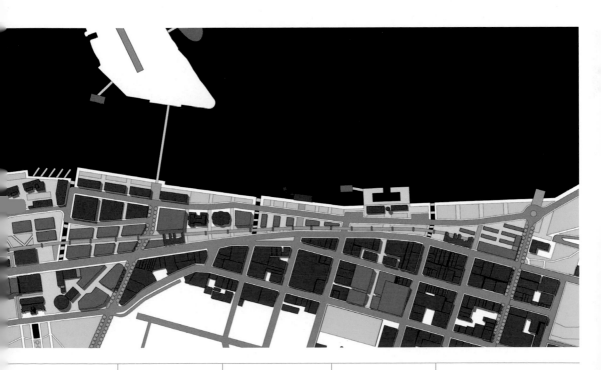

1 Sarah Maguire:
  Newcastle station
  bus interchange

2 Sarah Maguire:
  Newcastle station
  perspective

GREEN CORRIDOR: THE TRANSPORT AND KNOWLEDGE-BASED CITY

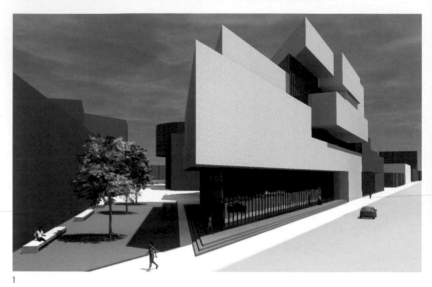

1

THE GREEN CORRIDOR

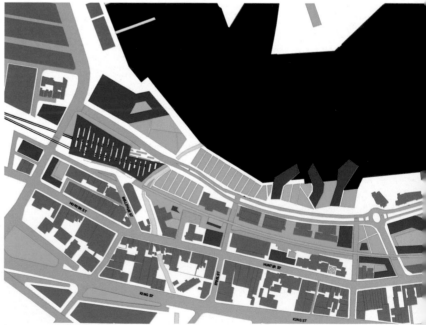

2

| 1 Cassandra Halpin-Smyth: Library, Hunter Street view | 2 Cassandra Halpin-Smyth: Masterplan | | |

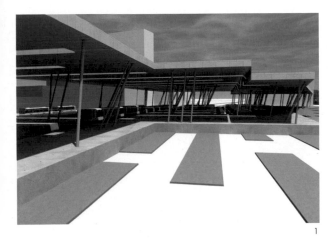

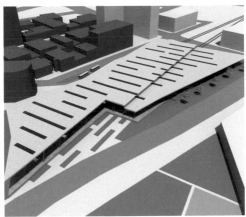

1 Cassandra
Halpin-Smyth:
Newcastle station

2 Cassandra
Halpin-Smyth:
Station aerial
and roof design

RESTRUCTURING THE WATERFRONT CITY

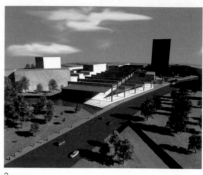

1

2

THE GREEN CORRIDOR

3

1 Kenneth Lau: City aerial and Newcastle station as gateway	2 Kenneth Lau: Station and Cottage Creek perspective	3 Kenneth Lau: Masterplan	

1

2

1 Kenneth Lau:
  Christie Place
  and Library
  perspective

2 Kenneth Lau:
  Library and Theatre,
  Hunter Street view

FOOD BOULEVARD AND AGRICULTURAL FIELDS

2

1

THE GREEN CORRIDOR

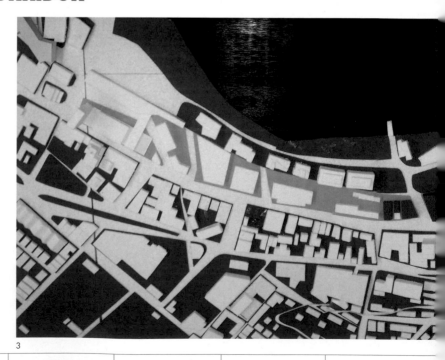

3

| 1 Kylie Burgess: Newcastle station and urban farming | 2 Urban Farming concept | 3 Kylie Burgess: Masterplan model | |

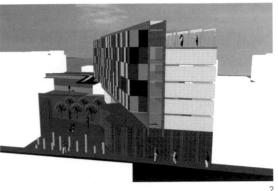

1

2

1 Kylie Burgess:
  Library
  plaza perspective

2 Kylie Burgess:
  Library perspective
  looking north

COURT HOUSE
3RD YEAR STUDIO: PUBLIC BUILDING DESIGN

In addition to students' *Green Campus / Green Corridor* design work in the Masters (MArch) programme, an assignment for 3rd year undergraduate students deals with the design of a public building within one of these developed masterplans. The building design is based on a realistic brief, in this case for a new court house, as part of the government's plans for a new legal precinct. The brief asked for a court house with 3 court rooms, combining district and local court facilities (3 court rooms, from 100 to 150 sqm in size). Questions of typology, civic form, the role of public buildings and public space, as well as the symbolism of a court house, are explored. Passive design strategies and active technologies are combined to achieve a carbon-neutral court house. A prominent urban site at Watt Street corner Wharf Road, next to the historical Newcastle Station, was selected to accommodate the complex brief. Once the heavy railway line has been removed and a new terminus station has been built at Wickham, the historical Newcastle Terminus will be available for adaptive re-use, for instance as an organic food market and conference centre.

THE GREEN CORRIDOR: Court House

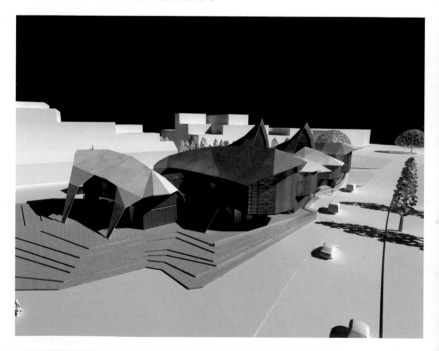

1 Ryan Bradley:
Court House,
perspective from
Wharf Road

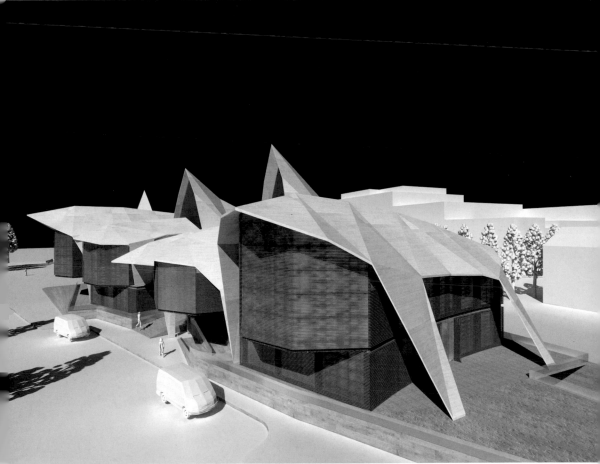

1

2

3

1 Ryan Bradley:
   Interior perspective
   of district court room
	2 Ryan Bradley:
	   Siteplan, showing
	   location at end of
	   Bolton Street
		3 Ryan Bradley:
		   Court House,
		   N/W perspective
		   showing expressive
		   roofscape

1

2

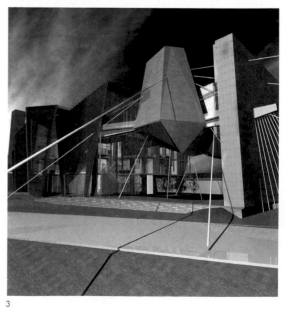

3

1 Reginald Baker:
Court House
model

2 Reginald Baker:
Court House
perspective

3 Reginald Baker:
Court House
perspective. The court
rooms are suspended
in the air

1

1 Reginald Baker:
   carbon neutral Court
   House, garden
   perspective

1 Matilda Watson:
Court House. Aerial
perspective with pedes-
trian link across former
Newcastle station.

2 Matilda Watson:
Court House,
internal perspective
of public waiting
area

1

2

1 Matilda Watson:
Court House,
perspective of pedes-
trian linkage

1 Matilda Watson:
Court House,
internal perspective
of circulation area

The Case Studies

The Manning Riverfront Masterplan for Taree

This part of Chapter 3 presents a real project, Case Study 4: the author's award-winning urban design project for the revitalization of the city of Taree, New South Wales, located around 300 km north of Sydney, at the Manning River. This project was developed as an interdisciplinary team and is planned to be Australia's first low-to-no-carbon urban development project.

From the beginning, the municipality expressed their desire for this project to be a showcase of sustainability initiatives and to transform the site into an inner-city urban village. The design team proposed to develop the site in a manner that incorporated sustainability throughout all stages of development, including masterplanning, design, construction and operation. Sustainability needs to be embedded during the masterplanning process, from project start, with a clear idea how to measure sustainability performance through quantifiable benefits. It's helpful to set 'macro targets' well before the start of design work that allow comparisons as the project progresses towards its defined goals.

A series of urban design principles were identified at an early stage to ensure a sustainable urban development. This project is a good example for possibilities in raising sustainability in a regional context, something often overlooked when there is too much focus on metropolitan capital cities.

Case Study 4
Taree Waterfront – Masterplanning Revitalisation of a Regional Town: A Sustainable Community in the Making

Vision statement for the masterplan

The Manning Riverside Precinct development presents a unique opportunity for the city of Taree (population: 65,000) for a high quality mixed-use development of broad regional importance, which connects the 1970s city centre with the riverfront.

There are various key issues critical to the success of an urban design strategy and masterplan, including:

- Density and yield
- Achievable mix of usage
- Land ownership
- Staging of the masterplan
- Integration of the new location with the existing town
- Relationship to surrounding areas and adjoining residential area
- View connections
- Management and operation of the development.

The Vision is to maintain the existing qualities and to create a vibrant and diverse community that is rich with the social, economic and environmental experiences of a fully realized urban tapestry. The Vision is a neighbourhood model based on a number of 'zero-carbon emission' strategies.

Fig. 01: Aerial photo of the 22 ha site in the city of Taree (NSW), on the Manning River. The site is partially brown-field, with three major land owners. The masterplan incorporates existing structures of a dairy farm.

Some of the key principles for low-to-no-carbon urban sustainability:

- low and medium-rise high density, mixed-use compact building typologies: over 50 dwellings per hectare of developed land
- building an almost self-contained urban village right on the river
- mixed-use: functional mix with local and culture-specific uses
- integration and re-use of existing buildings with elements of local identity
- fine grain and small street network, with attention to architectural detail
- a high quality public space network which always leads to the river edge
- improvement of public transport (bus system) and use of bicycles
- integration of a variety of urban greenery and filtration water gardens.

The identified urban design principles are:

1. Deliver sustainability of projected outcomes socially, economically and environmentally, with a high quality public domain.
2. Incorporate significant public open space, including a larger public green space along the Manning River as an integral design element that is linked and accessible to provide contiguous and permeable green space throughout the site.
3. Access the waterfront for public use. Include an integrated dominant pedestrian and cycle hierarchy precinct-wide, connected to adjacent existing pedestrian networks.
4. Enhance key view corridors to the river and surrounding areas to and from the site, with the ability to use the character of the native vegetation, landscape and riparian zones to create a connected and continuous (water-related) landscape.
5. Provide transport connections with an improved bus network to the centre of Taree, both private and public, that is responsive to community needs (express and mini buses).
6. Connect with the river setting, the unique vegetation on the river bank and the existing creek.

7. Design defined residential neighbourhoods providing varied housing typologies and relating to existing street patterning.
8. Build elements and urban form that respond to the human scale and reinforce a sense of place and site provenance in the local and broader regional context.
9. Respect the local context, and integrate the dairy farm related heritage into the over all final design of the masterplan.

Further masterplan objectives for regional waterfront development (the expanded key urban design principles):

1. Delivering sustainability

a. Social sustainability (People):
- Ensure opportunities exist for equitable participation in the structure of the proposed Manning Riverfront Precinct framework by a representative sample of the regional demographic; with significant involvement of the community
- A `quarter of short distances' with many small-scale meeting places
- Provision of accessible services for people to connect with their local community
- Provide partnerships with organizations and community groups
- Promotion of the arts, cultural, recreational and leisure activities. Provide fitness and sports facilities, in connection with the rowing club.

b. Economic sustainability (Profit):
- Ensure that the financial benefits of individual proposals translate to the whole community.
- Small-parceled land for sale of many individual lots.

c. Environmental sustainability (Planet and Place):
- Use accepted International Best Practice standards as an environmental benchmark for all building designs within the masterplan. Ensure optimal building orientation.
- Assess existing buildings for adaptive re-use and integrate existing structures in the masterplan. Retain significant heritage elements within the built environment and land scape (four buildings of the dairy farm were identified for adaptive re-use).
- Use energy efficient design parameters and urban water management strategies.
- Use recycled materials from de-construction of the diary farm related structures where possible. Locally sourced construction materials to be used.
- High insulation of all walls and roofs of all buildings. All buildings to use passive design principles, with good sun shading of western facades and natural cross-ventilation.
- Use of green power. Generate on-site power by installing PV photovoltaic collectors on 60 per cent of all roofs. Explore district-wide power supply through a new central plant, using combined heat-and-power energy supply (e.g. a wood-chip-fired CHP co-generation plant).
- Compulsory solar hot water for all buildings.

- Develop a district-wide energy strategy: Explore self-sufficient energy generation. All houses to use less than 30 kwh/sqm p.a. Each dwelling to have an energy display metre.
- Use of river water to cool buildings (chilled ceilings).
- Collect rainwater for irrigation and grey water use. Rainwater harvesting in localized tanks. Hard landscaping to be permeable where possible. Bio-filtration trenches.
- Use of stormwater and grey water re-use: Grey water to flush toilets and irrigate public spaces.
- Remediation of contaminated site areas.
- Promote use of public transport through circulation (e.g. easy access to bicycles, bicycle station and bus stops), reducing car dependency.
- Incorporate a local green waste and paper, domestic glass, metal recycle collection facility within the masterplan. Organic waste to be separated for biomass plant.
- Community garden using composting methods. Local food market.
- Design street profiles (widths) with sufficient space for large canopied trees to provide shade to pedestrians, cycle ways and building frontages. Provision of footways within the masterplan should reinforce dominant pedestrian networks on both sides of roads.
- Promote the use of bicycles through Free Bike Programme for all house buyers.
- Adopt City Council's *Urban Forest Policy* as an integral design tool for public domain and streetscape areas. Conserve existing trees where possible. 100 per cent native vegetation for new landscaping.
- All new services to be underground; stormwater harvesting for public spaces.
- Telecommunications fibre optics for 'home offices' ('tele-working' from home) to be explored.

2. Incorporating a diversity of public open spaces

- Introduce a car-reduced system, where parking in the streets is limited to short stops and car parking is underground or in a central 'solar garage'. Create memorable streetscapes through consistent height, scale and setbacks. No car parking in residential streets.
- Solar-powered LED street lighting.
- 'River Garden' – the major green site in the masterplan, and a significant contributor to the River Boardwalk public open space.
- Marina Square – the major civic public space connected to broader activities, such as restaurants, cafes, marina, markets; with space available for concerts, exhibitions (public art), street theatre.
- Pitt Street Park – A key terminus at the end of a major view corridor. Passive recreational space with views to the water.
- Riverfront edge – A continuous green ribbon along the river, as a pedestrian spine, linking all public spaces.
- Pocket Parks – More intimate small-scale green spaces.
- Along the River Boardwalk: Jetties for recreational fishing. The pool 'Floating River Bath' – this will allow safe swimming in varying weather conditions.

3. Enhancing key view corridors to the river

- Intensify the existing view corridors and plan for retention and improvement.
- Create opportunities for new view corridors. Develop building envelopes that allow view corridors to connect with various points along the Manning River.
- Create a regional park on the river bank to provide a green space that will be a key visual focus and attraction for the community to meet outdoors.

4. Providing strong connections to Taree city centre

- Road – Pitt Street to get dedicated cycleways.
- Bus – plan for an improved bus service with frequent, reliable connections from two locations that connect with the CBD.
- New pedestrian and cycle bridge connect with the Botanical Gardens to enhance movement along river.
- Water Taxi (to be explored).
- Cycle ways – ensure logical, well planned cycleway routes complete with a bike station, sufficient bike racks, bubblers, shade trees and seating for rest stops.
- Respect existing built form typology evident in Taree within new built form proposals.
- Ability to design for co-location of retail and community facilities in the precinct's centre to increase activity and minimize trip generation.
- Connect to river setting: Include infrastructure that promotes public and private water-craft use such as boat ramps, moorings, marina, a `Boatel' hotel, facilities for water skiing and rowing activities, and boat servicing opportunities.

5. Developing the design of five different residential precincts (zones)

- Locations and footprints of residential areas should be developed within the frame-work of public open space and aspects of community building.
- The masterplan includes a diversity of around 300 new residential units and a mix of commercial offices and retail outlets around a town centre concept.
- Medium-density developments should be located towards existing residential areas; 3- storey 'walk-up' typologies, such as townhouses, row houses and duplexes.
- Higher-density development (3 to 4, to max. 5-storey) should be restricted to the area along the street, with setbacks and numerous breaks for multiple access to the water front, incorporating commercial elements at ground level.
- Provide affordable housing (approx. 20 per cent of all housing to be affordable).
- Age care housing: Providing for suitable housing typologies for aged residents in two areas within the residential zones (approx. 20 per cent of all housing for seniors)
- `Urban Village' character: Relate proposed built form patterning to existing street patterning.
- Child care: one long day care centre is required (approx. 20 long day care places required per 1,000 population).

During the masterplanning phase, a baseline sustainability assessment of the concept plan was implemented by Arup, using their `SPeAR' (Sustainability Performance Appraisal Routine) process. This is a software tool providing indicators to assess the future sustainability performance of the masterplan against `best practice' standards.

As petrol costs will continue to rise, the efficiency of the almost self-contained, compact sustainable development, where walking to shops is possible, will continue to help keep living costs low. The project is expected to take ten to twelve years to complete, depending on market demand, with the first sites available for development in 2010. The masterplan includes urban design guidelines, and will act as a legally binding control plan prior to offering individual sites to private sector developers.

The Taree Masterplan project team (listed in full in the Appendix) found this project extremely helpful in identifying and formulating achievable and practical strategies for sustainable urban development in a regional city districts. Based on the success of the Taree Masterplan, the same team was commissioned to the Mildura Riverfront Masterplan, a very similar type of project in Victoria.

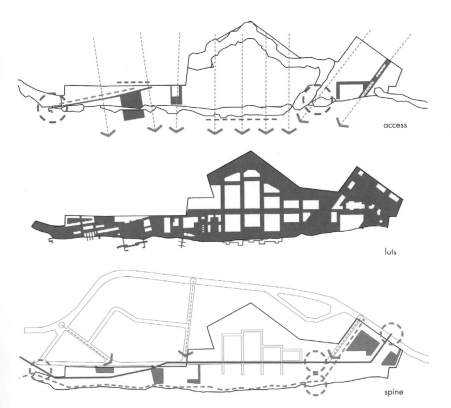

access

lots

spine

Fig. 02: Diagrams illustrating the key urban design principles of the Taree Waterfront Masterplan: Connectivity to the water, fine grain plot sizes, pedestrian and cycling spine for car-reduced district connecting all five precincts.

1

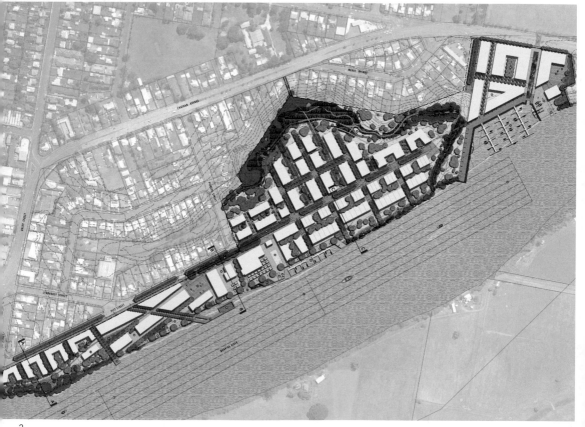

2

1 The 2.5 km long site along the Manning River and the adjacent residential neighbourhood

2 The Taree Waterfront Masteplan (2008), showing the existing creek and the new street lay-out.

It includes 300 units that cut CO_2 emissions by half, with almost 'Passive House' insulation standards, using less than 30 kWh/sqm p.a.

Sustainability is not a later add-on, but an integrated part of the first concept design.

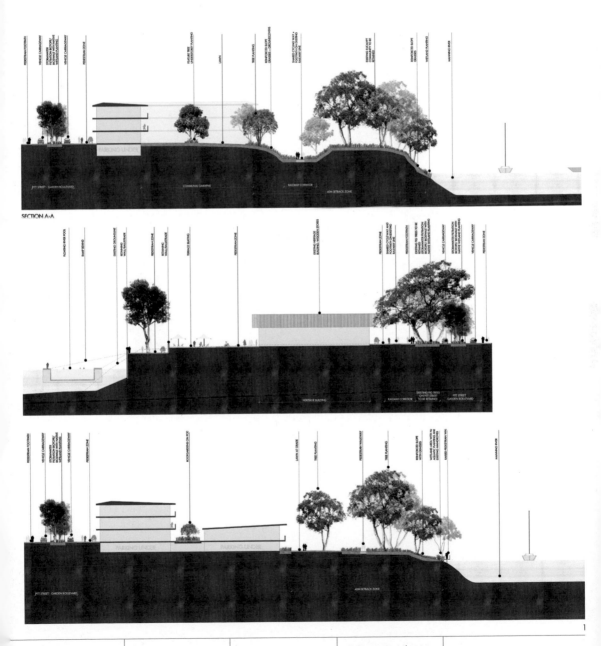

SECTION A-A

1 Site sections showing
the relationship of
building volumes to
the river

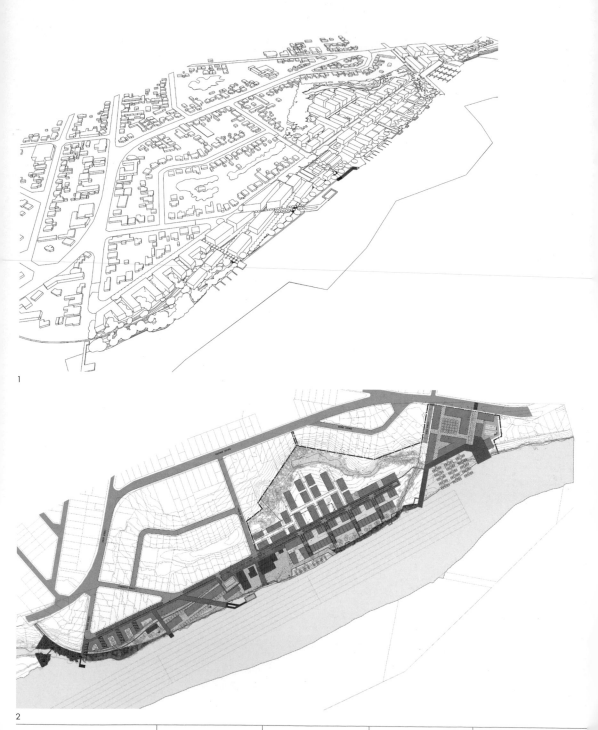

1

2

1 The perspective shows the medium-density of the master-plan, with row and town houses

2 Concept Plan, show-ing the landscaping and 5 distinct differ-ent, but complimen-tary precincts. This

Concept Plan was adopted by city council in October 2008.

1

Along the existing creek:
wetlands are used as natural
systems to filter and purify
water, processing wastewater.

2

| 1 The perspective shows the medium-density of the master-plan, with row and town houses | 2 The landscape includes bio-filtration fields for sensitive urban water manage-ment of stormwater. | The idea is to make the city's watertreat-ment process visible, informing the site planning. |

CHAPTER 4

Looking Ahead to a Low-to-No-Carbon Future

Rapid urbanization: developing future models of high-performance city districts

Urbanization is a defining feature of the 21st century, reshaping cities and communities in countries around the world. Between 2010 and 2030, over 80 per cent of total global urban growth will take place in developing countries – projected to triple their entire urban area (UN-Habitat, 2008; The World Bank, 2009). This unprecedented urban expansion poses a historic challenge and opportunity to cities, nations and the international development community, and provides a once in a lifetime opportunity to plan, develop, build and manage cities that are ecologically and economically sustainable, and socially more inclusive. As a more urban world emerges, we can see a historic shift occurring, one which will cause dramatic effects on human well-being and the environment. The world is undergoing a massive urbanization process – in certain areas it is happening rapidly – and the number of city dwellers is predicted to increase from 3 to over 4 billion within the next 15 years. Most of this increase will occur in the developing (transitional) world.

If backed with decisive action and governance, urbanization can lead to economic development and urban progress by improving living conditions, which will benefit everyone, including the urban poor. The alternative is to do nothing and wait for the inevitable de-

The Impact of Rapid Urbanization in the Asia-Pacific Region

struction and social unrest. The formulation of a more comprehensive and holistic theoretical model of sustainable urban development towards `eco-cities' will be of great benefit to most cities in the developing world, and there is an urgency to apply *green system thinking* and to make it take root in the collective mind. The Middle East and the Asia-Pacific regions are already home to 65 per cent of the world's population (2010). These are some of the fastest growing regions in the world in terms of growing energy demand, economic development, population growth and greenhouse gas emissions. How the leaders and populations of the Middle East and the Asia-Pacific regions respond to the challenge of sustainable urban development will affect the future of the entire world.

The 21st-century growth of cities occurs primarily in Asia and Africa, where the population is expected to double between 2000 and 2030.

With rapid change towards polycentric urban developments and ever-growing urban clusters, it's probably fair to say that the model of the `traditional city', with its historical core surrounded by suburbs and open countryside, has come to an end. Urban theorist Udo Greinacher comments on this shift: `In a time when infrastructures are becoming more important than structures, and the flow of materials and information is becoming more significant than static political and spatial boundaries, traditional planning methods are unlikely to succeed. As the emphasis shifts away from the design of enclosed objects, the design and manipulation of larger surfaces will move to the forefront,' and he continues, asking: 'what will replace the typical hierarchical parameters of urban design: control, optimization, predictability and comprehensibility?' (Greinacher, 2010)

By 2025, 16 out of 27 mega-cities in the world (cities with more than 10 mill. people) will be in Asia.

In the previous Chapter Two, we discussed principles to guide future urban design:
• Cities and urbanized areas need to be our focus, as it will be where most energy, water and materials are consumed and most waste is produced.
• Sustainability is most effective in urban areas when the development of those areas themselves is based on principles of sustainable urban development.
• Questions of urbanization patterns, density, public transport, sprawl, water management, solar orientation, day-lighting, construction systems, supply chains and waste management are all crucial in the process of urban design decisions.
• A mixed-use, compact city model represents the optimum use of space and of a city's future land use; increasing densities can lead to health gains and an increase in productivity.

Fig. 1a, b: The block model of the compact European city offers many advantages Around six- storey blocks, as we find them in Barcelona, Paris, Berlin (all energy-efficient cities), and many other cities, possess the urban characteristics of a compact city model with mixed-use buildings forming quiet courtyards. This aerial photo shows the *Cerda Plan* of Barcelona (1859), designed by the progressive urban planner Ildefonds Cerda. His modern plan transformed Barcelona: a city expansion based on a 113 x 113 metres grid of rectangular blocks. The *Cerda Plan* was celebrated as very innovative, integrating infrastructure, such as the gas network and the urban railway. (Similar to Otto Wagner's plan for Vienna, and Hobrecht's Berlin)

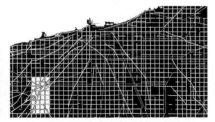

Fig. 2: The US-American urban grid: Chicago's orthogonal *gridiron* and the Great Lake's water edge meet. In 1871 a fire destroyed the city. The new regular grid system has a primary street every 4 city blocks. (Image: Courtesy M. Gandelsonas, 1991)

The Asia-Pacific and Middle East regions: two areas of rapid urbanization
Global greenhouse gas emissions have grown since pre-industrial times; alone, between 1970 and 2004, there has been an increase of 70 per cent of GHG emissions globally (IPCC, 2008). The UN Framework Convention on Climate Change (UNFCCC) was agreed in 1992. It declared that if global mean temperature increase was to be stabilized between 2.0 to 2.4° degrees Celsius, then CO_2 emissions would need to peak by 2015. Since the turn of the century, the Asia-Pacific and Middle East regions have emerged as places of rapid, uncontrolled, sometimes even traumatic urbanization, resulting in fast changing realities. Take, for instance, Shanghai: In 1980, the city of Shanghai had only 112 buildings taller than eight stories, now it has over 13,000 buildings in this category (data: 2009). Shanghai fits well with the fascination of living in a real *metropolis*, and it continues to grow, attracting droves of people from the countryside.

These regions are a major source of greenhouse gas emissions and are likely to be severely affected by the impact of global warming on regional economies, environment, society and the lives of ordinary citizens. The forecasts of UN-Habitat (UN Report, 2008) indicate that 90 per cent of urban growth over the next 15 years will occur primarily in developing countries, and there, mainly in cities. With such fast urbanization, by 2020, the Middle East and the Asia-Pacific regions will account for more than half of the world's urban population. Consequently, climate change presents tremendous challenges for these regions, probably more so than any other area on the globe. Therefore, a theoretical framework for action could help solve some of the pressing problems caused by rapid urbanization. One of the most critical areas of rapid urbanization is still the edge of the city, the peri-urban interface, home to industrial zones and hundreds of millions of people. This area, where the urban meets the rural, is always first to suffer from intense pressures on resources, lack of adequate services and amenities, poor planning and the danger of slum formation.

We have already a wide selection of well-developed technologies at our disposal for using the resources efficiently which Earth offers us, without spoiling her beauty.   **Manfred Hegger, 2007**

The scale and pace of growth and the level of ambition are quite extraordinary, especially in China, but with so much development, there have also been some positive examples where a real difference has been made; for instance, the cities of Dezhou and Rizhao, in south China, where 99 per cent of residential buildings use solar hot water systems, or in the city of Nanjing, where an intensive tree-planting programme has brought back impressive tree-lined boulevards, with wide bicycle lanes and a super-modern subway system that has boosted the use of public transport. Everywhere in China there are now huge investments made in public transport systems and the upgrading of the existing infrastructure. China currently has 50 new subway systems coming into operation in various cities to curb the growing car culture (McKinsey Global Institute study, data: 2007). To cope with an estimated increase of 350 to 400 million new urban dwellers, China will densify its existing cities and build hundreds of new cities from scratch. The Chinese government has also started to raise awareness of the need to drastically reduce overall consumption of goods with public education, awareness programmes and national campaigns.

Rapid, uncontrolled, sometimes even traumatic urbanization process in the developing world

It seems that global change is taking place at an ever-increasing (`run-away') speed. Throughout the 1980s and 1990s, `Asia's economies and cities, in particular, grew at a record rate and were catching up with the per capita levels of consumption in the previously developed countries, such as cities in the USA, Japan and Europe.' (Girardet, 2008) The United Nations is currently working with several governments in the Middle East and the Asia-Pacific region towards strategies for practical and achievable actions, to find solutions for:

- Reducing their vulnerability to natural disasters and the increasing intensity of extreme weather events (increased earth temperature, heat waves, storms and droughts).
- The threat of rising sea levels and flooding affecting coastal cities.
- The need for renewable energy solutions for reliable and clean energy supply.
- Better water management in the light of limited water resources.
- Growing population and high urbanization rates, with a lack of affordable housing.
- Material and waste flows: the need for better waste management and the problem of food security.
- Intelligent construction systems and an increase in local employment in the construction sector.
- Diversification of employment sectors that are not too dependent on one single area (e.g. on tourism only).
- In general, better education, research and training.

As a more urban world emerges, we can see a historic shift occurring, one which will cause dramatic effects on human well-being and the environment.
The world is undergoing a massive urbanization process – in certain areas it is happening rapidly – and the number of city dwellers is predicted to increase from 3 to over 4 billion within the next 15 years. Most of this increase will occur in the developing (transitional) world.

While rapid urbanization is at its most extreme in China, today, we can observe rapid urbanization in the Asia-Pacific, in Africa and in Latin America, all bringing similar challenges and environmental problems. This process is enabled by globalization, market forces, technological change, demographic change and the general move towards a global competitiveness. Rapid urban growth is also transforming the face of historic cities. Global processes have a deep impact on the integrity and community values of urban settlements and on the inhabitants. While urbanization can provide economic, social and cultural opportunities that enhance the quality of urban areas, it carries a threat to the sense of place, its identity, heritage and the uniqueness and integrity of the character of the urban fabric.

There is a wealth of information available from various scientific reports, for instance in the *Fourth Assessment Report* of the Intergovernmental Panel on Climate Change (IPCC, 2008), in the Stern Review (Stern, 2007), the McKinsey Report (McKinsey & Company, 2007), and science has given us some precise answers and robust conclusions. At the same time, scientific sources have graphically shown worldwide implications caused by climate change and the probable results of any inaction. Some examples of these possible impacts were noted by chief scientist Rachendra Pachauri (IPCC Report, 2008) as follows:

• `Small islands and coastal cities, whether located in the tropics or not, have characteristics which make them especially vulnerable to the effects of climate change, like sea level rises and extreme events (e.g. the Islands of Maldives).
• Sea level rise due to thermal expansion alone could be between 0.4 to 1.4 meters (IPCC, 2008); adding to this the melting of ice bodies, and we have serious effects of sea level rise on all low lying coastal areas and small islands.
• In some countries of Africa, yields from rain-fed agriculture could be significantly reduced and many people are likely to suffer additional losses to their livelihoods when climate change and variability occur together with other stresses, such as conflict. The effects of climate change will first and foremost affect the population in poor countries.
• Climate change could contribute to the dying out of 25 per cent of all species on Earth's ecosystem before the end of the 21st century. Climate change recognizes no borders and this is a global challenge, affecting everybody.' (Pachauri, 2008)

The vulnerability of small island states presents a special case. Particular issues of most small islands include the high dependency on tourism and the impact of seasonal population mobility on the resources and capacity for development. With limited possibilities of developing supporting infrastructures, small island states can usually not provide the resources required for maintaining a large seasonal tourist population, and, in many cases, basic requirements, such as water and energy, as well as agricultural produce, need to be imported.

The developing world cannot have the same debate and principles as the developed world. The developing world needs its own appropriate mechanisms and principles for sustainable urban development.

Integrating the developing, transitional world in a global agreement

To deal effectively and honestly with the challenges of pollution growth, climate change and energy inefficiency, we must focus our efforts on the developing (still much neglected) regions of the world, where the struggle for economic growth trumps all other concerns. Using hybrid automobiles in wealthy countries or installing more efficient refrigerators, while necessary, is not nearly enough. Funding from wealthy developed countries must help cities in the developing world to meet the new global standards for reducing carbon emissions.

Some of the measures required in a new post-Kyoto agreement will need to include:

• Knowledge transfer: sharing the knowledge in sustainable urban development internationally and freely.
• Funding from developed world to kick-start renewable energy projects in the developing world.
• Supporting cities in developing countries with better governance and management of their urban growth.

China alone has today around 21 per cent of the world's population. (2009)

Urban transport and public space as indicators

Particularly in rapidly growing cities, the quality of public space and urban transport planning is a good overall indicator of how the municipality struggles and deals with rapid growth. Transport problems are evidence of the city's management capacity to maintain the balance between sustainable growth and access to, and the affordability of, public transport. Cities in less economically developed regions frequently suffer from under-investment in infrastructure and the lack of green space. Consequently, the transport infrastructure is not able to keep pace with rapid urbanization. Singapore, Seoul and many Chinese cities have managed their growth very well. The Chinese government is now investing more in high-speed trains, railway projects, subway systems and bus rapid transit than any other nation worldwide. Since 2008, China has shown more leadership in climate change action than the US or Australia.

CHINA AND INDIA

China's particular situation

The two most populous countries in the world, China and India, still have some of the lowest gross domestic product (GDP) and some of the lowest energy consumption per head. However, both of these highly populated countries are currently striving to climb up the GDP ladder. In regard to China's emergence as a global power, Thomas Friedman argues: 'We cannot just be the consumer and China the producer, and neither of us can allow the goods produced and consumed to be made or used in ways that harm the environment on the scale that we have been. This way of growing standards of living is simply unsustainable – economically unsustainable and ecologically unsustainable.' (Friedman, 2008)

Blecher calls it 'the urbanization of the Third World' (Blecher, 1988), whereby the 21st-century challenge of urbanization in China and India concerns the entire world. In fact, the extreme rapid urbanization processes as they occur in both countries are already concerning and challenging the entire world on a daily basis, leading to epochal change, which forces us to rethink and understand architecture and urban design in a new way. In China, the industrialization and the increased need for energy has prompted the building of three new powerstations per week in recent years (mainly polluting coal-firing plants). Bicycles, formerly the most common and accepted form of transport in China, are now regarded as outdated and car ownership is fast rising. In this context, urban planning offers the greatest potential and is the low-hanging fruit of sustainable shaping of the country's future environment.

Until today, cities used to be the problem and the solution at the same time. However, this has now changed. As the urban slums of these mega-cities keep growing, it becomes obvious that our conventional instruments of urban design and planning appear to be of little use to counteract the increasing injustice or lack of appropriate living and working conditions. (Sassen, 2002; Herrle, 2009) Current rapid urbanization processes in the Asia-Pacific, Middle East and African regions are – in combination with the effects of globalization – leading to new types of urban agglomerations of (so far) unknown calibre. While in the past, cities were seen as the place of social integration and inclusion, the mega-cities of today have stopped providing such social inclusion for new urban dwellers.

For some time, China's leadership has made decisions that have fostered domestic economic growth at the expense of almost everything else, including the environment, and the country's massive economic and social upheaval has impacted negatively on the environment. As the world's second-largest economy, China's rapid economic growth and amazing rise has also changed global power realities. Given its size and growing profile, the world expects now that China does far more to demonstrate its global leadership, for example, by leading efforts to curb GHG emissions and starting to play a globally responsible role in shaping how a more sustainable future can unfold.

China is urbanizing faster than any other country ever before in history, requiring a huge amount of non-renewable materials, resources, energy and water.

China's unprecedented urbanization, since 1978

During the Cultural Revolution, especially from 1960 to 1977, China experienced de-urbanization and economic stagnation. It was only from 1978 that China's rapid urbanization started and then accelerated. Today, the country is almost 50 per cent urbanized, with around 600 million people living in cities (urbanization rate: National Bureau of Statistics China, 2009). New cities will emerge near existing cities and entire `urban networks' of cities are developing. City governments can, to a great extent, influence this process and guide how urbanization plays out. For instance, there are currently over 680 cities in China, all with municipalities concerned with sustainable urban development. In fact, 110 of them have recently announced some form of `eco-city' model development.

China's urban transformation started in 1978 when the then president Deng Xiaoping launched his economic reforms and an urban vision of the future, allowing for inner-China mobility. With mobility restrictions removed, the rural-urban migration started, which marks the beginning of rapid growth for Chinese cities. In fact, it started the greatest mass migration in human history, leading to urbanization at an unprecedented rate. Already, in

1979, the Chinese government had started to establish *Special Economic Zones* to allow for foreign investment. Due to the country's enormous economic growth over the following 30 years, approximately 300 million Chinese moved from the rural hinterlands to the towns and cities. This fundamental shift of populations can primarily be attributed to the effect of economic globalization, which was accompanied by significant changes in the labour market, the privatization of housing and the emergence of urban consumerism by a new Chinese middle class. The increase of urban population is expected to continue and rise to over 500 million by 2050 (data: *The Source*, February 2007). In this scenario, three mega-city regions have emerged as urban centres and economic powerhouses: the greater Pearl River Delta (the PRD, including Hong Kong, Shenzen and Guangzhou), the Yangtze River Delta Region (the YRD, including Shanghai, Suzhou and Hangzhou) and the Greater Beijing Economic Region (the GBER, including Beijing, Tianjin and Shijiazhuang). These are China's three powerful economic centres that drive the growth of the nation. Some of these regions, for instance the PRD, already have an urbanization rate of 75 per cent. However, the projection of China's urbanization for 2030, published in the *McKinsey Global Institute*'s report 'Preparing for China's Urban Billion' (released in March 2008), is even more striking:

China now has 120 cities with over one million people, 36 cities over two million, and continues its path of rapid urbanization. With climate change, much will depend on how these cities are managed.

It is predicted that by 2030 China will have an urban population of 1 billion people and 221 cities of more than 1 million.

The annual rate of increase of urban population is double that of total population increase. As a consequence, China now has the world's largest construction market and will build half of the world's new buildings over the next decade. The country is currently adding a staggering 2 billion sq metres of floor space per year. The roll-out of green buildings has started to receive much government support and stimulus money. The *China Green Building Council* recently reported that there has been a 50 per cent improvement in energy efficiency of buildings only in the last ten years. (CGBC, 2009)

The McKinsey Global Institute's report 'Preparing for China's Urban Billion' analyzes China's economic success and the rapidly rising standard of living of its people in great detail, and how it resulted in a historically unprecedented surge of urbanization, noting: 'If current trends hold, nearly one billion people will live in urban centres by 2025. China will have 221 cities with more than one million inhabitants – compared with 35 in Europe – of which 23 cities will have more than five million people. The urban economy will generate over 90 per cent of China's GDP by 2025,' and the analysis continues: 'of the slightly over 350 million people that China will add to its urban population by 2025, more than 240 million will be migrants.' (McKinsey, 2008) It is obvious that with such fast growth, it will be a major challenge for Chinese municipalities to secure sufficient public funding for the future provision of social services and the supply of water, energy and construction materials. The report also concludes that `a more concentrated pattern of urbanization is most likely to mitigate some pressures and increase the overall productivity of the urban system; concentrated urban growth scenarios could increase per capita GDP by up to 20 per cent over dispersed urban growth scenarios.'

The City of Shanghai, one of the largest of Chinese cities, is a good example of extreme change, enjoying over 10 per cent urban and economic growth per year (Shanghai inhabitants 1985: 6.7 mill.; inhabitants 2000: 13.6 mill. people). The metropolitan population density of Shanghai is around 16,500 inhabitants per sq km. Shanghai and some other Chinese cities, such as Chongqing, Shenzen, Guangzhou, Zhanjiang and Tianjin, have experienced exceptional economic growth, and continue to grow quickly because they are seen by the rural population as places of better job opportunities (especially in the construction and service sectors), and they are a symbol of the promise of higher income, easier access to affordable food and places of cheap energy supply. However, urban planning of this fast expansion has frequently proven to be inadequate, where infrastructure and housing provision have not kept up, and the early signs of urban sprawl (although at much higher densities) can be observed, pushing out city residents even further and leading to long commutes to work, thus deteriorating quality of life. For instance, there has been a rise in `gated community projects' for wealthier Chinese. This has increased sprawl and is an indication of a growing differentiation between the rich and the poor.

China's huge appetite for energy and materials

From 1978 to 1984, the Chinese government commissioned 78 new cities and redeveloped 32 existing cities; the total number of cities increased in 1998 to 668 (Lin, 2002). This dramatic urbanization has raised plenty of environmental and social challenges, as it has created social inequalities, urban wealth and urban poverty; the issues of air pollution, water shortages and lack of waste management are significant in all Chinese cities. Understandably, there are limits to social acceptance of such rapid change, and `shock urbanization' is taking place at a speed that the Chinese people often find difficult to cope with.

In 2008, China became the world's largest CO_2 emitter. Economic growth requires energy, and to get it China must install between 60 to 100 GW of new power generation capacity each year. In comparison, that's almost the equivalent of Germany's current total capacity. Much of this booming economy is fueled by cheap coal (which 80 years earlier enabled the fast industrialization of a booming Europe and US). Unfortunately, more than 70 per cent of the new, quickly rolled-out powerstations in China are coal-fired plants, which of course produce CO_2 emissions. In 2006, around 80 per cent of all energy generated in China was produced by coal-burning power plants (GTZ report, 2007). China put 174 coal-fired powerstations online in 2006 alone, which averages out to be one new plant every two days, significantly increasing the pressure on the environment, causing a `climate-change nightmare' (Scheer, 2007), especially when considering the fact that facilities built today will probably remain in operation for 30 years. China is (again) a place of extremes, where we find some of the most destructive and some of the most hopeful initiatives going on side by side. For instance, while coal-burning is a major contributor to air pollution, many cities in China have now banned combustion engine motorcycles, and only electric-powered ones are allowed (e.g. Nanjing).

Tackling urban environmental problems is one of the greatest challenges in the age of the city. Hardoy, Mitlin, Satterthwaite, 1992

According to the Chinese government's *11th Five-Year-Plan*, the situation of coal-fired powerstations is expected to change with a significant effort to boost renewable energy. In 2010, in an attempt to compensate for such development, China has limited new residential construction in large cities to buildings that require 65 per cent less energy than the level required by today's standard. In 2009, China's government set ambitious targets for renewable energy, which is scheduled to account for over 20 per cent of its total energy production by 2020. With its enormous land areas and a long coastline, China has exceptional potential for wind power. After hydro electric power, wind power is the cheapest (and most technologically mature) form of renewable energy.

The Global Wind Energy Council estimates that wind power will be responsible for 16.5 per cent of the world's electricity needs in 2020, and that this proportion can increase to as much as 34 per cent in 2050. Chinese wind power is to be boosted from 1 GW to 30 GW between 2006 and 2020. The USA, Spain, UK, Germany and Denmark are all leading wind power countries, however China has managed to double its wind power capacity each year for the last five years (2005-2009) and by 2011, will pass the US as the world's biggest wind power generator.

In 2008, the total share of energy generated from renewable energy sources in China was 8 per cent. However, by the end of 2010, the plan is for natural gas, water, wind, solar and nuclear energy to collectively account for 38 per cent of the country's energy production. By 2020, up to 20 per cent (290 GW) should be produced by hydropower alone (in 2006, the equivalent figure was 128 GW). China's hydropower potential is greater than that of any other country. The photovoltaic market in China is also growing. in 2006 it had reached 65 MW, around half of which powered households in remote, outlying regions. By 2020, some 1.8 GW is expected to be generated by photovoltaic installations.

China's appetite for energy will triple from 2010 to 2020, making it a key player in pushing up CO_2 emissions worldwide and accounting for a major share in future emissions. Overall, the level of energy efficiency in China is still low. It will take China many years to achieve the level of energy-efficiency now common among leading EU countries. China currently requires 3.5 times more energy than the global average to generate one dollar's worth of GDP.

Fig. 3 a, b: Left: Planning for China's rapid urbanization. Model photo of a new town network to be built in Hebei Province. (Photo: S. Lehmann, 2009) Right: Off-shore wind farms: In 2011, China will be the world's biggest wind power generator. For instance, in 2010 the Alpha Ventus wind park near Borkum Island (Germany) went online: twelve turbines located 30 km from the shoreline, each 150 metres high, deliver 220 GW p.a. – enough to power 50,000 households. Germany has currently 21,000 wind turbines in operation, and these deliver around 7 per cent of all electricity; 37 more large wind parks with 1,584 turbines are currently in planning (data: 2010). The German government guarantees the payment of 15 Eurocent p. kW for electricity generated by wind power for the first 12 years (this is three times the market price, which makes wind power compatible with fossil-fuel resources).

What kind of urbanization projects? From *New Towns* to *Urban Regeneration*

China's rapid urbanization process makes it an extremely interesting urban case study. Besides the planning of new towns, the urban renewal and revitalization of existing cities has become a major part in Chinese planning, with project categories such as:

• Brownfield and greyfield sites regeneration. For instance, in Shanghai, such adaptive re-use projects include the conversion of a former slaughterhouse into the '1933' arts factory.

• Historical district regeneration, with adaptive re-use projects. For instance, in Harbin, the Daowai Historical District regeneration.

• Mixed-use urban infill projects, such as the brownfield mixed-use development project in the Wangjiadun Business District in Wuhan.

• City campus developments, such as Tongji University campus in Shanghai.

• Urban waterfront and port city projects, such as Wuhan's waterfront development, and in Shanghai: Pudong and the 'Bund' redevelopment.

• Green corridor and public transport infrastructure projects, including green TODs, such as Zhenru Urban Sub-Centre in north-west Shanghai.

• Eco-city projects, such as the *Sino-Singaporean Tianjin Eco-City* and *Wanzhuang Eco-City* projects, both in Hebei Province. (See more information in the Appendix)

According to the Chinese government, around 400 million Chinese people will need new houses in the next 15 years. Cities like Chongqing and Shenzen have already grown at an unprecedented speed, by around 300,000 people annually (Data: 2006). There are also many new towns in planning, and between 2010 and 2025, China will need to continue to build over 10 new towns per year.

It will be important to take full advantage of this historic chance to realize the best city models possible. These new towns – currently being developed or under construction – offer unique opportunities for pilot 'total urban design concepts', where cities are built to the optimum density, with ideal ventilation and day-lighting conditions; where the design is based on masterplans for the integration of efficient public transport (including light railway systems); where each city block gains maximum solar exposure for renewable energy generation, combined with good shading devices for western facades. Indeed, if we were careful, this could be achieved for all those Chinese new towns.

The Indian case: growing slums and increasingly unaffordable housing

Despite Indian cities being among the largest and fastest growing in the world, the urbanization rate of India has still a long way to go to match the Chinese. Around 73 per cent of the subcontinent's population still lives in rural areas and villages spread across the countryside. India will add an additional 26 cities of one million or more by 2030 to its 42 one million plus cities today. India's population is forecast to overtake China's by 2030 (Data: McKinsey Global Institute Report, 2010).

However, with an economic growth (annual GDP growth) of around 9 per cent per annum, we are seeing cities like Mumbai, Delhi, Chennai and Bangalore continuing to grow while many smaller towns become cities in their own right. For instance, in the 1990s, the population of Bangalore grew by 38 per cent – mainly fuelled by the IT boom – and the population of Delhi by a massive 70 per cent (while, in contrast, Kolkata was almost stagnant with only 4 per cent growth). These Indian mega-cities are some of the fastest growing cities in the world. The urban densities are extreme. Mumbai, for instance, has an average population density of 27,000 people per sq km – higher than Manhattan or Hong Kong. (Data: *The Urban Age*, 2005). With over 18 million residents, the greater Mumbai metropolitan region is the world's fifth most populous; the city is predicted to overtake Tokyo as the world's largest city by 2030. However, 60 per cent of Mumbai's population lives in slums, with only informal access to water and electricity, which is a reflection of the city's lack of affordable housing and its high rental prices. (Data: 2009) Mumbai has one of the lowest levels of public space and green space per capita worldwide (the only exception in India is the administrative area of New Delhi, an urban masterpiece, with its formal, colonial layout and large public spaces, designed by Sir Edwin Lutyens and Herbert Baker, between 1912 and 1920). Mumbai only treats 35 per cent of its sewage, a constant cause of water pollution and disease.

By 2000, some 300 million Indians (this is around 30 per cent of the country's population) lived in around 3,500 cities and towns. In 2001, India counted 42 large cities of a million people or more. However, some 400 million people in India still do not have access to electricity (UN data: 2009). More than half of India's 203 million households still lack a toilet – a situation that spreads disease and undermines the nation's quest to become a global economic power. As an agricultural economy changes into an urban consumer society, the need for energy grows and consumption increases. What will this future urban society of India be like? In a country where 76 per cent of the population of 1.1 billion people still lives on less than US$2 a day, and where child malnutrition is on par with Sub-Saharan Africa, the contrast between rich and poor is sharp. The median age of India's population is only 25 years, so a major population increase can be expected over the next decade. The key challenges that Indian cities face include: out-dated infrastructure, traffic congestion, an increasing lack of affordable housing and public space, growing urban slums, lack of sewerage and sanitation and significant environmental degradation. All Indian cities are now under severe pressure to accommodate a fast growing increase in car ownership. (Rode and Chandra, 2008)

As far as CO$_2$ is concerned, India does not have any goals. And legitimately, there can't be any at this point, because our per capita emissions are about 1.2 tonnes per person per year, compared to around 20 for the US.
Developed countries are the big polluters and the ones who have caused the problem. It would be unethical and totally inequitable for India to make the first move.   **Rajendra Pachauri, IPCC, 2009**

All Indian cities share an extremely intense use of space. Overall, the environmental impact of these large cities and their (still) relatively small ecological footprint – given the number of people – is impressive. Indian cities share the following characteristics:

- high to extremely high population densities
- running on comparatively little energy use, and
- walking and public transit are the main means of travel.

Fig. 4: Figure ground plans of parts of districts of four Indian cities: Bagalore, Delhi, Kolkata, Mumbai. The urban morphology of each city is different in scale, density, typology and grain. (Source: *UN World Urbanization Prospects*, 2007)

India's case is very different from China's urbanization. In contrast to China, Indian cities are experiencing rapid, unplanned growth and the Indian government appears to be totally overwhelmed by the size of challenges and speed of transformation. As pointed out by the McKinsey Global Institute, there is a serious lack in urban governance, leadership at city level, long-term planning strategies and clear targets for sustainability, housing and infrastructure.

Informal settlements: slums upgrading programmes

Worldwide, approximately 2 billion people (this is 30 per cent of the current world population) live in substandard housing; 1 billion people reside in urban slums. In cities such as Kolkata, Mumbai, Manila or Jakarta, slums accommodate up to 60 per cent of the urban population. Today, there is a more differentiated understanding of slums and reasons for their formation and growth; the formation of slums cannot be explained by poverty alone. The emergence of slums in cities has much to do with misguided policies, outdated planning and poor governance by municipalities. Unplanned slums without basic services are not an inevitable consequence of urbanization, but most of the time they are caused by an inappropriate legal framework and a lack of political will. India's challenges are particularly significant. With rapid urban growth, we see a massive expansion of unplanned informal settlements in all Indian cities, falling short of meeting even the basic standards of living, such as in sanitation, sewage treatment and waste management. While India's slum population is around 24 per cent of the urban population, this amount is forecast to increase to 40 per cent by 2030. (McKinsey Global Institute Report, 2010)

Cities worldwide are moving step by step towards knowledge-based, service-oriented economies, whereas India, again a case of extremes, is jumping in a very short time-frame from a largely rural-based, agricultural society to a predominantly service-based economic model fuelled by the IT boom. In all Indian cities, hundreds of millions of low-skilled people are living in slums and informal squatter camps that have no sanitation but a high concentration of pollutants. Access to energy and clean water remains one of the essential keys to sustainable development in general, and to slum upgrading initiatives in particular. The informal habitat and urban slums of India's cities are also home to many marginalized social groups ignored by politicians (such as the 100 million people belonging to over 500 nomadic groups that cannot qualify for governmental benefits or welfare schemes). In the publication 'Slum-Upgrading: General Introduction and Compilation of Case Studies', the *Centre on Housing Rights and Evictions* (COHRE) explains what the problems of urban slums are and outlines strategies for slum upgrading. (COHRE, 2005) Unfortunately, between 2004 to 2009, urban poverty has risen in India by 100 million people. According to the UN, 410 million Indians lived in 2009 below the poverty line.

UN-Habitat defines slums as: informal habitat featuring a lack of durable housing, insufficient living area, lack of access to clean water, inadequate sanitation and insecure tenure. Slum upgrading, as opposed to slum redevelopment or slum clearance, is now widely acknowledged as one of the more effective means of improving the housing conditions of the poor and has been hailed as a linchpin of any urban poverty strategy. It has been defined by the *Cities Alliance* as consisting of 'physical, social, economic, organisational and environmental improvements undertaken cooperatively and locally among citizens, community groups, businesses and local authorities'. The improvement of slums is one of the United Nations' *Millennium Development Goals*, although the target of reaching 100 million slum dwellers with improvements seems somewhat low. The reduction of poverty was one of the *Millennium Development Goals* (MDGs) set by the UN at the turn of the century. This is a long way from being achieved, and sharply rising prices for fossil fuels and raw materials have made the achievement of the goals in the near future impossible.

Slum-upgrading can go beyond mere physical improvements and promote changes in policy at a city-wide or national level, recognizing that slums are not isolated problems but are indicative of an entire urban system that is not functioning and must be addressed through city-wide planning processes. (See more information at: www.cohre.org and www.citiesalliance.org) Following is a list of the most common issues being addressed by slum upgrading programmes:

• Legalization of tenure (ownership) status for sites and houses, including rental agreements to ensure improved tenure.

• Provision and improvement of technical services, e.g. water, waste and wastewater management, sanitation, electricity, road pavement, street lighting, etc.

• Provision and improvement of social infrastructure, such as schools, clinics, community centres, playgrounds, green areas, etc.

• Physical improvement of the built environment, including improvement of the existing housing stock.

• Construction of new housing units. (Housing construction might form part of upgrading schemes. Often enhancing and rehabilitating the existing housing stock is much more sensible and effective and can be achieved at little cost through legalisation of tenure status or regularization of rental agreements).

• Design of urban development plans (including, for example, the rearrangement of sites and street patterns according to infrastructural needs, although working within existing settlement patterns is generally less disruptive to community networks. This measure might entail resettlement of some residents).

• Changes in regulatory framework to better suit the needs and opportunities available to the poor, as far as possible keeping to existing settlement patterns.

• Densification measures (e.g. multiple-story houses), in order to protect fertile land from being occupied for settlement. Also possible: de-densification due to partial resettlement (COHRE, 2005).

• Ensuring all stakeholders are included and can participate in, and work towards, common visions, with policies and strategies flexible enough to adapt to changes.

Fig. 5: Informal habitat: Urban slum in Manila, Philippines. Some of most polluted metropolitan areas are Manila, Jakarta, Bangkok, Hong Kong, Cairo and various cities in China, India and Russia. (Source: Image Sharing Commons) One of the largest urban slums in Africa is Soweto Township, Johannesburg (South Africa), with over 3 million inhabitants.

With this background, it becomes obvious that the developing world cannot have the same debate and principles as the developed world. The developing world needs its own appropriate mechanisms and principles for sustainable urban development. Urban sustainability needs to be viewed through a different lens than in the developed world, and unique strategies for urban management and local actions need to be developed.

Renewable energy in developing countries

Mike Lindfield, of the Asian Development Bank, notes that `strategies for climate change in developing countries reveal competing priorities: short term poverty relief or long term global benefit.' (Lindfield, 2008) Knowledge transfer in sustainable urban development aims at ensuring that the mistakes of the developed world (e.g. urban development leading to increased dependency on fossil fuels and the automobile) are not repeated in developing countries during their rapid urbanization. For instance, developing countries have a great opportunity to directly construct an infrastructure for city districts based on renewable energy sources and strong public transport systems. However, in reality, this turns out to be rather difficult to achieve. The Copenhagen UN Climate Summit in 2009 revealed political tensions between the developed and the developing world, especially in regard to the question of how to tackle climate change in a cohesive way. Developing countries are confronted by a range of environmental threats – soil degradation, water shortages and air pollution, lack of waste management, deforestation and loss of biodiversity. All developing countries are affected by climate change on an increasing scale, affecting their economies and populations. In many of these countries, renewable energy technologies have enormous potential; for instance, India has enormous wind power potential, solar radiation and biomass in abundance.

Developing nations enjoy a greater potential for tapping solar power, wind power, biomass and geothermal power compared with most industrialized countries as they do not have the burden of 'old' industries and their infrastructure investments. These countries can move straight into the age of renewable energy. Therefore, renewable energy sources and technologies are of particular importance to developing countries, helping them to 'catch-up' with richer nations in a carbon-constrained future. While each country will have to develop its own *Post-Oil Strategy*, an abundance of clean energy gives a country an obvious strategic advantage in the 21st-century global economy. For instance, China increasingly benefits from its coastal winds, Africa from its solar radiation and Brazil from its bio-fuels.

According to a recent study of the *International Energy Agency* (IEA, 2005), 74 per cent of the increase in global primary energy consumption between 2010 and 2030 will take place in emerging economies, with China and India accounting for 45 per cent of this increase. New power plants and electricity transmission lines (entire new distribution networks) are very expensive and are often unaffordable for the poor nations, often due to their large land mass and distances between cities. The IEA estimates that expanding electrification to the extent that the number of people living in poverty worldwide is halved would cost over $16 billion a year for the next ten years. (IEA, 2008)

Renewable energy sources offer great potential for the developing world. In many areas of Africa, Latin America and Asia, electricity is still scarce, but small solar power units and hydropower plants can help to mitigate the effects of poverty. For instance, lack of lighting is one reason why millions of children in Africa still can't study at nighttime. In 2007, the World Bank launched the 'Lighting Africa' initiative, with the goal being to provide up to 250 million people in Sub-Saharan Africa with access to electric lighting.

We can find many examples of where off-grid renewable energy solutions are benefiting developing countries, leading to practical solutions for environmental projects in remote areas that are not connected to power grids at all. Technological advances are making 'eco-electricity' more affordable. India is already fifth in the world when it comes to installed wind power output. World Bank energy expert Amil Cabraal says that 'emerging markets are inspired by Europe's extensive investment in renewable energy sources and the EU's plans to meet 20 per cent of its requirements with environmentally-friendly power and heat by 2020.' (Cabraal, 2008) A couple of off-grid solutions that could help developing economies and their poorest citizens are currently in the testing phase. A mobile power plant that runs on coconut shells is being developed by Siemens in Africa – the plant's ash is used for water purification. Researchers in Bangalore, India, have developed a self-powered algae-based sewage treatment system that can remove 95 per cent of organic substances and up to 99 per cent of nitrogen and phosphates from effluent without any outside power source. Many of these sorts of off-grid developments are very affordable, reliable and ready to be scaled-up to any desired size and trucked into villages in Africa or Asia.

Rapid urbanization and climate change are inextricably linked.

Small energy systems for local use in developing countries
Today 1.6 billion people live without electricity. In India and China alone, over 600 million people are living below the poverty line. Eradicating poverty is the moral imperative in the developing world. So, any strategy in regards to climate change has to protect the capacity of poor countries to eradicate poverty. The leading US climate change economist, William Nordhaus, at Yale, has maintained for some time that if developing countries cut emissions too sharply and too soon (as advocated by many NGOs), they would run the risk of further impoverishing their people, because it would lower economic growth and hinder efforts to increase agricultural production in these places. A carefully balanced strategy is required.

It is important that developing countries go directly from no electricity to clean electricity. However, the need for clean energy should not come at the expense of growth in developing countries. It is, therefore, essential that financial mechanisms are established through which wealthy countries subsidize the associated costs of developing countries. Small energy systems are a great way to bring clean energy to all places. For instance, in Ethiopia, only 1 per cent of the population has access to electricity. Access to energy is a significant factor in lifting people out of poverty. But in Ethiopia, 80 per cent of the population live in villages far from the city and the country's power grid. The solution for rural, developing countries is small production units serving local demand, rather than large, centralized plants and grids.

CASE STUDY SHANGHAI ZHENRU URBAN SUB-CENTRE

Emergent urban patterns for Shanghai: new city sub-centres of the polycentric network city

The trend towards urban network configurations, away from the mono-centric city centre model, can be observed in many large cities around the world. It can be seen both in urban structures and their underlying patterns of activity and mobility, and also in relation to the increasingly pluri-centric nature of decision-making structures. It seems that the move towards polycentric network urbanization is a necessity for large cities when they grow beyond the 3 million people mark (as cities like Shanghai, Berlin, Sydney, Singapore, and so on, are all larger, the official planning targets have now moved towards polycentric models, away from the previous single city centre model). Polycentric structures are obviously the way to go for fast growing cities. However, there are unintended consequences that multi-clustered, polycentric structures bring along; for instance, one result could be a need for more journeys, therefore the existence of an efficient public transport system with high social acceptance is essential.

This part of the last chapter compares two cases of urban patterns for new sub-centres for polycentric city structures. It relates to the built development of new urban sub-centres in Berlin (Germany) and a proposed sub-centre in Shanghai (China), and the relationship of these sub-centres to the `Network City' theory. The aim of this part of the chapter is to serve as a practical guide to the process of developing a strategy for high-performance city districts. The case of Potsdamer Platz, Berlin and Zhenru Sub-Centre in Shanghai is discussed as evidence of cities moving towards more polycentric systems. Both are transit-oriented developments promoting mixed-usage, compact density and strong public transport systems. According to the documentation by Shanghai municipality, the new urban centre, which is currently in its planning phase, is to become a `sustainable sub-centre for a growing metropolis'. Based on the author's Potsdamer Platz design experience, where a `City within the City' was developed (like an island), a series of careful recommendations have been formulated for the design and development of Chinese urban sub-centres such as the Zhenru Sub-Centre, in full knowledge that it is difficult to translate from one case to another. Lessons from one project are not easily scalable or transferable to another, e.g. from Berlin to Shanghai. The context and cultural setting between Berlin and Shanghai is totally different, and so is the climate. For instance, high-density living has been accepted by the residents of Chinese cities for a long time and the automobile ownership per capita is much lower in China.

Nevertheless, an attempt has been made to transfer some important general observations for new urban districts. The conclusion includes five general recommendations from Potsdamer Platz for the urban design of such new sub-centres to ensure a delivery of economical, social and environmental sustainable outcomes.

George Gilder noted: `we are headed for the death of cities' (due to the continued growth of personal computing and distributed organizations advances) `cities are leftover baggage from the industrial era.' (Gilder, 1995) Since all major cities compete with each other to attract investment and a talented workforce, the development of specially branded metropolitan/urban sub-centres, separate from the historical city core, has emerged as a strategy to upgrade, diversify and increase the attractiveness of the metropolis. If these new sub-centres are developed as transit-oriented clusters, with a strong focus on public transport, compactness and achieving the right mix of programme, it may be possible to achieve sustainable outcomes for such developments. However, with greenhouse gas emissions escalating, the appropriate restructuring of our cities is crucial.

With rapid urbanization, a frequently posed question in China is: what urban models should we learn from? Are Stockholm, Barcelona, Freiburg or Singapore expressions of today's best practice, and could any of them be a model relevant for the future of, say, Chinese cities, with their entirely different constraints, contexts, scale, demographic change and speed of action? Successful urban design appears to be mainly a question of design quality and getting the right programme mix. Analyzing such urban mix, we need to be careful in deciding the proportions of new precincts in regards to:
• Public and cultural buildings, representing government and institutions.
• The integration of transport, where stations have previously been called `the cathedrals of the 19th century'.
• The percentage of commerce/retail/workplaces in the overall urban mix.
• The percentage of residences (with a wide range of typologies).
• Green spaces and open public spaces.

Urban transformations during the 1990s: case study Potsdamer Platz, Berlin
London, Paris and Berlin have all evolved as centres of civic architecture, each with its own variation on the theme of urban space and density. The development of these city centres owes much to the equilibrium between ideas about public and private spaces. We can easily identify their different approaches:

• **British**: `Long-life, low-energy, loose-fit' approach, as espoused by Alex Gordon in 1974, with a concern for a more humane built environment, against high-rise tower blocks (such as the much disliked The Barbican). The British approach is probably best exemplified by the work of Peter and Alison Smithson and by the residential complex `Byker Wall' in Newcastle-upon-Tyne (designed by the Swedish architect Ralph Erskine).

• **French**: `Grand gestures' of urban planning (e.g. from Haussmann to La Defense), with a Paris-centric focus even before Mitterrand's `Grands Projets', until the late 1980s (an example for this is Ricardo Bofill's theatrical public housing Abraxas in the *banlieues*).

• **German**: After World War II, most of the destroyed German cities (in East and West) were rebuilt according to the supposedly new guiding vision of rising car traffic, in an attempt to overcome not only the narrow old towns, but also its own dark history. It created the supposedly new idea of re-urbanization and the *Zwischenstadt* (peri-urban). This changed sharply with the 1973 *Oil Crisis*, when environmental performance started to emerge as a key generator of all urban form. Today, Germany's decentralized settlement structure is highly polycentric, following the fragmented structure of its federal states.

In Berlin, public discussion about urban development re-started in 1957 with two opposing models: the IBA in Tiergarten Hansaviertel (in the West), and the Stalin Allee model (in the Soviet-occupied East). During the entire 1990s and until today, the re-unified Berlin was guided by the rigid `Planwerk Innenstadt' and the backwards-looking principles of *Kritische Rekonstruktion* (critical reconstruction), developed and implemented by the *Senatsverwaltung* (these principles were formulated by Joseph Paul Kleihues and Hans Stimmann around 1991-92). The `critical reconstruction' principles included, besides other regulations, limiting all building heights to 22 metres and limiting volumes and plot sizes by preventing the amalgamation of sites, to retain the historic street pattern. One of the most acclaimed projects of large-scale urban renewal from this period, creating a new `city within the city', is the Potsdamer Platz development (built between 1994 and 2000 and based on the results of several design competitions).

With the fall of the *Wall* on 9th November 1989, the Potsdamer Platz site returned to being the centre of the city, taking on the role and symbol as the central area between Berlin East and Berlin West. The reconstruction of Berlin's centre in *Mitte* (heart), had quickly taken on the twin roles of:

• stitching together the two opposed political and urban systems (East and West), and
• re-introducing the quality of the compact, mixed-use European city model as a guiding typology, which was immediately understood as being a space of political manifestation (symbol of reunification).

Around 1990, by taking on its new role as a global city, Berlin identified the urgent need for large-scale commercial buildings, and speed of delivery was essential if Berlin was to again become the capital of a reunified Germany (as had been decided by the German Parliament, after heated debate, in 1991). The two leading developers – the high-tech companies Daimler and Sony – were, from the beginning, interested in energy-efficient buildings, as `green buildings' were already understood to be easier to let (usually yielding higher rents). The developers also understood, with rising energy and water costs, that the operational expenses of the new precinct were increasingly relevant. The explosion of demand of office space in Berlin around 1990 is partially comparable to the demand we see in China today (although on a much smaller scale). New urban sub-centres were

quickly needed to satisfy this demand. In Berlin, this coincided with a shift towards an urban architecture where buildings were seen as the new `stone palazzos' (`Das steinerne Berlin', Werner Hegemann, 1930), and where a well-distributed urban density meant delivering a sense of regained urbanity appropriate for the future capital of Germany.
Today, Potsdamer Platz has its own unique atmosphere. It is a place where contemporary architecture and a metropolitan urbanism gloss over Berlin's dark history. According to various media, the area has re-emerged as the symbol of the `New Berlin', whatever this means. The rediscovery of the compact, walkable `European City' model with its compact block typology and mixed-usage (as opposed to the American, mostly car-dependent model, with air-condition-dependent high-rise buildings) marked a sharp turning point in the urban design of the 1990s. It had a remarkable effect on the urban design discourse during the entire decade and it is fair to say Potsdamer Platz has had a huge influence and effect on urban designers worldwide. It was completed in 1999. The much quoted `rediscovery of the European compact mixed-use city model' was hereby connected to three main tendencies: Critical Reconstruction, Post-Modernism and Compact City Theory (as formulated by Aldo Rossi, Christopher Alexander, Heinrich Klotz, O.M. Ungers, Leon and Rob Krier, Charles Jencks, and others urban theorists).

In Germany, the 1973 *Oil Crisis* had an impact on rethinking cities, which were now understood as energy-hungry, stressed systems, out-of-balance with nature or ecological principles. During the 1990s, the cities of Curitiba, Copenhagen and Barcelona emerged as examples for innovative urban planning, as leaders of change and of new thinking about the future of regenerated city centres, and these were the models planners had in their heads when the Potsdamer Platz project took off. The district at Potsdamer Platz was the result of an extensive 2-stage competition process and an intensive public debate. One aim of the project was to have a diversity of architectural languages, and the 19 buildings in the Daimler area were the result of designs by ten international teams of archi-tects, under the artistic leadership of Italian architect Renzo Piano (and his office, Renzo Piano Building Workshop, RPBW). The Potsdamer Platz masterplan developed by RPBW in 1992-93, clearly followed the idea of the above mentioned traditional European city model. To ensure diversity in architectural language, the ten different offices involved in the design of the various parts of the masterplan were selected for their capacity to com-pose a vibrant part of the city. Regular `design charrette' meetings between all involved architects over four years ensured the integration and the coordination of diverse indi-vidual contributions. RPBW managed to translate the rigid design guidelines, which were set earlier by the Berlin Senate and the designers Hilmer & Sattler (the result of an earlier urban planning competition for the basic framework for the entire urban development), to give it a Mediterranean urban flavour.

It was clear that the proposed public space network of this district needed particular atten-tion. Piano's plans laid down the pattern of streets and blocks of the entire complex. It's worth remembering that the design starting point was an almost completely empty area with a large number of historical references, which, however, were no longer tangible; the few exceptions on the site being *Weinhaus Huth*, which had survived World War II unscathed, the Hotel *Metropol* and the remains of Potsdamer Street. Piano's concept established a convincing solution for the visual link with the nearby Kulturforum and the back of Scharoun's State Library building, as well as the inclusion of large water bodies in the development. All around Marlene-Dietrich-Platz, the architects grouped buildings with the most public of natures: the theatre, casino, restaurants, hotel, retail outlets and cinemas. This piazza was conceived of as the heart surrounded by an ensemble of independent buildings, thus ensuring a 24/7 public node.

Urban consistency and urban diversity

As a key element of a lively urban culture, the design of the *street* was given much attention (its profile, width, design quality materials, etc.). The streetscape was again regarded as an important public space, one that should not be dominated by vehicles, but by the pedestrian, the *Berlin Flaneur* (Walter Benjamin). Short distances between places within the quarter, achieved through strong pedestrian connectivity and arcades and variety in the architectural language of the individual buildings, helped achieve this goal. Other architects' offices were invited and commissioned to plan different buildings, including: Arata Isozaki and Steffen Lehmann (Tokyo/Berlin), Christoph Kohlbecker (Gaggenau), Hans Kollhoff (Berlin), Ulrike Lauber and Wolfram Wöhr (Munich), José Rafael Moneo (Madrid) and Richard Rogers (London). The authentic city is always the result of multiple authorship and a diversity of concepts. A set of design guidelines for the different blocks were agreed on in the design charrettes, such as the facades had to be primarily of terracotta, brick, ceramic or warm-coloured sandstone (no use of granite) so that the buildings would express a distinctive warm and inviting atmosphere. Nearly all the buildings were designed with wide arcades at ground level. Sidewalks up to eight meters wide provide enough space for various outdoor events.

The inclusion of water areas has had a positive impact on the microclimate; the water area of 1.2 hectares provides a balance to the district's urban density. In the phase of planning optimization, the usage ratio for offices, residential and commercial/retail was agreed as 50:20:30. The strategic arrangement of programmes within mixed-use urban blocks is much better understood today, however, in hindsight Potsdamer Platz was a `capstone project' in gaining better knowledge about the designing mixed-use sub-centres from scratch. Unrestricted access to the ground floors of all buildings was an important element in the concept of harmonious coexistence of public and private spaces. Invisible for residents, most deliveries to buildings in the district arrive underground (as does garbage collection) in order to keep the streets free of delivery vehicles and trucks. The Potsdamer Platz project was supported by experts in construction ecology right from the start. An ecological concept was developed and implemented, covering both the period of construction and the operation of the buildings following completion. Construction materials were chosen with due consideration for health and environmental aspects. Embodied energy, energy consumption and the emission of pollutants were minimized. What did we learn?

As urban designers, we need to respect the following basic and holistic approach:
• Not to cut-off the new centre from its surrounding context (not to create an 'island' or 'city within the city').
• Connectivity is everything, with a focus on pedestrians, cycling and public transport.
• Due to a general planning tendency towards systems and networks of centres, inter-linking and connectivity becomes crucial.
• There is a new understanding and valuing of public space; the high quality of public domain is again appreciated.
• A vibrant city needs large-scale and small-scale, bottom-up and top-down approaches, all at the same time, and an integrated set of solutions.

Fig. 6: Aerial photo, showing Potsdamer Platz Berlin: a new city district within the city, with the aim of stitching Berlin's two halves together; built 1993-1999; total 800,000 sq m floor space. Masterplans developed by Renzo Piano Building Workshop, Helmut Jahn, Giorgio Grassi, and others. An example of a privatized (quasi) public space at the heart of Berlin – a 'Ciy within the City' – a circumstance that had already received widespread debate in the mid 1990s. Potsdamer Platz and Leipziger Platz are in the north (upper part of aerial photo); the Landwehrkanal borders the site to the south. The large, elongated building on the left is Hans Scharoun's New State Library.
Such major metropolitan projects, like the Potsdamer Platz development, have often an overcomplicated planning process. (Images: Courtesy debis, 2002)

Fig. 7 a, b: Images showing Potsdamer Platz high rise towers, designed by Renzo Piano, Hans Kollhof and Helmut Jahn: overall, a new 'City within a City' emerged. Some figures: Around 75 per cent of all visitors arrive by public transport. There are over 10,000 work-places at Potsdamer Platz. Site area (Daimler site): around 80,000 sq m. Gross floor area, total: approximately 500,000 sq m.

There is an extensive body of research on the Potsdamer Platz project (some by leading authors and critics, such as Balford, Lampugnani, Zohlen, Bodenschatz, Buddensieg – to name just a few) so it is not the purpose of this chapter to repeat such a widely discussed body of work. What is of interest, however, is the conceptual parts of Berlin's regeneration project that might be relevant to China's current urbanization. These keys to high-performance city districts are: efficient transportation, energy systems, water systems and waste management systems, and the application of the holistic principles of Green Urbanism. At Potsdamer Platz, a set of simple concepts to achieve sustainability on the urban scale included:

• Solar: aiming to reduce solar gain in summer and heat loss in winter, through orientation, compaction and high insulation.

• Ventilation: maximizing natural ventilation and day-lighting (the end of deep plans), using passive design principles from the conceptual design stage and narrow, maximum 15 metres wide blocks. Operating all buildings with simple mixed-mode ventilation systems (partially natural ventilation) and automated opening windows for passive night purge (night flush cooling).

• Energy: developing an 'Energy Masterplan' right at the beginning, to map out the best strategy to harvest renewable energy sources and for positioning the BHK (*Blockheizkraftwerk*, a high-efficient gas/co-generation plant delivering district heating and energy, reusing waste heat).

• Materials and waste: using non-polluting materials and focusing on material flows, avoiding waste creation. Managing waste-streams in a better way, e.g. establishing waste recycling centres in the basement, where materials are sorted and separated; retaining rainwater run-offs in the district; water recycling through better urban water management systems.

• Public transport: reducing car-dependency through compact urban design and a strong focus on public transport, cycling and walkability, thereby minimizing the need to travel.

• Water and landscape: using greywater cycles and green roofs for rainwater capture by all buildings. Using wetlands and landscaping with a large water pond has been used around the buildings to recycle greywater and green spaces to ensure a comfortable urban micro-climate.

• Urban Regeneration: promoting the integration and reuse of existing buildings and brownfield sites within the existing built-up areas, thereby reducing urban sprawl and maintaining identity.

• Housing: supporting the provision of affordable housing solutions.

Creating sustainable transport systems that meet people's needs equitably and foster a healthy environment requires putting the automobile back into its useful place as a servant.
With a shift in priorities, cars can be part of a broad, balanced system in which public transport, cycling and walking are all viable options.
Marcia Lowe, 1990

For too long, sustainability has focused on 'green buildings'. At Potsdamer Platz we realized that to achieve sustainability targets, and in particular CO_2 reductions, we needed to better consider the urban scale and the district's supporting infrastructures, for instance by considering energy options at an early masterplanning stage. A series of targets were formulated during the design phase (see the five recommendations in the conclusion), supported by computer modeling to support informed decision-making:

• reducing operational energy demand,

• aiming for zero-carbon, de-carbonizing the energy supply, and

• reducing embodied energy and material transport.

Today, a decade after Potsdamer Platz's design phase, we can be much more ambitious about achieving better outcomes concerning 'Zero-Emissions - Zero-Waste' concepts, and concerning the social inclusion of all communities and residents. Most of the above mentioned concepts can be recommended for reuse at the Zhenru Urban Sub-Centre. In the last few years, more generic, universal building typologies have (re)emerged, in order to improve the longevity and flexibility of buildings. Simply by designing buildings that are fit for use for 60 years, instead of only for 30 years, helps to achieve environmental sustainability and significantly reduce greenhouse gas emissions. Flexible building typologies are the pathway to better longevity of buildings, making them more robust and adaptable to user changes.

Vibrant cities are highly complex and often messy places, and one of the prime principles for achieving vibrancy is to avoid the creation of mono-functional structures. Four types of preferred developments for sub-centres have emerged:
• Redevelopment of brownfield sites (instead of greenfield or greyfield), in central strategic locations, e.g. docklands, former industrial sites, military barracks – often urban waterfronts.
• Densification through urban infill, for the creation of new public space continuity, carefully inserted into the existing urban fabric.
• Intensification around transport nodes: more compact, transit-oriented developments.
• Retrofitting the existing city (instead of demolition and re-development), maximizing its mixed-use character and maintaining its existing community ties. The careful transformation through incremental steps, maintaining the identity and character of the place.

A series of interesting brownfield site regeneration and urban infill projects have been realized in China recently:
• In Wuhan: Brownfield and mixed-use development in the Wangjiadun Business District.
• In Harbin: Aijian New Town – Harbin Carriage Factory and Daowai Historical District Regeneration.
• In Shanghai: The two creative industries parks: `1933 Slaughterhouse' and `M50 Shanghai No. 12 Wool Mill' redevelopments, both located along an inner-city creek. (See: www.1933-shanghai.com and www.m50.com.cn)

The Potsdamer Platz development is not without critical voices. For instance, in his excellent essay, Dieter Hassenpflug explores the notion of the re-discovered *Europäische Stadt. Mythos und Wirklichkeit* (The European Town: Myths and Reality) and asks whether the European town model, such as Potsdamer Platz, could become a valuable example for global (especially Chinese) urban development or – as is more likely – if these cities are at risk of following the less-appropriate trend of the North American city model. (Hassenpflug, 2000)

Introducing the planning of Zhenru Urban Sub-Centre in Shanghai
Zhenru Urban Sub-Centre is one of the four new, large urban sub-centres of Shanghai. In the project brochure 'Shanghai Zhenru Subcenter', published in 2008 by Shanghai Zhenru

Subcenter Development Construction Investment Co. (a semi-public company), the project is introduced as 'Zhenru is Shanghai's last Subcenter, a Green Business District in complaisance with world-class green construction criteria, taking service industry as pillar industry, making full use of its location advantage as gateway to the Jangtze River Delta, to drive the CBD's sustainable development'. It continues in the marketing jargon: 'With the completion of the other three new subcenters, namely Xu Jiahui, Hua Mu and Jiang Wan-Wu Jiao Chang, how will Zhenru present itself as the last subcenter? It will be a model for Green City build-up, including the north-western transport hub, by adopting the standards for building a world-class e-friendly city in development, learning from many cities worldwide prestigious in preserving the ecological system and leveraging fully our own conditions and strengths, we will step onto a high stage for building an ecological city.' (sic). The City of Shanghai's main objectives are to optimize the distribution of urban space and to modernize the city's infrastructure (e.g. a major upgrade of the railway network).

Zhenru Urban Sub-Centre is one of Shanghai's most ambitious projects, with a site area of 6.2 sq kilometres, and therefore significantly larger than the Potsdamer Platz site (around 10 times). In contrast to Berlin, the development speed of Shanghai has been breathtaking. In 1980, Shanghai city had only 112 buildings taller than eight storeys, in 2009 there were over 13,000 buildings taller than eight storeys. The scale and pace of change and the level of ambition are quite extraordinary. The Chinese government has been reluctant for some time to fully commit to specific goals for emission cuts. In August 2009, China, for the first time, made public its target to cut greenhouse gas emissions by 2050 – the latest sign that the world's largest emitter wanted to make a green leap forward under a new agenda. A recent report by the Energy Research Institute and the Chinese State Council Development Research Centre even formulates that "it is expected policies will ensure greenhouse gas emissions of China to peak around 2030." (Report released Aug. 2009). This indicates that China will step-up policies for its urbanization process to curtail emissions growth and push the adoption of more green technology. China is now committed to transforming itself into a world leader in renewable energy industries. China already makes over a third of the world's solar cells and will soon unveil the world's first mass-produced electric car. The country has already become the largest market in the world for wind turbines. (Data: China Cleantech 2009)

Despite all this, the environmental impact of Zhenru sub-centre is likely to be immense. In addition, getting the usage mix right for the 6 million sq m floor area of the new sub-centre will be a huge challenge given its ambitious standards. Obviously, this new centre will need to be different from the Pudong New Area sub-centre in its mix of functions and ambience. Therefore, the government has suggested that it be more of a technological, industrial, logistic centre and service park (see also report by Shanghai Putuo District Government, 2008). The central business district has always contained the 'higher-level' functions of a city, for instance its cultural and administrative functions and its public green space for recreation. It is now necessary to think in terms of more than one core centre for the city; we cannot continue to flirt with the romantic idea that everything can be squeezed into one single centre.

The pivotal book by Manuel Castells, 'Network City: The Rise of the Network Society' (1996), has had an immense effect on how we understand and plan our city centres today. The end of the `object' has been proclaimed by many, in parallel with the rise of the `IT network'. There is clearly a movement away from mono-centric structures, towards polycentric cities. The `Network City' has emerged. The word `centre', of course, still implies a mono-centric organization; it indicates that a city or part of a city is organized in a hierarchical form. The use of the term `cluster' would be much better to describe a polycentric network system. Wouldn't the term *Zhenru City Cluster* be more appropriate?

The Network (`Networked') City: reinventing entire neighbourhoods

A new type of city is emerging worldwide: the *Network City*. We now find urban ag-glomerations the size of entire metropolitan regions, which may only with difficulty be recognized as cities. These agglomerations correspond to new social formations in a very direct manner, providing habitation for a more and more individualized, inter-connected society. The danger is a dramatically forced urbanization of the landscape without any urban qualities, cities without good public spaces, one-dimensional and lacking the rich complexity that cities always require in order to be vibrant. In this scenario, cities with traditionally centralized urban forms, through improved communication technologies, are increasingly linking with surrounding centres to create highly networked inter-linked met-ropolitan regions. As John Worthington points out, 'it appears that the twenty-first century city is a city of paradox: It has points of intense concentration whilst also being dispersed, forming a low-density city in a high-density (data) landscape.' (Worthington, 2009)

From the inclusive city, we have moved to exclusive enclaves. Joel Garreau, in 'Edge City', describes these emerging (sub-)urban centres, growing around transport intersections, where land is available to support new combinations of functions, such as retail, offices, education, services, logistics and leisure. These clusters are very much real estate market driven, invariably happening despite the planners. Location takes on a new significance in this dispersed, multi- or polycentred city. Worthington noted that significant places in the wider conurbation are 'growing at locations that are, simultaneously:

Hubs: Interchanges with different modes and levels (local, regional, international) of transport.
Nodes: Mix of functions – with overlapping functions over at least sixteen hours.
Places: Memorable gateways – accommodating a distinctive range of symbiotic functions.' (Worthington, 2009)

Faced with these paradoxes, planning has tended to focus on reinforcing traditional cen-tres. The discourse has been framed as a choice between centre or periphery, rather than recognizing it can be both central *and* dispersed, each finding their appropriate strengths, linked within a networked conurbation. Bill Mitchell puts this paradox succinctly in `City of Bits', when he notes: `We will gravitate to settings that offer particular cultural, scenic and climatic attractions... Sometimes we will network to avoid going places. But sometimes still, we will go places to network'. (Mitchell, 1996) These new centres, unlike traditional urban cores which have grown organically with a diverse mix of activities, are often uniform in their offering and are conceived of as precisely functional 'machines' to maximize the customer experience and the financial return to the operator. The new sub-centres are a reflection of the experience economy. The dilemma is that these 'instant environments' at the periphery, with their focus on efficiency, functionality and convenience, have frequently lost the chance encounters and unplanned authenticity of the experience they are aiming to create (as was pointed out previously by Smiley and Robbins, 2002). These super functional, themed locations have lost the qualities they set out to achieve. The public culture of a city is always strongly connected with the field and character of the public space the city provides. How can such differentiation be fully anticipated by the designer in the planning phase?

Newly built urban sub-centres run the danger of being too market driven rather than user led, designed to maximize efficiency and be 'over functionalized' within a semi-public co-coon. Maarten Hajer and the urban sociologist Arnold Reijndorp, in their essay 'In Search of New Public Domain', perceptively describe the new semi-public spaces and identify the need for a new language. (Hajer and Reijndorp, 2004) They describe these new places as `a consumer commodity and the urban field as an archipelago of enclaves.'

Fig. 8 a, b: Architect's impressions of the proposal for the new Zhenru Sub-Centre, to be built in Shanghai's northwest. It is one of the four new, large urban sub-centres of Shanghai, consisting of 6 million sq m floor area. Image b shows the central axis, the space between the flanking high-rise buildings; proposal for the new Zhenru Sub-Centre in Shanghai, where an entire neighbourhood is reinvented from scratch. (Images: Courtesy Zhenru Development Corporation, 2008) Today, urban designers understand that a purely pedestrianized city doesn't work and is not practical; the electro-car can be part of the urban, mixed-use environment; however, the automobile has to play a less important role in the city of the future.

To overcome the lack of space and diminishing car accessibility in traditional cities, more and more businesses are moving to the urban periphery or are locating along infrastructure routes and corridors. A recent report by VROM (the Dutch Ministry for Planning and Housing, 2004) concludes 'the development into a network society is evidenced spatially by the emergence of new urban networks; no longer is everything centred around one city or one conurbation. Instead, various sub-centres are developing and citizens are zigzagging across greater distances based on their individual choices and desires.' The Randstad region in the Netherlands, for instance, has become such a laboratory for emerging urban nodes, with Schiphol Airport and its surrounding sites arguably one of the main urban nodes. The Randstad and the Ruhr metropolitan region in Germany are now both highly urbanized, polycentric networks of urban density clusters with a total population higher than that of Greater Paris.

The challenge for today's urban designers, perhaps, is to understand the attributes of these peripheral nodes, to give meaning to both centre and periphery, and to offer coherence to the journey between the points. New typologies, such as `urban sub-centres', are continuing to emerge, while existing nodes will need further intensification, urban infill and retrofitting. Both, if they are to become embedded in the community, will require intelligent programming (briefing) and imaginative urban design (strategy).

The *Zhenru Declaration for Green Environment* (part of the report by Shanghai Putuo District, 2008) was an important step in the right direction for Shanghai's last sub-centre. It will be important to further consider:

• new criteria for vision, construction and urban management,

• integration and connectivity as a driver,

• urban governance and social inclusion.

We need to connect our systems; however, we have very little time to do so as our fossilized regulations prevent us from doing things differently. It is not a technical crisis; most of the time, the issue is institutional and requires behavioural change. To ensure authenticity, rather than having a themed *Disneyesque* environment, we should search for a dominant culture around which informal sub-cultures can flourish. Worthington suggests `more flexible frameworks that set infrastructure, typologies and value systems, within which a programme of built projects and events can unfold, are superseding *Masterplans* as blueprints.' The *Networked City* offers a challenging canvas for urban designers.

Fig. 9 a, b: Is this an appropriate response to `tropical urbanism'? The site: Site preparations have started for the new Zhenru Urban Sub-Centre in Shanghai's north-western area. Model photo: The early conceptual masterplan is now in the phase of revision. An International Advisory Panel has been established, including urban designers Qingyun Ma, Ralph Lerner and Steffen Lehmann. (Photos by the author: July 2009)

Some recommendations and strategies for re-conceptualizing urban sub-centres
UNESCO, the UN nodal organization for education, science, culture and architecture, has made urban sustainability a key topic in its development oriented activities, and has launched an initiative to address the increasing concern of non-sustainable urbanization, which currently occurs too often in the Asia-Pacific Region. From the United Nations' side, there has always been a strong interest in holistic approaches and a focus on social sustainability. The Asia-Pacific is a region of rapid change, cultural alienation and environmental crisis, with a threatening divide between city and countryside. In the face of mounting challenges, there is a need to identify effective strategies and to propose practical solutions to support sustainable urban development based on the conditions specific to each area of the region and characterized by great diversity in terms of economy, politics, culture, climate and the natural environment. We need innovative, interdisciplinary planning methodologies for sustainable urban growth. To be able to house the growing urban population, there is an urgent need to build more energy-efficient cities and neighbourhoods based on renewable energy sources. Sustainable Cities was a key theme of the UNESCO Chair's platform, especially ahead of the UN's Climate Change Conference in Copenhagen in December 2009. The UNESCO Chair promoted binding emissions targets and the message 'let's get started', and that progressive change will lead to ever greater change. There are many examples of increasing worldwide market demand for 'green' architecture for commercial offices and the existing commercial building stock. There is a direct link between climate change and urbanization, the design of buildings, districts (such as urban sub-centres) and cities. The global environmental crisis is, in large, tied to the cities we live in.

Conclusion and five recommendations from the Berlin case
Aspiring to become (again) a *World City*, Shanghai has mapped out a new ambitious plan to transform the city through large-scale reurbanization into an international economic and trade centre. However, the city's explosive growth in such a short time has 'mainly been the result of ad hoc decisions by different bodies with divergent interests.' (Chen and Hu, 2009) The challenge today is to bring the over-technicalized and over-socialized responses together, to manage the transition of urban infrastructure to new decentralized infrastructure, and to the Zhenru masterplan. To meet its ambitious goals – a 20 per cent increase in energy productivity and a 10 per cent decrease in emissions compared to 2005 levels by the end of 2010 – China will need to rely on strong national policies, like the so-called 'green stimulus package'. It will also require the determination and leadership of the officials that oversee the country's ferocious, unprecedented urbanization – China's mayors and planning directors in the municipalities. Zhenru Sub-Centre is a major urban development project for Shanghai at a time when China is rethinking ways to develop its cities. After a period of strong interest in the formal qualities of new prestige projects, there is now a growing interest in combining practical and efficient planning layout with renewable energy technologies that both passively and actively reduce the energy consumption of the buildings, reducing the overall emissions of new developments. Zhenru Sub-Centre is currently under construction and the author was asked to make recommendations for its

sustainable development, based on his experiences from the Potsdamer Platz development. Such large-scale projects and new quarters, once finished, can be strangely discomforting due to their newness, semi-private corporate sphere and lack of grown authenticity. The community needs responsive spaces for appropriation – something often forgotten or lost in the predetermined vision of new city centres. New technologies and concepts need always to be evaluated and judged on their appropriateness to the place. In general, great districts and city centres are never the result of one single author or designer; they are the outcome of multiple authors and a diversity of design concepts.

Holistic strategies and integrated approaches to urban development

The following are five recommendations for the design of new sub-centres to ensure they deliver economically, socially and environmentally sustainable outcomes:

1 – Develop compact urban form at transport nodes: a resilient network

Land use, planning and design controls, together with building codes, require more consist application by all levels of government to ensure that housing location and types deliver a compact urban form with higher densities around transport networks. This will require an integrated framework cascading from national to district government levels, with rigorous implementation. I dare to argue that we still have not seen a convincing urban planning model fully appropriate for the tropical, humid city, such as Shanghai. There is a danger of increasing density too much and changing land-cover through development, thus reducing natural urban ventilation and increasing the risk of the *Urban Heat Island* effect. A balance is necessary (e.g. the Hong Kong government had to develop the *Air-Ventilation Assessment System*, adopted in 2008, with the aim of creating better airflow and breezeway corridors). The type of hyper-tall urban environment, as found in Hong Kong, is an extreme, relatively rare case where many of the sidewalk levels are shaded from direct sunlight during most daylight hours. Trying to fix the impact of overdevelopment is very difficult. Hong Kong is now engaged in the identification of major air flow corridors which will receive special protection to ensure the remaining natural ventilation is not entirely lost to overdevelopment. We need to favour inner urban diversity and density, including the reinvigoration of existing inner urban shops, schools and community facilities, and developments should favour boulevards and transport corridors, in support of public transport and walkable cities. Eco-districts include the integration of agricultural fields into the city for urban farming – from allotment and community gardens, to food boulevards, to urban neighbourhood farms. The advantage of urban agriculture is a local, short food supply and the reuse of nutrients from the urban metabolism (nutrient recycling). (Viljoen, 2005)

2 – Evolve towards `eco-infrastructure', implemented in unison with climate responsive built form

Currently, legislation discourages an integrated precinct resource management. Regulations need to be changed to allow distributed renewable energy networks and non-traditional water supply systems to be implemented. It is important to develop nationally recognized equitable contracts for ESCo, energy and water supply services that cover all stakeholders, to avoid transactional cost issues. Precinct prototyping of smart grid systems is an immediate need due to the lead-time, and they must be incentivized. Methods for assessing climate change resilience must be implemented by district regulations. Current policy tools, such as the LEED, CASBEE, GreenStar, or BREEAM assessment tools, must be used to affect landscape design, site resilience and resource management.

De-carbonizing the energy supply on the district scale is a necessity. Low-emission energy generation technologies can turn city districts and sub-centres themselves into powerstations, where energy is generated close to the point of consumption. Localized energy generation using renewable energy sources (solar, wind, biomass, geothermal) and complemented by distributed heating and cooling systems, has the potential to reduce the built environment's energy demand and emissions. Such decentralized, distributed systems, where every citizen can generate the energy they need, will eliminate transmission losses and transmission costs (which always occur with a large grid and inefficient base-load powerstations) for the local consumer. The concept works for both existing and new buildings. Small power generators are positioned within communities to provide electricity for local consumption, and the waste heat they produce is captured for co-generation (for CHP; or for tri-generation, when waste heat also produces chilled water for cooling). It is also used for space conditioning via a local district heating or district cooling system. New exergy principles look at capturing and harvesting waste heat and wastewater streams, and the strategic arrangement of programmes within mixed-use urban blocks can lead to the unleashing of such unused energy potential. Urban greenery can be used to reduce and mitigate against the Urban Heat Island effect.

3 – Develop a policy pathway to zero-carbon and zero-waste: targets that are more ambitious

A trajectory to a de-carbonized energy supply for Zhenru Sub-Centre needs to be established. This should involve long-term overall targets, together with medium and short-term targets, subdivided into sectoral responsibilities. Evolving policy and regulatory frameworks need to reflect this trajectory. Given the relatively long life of buildings, their targets (for both refurbished and newly built urban developments) need to reflect their longer-term contributions to the trajectory (buildings that last longer). Assessment ratings should consider the requisite energy standards, with zero-carbon emissions attracting the highest rating.

4 – Develop a holistic pathway to climate-adaptive buildings

A clear vision of what constitutes a climate adaptable and resilient building needs to be established, with appropriate overall regional variations. These adaptive measures need to be embedded within assessment tools and be progressively introduced, as experience grows, into the regulatory framework. Examples of such measures (suitably quantified) might include:

• Extending the life of buildings, giving them the ability to accept change of uses ('long life, loose fit'). Among other aspects this impacts on depth and massing of buildings.

• Using thermal mass (heat storing) materials into building structures.

• Operating buildings completely passively (without any energy consuming systems operating) for large proportions of the year.

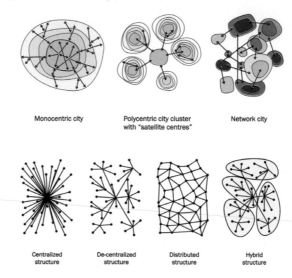

Monocentric city	Polycentric city cluster with "satellite centres"	Network city

Centralized structure	De-centralized structure	Distributed structure	Hybrid structure

Fig. 10: Different city structures: monocentric, polycentric and nnetwork city. The unique connectivity patterns, scale and spatial characteristic make up individual experiences of cities and public space networks. (top: Chr. de Portzamparc. Below: after P. Rand)

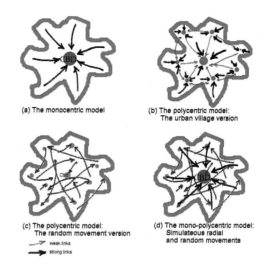

(a) The monocentric model

(b) The polycentric model: The urban village version

(c) The polycentric model: The random movement version

----▷ weak links
━━▶ strong links

(d) The mono-polycentric model: Simulateous radial and random movements

Fig. 11: Diagram: Schematic representation of trip patterns within monocentric and polycentric metropolitan areas. (Diagram: Courtesy Alain Bertaud, 2003). (a) The `classical monocentric' model has a single strong centre (CBD) with a high concentration of jobs. (b) In the `urban village' model, people can walk or cycle to work, even if its a large metropolis. However, this model is difficult to achieve. (c) In the `polycentric' model there is not one dominant centre, but sub-centres. (d) The `composite model' has a dominant centre and some sub-centres.

• Reducing the volume of materials needed by buildings, particularly the frequently re-placed components. Urban Heat Island reduction measures are required to allow reduced energy consumption in building systems (electric vehicles, transport modal switching, extensive urban vegetation to mitigate UHI, and associated urban rainwater retention).

5 – Built environment education, training and research must take *climate change mitigation and adaptation* as a main intent

The building industry is currently not trained to renovate existing buildings into new low carbon and climate adaptable buildings, nor is it trained to deliver new ones. In addition, professional education does not sufficiently prioritize, or effectively deliver, curricula that empower graduates to shape a zero-carbon and climate adaptable urban environment. Reform and expansion of built environment education and training with climate change mitigation and adaptation as its main intent must occur within the next five to ten years. Potsdamer Platz was at a time when architects and planners started to become aware of this; Zhenru Sub-Centre is happening ten years later and there has been a huge shift in awareness over this period.

Mass industry re-training over the next ten years is required to provide the necessary leadership and the capacity to engage in the mass renovation of existing buildings. Intensified interdisciplinary research to deliver the framework for the transition to a zero-carbon building sector is necessary. Much of our housing and workplace models (existing stock and current production) are inadequate and repeat out-dated models instead of dealing with the immense challenges we face. Research with a focus on future-proofing urban design, architecture and the entire building sector, and celebrating diversity, is needed. Therefore, research has to identify best practice and its application in a holistic way, developing performance-based principles for compact urban form, energy-effective buildings and more flexible, adaptable building typologies, in order to re-conceptualize a new generation of housing and workplaces. Better methodologies for measuring sustainability, resource management and material flows need to be researched and developed.

Changing Chinese and Indian cities: from vernacular to global in 10 years

In Chinese and Indian society, there is an expanding middle class with new requirements and expectations what the city has to be like and to offer. However, the fast urbanization process is a threat to unique local qualities and character: what often emerges, after massive demolition of traditional buildings and districts, is an architecture of 'non-places', which communicates a soul-less global image that has become the basis of much of Asia's rapid urbanization, disregarding the local and everyday life. For instance, Shanghai's Pudong district has become the symbol of China's spectacular urban revolution, and this process is accompanied with global events, such as the Beijing Olympics (2008) or the Shanghai World Expo (2010); and Shenzen, the new 'Instant City' that has grown from village size to 9 million people in only twenty years, is a city devoid of any local character, representing Rem Koolhaas' 'Generic City'. It becomes clear, with rapid urbanization, it's essential to design public spaces that are more local in their character, allowing a high level of community participation and urban governance.

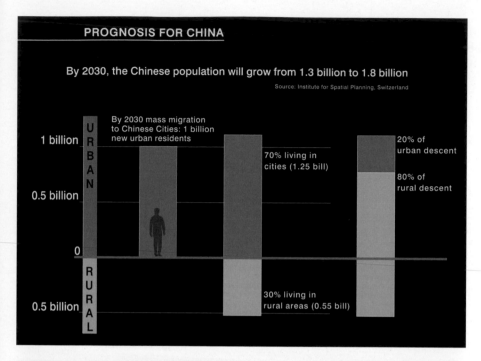

PROGNOSIS FOR CHINA

By 2030, the Chinese population will grow from 1.3 billion to 1.8 billion

Source: Institute for Spatial Planning, Switzerland

1 billion

URBAN

By 2030 mass migration to Chinese Cities: 1 billion new urban residents

70% living in cities (1.25 bill)

20% of urban descent

80% of rural descent

0.5 billion

0

0.5 billion

RURAL

30% living in rural areas (0.55 bill)

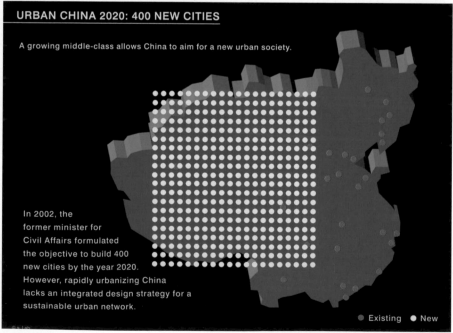

URBAN CHINA 2020: 400 NEW CITIES

A growing middle-class allows China to aim for a new urban society.

In 2002, the former minister for Civil Affairs formulated the objective to build 400 new cities by the year 2020. However, rapidly urbanizing China lacks an integrated design strategy for a sustainable urban network.

● Existing ● New

China's rapid urbanization started around 1978. Top: A prognosis indicates that with mass migration from rural to urban China could see up to 1 billion new urban residents by 2030. This will require the densification and retrofitting of existing Chinese cities and, in addition, to building up to 400 new cities for the new urban residents within the next two decades. Where will these cities be located?

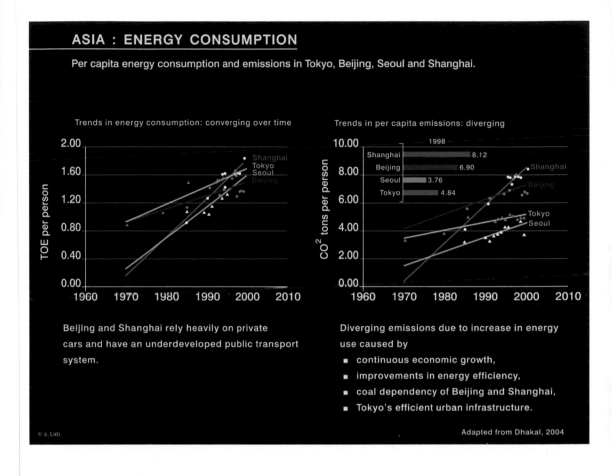

ASIA : ENERGY CONSUMPTION

Per capita energy consumption and emissions in Tokyo, Beijing, Seoul and Shanghai.

Trends in energy consumption: converging over time

Trends in per capita emissions: diverging

Beijing and Shanghai rely heavily on private cars and have an underdeveloped public transport system.

Diverging emissions due to increase in energy use caused by

- continuous economic growth,
- improvements in energy efficiency,
- coal dependency of Beijing and Shanghai,
- Tokyo's efficient urban infrastructure.

© s_Lab

Adapted from Dhakal, 2004

China's rapid development

In only the last ten years, China has emerged as the new dominant, urbanized world power. There are now over 110 cities with more than 1 million inhabitants. China is placed in a unique position in history, to define and shape new forward-thinking ideas of urbanization that do not simply repeat the mistakes of the 20th-century Western industrialized world. It is widely acknowledged that the majority of global emissions has previously been caused by, and are the responsibility of, the developed Western nations. Unfortunately, this cannot be undone. However, China has now the opportunity to act quickly, with bold and visionary policies, to build an energy-efficient, low-carbon economy and to realize true eco-cities and eco-districts. It is estimated that China's CO_2 emissions will have to peak by 2025 to avoid catastrophic consequences. The Chinese government's 'White Paper on China's Policies and Actions on Climate Change' (published in 2008) outlines substantial efforts to improve energy-efficiency and to reduce emissions. In 2009, China started to actively promote sustainable economic development and commit to greenhouse gas emissions reductions, focusing on specific industrial sectors, urbanization, transport systems and energy transformation. The aim is to move away from conventional fossil-fuel (mostly coal-burning) power generation and towards the increasing use of renewable energy sources and energy conservation measures. It is estimated that by 2012, China will be the world's largest windpower nation.

A comparison of energy consumption and emissions of 4 Asian mega-cities: Tokyo, Seoul, Beijing and Shanghai. The energy consumption of all cities has been rapidly converging over the last 40 years; however, due to a lack of efficient public transport, Shanghai and Beijing are now causing much larger emissions than Tokyo and Seoul. (Diagram after: Dhakal, 2004)

Benefits of density and compactness as key issues

For hundreds of years, the search for the *Ideal City* has been a concern to many planners, architects and philosophers. Today, most urban designers agree that more compact, denser living is a more sustainable, and therefore 'ideal', way of living. However, it's important that the question of urban density is looked at closely and more research is conducted on this topic. Timothy Beatley and Mike Jenks have extensively researched the benefits and detriments of more dense, compact cities. They found that high-density cities encourage reduced transit through shorter trip lengths, since amenities are more closely located; and they encourage the use of public transport (thereby reducing transport energy costs and CO_2 emissions). The *Compact City* also increases efficiencies in urban infrastructure and services (through shorter distribution networks), reduces the spread of suburbs into precious agricultural land, and has, in general, the potential to support a higher quality of urban life. This is why many cities around the world have started to encourage, even require, higher densities in urban developments, as part of their growth management policy.

Density directly influences the urban climate. So, to what density should we build? Is the unorganized city (with its slowly grown, random street pattern) better and more livable than a grid-planned man-made city structure?

Density and Compact Communities

City blocks too close together shade each other – something only desirable in (sub)tropical cities such as Singapore, Manila or Bangkok. The urban design principles that apply to cities in hot, humid and tropical conditions (not only in South East Asia, but also to parts of Australia, India, Africa, US and Latin America) are obviously different from the urban design principles in temperate climates.

As Bay and Ong have pointed out, the effects of urban canyons, natural ventilation and heat entrapment in the city are different for the tropics: 'While sunlight is welcome in the temperate city and buildings are set back to allow sunlight to penetrate to the road level, shade is preferred in the tropics; (…) however, more wind and ventilation are always welcome in the tropical city.' (Bay and Ong, 2006). In tropical conditions we want to create shade and over-shading between buildings, as long as we ensure sufficient day-lighting and efficient natural ventilation of the spaces between the buildings.

The redevelopment of the existing city and the regeneration of formerly industrially used sites and docklands (the careful redevelopment of disused urban brownfield sites) are basic principles of sustainable urban development.

Fig. 1: Hong Kong is already a city of extremely high density (some cities in India are more dense). In addition, informal settlements have been built in the form of roof slums, emerging on top of numerous public housing estates from the 1950s. Entire two-storey 'roof villages' have grown on the unused roof space, thus further densifying the city. The occupants of these informal habitats are mainly immigrant workers from central China or Pakistan. Similar roof slums can be found in Cairo, another fast-growing city where inner-city housing is very expensive. (Photo: S. Canham, 2009)

Green urban density: Many findings indicate that a denser, more compact city is a better city.
The compact city with five to seven stories represents the optimum use of space and, in combination with efficient public transport, forms transit-oriented developments as highly serviced urban activity centres. So, what about the social acceptability of higher densities?

Conventional patterns of urban development (that have frequently led to suburbs with lower densities and greater infrastructure costs) are unlikely to remain economically feasible, as the greater dispersion of activity centres leads to increased automobile dependence. The necessary technical infrastructure and the provision of local public transport can only be guaranteed in densely populated areas. Therefore, it is imperative to ensure appropriate urban densities, meaning when the distances to facilities are short enough for pedestrians and there is enough purchasing power concentrated in one area to ensure effective mixed-use functions (e.g. retail facilities) and concentration of urban diversity. Low density suburbs are incapable of sustaining a public transport infrastructure. Densification and intensification is the key. Densification through mixed-use urban infill is a good strategy, and no inner-city site is too small for such new architecture. Density is related to mixed uses. However, as Gissen notes, 'there is no one formula for a mix of culture and technology that makes cities vibrant and more liveable.' (Gissen, 2003)

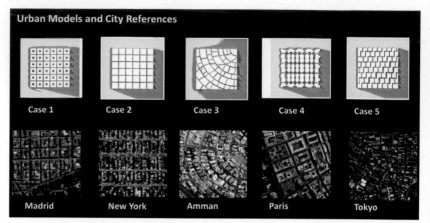

Urban Models and City References

| Case 1 | Case 2 | Case 3 | Case 4 | Case 5 |

| Madrid | New York | Amman | Paris | Tokyo |

Fig. 2: Diagram: Different urban structures compared (Diagram: Courtesy WSP, 2008). Low density is seen as principal contributor to CO2 emissions, while compact development fosters less driving.

The *Low-to-No-Carbon City* (LTNCC_city)

Clearly, the intensified and densified city district with a mix of uses on the neighbourhood scale is the way to arrive at a more sustainable city form. According to researchers from Michael Breheney to Jan Gehl and Elizabeth Brown, the *Compact City* with five to seven stories offers a wide series of benefits, such as (Breheney, 1992; Gehl, 2000; Brown, 2000):

- greater scope for walking and cycling
- reduced greenhouse gas emission
- reduced need to travel
- improved public transport use
- improved energy efficiencies
- reduced social segregation
- better job opportunities for the lower skilled
- better access to facilities
- increased opportunities for social interaction and contacts, and
- lower death rate from mental illness and depression.

The researchers conclude in their findings that urban compactness (the *Compact City*) is positive in several respects in terms of social equity and better mix of land uses. However, they also point towards the risks: poorly planned and badly managed density, leading to overcrowded apartments, of them being too compressed, with dark and over-furnished living spaces and a loss of privacy; a lack of affordable housing (as urban infill frequently leads to up-market developments); and the loss of greenery (the effective protection of green space and the development of new housing typologies, with green roofs and private and public outdoor spaces is necessary). As we move towards higher densities, it becomes a necessity that innovative design solutions for new, denser housing typologies are developed to incorporate sufficient privacy and living space, as well as integrating green space and good public space. While intensification can, if not carefully managed, lead to loss of green space, the urban designer can avoid such threats by making landscaping and the public domain important elements of the development from the outset, and by adhering to policies that are more prescriptive about standards of public space.

Green density and urban livability: the city's spatial structure matters

The efficiency of a city's spatial structure has a significant impact on urban livability and quality of life. Urban density is a key factor in determining urban livability. Cities' urban structures are rarely the result of design considerations; rather they are shaped by economic forces. The spatial structure of a city is determined by the spatial distribution of the population (the profile of population densities) and the pattern of daily trips. Alain Bertaud argues that these factors are a result of government policies and strategies (e.g. land use regulations regarding floor space ratio, controls of supply of land, infrastructure investment, effectiveness of public transport, planning of road widths, etc), the real estate market and cultural preferences. (Bertaud, 2003) Overall, urban intensification represents the most sustainable use of land, protecting rural and agricultural land from sprawling suburbs. The protection of the city's greenbelt levers developments towards brownfield sites and derelict land within the growth boundary, therefore contributing to urban regeneration and the vibrancy of the city. John Gray puts it this way: `More than ever the world requires housing that costs little to make and maintain, thereby reducing expenditure on resources as well as conserving diminishing resources. Crucially, it also means a wider range of flexible housing models to allow for change in use over the life of the buildings and different types of occupancy.' (Gray, 2010)

	8 separate houses (ground floor plus basement)	2 terraces of 4 houses (ground floor plus basement)	block of 8 flats (2 storeys plus basement)
Site area	100 %	70 %	34 %
Envelope surface area	100 %	74 %	35 %
Heating energy	100 %	89 %	68 %
Construction costs	100 %	87 %	58 %

Fig. 3: Diagram: Comparison of surface area, heating energy consumed and construction costs for eight housing units, in different configurations: eight separate houses, two terraces (row houses) of four houses each; and a block of eight flats. (Diagram: Courtesy H. R. Preisig, Zurich, in: Oekologische Baukompetenz, 1999) *Urban infill* is used to fill in the city's gaps left by demolition, where buildings are squeezed into narrow plots, which were previously considered unsuitable for development.

Kirk Shanks has intensively researched and measured low-energy housing designs in the UK and Ireland. He argues in support of increasing densities and the compact city model, that `living near to one's place of work and having all the social and functional requirements of modern life on the doorstep is intrinsically more sustainable than the high carbon, car intensive lifestyles inherent in edge-of-city suburban housing developments.

City centre living patterns not only reduce the carbon footprint of individuals and therefore housing communities, but more importantly help to reinforce the complex urban cultures ingrained in the historical compact city.' (Shanks, 2010) In a similar vein, urban designer Simon Guy argues that the inputs of resources and outputs of waste of the `Self-Reliant City' model are closely linked, since this model is based on circular urban metabolism. The sphere of influence is hereby reduced to an appropriate bio-region within which resources flow, and consumption and waste flows can be minimized and better managed. Guy notes that in the `Self-Reliant City' model, `decision making is shifted towards more localized and community-based styles and residents are more closely involved in a transition from centralized to decentralized technologies.' (Guy, 2000)

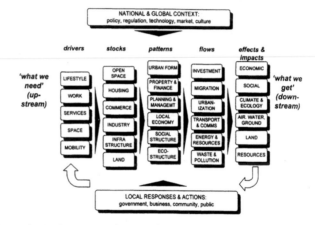

Fig. 4: Diagram showing the comparison between `what we need' and `what we get', within the complex dependencies between the national/global context and the need for local responses and actions. (Diagram: Courtesy Joe Ravetz, Manchester, 2000)

The green roof as 5th facade and field of city expansion

The continuous demand for development land can be met by the increased reuse of brownfield properties and derelict land that has been abandoned due to heavy industry moving away or closing down. While many of these brownfield sites have deteriorated or are contaminated, one of the first priorities of environmental and spatial planning based on green urbanism is the rehabilitation and redevelopment of brownfield sites to find appropriate new uses for them (therefore avoiding the further expansion of the urban footprint).

Given the need for urban heat island mitigation and despite the many benefits of green, cool roofs, it is hard to understand why we do not see more use of rooftop gardens. For instance, in a warm or hot climate, green roofs are proven to provide significant reductions to the urban heat island effect. They insulate and reduce the energy demands of the building, aid storm water management and the collection of rainwater, provide important extensions to habitat, as well as providing social and amenity value to the building's users. Urban parks are developing along this path; much urban design is about creating new models for park systems, characterized by an innovative intertwining of natural and designed environments.

In this regard, Japanese architect Toyo Ito notes that 'architectural and urban space will have to increasingly relate to, and integrate with, the natural world. In this world, the architect will be able to create buildings that serve many different functions reflecting the 21st-century condition where living, working, and playing are all intermingled,' Ito predicts. (Ito, 2009)

It is necessary to develop a database for 'international best practice in sustainable urban development', a holistic and systematic evaluation framework, to compare the different urban models and case studies.

Density and compactness: preserving agricultural land

Future development will need to occur in the city centre, with compact typologies between four and seven storeys high, with a very high quality design of street frontage at the pedestrian level, and a focus on inner-city brownfield sites. Keeping within the recognized footprint of the city and establishing strict growth boundaries can ensure that no more farmland and precious biodiversity is lost to the suburbs, to the sprawl of detached bungalows and other low-density, car-dependent, mono-functional development. Preserving farmland, forests and open landscape from such unsustainable development is crucial for food security and recreational aspects. In regard to the Australian suburbanization and its consequences, the City of Melbourne urban planning director Rob Adams noted: 'The cost of locating more and more people on city fringes is of serious concern. Many people living in these suburbs suffer real financial difficulties. While the house and land package may initially come with an attractive price, the suburb residents will spend up to 25 per cent of their income for getting to and from work and getting the milk. Our research shows that locating 1000 houses on a city fringe costs $300 million more over 50 years than the same number of houses in existing areas. While $85 million of that difference in cost is the hard infrastructure, the main part is the impost of people living in the suburbs in terms of the lifestyle they have chosen and things they have not factored in when buying the house, such as: one-and-a-half hours commuting in a car instead of walking, and the issues of health and obesity; and the rising cost of petrol to get to work.' (Rob Adams, in an interview, 2009)

Very dense high-rise cities are not the best option. Medium density, compact developments as 'green TODs' are the preferred development option and would be a useful model for much of China's urbanization.

Medium-rise, high-density: learning to live in more compact communities

Urban districts have a significant complexity about them and there we need to accumulate knowledge and expertise in urban governance issues for the compact city. It is therefore necessary to test and develop new urban patterns and typologies for compact precincts, where all energy, water and waste systems are integrated, and the potential for renewable energy and greenery is maximized. All over the world, new models of high-density housing developments are being explored, where buildings and greenery, and public and private spaces are convincingly being combined and intertwined. Grouping together several units in a simple, compact volume can offer considerable environmental and economic benefits. As the examples in Chapter 2 illustrate, Germany, Austria and Scandinavia have been, since the 1990s, leading the way in low energy housing design, especially with the development of the 'Passivhaus Standard' (energy requirement of a Passivhaus is a maximum 15 kWh/sqm p.a. for heating, with a total maximum energy demand of 120 kWh/sqm p.a.). However, developments like Freiburg-Vauban or Hannover-Kronsberg are usually considered to be part of the medium-density category, not in the high-density category; high-density buildings are more problematical as the requirements for good internal and external spaces often pose a serious challenge to the conflicting demands of compactness and access to greenery (for further research on the topic of residential density, see the work on high-density living by Edward Ng and Christian Schittich).

The city centre needs a rich mix of all types of inner-city uses: office buildings, hotels, department stores, university buildings, residential buildings, shops, cinemas, squares, good landscaping, and so on. The aim of a significant amount of new development is to get the right mix and balance between usage programme, scale and density to create a city centre with a compact but spatially complex model. This model will always rely heavily on public transport, and 'green TODs' are a good way of combining several of these criteria. Grouping residential units or townhouses together into compact volumes of around five to seven storeys in height – similar to the 19th-century 'compact city block' model found in Paris, Barcelona, Athens, Amsterdam or Berlin – would bring considerable environmental benefits, such as:
• smaller building envelopes, therefore less land use and less heat gain in summer;
• less materials used, therefore lower construction costs; and
• sharing fire walls, therefore reduced energy consumption and less heat loss in winter.

We have reached a tipping point, where our larger agenda of sustainable urban development requires the planning and urban design professions to take a key role in working to reduce patterns of high consumption and CO$_2$ emissions.

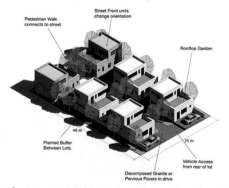

Fig. 5: Housing typologies for 'Nano City', India: 3-storey walk-ups with residential lane and stepping green roofs. (Image: Courtesy BgAP Group, Nazar Al Sayyad, Berkeley, 2006)

Compactness and density: the A/V ratio

The compactness of the urban shape of a development and its density ratio decide the efficiency of land use (a site, a natural area) and the resulting level of urban dispersion. For instance, if the development is more dispersed due to lower compactness and density, it results in a greater need for energy for infrastructure and movement of people and goods.

The A/V ratio is the ratio of the surface area of a building to the enclosed (heated/cooled) volume. The A/V ratio is an important factor in the calculation of energy consumption. Typical A/V ratio values vary from 0.4 for compact multi-storey buildings to 1.1 for inefficient, detached bungalows in suburbs. The more compact the urban form (with smaller facade surfaces), the more energy-efficient it is. There is a wide field between low-density suburbs (e.g. the US or Australian suburb, with less than 1,000 people per sq km) and the areas of high concentration that can be found in Asia (e.g. areas in Mumbai are even twice as dense as New York City, with far over 10,000 people per sq km); the densities of Paris, Berlin and Barcelona, in a range of 3,500 to 5,000 people per sq km, would be a good target.

Energy simulations have shown that multi-storey buildings can lead to reduced energy losses. More compact typologies, combined with higher densities and direct access to public transport (green TOD), allow for a high flexibility of choice in the energy supply system and for integrated energy concepts. For instance, the classical courtyard block typology is one of the most compact urban forms, with the smallest outside surfaces. The internal courtyards are quiet and protected from noise; hence natural ventilation through windows is possible even in noisy inner-city areas. The ideal compactness of the residential courtyard block makes common energy generation on the district-scale (using decentralized systems and small CHP plants) very attractive. Even within multi-storey apartment buildings we find a large variety in energy consumption between individual units. The climatic characteristics of individual units – such as solar gain or energy requirements for ventilation – depend to a high degree on the urban geometry of the building (for instance, is the building a linear slab type, or courtyard, or point tower typology?), as well as the orientation of the building and unit.

Cities where the residents don't need to drive much and efficient public transport is available have many advantages. For instance, in Australian cities, the need to drive from low density suburbs to inner-city workplaces rob the nation of $11.1 billion in lost time, environmental and social costs every year (data: IBM, 2010). Some conflicting demands, however, will need to be balanced through convincing design solutions. For instance, with increased densities there is always the danger of encountering the Urban Heat Island effect. Mitigation of the UHI effect is particularly important for large tropical and subtropical cities located in developing countries such as Bangkok, Jakarta or Hong Kong. The choice of materials (thermal mass), colour of surfaces (albedo reflective effect) and application of green roofs becomes essential.

Large-scale cultivation of algae for future energy and environmental solutions

Biological material for energy production, such as algae and seaweed, can be an important, inexpensive contribution to the low-emission city of the future. Seaweed (a macro-algae) is already used to produce bioplastics as material for the post-oil age. There are over 10,000 different types of algae, and they can be used to produce energy, nutrients for food, oil, algae-based fuel for aviation, and many other applications. Algae are amongst the fastest-growing organisms; they grow well in areas that are unsuitable for growing food, and therefore do not come into conflict with food production or conservation areas.

Lightweight rooftop extensions are a way forward to offer affordable inner-city housing (e.g. student housing) and activate the full site potential, without building on greenfield sites. Building the 'city above the city', it's important to apply only a minimum of additional loads to the existing structure. Left: Rooftop houses by DMA, South London (2008). Right: Ultralight extension by A4-Architects, Stuttgart (2007).

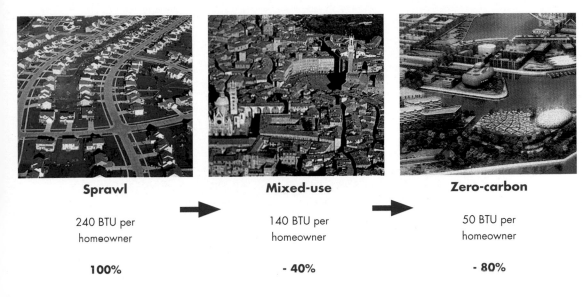

Sprawl

240 BTU per
homeowner

100%

Mixed-use

140 BTU per
homeowner

- 40%

Zero-carbon

50 BTU per
homeowner

- 80%

Transforming the city – achieving sustainable urban form

Diagram above: Transforming cities through CO_2-reduced districts and more compact urban form. Transforming banal sprawl to mixed-use compact urban form reduces the energy consumption by 40 per cent. Moving to zero-carbon models can bring further significant energy use reductions (one BTU is the amount of energy needed to heat one pound of water one degree Fahrenheit). For a long time, the high infrastructure costs and inefficiencies caused by sprawl have somehow been accepted on the wrong assumption that sprawl would provide affordable housing. Now we need to increase the suburbs' densities and transform out-dated urban values towards the acceptance of higher density, mixed-use and public transport.

Densification of existing city districts: building 'the city above the city', by extending existing buildings in the city, adding two floors in lightweight structure. Land prices in urban areas are very high, so multi-storey housing that does not require additional land (sites) is an effective way to densify the city. (Image: roof extension in Germany, courtesy architect, 2004)

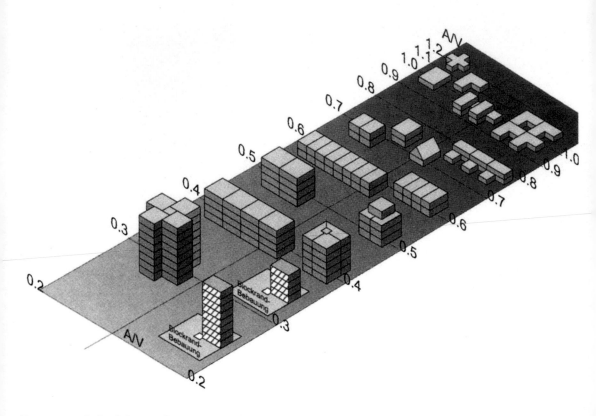

Recommended minimum densities and compactness

As an important benchmark for minimum densities of new urban developments, we can often find in the literature the figure of a minimum 50 to 70 homes (dwellings) per hectare. Sustainable districts are only viable on developments over 70 households (dwellings) per hectare, as densities below this do not sufficiently support public transport, the integration of mixed-use programmes and the energy generation with common district-based systems (e.g. using a CHP plant).

Based on their densities, Eco-Cities and Eco-Districts reduce the need to travel, providing sustainable mobility options and alternatives to the use of private automobiles. Developments with reasonable density will have workplaces and community facilities within easy cycling, or walking, distance. An average density of no less than 70 dwellings per hectare, preferably closer to 100 to 115 dwellings per hectare in central built-up areas and along transport corridors, will enable easy walking and cycling to key local facilities. Consequently, the key issues that should guide the masterplan are layout, solar orientation, prevailing wind direction, pedestrian and cycling connectivity, building blocks for the use of natural ventilation, and density (developments of five to seven stories) – all considered in relation to public transport nodes. This will involve working with the landscape, topography and the renewable resources available that are particular to the site.

There is now a growing awareness of the many advantages of compact developments and *green quality density* (as promoted by the cities of Melbourne, Singapore, Vancouver and Barcelona, just to name a few), and the positive outcomes, which often helps to convince concerned residents to give up their 'not-in-my-backyard' (NIMBY) attitude.

Density studies: This diagram illustrates the changing ratio between floor space and volume, which is an indicator of compactness, relevant for potential heat gain in summer and heat loss in winter. The comparison of the ratio of building envelope area to usable space can help to optimize the building shape. The lower the value, the more energy-efficient is the shape. (Courtesy: Solarbuero, D. Goretzki, 1997)

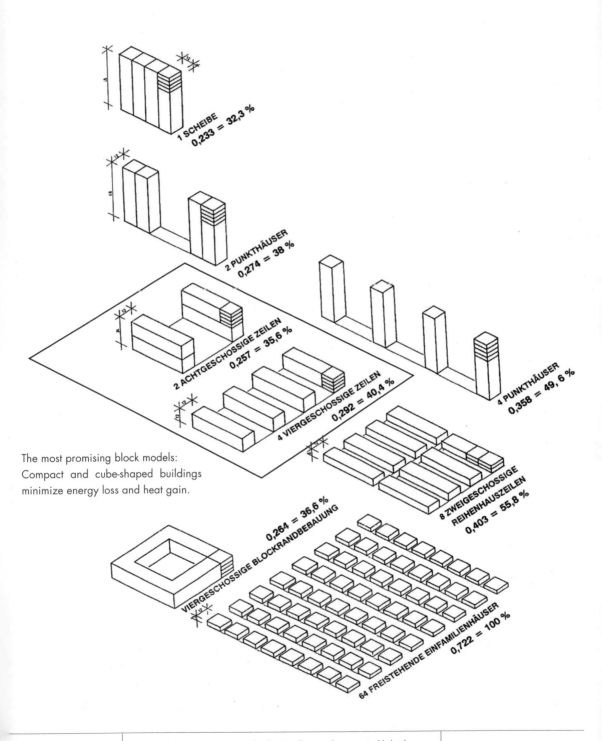

1 SCHEIBE
0,233 = 32,3 %

2 PUNKTHÄUSER
0,274 = 38 %

2 ACHTGESCHOSSIGE ZEILEN
0,257 = 35,6 %

4 VIERGESCHOSSIGE ZEILEN
0,292 = 40,4 %

4 PUNKTHÄUSER
0,358 = 49, 6 %

8 ZWEIGESCHOSSIGE
REIHENHAUSZEILEN
0,403 = 55,8 %

VIERGESCHOSSIGE BLOCKRANDBEBAUUNG
0,264 = 36,6 %

64 FREISTEHENDE EINFAMILIENHÄUSER
0,722 = 100 %

The most promising block models:
Compact and cube-shaped buildings
minimize energy loss and heat gain.

A/V-ratio and density comparison: This diagram illustrates the unsustainable land-con-
sumption which is needed to build 64 free-standing family houses, compared to block
and slab models; it also shows the solution to accommodate 64 families in point towers.
The most promising models in terms of energy-efficiency and ratio between facade
surface and floor area are 5 to 7-storey block models (Courtesy: G. Moewes, 1995)

Design professionals making a difference: from using recycled materials to empowering community

Over the last few years social concepts in architecture have made a strong comeback and an increase in interdisciplinary attempts to address the complex problems facing today's societies and communities. Cumberlidge and Musgrave note that 'recent projects often use minimal resources to effect the maximum possible change in people's lives... encouraging communities to take responsibility for their own environments.' (Cumberlidge and Musgrave, 2007) The projects featured in the following pages are interesting for their social impact. They range from a school building in Goa that follows migrant work-ers' families, to a mobile farm in Chicago that turns vacant lots into a source of food and employment. Some of these small-scale projects have changed their immediate social landscape through involving citizens and grassroots organizations. As a result, local liv-ing conditions have improved and new attitudes have been developed. In this regard, Cumberlidge and Musgrave observe that 'a campaign to build new homes for the urban poor resulted in the acquisition of new skills by local residents, enabling them to take on increased responsibility for future neighbourhood planning while altering their percep-tions about their ability to engineer significant change in their own environment.'

Socially-Engaged Architects Working in the Developing World

The effectiveness of small-scale action shows that change can often be settled and inte-grated and is not always radical or large-scale.

In future, our expertise will need to be about combining low-carbon de-sign solutions with material and energy-efficient technological systems and social innovations. This will facilitate more sustainable communities.

Material flows: designing with reused building components and materials

Currently, much innovation is about the better reuse of underutilized resources. The growing constraint in the use of materials and the scarcity of resources such as metals, require a new way to think about our profession. A new economy around recycling has emerged and a good example for this is the work of the *Rural Studio* in Alabama, where a group of architects and architecture students carry out low-cost recycling design projects in the impoverished community that result in tangible physical and economic change. In this context, new ideas and tools are evolving through the minimization of waste, through recycling and reusing building components – all important responses to addressing environmental problems, and all trespassing over the fields of architecture, urban design, community development, environ-mental planning, industrial and landscape design, etc. New products emerge from recycling of production waste products and the move towards biodegradable, compostable plastics.

The construction sector is a huge consumer of materials and much waste is derived from the construction and demolition sector. Reusing salvaged and reclaimed materials is an effective way of addressing waste minimization and inventing solutions for effective waste management. For instance, the Australian construction industry generates more than 32 mill. tonnes of waste each year and accounts for 42 per cent of all waste (data: ABS, 2008). The construction and demolition sector produces a significant amount of waste for landfill. In Australia 40 per cent of all landfill comes from the construction sector (Hyder Consulting, 2006). *Zero Waste South Australia* has set a target of eliminating waste and reducing waste to landfill by 25 per cent by 2014 (using 2002 data as the baseline; *Zero Waste SA*, 2005) In addition, existing buildings deliver huge reservoirs of materials and components, and these can potentially be mined to provide much needed resources. Designs for new projects using reclaimed components and recycled materials has a low environmental impact, but its uptake by building professionals is slow, as it requires research by the design team, which may be costly and time-consuming, and clear standards are lacking and it can be difficult to locate and source the exact quality of material the designer is looking for.

It is not unrealistic for projects to use 25 to 40 per cent in salvaged materials. Mark Gorgolewski notes that the factors deciding what to select for reuse should be based on its embodied energy content. He recommends 'concentrating on reusing materials and components with high embodied energy, such as metals and bricks, as these will have the greatest potential energy saving impact.' Gorgolewski has categorized reclaimed and salvaged materials in four general categories:
• On-site components, such as bricks from an old building reused into a new building (no transport), most efficiently used in smaller projects.
• Entire components salvaged from other sites, such as timber elements or dismantled steel structures from a demolition site of another project, and thus requiring little reprocessing.
• Reconditioned components taken from a demolished building for use in a new location, which require some improvement, such as doors, windows or staircases.
• *Recycled content building products* (RCBPs), including significant amounts of feedstock material that is taken from demolition to produce new products. (Gorgolewski, 2008).

Balancing new developments with upgrades and considering the value of the embodied energy represented in the existing built form, will lead to a better understanding of our cities. Reuse and retrofitting raises general considerations in regard to social sustainability; the real challenge seems to be in regard to consumer behaviour, which some researchers have termed *retrofitting lifestyles*. But how might changes in consumer attitudes and preferences best be initiated? A solution may be schemes that provide consumers with access to bulk purchase of green energy, materials and technologies, reducing the overall purchasing costs. Such schemes can be a genuine stimulus for changing behaviour. Achieving a maximum effect with minimal means has been a virtue of design and architecture for many centuries. In fact, it seems that pressure on materials and limited availability of resources often results in increased inventiveness and appreciation of the value of materials or existing buildings. Designers with an emphasis on reuse and reduction of waste are giving more value to salvaged materials, which are otherwise discounted as 'low-grade' or unattractive. *Design for disassembly* and the application of *modular prefabrication* allows for deconstruction and reuse of entire building components at a later stage. However, there are still several barriers to the fast uptake and integration of reuse practices, such as: rigid perceptions and consumer tastes concerning recycled building materials; the additional time required to carefully dismantle buildings; the lack of markets for used components; and the fact that building codes do not yet address the recycling and reusing of components. Some architects have already specialized on the reuse of materials and building components, for instance *2012 Architects'* (from Delft, The Netherlands) design of waste-based architecture where everything is reused in inventive ways. (For further information, see these web sites: www.superuse.org and www.recyclicity.net).

Material flow, recycling and remanufacturing

Improved recycling processes are crucial. Material flows and circular urban metabolism are increasingly recognized as major issues in any survival strategy, at least equal in importance as the energy, water and transport questions. For instance, electronic waste (e-waste) alone poses dramatic challenges: e-waste from developing countries is forecast to overtake that of the developed world, as increasingly wealthy consumers in countries such as China, India, South Africa and Brazil dump their massive amounts of domestic e-waste due to lack of recycling centres, regulations and policies, and this is poisoning water and soil. To illustrate the seriousness of this problem, a recent research study found that 'within six to eight years, developing countries will be disposing of more old computers, refrigerators and mobile phones than the developed world today', leading to serious public-health problems and environmental degradation on a massive scale. (Yu, Williams, Yang, 2010) More responsible recycling within the computer industry, including take-back regulations for an 'extended producer responsibility', is necessary. The study predicts that 'by 2030, these nations will be disposing of two to three times as many computers as the developed world, perhaps resulting in up to 1 billion computers being dumped worldwide every year – up from a global total of around 180 million units per year now.' (Yu, Williams, Yang, 2010) Estimating how many domestic computers the developing world will be adding to the current stream of electronic waste from the developed world is not too difficult; one just needs to look at computer sales data from the International Telecommunication Union (an agency of the United Nations headquartered in Geneva, Switzerland) and factor in the average computer's lifespan.[1]

Reclaiming metals from illegially shipped e-waste to China and India

A large amount of e-waste from developed countries ends up in the developing world anyway, as it is shipped there (partially legally, partially illegally), for disassembly. However, the methods applied by developing world recyclers to take the toxic materials out of these computers are highly unsave and environmentally problematic. The feedstock for the informal recycling is massive exports from developed countries, mostly against the *Basel Convention* (the international agreement that controls trade in hazardous waste). The recycling process by informal `backyard recyclers' to reclaim precious metals from circuit boards and wires inside the computers, copy machines and televisions is rather primitive: `they simply burn off the insulation, producing a host of toxic chemicals from the burning plastic; and to obtain gold and other metals from circuit boards, they simply treat them with litres of nitric acid and cyanide, which ends up being dumped into local water or soils,' researcher Eric Williams notes. (Yu, Williams, Yang, 2010) Bio-degradation of e-waste with microorganisms could be one future solution. Today, China is still not doing enough to tackle this threat, especially in rural China, where chemical plants and cement factories are everywhere, emmitting toxic pollutants into rivers. The recycling and e-waste topic has still not arrived. In Delhi, India, it is estimated that about 80,000 waste collectors comb the city's streets each day in search of things – like paper, plastics, bottles, metals – to sell to more than 25,000 small scrap dealers. This army of recyclers intercepts tonnes of reusable items before they end up as landfill. In addition, millions of tonnes of toxic e-waste is imported to India, from the US and Europe. What is needed to deal with this massive problem, is better governance and improved recycling processes globally, and better waste management infratructures in the developing world.

Jane Jacobs: promoting diversity and the value of urban complexity

American writer Jane Jacobs was one of the early activists to point out the need for diversity, urban complexity and social inclusion, through her pivotal book *The Death and Life of Great American Cities* (1961). This much celebrated urban manifesto encapsulates a practical philosophy for community-based activism that relies on street-level observations. It is a manifesto that was much needed in New York City in the 1960s to protect local neighbourhoods and the character of districts that were under threat of demolition due to insensitive developments. Today, more than ever, the principles of social sustainability again need to be part of the architect's and the urban designer's toolbox, be it in the developed or the developing world. The legacy of Jane Jacobs is continued by Amanda Burden, urban planner, civic activist and New York City's Director of City Planning (since 2002).

Cities have the capability of providing something for everybody, only because, and only when, they are created by everybody.
Jane Jacobs, 1961

Ethical, local answers to global problems

With the focus strongly on environmental sustainability, let's not forget other global challenges, such as poverty, housing affordability and social injustice. The most pressing issues in the developing world still include the basics of living – water supply, sanitation and shelter – whereas the wider issues for cities in the 21st century are climate change resilience and how to design for a sustainable urban future in a carbon-constrained world. Since Jane Jacobs, we have known that inexpensive, community-based, small-scale projects and site-specific interventions can trigger big change. This is also present in the work of Sheila Dikshit in Delhi, India, and Jaime Lerner in Curitiba, Brazil. Working with urban and rural communities in slums in India or in places such as Bangladesh and *favelas* in Brazil, `testing the limits of architecture' (Pallasmaa, 2009), Lerner has given a new form of social engagement to architecture. Beyond a culture of consumerism and entrenched conventions of the profession in the developed world, architects and engineers have been able to offer many innovative solutions to improve lives, reminding us of the early endeavours of modern architecture, when ideas of a social utopian and mass production were part of the profession and the driver for innovation (Gropius' social agenda, before *Modernism* emerged as a *style*, called the `International Style', reduced to merely stylistic aspects, articulated by Johnson and Hitchcock, 1932).

But what kind of change is exactly `small inexpensive change, which can cause big improvements'? Nabeel Hamdi defines it like this: 'Build a bus stop in an urban slum and a vibrant community sprouts and grows around it. This shows the power of small change that can have huge positive effects.' (Hamdi, 2004). In his book on `Urban Participatory Development', Hamdi argues for `the wisdom of the street, the lessons from the informal city, the ingenuity of the improvisers and the long-term effectiveness that immediate, small-scale actions can have in improving social and urban living conditions.' For instance, the introduction of community-based waste management and recycling programmes in Curitiba has led to the empowerment of the poor, the increased use of public transport and a cleaner public domain – all in a very short time and without the municipality spending much money.

New forms of locally distributed energy generation through co-generation offers opportunities for neighbourhood-level action by residents and businesses, providing energy needs as well as generating income through feeding energy into the grid.

Architecture's shift to a more social agenda

Let's look at some of the `socially-engaged' architects and the political-social contexts they are working in: Diebedo Francis Kéré in Burkina Faso (Africa), Nina Maritz in Namibia (Africa), Mette Lang in Goa (India), Andrew Freear of *Rural Studio* in Alabama (USA), Cameron Sinclair of *Architecture for Humanity* (USA) in Africa and Asia, Urban Think Tank in Caracas (Venezuela), Tom Blaxham in Manchester (UK), Chelvadurai Anjalendran from Sri Lanka (Asia), Anna Heringer in Bangladesh (Asia), or Dipal Barua in Bangladesh (Asia). New ideas are reactivating derelict communities in many different places. Socially-engaged architects are identifying future tasks for the profession, tasks that deal directly with community; and tasks that have been seen as marginal for decades and which are mainly concerned with aesthetics. Architecture can be a powerful means of changing social conditions. Architects can confront inequality using the tools of design to engage in social, economic and political conditions. Architectural solutions can emerge from close collaborations with future users and sustained research into local conditions, wherein the architect's roles, methods and responsibilities are dramatically reconsidered and reconstituted. `Sustainable' in the local context of African or Asian cities often means `affordable' and some low-cost projects are built entirely of salvaged materials. Constructing at remote places in Africa or Bangladesh, with no maintenance, means that the choice of materials and the detailing of a project is very important.

The architect as moderator of social processes and as agent of social change
Architectural historian Andres Lepik has documented how architects can work within small budgets but still effect significant positive impact on social conditions. He points to the high level of community engagement as a basis for *small scale, big change* projects: `Even with a very low budget, you can achieve a very high aesthetic standard and social engagement. Still, these projects are all beautifully designed, keeping in line with the history of modern architecture. Many of the socially-engaged architects are tired of architectural utopias. They are not interested in politics particularly; rather they are interested in addressing specific local problems.' (Lepik, 2010)

For instance, socially-engaged architects are genuinely improving living conditions in favelas and slums in projects such as slum upgrading, improving standards of living for the poor, and empowering underrepresented communities, creating places and spaces that are formed by local climatic conditions, materials, resources and technologies. For these architects, the challenges of working in harsh environments with limited means and reusing materials are already an everyday reality. Their work presents models for making compelling buildings despite the lack of resources. This is what Cumberlidge and Musgrave have called `the professional operating outside their normal sphere of practice, where the practitioner has moved outside their own discipline to work in a broader, more strategic and critical role. This may be allied to a renewed recognition that *regeneration* or *renewal* is not merely a task for city planners, economists, architects or politicians.' (Cumberlidge and Musgrave, 2007) Defining an ethically correct design answer has become a major mission for engaged architects and engineers, which includes supporting local inhabitants, or training young architects and builders in Bangladesh, Burkina Faso, India, Venezuela, and South Africa and so on. New models of participation, sustainable prototypes of climate-responsive design and new infrastructural concepts are all socially-relevant projects.

The challenges posed by climate change are complex – but as a society we have the skills, knowledge and determination to achieve the necessary changes.

Empowering local communities: architecture beyond architecture
The links between environmental, social and climate challenges are so strong that we need integrated solutions. We also need a different approach that embraces a form of globalization that empowers local communities and regional cultures and utilizes their accumulated wisdom. For instance, urban farming to grow food locally, or decentralized electricity generation close to the point where it is consumed, are useful strategies for enabling citizens to produce a significant part of the energy and food they require for themselves. These challenges have formed a new breed of architect and engineer who is not interested in imposing an idealized rationalism or a modernist utopia on locals, but, instead, who wants to share an understanding of the present threat of climate change and the destabilizing effects that globalization has had on communities. Such initiatives demand creative engagement

and practical, concrete proposals. A `can-do' attitude drives these socially engaged architects and engineers to implement *micro-revolutions*; their motivation is based in social ideals and pragmatic concerns, the desire to end poverty and to improve substandard living conditions.

Some examples of school, community centre, housing and infrastructure interventions are:
• Primary School in Gando, Burkina Faso (Diébédo Francis Kéré).
• `METI – Handmade School' in Rudrapur, Bangladesh (Anna Heringer).
• The `$20K House' in Hale County, Alabama (Rural Studio).
• `Living Rooms at the Border' and Senior Housing with Childcare in San Ysidro, California (Estudio Teddy Cruz).
• The work by `Urban Splash' in North England.
• `Grameen Shakti' NGO for micro-credits and energy technology, Bangladesh.

The adaptive reuse of buildings (rather than their demolition) and the regeneration of the city centre saves energy and materials. Not only is it environmentally sustainable to reuse structures that already exist, but it is socially responsible to regenerate urban areas that have fallen into decay and to help maintain the city's identity.

• Primary School in Gando, Burkina Faso (by Diébédo Francis Kéré, 1999–2002): Francis Kéré is an architect from Burkina Faso, based in Berlin. As an architecture student he founded the 'Schulbausteine for Gando Association' to raise funds for the construction of his first building, a village school in his home town. This building was later honoured with the Aga Khan Award for Architecture in 2004. He designs site-specific buildings that meet climatic demands and support Burkina Faso's inhabitants in their development. The need to enlarge the existing school building in Dano, another small African town, led to similar local solutions. The building truly belongs to the place, as its materials are resourced from the site and are available locally. The walls are made with blocks of clay taken from the site; the roofing structure consists of iron bars welded on the spot and assembled in situ; and local labour was used for its construction. Throughout the entire construction process, local workmen were trained to use simple building techniques, ensuring that they learned the required methods for future community projects. The building's basic design is based on careful analysis of the local microclimate, providing a direct answer to the need for functional space in conditions of poverty and material constraints.

• `METI – Handmade School' in Rudrapur, Bangladesh (by Anna Heringer, 2004–06): Anna Heringer's school building in Rudrapur exemplifies how the use of local resources and traditional technologies can be applied in an innovative way. The building was constructed by hand in four months, out of simple, locally-sourced materials such as clay, straw, bamboo and nylon lashing. The architects engaged local craftsmen in the project, helping them to refine their processes and training them in new techniques that they might apply to local housing projects.

• The `$20K House' in Hale County, Alabama (by Rural Studio, 2003–present):

Founded 1993 by Samuel Mockbee, the Rural Studio is Auburn University's outreach programme in impoverished south-east Alabama, where students design and build low-income affordable housing for only $20k in materials and labour per house. The modest dwellings are of surprisingly high spatial quality and simplicity, applying passive design principles. More info on the Rural Studio can be found at: www.cadc.auburn.edu/rural-studio.

• `Living Rooms at the Border' and Senior Housing with Childcare in San Ysidro, California (by Estudio Teddy Cruz, 2001–present): Teddy Cruz from San Diego initiated the `Border Postcard: Chronicles from the Edge' project in 2004, exploring new urban strategies for the contested zone spanning the US-Mexican (San Diego-Tijuana) border. He designed new mixed-use developments and low-cost housing that reused, adapted existing structures using recycled materials.

• Urban regeneration and adaptive-reuse projects by `Urban Splash', Manchester (1993–present): Tom Bloxham was the co-founder of `Urban Splash' in 1993, which initially converted redundant properties in north-west England (mainly inner-city structures in recession-hit Manchester and Liverpool) into affordable city centre residential loft apartments and studios for creative industries. `Urban Splash' has established a reputation for taking on projects that conventional developers would not touch, and has played a significant role in the revitalization of otherwise obsolete, overlooked spaces and the urban renewal of cities in northern England, including the creation of local employment. Today, Bloxham is known for the adaptive reuse of unused buildings and industrial sites creating vibrant, mixed-use spaces, revitalizing city centres and communities. Bloxham has become something of an urban regeneration pioneer, seeing himself more of a *regenerator* than a developer.

• `Grameen Shakti' NGO for micro-credits and energy technology, Bangladesh (1985–present): Dipal Barua is the founding Managing Director of the NGO initiative `Grameen Shakti'. Barua has worked tirelessly over the last few decades to bring renewable energy solutions to the rural population of Bangladesh. His organization, Grameen Shakti (GS), has installed more than 200,000 solar PV systems that currently provide power to more than two million rural people. Under Barua's leadership, GS has developed a number of other innovative initiatives, including a biogas plant technology that converts cow and poultry waste into gas for cooking, lighting and fertilizer. GS has installed more than 6,000 biogas mini-plants (data: 2009) and intends to construct 50,000 more by 2012. In addition, GS has trained rural women to be solar technicians, thereby enabling them to become green entrepreneurs through a highly successful micro-credit programme. With Barua's help, the rural people of Bangladesh have demonstrated significant ambition in adopting clean, renewable technologies to solve their daily energy challenges.

These projects give us hope, as they exemplify that architecture and urban design can be a powerful means of changing social conditions and improving living conditions. Designers confront inequality globally, using the tools of design to engage in social, economic and political conditions.

Source: Courtesy D.F. Kéré

Small projects - big impact: New sustainable architecture in Burkina Faso, by Diebedo Francis Kéré. A school building in Gando, built together with the local community (Aga Khan Award for Architecture in 2004). Kéré has, since then, built several other schools and health centres in Burkina Faso, for which he found sponsors himself and trained local people in construction methods with clay and mud. www.kere-architecture.com

The challenges of the developing world: buildings made from recycled materials

The challenges posed by the urbanization in developing countries are redefining all our established strategies of urban design for the developed world. By 2050 we can expect 200 mill. people will have to be re-settled due to climate change. The 'Moving School' initiative in India (below) is a clever project in the category: *Small budget - big impact*. When the children move with their migrant parents, the school moves with them; these children of temporary settlers would otherwise be exluded from education.

Source: Courtesy M. Lange

It's clear that the urban design strategies for sustainable development need to be different for developed countries and for developing countries. With around one billion people worldwide living in slums, without access to sanitation and clean drinking water, it has become a moral issue to act quickly. Below: The 'Moving School' project in Goa, India, providing basic facilities for neglected children of the moving labour groups. (architect: Mette Lange) www.movingschool.org

Challenges ahead: research in *Speculative Green Urbanism*

As we have seen in earlier chapters and case studies, it is important to consider the broader region-wide and city-wide context of sustainable development and the general concept of imagining communities beyond the narrow confines of *projects* and *buildings*. There has been a positive shift in emphasis, in recent years, away from formalistic aesthetics and towards a set of broader shared values as the basis for the critique of urban design and architectural work. Globally, the task on the urban scale is in re-housing one billion people who currently live in absolutely inadequate slum conditions and in housing some three billion additional people due to global population growth in the coming forty years. In Europe, dealing with large-scale residential districts and public mass housing on such a scale hasn't been a topic since post-war reconstruction under the auspices of Constantinos Doxiadis and other urbanists. We are not used to thinking about urban development in terms of entire new cities, yet Chinese urbanization alone will require new cities for up to 350 million people as its rural population moves to urban centres. These new cities need to be built in the next two decades. What kind of housing products will need to be on offer for the required low-carbon lifestyle?

With an increase in income, China's city dwellers will want to increase their living space; this will only be possible in a sustainable way by constructing standardized mass housing of

The Challenges Ahead:
A Research Agenda in Green Urbanism, Transforming our Cities

high quality. It's a good strategy to develop models for zero-emission city districts and new mixed-use block typologies first, so that they can then be combined and added (as the *Stadtbaustein*) to eco-city configurations of different sizes. This doesn't, of course, mean repetitive uniformity, nor does it mean an aesthetic like Russia's 1970s industrialized, standardized mass production housing. In this context, the question is about diversity, modularity, construction process, flexibility, adaptability, materials flow, user participation and affordability. For all this to happen, design and planning disciplines will need to expand their traditionally compartmentalized roles and become far-reaching, interdisciplinary efforts envisioning holistic, city-scale proposals that are capable of producing ecologically transformative green city districts.

The city is justifiably regarded as the most precious invention of civilization, second only to language in its role as a mediator of culture.
Lewis Mumford, 1961

Measuring *Eco-City* performance

The Swedish government has set a national goal for the entire country of being free from oil by 2020. This has already been achieved by several cities, such as Overturnea. Havana, in Cuba, has successfully dealt with its 50-year trade embargo and negotiated its early *Peak*

Oil experience by becoming virtually self-sufficient in food. Today, Havana is a leading example of local food production through community gardens and urban agriculture. Curitiba in Brazil, Copenhagen in Denmark, and Malmo in Sweden have demonstrated how to make cities close to independent of private automobiles by improving public transport and cycling. However, there is still very little by way of scientific evidence in the assessment of these projects.

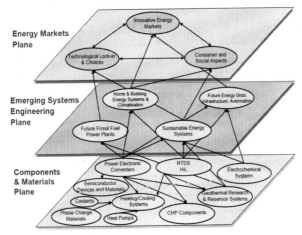

Fig. 1: New research centres for sustainability research emerge at universities worldwide, with their interdisciplinary research agendas. For instance, this diagram shows the research planes identified by a research centre (E.ON Energy Research Centre, Germany, 2009). Key research topics can be allocated to one of the planes, which structure the research activities. Interactions between disciplines and across different planes encourage and accelerate innovative work. (Diagram: courtesy R. De Doncker, 2009)

If we want to compare the merits of initiatives around the world, we will need to establish a data base of valid *Eco-City* strategies and produce tangible, measurable outcomes using a scientific basis for comparing different approaches (comparing smaller cities with each other). There are leading eco-communities – Vauban and Kronsberg in Germany, Gussing in Austria, Samso in Denmark, Overturnea in Sweden, or Woking in the UK – that have all achieved the goal of being net exporters of renewable energy, feeding more energy into the grid than they consume. There needs to be a mechanism whereby the overall successes of these communities can be better quantified.

For instance, the 'Ecological Footprint' method, developed by Wackernagel and Rees, is a candidate for being one such reliable way to establish a city ranking based on facts and data. This method includes comparing some basic facts for each district, such as:
- overall population density and ratio of green space in the city
- amount of renewable energy generated and consumed
- amount of water used per capita and amount of water recycled
- amount of waste recycled or composted, and amount of waste going to landfill
- percentage of food produced within a 200 km radius ('foodprint')
- amount of car ownership per capita and percentage of journeys by public transport
- amount of sq m of public space per capita, and
- similar data, relevant to analyze the environmental performance.

Measuring the *Ecological Footprint* (EF) and evaluating embodied energy
The Ecological Footprint's unit of measurement is in global hectares (gha); these are hectares (ha) with world-average productivity for all productive land and water areas in a
given year (as defined by the Global Footprints Network; for more information, see www.
footprintstandards.org). On this scale, China's growing population and per capita wealth
is creating an ever larger Ecological Footprint (e.g. Arup's Ecological Footprint research,
2008, calculated that in all China, in 2008, it had a value of 1.6 gha per capita; however,
Shanghai is already using 4.7 gha per capita). If all future urban developments were based
on principles of green urbanism and large-scale retro-fitting of existing cities occurred, we
could ensure that people living in urban areas enjoyed a modern lifestyle with an Ecological Footprint stabilized at around 2 gha per capita. With the right legal framework and
theoretical knowledge base we would be able to turn rapid urbanization in the Asia-Pacific
Region into a great opportunity.

Assessing the embodied energy of building components can be very complex and is often
difficult. In its report 'Towards Sustainable and Smart Eco-Buildings. Summary Report:
Smart Eco-Buildings in the EU', the International Council for Research and Innovation in
Building and Construction (CIB) found that: 'Material sourcing and manufacturing of components are often the most resource intensive phases of the construction process and generally have an energy or carbon footprint larger than site works, demolition and recycling
activities. In the UK, the carbon emissions associated with running buildings are currently
four to five times greater than the emissions generated from material sourcing and manufacture. However with more buildings constructed to high operational efficiency standards,
the impact of material sourcing and manufacture is becoming even more significant.' (CIB,
2010) The report goes on to suggest key parameters for identifying the energy required to
manufacture and supply materials or services, its 'embodied energy'. The report explains,
'Embodied carbon dioxide is defined as the CO_2 emitted during these processes. The CO_2
emissions associated with the energy used in the manufacture and supply of materials may
vary depending on the energy source and manufacturing processes involved. For example
any material that uses electricity in its manufacturing process will have an embodied CO_2
that is dependent on the fuel mix for the electricity supply. The same material manufactured
in France and the UK could have different embodied CO_2 values. Concrete can be pre-cast
or in situ and contains a number of constituents (cement, aggregate, water, sand, admix-
tures) in an infinite variation of ratios and type and amount of steel reinforcement. Accessible, reliable and objective data sources are critical to assess the impact of a particular
design, manufacturing or construction decision on energy and water use, waste and use
of by-products, recycling opportunities, resource depletion, human toxicity and pollution of
soil, water or air.' (CIB, 2010)

Luckily, innovative and inspiring environmental initiatives are now emerging everywhere, not
only in the architecture and urban design field. For instance, in 2010 David de Rothschild
is sailing a boat, the *Plastiki*, made of recycled plastic bottles across the Pacific, to advocate

ethical waste management and recycling, and to inform about the dangers of dumping plastic waste into the oceans. 'Plastic is not the enemy as long as it is used responsibly and repeatedly,' he says. His catamaran is constructed from 12,500 recycled PET water bottles (polyethylene terephthalate), designed into the hulls of the boat, using solar energy. The mast of the boat is made of a recycled aluminium pipe and the sail is made of recycled PET textile bonded with a specially developed organic glue made from sugar cane. (See: Fig. 3) PET water bottles are a particular problem: globally, more than 2.7 million tonnes of plastic are used for bottling water alone, but only 23 per cent of these plastic bottles are recycled. However, it would be twice as energy-effective to recycle these bottles as it does to inciner-ate them. Recycling one tonne of plastic saves enough energy to power a refrigerator for a month (Data: Australia's Sustainable Choice, 2009). Giving plastic bottles a useful second life is relatively easy: Up-cycling PET is one of the easiest treatments of consumer plastics, and has recently been used successfully by Nike, Coca Cola and other brands.

Biodiversity is being lost at a pace never seen before, undermining the capacity of ecosystems to provide essential services and goods that un-derpin the livelihoods of millions of people and the global economy.

The underlying causes of this problem have not been addressed ad-equately, because current economic and governance systems and policies are promoting the over consumption of natural resources to an unsustainable level. We are seeing the degradation of nature right before our eyes, and the responses have been inadequate so far.
UN-Habitat, 2010

Transforming regions: a research agenda in Australian regional urban communities

While city centres in the developed world have been in decline for a long time, there is now a need for more research on the reasons for this decline and on possible ways to turn such anti-urban developments around. Australian cities are an interesting case study. Australia is the 18th most urbanised of the world's 204 countries, according to UN statistics, with an urbanization rate of almost 90 per cent (UN, 2009). The Australian Bureau of Statistics says that 69 per cent of the Australian population live in 7 big cities: nearly everybody lives in the 7 capital cit-ies (Sydney, Melbourne, Brisbane, Adelaide, Perth, Hobart and Canberra). These cities grew in average at a rate of 2.3 per cent in 2008–09, compared with 1.9 per cent for the rest of Australia. Australia is becoming still more urbanised and population is predicted to grow from 21 million to 36 million people by 2050. Australian cities can deal with more people, as long as the infrastructure is renewed, existing districts are retrofitted and sufficient affordable housing is supplied. Around 20 per cent of Australia's population live in regional urban areas and many regional Australian cities have a slow growth rate, sometimes well below the aver-age capital city growth (ABS, 2008). In Australia, local governments espouse sustainable development and adaptation, but lack appropriate strategies for decision-making.

While much research has been done on the capital cities, regional cities have not received the required attention. We also have to focus on research projects that will deliver strategies and tools to develop highly sustainable regional cities and healthy communities to meet the challenges of peak oil and climate change (IEA/OECD, 2008). The findings from such research will be of particular relevance to post-industrial cities, city councils, communities and towns along the coast, where new urban identities around tourism and the service sector emerge. They will also be relevant to those cities whose centres require sustainable regeneration and re-engineering. While some research has been undertaken into the sustainable development of larger cities and metropolitan centres, there has, so far, been little systematic research into the sustainable development of regional urban settlements.

Suitable development strategies could be applied to regional cities, both nationally and globally. For instance, regional Australian cities are characterized by such unsustainable trends as:
• a city centre in need of regeneration, often with disused brownfield (former industrial) sites,
• the existing building stock is old and not energy-efficient,
• structural problems e.g. CBD retail closure, often due to the expansion of large suburban shopping malls and lack of catalytic inner-city projects,
• high carbon energy supply and transport modes,
• inefficient water, waste and transport operations, and
• low population growth, combined with job losses.

The challenge is now to bring the over-technicalized and over-socialized responses together, to manage the fast transition of urban infrastructure to a new decentralized infrastructure, and to develop more expertise in retrofitting the existing city.

However, regional cities also share the more resilient characteristics of lesser impact on the surrounding land for food and waste, compared to larger cities, and closer community ties, with a strong attachment to history and place. Such research would deliver much needed urban adaptation elements, such as:
• A range of community expectations for Australian regional cities (e.g. values, desired services and cultural assets, degree of public and private ownership).
• Approaches to sustainably regenerate safe and healthy downtown environments.
• The social, economic and environmental impact on the regional city district, measured by Neighbourhood Ecological Footprint and neighbourhood well-being.
• Climate-sensitive sustainably built forms (e.g. definition of densities; compactness; orientation; architectural principles); better zonings e.g. mixed-usage and multi-storey and compact residential typologies; this maximizes green space and avoids sprawl.
• Adaptive re-use of existing buildings (for low greenhouse gas emission) near public transport for transit-oriented development (TOD), including sustainable energy, water and food facilities.
• Urban consolidation to ensure that new homes are close to public transport, employment, education, shopping, health services, etc. giving the option to walk, bike, or take public transport.

• A high proportion of building materials designed for reuse and recycling.

There is now comprehensive evidence of a direct connection between urban development and climate change (ULI, 2007, Breheny, 1992; Blakely and Bradshaw, 2002). The *Sydney Metropolitan Strategy* (DOP, 2005) has already outlined a future in which only 30, to a maximum of 40, per cent of new housing is developed in new greenfield land release areas, with the remaining 60 to 70 per cent accommodated through increased densities in existing urban areas and urban infill.

The European Parliament has asked the European Commission to create a shared method of calculating the overall energy-efficiency of buildings by 2010.

New EU policies for net zero-energy buildings

Europe is ahead: In 2009, the parliament of the European Union decided that from 2018 onwards, all new buildings in the EU had to cover their own energy requirements. Moreover, they decided that an agreed method for calculating overall energy efficiency of buildings was to be developed in 2010 and would become uniform throughout Europe. It is a good example of how policy can drive the uptake of energy-efficiency. Since 2002, the 'Directive on the Energy Performance of Buildings' (2002/91/EC), which is applicable throughout Europe, has been the basis of national legislation in the EU. In 2009, the European Parliament ratified a new version of the directive. According to this new version, EU member states must ensure that by 2018 all newly constructed buildings will generate as much energy as they consume – for example, by means of solar collectors or heat pumps. The member states are required to develop national plans for increasing the number of 'net zero-energy buildings'. In addition, governments are to specify how high the proportion of zero-energy houses among existing buildings is to be for the years 2015 to 2020. In this context, public institutions in Europe are taking the lead in implementing the changes in their own building stock. The primary aim is to remove legal obstacles and market barriers for energy-efficiency and to introduce new tax-related and financial instruments. One proposal, for example, is to reduce value added tax on goods and services that are purchased for energy saving purposes. The EU hopes that the policy amendment to the directive will result in overall energy consumption being reduced by 6 per cent and CO_2 emissions being lowered by 5 per cent by the year 2020.

Education, training and research

In order to implement the changes implied by Chapters 1 and 2, there will need to be substantial changes in the understanding and attitudes of people at all levels of government, the building professions and the general community. Thus communication, in the forms of education, training and research, will need to be a major element of the overall policy required to bring about changes associated with adapting to, and the mitigation of, the impact of climate change. Changes in understanding are needed in order to avoid the continuation of unsustainable practices currently used in architectural and urban design and construction, which are too blindly accepted by government and the community.

The building industry is currently not trained to deliver climate-adaptable and zero-carbon cities and buildings as either renovations or new developments. In addition, professional education generally does not sufficiently prioritize or effectively deliver curricula that empowers graduates to shape a zero-carbon and climate adaptable urban environment. Reform and expansion of built-environment education and training with climate change mitigation and adaptation as a primary focus should occur within the next ten years to ensure that the workforce develops the needed expertise in a reasonable time frame. Specific actions to achieve these changes include:

• Reorientation of professional education to eliminate curricula that reproduce modes of practice that increase the impact of buildings and cities on climate change.

• Development and implementation of interdisciplinary curricula for professional courses.

• Refocusing of accreditation criteria for professional courses on climate change mitigation and adaptation.

• Re-training of the industry to provide the necessary leadership and capacity to engage in the mass renovation of existing buildings and retrofitting of districts.

• Public and formal learning informed by pedagogies oriented towards reflection-in-action. Formal education should be informed by detailed and continual analysis of the climate performance of buildings and cities. There should be public feedback on climate performance.

• Renovation of formal settings for schools and universities should be prioritized to provide learning environments that exemplify climate-sensitive built environments.

Education, training and research will need to be major elements of the overall policy required to bring about the changes associated with adapting to, and mitigation of, the impact of climate change.

Looking ahead: a research agenda in *Low-to-No-Carbon urban design*

More research in green urbanism is still necessary. However, research in architecture and urban design is multi-faceted. As the *EAAE Charter* 2010 (the Charter for Architectural Education in Europe) notes: `architecture is a discipline focusing on the physical articulation of space on different scale levels, which deeply affects our life environment. It involves bodies of knowledge and practices that are wide-ranging in nature and scope, as was already noticed, for example, by Vitruvius, when he pointed towards *firmitas, utilitas* and *venustas* – firmness, commodity and delight – as basic dimensions of architecture.' (EAAE, 2010)

The public and professional education on sustainable built environments needs to be based on sound research results. In particular, research should be focused on integrated building design and construction, supporting whole-system approaches and innovation and aimed at unlocking knowledge from existing projects and best practices to facilitate the transition to a zero-carbon building sector. Many of our current housing and workplace models are inadequate and outdated, and they do not deal with the immense challenge of transforming the built environment.

There needs to be increased support for research activity that:

• Identifies best practice and its application in a holistic way and which develops performance-based principles for a more compact urban form, energy-efficient districts and more flexible, adaptable building typologies in order to re-conceptualize our housing and workplaces.

• Generates better methodologies for measuring sustainability and resource management, where material flows are identified, analyzed and communicated.

• Develops strategies for achieving a close to zero-carbon built environment, with a focus on identifying the relevant questions needed to future-proof the building sector and to develop pathways to a low-to-no-carbon society.

Significant behavioural changes, based on improved understanding of the complexities involved and our extended knowledge of the situation, are needed to create an energy-aware culture that allows decision-makers to better understand the opportunities for energy-efficient buildings and cities. These changes should be based on sound research to provide clear information about new and emerging technologies. A broad research programme should be fostered within and across built-environment disciplines to promote a seamless connection between research, practice and teaching. We therefore need more research that meets the highest standards of excellence in its field and makes an equally excellent contribution to the practice of the built-environment professions. Required activities include:

• contributing to capacity building and raising awareness

• conducting quantitative and qualitative scientific research into passive design principles and developing new concepts on how to create sustainable cities, districts and buildings

• enhancing international research cooperation to develop knowledge of international research-based best practice, focusing on the chief challenges of our time

• publishing and disseminating knowledge and best practice principles for re-engineering buildings, districts and cities

• knowledge-sharing: transferring knowledge to developing countries, up-skilling and training professionals and offering wider access to information networks and databases

• observing how buildings, districts and urban environments actually perform

• developing baselines and consistent methodologies for measuring progress and return on investment in carbon markets, and

• researching and developing component prefabrication and modular construction to facilitate resource efficiency and adaptable design.

Sustainable urban strategy = Urban design strategy + Process design strategy
Kees Christiaanse, 2008

Research as 'Community Engagement' needs to involve the development of partnerships that bring real benefits to communities. Such engaged scholarship integrates student learning with research that is undertaken in collaboration with professional partners who are involved in all stages of the discovery activities. Such research calls on many disciplines, is highly collaborative, strongly applied and is problem-driven. Today, research in the built environment is in the process of transforming through networks of strong interdisciplinary teams in which all disciplines make specific contributions. Architecture and urban design should be understood as exciting fields of open research, rather than as fields of orthodoxy with fixed solutions. The resources that contemporary architects and planners can draw on are no longer a closed body of knowledge; what must be explored, taught and learnt is the result of a continuous research process. The constant changes in the field of built-environment technology and science, with new relationships between work and leisure, public and private space, heritage values and the demands of tourism, the establishment of roots and the lure of mobility, mean there is no longer a limited set of rules that defines what research is or what it can be. Research and knowledge-sharing are truly globalized.

The *Zero Waste Research Centre* and UNESCO Chair

New research centres dedicated to such forward-looking research agendas are now emerging at universities worldwide. For instance, the *Zero Waste SA Research Centre for Sustainable Design and Behaviour* at the University of South Australia is an internationally recognized research centre and a focal point for sustainability and material/waste-related research. The UNESCO Chair and the Zero Waste SA Research Centre are building long-term collaborative partnerships with industry, business, government and the community to promote environmental sustainability and to develop regional solutions for Australia, focusing on reducing waste, avoiding consumption and optimizing material flows. The centre builds long term capacity in research and conducts scholarly research in the following priority research areas:

• Environmental sustainability and infrastructure planning for climate change.
• Sustainable, resilient cities based on energy and material-efficient architecture and urbanism.
• Social sustainability and its relation to urban ecology, technology and design issues.
• Resource efficiency: material flows, circular urban metabolism and value chains.
• Waste avoidance, waste management and recycling towards a truly sustainable society.

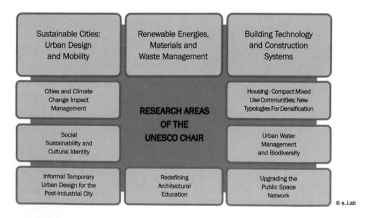

Fig. 2: The Zero Waste Research Centre for Sustainable Design and UNESCO Chair in Sustainable Cities for Asia and the Pacific have a focus on the listed research areas. (Diagram: S. Lehmann, 2010)

• Sustainable design and behaviour that addresses issues of reduced or modified consumption.
• Sociological and technological innovations in sustainable practices and design.
• Development of innovative design solutions and technological change leading to reduction in material use, energy use and waste creation.
• Prefabricated, lightweight construction systems for material efficiency and durability.
• Measuring embodied energy, consumption and the ecological footprint of urban environments.

This kind of interdisciplinary research is carried out in partnerships and through collaborations. In addition, the UNESCO Chair has the international mission to:
• Share knowledge, support capacity building for sustainable urban futures and advise governments.
• Involve developing countries in the Asia-Pacific Region in working towards a global agenda to harmonize rapid urbanization.
• Supporting and mentoring higher degree researchers and young academics from the Asia-Pacific Region.

City is not a problem, city is solution!   *Jaime Lerner*

Fig. 3: The *Plastiki* is a catamaran sailing boat made of 12,500 recycled PET plastic bottles. It's journey across the Pacific (in 2010) is part of an initiative to advocate ethical waste management and recycling of plastic consumer items. (Photo: Courtesy D. de Rothschild, 2010)

Acknowledgement:
Regarding the text on a proposed `Research Agenda', I acknowledge the discussions and collaboration with the following colleagues and the support from the *Australian Academy of Science/ATSE*: Chris Twinn, Ken Maher, Haico Schepers and Peter Graham, 2009.

References

ABS, *Year Book Australia* 2008 (2008): Australian Bureau of Statistics, Australia

Air Ventilation Assessment Method for urban climatic mapping: *The comprehensive study* (2007): *Feasibility study for the establishment of Air Ventilation Assessment (AVA) Method in Hong Kong*; published by CUHK, commissioned by the HK SAR Government (2003-06); including the development of an Urban Climatic Map and Wind Standards for HK. See: www.hkia.net

Arup-1. Website (2009): www.arup.com/eastasia/project.cfm?pageid=7047, accessed May 2009

Arup-2. Website (2009): www.arup.com/arup/feature.cfm?pageid=11227, accessed May 2009

Aslin, H.J. & Brown, V.A. (2002): *Terms of engagement: a toolkit for community engagement for the Murray-Darling Basin*. Bureau of Rural Sciences, Canberra.

Balford, Alan (1990): *Berlin: The Politics of Order, 1737–1989*; Rizzoli, New York.

BASIX – *Building Sustainability Index*, NSW Department of Planning, Sydney. At: www.basix.nsw.gov.au, accessed Oct. 2009.

Beatley, Timothy; Wheeler, Stephen (2004): *The Sustainable Urban Development Reader*; Routledge, Taylor and Francis Group, London, UK.

Blakely, Ed J., Bradshaw, T.K. (2002): *Planning local economic development: theory and practice*. Sage Publications, Thousand Oaks.

Bertaud, Alain (2003): *Metropolitan Structures around the World*; presentation May 2003; available online at: www.alain-bertaud.com

Breheny, Michael J. (1992): *Sustainable Development and Urban Form*. Pion, London, UK.

Calthorpe, Peter (1993): *The next American Metropolis: Ecology and Urban Form*; Princeton Architectural Press, New Jersey, USA.

Castells, Manuel (1996): *Network City: The Rise of the Network Society*; Blackwell Press, Oxford, UK.

Carson, L. (2003): *Building Sustainable Democracies*; Now We the People Conference, University of Technology: www.activedemocracy. net/articles/building_sustainable_democracies.pdf; accessed, May 2009.

Chandler, T. (1987): *Four Thousand Years of Urban Growth*; St. Davids University Press, Lewiston, New York.

Chen, Yawei and Hu, Hao (2009): *Shanghai*; in: Carmona, M; Burgess, R. (2009): *Planning through Projects. Mov-*

References for Chapter 4

ing from Master Planning to Strategic Planning; Techne Press, Amsterdam, The Netherlands.

CIB Report (2010): *Towards Sustainable and Smart Eco-Buildings. Summary Report: Smart ECO-Buildings in the EU*; report by the International Council for Research and Innovation in Building and Construction (CIB), London, UK.

Cities Alliance (1999): *Cities Without Slums: Action Plan for Moving Slum Upgrading to Scale*; published by The World Bank and UN Centre For Human Settlements (UNCHS; UN-Habitat), Special Summary Edition, 1999), p. 4; available online: www.citiesalliance.org

COHRE (2005): *Slum-Upgrading. General Introduction and Compilation of Case Studies*; published by the Centre on Housing Rights and Evictions (COHRE, Geneva, CH, 2005)

Cumberlidge, Clare; Musgrave, Lucy (2007): *Design and Landscape for People*; Thames & Hudson, London, UK.

Department of Planning, NSW (2005): *Sydney Metropolitan Strategy*; plan for Sydney and the greater metropolitan region, NSW Government, Sydney www.metrostrategy.nsw.gov.au, accessed Jan. 2009 (released 2005)

Droege, Peter (2007): *The Renewable City*. Wiley, www.renewablecity.org, accessed Oct. 2009; and in private conversation with the author.

Dunster, B; Simmons, C; Gilbert, B. (2008): *The ZED Book – Solutions for a Shrinking World*; Taylor and Francis, London, UK.

EnergyPlus: free energy simulation tool (software) for buildings, developed by US-Department of Energy www.energyplus.gov accessed Oct. 2009 (version 2008).

Frumkin, H.; Frank, L; and Jackson, R. (2004): *Urban sprawl and public health. Designing, planning and building for healthy communities*. Island Press, Washington, USA.

Garreau, Joel (1991): *Edge City: Life on the New Frontier*, Doubleday, New York.

Garnaut, Ross (2008): *The Garnaut Climate Change Review*, Cambridge University Press, UK.

GBCA, 'GreenStar' is the rating system of the Green Building Council of Australia; www.gbca.org.au ; accessed Oct. 2009.

Gehl, Jan (1971): *Life between Buildings. Using Public Space*; Danish Architectural Press, Copenhagen, Denmark.

Girardet, Herbert (2008): *Cities, People, Planet*. John Wiley and Sons, UK; and in private conversation with the author.

Gissen, David. (ed.) (2002): *Big & Green: Toward Sustainable Architecture in the 21st Century*. Princeton Architectural Press

Gorgolewski, Mark; Morettin, Lawrence (2008): *Designing with reused building components*; in: proceedings of *SB08 World Conference*, Melbourne, Australia.

Gray, J.; McIntosh, J.; Maher, S. (2010): *In praise of sharing as a strategy for sustainable housing*; in: *Journal of*

Green Building, Vol. 5, No. 1, Winter 2010, College Publishing, Virginia, USA.

Greinacher, Udo (2010): *Developing future models of the city.* Statement prepared for ACSA 2011 conference. Washington, USA.

Guy, Simon (2000): *Models and Pathways: The Diversity of Sustainable Urban Futures;* in: *Achieving sustainable urban form,* by: Williams, K; Burton, E; Jenks, M (2000); Spon Press/Taylor and Francis, London, UK.

Habermas, Jürgen (1989): *Structural Transformation of the Public Sphere,* MIT Press,Cambridge, MA

Hajer, M. and Reijndorp, A. (2004): *In Search of New Public Domain, Analysis and Strategy,* NAI Publishers, Rotterdam

Hall, Peter (2005): *The Sustainable City: A Mythical Beast,* Keynote L'Enfant Lecture, American Planning Association and National Building Museum, Washington

Hamdi, Nabeel (2004): *Small Change. Urban Participatory Development.* Earthscan, London, UK.

Hassenpflug, Dieter (ed.). (2000): *Die Europäische Stadt. Mythos und Wirklichkeit* (The European Town: Myths and Reality). Bauhaus-University Weimar and LIT Verlag, Muenster

Hardoy, J., Mitlin, D., Satterthwaite, D. (1992). *Environmental Problems in Third World Cities.* Earthscan, London.

Hoyer, Karl, and Holden, Erling (2003): *Household Consumption and Ecological Footprints in Norway – Does Urban Form Matter?* In: *Journal of Consumer Policy,* 2003, p. 327-349

Hyde, Richard (2000). *Climate Responsive Design: A Study of Buildings in Moderate and Hot Humid Climates;* Spon Press, London, UK.

Hyder Consulting (2006): paper: *Waste and Recycling in Australia;* WA Department of Environment and Heritage, Perth, Australia.

IEA/OECD (2008): *World Energy Outlook – Executive Summary,* www.iea.org/Textbase/npsum/WEO2008SUM.pdf, accessed May 2009

IPCC Intergovernmental Panel for Climate Change; *Climate Change Report, Mitigation* (2007): *Fourth Assessment Report of the IPCC – Technical Summary,* UN's Intergovernmental Panel on Climate Change, Cambridge University Press, UK

Jacobs, Jane (1961): *The Death and Life of Great American Cities,* Random House, New York.

James, H. (2001): *The End of Globalization;* Harvard Press, Cambridge, USA.

Jenks, M; Burton, E; Williams, K. (eds) (1996): *The Compact City: A Sustainable Urban Form;* Spon Press/Chapman and Hall, London, UK

Kuts, Greg, et al. (2003): *The Costs and Financial Benefits of Green Buildings;* report to California's Sustainable Building Task Force (released Oct. 2003)

Kenworthy, J; Laube F; Newman, P; Barter, P; Raad, T; et al (1999): *An International Sourcebook of Automobile Dependence in Cities 1960-1990;* University Press of Colorado, Boulder, USA.

Koolhaas, Rem; Mau, Bruce (ed. Siegler, J.) (1994): *What Ever Happened to Urbanism?,* in: *Small, Medium, Large, Extra-Large* (1995); 010 Publisher/The Monacelli Press, Rotterdam, The Netherlands.

Kurokawa, Kisho (1992): *From Metabolism to Symbiosis;* Academy Edition, London, UK.

Lehmann, S. (2006): *Towards a Sustainable City Centre: Integrating Ecologically Sustainable Development (ESD) Principles into Urban Renewal.* In: *Journal of Green Building,* College Publishing, Vol. 1, Number 3 (Summer 2006) p. 85-104

Lehmann, S. (2009): *Regenerating the City;* in: *Back to the City. Strategies for Informal Urban Interventions* (ed. S. Lehmann); www.backtothecity.com.au, accessed May 2009.

Lehmann, S. (2008): *UNESCO Chair Brochure,* Australia

Lehmann, S. (2009): *UNESCO Chair for Sustainable Urban Development,* www.slab.com.au/unescoslab.php, accessed Oct. 2009.

Lehmann, S. (2009): *Interdisciplinary models for collaboration: empowering community, inspiring urban renewal;* in: *UNESCO Observatory* (e-Journal), Vol. 1, Issue 4, June 2009; the University of Melbourne, Australia.

Lerup, Lars (2000): *After the City.* The MIT Press, Cambridge, USA.

Lepik, Andres (2010): *Small Scale, Big Change: New Architectures for Social Engagement;* MOMA catalogue, Oct. 2010, New York, USA; and in private conversation with the author.

Lin, G. (2002): *The growth and structural change of Chinese cities: A contextual and geographical analysis;* in: *Cities,* Vol. 19(5).

Lowe, Marcia (1990): *Alternatives to the Automobile. Transport for Livable Cities;* Worldwatch Paper 98, Worldwatch Institute; available online www.thesource.com , accessed May 2009

Mackay, David (2008): *Sustainable Energy – Without the Hot Air,* UIT Cambridge, UK.

Madanipour, A. (2003): *Public and Private Spaces of the City;* Routledge, Taylor and Fracis, London/New York.

Marvin, Simon; Hodson, Mike (2009): *The right to the City – energy and climate change;* in: *Critical Currents,* No. 6, Oct. 2009, Dag Hammarskjoeld Foundation, Uppsala, Sweden; available online at: www.dhf.uu.se

Mitchell, William (1996): *City of Bits. Space, Place and the Infobahn;* MIT Press, Massachusetts, USA; and in private conversation with the author.

McCurdy, R. (2008): *Grounding Vision – Empowering Culture. How to Build and Sustain Community Together,* Institute of Earthcare Education, NZ

McGregor, Duncan; Simon, David; Thompson, Donald (eds.) (2008): *The Peri-Urban Interface. Approaches to Sustainable Natural and Human Resource Use.* University of London/Earthscan, London, UK.

McKinsey & Company (2007): *Pathways to a Low-carbon Economy.* Report released 2007, available online: www.mckinsey.com ; www.lowcarboneconomy.com (Version II, 2009), accessed May 2009

McKinsey Global Institute (2008): *Preparing for China's Urban Billion*. Report available online; report released in March 2008; Shanghai, China.

McKinsey Global Institute (2010): *India's Urban Awakening*. Report available online.

Mumford, Lewis (1961): *The City in History. Its Origins, its Transformations, its Prospects*; Penguin Books, London, UK.

Newman, P. and Kenworthy, J. (1989/1999): *Cities and automobile dependence: An international source book*. Gower, Aldershot (1989); and: *Sustainability and cities: overcoming automobile dependence*. Island Press, Washington DC (1999); and in private conversation with the author.

Newman, P., Beatley, T., Boyer, H. (2009): *Resilient Cities. Responding to Peak Oil and Climate Change*. Island Press, Washington DC, USA.

Ng, Edward (ed.) (2009): *Designing High-Density Cities for Social and Environmental Sustainability*. Earthscan, London, UK.

Ravetz, Joe (2000): *Urban form and the sustainability of urban systems*; in: *Achieving sustainable urban form*; Williams, K; Burton, E; Jenks, M (eds) (2000); Spon Press/Taylor & Francis, London, UK.

Rees, William, and Wackernagel, Mathias (1995): *Our Ecological Footprint: Reducing Human Impact on the Earth*. New Society Publishers, Philadelphia.

Rode, Philipp; Chandra, Rit (2008): *Urban India: Comparing Mumbai, Delhi, Kolkata and Bangalore*; in: *Connecting Cities: India. A Research Publication for the 2008 Metropolis Congress*; Johnson, Chris (ed.); Metropolis, Sydney, Australia.

Sassen, Saskia (2001): *The Global City*; Princeton University Press, New Jersey, USA.

Satterthwaite, David (ed.) (1999): *The Earthscan Reader in Sustainable Cities*. Earthscan, London, UK.

Schittich, Christian (ed.) (2004): *High-density Housing. Concepts, Planning, Constructions*. Edition Detail, Birkhaeuser, Boston, Basel, Berlin, Germany.

Schroepfer, T. and Hee, Limin (2007): *Emerging Forms of Sustainable Urban Housing*, ENHR Conference Proceedings, Rotterdam, NL; and in private conversation with the author.

Shanks, Kirk; Daly, Patrick (2008): *Strategic Energy Planning for Decision-Making*; in: *Proceedings PLEA 2008* Conference, Singapore.

Shiel, J., Lehmann, S., Mackee, J. (2008): *Strategies for practical greenhouse gas reductions in the existing building stock*, Proceedings ANZAScA 2008, University of Newcastle, Australia; and in private conversation with the author.

Smiley and Robbins (2002): *Sprawl and Public Space: Redressing the Mall*, Princeton Architectural Press, USA.

Notes and Web Sites for Chapter 4

Szokolay, Steven V. (2004): *Introduction to Architectural Science, the basis of sustainable design*. Architectural Press

Urban Land Institute (ULI) (2007): *Growing Cooler. The Evidence on Urban Development and Climate Change*. Urban Land Institute, Washington, www.uli.org, accessed May 2009.

UNDP (2008): *Human Development Indices*; available online: http://hdr.undp.org/en/statistics/

UNEP (2007): *Buildings and Climate Change – Status, Challenges and Opportunities Sustainable Construction and Building Initiative of United Nations Environment Programme* (UNEP): France, www.unep.fr/pc/sbc/documents/Buildings_and_climate_change.pdf , accessed May 2009.

VicUrban (2006): *Melbourne Docklands ESD Guide*; VicUrban, Mercedes Waratah Press, Melbourne, Australia.

Viljoen, A; Bohn, K; Howe, J. (2005): *Continuous productive urban landscape. Designing urban agriculture for sustainable cities*; Elsevier, Amsterdam, NL.

VROM Report (Dutch Spatial Planning and Environmental Communication Directorate) (2004): See also in: Graham and Martin (2004): *Splintering Urbanism*; Spon Press, London, UK.

WHO (World Health Organization) (1992): *Report of the Panel on Urbanization*, WHO Commission on Health and Environment, Geneva, Switzerland.

Wood, Brian (2003): *Building Care*; Blackwell, Oxford (Brian Wood describes Alex Gordon's approach to urban planning)

Worthington, J. (2009): *Urban Form for a Sustainable Future*. Paper presented at SASBE'09 Conference in Delft, The Netherlands, in June 2009 (published in proceedings): www.sasbe2009.com; and in private conversation with the author.

WFES (2009): *Today's Source for Tomorrow's Energy*, World Future Energy Summit, Abu Dhabi, UAE.

Worldwatch Institute (2010): *State of Our World 2010: Transforming Cultures from Consumerism to Sustainability*. Worldwatch Institute / Earthscan, London, UK.

Yu, J; Williams, E; Ju, M; Yang, Y. (2010): *Forecasting Global Generation of Obsolete Personal Computers*, study published in: *Environmental Science & Technology*, online publication doi:10.1021/es903350q; ACS Publication/ Univ. of Iowa, USA (March 2010).

Web Sites and Online Sources (Accessed January 2010)

www.bts.gov — Bureau of Transportation Statistics
www.demographia.com — Site of Demographia Network
www.forbes.com — Site of Forbes Online

www.un.org	The United Nations
www.census.gov	United States Census Bureau
www.worldbank.org	World Bank
www.recyclicity.net	Source for recycled materials
www.superuse.org	Site of architects working with recycled materials
www.chinasolarcity.cn	Chinese Solar City initiative site
www.gtz.de	German Government's technology transfer/development initiative
www.worldchanging.com	Future Materials research site
www.footprintstandards.org	Global Footprints Network
www.urbaner-metabolismus.de/link	Site (Uni Kassel) with plenty of resources on Sustainability
www.worldwatch.org	Worldwatch Institute site
www.nachhaltigkeit.at	Sustainability site from Austria
www.energie-cities.org	Informative site on urban energy topics
www.c40cities.org	C40 is a group of the 40 world's largest city
www.mvrdv.nl	Dutch visionary architects
www.dcue.dk	Danish Centre for City Ecology
www.passivhus.dk	Danish Passive House Association
www.ecobuilding.dk	Danish eco-building project
www.ecocity-project.eu	Scandinavian-Spanish initiative
www.urbanecology.org.au	Australian site, Adelaide-based initiative
www.oekosiedlungen.de	German site: overview of 180 eco-projects
www.clintonfoundation.org	Clinton Climate Initiative
www.ecocitybuilders.org	US site of Californian initiative
www.worldchanging.com	Site on innovative developments, materials

Notes

1 Kellyn Bets added the following commentary on the study on e-waste recycling, by Yu, J; Williams, E; Ju, M; Yang, Y., published in *Environmental Science & Technology* (March 2010): 'This new study published in Environmental Science & Technology presents the first estimate of the worldwide volume of obsolete personal computers (PCs). The authors, who are based in China and the US, show that developing world nations will be disposing of more old computers than developed countries by 2018 – or sooner. This is significant because uncontrolled toxic emissions result from the informal recycling practices that are often used to deal with e-waste in the developing world. Informal recycling practices documented in China and other developing nations over the past decade include burning plastic computer materials and using crude methods to recover precious metals such as copper and gold by using acids and cyanide. The resulting emissions, which can include dioxins, furans, and cyanide, can harm the recycling workers and pollute local environments. Up until now, the main approach to mitigating the impacts from informal recycling has focused on reducing the amount of e-waste that developed nations export to developing countries. The EU's Waste Electrical and Electronic Equipment (WEEE) directive is intended to ensure that the Union's e-waste is not processed informally. Current U.S. federal regulations target only e-waste that contains a cathode ray tube (CRT) or mercury (Hg), but 20 U.S. states, plus New York City, have passed legislation mandating e-waste recycling, according to the Electronics TakeBack Coalition (ETBC). The United Nations Environment Program's (UNEP) Basel Convention also prohibits the transport of hazardous waste, including e-waste, between countries. In their new paper, Eric Williams and his colleagues at Arizona State University's School of Sustainable Engineering and Nankai University (China) write that 'the prevailing assumption that trade is the main driver of informal recycling will soon become obsolete.' Their paper is the first to break out the volumes of e-waste arising in the developed and developing worlds. However, some of the same issues were raised in a recent UNEP report, which noted that the volume of e-waste was rising exponentially in developing nations, such as India, China, and South Africa. By failing to consider the whole range of consumer electronics that end up as e-waste, Williams is missing 'a huge part of the story,' charges Barbara Kyle, ETBC's national coordinator. The worldwide volume is steadily increasing in part due to the rapid emergence of new technologies in televisions, computer displays, and cell phones, she points out. The new analysis focuses on PCs because that is the technology for which the most robust database on global adoption is available, Williams says.' (Bets, 2010)

Further research

The following pages show a collection of images and diagrams in regard to the topics raised in Chapter 4, to introduce a wider context and inspire the reader to conduct further research in these fields.

Floor Space - Volume: Comparison of Building Typologies and Energy-related Characteristics

TYPOLOGICAL COMPARISON		A/V RATIO
	Detached House	0.78
	Terrace House	0.65
	Apartment Block	0.43
	High-rise Building	0.49
	Stepped Arrangement	0.78

After: Energy Manual (2008)

Diagram illustrating the comparison between volume, building typologies and energy-related characteristics. The block structure of the apartment slab or row (terrace) housing typologies, sharing walls and circulation, have clear energetic advantages compared to high-rise, through their more compact form. Are there any new block typologies emerging?

Research areas of the UNESCO Chair

Sustainable Cities: Urban Design and Mobility	Renewable Energies, Materials and Waste Management	Building Technology and Construction Systems

Cities and Climate Change Impact Management		Housing - Compact Mixed Use Communities; New Typologies For Densification
Social Sustainability and Cultural Identity	**RESEARCH AREAS OF THE UNESCO CHAIR**	Urban Water Management and Biodiversity

Informal Temporary Urban Design for the Post-Industrial City	Redefining Architectural Education	Upgrading the Public Space Network

© s_Lab

Above: The ten priority research areas of the UNESCO Chair in Sustainable Urban Development for Asia and the Pacific. Most doctoral research is conducted in the areas of sustainable cities, district-wide integration of renewable energy sources, food security and sustainable construction systems using modular prefabrication. (Diagram UNESCO Chair, 2008)

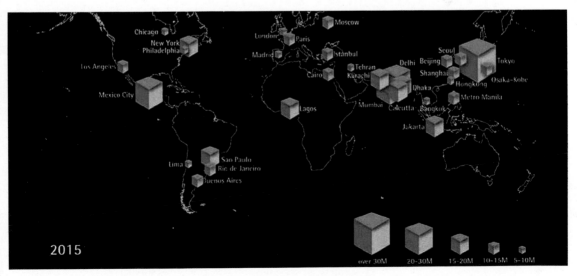

Energy consumption by 2015: Asia will be the place of immense energy consumption, as shown by this diagram. It is in China, India, Indonesia, and around South-East Asia where most energy will be consumed. The two largest countries, China and India together, represent over 2.5 billion people. Other focus points will be in Latin America, Mexico City and Sao Paulo. In the same way, the centre of gravity of global scientific research is moving slowly to Asia.

Diagrams: Different Infill Arrangements

EXTRA STOREY

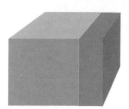

EXPANSION

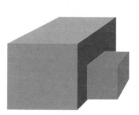

EXTENSION

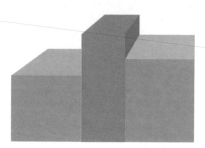

URBAN INFILL

PERIMETER BLOCK INFILL

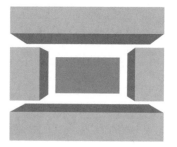

INNER COURTYARD INFILL

After: Energy Manual (2008)

Diagram illustrating some different densification and urban infill concepts. As we need to increase densities and compactness, and improve the intensification of existing inner-city building ensembles (especially around transport nodes), many opportunities exist for implanting mixed-use programmes into these existing block arrangements. (UNESCO Chair, S. Lehmann; after: Energy Manual, 2008)

Optimum compactness: the ideal building shape does not exist;
only optimization processes depending on location, orientation and climate.

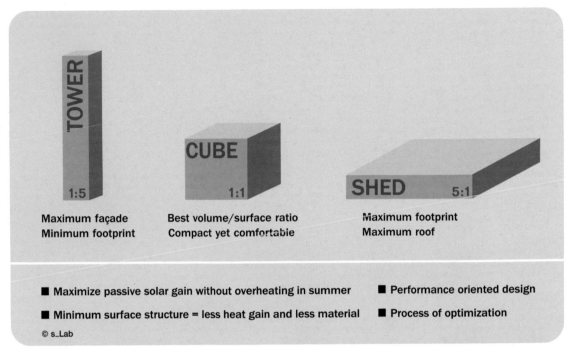

TOWER 1:5

Maximum façade
Minimum footprint

CUBE 1:1

Best volume/surface ratio
Compact yet comfortable

SHED 5:1

Maximum footprint
Maximum roof

■ Maximize passive solar gain without overheating in summer

■ Minimum surface structure = less heat gain and less material

■ Performance oriented design

■ Process of optimization

© s_Lab

The compactness of the cube has many energy-related advantages, especially when combined with a naturally-ventilated atrium, for cross-ventilation and day-lighting strategies. As Asian cities change their scale, Chinese cities are fully embracing the residential tower as preferred typology, despite its thermical disadvantage of maximum solar gain. (Photos: S. Lehmann; left: Singapore, 2009; right: Shanghai, 2006)

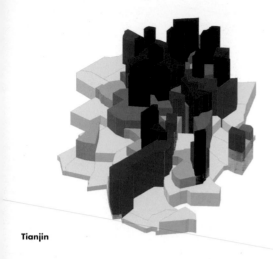

Tianjin

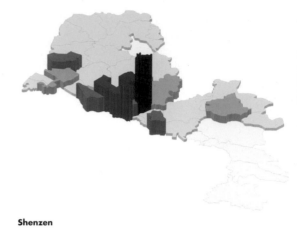

Shenzen

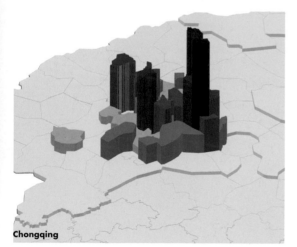

Chongqing

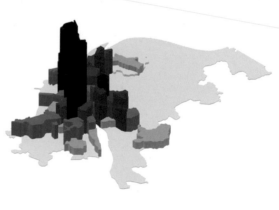

Wuhan

Global population growth means growing cities (and growing urban slums)

It is estimated that over one billion people are now living worldwide in slums (data: UN-Habitat, 2009). Every year, around 25 million people are added to the slum population. With global population growth, around 80 million people p.a. are added to the world population; and a majority of them is added to cities. This means that every week a city of 1 million people has to be built. In other words, 4,000 houses must be built every hour to meet the global demand. The UN has identified poverty alleviation and upgrading of slums as some of their main goals for the 21st century. Rather than forcefully evicting slum dwellers (as was normal policy in the past), most governments and cities have changed their attitude to slum dwellers; upgrading slums is crucial to a point where they merge with the rest of the city. Investing in sustainable frameworks for human life is a moral and worthwhile project. For instance, every dollar invested in sanitary infrastructure gives an immediate return of seven dollars. Mumbai is called the 'global capital of slum dwelling', with Dharavi being the largest slum in Asia.

Study of population densities of 4 large, second-tier cities in China: The population distribution of Shenzen, Wuhan, Tianjin and Chongqing is visualized; the distribution of residents appears unbalanced (especially in Chongqing and Shenzen) where population is concentrated in a mono-centric way. Many Chinese cities are still too mono-centric and centralized, given their size. (Source: Wenli Dong, UNESCO Chair, 2009)

Growing urban slums in India. Top: In Mumbai, Asia's largest slum, Dharavi. An informal habitat for an estimated 700,000 to 1 million people without basic sanitation and supply of drinking water. With an area of 175 hectares it is probably the most densely populated neighbourhood in the world. Below: Smaller slum clusters in Mumbai Bandra, for construction workers. (Photos: S. Lehmann, March 2006)

Low-lying coastal cities

Frequent flooding caused by changing weather patterns as a result of global warming leads to a large amount of people being displaced and made homeless. Bangladesh, for instance, is particularly affected, and many of the country's population have become climate change refugees. It is expected that we will see a dramatic increase in climate refugees from low-lying coastal cities in the mid-21st century, such as Dhakar, as rising sea levels and flooding force people permanently from their homelands. Bangladesh has recently experienced more frequent flooding, caused by an increase in intensive rain periods. It is estimated that, due to global warming, Bangladesh could have over hundred million climate change refugees by the end of the century. (Photo: Flooded Dhakar, 2007; source: Flickr Commons, open source online)

China's economic development often comes at the cost of air and water pollution and land degradation. From the Benxi steel mill (left) to coal-firing powerstations in Hebei (right), are contributing to China's CO_2 emissions, the largest in the world. (Source: Flickr Image Sharing Commons, open source online, 2008)

Source: Image Sharing Commons

Scaleless high-rises of banal mediocrity

As cities worldwide lose their distinctive identity and unique qualities, they become more interchangeable; an impact of globalization. Uncoordinated, randomly dispersed high-rise buildings – this phenomenon can be observed in Shanghai, in Sao Paulo, in Bangkok and many other cities. While the high-rise tower typology is practical for office space, it is less practical for housing. Apartment towers can only work well in particular circumstances and when they are designed, built and maintained at a very high quality level.

Top: Over-development and lack of diversity might create social issues in such new estates like this one in Kowloon: housing project, Hong Kong (2006). Skyline: Sao Paulo, the financial capital of Brazil, has around 18 mill. people and is an endless agglomeration of modernistic apartment towers. Endless city: the municipality of Sao Paulo is approximately the size of Shanghai, with an area of over 1.5 mill. sq km.

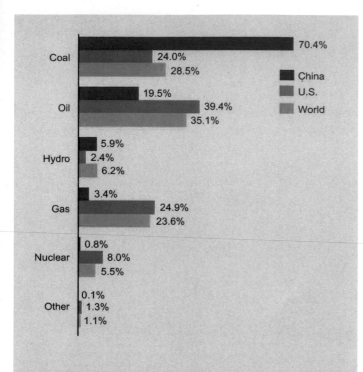

Coal
- 70.4%
- 24.0%
- 28.5%

Oil
- 19.5%
- 39.4%
- 35.1%

Hydro
- 5.9%
- 2.4%
- 6.2%

Gas
- 3.4%
- 24.9%
- 23.6%

Nuclear
- 0.8%
- 8.0%
- 5.5%

Other
- 0.1%
- 1.3%
- 1.1%

■ China
■ U.S.
■ World

Note: *"Other" includes electric power generated from geothermal, solar, wind, and wood and waste sources*
Sources:
1. BP, "BP Statistical Review of World Energy June 2009"
2. Energy Information Administration, "International Energy Annual 2006" Table F.8
3. The China Greentech Initiative analysis

Huge opportunities for renewables

The Asia-Pacific Region is likely to be significantly affected by energy mismanagement, despite its growing market for renewable energy products and its huge manufacturing capacities. Large-scale implementation of renewable energy technologies would be an effective way to address energy supply and energy security challenges. Recent policies by China (since 2009) acknowledge this fact and they have started to support the large-scale roll-out of wind-power and solar power plants. Developing nations can enjoy a greater potential for harnessing solar power, wind power, biomass and geothermal power, compared with most industrialized countries, as they do not have the burden of `old' industries and their infrastructure investments. These countries can move straight into the age of renewable energy. Therefore, renewable energy sources and technologies are of particular importance to developing countries, helping them to `catch-up' with richer nations in a carbon-constrained future.

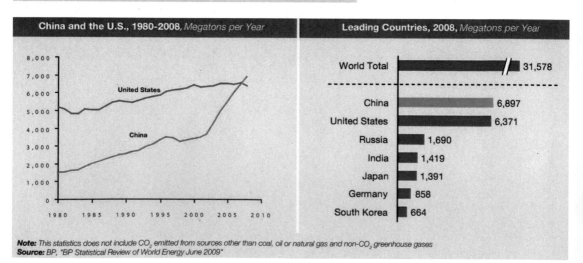

China and the U.S., 1980-2008, *Megatons per Year*

United States

China

Leading Countries, 2008, *Megatons per Year*

World Total	31,578
China	6,897
United States	6,371
Russia	1,690
India	1,419
Japan	1,391
Germany	858
South Korea	664

Note: *This statistics does not include CO_2 emitted from sources other than coal, oil or natural gas and non-CO_2 greenhouse gases*
Source: *BP, "BP Statistical Review of World Energy June 2009"*

Top diagram: China's primary energy mix compared to the US and World, 2007 (% of total energy consumption).
Below: CO_2 emissions from consumption of Coal, Oil, Gas, by different countries. (Source: Both diagrams courtesy BP `Statistical Review of World Energy', June 2009)

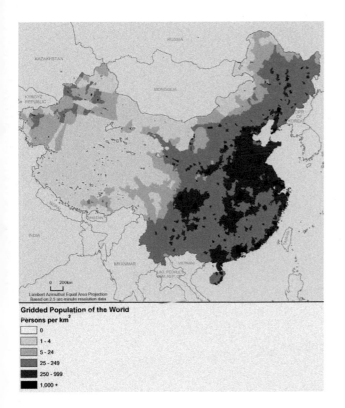

Gridded Population of the World
Persons per km^2

- 0
- 1 - 4
- 5 - 24
- 25 - 249
- 250 - 999
- 1,000 +

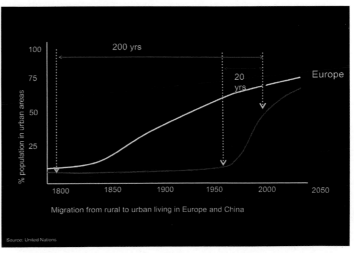

China is characterized by a very uneven distribution of population density, with most people living in the eastern provinces. China has also very different climatic conditions, ranging from severe cold in the north to hot and humid in the south. (Source: 'China Population Density 2000' by Sedac, NY). Diagram: China has urbanized in 20 years to the degree that has taken Europe 200 years.

European city typology
compact, mixed-use block

Chinese city typology
dispersed high-rise

American / Australian typology
flat suburb, dense business core

Impact of globalization on urbanism: losing distinctive difference

With globalization, the distinctive typologies of the city in Europe (Paris, Barcelona), Asia (Shanghai, Seoul), and the US / Australia (Houston, Brisbane) have become increasingly similar. In fact, we can frequently find the same designers doing similar projects in totally different contexts. In the US and Australia, cities are much younger, without any pre-industrial history. How will we manage to maintain the unique, distinctive characters of the various places?

Housing in Singapore

The tropical city-state of Singapore is a small island without much natural resources, noted as a 'Garden City'. Singapore has managed to develop in short time to a global city, and is now on the way to becoming a model of sustainable development for the Asia-Pacific Region. The city has a population of 4.48 million people (date: Jan. 2009). The concept of high-rise city living has been well introduced, and an astonishing 95 per cent of Singaporeans own their own flat. Over 85 per cent live in Housing Development Board (HDB) flats, developed by the Singaporean government. The average floor area of a 4-room HDB unit is 90 sqm. The high degree of home ownership has been an advantage, as home owners usually take better care of their neighbourhood. Many of the mature housing estates, mostly modernistic slab, coutyard, or point tower types, now require rejuvenation and transformation.

Top: With globalization, different city typologies are becoming increasingly similar. Which typology offers the most sustainable form? What are the advantages of the compact, mixed-use European block model (let's say, of Barcelona and Paris), as compared to the current high-rise model which is applied by China for its rapid urbanization? Below: Bukit Batok Estate and Dawson Estate in Singapore, developed in the 1970s.

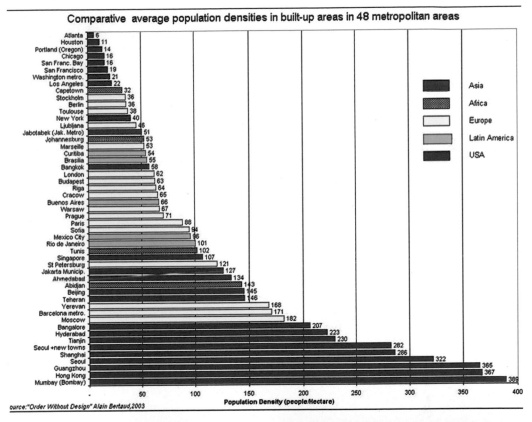

Comparative average population densities in built-up areas in 48 metropolitan areas

City	Density
Atlanta	6
Houston	11
Portland (Oregon)	14
Chicago	16
San Franc. Bay	16
San Francisco	19
Washington metro.	21
Los Angeles	22
Capetown	32
Stockholm	36
Berlin	36
Toulouse	38
New York	40
Ljubljana	46
Jabotabek (Jak. Metro)	51
Johannesburg	53
Marseille	53
Curitiba	54
Brasilia	55
Bangkok	58
London	62
Budapest	63
Riga	64
Cracow	65
Buenos Aires	66
Warsaw	67
Prague	71
Paris	88
Sofia	94
Mexico City	96
Rio de Janeiro	101
Tunis	102
Singapore	107
St Petersburg	121
Jakarta Municip.	127
Ahmedabad	134
Abidjan	143
Beijing	145
Teheran	146
Yerevan	168
Barcelona metro.	171
Moscow	182
Bangalore	207
Hyderabad	223
Tianjin	230
Seoul +new towns	282
Shanghai	286
Seoul	322
Guangzhou	365
Hong Kong	367
Mumbay (Bombay)	389

Legend:
- Asia
- Africa
- Europe
- Latin America
- USA

Population Density (people/Hectare)

Source:"Order Without Design" Alain Bertaud,2003

More comparative research of metropolitan densities is necessary. (Diagram: courtesy A. Bertaud, 2003) Singapore's urbanization is in need of sustainable models for its mature housing estates: Every time, the government demolishes entire housing estates, the existing community ties are lost. Wouldn't it be better to keep the existing structures and integrate them in a 'densification strategy' that introduces mixed-use programmes?

Above: *Elmpark Green Urban Quarter*, Dublin (Ireland) is a mixed-use development with residential and office blocks; architects: Buchholz McEvoy, 2008: www.bmcea.com

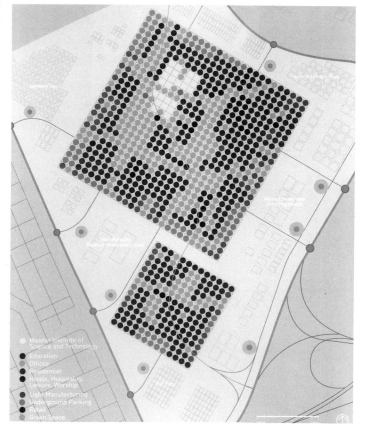

Masdar City, a mixed-use, self-contained, car-free business park for working, living and learning (left).

The mixed-use city is an important concept, as it is the prerequisie for social contacts. The diagram left illustrates Masdar City's planning concept to integrate a diversity of functions. Every dot in the diagram represents another functional use: there will be an Institute of Science and Technology campus with research incubators, office workplaces, residential, hotels with conference centre, light manufacturing, retail and leisure facilities, combined with green space and underground parking. The city is surrounded by a new infrastructural landscape, including: solar farm (a 10 MW PV plant), water treatment plant, waste transfer and recycling station, CSP solar plant and sports facilities for fitness and well-being. (Diagram: Courtesy Masdar City, 2009) Great city districts and quarters have always multiple design authors and a diversity of design concepts.

Top left: Terraced houses at Loorestreet, Affoltern (Switzerland, 1997-99), by Metron Architects. These are ten low-cost, medium-density terraces of four houses each, with standardized structure and prefabricated, large-scale wall and facade systems. External cladding is in local douglas timber; there are green roofs with rainwater retention and solar hot water systems. (Photos: Courtesy Metron Architektur, 2005; BMCEA, 2008)

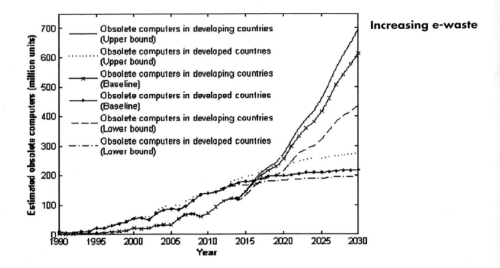

Increasing e-waste

Global Hunger Index, 1990-2009

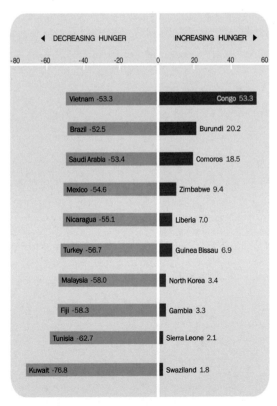

Above: Diagram illustrating the massive increase expected in e-waste in developing countries. (Courtesy: Yu, J; Williams, E; Ju, M; Yang, Y.: *Forecasting Global Generation of Obsolete Personal Computers,* study published in: *Environmental Science & Technology,* USA (March 2010). Below: Diagram of the Global Hunger Index, 1990-2009. An increase in ranking identifies the worsening of a country's hunger situation. (Source: UN, 2009)

Transition from carbon-intensive fossil fuel cities and industries to green urbanism and a green society

At the start of the 21st century we are faced with human activities having an enormous effect on the environment, ecological systems and on humanity itself. We are now at a critical stage and need to make some difficult decisions, choices and changes in behaviour and lifestyle. We are at the point where we have to adopt integrated technical and social approaches to building a more sustainable society. Governments need to continue investing in the research and development of low-emission technologies and support the transition towards a zero-carbon society by opting out of fossil fuel based industries and practices.

In the US and Australia, where there is still a lack of real commitment to renewable energy sources, coal and other fossil fuels continue to be the main energy sources (and in the case of Australia, its biggest export earner). It is likely that these fuels will remain the major sources of power generation for another decade. Based on climate change and resource constraints, the necessary rapid and far-reaching process of transforming our existing cities requires a clear framework for managing the transition; for instance, a framework for the way we replace existing urban infrastructure with a new, localized, decentralized infrastructure. In this process, we must phase out coal-fired powerstations

Epilogue: How does Urbanism and Urban Design need to Change?

and start generating energy in different, cleaner ways, and we need to rethink material cycles. Unfortunately, governments won't act unless they are forced to. We don't have time to take tiny steps; we need a decisive phase-out plan for coal, to close the coal industry by 2030. To be able to do so, we need a transition plan for green jobs – including new positions for those currently employed in the mining industry.

About a fifth of CO_2 emissions arise from deforestation, so it is essential that we massively reduce the rate of deforestation, especially the clearing of tropical rainforests. Every year, rainforests absorb about 15 per cent of emissions from fossil-fuels, therefore by conserving them and planting more trees we will take a huge step in rectifying one of the causes of our climate problem. Rainforests produce much of the world's rainfall. Deforestation obviously reduces this and changes precipitation patterns across the world, thus contributing to food shortages.

The future is not something we enter. The future is something we create.
Leonard Sweet

In Chapter 1 the challenge of re-engineering our cities was introduced, while Chapter 2 outlined the *15 Principles of Green Urbanism* in detail. This holistic framework gives replicable strategies and guidance to urban design. Much of *Green Urbanism* is common sense urbanism. Chapter 2 described the available and emerging most promising concepts and technologies, and Chapter 3 went on to translate and apply these concepts and technologies into a series of realistic design proposals. Chapter 3 illustrated the application of these principles in different urban designs: the *City Campus, Port City, Green Corridor* and *Taree Waterfront* projects were documented – all outcomes of the author's design studios over the last five years. These studios reconsidered how buildings are part of a green district or quarter, and how holistic strategies and integrated approaches can guide urban development.

It was helpful to have a case study city such as the city of Newcastle, as the potential for the prinicples' application needed to be tested in real life conditions, and the chosen case study city is a useful model for many other post-industrial cities – in size somewhere between a large metropolitan centre (such as Sydney) and a regional urban centre. In addition, the phenomenon of a regional city of around 200,000 to 500,000 people has previously not yet been looked at properly. In Chapter 4 the view was widened and the perspective included Asia's rapid urbanization and its consequences. We looked at cities, with their complex layering over time, as meaningful compositions.

This study does not intend to tell the reader what to do. It is a voluminous compilation of information, a resource and reference book, out of which questions and new urban strategies might evolve. In 'Whatever happened to Urbanism?', Rem Koolhaas explored the paradox that 'urbanism as a profession, has disappeared at the moment when urbanization everywhere is on its way to establishing a definitive, global *triumph* of the urban condition... Now we are left with a world without urbanism, only architecture, ever more architecture' (Koolhaas, 1995), and he continues to point out that 'Modernism, its ideas, aesthetics and strategies are finished.' As a result of the new condition caused by climate change and resource depletion, the *Principles of Green Urbanism* could lead to a new, revised understanding of the important role of urbanism, offering an opportunity to reconnect with city-making in a meaningful way.

Issues were identified as significant for the pathway towards a low-to-no-carbon society

Behavioural change and a shift of attitude by city dwellers were identified as essential issues to address. However, introducing behavioural change is always difficult – it requires seriously engaging the users and is a question about resources and material futures. Changing behaviour of a 'throw-away society' and aiming for zero waste will not be easy.

Another issue identified is the need for a more conscious use of waste, materials, metals, resources and products must be achieved. This requires general support by all stakeholders in reusing and recycling materials and end-of-life products. This is an imperative for the preservation of resources. Energy and material recovery requires changes in production systems, an optimization of processes and a shift in the way we design, construct/produce and operate cities, districts, buildings and products.

Improved recycling processes are crucial. Material flows and circular urban metabolism are increasingly recognized as major issues in our survival strategy, at least equal in importance with the energy, water and transport questions. For instance (as discussed in Chapter 4), electronic waste (e-waste) alone poses dramatic challenges: e-waste from developing countries is forecast to overtake that from the developed world, as increasingly wealthy consumers in countries such as China, India and Brazil dump their e-waste, which is poisoning water and soil. To illustrate the seriousness of this problem: recent research found that within six to eight years, developing countries will be disposing of more old computers, refrigerators and mobile phones than the developed world (Yu, Williams, Yang, 2010). Our system of subsidies even encourages the wasteful consumption of resources. So, how can we influence global consumption and achieve behavioural change before it's too late?

Richard Buckminster Fuller 40 years ago noted in regard to behavioural change: 'If you want to change how someone thinks, give up; you cannot change how another thinks. Give them a tool, the use of which will lead them to think differently.' (Buckminster Fuller, 1970)

The city is dead – long live the city

Urban design and urban energy transition offer important keys to combating climate change. We already have most of the answers about how to achieve the necessary transition and we posses the technological know-how to do it, but decision-makers are strangely reluctant to apply these solutions. I fear that we will fail (again) to recognize the urgency of the situation, and that this hesitation will have serious lasting consequences for the environment. The re-engineering of city districts will take some time, so the task cannot be postponed any longer. The *Principles of Green Urbanism* need to become the standard for all urban design, for applying a holistic framework that can easily be adapted to local conditions, and for following practical steps to rapidly turn all urban settlements into eco-districts and eco-cities.

As conclusion, it is fair to summarize: in terms of urban form, best is the incremental development of an urban form that is compact, pedestrianized, highly mixed-use and network-based.

The most recent research from scientists at the *Potsdam Institute for Climate Impact Research* (PIK Report, 2009) has produced further evidence that it will take the climate and the environment much longer to recover from excessive warming than had previously been thought, and that we need to ensure greenhouse gas emissions reach their absolute peak by 2015, otherwise it may well be too late to stop temperatures rising beyond critical levels. The PIK report states that 'this would render unbelievably large parts of the world uninhabitable as sea levels rise, bringing massive disruption to global food and freshwater supplies, and eventually lead to hundreds of millions of environmental refugees.' We are at a turning point. Fundamental change in urban development practice is urgently required, where society has a new vision that better links socio-economic and environmental policy.

This is undoubtedly the greatest challenge of our time.

The following pages list relevant *City Data* on urban density and growth

Metropolitan population and residential densities

a. Comparison of selected metropolitan population densities in terms of number of inhabitants per sq km of built-up area in the year 2000.

Cairo	27,490	Beijing	14,479
Taipei	23,012	Bangkok	13,869
Mumbai	19,377	Mexico City	11,687
New Delhi	17,677	Sao Paulo	8,945
Seoul	16,725	Barcelona	5,388
Shanghai	16,393	Paris	3,545

b. Comparison of selected residential population densities in terms of number of inhabitants per sq km of inner-city residential area in the year 1985.

Hong Kong	104,135	New Delhi	19,588
Mumbai	49,191	Barcelona	16,480
Lagos	41,752	Beijing	14,343
Jakarta	41,228	Tokyo-Yokohama	9,022
Tianjin	36,394	Berelin	4,278
Cairo	31,952	Sydney	3,881

(Source: Metropolitan World Atlas, 2009)

Another hot-spot of rapid urbanization is Dubai. Hundreds of thousands of migrant workers from India and Pakistan are working on construction sites in the United Arab Emirates. Behind the opulence and dizzying skyscrapers of Dubai and Abu Dhabi, there is often an exploited army of migrant workers living in squalor. The applied models of urbanization are dated from a fossil-fuel era of 'endless oil', depending on fully air-conditioned spaces.

City population by country: the 30 largest cities worldwide

In 2000 there were 200 cities with 1 million people on Earth, 100 cities of between 1 and 10 million people, and only 10 mega-cities (cities with more than 10 mill. population). In the meantime, the world's fastest growing cities are emerging in South-East Asia, the Middle East, Latin America and in Africa.

In 2035 it is estimated that there will be 35 mega-cities, with most urban growth predicted for Asian and Indian cities, such as Dhaka, Lagos and Jakarta. To which extend can the city be a self-organising system?

	2010	2020
Africa (3)		
Cairo, Egypt	12.5 mill.	14.4 mill.
Kinshasa, D.R. of Congo	9.0 mill.	13.8 mill.
Lagos, Nigeria	10.5 mill.	14.1 mill.
Asia (19)		
Dhaka, Bangladesh	14.8 mill.	19.4 mill.
Beijing, China	11.7 mill.	13.8 mill.
Guangzhou, China	9.5 mill.	11.2 mill.
Shanghai, China	15.8 mill.	18.5 mill.
Shenzen, China	8.6 mill.	9.6 mill.
Hong Kong, China SAR	7.6 mill.	8.1 mill.
Calcutta, India	15.6 mill.	18.7 mill.
Delhi, India	17.0 mill.	20.5 mill.
Chennai, India	7.6 mill.	9.2 mill.
Mumbai, India	20.0 mill.	24.1 mill.
Jakarta, Indonesia	9.7 mill.	11.7 mill.
Teheran, Iran	8.2 mill.	9.4 mill.
Osaka-Kobe, Japan	11.3 mill.	11.3 mill.
Tokyo, Japan	36.0 mill.	36.4 mill.
Karachi, Pakistan	13.0 mill.	16.9 mill.
Lahore, Pakistan	7.1 mill.	9.2 mill.
Manila, Philippines	11.6 mill.	13.8 mill.
Seoul, Korea	9.7 mill.	9.7 mill.
Istanbul, Turkey	10.5 mill.	11.7 mill.
Europe (3)		
Paris, France	9.9 mill.	10.0 mill.
Moscow, Russia	10.4 mill.	10.5 mill.
London, UK	8.6 mill.	8.6 mill.

	2010	2020
Latin America (6)		
Buenos Aires, Argentina	13.0 mill.	13.6 mill.
Rio de Janeiro, Brazil	12.1 mill.	13.2 mill.
Sao Paulo, Brazil	19.5 mill.	21.1 mill.
Bogota, Colombia	8.3 mill.	9.3 mill.
Mexico City, Mexico	19.5 mill.	20.7 mill.
Lima, Peru	8.4 mill.	9.2 mill.
North America (3)		
Chicago, USA	9.2 mill.	9.7 mill.
Los Angeles, USA	12.7 mill.	13.5 mill.
New York-Newark, USA	19.4 mill.	20.3 mill.

(Source: United Nations, Department of Economic and Social Affairs, 2008)

The highest population densities of inhabitants per sq km

Kolkata, India	43,752
Dhaka, Bangladesh	37,136
Chennai, India	27,462
Delhi, India	26,276
Hyderabad, India	24,547
Lagos, Nigeria	23,403
Mumbai, India	23,088
Ahmedabad, India	19,185
Seoul, Korea	17,215

Slum population by country in urban areas: largest slums worldwide

The highest percentage of urban population living in slums is in Africa, Asia and Latin America. In African cities, this percentage can be up to 95 per cent of the urban population. For instance, in sub-Saharan Africa, urbanization has become virtually synonymous with slum growth: 72 per cent of the region's urban population lives in slums.

Slums are defined as poor areas that lack basic services or access to clean water, where housing is poorly built and overcrowded. About a sixth of the world's population – over 1 billion people – are living in slums, and that number could double by 2030 if developed nations don't reverse course and start giving the issue serious attention, according to the United Nations. (The UN Human Settlements Program's report, 2008) The report says that the worldwide number of slum dwellers increased by 36 per cent in the 1990s, to 923 million people. At its current pace, the number is likely to double to 2 billion people by 2030.

Slum population

A main concern are the informal squatter settlements in the developing nations in Asia and Africa, because the migration from rural areas to cities in Europe and the Americas has largely played out.

Today, Asia has the largest number of slum dwellers overall, with 554 million, while sub-Saharan Africa has the largest percentage of its urban population living in slums – about 71 per cent of the population live without adequate sewage systems and water supplies. Developed nations are not immune. According to the UN report, 54 million people who live in cities in richer nations live in slum-like conditions.

	Slum population in urban areas	as % of urban population
Africa		
Angola	4.7 mill.	86.5 %
Benin	2.4 mill.	71.8 %
Burkina Faso	1.4 mill.	59.5 %
Burundi	0.5 mill.	64.3 %
Central African Republic	1.4 mill.	94.1 %
Chad	2.2 mill.	91.3 %
Cote d'Ivoire	4.6 mill.	56.2 %
D. Rep. of Congo	14.1 mill.	76.4 %
Ethiopia	10.1 mill.	81.8 %
Ghana	4.8 mill.	45.4 %
Kenya	3.9 mill.	54.8 %
Madagascar	4.0 mill.	80.6 %
Mali	2.7 mill.	66.0 %
Mozambique	5.4 mill.	79.5 %
Niger	1.9 mill.	82.6 %
Nigeria	41.6 mill.	65.8 %
Sierra Leone	2.2 mill.	97.0 %
Somalia	2.8 mill.	73.5 %
Sudan	13.9 mill.	94.2 %
Tanzania	6.2 mill.	66.4 %
Uganda	2.4 mill.	66.7 %
Asia		
Bangladesh	25.2 mill.	70.8 %
Cambodia	2.3 mill.	78.9 %
China	174.7 mill.	32.9 %
India	110.2 mill.	34.8 %
Indonesia	28.1 mill.	26.3 %
Iran	14.5 mill.	30.3 %

Iraq	9.6 mill.	52.8 %
Lebanon	1.7 mill.	53.1 %
Myanmar	7.1 mill.	45.6 %
Nepal	2.6 mill.	60.7 %
Pakistan	26.6 mill.	47.5 %
Philippines	22.8 mill.	43.7 %
Vietnam	9.2 mill.	41.3 %
Latin America		
Argentina	9.3 mill.	26.2 %
Bolivia	2.9 mill.	50.4 %
Brazil	45.5 mill.	29.0 %
Haiti	2.3 mill.	70.1 %
Mexico	11.7 mill.	14.4 %
Peru	7.3 mill.	36.1 %
Venezuela	7.5 mill.	32.0 %

(Source: UN-Habitat, Urban Info database, 2006)

So far, politicians and scientists have failed to clearly tell humanity what it faces if global temperatures reach the upper range of forecasts made by the IPCC. The full impact of global warming has been grossly underestimated.

The difference between rich and poor is increasing worldwide

The United Nations Development Programme (UNDP) index, published in 2009, was compiled using 2007 data on GDP per capita, education and life expectancy, and showed marked differences between the developed and developing world. Norway has retained its status as the world's most desirable country to live in, followed by Australia and Switzerland. The sub-Saharan African states afflicted by war and HIV/AIDS are ranked as the least attractive places. Niger, Afghanistan and Sierra Leone scored worst in terms of human development. Life expectancy in Niger was only 50 years, about 30 years shorter than in Norway, according to the UNDP index. 72 million kids are not receiving any education at all and do not have the chance to attend school, mainly in sub-Saharan Africa. Education, life expectancy and income are here used as indicators. For instance, half the people in the poorest 24 countries are illiterate, compared to 20 per cent in nations classified as having medium levels of human development. Japanese people live longer than others, to 82.7 years on average, with life expectancy in war-ravaged Afghanistan just 43.6 years. People are poorest in the Democratic Republic of Congo, where average income per person is $298 per year. For every dollar earned per person in Niger, $85 is earned in Norway. Liechtenstein has the highest GDP per capita at $85,383; this tiny principality is home to 35,000 people, 15 banks and more than 100 wealth management companies.

More city data

In developing countries, climate change has a direct impact on each person's right to the essentials of life, such as food, water, shelter and security. A recent study by Oxfam predicts that 375 mill. people worldwide will be affected by climate disasters by 2015, pointing out the connection between the impact of climate change and poverty (report by Oxfam Australia, 2009). The report points out: `Unless the climate change debate is framed around people and not economics, people in developing nations will be pushed further into poverty. As climate change is the emerging human rights issue of our time, without immediate action, fifty years of development gains in poor countries will be permanently lost.'

Countries with largest proportion of multi-apartment living

Hong Kong SAR	82%	of population living in apartments
Singapore	72%	
Russia	72%	
Baltic States	68%	
Ukraine	65%	
Spain	62%	
Germany	57%	
Sweden	54%	
Italy	54%	
Austria	50%	

Average building heights in different cities

Hong Kong	26	Number of storeys
Shenzen	23	
New York	20	
Dubai	19	
Singapore	18	
Moscow	14	
Paris	5	
Berlin	4	
London	3	
Amsterdam	2	
Los Angeles	2	
Dar es Salaam	1	

Some of the fastest growing cities worldwide

Beihai, China	10.58% Annual growth rate
Ghaziabad, India	5.20%
Sana'a, Yemen	5.00%
Surat, India	4.99%
Kabul, Afghanistan	4.74%
Bamako, Bali	4.45%
Lagos, Nigeria	4.44%
Dar es Salaam, Tanzania	4.39%

(Source: Research by S. Pennec, based on National Housing Consensuses, 2009)

World population data (2009)

	Population		Life expectancy	Urbanization rate	Density
World	6.625 mill.	100%	68 years	49%	49 / sq km
Asia	4.010	61%	68	41%	126
Africa	944	14%	53	37%	31
Europe	733	11%	75	72%	32
North America	523	8%	78	79%	15
South America	381	6%	73	76%	28
Oceania	36	1%	81	91%	4
China	1.322	%	73	44%	138
India	1.132	%	69	28%	344
Indonesia	235	%	70	42%	122
Bangladesh	150	%	62	23%	1.035

(Source: Metropolitan World Atlas, 2009)

APPENDICES

Conversation 1 – Meeting the Green Urban Planner

Eco-Masterplanning for Green Cities

Malaysian architect Dr. Ken Yeang is an architect-planner and is frequently described as one of the foremost eco-designers, theoreticians and thinkers in the field of green design. He has been described as one of the world's leading advocates in ecological and passive low-energy design. He has designed over one hundred projects and his theory of 'bio-climatic' towers has had an impact around the world, fusing high-tech with organic principles. He was born in Penang, Malaysia, in 1948, and was educated in Penang, the United States and at the Architectural Association in London. He received his doctorate in Architecture from Cambridge University in 1974. He is the author of a number of books on the topic of ecological planning and high-rise design (e.g. 'The Skyscraper: Bio-climatically Considered', 1996; 'Eco-Masterplanning', 2009). According to Yeang, the 'bioclimatic' high-rise tower is a low-energy tower that is based on bioclimatic design principles and designed as a vertical urban design typology crossed by air and light wells and protected by sun shading devices. 'Bio-climatic' in architecture means responding to the climate with minimal reliance on fossil-fuel energy for achieving comfort.

Conversation with Ken Yeang on Eco-Masterplanning

Ken Yeang's definition of 'bio-climatic' is based on five concepts: The integration of the grey (engineering), blue (water), red (human), and green (landscape) infrastructures in projects of all scales; the bio-integration of the building as an artificial element into the biosphere; the eco-mimesis, repeating nature's patterns such as solar energy and waste equals food; the re-linking of ecosystems by bridging the existing natural areas; and, finally, the monitoring for rectifying and improving the existing built environment. His single-minded pursuit of eco-design through his own architectural and planning practice and writing for over 35 years has influenced countless architects around the world. Major works by Ken Yeang include:
• The IBM Malaysia Tower in Kuala Lumpur (1989-1992).
• The National Library Building in Singapore (2000-2005).

The National Library is the first building in Singapore to obtain the 'Green Mark Platinum' award. It incorporates many passive and active design strategies, e.g., a large naturally-ventilated and lit atrium space; the use of external sun-shading louvers; integrated greenery for thermal benefits. The total embodiment of the building (being its 'first costs') was calculated to be 17GJ/sqm, an impressive result achieved through carbon footprint considerations in the selection of all building materials.
The author met with Ken Yeang at the SASBE Conference in Delft, in June 2009 (where they were both invited as speakers) , to discuss the future of sustainable urbanism and why our cities need to change. Here are excerpts from their conversation.

Steffen Lehmann (SL)

Ken, at the beginning I would like to talk with you about the challenges of designing sustainability at the scale of the district, not at the individual building or façade level, so that we can focus on potential strategies that you might bring to projects in the light of the huge challenges we are facing. For instance, how can we best address the broader requirements for the transformation of cities and their energy landscape?

Ken Yeang (KY)

I think it is not so much a matter of scale, but rather a matter of relationships between our human built environment and our activities with the natural environment, regardless of scale. Our human built environment needs to bio-integrate with the natural environment seamlessly and benignly at three levels: physically, systemically and temporally.

SL

The concept of 'ecological land use layers' is of particular relevance to the eco-master-planning process. Could you please explain the key principles of this approach?

KY

The ecological land-use mapping approach is a useful and quick way to understand the ecology of any location prior to making site layout designs and planning decisions. However, it is a simplistic reductionist method, and in addition to this a series of ecological cross-checking needs to be done. The ecological land-use method, for example, does not take into account the state of ecological succession, or the energy flows through the ecosystem, the level of biodiversity, and so on. The key principle of this approach is the integration of all layers, which represent the grey, blue, red and green infrastructures.

SL

Because eco-design in the 1970s did not have the benefit of research or academic theoretical models, you had to do your own research. Much of your design work is research-led and is based on in-house knowledge that you have built up over years, from one project to the next, where one project builds on the previous one. Design which is led by research and ongoing explorations – for instance in recycled material research, innovative technology for prefabrication of building systems, or energy-modeling – has increasingly been recognized as a driver for achieving a higher quality of work. Besides doing the daily project work, many practices now have a research and development division engaged in building special prototypes or other independent experiments that feed-back into the daily office work. Given that you are now involved in projects from London to Dubai to Bangalore, how do you feel about exporting this know-how globally? How is the office driving the design of the master-planning projects? Is the client usually willing to reimburse the research activities or are they simply expecting an architect to do such research as the basis for a commission?

KY

We have no problem with disseminating our knowledge and skills globally – in fact we present all our discoveries and ideas in our books and publications. Regarding the in-house research, most of our clients will not offer extra reimbursement to the research activities. They expect an architect to do such research as the basis for a commission. Our clients are mostly interested in the end result and the output, not so much in the process.

In future, we will see much more need for ongoing in-house research activities simply to stay ahead of the developments.

SL

Sustainable design is always about holistic approaches and about seeing things, systemically exploring and understanding the variety of solutions that are usually available to any problem. You frequently use large glass panels to achieve transparency in your designs, even in projects located in hot and humid climates such as in Kuwait, Kuala Lumpur or Bangalore. In building design, there are different ways to avoid heat gain; for instance, by reducing the glass surface. In your architecture there is a desire to build transparency similar to the early modernists. How can it be climatically controlled?

KY

We generally like to achieve a more natural and unobstructed relationship between the interior and the exterior, which is why we use high-performance glass. We also try to bring in as much natural daylight to the insides of buildings as possible, to reduce the use of artificial lighting. To climatically control the building and to avoid overheating, it is necessary to use cool roofs and facade materials with reflective or white surfaces to avoid heat storage, and to integrate greenery and effective sun-shading devices.

SL

In your recent book 'Eco-Masterplanning', published in 2009, you present nothing less than twenty huge masterplanning projects based on your particular approach and design process. I want to talk with you about the question of density in urban design, and the idea of high-rise. Firstly, does the notion of 'green high-rise tower' actually exist? Secondly, if yes, how can a high-rise ever be truly green? Finally, in regard to transport-oriented developments close to public transport and mixed-use neighbourhoods, which densities should we aspire to in our urban design?

KY

At the start, we need to determine the carrying capacity of a particular location or site and its permissible ecological footprint. We have demonstrated that we can build bioclimatical, sustainable high-rise towers, for instance in KL. To stop sprawl and the further consumption of precious land, we need to build more densely, employing vertical typologies. There is no need to be scared by higher densities.

SL

But many of the buildings you design are large mono-functional 'machines'; for instance, the large office towers which are used as headquarters of banks and global corporations are huge complexes – and I know the brief is asking for these mono-functional towers. Do you see new mixed-use typologies emerging? In this regard, what is, then, the future of Asian cities and where we are currently experiencing the most rapid urbanization processes?

KY

On the contrary, I usually design buildings like cities-in-the-sky or as vertical urban design, as illustrated in my earlier book: 'Reinventing the Skyscraper: A Vertical Theory of Urban Design', published in 2002. For instance, my BATC project from 1997, which is part of a much larger urban idea, is a classic model of mixed-use, multiple accessibility and vertical urban design. Asian cities will continue to grow and build high-rise towers. So our task is to ensure that these towers are bio-climatic, energy-efficient towers. Bio-climatic design achieves two outcomes: it results in a design that is passive-mode and low energy; and, secondly, by being tied to the climate of the locality, it is a more regionalist in its design.

SL

In order to reduce car-dependency, Barcelona and Copenhagen are regarded as robust models, where walking is very pleasant and is well supported by an inter-linked public space network. However, Barcelona has about double the population density per square kilometre compared to, for instance, Sydney or Houston. A lot of new research indicates that compact 4 to 6-storey buildings are more likely to deliver social and environmental sustainability. But we rarely build new cities from scratch today, outside of China. So, what should we do with the existing cities and existing building stock? And what should happen with low-density suburbs?

KY

We should retrofit existing cities and existing building stock and transform them into green eco-cities and green buildings, thereby avoiding sprawl and reconnecting existent low-density suburbs with its green hinterland. The disconnect between the rural and the urban needs to be better considered. If people abandon suburbs and living in these suburbs is not cost-effective, we will need to consider demolishing them and returning the land to nature.

SL

All experts agree that cities will play a major role in reducing the negative effects of climate change. In the past few years this role has been actively debated at all levels and some experts have expressed a very clear and progressive view of what cities could do to tackle climate change related issues. For instance, we could start with city-wide, urban-scale transformations of existing districts – the technology and concepts for holistic solutions are available – however, not much of it has really been taken up so far. In the meantime, some cities have grown considerably and have further increased their ecological footprint. A high percentage of environmental problems are produced by the uncontrolled expansion of cities. How can a more sustainable, more compact, form of urban design be achieved?

KY

A more compact form of urban design should be implemented and designed at the outset. Retrofitting existent layouts are often costly to implement and difficult to achieve,

Ken Yeang and Steffen
Lehmann in conversa-
tion, Delft, June 2009

due to multiple land ownership issues. We should work towards creating more compact and intense urban developments, instead of dispersed, low-density models. The more compact, mixed-use, multicultural and diverse a city is the more effective and sustainable it becomes. Most cities lack a growth boundary and allow uncontrolled sprawl into the precious landscape. Sustainability, of course, deals with all human activity; it is not just a concept of energy, but it has to do with environmental, as well as social and economic issues. A responsible design from an energy point of view is a good start, but is, in itself, not enough. The quality of public space around and between buildings is extremely important; it impacts the quality of life for citizens, as well as enabling social sustainability. Ideally, all individuals and institutions would participate and, in the process, citizens would play an active role in the creation of public space. It is important to consider the broader city-wide context of sustainable development, and the general idea of imagining communities outside of the narrow confines of 'building projects'. I call it 'eco-masterplanning'.

SL

Sustainability has a long history and there are multiple examples of traditional solutions in vernacular architecture throughout the world, where passive design principles have been convincingly applied. However, over the last fifty years, with the introduction of mechanical air-conditioning systems and other 'techno-fix' solutions, it seems like we have forgotten about the most basic and elementary design concepts. Are these passive design principles still relevant today?

KY

Buildings often do not respond well to their environment and context. A good building design guarantees a better life for its users and lower maintenance costs throughout its life-cycle, making sustainable buildings more economically efficient. There are active systems, such as the implementation of new technologies and new materials, as well as passive ones, which are based on the design criteria and don't require a budget increase. Firstly, we need to focus on using the passive systems, such as cross-ventilation or sun-shading systems. By doing so, we are already improving the energy efficiency of the building.

SL

As a consequence, should buildings be simpler and more generic, less specific, to make them more flexible and to integrate newly-developed systems easier?

KY

Yes, buildings could be simpler, more flexible, with its newly-developed sustainable systems better integrated with the natural environment. If buildings are complex, it is often difficult and expensive to change things or integrate them with the sustainability systems, which has an effect on the life-cycle of the buildings. The need for buildings to be recyclable, to be assembled and disassembled easily, has already pressured the architecture community to think differently.

SL

With the *Solaris* office building in Singapore you are currently realizing `the ideal manifestation of a human-made eco-system'. Can you please explain what you mean by this?

KY

The *Solaris* building features a spiral ramp, like a green ribbon on the outside of the building, more than 3 metres wide and running over an entire kilometre long. This means the amount of planted area, winding its way up the building, has a larger square footage, of about 9,000 square metres, than the footprint of the site itself, which is only 7,500 square metres in size. In this way the building will act like a human-made eco-system, maximizing the amount of landscaping provided to cool the air and to absorb CO_2.

SL

It seems that many of our leading philosophers and thinkers today have not yet started to embrace the life-shaping issues around sustainability. There is not enough discourse about the future of the city, about the question why we need 'urbanity'. Brazilian urban planner Jaime Lerner said, that 'it is possible to change and transform a city in just two years'. Curitiba is a good example, which illustrates that even small, inexpensive initiatives are able to generate big transformations and improve the urban complexity as a whole. How do you see the future of our cities and the development of urban models in the next twenty years?

KY

Cities are complex systems that are already stressed, and very inefficient in some aspects, for example in relation to the management of resources. Not enough has been done to explore new urban models to improve the efficiency of cities in the past few decades. I believe this is, increasingly, a lost opportunity, and we are losing precious time in the battle against climate change. Many times it has been pointed out that cities are both the problem and the solution. Indeed, many things could be done immediately; for instance, implementing new solutions for mobility, waste management, water treatment, installation of smart grid technology, energy or environmental education, and so on. All these ideas would improve the existing city and set a new standard for a very different future. More needs to be done by architects and designers, to make sustainable design the standard, not an option.

SL

Ken, thank you for the conversation.

Ken Yeang's web sites:
www.ldavies.com
and
www.trhamzahyeang.com

The National Library Building in Singapore (2000–2005), which is a 14-storey library, regarded as one of

the most energy-effective buildings in South East Asia. (Photos: S. Lehmann, July 2009)

Conversation 2 – Meeting the Green Architect

Beauty in Necessity. The Future is Green

Christoph Ingenhoven was born in 1960, the son of an architect. He founded his practice, Ingenhoven Architekten, in 1985, and is an advocate of sustainable design and low energy architecture. He is considered Germany's most successful architect of his generation and a leader in the application of an ecological approach to design. The central themes of his work are: future work environments, ecology, mobility and urban landscapes. He achieves his aims through the use of conceptual strategies and innovative solutions, and by using integrated approaches with a dedication to optimizing and implementing his ideas. Ingenhoven is influenced by the work of other modern German architects, such as Egon Eiermann, Frei Otto, Thomas Herzog, and Guenther Behnisch, all of whom understood so well the relationship and tension between architecture and engineering.

Christoph Ingenhoven is involved in projects all over the world and is increasingly involved in the design of major buildings in Australia. After winning the design competition for a new high rise tower in Sydney's central business district in 2006, his new 'Space' high rise office tower (to be completed in 2011; ground breaking was in May 2009) and his

Conversation with Christoph Ingenhoven on Sustainable Urbanism

recent involvement with the urban and architectural design of the *Barangaroo* waterfront development might bring him to Australia on a regular basis. Sydney will gain a prominent addition to its skyline with this new (6-star GreenStar rated) office tower on Bligh Street.

Other major works by Christoph Ingenhoven include:
• The RWE Tower, the cylindrical high rise headquarters in Essen for one of the biggest energy suppliers in Europe, designed in 1991 and completed in 1997, was one of the first ecologically orientated high-rise buildings that – with its double façade technology – allows each floor to be naturally ventilated.
• The Lufthansa Headquarters at Frankfurt Airport, completed in 2006, which requires only one-third of the energy of a conventional office building.
• The new Main Station in Stuttgart, to be built over the next ten years, was awarded the Gold Global Holcim Award in 2006 for its sustainable design. As a carbon-free and zero energy railway station, it will require no heating, cooling or mechanical ventilation (described as 'the 21st century underground version of a 19th century railway cathedral'; Walsh, 2008).

The author met with Christoph Ingenhoven in Sydney, in May 2009, to discuss the future of green design. Here are excerpts from their conversation.

Steffen Lehmann (SL)

Christoph, at the beginning I would like to talk with you about the challenges of designing for sustainability at an urban scale – let's say for the *Barangaroo* waterfront development in Sydney, but also more generally. I feel we have moved on from the scale of the individual building or from the sophisticated façade solution, to a broader scale that deals with the entire city. Discussing sustainability on the scale of districts and neighbourhoods, rather than on the eco-facade scale, means that we can focus on potential strategies that you might bring to Sydney projects in the light of the huge challenges we are facing. For instance: How can we best address the broader requirements for the necessary transformation of cities and their energy landscape?

Christoph Ingenhoven (CI)

Public spaces, and the city as a whole, are always much more important than a single building. If we think about sustainability as a necessity, it's still very complex, but not impossible, to build city districts entirely without CO_2 emissions and zero waste to landfill. Mixed-use is thereby one of the most important aspects, because it is a prerequisite for achieving social sustainability. For example, at the new *Gateway* university campus in Dublin, which we are currently planning, we are incorporating a series of existing buildings in the masterplan. New campus structures will have large sophisticated roof shells with building-integrated photovoltaic panels and wind turbines. Supported by geo-thermal power, these buildings will provide more energy than the campus will actually need to operate.

SL

What exactly is your involvement with the Barangaroo waterfront development in Sydney?

CI

We have been invited to be part of a large international team, with JPW and landscape architect Peter Walker, Leighton Properties, MIRVAC and Macquarie Bank, and we are competing here with the team of Richard Rogers. I see the Barangaroo project as Sydney's last chance to significantly expand and transform its CBD through genuinely mixed-use sustainable strategies. Sydney will need to keep up with changes to stay competitive with other cities, such as Singapore or Shanghai. At the same time, Sydney needs a very good, long-term plan to improve its sustainability performance. The city must continue to evolve in order to remain competitive, by integrating density in commercial and living spaces, bringing people back to live in the city centre. Efficient public transport will play a major role in this transformation process. For *Barangaroo*, we developed the idea of 'energy islands', where much of the required energy is generated locally on-site, or at least as close-by as possible, using solar-PV and wind turbines along the harbour. The idea of autonomous energy production with small units on-site is very interesting, and we also propose to re-use an existing wharf building that is already there. Our concept for Barangaroo hopes to extend the CBD by improving and complementing the setting, and reducing the energy needed for this new district by having the right volume, exposure, façade and, of course, by having the right systems in place. A better life-cycle and potential re-use, allowing for changes of structures in future, means more flexibility. Barangaroo is Sydney's great chance to be one of the sustainable 21st-century cities.

SL

A lot of your design work is research-led and based on in-house knowledge that you have built up from one project to the next, an aspect not dissimilar to the practices of Norman Foster or Renzo Piano, where we can find technologically focused details, with a constantly expanding knowledge base that is nurtured inside the office, for instance in the fields of prefabrication and façade technology. One project builds on the previous one. Given that you are now involved in projects from Osaka to Sydney to Luxemburg, how do you feel about exporting this German know-how globally?

CI

It seems to me natural to export this know-how. As you know, German architecture has been very committed to green buildings for a long time, and this has presumably some-thing to do with what others call *German angst*, which could also be described as being scared about environmental pollution and destruction, health issues and security prob-lems, which we can see everywhere today. This development started around 25 years ago, but it is more than just a question of technology or detail – it has grown to a unique approach and attitude. I do not think it is possible to export the solution, but it is possible to bring a philosophical approach and commitment to another place, never the solution as such. The final solution emerges from climatic considerations and the local contextual circumstances, which in every project needs to be carefully analyzed at the beginning.

SL

Sustainable design is always about holistic approaches, about seeing things systemically and with regard to all the connections – and implications – of what we do, exploring and understanding the variety of solutions that are usually available to any problem. You frequently use large glass panels to achieve transparency in your designs, even in hot and humid climates such as Singapore or Osaka. Wouldn't it be more helpful to use prefabricated concrete panels to reduce the amount of heat gain? There are many ways to avoid heat gain. One is by choosing appropriate materials and surfaces, but a glass tower might lack thermal mass. I know that you do not use glass wherever you build, but there is clearly a desire to build transparency, similar to the early modernists. Where does this urge come from?

CI

This desire for transparency has to do with the human experience. Humans used to live outside before we started to settle, and for me this has something to do with an instinc-tive wish to live outdoors, directly experiencing the change of seasons and sunlight. Yes, transparency is difficult to achieve, because it's a question of energy saving too, but even in a building like the Osaka tower, if you calculate the amount of glass, it's less than 50 per cent, because you have the metal cladding and core areas which are closed. We are always restricted by orientation and views, trying to keep out the steep summer sun with sophisticated sun shading devices. For instance, at the Bligh Street tower, the naturally-ventilated atrium is completely oriented to the south, shielded from the sun. To ensure energy-efficiency, we provide a double-skin façade with efficient sun shading in the space between. I don't want to be ideological about the question of materials and transparency. Beautiful architecture is not driven by aesthetics, but by efficient engineering. We have also done wooden facades and brick facades. For instance, the university building in Duesseldorf is nearly closed, without windows on the colder façade; only the sunny side is open, using passive design principles, and wide cantilevering roofs to keep the summer sun away. The traditional house, with verandahs around it, is actually quite transparent too. If you think of the traditional examples in Singapore, these provide flexible envelopes.

SL

So the double-skin façade is a modern interpretation of the traditional verandah? That's quite a poetic way to look at it...

CI

Maybe it's more like the modern interpretation of a multi-layered window. I remember I was very impressed as a kid when I visited, with my father, an old house on Lake Geneva, an area which has a mild climate. An old villa there had shutters outside the window for security reasons, then the window itself, which they called a 'winter window', had an inner window, and in between these two wooden framed windows was an inside shutter for glare control. In addition, they had two different layers of curtains on the inside – one translucent and one for blacking-out. So, they ended up with six layers.

SL

And you have only three!

CI

Exactly! *[laughs]* But you see the technology is quite old. You can find it in vernacular architecture in the Alps, for instance at old farmhouses. These frequently have so-called 'winter glasses', and they just put these in as is necessary.

SL

I want to talk with you about the question of density in urban design, and the idea of high rise. Does the notion of 'green high-rise tower' actually exist? Can a high-rise ever be truly green?

Christoph Ingenhoven and Steffen Lehmann in conversation, Sydney, May 2009. (Photos: Cida de Aragon)

CI

They have to be green! In the future there will be no modern city without high rises. Many German cities are shrinking because their population is in decline; they don't need high rise buildings. But globally, Asian cities are rapidly growing, and we find there they have hundreds, even thousands, of high rise buildings for working and living – just think of Hong Kong. We need high rise towers on the global scale. So, why shouldn't we develop better high rise models? The denser city is certainly the better city, but this doesn't depend on high rise. Take, for example, Houston in the US, which has high rise but an appalling low overall density. It depends on the whole city scale. Sydney has an extremely low density and is one of the biggest energy consumers per capita. On the opposite side, the city of Copenhagen, which has no high rise at all, is one of the best cities in terms of energy-efficiency. What does this tell us? It's not about high rise, but about other elements; for instance the extensive use of the automobile has become a major problem, and it is essential for understanding the need for more public transport and mixed-use neighbourhoods. Even in the European context, a single person commuting every morning and evening alone in a car uses more energy than a four-person family in a house. Sustainable urban design depends on the right mix of uses, the right densities and efficient public transport. We can reduce the energy consumption of a city by combining living and working, and by reducing the distances in between and therefore reducing traffic.

SL

But all buildings you design are large mono-functional 'machines'. For instance, the Lufthansa Headquarters is a huge complex – and I know the brief has asked for this. Are there any new mixed-use typologies that are emerging? In this regard, what is, then, the future of Asian cities that are currently experiencing rapid urbanization?

CI

The city needs to be planned in a way that reduces dependence on the automobile. The land use in the city and public transport needs to be intensified. We need to upgrade on all levels, from new bus-based routes to light rail networks and cycle paths, if we seriously want to enhance mass transit. Of course, it's still very difficult to do a real mixed-use high rise typology. The bigger a single building is, the more difficult and unsafe it becomes. To be honest, the better solution might be to have office high rises and residential towers side-by-side, not mixed in one building. Structure and service-wise it's really difficult to do an environmentally sustainable project for both users. I would like to be realistic, it's not about a single piece of architecture, it's about the city's overall structure and intensification of use.

SL

Barcelona has been looked at as a robust model, where walking is very pleasant and is well supported by a memorable public space network. However, Barcelona has about double the population density per square kilometre compared to Sydney. We don't build new cities from scratch, so what should we do with the existing cities and existing building stock? And what should we do with the suburbs? A lot of new research indicates that compact 4- to 6-storey buildings are more likely to deliver social and environmental sustainability. For instance, Thomas Herzog always says that if there is a black-out a 30-storey building is dysfunctional, but a 5 or 6-storey building can still be used. Isn't there an over-dependency of architecture, especially high-rises, on technical systems?

CI

We need to increase the density, compactness and intensity in the suburbs too, maybe even give some of it back to nature by demolishing inefficient suburbs. The city is about being able to deal with technology on many levels. A smaller grain of decisions and function is much better than large complexes. I agree that we need a clear step towards compactness and small-scale technical systems.

SL

Many planners predict that the suburb is an outdated model and urban sprawl will soon out-run and stop by itself, as no one wants to live in isolated houses far from the city anymore.

CI

This will require a shift in public thinking. At the moment most of us live in the suburbs, which are still growing into the landscape, consuming precious landscape and agricultural land. But I agree, the ineffectiveness of low-density suburbs makes it an outdated model. Several developers, who used to develop suburbs, are now talking to us about inner-city residential buildings and ways to make their products green. To communicate good green design and to convince the client is not the problem. You can always explain things. The main problem is that the public is not yet really behind it. There is a lot of public desire for sustainable architecture, but I often find that people are not really interested.

SL

It seems today, a building's sustainability rating correlates to its letability and therefore to its value on the real estate market. I would like to talk about the new tower in Bligh Street, which has been hailed as a 'benchmark building' in integrative environmental design and construction in Australia, even before it's completed. It's an elliptical tower, similar to Harry Seidler's cylindrical *Australia Square* tower from 1961, which, in fact, is just next-door. How can you ensure it is truly a new generation of green high rise, without knowing the tenants and their fit-out plans?

CI

The Bligh Street tower – also known as `Space' – will feature a transparent elliptical shape, with 29 storeys and around 140 metres high. It has a range of progressive environmental design features, including a double skin façade with potential for natural ventilation, an atrium and a range of energy and water initiatives. Our work is based on innovative and holistic solutions in terms of energy, sun shading and thermal comfort. The use of regen-erative energies and resources, like geothermal energy and rainwater, plays an important role in all our building concepts, and so does the intensive integration of daylight, as well natural cross-ventilation. With a minimum consumption of energy and resources we aim for the highest degree of user comfort. Our first eco-high rise was the RWE Tower in Es-sen, twenty-five years ago, which was all about the building's envelope. Since then, we have done over 40 buildings with dual glass skin facades, and the technology has greatly evolved over this time. The Bligh Street tower will be the first high-rise to receive a 6-star certificate on the GreenStar rating system. This tower will be equipped with a real double-skin façade and will be ventilated by an atrium stretching the whole height of the tower. 50 per cent of the ventilation will be provided by the double-skin façade, as mixed-mode system. The building will capture great gap views to Circular Quay, and there is a whole range of things we have introduced that will make the project work well. For instance, the façade will allow us to have a 100 per cent shading solution and glare protection, with perforated internally adjustable blinds within the 600 mm double-skin cavity. The sun protection is very efficient, while maintaining the views, so we can use non-tinted glass on the outer skin. This makes the building extremely transparent and will offer the user a different experience. The ventilated outer skin is made of clear glass, which will ensure a highly transparent building.

The treatment of water has also been made a priority. It has an on-site black-water treatment of 25,000 litres of sewage and recycling. In addition, we're tapping into the city sewer and will be treating another 75,000 litres a day and using the water for landscape features, such as the green walls in the ground floor plaza, and also for toilet flushing. In addition, there is a gas-fired co-generation plant in the basement, and solar tubes with absorption chillers are used for creating solar cooling. The tri-generation system uses gas and solar energy to generate cooling, heating and electricity. 500 sqm of roof mounted solar panels will provide energy to directly power the absorption chiller. Solar cooling is great new technology, invented in Germany. Free heating is provided by in-slab pipe work supplied with the heat that is normally rejected through the cooling towers. A hybrid air-conditioning system consists of chilled beam cooling for the façade and a low temperature variable air volume (VAV) system for the central zones. Also in regard to construction methods, we will exceed the standards: the concrete which will be used contains a much higher percentage of recyclable materials than usual, site amenities are solar powered and 90 per cent of the rubble from demolition will be put back into the site.

SL

Interestingly, the tower has a compact single shape. Frei Otto, the pioneer of light building, used to say that `the human eye perceives those shapes, which are the product of a successful natural evolution towards the most optimal form, as especially beautiful'. You can be quoted as saying that `Beauty is the logical consequence of necessity, logic, truthfulness, efficiency, simplicity and minimalization' (2005). It seems to me that the building's highly refined elliptical shape – a distorted circle in plan – deals well with the diagonal shift that occurs here in the main city grid, the angle of Bligh Street and the curve along Bent Street. In addition, the flattened shape maximizes harbour views from offices inside. I read that the tower's elliptical plan is 12 per cent more efficient than a rectangular building in its façade surface to floor area ratio, so it also delivers economic efficiency. What you propose for the ground floor is interesting. The office floors are pushed up to provide an open public space on the ground floor, with the tower above. This publicly accessible urban undercroft will make it easier to relate to the street level and surrounding context, and allows for more responsible city-making, I suppose.

CI

Exactly. Maximizing the view, while eliminating solar gain. The atrium is hereby another key element of the building and it allows natural light to penetrate deep into the floor plate. Ventilating through the atrium also means that the offices stay noise protected. It creates a social hub for office workers and has balconies that project into the atrium void to provide naturally ventilated break-out spaces, which is important when we think of the next generation workspace. What interests me first and foremost is how people will prefer to work in the next decade and how they envision an optimal work environment. Each floor in this tower will have balconies projecting into the atrium, creating social spaces and opportunities for interaction between tenancies. Sustainability has also a strong social component, and this part is about creating human public spaces and healthy working spaces.

SL

I agree, human public workspaces include optimal air and light conditions. For instance, windows which can be opened and lot's of daylighting, achieved by higher ceilings around the buildings perimeter. What are the other challenges with this project, for instance the `unknown' user requirements for the internal fit-out?

CI

With rental office buildings there is often a disconnect with the end user of the offices, the unspecified tenant that will occupy the building. This has the disadvantage that we cannot communicate with the future users during the design phase and need to make decisions based on assumptions. We try to predict future tenant requirements and focus on indoor environmental qualities and energy-efficiency. Of course, the performance of the design is also dependent on the fit-out and how the tenants will operate the building. While the tower has the potential to be fully naturally ventilated, it depends on the final fit-out from the tenant. Much of the cooling will be provided passively, by activating the thermal mass of the concrete slab. If realized to a high standard, our double-glazed façade concept will allow naturally ventilated floor space for high rise offices, something that is possible even in extreme climatic conditions – like during summer in Sydney, when the temperature outside can reach 35 degrees Celsius.

SL

Clearly, the future is green. Christoph, thank you for the inspiring conversation.

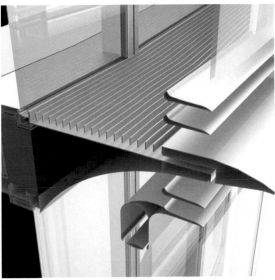

Christoph Ingenhoven's web site: www.ingenhovenund-partner.com	The green high rise tower 'Space' at 1 Bligh Street, Sydney, by Ingenhoven (2007–2011); facade detail.	Natural ventilation is achieved through clever design of the double-skin facade.

Conversation 3 – Meeting the Green Engineer

Beyond Eco-Buildings. Entering the Ecological Age

Arup, the global design, engineering and business consultancy, is the creative force behind many of the world's most innovative and sustainable buildings, transport and civil engineering projects. Founded over 60 years ago in London (1946), Arup has operated in China for more than three decades, and almost a quarter of their worldwide staff of 9,000 is based in Hong Kong and China. Arup was initially commissioned by the Shanghai Industrial Investment Corporation in 2006 to put forward concept proposals for a new sustainable city, *Wanzhuang Eco-City*, located in Hebei Province. Plans for the 80 sq km site are now being guided by a Development Strategy, the Preliminary Control Plan and Sustainability Design Guidelines.

British engineer Peter Head has been a director at Arup since 2004 and is based in London. He is chairman of global planning and leads the company's planning and integrated urbanism business, which includes development planning, economics and policy, integrated urbanism, transport and environmental consulting and sustainable development. In his early career, Peter worked at the forefront of steel bridge technology and in 1998 he was awarded

Conversation with Peter Head on Entering the Ecological Age

an OBE for his services to bridge engineering. He is also chairman of the Steel Construction Institute. Peter was appointed a Commissioner on the *London Sustainable Development Commission* in 2002, representing the construction sector. There, he was a member of the group that drafted the 'Sustainable Development Framework' for London, which led an initiative to create a voluntary code of practise for sustainable planning, design and construction of London's built environment. For the last decade or so, Peter has been dedicated to overthrowing the notion that urbanization is inevitably the fast track to environmental collapse. Specifically, he is fighting to ensure that a growing number of the world's mega cities, and the associated mega projects, embrace sustainability principles from the outset.

From 2004 to 2008 he was project director for the *Dongtan Eco-City* project near Shanghai, a project that has recently stalled. Over the last five years, Peter Head has lectured all over the world on sustainable development and the transformation of cities. He gave the 2008-09 *Brunel Lecture Series* for the Institution of Civil Engineers, titled 'Entering the Ecological Age', which he presented in twenty countries. The Brunel Lecture looked in detail, as to whether there is a model that would enable 9 billion people to live sustainably on Earth in 2050. It asked which policies and investments would be needed to achieve this, and whether it could be done without damaging the economy. In focusing on this ecological transition Peter developed retrofit scenarios for existing buildings and districts.

Steffen Lehmann met with Peter Head at the IGBC Conference in Singapore in October 2009 (where they were both invited as speakers), which discussed the world crises caused by climate change, food, energy and water shortages and resource constraint problems. He asked him what the planner's and engineer's role will be in the cities' transformation to sustainable urbanism. Particularly, how such urban concepts and technologies could be scaled to fit the world's most populous country, China? Here are excerpts from their conversation.

Steffen Lehmann (SL)

Peter, with the economic and financial crisis it has become obvious that our industrial model of development is failing and we quickly need to move towards a new model based on efficient use of renewable resources and materials. I would like to talk with you about the challenges of designing sustainability at the scale of the city district; for instance, how can we best address the broader requirements for a transformation of existing cities, city districts and their energy landscape?

Peter Head (PH)

A significant paradigm shift in architecture, urban planning and engineering is required, and has started to happen, with the aim being to achieve a fair distribution of resources and to encourage a reduction in non-renewable resource consumption. To make real progress, we need to think on the level of the entire city and of complete systems. The main parts of such a holistic approach are food, energy, water and raw materials. Especially important is to include food production as part of a harmonious ecological development. The answer for water is probably in energy, because if we have enough energy we can desalinate water. We need strategies based on 'smart responsive simplicity'. By this, I mean we should keep systems simple, instead of building more and more complex systems; for instance, to use small distributed, decentralized systems, rather than large central ones. This includes collecting energy from the building and district scale, where every building itself produces the energy it requires to operate and feeding surplus energy into the grid, and also, generating energy from waste and reducing energy used in transport and water supply. The solar energy *feed-in tariff*, which was introduced by Germany in 1999, allows every citizen to produce their own energy, and has been a great success story. This policy is about to get replicated and adapted by fifty other countries.

SL

It looks like we need a dramatic rethink and a different approach to town planning and urban design. I imagine, we will probably see more buildings that are simpler and more generic, less specific, to make them more flexible and to integrate any newly-developed systems easier. Technology and design are now drivers for our modern economies. It is particularly exciting to think of the domain of sustainable technology and design as an emerging force rather than an established, already defined practice. Given that you are involved in projects from London to Shanghai to Mumbai, how do you feel about exporting this know-how globally? How is the office driving the design of masterplanning projects, especially sustainable developments for China?

PH

Arup has always been active globally. In China, the ecological footprint is currently grow-ing at a rate of around 3 per cent annually, which means finding an extra 90 mill. hectares of new land each year. The situation in China is quite unique, and the Chinese people are now beginning to embrace a fundamentally different paradigm in urban development, one which starts to reduce this unsustainable demand. Quite apart from the demographic and environmental pressures, there are commercial incentives too. They are also saying that if we get it right, we can sell this success, with its urban solutions and technology, to the rest of the world. Every year for the next twenty years it is estimated that up to 10 million people will move from China's countryside to its urban areas. This unprecedented rural urban migration is placing huge demands on existing cities. To accommodate the new urban population, the Chinese Government plans to build over 50 new cities by 2020. China's leaders recognize the environmental consequences of such growth and have placed an emphasis on economic development based on social harmony, environ-mental protection and energy conservation. The volume of people is so large that there is no one answer for how to accommodate them in a sustainable way; however, we are now working on several initiatives with the Chinese Government, private developers and research institutes that will form part of the solution.

Wanzhuang Eco-City is one such initiative that transforms a number of existing com-munities into an eco-community. Eco-cities deliver significant, tangible and measurable environmental, social and economic gains versus the 'business as usual' case for urban development. They demonstrate greater energy efficiency, better land usage, reduced resource consumption and reduced emissions. We believe that to be truly sustainable, a city must not only be environmentally sustainable, but also be socially, economically and culturally sustainable too.

SL

Could you elaborate on the different social and technological strategies you are using for Wanzhuang Eco-City?

PH

The site of Wanzhuang Eco-City is in Hebei Province, 50 kilometres south east of Beijing and halfway between the nation's capital and the port city of Tianjin. It is close to the city of Langfang, which some have dubbed 'China's Silicon Valley' due to its fast developing economy based on computing and technology. The 80 sq km site includes 15 villages with a total existing population of 100,000. The area has been selected by the Chinese Government for development into a city that will accommodate a population of 400,000 people by 2025. We found that geothermal power is available at this location and plan to tap into this wonderful renewable energy resource for a power supply. Prior to our involvement, the plan for the city was a Los Angeles-style grid of roads based on *super blocks* – gated communities on a mammoth scale, typically over one kilometre square, that cause social segregation, encourage car use and rely on centralized services – electric power lines, sewage treatment plants, sewers and sanitary water supply. The design swallowed existing villages and would have relied heavily on private cars for transport.

Our masterplan is very different. We argued that the American model is much less useful for China's urbanization compared to the European one, with its compact, mixed-use model. The design proposal begins with the simple proposition of retaining and enhancing existing communities through selective renovation and regeneration. Historic buildings and more organic-shaped street patterns are retained as a footprint for the new city, and the villages are expanded as mixed–use communities that connect with walking, cycling and public transport to create the city. Jobs will be created for residents in a range of different zones. Expansive historic pear orchards, which are a key feature of the region, will be preserved. We proposed that the standard of living and environmental quality of the existing villages should be improved, as well as them having new opportunities through education and jobs. A community consultation was carried out with villagers to ensure that the project priorities of addressing culture, water transport and green space were correct. We found that the existing villages in the Wanzhuang area are culturally diverse and could become distinct neighbourhoods. In a cultural workshop with villagers, they expressed the type of cultural spaces the residents would like within Wanzhuang: for example, areas for 'pole walking' and public squares for dancing. The aim of these consultations was to encourage local identity and ownership of place. Arup was using the STEEP evaluation system, which stands for five categories: the social, technological, economic, environmental and political domains.

We gained much experience with the earlier *Dongtan Eco-City* project, a similar project close to Shanghai, designed for 500,000 people. While this masterplanning project was halted in 2008, it created a large knowledge pool for similar projects in China.

SL

With such large-scale projects in China or India, I believe it's of prime importance to understand and translate local cultural traditions. Such a careful renewal approach, which

Peter Head and Steffen
Lehmann in converstion,
Singapore, October
2009

you describe, marks a clear change in attitude. Public consultation and grassroots participation, such as running workshops with village leaders to make sure that the planners have the objectives correct from the start to ensure people-sensitive urban design, is a new approach in China. It's about doing things differently. However, I think such strategies are increasingly important for slowing down and harmonizing the negative effects of rapid, high-speed urbanization, which is frequently lacking long-term planning frameworks and guidance for cooperative process. Sustainable design is about holistic approaches and about seeing things, systemically exploring and understanding the variety of solutions that are usually available to any problem. What about the technological strategies for water, energy and transport in the Wanzhuang project? For instance, in regard to transport-oriented developments close to public transport and mixed-use neighbourhoods, how do you deal with the need for higher density in the urban design?

PH

To determine the best relationship between population density, land value, building density, water management, transport models, and so on, is always very difficult. For instance, water scarcity is a serious concern in neighbouring Langfang, and we have, therefore, suggested a range of methods for reclaiming and distributing water for drinking and non-drinking (grey water) use. Drinking water will be harnessed from underground reserves, and non-potable water will be made available through the treatment and recycling of alternative sources of water. This water will also be used to recharge the underground reserves. By recycling all the existing waste water from the area and recycling it as grey water, there will be enough water to irrigate the farmland for the first time. This, in turn, will increase food yield. In the landscaping, we reintroduce techniques from the past, slopes which cause erosion and water run-off will be replaced by terracing. The flat surfaces contain and soak away rainfall. Water will be harnessed in the existing canal network, but significant improvements have first to be made to the currently polluted network. In addition, we propose that a new water and waste management system be incorporated into the canal network, including new pedestrian paths for improved access, and tree planting schemes to improve shading and reduce water evaporation.

In terms of transport, the Government has proposed a new high-speed rail link that passes through adjacent Langfang. The site is intersected by an existing freight and passenger railway linking Beijing and Tianjin. We are suggesting a new electric public bus or tram network linking all the villages to Langfang and this new high-speed rail station. A network of direct paths will connect the villages to encourage walking and cycling, and the city centre will be a dedicated pedestrian zone. Cars will have to follow protracted routes along the canals in order to avoid crossing the pear orchards and the cycling and pedestrian paths. Fossil fuel vehicles will be restricted and a programme of extending the use of cleaner vehicle technologies will be promoted. Social infrastructure such as schools, offices, medical centres and shops will be spread throughout the city to reduce the need to travel and to minimize use of private cars. In regard to density, despite the compact planning, we provide a large amount of green space. Historic pear orchards and poplar forests will be retained and enhanced to become an expansive city park stretching all the way to Langfang town centre. The new park defines the limits of each development area around the villages and reinforces the city edges with high density development. These city parks will provide additional visual and physical amenity to residents living along its edges, thereby increasing its value. Efficient public transport is crucial, as it means better economic growth and a healthier city. By the way, the city state of Singapore is a good example of this. Transport energy in Singapore is really low and the government continuously invests a relatively large 3 per cent of its GDP annually into the public transport system. Singapore is also on the way to becoming a great model for new eco-mobility, as an island state with only 5 million people it can move more quickly to introduce and implement new policies compared to larger countries.

SL

From what you say it's clear, the fossil-fuel powered energy and transportation systems that currently support our cities must be rapidly turned into systems using renewable energy. If we look at infrastructure, we find that cities have always been planned and built in direct relationship to their urban infrastructure systems. Transforming our urban environments through better integrated infrastructure and land-use planning will be vital in making the transition to sustainable city districts. Talking about systems, I know you are very interested in *biomimicry* principles, as defined by Janine Benyus and others.

PH

Yes, nature teaches us some important lessons. For instance, to use waste as a resource, to optimize not maximize, and to use local resources and materials. These are all great principles which can be applied to urban design, such as looking at circular rather than linear systems. It's not about copying or imitating nature, but about understanding the principles and applying them abstractly. This is performance-led design. I have already described the principle of collecting and using energy efficiently in buildings, but there is also the matter of information; whereby people can live a more sustainable lifestyle through having access to real time information on things like public transport and local services.

SL

In order to reduce car-dependency, many cities have taken action; from Barcelona to Vancouver, from Curitiba to Copenhagen, cities everywhere have adapted robust models, where walking and cycling is made more pleasant and is well supported by an inter-linked public space network. The concept of 'cities of short distances' is about new ways of connecting buildings and precincts to each other that makes better use of existing infrastructure and moves living spaces closer to where we work, closer to transport nodes and community facilities. What do you think will be the effect of the electric car on urban design?

PH

That's an interesting question, as we do not know yet if we will need to build more roads to facilitate a new form of transport. I am convinced that very soon we will see the large-scale roll-out of electric vehicles, and this will have important positive side effects on the urban environment; for instance, by reducing air pollution, we will get a quiet and clean environment in the city, which will again deliver us the opportunity to increase natural cross-ventilation of buildings by simply opening the window. This means, that the electric vehicle will enable us to build a city district based on natural ventilation and reduced air-conditioning dependency, which is all very positive. On the other hand, inter-connecting cities and city centres with high-speed railway will be the future, combined with a policy of public transport-led urban planning.

SL

Most experts agree that sustainable city planning will play a major role in reducing the negative effects of climate change. In the past few years, this role has been actively debated at all levels and some experts have expressed a very clear and progressive view of what cities could do to tackle climate change related issues. For instance, it has been suggested that we start with city-wide, urban-scale transformations of existing districts, re-engineering and retrofitting the existing building stock to make them energy-efficient buildings. Today, the technology and concepts for holistic solutions are mostly available; however, not much of it has really been taken up so far. In the meantime, some cities have grown considerably and have further increased their ecological footprint. A high percentage of environmental problems are produced by the uncontrolled expansion of cities. How can a more sustainable, more compact form of urban design be achieved? Shouldn't we establish strict growth boundaries and clearly focus on densifying the existing footprint?

PH

New urban–rural linkages need to be considered, where we reconnect the urban–rural resource flows to establish a better rural–urban economy, in order to develop the urban and the rural together. Not enough work has been done in improving the relationship between the urban and its rural hinterland. We will also need to consider the important role of brownfield sites, to stop building on greenfield sites, and focus on densifying the existing city.

There are now a series of so-called eco-city projects under way, which are build on greenfield sites and which are in need of further critical assessment. I am still skeptical of the *Masdar-City* project outside Abu Dhabi. Will it be a model that can be replicated? Is it at the right location? Will it attract communities and people to live there? Another much published project is *Tianjin Eco-City*. Unfortunately, its energy supply is based on a coal-burning power station. The energy generation is, of course, a major aspect and in the case of Tianjin Eco-City this has not been shifted to renewable energy, so it's a limited model. We also have to remember that much of sustainability is ongoing, still evolving, and 'learning by doing'. I agree that we need to put higher density mixed-use developments around existing or new transport hubs in cities and suburbs, so that public transport is more affordable and people can get to work more easily. In some sprawling cities, some suburbs will have to be abandoned.

SL

Sustainability has a long history and there are multiple examples of traditional solutions in vernacular architecture throughout the world, where passive design principles have been convincingly applied. However, over the last fifty years, with the introduction of mechanical air-conditioning systems and other *techno-fix* solutions, it seems like we have forgotten about the most basic and elementary design concepts. Buildings often do not respond well to their environment, climate and context. How can we better reintroduce passive design principles into planning and architectural design?

PH

It's important to quantify and evaluate the effect of these passive design principles to better understand how they can be applied most effectively. The combination of thermal mass and greening of walls, roofs and surrounding spaces to shade and cool the building are all important techniques that can improve the overall efficiency and working and living environment, and they can be much cheaper and more attractive than current designs.

SL

You mentioned that solving the energy question by de-carbonizing the energy supply and introducing decentralized systems to generate energy and supply water is of prime importance. What about the large solar thermal projects like *Desertec*, which plan to build gigantic solar fields in the desert?

PH

There is enough solar energy in desert regions to power the entire world's energy needs 10 times over. The issue is, of course, how to get the energy from the desert to the cities. I would think hydrogen is a better solution for some situations, like taking energy from the Australian continent for use in Japan. Ships could transport the hydrogen power stored in cells, and the ships themselves could be powered by hydrogen, transporting the power from places with plenty of sun, such as Africa and Australia, to places of consumption. Africa and Australia could become main producers of hydrogen energy and supply it to large cities in Asia and Europe. However, low conductivity grids and the use of wind, waves, hydro and stream power will also play their part.

SL

Things are moving quickly now, and it seems important that we keep people engaged in sustainability efforts without overloading them with technical information and causing them to lose interest.

Peter, thank you very much for the interesting and optimistic conversation.

Arup's web site: www. arup.com and London's Sustainable Development Commision: www.londonsdc.org

Artist's impression of Wanzhuang Eco-City, located near Langfang (in Hebei Province, China). It's an urban development that is predicted to grow from 100,000 to 400,000 people in the next 15 years. (Courtesy: Arup, London; 2009)

The San Francisco Eco-City Declaration, 2008

An Eco-City is an ecologically healthy city. Into the deep future, the cities in which we live must enable people to thrive in harmony with nature and achieve sustainable development. People oriented, Eco-City development requires the comprehensive understanding of complex interactions between environmental, economical, political and socio-cultural factors based on ecological principles.

Cities, towns and villages should be designed to enhance the health and quality of life of their inhabitants and maintain the ecosystems on which they depend. Eco-City development integrates vision, citizen initiative, public administration, ecologically efficient industry, people's needs and aspirations, harmonious culture, and landscapes where nature, agriculture and the built environment are functionally integrated in a healthy way.

Eco-City development

Eco-City development requires:

a. Ecological security – clean air, safe and reliable water supplies, food, healthy housing and workplaces, municipal services and protection against disasters.

Excerpt from the `Eco-City Declaration', 2008

b. Ecological sanitation – efficient, cost-effective eco-engineering for treating and recycling human excreta, grey water, and all wastes.
c. Ecological industrial metabolism – resource conservation and environmental protection through industrial transition, emphasizing materials re-use, life-cycle production, renewable energy, efficient transportation, and meeting human needs.
d. Ecoscape (ecological-landscape) integrity – arrange built structures, open spaces such as parks and plazas, connectors such as streets and bridges, and natural features such as waterways and ridge lines, to maximize biodiversity and accessibility of the city for all citizens, while conserving energy and resources and alleviating such problems as automobile accidents, air pollution, hydrological deterioration, heat island effects and global warming.
e. Ecological awareness – help people understand their place in nature, cultural identity, responsibility for the environment, and help them change their consumption behavior and enhance their ability to contribute to maintaining high quality urban ecosystems.

Key actions needed

1. Provide safe shelter, water, sanitation, security of tenure and food security for all citizens, and give priority to the urban and rural poor in an ecologically sound manner to improve the quality of lives and human health.

2. Build cities for people, not cars. Roll back sprawl development. Minimize the loss of rural land by all effective measures, including regional urban and peri-urban ecological planning.

3. With 'Eco-City mapping' identify ecologically sensitive areas, define the carrying capacity of regional life-support systems, and identify areas where nature, agriculture and the built environment should be restored. Also identify those areas where more dense and diverse development should be focused in centres of social and economic vitality.

4. Design cities for energy conservation, renewable energy uses, and the reduction, re-use and recycling of materials.

5. Build cities for safe pedestrian and non-motorized transport use with efficient, convenient and low-cost public transportation. End automobile subsidies, increase taxation on vehicle fuels and cars, and spend the revenue on Eco-City projects and public transport.

6. Provide strong economic incentives to businesses for Eco-City building and rebuilding. Tax activities that work against ecologically healthy development, including those that produce greenhouse gases and other emissions. Develop and enhance government policies that encourage investment in Eco-City building.

7. Provide adequate, accessible education and training programs, capacity building and local skills development to increase community participation and awareness of Eco-City design and management, and of the restoration of the natural environment. Support community initiatives in Eco-City building.

8. Create a government agency at each level – village, city, regional, national and international – to craft and execute policy to build the Eco-City and promote associated ecological development. The agency will coordinate and monitor functions such as transportation, energy, water and land-use, using holistic planning and management, and facilitating projects and plans.

9. In policy at all levels of government and in the decision-making bodies of all institutions – universities, businesses, non-governmental organizations, professional associations and so on – address in the plans and actions of those institutions specifically what can be done through the institutions' physical design and layout relative to its local community to address global warming, the coming end of fossil fuel use and the global crisis of species extinction.

10. Encourage and initiate international, inter-city and community-to-community cooperation to share experiences, lessons and resources in Eco-City development and promote Eco-City practice in developing and developed countries.

Source: *The Eco-City Declaration* (first formulated by **Richard Register** and others, at the Eco-City Summit in Bangalore, in 2006) was further developed and agreed on at the Eco-City Summit in San Francisco, in April 2008. Signatories of the original text included: David Suzuki, Richard Register, Jaime Lerner, Tim Beatley, Peter Head, Jeff Kenworthy, Ken Yeang, Mathias Wackernagel, Brent Toderian, Wulf Daseking, and many other leading thinkers and urbanists.

Charter for Solar Energy in Architecture and Urban Planning, 2007: The City

Renewable forms of energy present an opportunity to make life in cities more attractive. In the realms of energy supply and transport infrastructure, the use of these kinds of energy should be maximized through the actual form of the building. The existing building fabric should be used as far as is practical and possible. The combustion of fossil fuels must be drastically reduced.

The relationship between cities and nature should be developed to achieve a symbiosis between the two. Alterations and other measures carried out in public spaces or existing buildings, or caused by new construction, must take account of the historical and cultural identity of a location and the geographic and climatic conditions of the landscape. The city must be comprehended in its entirety as a self-contained long-living organism. It must be possible to control the constant changes in its use and appearance, as well as in technology, in order to ensure a minimum of disturbance and a maximum conservation of resources.

Cities are resources in built form and have a high primary energy content. To achieve a closer integration with the overall balance of nature, various neighbourhoods, buildings and open spaces,

Excerpt from the `Charter for Solar Energy', 2007

their infrastructures, and their functional, transport and communication systems must be subject to a constant process of modification and reconstruction that follows natural cycles of renewal.

The form of the urban and landscape structures that man creates must be governed by the following environmental and bio-climatic factors:

• orientation of streets and building structures to the sun;
• temperature control and use of daylight in the public realm;
• topography (land form, overall exposure, general situation);
• direction and intensity of wind (alignment of streets, sheltered public spaces, systematic ventilation, cold-air corridors);
• vegetation and distribution of planted areas (oxygen supply, dust consolidation, temperature balance, shading, windbreaks); and
• hydro-geology (relationship to water and waterway systems).

Source 1: Thomas Herzog (Ed.): 'European Charter for Solar Energy in Architecture and Urban Planning', Prestel Publishing, London and Munich (1995/reprinted 2007 in ten languages), p. 46-47.

This document was first drawn up by Professor **Thomas Herzog** in 1994-95 in the context of the READ project supported by the European Commission DG XII, and further formulated by the *READ Group* (Renewable Forms of Energy in Architecture and Design), which included Thomas Herzog, Norman Foster, Stefan Behling and Norbert Kaiser. Signatories of the original text (formulated in 1995) included: Frei Otto, Norman Foster, Renzo Piano, Richard Rogers, Thomas Herzog, Ralph Erskine, Herman Hertzberger, Thomas Sieverts, Gustav Peichl, Victor Lopez Cotelo, and many other leading green architects. Courtesy: Thomas Herzog, Munich.

Some Thoughts about the City

We need building structures, which in their development, land use and use of space are considerably more neutral than is typically the case for most residential buildings – particularly the publicly funded ones. One of the consequences here would be to build as densely as possible. It is only when there is enough purchasing power in an area and the distances to facilities needed for daily needs are short enough for pedestrians that an effective mixture of operations is possible. At the same time, motor traffic can be reduced by a noteworthy order of magnitude. A reduction in land use and infrastructure costs naturally goes hand in hand with this, which is significant for the communities in regard to investment and maintenance.

It is exactly here that new models are needed that are socially acceptable. The ideal of living in the countryside awakens the totally wrong impression of being an ecologically sensible strategy. Your own home on the edge of town in a low-density development does give you as an individual the feeling of being close to nature, but it makes you dependent on transport, increases fuel consumption and pollution, and has devastating social repercussions.

Source 2: Thomas Herzog: 'Solar Architecture', originally published in *Detail*, No. 3, 1999, Munich.

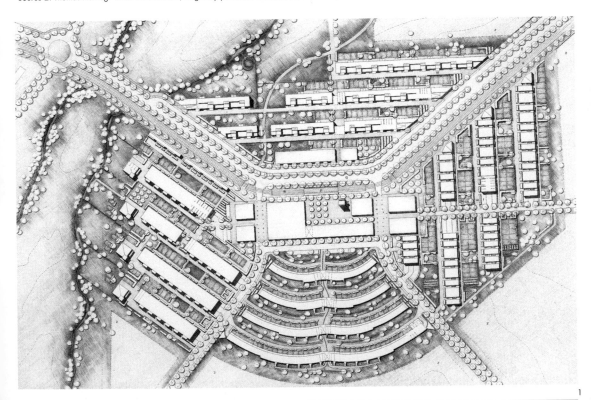

1

1 'SolarCity' at Linz Pichling, Austria, a sustainable development that now accommodates over 3,000 residents.

A new eco-district built between 1994 and 2005; masterplan by Roland Rainer, Thomas Herzog, Martin Treberspurg, et al.

Ten-Point Checklist for Healthy Communities and Cities, 2008
This text identifies a Ten-Point Checklist for the planning and development of healthy and sustainable communities. The 10 domains in the checklist are essentially physical characteristics of places. Each domain has relevance to the health of people living in the place, and to the sustainability of the environment. The checklist is intended as a tool for those who plan, develop and manage urban environments. Such tools can be valuable for assessing the health and environmental impacts of decisions made by urban and transport planners, and businesses engaged in land development and infrastructure projects.

The urban environment is an important determinant of health. Obesity is a good example of how environmental factors can affect health. Obesity results from an energy imbalance: consuming more energy (food) than is expended through physical activity. In developed countries, there is an increasing reliance on highly processed and convenience foods, which often have high energy content. The integration of human health considerations with environmental considerations when developing policy for urban and regional planning is essential. This Ten-Point Checklist is a guide for the development of healthy human habitat. The goal should be to minimize ecological impact while maximizing the human experience, including

A Checklist for Healthy Communities and Cities, 2008

health and well-being. The checklist focuses on characteristics and attributes of places rather than people, because planners and developers can influence such characteristics.

1. Outdoor air quality
Air pollution in most cities is known to exacerbate asthma. The main source of outdoor air pollutants in urban environments is motor vehicle emissions. Improved motor vehicle emission controls have reduced emissions per kilometre travelled; however, the total number of kilometres travelled is increasing. Until there is a reduction in the total number of kilometres travelled, air pollution will remain a health issue. Urban planning and public health interventions to reduce motor vehicle dependence and improve air quality include:
- locating jobs, services, schools and shops close to where people live;
- promoting active modes of transport (walking and cycling); and
- providing mass transit (public transport) options.

2. Water supply and sanitation
Ensuring safe drinking water is a traditional public health function. The warming and drying of the climate in many countries has focused attention on water supply and demand. Governments have issued policies to reduce household water consumption (including restrictions on watering of gardens and promotion of dual-flush toilets and low-flow shower

heads). New water supply options are being considered everywhere. Recycled water can be safely used in drinking water supplies. Public health professionals have roles in the risk assessment, management and communication about water re-use.

3. Housing and buildings

Housing is an important determinant of the ecological footprint of a city. The number of people living in apartments and town houses in Australian cities has increased exponentially since the 1970s. This has been driven by lifestyle choices, increasing land costs and the trend towards single households. Governments have issued policies to reduce energy and water use in new and renovated homes to guide new and retro-fit developments at both the building and the neighbourhood levels. Housing and building characteristics with implications for the health of people and the environment include: Solar access; indoor air quality; natural ventilation to minimize the need for air-conditioning; re-use of building materials; sustainable materials; avoidance of harmful chemical exposures; on-site re-use of water and alternative sanitation options (such as composting toilets). There are benefits in having a mix of housing types and prices in any community. This ensures there are housing options suitable throughout the life-cycle (including options for those with disabilities), allowing elderly people to move within their community as their housing needs change. They need not leave their established social network (*aging in place*).

4. Food

A public culture of food brings vitality and conviviality to urban life. There are health benefits from food shops (fruit and vegetables, meat and fish, daily grocery items) and cafes in close proximity to where people live. People can walk or cycle to such food outlets, and they can connect with others in the community around the food outlets. This is particularly important for elderly and unemployed people who may not have access to motor vehicles. Bringing food to people, rather than expecting people to travel by car to a regional shopping centre to purchase food, can reduce emissions. Such food businesses need a customer base to be financially viable. Locating the businesses on mass transit routes will bring customers to the shops. Economic viability may also be improved by increases in residential density. Food production in urban areas will be increasingly important as liquid fossil-fuels become more expensive (urban farming). Local production reduces transport costs. It can also enable city dwellers to learn about food production and have closer contact with nature. Urban agriculture can reduce the intensity of urban heat islands. Growing food in a communal way, in community gardens and city farms, breaks down barriers between people and stimulates a sense of pride in the local environment. Every jurisdiction should have a food policy to promote local food production and improve healthy food access.

5. Shops and services

In addition to food shops, there are benefits from access to other shops and services in the local area, including primary health care. Shops, services and other destinations can encourage physical activity, social interaction and conviviality. They can also reduce motor vehicle use. The emergence of large, stand-alone, regional shopping centers since the 1960s has affected the economic viability of local shops and services. The impact of these changes on our health and well-being warrant further investigation.

6. Schools and other educational institutions

Quite apart from what is learnt in schools, including life skills and health literacy, there are health benefits associated with the physical presence of schools in communities. Schools can provide an important social focus in communities. Children, parents and grandparents can develop a social network around the school. Schools present an unparalleled opportunity to promote children's health. When schools are located close to children's homes, and when there are safe pathways to the school, children are more likely to walk or cycle to school.

7. Community spaces

Spaces (both outdoor and indoor) for recreation and social interaction are a valuable community resource. Parks and community halls are places where groups can meet, play and organize themselves to work together on projects and activities. People who have good access to attractive open spaces are more likely to be physically active. Governments and planners should place more emphasis on the public domain, as increasing numbers of people live in apartments and town houses. Care should be taken to avoid over-regulation of public spaces. While rising public indemnity insurance costs are an issue for governments and municipalities, regulations can reduce fun, informality and spontaneity.

8. Transport and street connectivity

Active transport (walking and cycling) is good for our physical and mental health. It also reduces carbon dioxide emissions. People are more likely to walk or cycle if there are destinations of interest in the community, such as shops, services and parks. A network of good connectivity is another determinant of the likelihood of walking. Safe pathways to walk and cycle are essential. Pathways should be well maintained and appropriately lit. Mass transit is good public policy. It is good for health (because it is possible to walk to the bus, tram or train stop), good for the environment (because it reduces carbon dioxide emissions) and good for business (because it reduces the cost of traffic congestion). Mass transit is particularly good for young people, the elderly and the disabled, who may not have a license or access to a motor vehicle.

9. Communication technology

Modern communication technologies are essential urban infrastructure. The mobile phone and laptop have started social networks and create mobile business opportunities. High-speed internet services enable access to information for work, education and recreation, in public space or at home. New forms of communication have changed the way we work and communicate; they will reshape our built environment and, as a consequence, new forms of public space will emerge. The impact of these changes on our health and well-being warrant further investigation.

10. Economy and employment

Historically, there was a public health imperative to separate residential areas from employment zones in cities. Industrial point-sources of air pollution were adversely affecting health. In post-industrial societies this is no longer the case, since conditions have fundamentally improved over the last fifty years. Nowadays, physically separating industrial and commercial areas from residential areas is no longer insisted on. Urban planners have started to value intertwinement, urban diversity and the mixing of functions. Arguably there are now public health and environmental imperatives to reintegrate and intertwine life and work. If people live close to where they work, there can be benefits to their health and the health of the environment. Long commuting times can be a source of stress, can adversely affect health and increase carbon dioxide emissions. Local economic development is a tool to create locally based jobs. Each community needs to find ways to incubate new ideas and new jobs. Communities should have local job generation programs and measure job creation as a central tenet of community well-being, not simply the number of people employed.

Affecting the health of people

The 10 domains in the checklist are essentially physical attributes of places. These attributes affect our health by influencing:

- levels of physical activity;
- food choices;
- safety and sense of security;
- sound and noise exposure;
- thermal exposure (heat and cold);
- exposure to air and water pollutants and contaminated land;
- access and participation (especially for youth, disabled people, elderly);
- social connection and conviviality;
- opportunities for contact with nature; and
- time use (commuting, with family, for recreation, in community).

This *Ten-Point Checklist* is a guide for the development of healthy human habitat, focusing on characteristics and attributes of places rather than people. Designers, planners and developers can influence such characteristics.

Professor **Anthony Capon** is a public health physician and a visiting fellow with the National Centre for Epidemiology and Population Health at the Australian National University, Canberra. He is a former director of public health with Sydney West Area Health Service.
This checklist was compiled by Anthony Capon, with input from Ed J. Blakely and Steffen Lehmann, Sydney 2008.

Transcript of Speech, 2009
Keynote address delivered by Steffen Lehmann in September 2009, at the 'International Conference on Sustainable Energy Technologies, SET 2009' in Aachen, Germany. (www.set2009.org)

Green Districts: The City as a Powerstation

Honourable Ministers, Excellencies, Distinguished Ladies and Gentlemen,
Sehr geehrte Damen und Herren,

This is a significant international conference, so please allow me to address you in English today. Firstly, I would like to say how honoured and delighted I am to be delivering this speech at such an important conference. I would like to compliment and thank the organizers – the Government of the State of NRW, the City of Aachen, the University of Duisburg-Essen and the World Society of Sustainable Energy Technologies – for putting together such an excellent programme over the next three days, in the historic city of Aachen.

This city is over 1200 years old. I am currently living in Sydney, and for Australian condi-

Keynote Address: `Green City Districts'

tions, where no city is older than two hundred years, this is indeed a very long history. I want to invite you to see the famous cathedral of Aachen, which has been designated as a UNESCO World Heritage site. Some of our cities have existed over such a very long time and I would like to suggest that we can learn a great deal from their history; for instance, in how cities have become resilient against extreme situations and challenges, and how cities have been built and extended with sustainability in mind.

Cities and urbanization play a major role in the battle against climate change
Today we stand at a crossroads in history concerning the future of our cities. The warnings from our most respected scientists are loud and clear. SET 2009 is an international conference and an important platform for focusing on solutions for both the adaptation and the mitigation of climate change challenges. Over the next few days, you will exchange ideas and think about how our cities and urban infrastructures can become more resilient to the changing conditions of global warming.

I was asked to speak on 'Green Districts' and how cities themselves will become the powerstations of the future, creating their own energy, cleaning water and growing food locally. As the holder of the UNESCO Chair in Sustainable Urban Development for Asia and the Pacific, my main focus is on the rapid (and often traumatic) urbanization processes in Asia. No doubt, it is in Asian cities where we will see most urban development over the next twenty years, and consequently there are increasingly serious concerns regarding energy security, water management and food supply, not only in regard to Asian cities but to Asia in general.

Cities are resource-intensive

By 2030 we will need to produce 50 per cent more energy and 30 per cent more food on less land, with less water and fewer pesticides if we want to avoid catastrophic consequences. The world situation is deteriorating faster than we had previously anticipated.

If global mean temperature increase is to be stabilized at about 2° Celsius, then CO_2 emissions must peak by 2015. However, we need to consider whether the effort to limit an increase in global mean temperature to about 2° Celsius would be adequate, because sea level rise due to thermal expansion alone would be between 0.4 to 1.2 metres by the end of this century. Add to this the melting of ice bodies and we have serious effects in terms of sea level rise on low-lying coastal areas and small island states. CO_2 concentration, temperature and sea level will continue to rise long after emissions are reduced.

It is clear that our increasing energy needs must be covered, to a large degree, by renewable energy sources. Renewable energy sources will need to provide sufficient energy for an ever-increasing world population, if we want to maintain today's lifestyle. This must include the phasing-out of risky nuclear power technology and an end to the construction of new coal-fired powerstations.

It is not as if this is a sudden or unexpected crisis; we have known the damaging consequences of fossil-fuels for forty years. However, it appears that some government leaders continue to ignore the scale of the threat and want to see the impact of climate change as distant and undefined so that they do not have to give it the attention it requires.

The fact is, climate change has created a sense of urgency for all of us in the design, planning and engineering disciplines. This is why we need to rethink urbanism and architecture, and the way how we design, build and manage cities in the future. We are now engaged in nothing less than a peaceful cultural revolution, where all our standards and values in architecture and urban design are being transformed and redefined. Climate change offers us the opportunity to embark on a renewable energy revolution.

Cities are in constant change

But are they heading in the right direction? My presentation will suggest they are not. At the same time I would like to point to the numerous examples of what cities around the world are currently doing to create a more resilient and compact urban form – something that we can, and must, do. Green urbanism has to become the norm for all developments.

Luckily, there are many innovative and exciting developments all over the world that give us cause to hope; for instance, organic photovoltaics are a new technology that could, very soon, make energy from solar cells as cheap as energy from fossil fuels; and research that studies how we can harvest energy from civil infrastructures, such as road surfaces and bridges, which heat up and have the capacity to store energy; or solar cooling technology that runs off-grid and has the potential to replace mechanical (electrical) air-condition systems in the very near future. For 2020, it is predicted that, worldwide, seven million electric vehicles will be on the road (McKinsey study, 2009), and one million of these, it is estimated, will be 'made in Germany' and 600,000 of them will be driven in German cities.

Cities are systems already under stress

This is a time where we need to engage in yet more change in order to adapt to our social, economic and environmental dilemmas.

Green districts require strategies on the neighbourhood scale for urban areas to be more sustainable, with new types of infrastructure systems that no longer provide resources such as power, water and waste through centralized systems, managed by large distant companies. Instead, district systems will supply energy and water, and will manage waste locally at the neighbourhood and district scale, turning existing districts themselves into self-sufficient powerstations.

Cities need to be re-engineered to become more sustainable and resilient

Some of the built environment principles of resilient city districts include:
• transit-oriented, pedestrian-friendly, mixed-use neighbourhoods, with a public space network that makes walking and cycling pleasant;
• urban areas powered by renewable energy – at all scales from the district-level to individual buildings – arranged in compact communities;
• power, water and waste systems that are small-scale and neighbourhood-based, not large and centralized;
• the de-carbonization of the energy supply, where renewable energy is harnessed locally, at the point of consumption, by building-integrated PV and other measures;
• a high proportion of energy and material needs being provided from re-used waste, in closed-loop systems;
• urban food production to help grow vegetables and fruits locally, through urban farming;
• every home, business and neighbourhood being carbon neutral, and all of it contributing to building local economies and a sense of place; and
• urban layouts that allow transport to be by walking, cycling and public mass transit, supplemented by electric vehicles, whereby public mass transit will always be faster than vehicle traffic in all major urban corridors.

Retrofitting the existing city on the district scale requires the integration of low and zero-emission energy generation technologies, complemented by distributed district heating and cooling systems. Every citizen can generate locally the energy they need, which will eliminate transmission losses and costs that otherwise occur for the consumer where the services are provided by a large grid and inefficient base-load powerstations. Therefore, small power generators need to be positioned within communities to provide electricity, while waste heat is captured for combined heat–power (CHP) co-generation, and used for space conditioning.

We need to consider new exergy principles, which look at capturing and harvesting waste heat and waste water streams, and how the strategic arrangement of programmes within mixed-use blocks can lead to unleashing such unused energy potential.

I strongly urge the implementation of these principles and concepts to become mainstream public policy for all urban design, and all cities, especially in regard to high-speed urbanism scenarios in Asian cities. Many good initiatives are already under way, and most of the afore-mentioned principles are eminently achievable, as most of the required technology is already on the market. The communities that are most responsive to change will best survive the challenges of the future. In an ideal world, every development, every building, is energy-efficient, using the best know-how to avoid the wasting of energy, water and materials.

Each country will need to work out its own 'post fossil-fuel energy plan', and that will depend on that country's energy consumption, anticipated lifestyles, population densities and geographical and climatic conditions.

Concluding remarks

My plea to this audience is to please listen to and reflect on the voices of science and the valuable expertise available at this conference over the next days, and to act with determination and a sense of urgency.

The United Nations does not prescribe any specific action, as there are various ways we can take action, but action is a must. Business as usual is not good enough anymore.
Climate change is no longer just an environmental issue; it touches every part of our lives: peace, hunger, health, security, human rights, poverty, mass migration and economics.
Sustainable development of cities must happen along the principles of 'international best practice' in urban planning, architecture and engineering.
Europe is part of a larger system, and part of a globalized world. We cannot look at Germany, or the UK, or at Europe, Australia, or China, as isolated cases. Similar developments have started everywhere and only an internationally coordinated, combined interdisciplinary effort will be strong enough to combat climate change.

I would like to finish by reminding you that with the Copenhagen meeting fast approaching, in December of this year, there is no time for further excuses or postponement. This is a time for leadership and immediate action.

I wish you all a productive and successful conference. Thank you for your attention.

Who's Who? 101 Leaders in Sustainable City-Making and Theory
The following list is a selection of 101 urban experts who made a name in green urbanism and sustainable design theory, and who have discussed the need to transform our
cities and renew outdated principles of urban design earlier than most others. These
leaders and visionaries all share a passion for confronting the threats facing the earth,
by introducing new principles of environmentally sustainable development, and by ensuring that green urbanism doesn't remain an empty slogan. Some of the featured people
are globally well-known, others are less known. However, what counts is their ideals,
persistence and early start in leading research and action in the field.
Leadership is about making decisions, setting new benchmarks, being prepared to take risks,
and learning from each other. The featured 101 leaders can be planners, architects, community activists, mayors, and so on. They are all key proponents of urban sustainability. They
are all aware that no one person or organization can solve climate change alone, and have,
therefore, been working in interdisciplinary teams and networks, developing action plans for
a sustainable future of our cities. Only multidisciplinary international efforts will deliver the necessary solutions to combat climate change. The following experts are therefore representative
of all thinkers in sustainable design and urban development in general, imagining possible
futures of a low-carbon society. Many more leaders could have been selected for listing.

Who's Who in Sustainable City Making and Theory

From A to Z, the 101 selected leaders in sustainable city-making are:

Adnan H. Aliani, UNESCAP Sustainable Urban Development Unit (Bangkok, Thailand).
Aliani is the Human Settlements Officer in the poverty reduction section of UNESCAP and the
founder of a community-based, decentralized composting strategy, which minimizes waste whilst
helping to reduce extreme poverty. The method he introduced is a cycle where organic waste is
broken down into compost (fertilizer), which is used in agriculture and then returned to urban areas as organic food products. This creates a sustainable closed-loop cycle. www.unescap.org

Sultan Ahmed Al Jaber, Masdar Eco-City developer (Abu Dhabi, UAE).
Dr. Sultan Ahmed Al Jaber is CEO of the Abu Dhabi Future Energy Company (ADFEC),
which is undertaking the Masdar initiative, Abu Dhabi's vision and investment in the future of
energy and environmental sustainability, a response to the need for a focus on the development of advanced energies and sustainability-related technologies. He is also an advisor to
Mubadala Development Company, where he holds broad-based responsibilities that include
direct project execution in the energy, industry and utilities sectors as well as relationship
management with key multinational companies and government institutions. Al Jaber holds
a PhD in Economics from Coventry University, UK. Masdar City was selected by the International Renewable Energy Agency (IRENA) for its global headquarters. www.masdar.ae

Rob Adams, former urban planning director (Melbourne, Australia).

Rob Adams is the director of design and urban environment at Melbourne City Council, where he has developed *Council House 2* building (called *CH2*, completed in 2006), the new green headquarters for council staff. His strategic plan 'Transforming Australian Cities', for the densification of Melbourne along transport corridors, won the 2009 National Award for Urban Design. In the 1990s he engineered the turnaround of Melbourne's moribund city centre with the 'Postcode 3000' initiative, introducing inner-city living to Melbourne and turning the CBD into a vibrant place to live and work. The scheme provided the impetus for a surge of residents into the centre, along with a multitude of small cafes, bars and a rejuvenated nightlife. 'There are some basic rules for good urbanism. Each locality should include mixed-use, reasonable housing density, good connections to the city centre and a high-quality public realm,' he said recently. In 2008, Adams delivered a visionary urban consolidation report to the Victorian state government on how to accommodate an additional 2 million people in Melbourne by 2030, without extending its urban fringe. The plan proposes to develop thousands of sites along key public transport corridors into medium and high-density housing precincts and TODs.
www.melbourne.vic.gov.au www.sustainablemolbourne.com

Gregg D. Ander, chief architect of Southern California Edison (Irwindale CA, USA).

Mr. Ander was the executive producer of six environmentally focused television programmes, including 'Greener Buildings/Bluer Skies', which won a 2006 Emmy award. He is a member of American Institute of Architects (AIA) and serves on the Board of Directors of the Sustainable Building Industry Council (SBIC), the New Buildings Institute (NBI), the Collaborative for High Performance Schools (CHPS) and the California Commissioning Collaborative (CCC). He is the author of 'Daylighting Performance and Design' (2008). www.sce.com

Marc M. Angélil, educator and architect at the ETH (Zurich, Switzerland).

Dr. Marc Angélil is professor and dean of the Department of Architecture, at the Swiss Federal Institute of Technology (ETH Zurich), Switzerland. His research at the newly formed ETH-Center 'Network City and Landscape' (NSL) addresses recent developments at the periphery of large metropolitan regions. He is the author of several books, and completed his PhD at the ETH Zurich. He was an Assistant Professor at Harvard University, and subsequently Associate Professor at the University of Southern California. He is a member of the Management Board of the Holcim Foundation. Angélil practices architecture with four partners, as the architectural cooperative agps.architecture, with offices in Los Angeles and Zurich. Their built projects include the new Terminal at Zurich Airport; the town center and light-rail station of Esslingen/Zurich; the remodeling of a factory for housing and commercial uses; the extension of the headquarters of the World Conservation Union (IUCN) near Geneva; an aerial tram infrastructure project in Portland, Oregon; and sports facilities for Adidas in Herzogenaurach, Germany.
www.agps.ch and www.ethz.ch

Dipal Barua, green entrepreneur and activist (Dhaka, Bangladesh).
Mr Barua is managing director of Grammen Shakti. He has developed a system whereby his non-profit organization gives micro-loans to Bangladeshi women and trains them to assemble and re-pair photovoltaic lights (PV lanterns), which bring electricity to rural villages. The organization has a focus on empowering women, as they see them as implementer of change. www.gshakti.org

Guy Battle and **Christopher McCarthy**, environmental engineers (London, UK).
Founding partners of the consultancy engineering practice Battle McCarthy Engineers and Land-scape Architects (founded 1993.) As environmental and building engineers they specialize in the design of low-energy, sustainable buildings and urban environments, dwelling in the interac-tion between structure and the natural environment. Battle-McCarthy is increasingly involved in sustainable masterplanning projects. Publications include: 'Sustainable Ecosystems and the Built Environment' (2001), 'Wind Towers: Detail in Building' (1999) and 'Green Architecture' (2002). Battle and McCarthy constantly develop new ways to make the built environment more efficient, considering economic, social and environmental parameters. www.battlemccarthy.com

Tim Beatley, university educator and author (Virginia, USA).
Professor Timothy Beatley has been teaching at the University of Virginia, School of Architecture since 1989, and has written several books and papers on urban sustainability and livability. His book 'The Ecology of Place' (co-authored with Kristy Manning) is a planning guide for environment, economy and community that has been used in college classrooms across the US since 1977. www.arch.virginia.edu

Joo-Hwa (Philip) BAY, and **Boon Lay ONG**, founders and chairmen of the Interna-tional Network for Tropical Architecture (iNTA), (Singapore and Perth, Australia).
Both are currently senior lecturers: Associate Professor Philip BAY has a particular focus on tropical climate and tropical architecture, at the University of Western Australia. He holds a PhD on design thinking in environmental architecture from the TU-Delft. His publications in-clude: 'Beyond environmental comfort' (2009), 'Tropical Sustainable Architecture: Social and Environmental Dimensions' (2006), 'Sustainable Cities in the 21st Century' (1998), and 'Naturally Ventilated Buildings' (1997). He co-authored a book with Boon Lay ONG, who holds a PhD from Cambridge University. Dr. Ong has a particular interest in ecologi-cal design in the tropics and in urban greenery. He teaches at the University of Melbourne and the National University of Singapore. www.uwa.edu.au, www.nus.edu.sg

BgAP, The Berkeley Group for Architecture and Planning (San Francisco, USA).
BgAP is a group of faculty members, professionals and students affiliated with the Uni-versity of California at Berkeley who develop sustainable city projects. Their 'NanoCity Project', a development of a future city near Chandigarh in India, started in 2007. www.ced.berkeley.edu/research/projects/bgap/nanocity

Bjorn Berge, architect, researcher and author (Oslo, Norway).
Bjorn Berge is a practicing architect with Gaia Architects and has, since 1970, written several

books on materials, such as: *The Ecology of Building Materials* (1992). www.gaiaarkitekter.no

Peter Brandon, researcher, educator and author (Manchester, UK).
Professor Emeritus Peter Brandon is director of the Salford Think Lab (where he collaborates with Prof. T. Fernando), researching sustainable development in construction management, with a focus on knowledge-based systems for sustainable development. He is the former Pro-Vice Chancellor for Research of the University of Salford and has published over 20 books. His latest book is co-authored with Dr Patrizia Lombardi (Torino): *Evaluation of the Built Environment for Sustainability* (2010), which offers a new structure for sustainable development based on the 'Philosophy of the Cosmos' by Herman Dooyeweerd, encouraging a holistic and integrated systems approach. www.thinklab.salford.ac.uk

Michael J. Breheny, urban and regional planner (University of Reading, UK).
Prof. Breheny has contributed to the idea of the sustainable city through research in measuring the compactness of cities, and the difficulties of planning relating to such issues as land consumption and travel behaviours. 'Sustainabile Development and Urban Form', published by Breheny in 1993, was important research for raising issues of sustainable design through urban planning. The book discusses transport and urban form, to reduce energy consumption, with particular interest on the compact city typology. Michael Breheny was Professor of Planning in the Department of Land Management at the University of Reading. He died tragically in 2003, aged 54.

Lester R. Brown, environmental activist and author (Washington DC, USA).
Lester Brown launched the Worldwatch Papers, the annual State of the World reports, World Watch magazine, a second annual entitled *Vital Signs: The Trends That are Shaping Our Future*, and the *Environmental Alert* book series. In 1974, he founded Worldwatch Institute, of which he was President for its first 26 years; it's the first research institute devoted to the analysis of global environmental issues. He has authored or co-authored 50 books, and his books have appeared in some 40 languages. Among his earlier books are 'Man, Land and Food' (1963) and 'Building a Sustainable Society' (1981). His 1995 book 'Who Will Feed China?' challenged the official view of China's food prospects, spawning hundreds of conferences and seminars. In 2001, he founded the Earth Policy Institute (EPI) to provide a vision and a road map for achieving an environmentally sustainable economy. In 2001, he published 'Eco-Economy: Building an Economy for the Earth', which was hailed by E.O. Wilson as "an instant classic." His most recent book is 'Plan B 3.0: Mobilizing to Save Civilization'. His principal research areas include food, population, water, climate change, and renewable energy. www.earthpolicy.org

Blaine Brownell, 'Transmaterial' researcher and university educator (Minneapolis, USA).
Brownell is an architect with expertise in how innovative eco-materials have the potential to facilitate sustainable building design. He researches the use of the latest materials to transform the way buildings react to the natural environment. His research in materials dwells on innovations affecting the physical qualities of structure. Brownell uses the latest technology products and building materials in a sense of promoting sustainable design. At the University of Minnesota, he collabo-

rates with Dr. **John Carmody**, Director of the Center for Sustainability. www.transstudio.com

Jeb Brugmann, urban strategy expert and founder of ICLEI (Toronto, Canada).
Jeb Brugmann is a partner of *The Next Practice* (TNP), and is an economist and public administrator by education. A leading practitioner in devising localized solutions for business, government and international development agencies, he served as founding Secretary General of the International Council for Local Environmental Initiatives (ICLEI). His work has ranged the fields of economic development, urban development, transportation and infrastructure, climate change and natural resources management, refugees and disaster reconstruction. Some other initiatives he has pioneered include: The *Local Agenda 21* initiative, launched at the 1992 UN Earth-Summit and involving more than 6,500 local communities to prepare local measures to address their sustainable development priorities; *The Cities for Climate Protection Campaign*, a programme in alliance with multiple national governments; and the Conference of Parties to the Kyoto Protocol, involving more than 500 cities in a uniform process to identify and implement local measures for greenhouse gas emission reductions. His latest book is entitled 'Welcome to the Urban Revolution' (2009). www.iclei.org

Richard Burdett, researcher at the London School of Economics (London, UK).
Prof. Ricky Burdett believes that flexible and adaptive urban systems must go hand in hand with environmental strategies to achieve a sustainable urban environment. He identifies the need for cities to be more compact to make the most of their urban assets, and wants to address issue about the speed of urban change using intelligent infrastructure systems; he also wants to eradicate social exclusion and introduce proper forms of urban governance. Burdett was the curator of the Venice Architecture Biennale in 2006. He is the director of *Urban Age* and an advisor on architecture and urbanism for the London 2012 Olympics. www.urban-age.net

Federico M. Butera, zero-carbon urbanist and researcher (Milan, Italy).
Professor Butera teaches at the Milano Politecnico, Faculty of Architecture, where he holds the chair of the Department of Applied Environmental Physics. At the University of Palermo, he is the head of the Department of Energy and Applied Physics. He is an urban planner, researcher, scientist and author, and has become an active scientific promoter of renewable energies. Butera's publications include: 'Automation and Work Design', 'Renewable Energy Sources in developing countries: Successes and failures in technology and transfer', 'From the cave to the ecological house - a history of comfort and energy', and 'Which Energy for Which Society?' He worked with architect Mario Cucinella on the SIEEB project in Beijing. www.polimi.it

Fabio Casiroli, **Luca Guala** and **Federico Parolotto**, transport and urban planners (Cagliari/Milan, Italy).
Their company Systematica (founded in 1989) consults on environmentally friendly transport solutions and planning. Prof. Casiroli is the author of a book and theoretical urban

project: 'Khronopolis: Accessible City, Feasible City' (2009). Casiroli is a professor in Transport Planning at Milano Politecnico, in the Faculty of Civil Architecture; he is the founder of Systematica and has been researching transport planning and high-speed networks since 1980. The group is now developing the Personal Rapid Transit System for Masdar Eco-City. www.systematica.net

HRH Charles, The Prince of Wales (UK); and **HRH Willem-Alexander, The Prince of Orange** (Netherlands).
Monarchs joining the battle to save the planet. These aristocrats are personally involved with issues of climate change, water management and climate adaptation. Their influence on public opinion is still immense, so they make an important contribution. Both Prince Charles and Prince Willem Alexander are eldest children and are heirs to their respective British and Dutch thrones. Both are engaged in spatial planning issues. The Prince of Orange has, since 1997, had a particular concern with water management.

Raymond J. Cole, researcher and educator (Vancouver, Canada).
Professor Cole is the leader of the Environmental Research Group at the School of Architecture at the University of British Columbia in Vancouver. He is co-founder of the Green Building Challenge, benchmarking building performance and assessment method.
www.architecture.ubc.ca

Klaus Daniels, engineer, author and researcher (Munich / Zurich, Switzerland).
Professor Klaus Daniels (born 1939) has devoted four decades to advanced engineering solutions as a consulting engineer and educator. From 1991 to 2006 he taught at the Eidgenössische Technische Hochschule (ETH) in Zurich, where he held the Chair of Building Services. In 2006, the Technische Universität, in Munich, celebrated his work with an honorary doctorate in engineering. Over the past 20 years, Daniels and the engineers of his engineering consultancy, HL Technik AG, have published four volumes of seminal work related to the subject, and their work is continuously being updated. His main interest is in how modern architecture needs to be adaptive to energy conditions and how design and technology can be blended successfully.
www.hl-technik.de

Jean-Francois Deceaux and **Jean-Charles Decaux**, eco-entrepreneurs and bicycle system managers (Paris, France).
Bikes are an important part of any attempt to green and transform a city. The Decaux brothers are the green entrepreneurs behind Paris's public bike-rental and sharing scheme (Velib) introduced in 2007 (after a successful start in Lyon) and which has transformed the city's streetscape by offering, city-wide, 25,000 bikes for use. Now ready to be rolled-out worldwide, over 50 municipalities have adopted the concept. It does not require tax payers' money; it is financed through exclusive advertising rights in prime places granted by the municipality. www.jcdecaux.com

Shobhakar Dhakal, researcher and director of the 'Global Carbon Project' (Tsukuba, Japan). Dr. Dhakal is the senior policy researcher for the Institute for Global Environment Strategies (IGES), Japan, and has a special interest in the ecological footprint of Asian cities. He holds a PhD in Urban Environmental Management from the University of Tokyo, and has a Masters degree in Energy Economics and Planning from the Asian Institute of Technology, Bangkok. His core interests are: energy use and emissions in an urban context, management strategies, local climate policies and air pollution. His current involvement is in research dealing with the integration of energy-related policies in Asia, with a focus on urban transport. www.iges.or.jp

Rolf Disch, eco-architect and inventor (Freiburg, Germany).
Rolf Disch's pioneering Office for Solar Architecture has been working on passive energy concepts since 1969. His idea of the *Plus Energy House*, a building that generates more energy than it needs to operate, has been widely published. He is also the urban designer of the Solar-Siedlung in Freiburg. www.plusenergiehaus.de and www.rolfdisch.de

Andy van den Dobbelsteen, researcher and educator, TU-Delft (The Netherlands).
Professor van den Dobbelsteen is an expert in 'Low-ex planning' and does research in exergy on the scale of regional planning at the TU-Delft, in the division of Climate Design & Sustainability in the Faculty of Architecture, where he leads the Climate Design section. Exergy, the local potential of unused energy sources ('energy potential mapping'), is used as a starting-point for a new urban and regional planning theory. Andy is chair of the Advisory Group of the Dutch Green Building Council and organized the 3rd CIB International Conference on *Smart and Sustainable Environments* (SASBE) in 2009. In 2008 he developed the REAP approach (Rotterdam Energy Approach and Planning), a climate and energy planning methodology for the city of Rotterdam, aiming towards CO_2-neutral urban development. It advocates the strategic combination of building programmes that complement each other in terms of energy exchange and storage (a methodology developed with N. Tillie and D. Doepel). http://bk.faculteiten.tudelft.nl, www.sasbe2009.com

Paul F. Downton, 'Ecopolis' architect (Adelaide, Australia).
Paul Downton is director of Ecopolis Architects. In 1991 he formed, with two partners, the non-profit urban environmental community group *Urban Ecology Australia* (UEA), which has been actively promoting ecological developments ever since. Paul has been an important voice in developing an eco-city theory and has realized building projects (such as *Christie Walk* in Adelaide) based on this theory. www.ecopolis.com.au and wwwurbanecology.org.au

Russell Drinker, architect and urban designer (San Francisco, USA).
Mr Drinker is a director at Perkins+Will Architects, where he leads teams for architecture and planning on a broad range of large-scale, technically challenging projects with an emphasis on sustainable design. His portfolio is notable for its research in the design of academic campuses, including master planning for six of the University of California's

campuses and multiple projects at Stanford University. He is currently leading the Campus for Research Excellence and Technological Enterprise (CREATE) project for the National Research Foundation in Singapore, and the Princess Noura University project in Riyadh, Saudi Arabia. CREATE will be a multi-national, multi-disciplinary research enterprise dedicated to stimulating innovation, discovery and sustainability. Mr Drinker is a leader in integrated project delivery and has a focus on developing strategic, collaborative solutions. www.perekinswill.com

Peter Droege, urban planner and author (Sydney, Austalia; and Vaduz, Lichtenstein); and **Hermann Scheer**, politician and 'Eurosolar' activist (Berlin/Bonn, Germany).

Dr. Peter Droege is an expert in renewable energy within the fields of urban planning and infrastructure. He has directed and developed a 'Solar City' project as a research development effort conducted under the auspices of the International Energy Agency. Droege has performed academic roles at major universities in the United States, Australia and Japan. He is a Chair of the World Council for Renewable Energy (WCRC) for the Asia Pacific, and directs Epolis, a Sydney-based consultancy active in sustainable urban planning. He is the author of the 'Renewable City' book (2006), and currently teaches at the Hochschule Liechtenstein.

Dr. Hermann Scheer (born 1944) is a member of the German Parliament (since 1980), president of EuroSolar (a Bonn-based environmental organization), and chairman of the World Council for Renewable Energy (WCRC) in Berlin. He is also the president of the International Parliamentary Forum on Renewable Energies, and the founder of IRENA, the International Renewable Energy Agency. For many years, **Hans-Josef Fell** and him have been policy innovators and outspoken supporters of the system of subsidies for solar power (the feed-in tariff) that the German government pays to citizens to install solar panels and feed their locally produced energy in the grid. Scheer's latest book is 'Energy Autonomy' (Earthscan, 2007). www.epolis.com.au, www.solarcity.org, www.eurosolar.de, www.hermannscheer.de

Bill Dunster, BEDZed/ZEDfactory, architect (Surrey, south of London, UK).

Bill Dunster, and his former partner **Pooran Desai**, are both leaders in the UK in the field of zero-carbon design and development. Dunster's office in the ZEDfactory is located south of London, in Wallington, Surrey; *BEDZed* means Beddington Zero Energy Development. After splitting from Dunster, Desai initiated the *One Planet Living* initiative. Dunster first worked for Michael Hopkins and Partners, where he was project architect for the Nottingham University Campus. He also taught part-time at the Architectural Association and Kingston University. In 1995 he built his own house, Hope House, which is a prototype low-energy live/work unit, in which he and his family live. Dunster founded 'the ZEDfactory' in 1999; it's now a multidisciplinary group of architects, project managers, engineers, physicists and financial expertise, all dedicated to providing viable low and zero-carbon development solutions. The company aims to demonstrate that a step change reduction in carbon footprint is achievable at the same time as an increase in overall quality of life – with a zero-carbon and zero-waste lifestyle, and work-style achieved by synchronizing urban ZEDs with zero-fossil energy farming and food distribution. The practice has de-

veloped its own building physics models tunable to different climatic regions, and has its own low cost bulk purchasing supply chain with specially developed building integrated renewable energy systems. The ZEDfactory is best known for the BedZED project, a 100 home mixed-use community with workspace and social facilities; the SkyZed high-rise proposal in Wandsworth, and the RuralZED zero-carbon kit house – recently in manufacture for projects up to 50 homes / ha. A similar approach using the retrofitting of low carbon construction techniques is being used to extend the useful life of existing 1970s social housing in East London. ZEDfactory are now working on eco-town masterplans, and a number of larger urban projects in China and France, with particular emphasis on the holistic integration of zero-carbon thinking into the place-making and transportation agenda. Bill has co-written the `ZEDbook' (2008) with eco-footprint expert Craig Simmons and building physicist Bobby Gilbert – a manual for achieving zero carbon development at different densities and scales.
www.zedfactory.com, www.ruralzed.com, www.oneplanetliving.org

Joachim Eble, urban designer and architect (Tübingen, Germany).
Eble is principal of the firm Joachim Eble Architektur, Tübingen, based in Germany, and lectures at various international universities. Eble has a focus on creating sustainability in an urban context. He aims to achieve this through public space that is designed to prioritize the pedestrian, city farms producing organic local foods, higher densities, mixed-use housing, car reductions, preventing urban sprawl, and reducing land consumption. Based on these strategies and the idea of Eco-City, he realized the concept of the 'City of Short Distances.' www.eble-architektur.de

Karl Otto Ellefsen and **Anne Grete Hestnes**, university teachers and sustainability researchers (Oslo and Trondheim, Norway).
Professor Ellefsen is currently dean of the Oslo School of Architecture and Design (AHO) in Oslo. He has a particular interest in sustainable cities. Professor Anne Grete Hestnes is an architect with degrees from MIT and UC Berkeley. She has been full professor at the Norwegian University of Science and Technology since 1985. Her main scientific interest is in the areas of energy conservation and the use of solar energy in buildings. In 2005 she was awarded an honorary doctorate by Chalmers University for her work within the field of sustainable development. She is part of the Department of Architecture at the Norwegian University of Science and Technology (NTNU) in Trondheim, where she is leading the Research Centre on Zero-Emission Buildings. She works with Associate Professor **Matthias Haase** (formerly from SINTEF) and others. www.aho.no, www.ntnu.no

Reid Ewing, university researcher and author (Maryland, USA).
Professor Ewing teaches urban studies and planning in the National Center for Smart Growth, at the University of Maryland, and his study of sprawl and obesity has received widespread media coverage. Ewing holds degrees in engineering and city planning from Harvard University and MIT. He is lead author of 'Growing Cooler: The Evidence on Ur-

ban Development and Climate Change', which makes an important connection between low-density sprawl and CO_2 emissions. www.smartgrowth.umd.edu

Douglas Farr, architect and urban planner (Chicago, USA).
Farr is the founding principal of Farr Associates, an architecture and urban planning firm based in Chicago, described by the *New York Times* as "the most prominent of the city's cadre of ecologically sensitive architects in the US." Farr Associates have designed several LEED Platinum buildings. Doug is on the board of the Congress of New Urbanism, serves on the BioRegional Development Group board of directors, and was the founding chair of the LEED for the Neighborhood Development project. www.farrside.com

Roger Fay, university researcher and architect (Launceston, Australia).
Professor Fay is Head of the School of Architecture and Design at the University of Tasmania. His research interests are in assessment of sustainable design, life-cycle energy analysis and simulation, and affordable housing. He collaborates with Dr. Dominique Hes and Dr. Ceridwen Owen in the area of sustainable design. www.utas.edu.au

M. Norbert Fisch, solar technology engineer (Braunschweig/Stuttgart, Germany and Shanghai, China).
Professor Norbert Fisch teaches at the TU-Braunschweig, where he leads the Institute of Building Services and Energy Design (IGS), since 1996. He has been involved with the 'Solar City' scheme, which is a German initiative aiming to broadly advance renewable energy technologies globally. With the 'Solar-Stadt' projects he works towards reducing long-term urban greenhouse emissions, and is now working on urban projects in Asia and the Middle-East. www.igs.bau.tu-bs.de

Tim Flannery, global warming activist and scientist (Sydney/Canberra, Australia).
Professor Flannery is one of Australia's most well-known scientists and advocate for sustainable energy. He argues that the technology required to avoid an unpleasantly hot future is not difficult to implement. He has been concerned with the threat of global warming for a long time, and has been researching: how to reduce warming on the urban scale; the impact of population increases worldwide and how it will affect our planet; strategies to increase industries in solar, wind, water treatment and transport design for a globally sustainable future. He is a best-selling author, and his most popular book is 'The Weather Makers' (2004). His views are often provocative, both intellectually and socially. Prof. Flannery is the principal research scientist at the Australian Museum in Sydney. He has a PhD from the Zoology department at UNSW. He is one of Australia's leading thinkers and writers, and an internationally acclaimed scientist, explorer and conservationist. Tim's books include the definitive ecological histories of Australia (*The Future Eaters*) and North America (*The Eternal Frontier*). He is a leading member of the Wentworth Group of Concerned Scientists, which reports independently to government on sustainability issues. He currently holds a position at Sydney's Macquarie University.
www.theweathermakers.org

Colin Fournier, urban designer and 'hyper-density' researcher (London, UK).
Professor Fournier teaches urban design at the Bartlett School of Architecture and Planning, University College, London (since 1998), with a special focus on hyper-density, sustainable urbanism and generative systems. He built the Kunsthaus Graz, with Sir Peter Cook (2004). A colleague of Fournier at the Bartlett is Professor Bill Hillier, who carries out spatial research on sustainable urban form in his research centre, Space Syntax.
www.bartlett.ucl.ac.uk and www.spacesyntax.org

Norman Foster and colleagues, Foster and Partners architects (London, UK).
Lord Norman Foster is one of the most eminent architects of the late 20th-century; his practice has won over 500 awards. His urban design for Masdar Eco-City in Abu Dhabi, United Arab Emirates (construction started in 2008) is setting a new benchmark for masterplanned sustainable urban development. Foster graduated from Manchester University, School of Architecture and City Planning in 1961 and gained his Masters degree at Yale University. He founded Foster and Partners in London in 1967, which now has offices in over 20 countries and projects worldwide. Foster and Partners addresses the need to take action in regard to sustainability, realizing the role that architects and urban planners play in designing energy-efficient and socially-responsible buildings and cities. *"Sustainability requires us to think holistically…"* (Foster). Lord Foster is assisted in his work on eco-cities by many colleagues, such as by senior partner David Nelson. Another of his partners is the German-born architect Stefan Behling, who joined Foster and Partners in 1987. Initially, he worked on masterplans for Kings Cross Station, London, and later became a director of the practice as well as managing director of Foster and Partners' German office in 1996. A specialist in ecology, sustainability and energy conservation, he has worked on a number of projects that have pioneered new techniques for energy management, including the masterplanning and regeneration of Duisburg's Inner Harbour, the new German Parliament at the Reichstag in Berlin, and the headquarters for Commerzbank in Frankfurt. More recent projects include City Hall, the Greater London Authority headquarters; the library of the Free University of Berlin; and the headquarters for McLaren in Surrey. At Foster and Partners, Behling leads research and development of new sustainable designs and the use of new materials and methods in construction, establishing a materials resource centre which is available practice-wide. Since 1995, he has been a professor at the University of Stuttgart, Germany, holding the Chair for Building Construction, Technology and Design. He has led several research projects in this field, some of which were funded by the European Commission. His books include 'Sol Power', discussing the use of solar energy in architecture. As Senior Partner at Foster and Partners, he is working on a number of large projects, including a sustainable masterplan for four plots within the Masdar Eco-City initiative in Abu Dhabi.
www.fosterandpartners.com and www.masdar.ae

Karl Ganser, urban planner and geographer (Cologne/Bochum, Germany).
Dr Karl Ganser, born 1937, was the director of the international building exhibition

IBA Emscher Park, in the former coal-mining area in the state of North Rhein Westphalia (NRW) in Germany. He is one of the pioneers of environmentally sustainable urban renewal and the transformation of formerly industrially used brownfield sites, promoting the careful adaptive re-use and integration of existing structures. He was responsible for saving the industrial landscape of the Zeche Zollverein in Essen (today a landscape park with design school and museum), and the former steel manufacturing plant of Duisburg. The successful revitalization of these large structures in the early 1990s introduced the concept of interim-usage and adaptive re-use of large industrial heritage sites to many other cities in Europe. Ganser worked as an urban planner for the city of Munich before joining the federal Ministry for Planning in Bonn in 1971, where he subsequently led the urban research institute. Until 1989 he was Director of Urban Planning at the Ministry for Planning in NRW. He became director of the IBA Emscher Park in 1989, a position he had until 1999. In 1999 he retired and is now active as an urban consultant. He coined the notion of 'Structural Change without Growth' (Strukturwandel ohne Wachstum) and was involved in research on the 'shrinking cities' phenomenon. wwwiba.nrw.de

Nicky Gavron, **Ken Livingstone** and **Allan Jones**, Greater London Authority (London, UK).
Both British politicians, Gavron and Livingstone use their political positions to shape the London Plan for a sustainable future. In 2005, they founded the 'C40' initiative, which includes 40 of the world's largest cities and binds them in a commitment to sustainable urban development; it is a worldwide climate change action group. Gavron and Livingstone had a significant impact in London's environment and planning policies, spatial development and strategic planning. They are key players in the battle against greenhouse gas emissions and in fighting climate change in the UK. Nicky Gavron is a member of the London Assembly and former Deputy Mayor of London; she has been a member of the Labour Party for 35 years. In 2000, former Mayor Ken Livingstone made Nicky Deputy Mayor of London, a post she has held for eight years. In this position, she has led for the Mayor on environment and planning policy, overseeing the new 'green' London Plan. Nicky is internationally recognised for her environmental expertise, and she was a key figure in the establishment of the *London Climate Change Agency* and the *C40*. Allan Jones has turned the city of Woking onto tri-generated power and heating. He now heads up London's Climate Change Agency, with the aim of taking London off the coal-fired power grid through alternative localized power generation systems. www.nickygavron.com, www.london.gov.uk, www.c40cities.org

Jan Gehl, urban planner and livability researcher (Copenhagen, Denmark).
Professor Jan Gehl (born 1936) is an internationally renowned Danish architect and urban design consultant who has focused his career on livability and improving the quality of urban pedestrian life. Gehl's books include 'Life Between Buildings' (1987), and 'Public Space, Public Life', which tells how improvements in the urban context have transformed Copenhagen from a car-dominated city into a pedestrian orientated society. He calls himself an Urban Quality Consultant and his research has been applied in cities across Europe, North America and Asia. Gehl strongly believes in the 'bicycle culture' and a city where the use of cars and CO_2 emissions are reduced. Gehl has advised cities on urban design and public projects worldwide.

Helle Soeholt, David Sim, Henning Thomsen and others are working with Jan Gehl as associates. www.gehlarchitects.dk

Herbert Girardet, author and Director of Programmes, *World Future Council* (London, UK). A recipient of the UN Global 500 Award for outstanding environmental achievement as filmmaker, social anthropologist and a leading author, Professor Herbert Girardet is the Director of Programmes at the World Future Council (WFC), where he is assisted by Stefan Schurig. He has produced more than 50 TV-documentaries on human environmental impacts and has been a consultant to many clients, including UNEP, UN-Habitat, the Greater London Authority, The London Development Agency, and the city of Vienna. He is an honorary fellow of the Royal Institute of British Architects, is author of 12 books and is a visiting professor at the University of the West of England. In recent years his main focus has been in sustainable urban development, and he has been called the world's foremost urban ecologist. In 2003, as `Thinker in Residence' in Adelaide, he developed sustainability strategies for South Australia that are now being implemented. His book `Cities, People Planet – Urban Development and Climate Change', was published in 2004 and 2008. Most recently he edited `Surviving the Century – Facing Climate Chaos and Other Global Challenges' (2007), and authored 'A Renewable World – Policies, Practices, Technologies' (2009). www.worldfuturecouncil.org and www.adelaidegreencity.com

Leon Glicksmann, Massachusetts Institute of Technology (Cambridge, USA).
Professor Glicksman has been the head of the Building Technology Programme in the MIT Department of Architecture since 1990. He is a professor of Building Technology and Mechanical Engineering, researching energy efficient building components and design, and residential buildings' indoor air quality. Glicksman and co-workers are developing a web site for advanced envelope systems that can be easily used by architects and developers in the early stages of design, and guidelines for sustainable buildings for the MIT campus are being defined. www.mit.edu

Joana C. Goncalves, Laboratory of Environment and Energy-Efficiency, at the University of Sao Paulo, FAU (Sao Paulo, Brazil).
Professor Joana C. Goncalves works with Dr. Denise Duarte, leading the Laboratory of Environment and Energy-Efficiency Studies (LABAUT), in the Department of Technology, in the Faculty of Architecture and Urbanism (FAU) of the University of Sao Paulo (USP). They are researching urban micro-climates and the energy use of urban spaces; the latest book is entitled 'The Environmental Performance of Tall Buildings'. At the same university in Sao Paulo is Prof. Raquel Rolnik, teaching sustainable urban planning with a focus on affordable housing. www.usp.br/fau/labaut/

Al Gore, Bill Clinton, and **Arnold Schwarzenegger**, all politicians, policy-makers and leaders in environmental thinking (USA).
While they couldn't be more different, all three are global leaders and influential environ-

mental advocates tackling climate change and spreading the message. They are three powerful voices for green cities and reduction of carbon emissions. Former Vice-President Al Gore was awarded the 'Nobel Peace Prize' for 2007. Al Gore is an articulate transla-tor of complex scientific facts and ideas, and is able to explain complexity in terms easily understood by everybody. His film 'An Inconvenient Truth' (2006) became a Hollywood success. Schwarzenegger has influenced environmental policy and led California, in his role as Governor, to becoming the greenest state in the entire US. He is a tireless advocate for environmental sustainability and is responsible for ensuring the passage of crucial legis-lation for improving environmental protection and educating the public on issues of global warming. The William J. Clinton Foundation launched the Clinton Climate Initiative (CCI) to create and advance solutions to the core issues driving climate change, taking a holistic approach, addressing the major sources of greenhouse gas emissions and the people, policies and practices that impact them. Working with governments and businesses around the world, CCI focuses on three strategic programme areas: increasing energy efficiency in cities, the large-scale supply of clean energy, and working to stop deforestation. www. climatecrisis.net, www.gov.ca.gov, wwwsmud.org, www.clintonfoundation.org

David J. Greenwood, research director and educator (Newcastle-Upon-Tyne, UK).
Dr. Greenwood is the professor of Construction Management at Northumbria University, where he leads the Sustainable Cities Research Institute (SCRI), and works with Prof. Bob Giddings and others. www.sustainable-cities.org.uk

Susannah Hagan, researcher (Brighton/London, UK).
Professor Hagan is director of the interdisciplinary group R/E/D (Research into Environment and Design) and teaches at the University of Brighton. She studied architecture at Columbia University and the Architectural Association, and was head of the MA Sustainable Design programme at the University of East London. Her written work includes 'Taking Shape: The new contract between architecture and nature' (2001). Her work centres on environmen-tally-led urban design and the social and economic benefits it can bring to cities, whether shrinking (EMPTYing CITIES project, Wuppertal, Germany), or exponentially growing (En-LUDe 2 project, an urban design project for Sao Paulo, Brazil). www.theredgroup.org

Ekhart Hahn, engineer, planner and researcher (Dortmund/Berlin, Germany).
Professor Hahn (born 1942) is a prominant urban planner and pioneer in dealing with both urban and regional ecological solutions. His books include: 'A Green Corridor between town and country' (1996) and 'Ecological Urban Restructuring - Theoretical Foundation and Con-cept for Action' (1991). His theories dwell in ecological concepts of the eco-station, ecological neighbourhood development on the urban scale, urban restructuring, and heating and water strategies designed to complement the central city system. He emphasizes socio-ecological ap-proaches in realizing environmental sustainability in the urban context. He teaches in the Faculty of Spatial Planning at the University of Dortmund.
www.oeko-city.de and www.raumplanung.uni-dortmund.de

Peter Hall, researcher and urban planner (London, UK).
Sir Peter Hall (born 1932) is a world-known town planner, urbanist and Professor of Planning and Regeneration at the Bartlett School of Architecture and Planning, University College, London; and President of the British Town and Country Planning Association. From 1991-1994 he was Special Adviser on Strategic Planning to the Secretary of State for the Environment, with special reference to issues in London and South East regional planning. Professor Hall was also an advisor to the Bannon Government's 'Planning Review' in South Australia between 1990 and 1992. In 1998-1999 he was a member of the Deputy Prime Minister's Urban Task Force. From 2004 to 2008 he was Chair of *ReBlackpool*, the Blackpool Urban Regeneration Company. He is author, co-author or editor of over 35 books on sustainable urban and regional planning and related topics, most recently: 'London Voices - London Lives', published in 2007. Peter Hall received the *Gold Medal* of the Royal Town Planning Institute in 2003 and the Sir Patrick Abercrombie Prize of the International Union of Architects (UIA) in 2008. www.bartlett.ucl.ac.uk

Steve A. Hammer, urban climate change researcher (New York, USA).
Dr. Steve Hammer is director of the Urban Climate Change Research Network (UCCRN), and director of the Urban Energy Programme at Columbia University's Centre for Energy, Marine Transportation and Public Policy. He has a particular focus on city-level impact assessment. At UCCRN, he works with Dr. Albert Bressand. He teaches a course on Urban Energy Systems and Policy, and oversees the Urban Energy workshop at Columbia's School of International and Public Affairs. He lectures internationally on energy issues and collaborates with the *Joint U.S.-China Cooperation on Clean Energy* (JUCCCE), which was founded by Peggy Liu in Shanghai. Prof. **Nickolas Themelis** researches sustainable waste management at Columbia University. www.uccrn.org, www.juccce.com and www.columbia.edu

Bob Harvey, Mayor of the City of Waitakere, close to Auckland (New Zealand)
Bob Harvey has been re-elected as mayor for six terms (since 1992), and has been seminal in his long-term championing of the Waitakere Eco-City principles established at the UN's Rio Earth Summit in 1992. www.waitakere.govt.nz

Gerhard Hausladen, engineer, educator and researcher (Munich, Germany).
Professor Hausladen (born 1947) has held the Chair of Building Climate and Technology, at the Technical University of Munich since 2001, where he collaborates with colleagues, including Prof. Dietrich Fink and Prof. Richard Horden on new energy-efficient building concepts. His latest books are 'Climate Design', 'Climate Skin', and the 'Ausbau Atlas' (2009). www.climadesign.de

Peter Head, Tristram Carfrae, Roger Wood, Haico Schepers, Mahadev Raman, Chris Twinn, Raymond Yau, Paul Sloman, Alistair Guthrie, and colleagues; environmental engineers (London, New York, Sydney, Hong Kong / Arup offices, globally). These leading engineers work for the global interdisciplinary consulting firm Arup, a Brit-

ish design and engineering firm based in London. Just to introduce a few of them:
Peter Head leads Arup's planning and integrated urbanism section, and is working on entire new eco-cities in China (for instance, Dongtan, near Shanghai; Wanzhuang, near Beijing) and in the UK. The *Dongtan Eco-City* project was a masterplanned development on Chongming Island near Shanghai. Mr Head is a champion for developing global practise that demonstrates that the way we invest public and private money in the built environment could be made much more effective if the public and private sector adopted sustainable development principles. He is a civil and structural engineer who has become a recognized world leader in the construction of bridges and in sustainable development of cities. Head joined Arup in 2004 to create and lead their Planning and Integrated Urbanism Group and now heads this team globally. He was appointed, in 2002, by the Mayor of London as an independent commissioner on the London Sustainable Development Commission. Peter Head is also chairman of the Steel Construction Institute. He was awarded the 2008 Sir Frank Whittle Medal by the Royal Academy of Engineering for his efforts in delivering an environmentally sustainable built environment in a rapidly urbanizing world. Peter Head is making his way around the world explaining to governments and public forums how it's possible and realistic to make 80 per cent cuts in greenhouse emissions by 2050 (using Manchester in the UK as the demonstration city).
Haico Schepers is Arup's leader of the Sustainable Technologies Group, combining his training as an engineer and architect specializing in sustainable building design. He has a focus on the integration of passive thermal strategies, natural daylight and building systems, with the aim of achieving real change. Malcolm Smith is director of Integrated Urbanism. Chris Twinn is director of the Building Engineering Sustainability Group based in Arup London. With a background in both building services and building physics, he has a particular interest in integrating building fabric and systems to create appropriate indoor and outdoor environments with the minimum impact on the wider environment. Dr. Raymond Yau is head of Arup's Building Physics Group in the East-Asia Region and was Arup's Global Buildings Sector leader between 2003 and 2008. He is now based in Hong Kong, where he works closely with the government in formulating a roadmap for the local sustainability agenda. Mahadev Raman leads the Arup building section for the Americas. Based in New York, he has been with Arup since 1978 providing engineering design leadership for multi-disciplinary teams on a wide variety of projects in North America and beyond. Bringing particular expertise in the design of high performance buildings, Mahadev has pioneered the use of sophisticated analytical techniques to validate the design of, and to optimize the performance of, low-energy buildings. He is a faculty member at both Princeton and Columbia Universities. Dr. Chris Luebkeman is director of the Foresight and Innovation Group, exploring the drivers of global change.
Arup employs many more experts on green design and engineering. www.arup.com
(see interview in this Appendix)

Chye Kiang HENG, and colleagues, university researchers at NUS (Singapore).
Professor Heng is currently Dean of the School of Design and Environment at the National University of Singapore (NUS). The research centre CSAC 'Centre for Sustainable Asian

Cities' at NUS has a special focus on urban spaces and development of cities in Asia; research covers areas of density, heritage and growth of cities. CSAC connects a series of NUS colleagues, such as Associate Professor Yunn Chii WONG, Associate Professor Nyuk Hien WONG, Associate Professor Johannes WIDODO, Dr. Lai Choo MALONE-LEE, Dr. Limin HEE, Dr. Beng Kiang TAN, and others members of this research cluster. Dr. Heng studied architecture in Paris and holds a PhD from the University of California. He is a board member of the Singapore's Urban Redevelopment Authority (URA). www.nus.edu.sg

Peter Herrle, university educator, architect and urban designer (Berlin, Germany).
Professor Herrle holds, since 1995, the Chair of the Habitat-Unit for International Urbanism at the Technical University of Berlin (TU-B), a teaching and research unit with a special focus on socio-cultural issues of urbanization. At TU-Berlin he collaborates with Prof. Claus Steffan and others; he is an Advisory Professor at Tongji University in Shanghai. He is the author of a series of books exploring social sustainability, informal habitat, and identity in urban design. www.habitat-unit.de

Richard Hyde, university researcher and author (Sydney, Australia).
Professor Richard Hyde studied in England before moving to Australia. His research interests are in technology, computer simulations and building construction, and new green building materials. He teaches at the University of Sydney, in the Faculty of Architecture, Design and Planning, where he is Head of Architectural and Design Science. He is currently editor of the journal *Architectural Science Review*. www.arch.usyd.edu.au

Mike Jenks, university researcher and educator (Oxford, UK).
Professor Jenks is head of research in the School of the Built Environment at Oxford Brookes University, and is founding director of the Oxford Institute of Sustainable Development (OISD), where he has, together with Elizabeth Burton, edited two books on sustainable urban form and compact city theory. www.city-form.org and www.brookes.ac.uk

Françoise-Hélène Jourda (Lyon, France), and **Manfred Hegger,** architect and university educator (Darmstadt/Kassel, Germany).
Architect Françoise-Hélène Jourda states that she tries to take her efforts as far as they will go, "to work with renewable materials, soft tech and bio-climatology, whilst taking along the partners and clients." Her goal is to encourage a different way of living and working. One of her major works is the Mt. Cenis-Training Academy Building in Herne (Germany), where she has been able to realize a radically new concept: a large micro-climatic glass envelope (1999-2007). It took almost ten years to complete. It is part of the ecological and economic renewal of the region, and started with a two stage competition in 1991 for the International Building Exhibition IBA Emscher Park (originally won by French architects Jourda & Perraudin).
In the second stage, the German architects Hegger-Hegger-Schleif (HHS, Kassel) joined the design team. Led by Professor Manfred Hegger, this innovative building has set new benchmarks in sustainable design. Hegger is co-author of the book 'Energy Manual'

(2008), and he teaches energy-efficient design at the TU Darmstadt.
www.jourda-architectes.com and www.architecture.tu-darmstadt.de

Soren Hermansen, Managing Director of Samso Energy Academy (Samso, Denmark). Thanks to the irrepressible determination of Soren Hermansen and the 4200 residents of the small Danish island of Samso, the island has become, within 12 years, self-sufficient, using renewable energy. 20 windmills and 4 district heating plants provide all of the island's electricity and heating consumption. In fact, they produce more electricity than is needed and are able to export as much as 80mill. kWh p.a. to the mainland. This is the equivalent of the total energy requirements of 4,000 Danish households. Mr Hermansen has ensured that the project is meaningful for the residents and that their investment in renewable energy is profitable. The Samso Municipality has acted as borrower on the investment loans and provided guarantees for the loans for the island's four centralized heating plants. In 2009, Mr Hermansen received the Gothenburg Prize for his work and leadership on the project. www.samso.com.dk

Thomas Herzog, architect, urban designer and researcher (Munich, Germany).
Professor Thomas Herzog (born 1941) is one of the most prominent German architects, recognized for his pioneering sustainable approach. In 1973 he became Germany's youngest Professor in Architecture, and 10 years later established his firm Herzog and Partner. His 'Richter Residential Complex' in Munich is regarded as an icon of modern sustainable architecture. His architectural approach is a response to issues of zoning, natural infrastructure, economics, site restraints, solar energy and the thermal qualities of building materials; aiming for a truly sustainable architecture of the future. He is one of the masterplanners of 'SolarCity' in Linz (Austria), and the author of many books, including the 'Charter for Solar Energy in Architecture and Urban Planning' (1995/2007). He has been the Dean of the Faculty of Architecture at the TU-Munich (2000-2006), where today he holds the position of 'Emeritus of Excellence'. His latest energy-efficient building is the *Oskar-von-Miller-Forum* in Munich (completed in 2009). Prof. Herzog has co-authored the 'Fassaden Atlas' (2004), with Dr Werner Lang and others. Associate Prof. Lang teaches sustainable Architecture at the University of Texas and at TU-Munich.
www.herzog-und partner.de, www.ar.tum.de

Arab Hoballah, sustainable development expert at UNEP (Paris, France).
Dr. Hoballah has been Chief of Sustainable Consumption and Production Branch in the Division of Technology, Industry and Economics, at the United Nations Environment Programme (UNEP) since 2005. He is convinced that sustainable development depends on consumption and production patterns through individual and collective behaviour. He promotes a culture of change and adequate policy reforms, and a multi-stakeholders approach. 'Sustainable development depends on consumption and production patterns through individual or collective behaviour, promotion of a culture of change, adequate policy reforms and a multi-stakeholder approach.' (A. Hoballah, 2009) www.unepsbci.org

Christoph Ingenhoven, architect (Duesseldorf, Germany; and Zurich, Switzerland). German architect Christoph Ingenhoven (born 1960) is a leading architect and urban designer who has been much involved in sustainable design since the foundation of his studio in 1985. He is lead designer of major projects in Sydney, Osaka, Den Hague, Luxembourg, Stuttgart and Shanghai. His new 'supergreen' high-rise office building 'Space' in Sydney's central business district (to be completed in 2011) has been the first 6-star Green Star rated office tower (the highest rating possible). His Stuttgart Bahnhof railway station is a zero-emission complex which does not need any mechanical ventilation, heating or cooling.
www.ingenhovenundpartner.de, www.ingenhovenarchitects.com
(see interview in this Appendix)

Kazuo Iwamura, architect and researcher at Musashi Institute of Technology (Yokohama, Japan). Professor Iwamura is the principal and founder of Iwamura Atelier in Tokyo, a practice focusing on architectural and urban research based on holistic environmental design approaches by networking related experts or organizations. Iwamura graduated in 1973 from Waseda University and worked in Germany and in Paris. He co-founded AG5 (Arbeitsgemeinschaft für Architektur und Städtebau, 1977-80) implementing the "Baubiologie" (Building and Biology) approach to town planning. Since 1988 Iwamura has been a Professor at the Faculty of Urban Life Studies, as well as the Graduate School of Environmental & Information Studies, at Tokyo City University in Yokohama. He is vice-president of the International Union of Architects (UIA), past vice-president of the Japan Institute of Architects, co-director of the UIA work programme 'Architecture for a Sustainable Future', and a member of the board of directors of the World Green Building Council (WGBC). He was awarded the World Habitat Award in 2002 by UN-Habitat and is recognized for his 'Environmentally Symbiotic Housing' project.
www.iwamura-at.com

Rita Justesen, Head of City Planning of Copenhagen City and Port, By & Havn (Copenhagen, Denmark).
Ms Justesen and Jan Christiansen, City architect of the municipality of Copenhagen, are overseeing the development of the Copenhagen North Harbour (Nordhavnen) project, which in the coming decades is being expanded to accommodate housing and workplaces for up to 40,000 people. They have developed policies on sustainability, public space for waterfront and urban identity, with support from then Danish Minister for Climate and Energy, Ms Connie Hedegaard. The Nordhavnen area will undergo an enormous transformation that will give Copenhagen a completely new urban district, in which water and the harbour will be essential elements. www.english.dac.dk/

Manabu Kanda, university researcher at the Tokyo Institute of Technology (Tokyo, Japan). Professor Kanda is a board member of the International Association for Urban Climate (IAUC), an organization with scientific, scholarly and technical interests in the climatology and meteorology of built-up urban areas, urban air quality, and wind and turbulence in the city. He has been a leader in the representation of urban landscapes in models of climate at meso-scales, and the Kanda Lab is concerned with comfort in urban space. www.urban-climate.org and www.ide.titech.ac.jp/~kandalab

Hermann Kaufmann, architect and university educator (Munich / Dornbirn).
Professor Kaufmann holds the Chair in Timber Architecture at the Technical University of Munich in Germany (since 2002), where he is assisted by Frank Lattke and others. Kaufmann is a leading architect and university educator, coming from an Austrian family of timber building components manufacturers. He has a particular interest in the prefabri- cation of structural timber elements and energy-efficient wall systems, and building sustain- able multi-storey timber buildings. www.holz.ar.tum.de, www.kaufmann.archbuero.com

Jeffrey R. Kenworthy, author and transport researcher (Perth, Australia), and
Peter W. Newman, author and transport researcher (Sydney, Australia).
Jeff Kenworthy was a Professor at Murdoch University, but is now Professor in Sustain- ability in Curtin University's Sustainability Policy Institute, Perth, Western Australia. Jeff has worked in the transportation and planning field since the mid 1980s and conducts comparative urban research. He studies international comparisons of transport and land use in cities, and its impact on urban form and development patterns. Both Kenworthy and Newman have co-authored a number of articles and books, including the pivotal book 'Sustainability and Cities: Overcoming Automobile Dependency' (1999), where they out- line the concept of a new urban transportation policy. Both are members of the CUSP Research Institute. Peter Newman is the Professor of Sustainability at Curtin University and is on the Board of *Infrastructure Australia* that is funding infrastructure for the long term sustainability of Australian cities. Their recent books include: 'Resilient Cities: Responding to Peak Oil and Climate Change' (2009) and 'Green Urbanism Down Under', both co- authored with Tim Beatley. In Perth, Peter Newman is best known for his work in reviving and extending the city's rail system. Peter claims to have invented the term 'automobile dependence' to describe how we have created cities where we have to drive everywhere. For 30 years, since he attended Stanford University during the first oil crisis, he has been warning cities about preparing for peak oil.
www.sustainability.curtin.edu.au, www.urbancity.org and www.resilientcitiesbook.org

Yuichiro Kodama, eco-architect and educator (Kobe, Japan).
Dr. Kodama is a Professor at Kobe Design University (since 1998), where he teaches bio- climatic design. He has been engaged in research and design practice in passive heating and cooling systems at the Building Research Institute at the Ministry of Construction, Japan. He is known as a programmer of interactive design tools for passive design and for life-cycle analysis of buildings. He is the author of the book 'Bio-climatic design, Passive Design and Sustainable Design', and has been awarded the Good Design Award of Japan, for his house in Motoyama (2003). Internationally, he is active with PLEA (Passive and Low Energy Archi-

tecture Network), *iNTA* (International Tropical Architecture Network), and with IEA (Energy Conservation in Building and Community Systems Programme). www.kobe-du.ac.jp

Arvind Krishan, architect, researcher at School of Planning and Architecture (New Delhi, India). Professor Krishan is a qualified structural engineer and architect. He is one of the leading architects in the field of climate responsive and energy efficient architecture in India, with his designs aiming to integrate renewable resource strategies. Through this he hopes to optimize embodied energy in materials and enhance thermal performance and natural day-lighting in architecture. Dr. Krishan is the former Head of Department at SPA, a consultant to the World Bank, and a member of UNEP's expert group on eco-cities. www.spa.ac.in

Aniruddha Kumar, Director (JNNURM, the Nehru National Urban Renewal Mission) in the Ministry of Urban Development (New Delhi, India).
Mr Kumar heads the JNNURM, whose mission it is to upgrade city infrastructure and improve living standards in all Indian cities, with a focus on the 68 largest cities in India. Kumar also heads the National Urban Renewal Mission (NURM), a mission for integrated development of urban infrastructure services with the assistance of the centre, state and local bodies. The JNNURM is directed by the Minister for Urban Development, A.K. Walia. www.indiaenvironmentportal.org.in

Alison G. Kwok, University of Oregon (Oregon, USA).
Professor Kwok teaches design studios, gives seminars in climatic design, lighting and building performance, as well as giving classes in environmental technology, in the Department of Architecture at the University of Oregon. She holds a PhD from the University of California, Berkeley, and is the co-author of the 'Green Studio Handbook' (2007). Her research areas include thermal comfort, day-lighting, and building performance. Active in professional service, Dr. Kwok has served as treasurer, secretary and board member on the Architectural Research Centers Consortium, is a past-president of the Society of Building Science Educators, and is a member of several technical committees. She is the recipient of the American Solar Energy Society's WISE (Women in Solar Energy) Award in 2008. www. uoregon.edu

Nils Larsson, architect and CEO of the non-profit organization iiSBE (Paris, France).
Swedish architect Nils Larsson is director of the *International Initiative for a Sustainable Built Environment* (iiSBE), where he collaborates with Prof. Thomas Luetzkendorf. He developed the *SBTool* assessment method, focusing on R&D in green buildings, and managed a demonstration programme for high-performance buildings in Canada. Larsson is now based in Paris, from where he has been instrumental in the organization of the SB Conferences. In 1994, the *International Council for Research and Innovation in Building and Construction* (CIB) held the first international green building conference in London. As a part of the Green Building Challenge process, now operated by iiSBE, Larsson organized the international conference on green building in Vancouver in 1998. Following these initial ground-breaking events, CIB and iiSBE joined forces to co-organise conferences on sustainable building in Maastricht, Oslo, Tokyo, Melbourne, and, in 2010, in Madrid and London. www.iisbe.org

Norbert M. Lechner, researcher and university educator (Auburn, Alabama, USA). Architect and Emeritus Professor Norbert M. Lechner is the author of the seminal book 'Heating, Cooling, Lighting. Design Methods for Architects' (2001), which is used by more than one-third of all architecture schools in the US and has been translated into many languages. He is an expert in solar architecture and heliodoms and has been teaching sustainable design at the architecture school at Auburn University for over 30 years. In 2009, Professor Lechner was named *Fulbright Senior Specialist* by the Council for International Exchange of Scholars. Since 2007, he has been teaching energy responsive design in Thailand. "There is no way that the world could ever produce enough clean energy if buildings keep wasting energy as they are doing now. We have already the technical know-how to make buildings very energy-efficient. We are presently building zero-energy buildings. Such buildings import zero net-energy during a year. At night they import energy and during the day they export energy." (Lechner, 2009). www.cadc.auburn.edu

Steffen Lehmann, architect, urban designer and UNESCO Chair (Adelaide / Berlin). Professor Steffen Lehmann (born 1963) is a German architect, author and urban designer who has been involved in environmental design research and consultancy since the late 1980s. He holds the UNESCO Chair in Sustainable Urban Development for Asia and the Pacific, and, from August 2010, is Professor of Sustainable Design and Founding Director of a major research centre, exploring material flows and low carbon design at the University of South Australia, in Adelaide. He has held the Professorial Chair of Architectural Design in the School of Architecture and Built Environment at the University of Newcastle (NSW), where he was the leader of the *Sustainable Design Research Group*. From 2003 to 2006 he was Chair, Head of Architecture at the Queensland University of Technology in Brisbane. He is founding director of the s_Lab Space Laboratory for Architectural Research and Design (Sydney-Berlin), an international interdisciplinary research cluster. The s_Lab was founded in 1993 in Berlin to combine practice with research and teaching in pursuit of a sustainable design ethic. He has run his own practice in Berlin for over ten years and built award-winning buildings. Steffen works closely with the architectural profession and the building industry. He has taught at leading universities, such as NUS in Singapore, TU-Munich, Art Academy Berlin-Weissensee, TU-Berlin and Tongji University in Shanghai. He studied at the Architectural Association in London, holds a PhD from the TU-Berlin, and is primarily interested in the relationship between urban form and environmental performance, strategies for compact cities and emerging models of public space. He is the General Editor of the US-based *Journal of Green Building,* and an advisor to government, city councils and industry in Europe, Asia and Australia. He developed frameworks for sustainable development for the governments of Jordan, Mauritius, the City of Shanghai, and several other municipalities in the Asia-Pacific region. His latest book is 'Back to the City' (2009). www.slab.com.au

Claude Lenglet, urban planner and engineer (Bruxelles, Belgium). Mr Lenglet is a member of the European Construction Technology Platform, a European Union initiative to promote the construction of sustainable urban districts. He is an engineer at the construction company Bouygues Construction and co-leader of the E2B project. www.norpac.fr

Jaime Lerner and **Enrique Penalosa**, both are urban planners and former mayors of Latin American cities (Lerner: in Curitiba, Brazil; Penalosa: in Bogota, Colombia).
The two former mayors (of Curitiba in Brazil and Bogota in Colombia) are carrying their message of sustainability to the world's burgeoning cities. Lesson one: *Get rid of your car!* Jaime Lerner is the architect and planner who led the work to transform his city, starting in 1972, into a world model of ecological and social policies, designs and built projects. Lerner's concept of 'Urban Acupuncture' has been widely published, suggesting inexpensive, small-scale, community-supported initiatives to initiate change: 'Go to the place, work with people locally for a week, propose one or two ideas, and if they like, they can make it happen.'
Enrique Penalosa has taken the forward-thinking schemes on board and managed to initiate similar ground breaking, rapid changes in his city: Reducing car congestion, improving the pedestrian usability of public space, and introducing the Rede Integrada de Transporte (RIT), an integrated transport system. The network was replicated in Los Angeles, Panama City and other cities. Jaime Lerner's work is now continued by Clever Almeida, President of IPPUC, the Institute of Research and Urban Planning of Curitiba. www.ted.com/talks, www.jaimelerner.com, www.cidadesinovadoras.org.br

Richard S. Levine, researcher and university educator (Lexington, Kentucky, USA).
Professor Levine heads the Center for Sustainable Cities at the University Kentucky and has a 30-year long interest in urban form and density research. He is the director of the Center for Sustainable Cities (CSC) in Lexington and has been a pioneer for sustainability-oriented urban design in the US. He has authored over 200 publications on solar energy and sustainability research and conducted sustainable city research projects in Italy, Austria, China, the Middle East as well as in Kentucky. In the mid 1980s, Prof. Levine, along with his colleague Ernest J. Yanarella, started the Center for Sustainable Cities at the University of Kentucky, to study and advance the theory of sustainability. The `City-as-a-Hill' urban form, the Sustainable Urban Implantation, the Partnerland Principle, the Sustainable Area Budget, and other sustainable urban design principles were bolstered by the Vienna Westbahnhof project (in collaboration with Dr. Heidi Dumreicher) and continue to be studied and expanded upon today. www.uky.edu/Design, www.centerforsustainablecities.com

J. Owen Lewis, university educator, author and researcher (Dublin, Ireland).
Dr. Lewis is Professor of Architectural Science at the University College Dublin (UCD) and Director of the Energy Research Group (ERG). His sustainable projects and research include: Energy utilization and sustainability in the built environment, indoor environmental quality, technical change in the construction industry, solar energy and renewable energy sources, energy efficient design. He is currently focusing on zero-energy buildings. Lewis is also the chief executive officer of Sustainable Energy, Ireland. www.ucd.ie

Borong LIN, researcher and editor of building standards (Beijing, P. R. China).
Dr Lin is currently an associate professor and the vice-director of the Institute of Building Technology, School of Architecture, Tsinghua University. He also worked in the BERC (Building Energy Research Center), and the Key Lab of Eco-planning and Green Building, Ministry of Education. Lin is a member of high profile government-funded project teams, including 10th and 11th Five-year National Plan Research Projects and Beijing Olympic projects, including green building assessment system (GOBAS), and Olympic building energy efficiency evaluation. He is the editor for several governmental standards for green buildings and received a number of awards for sustainable building research and practice. He is the Deputy Chairman of the Green Building Labeling Committee, Ministry of Urban Housing and Construction, Deputy Secretarial of Beijing Green Building Council, Deputy Secretarial of Beijing Sustainable Council, and Green Building Consultant for Shenzhen Building Energy Research Centre. www.tsinghua.edu.cn

Nina-Marie Lister, planner and researcher (Toronto, Canada).
Associate Professor Lister teaches Urban and Regional Planning at Ryerson University in Toronto. A registered planner with a background in resource management, field ecology and environmental science; she is the founder of *Plandform*, a creative studio practice exploring the relationship between landscape, ecology and urbanism. Her research, teaching and practice focus on the confluence of landscape infrastructure and ecological processes within contemporary metropolitan regions, and on adaptive ecological design for ecosystem complexity and biodiversity conservation, waterfronts in post-industrial landscapes, and urban food systems and productive landscapes. She is co-editor of 'The Ecosystem Approach: Complexity, Uncertainty, and Managing for Sustainability' (2008). www.ryerson.ca/surp/

Vivian E. Loftness, researcher and Head of School (Pittsburgh, USA).
Professor Loftness, at Carnegie Mellon University, researches with German-born Volker Hartkopf and others, in the Centre for Building Performance. She has a particular focus on advanced building systems and workplaces of the future. www.cmu.edu/architecture

Amory B. Lovins, scientist and institute co-founder, Rocky Mountain Institute (Snowmass, Boulder, Colorado, USA).
The Rocky Mountain Institute (RMI) has been an important, independent, non-profit research nexus since its foundation in 1982. Dr. Lovins, CEO of the RMI, has lately led the redesign of over US$30 billion worth of facilities in 29 sectors for radical energy and resource efficiency. Amory Lovins co-founded the RMI in 1982, advising firms and governments worldwide on advanced resource productivity and environmental issues. Lovins studied physics at Harvard and Oxford Universties, and has received nine honorary doctorates. He was named by *NewsWeek* as "one of the Western world's most influential energy thinkers". He has briefed nineteen heads of state, held several visiting academic chairs (most recently, 2007 at Stanford), written twenty-nine books, and consulted for scores of industries and governments worldwide. His work focuses on transforming the

car, real estate, electricity, water, and semiconductor sectors of the economy, toward advanced resource productivity. He is the recipient of the Right Livelihood Award (the 'Alternative Nobel Prize'), amongst many other awards. His latest books are 'Natural Capitalism: Creating the Next Industrial Revolution' (1999), and 'Small is Profitable: the Hidden Economic Benefits of Making Electrical Resources the Right Size' (2002). The institute's US$8 million income is mainly earned by programmatic enterprises such as private sector consultancy; the rest comes from grants and donations. Stephen Doig is Vice President of the RMI, while Michael Kinsley and James Scott Brew are RMI Senior Consultants, heading the section concerned with sustainable cities. www.rmi.org

Ian Lowe, environmental activist (Griffith University, Brisbane/Noosa, Australia).
Emeritus Professor Lowe is a prominent figure in the environmental debate and as president, he heads the Australian Conservation Foundation (ACF). His efforts and research in sustainablity include: energy use in industrialized countries, energy policy options, large scale environmental issues and sustainable development, fossil fuels and carbon emissions, protection of forests, prevention of climate change and overall energy efficiency. www.acfonline.org.au

Thomas Luetzkendorf, researcher, engineer and educator (Karlsruhe, Germany).
Professor Luetzkendorf is a member of the iiSBE group and holds the Chair in Sustainable Management of Housing and Real Estate at the Karlsruhe Institute of Technology (foremerly University of Karlsruhe), where he researches in strategies for affordable, sustainable housing. www.wiwikit.edu

Joachim Luther, scientist and researcher (Freiburg, Germany, and Singapore).
Dr. Luther promoted regenerative energy sources like solar and wind as early as the 1970s. From 1993 to 2006, he was head of the Fraunhofer Institute for Solar Energy Systems (ISE) in Freiburg, working on real-world applications to run entire cities and air-conditioning systems on solar power, all vitally important to slowing the effects of climate change. Professor Luther has over thirty years of experience in physics and the development of renewable energies. Since 2008 he has been the Chief Executive Officer of the Solar Energy Research Institute of Singapore (SERIS), where he works with Professor Armin Aberle and Dr. Stephen Wittkopf. This new institute is located at the National University of Singapore. SERIS conducts industry-oriented research and development as well as use-inspired basic research in the fields of: solar energy conversion, PV-devices and modules, energy-efficient buildings. Luther holds a PhD in atomic physics from the University of Hannover. From 1997 to 2002, he was president of the European Association of Renewable Energy Research Centres, and from 1999 to 2002 editor-in-chief of the *Solar Energy* journal. From 2000 to 2004 he was a member of the Advisory Council to the German Government on Global Change. Since 2005 he has served as vice-chairman of the European Union Photovoltaic Technology Platform. In 2007 he joined the Expert Committee of the German Government on Science and Innovation, and in 2008 he became a member of the International Panel of Experts (IPE) on Sustainability of the Built Environment for the Building and Construction Authority of Singapore (BCA). www.seris.nus.edu.sg

Winy Maas, **Nathalie De Vries**, and **Jacob Van Rijs**, **(MVRDV)**, architects and urban designers (Rotterdam, The Netherlands).

MVRDV is one of the leading architectural and urban design offices in the Netherlands (and Europe). The practice was set up in 1993 by the three architects with a strong interest in the conceptual futures of urbanism and landscape architecture. MVRDV have published many books on urban conceptual ideas, such as `Meta-City - Data Town' (2004). They have designed eco-cities, such as for the Rioja region in Spain. In 2009 they developed 'The Green City Calcultor', an assessment tool to facilitate better sustainable performance of existing cities, and developed a sustainable urban vision for greater Paris.
www.mvrdv.nl

Bow Tan MAH and colleagues, Singaporean Ministry for National Development, driver behind Tianjin Eco-City project in China (Singapore).

The *Sino-Singapore Tianjin Eco-City*, located 150 km (around 100 miles) from Beijing, in the Tianjin Binhai New Area, is the result of a collaborative agreement between the governments of China and Singapore to jointly develop an environmentally friendly and resource-conserving city in China. The Tianjin Eco-City is meant to demonstrate the determination of both countries in tackling environmental protection, resource and energy conservation, and sustainable development, and is meant to become a model for sustainable development for other cities. When fully developed (by 2020), Tianjin Eco-City will be home to about 350,000 residents on an area of 3,000 ha, with a population density of 150 pers./ha. The masterplan was jointly developed by the China Academy of Urban Planning and Design, the Tianjin Urban Planning and Design Institute and the Singapore planning team led by the Urban Redevelopment Authority of Singapore, led by the Minister, Bow Tan MAH. It is based on the module of an Eco-Cell (400x400m) as community module, and 4 Eco-Cells create 1 Eco-Neighbourhood. The idea is that each Eco-District has 16 Eco-Cells.

Mr. Beng Lee ONG is the director of the Tianjin Eco-City Project Office in the Ministry of National Development, where he formulated policies and programmes for the Tianjin project, and oversees its implementation in close partnership with the relevant Chinese authorities. Mr. Tian YE is Vice-Director of the Tianjin Urban Planning & Design Institute. He holds a PhD from the Architecture School at Tsinghua University, with a major in Urban Planning and Architecture. Mr. Lay Bee YAP is the Head of Urban Design at the *Urban Redevelopment Authority* (URA), where he is assisted by Larry Lye Hook NG and others. From 2007, Mr. Siong Leng TAN (Deputy-CEO of URA) participated in the site assessment and selection for the Tianjin Eco-city and subsequently led a Singapore Planning Team to work with Chinese planners to draw up the masterplan as well as the Urban Design and detailed plan of the 4 sqkm Start-up Area of the Tianjin Eco-city. Mr TAN is currently the Deputy Chief Executive Officer of the Urban Redevelopment Authority responsible for the URA Consulting Group and the Corporate Development Group.

A Green Building Masterplan and the Green Mark assessment tool have been developed by Singapore's *Building and Construction Authority* (BCA), under the leadership of Lin Ji KOH and Kian Seng ANG, and their team. Siew Wah LAM is Deputy Chief Executive

Officer of the Building and Construction Authority, where he is co-responsible for shaping Singapore's built environment in the areas of sustainability and quality. Mr LAM played a key role in the development of Singapore's green building rating system – the Green Mark tool – which was launched in 2005, and he spearheaded the development of the first Green Building Masterplans, which offer monetary incentives to encourage developers to achieve higher Green Mark ratings. www.tianjinecocity.gov.sg, www.eco-city.gov.cn, www.bca.gov.sg, www.sustainablesingapore.gov.sg

Ken Maher, urban designer and landscape architect (Sydney, Australia).
Ken Maher is chairman of the multi-disciplinary practice Hassell, which has offices in Australia and China, and teaches architecture at the University of New South Wales, Faculty of the Built Environment, in Sydney. He has been involved in major urban projects and high density housing design. He was a founding member of the Green Building Council in Australia. In 2009, he was awarded the Australian Institute of Architects Gold Medal. www.hassell.com.au

Mokena Makeka, architect in Cape Town (Cape Town, South Africa).
Mr Makeka graduated from the University of Cape Town, South Africa. He embodies the holistic lateral thinking in architecture and urban design that is quickly becoming the standard for design excellence across the globe. He researches in the field of `Sustainable transport and public space for social stability'. He is the founder of Makeka Design Lab (MDL). The purpose of MDL is 'to problematise the nature of praxis in a meaningful manner and make cognate new cultural trajectories in spatial terms. This mission requires a method, which is both urban and architectural and overlaps with industrial design and even film and media.' He also argues that 'neglecting the importance and relevance of transport infrastructure and public space results in inequitable access and distribution of resources in our society. Transport is the backbone of the economy that connects people to place.' (2009) www.makekadesignlab.com

Volker Martin, educator and urban designer (Cottbus/Berlin, Germany/HCMC Vietnam).
Professor Emeritus Martin (born 1944) was head of the department of Urban Planning and Spatial Design, part of INSL at the Brandenburg University of Technology, Germany. Martin heads the EU-funded Mega-City project in Ho Chi Minh City (HCMC). His research is in `the balance of urban growth and redevelopment in HCMC – sustainable housing policies for mega cities of tomorrow', with the aim being to identify impacts of climate change and to develop strategies to reduce effects through urban planning decisions, with a particular focus on Asia. For the HCMC-Mega-City research project, he collaborates with Prof. Michael Schmidt and Prof. Nguyen Trong Hoa. www.emerging-megacities.org, www.tu-cottbus.de/megacity-hcmc

Edward Mazria, architect and environmental activist (Santa Fe, New Mexico, USA).
'Architecture 2030' is a non-profit, independent organization, established in response to the global-warming crisis by architect Mazria in 2002. Today, Mazria is a prominent voice and consultant to government. His mission is to rapidly transform US-cities and global building sector from being the major contributor of greenhouse gas emissions to becoming a

central part of the solution to the global-warming crisis. www.architecture2030.org

William McDonough, eco-architect and urban designer (Charlottesville, Virginia, USA); and
Michael Braungart, environmental chemist of Process Engineering (Lüneburg/Germany).
William McDonough is an American architect who founded William McDonough and Partners. His career is focused on designing environmentally sustainable buildings and transforming industrial manufacturing processes. He co-authored, with Michael Braungart, the book
'Cradle to Cradle: Remaking the Way we make things' (2002) which uncovered the 'Cradle
to Cradle' concept in design. *Time Magazine* recognized McDonough and Braungart as *He-
roes of the Environment* in 2007. In 1996, Mr. McDonough received the *Presidential Award
for Sustainable Development*, the nation's highest environmental honor, and in 2004 the National Design Award. He is also principal of MBDC, a product and systems development firm
assisting client companies in designing profitable and environmentally intelligent solutions.
He is an Alumni Research Professor at the University of Virginia's Darden Graduate School of
Business Administration, and a Consulting Professor of Civil and Environmental Engineering
at Stanford University. From 1994-1999, he was a Professor of Architecture and Dean of the
School of Architecture at the University of Virginia. Mr. McDonough's leadership in sustainable
development is recognized widely, both in the U.S. and internationally, and he has written
and lectured extensively on his design philosophy (e.g. see: Ted Talks). He was commissioned
in 1991 to write 'The Hanover Principles: Design for Sustainability' as guidelines for the City
of Hannover's EXPO 2000; in 2005 he developed the Liuzhou Eco-City project for China.
Professor Michael Braungart is a chemist and founder of EPEA International Umweltforschung
GmbH in Hamburg, Germany. He is also co-founder of the interdisciplinary firm McDonough
Braungart Design Chemistry (MBDC) in Charlottesville, Virginia, USA. After completing his studies in Process Engineering in Darmstadt, Dr. Braungart went on to explore the chemical process
of industrial production techniques with the Chemistry Department at Konstanz, Germany. He
subsequently spearheaded the formation of the Chemistry Section of Greenpeace International,
assuming leadership of Greenpeace Chemistry by 1985. He is currently Professor of Process
Engineering at the University Lüneburg, in Germany, and (since 2008) at the Erasmus University
in Rotterdam, lecturing on such topics as eco-effectiveness, cradle-to-cradle (the *C2C* health initiative) design principles, intelligent materials pooling, material flows and resource management. In
1987 he founded the Environmental Protection Encouragement Agency (EPEA), which developed
the 'Intelligent Products System' (IPS), creating products oriented toward a life-cycle economy and
eco-effectiveness. "We can never be carbon-neutral; but we can learn from nature. Nature only
uses what it needs and doesn't leave waste; it's effective rather than efficient." (Braungart, 2009).
www.mcdonough.com, www.mbdc.com, www.epea.com, www.worldgbc.org

Adrian McGregor, landscape architect and urban designer (Sydney, Australia).
Adrian McGregor is a landscape architect and director of Mcgregor+Coxall, a Sydney-
based environmental design studio. After graduating in 1988, he began work in Sydney
and then moved to North America and the UK to work on a range of environmental projects. He founded Mcgregor+Coxall in 1998 and the *Biocity Studio* in 2006, to combine

practice with research based on a sustainable design ethic. The practice received the international Topos Landscape Award 2009 in recognition of its environmental design work. The *Biocity Studio* is a theoretical urban design model that proposes cities be re-conceptualized as interconnected eco-systems. By embracing an envirocentric agenda, it aims to introduce new paradigms for restorative urban programmes through apply-ing equal planning weight to cultural and environmental processes. "Biocity respects the earth's abundance promoting recognition that humans are not divorced from natural sys-tems. By looking to ecological systems for design inspiration, the model actively strives to go beyond the minimisation of development impact to produce regenerative legacies. By encouraging networks of human activity that are purposefully restorative, Biocity aspires to nurture positive change, not just be less negative." (McGregor, 2009) www.mcgregorpartners.com.au, www.biocitystudio.com

Hans Mönninghoff and **Wulf Daseking**, both are city councilors and drivers of new sustain-able districts in two German 'green' cities (Mönninghoff in Hannover; and Daseking in Freiburg). The new city district 'Kronsberg' in Hannover, and the green transformation of the city of Freiburg im Breisgau (a city of 220,000 people) are both great examples of what a munici-pality can do with the existing urban fabric, for instance in regard to distributed energy gen-eration and sustainable urban water management. Freiburg is now almost fossil-fuel energy independent, using many of its buildings' facades and roofs to generate electricity locally, with building-integrated photovoltaic panels (over 500 installations). The constant carbon reduc-tion initiatives of both cities over the last 20 years are remarkable. Municipalities need such champions who persistently drive their environmental goals, like Hans Mönninghoff and Dr. Axel Priebs (Director of Planning and Environmental Protection) in Hannover. The ecologically oriented new districts and experimental housing estates `Vauban' and `Rieselfeld', both in Freiburg, have set new benchmarks for best practice in eco-city districts. At Vauban, the new ecologically designed settlement of 2,500 units was built on the site of an abandoned French military base, a `Solar Village' – probably Europe's most modern solar housing project, with 50 `Solar Energy+' houses that produce more energy than they consume. It was designed by Rolf Disch.

Wulf Daseking has been the director of City Planning in Freiburg since 1984. He has been responsible for urban development, land development, landscape planning and masterplan-ning. He is a lecturer in city planning at Freiburg University and at Darmstadt University. Hans Mönninghoff has been the managing director of Environmental Services of the City of Hannover since 1989. As a member of City Council, he led the green district 'Kronsberg' project and Hannover's Carbon Reduction Initiatives, which led to a 80 per cent reduction in CO_2 emissions compared to conventional urban development projects. Today, Freiburg and Hannover are two of the greenest cities in Europe. The Solar Info Centre in Freiburg is a competence centre that hosts companies and research institutes and facilitates collaboration with leading research institutes, such as the Fraunhofer Institute. The supportive Mayor of the City of Freiburg, since 2002, is Dr. Dieter Salomon.   www.sustainable-hannover.de, www.hannover-stadt.de, www.solarregion.freiburg.de, www.solar-info-center.de

Helmut F. O. Müller, university educator and researcher (Dortmund, Germany). Emeritus Professor Müller is the former Chair of Climate-Design and Environmental Architecture at the Technical University of Dortmund, Faculty of Architecture. He has researched energy-efficient buildings for several decades and has a particular interest in facade and day-lighting technology. www.bauwesen.uni-dortmund.de

Ravi Naidoo, designer and social entrepreneur (Cape Town, South Africa). Dr. Naidoo is the founder of Design Indaba (a magazine and conference), and is CEO of Interactive Africa and the Far East Organization. He has a particular focus on urban farming, social entrepreneurship and the future of African cities. Architect Gita Goven of ARG Design researches in informal settlements of townships. www.designindaba.com

Edward NG, The Chinese University of Hong Kong (CUHK), (Shantin, HK, China). Professor Ng is the author of the book 'Designing High Density Cities' (2009) and Director of the Sustainable and Environmental Design Programme at CUHK in Shatin. He holds a PhD from Cambridge University, and is involved in the Air Ventilation Assessment (AVA) Guidelines for city planning in Hong Kong. www.edwardng.com

Malin Olsson, Head of Urban Planning, at the City of Stockholm (Stockholm, Sweden). Mr. Olsson is the head of the Planning Division at the City of Stockholm. The Hammarby-Sjostad eco-district is a good example of what a municipality can do when they have a local champion such as Olsson. Stockholm has demonstrated how integrated planning and urban governance can transform an older inner-city industrial area into a new sustainable eco-district. The Hammarby district is a green neighbourhood based on cyclical urban metabolism and effective public transport that has led to a 30 per cent reduction in non-renewable energy use and a 40 per cent reduction in water use. www.stockholm.se/hammarbysjostad

Rajendra K. Pachauri, chief scientist and environmental activist (New Delhi, India). Dr. Pachauri has been the elected chair of the United Nation's *Intergovernmental Panel on Climate Change* (IPCC) since 2002. He won the 2007 Nobel Peace Prize, alongside Al Gore. Since 1982, Dr. Pachauri has led the international research organization *TERI* (The Energy and Resources Institute) in Delhi, where he is assisted by architect Ms Mili Majumdar, Director of Sustainable Building Science, amongst others. Dr. Pachauri assumed his current responsibilities as the Chief Executive of TERI in 1982, first as Director and, since 2001, as Director-General. TERI conducts research and provides knowledge in the areas of energy, environment, forestry, biotechnology and the conservation of natural resources to governments, institutions and corporate organizations worldwide. The IPCC was established by the World Meteorological Organization and the United Nations Environment Programme in 1988. Dr. Pachauri holds a PhD in industrial engineering and in economics (1974). His wide-ranging expertise in energy has resulted in his membership of various international and national committees and boards. He joined the board of the Global Humanitarian Forum, founded by former United Nations Secretary-General Kofi Annan. Currently he is member of the Indian Prime Minister's Advisory

Council on Climate Change. Dr Pachauri taught at the School of Forestry and Environmental Studies, Yale University, USA, and has also authored 23 books. Dr. Pachauri was appointed as Director of the Yale Climate and Energy Institute, in 2009. www.teriin.org, www.ipcc.ch

Renzo Piano and R.P.B.W. architects and urban designers (Genova/Paris).
Renzo Piano (born 1937) is one of the most eminent architects of the late 20th-century. For many years his practice, the Renzo Piano Building Workshop, has been at the forefront of sustainable design worldwide, with masterplans for the revitalization of Genova Waterfront, Berlin Potsdamer Platz, and North Milan Sesto San Giovanni area. Piano was one of the first architects (together with Norman Foster) to show that ecological-driven architecture can look elegant and stylish. www.rpbw.r.ui-pro.com, www.potsdamerplatz.de

Jonathon Porritt, environmental writer, broadcaster and commentator (London, UK).
Jonathon Porritt is founding director of the *Forum for the Future* and, since 2000, he has been Chairman of the UK Sustainable Development Commission. Established in 1996, *Forum for the Future* is now the UK's leading sustainable development charity, with over 100 partner organizations. The UK Sustainable Development Commission is the government's principal source of independent advice across the whole sustainable development agenda. Jonathan has been a member of The Board of the South West Regional Development Agency since December 1999, and is co-director of The Prince of Wales's Business and Environment Programme. He was formerly Director of Friends of the Earth (1984-90) and co-chair of the Green Party (1980-83).
www.jonathonporritt.com, www.sd-commission.org.uk, www.forumforthefuture.org.uk

Gerry Post, Planner and Director of the Amman Institute (Amman, Jordan).
Dutch-Canadian planner Gerry Post is the General Manager of the Amman Institute for Urban Development in Jordan, where he works on large-scale urban developments in the Middle-East. He has developed an Action Plan for Amman, which was published as 'The Amman Plan. Metropolitan Growth' (2008). www.ammaninstitute.org

Darko Radovic, researcher, university educator and author (Melbourne, Australia).
Associate Professor Darko Radovic received his doctorate from the University of Belgrade. He teaches sustainable design at the University of Melbourne and is (since 2009) a Visiting Professor at Keio University in Yokohama, Japan. He has co-published several books, including: 'Green City' (2005), 'Cross-Cultural Urban Design' (2007), and 'Eco-urbanity' (2008). His research "focuses at situations where architecture and urban design overlap, where traditional 'architectural' and 'urban' scales blur, where social starts to acquire physical form." www.ecourbanity.org

Fernando Ramos, university educator and researcher (Barcelona, Spain).
Professor Ramos is an architect and former collaborator of Ignasi Sola-Morales. He is the coordinator of the *University Network for Architectural and Urban Sustainability* at the Catalan University Politechnic (UPC) in Barcelona, where he works with Prof. Joseph Puig, Prof. Albert Cuchi

i Burgos, and is assisted by Dr. Katarina Mrkonjic and others. Dr Zaida Muxi is professor of urbanism at UPC, where she works with Josep M. Montaner. www.asiasustainabilitynet.upc.edu, www.etsab.upc.es and www.laboratoriovivienda21.com

Ulf Ranhagen, architect, urban planner and researcher at KTH (Stockholm, Sweden). Professor Ranhagen teaches sustainable design at the KTH Royal Institute of Technology in Stockholm. He is involved in the urban design of parts of the new eco-city Tianjin in China, to be developed in the Tangshan Region, 250 kilometers east of Beijing. In the future, it is envisaged that up to a quarter of a million people will live in this eco-city. Sweco, the multidisciplinary company Ulf Ranhagen and Jan Mattsson are working for, has established a sustainability strategy for the first stage of the construction, to be completed by 2020. The focus is on integrated solutions for energy supply and urban form. The Dongtuo area will act as the urban innovation engine for the development of *Hangu Eco-City*. The Swedish-Chinese collaboration is based on an agreement that the Chinese and Swedish governments signed in 2007. Sweco is one of the most innovative Scandinavian engineering companies in sustainable development. www.sweco.se

Manit Rastogi, emerging eco-architect (New Delhi, India). Mr Rastogi is a co-founder member of Morphogenesis, which was formed in 1996, after completing his studies in Sustainable Energy Design at the Architectural Association in London. He has taught at various schools and is a member of the Technical Advisory Committee to the Ministry of Renewable Energy, Government of India. Morphogenesis works out of New Delhi and handles projects across varied and complex typologies, where sustainability is seen as a core creative value and is part of the evolution of the design. The work of the practice has been published internationally. www.morphogenesis.org

K. T. Ravindran and **Ashok Lall**, forward-thinking urban designers New Delhi, India). Both Professor Ravindran and Professor Lall teach urban design at the School of Planning and Architecture (SPA) in New Delhi. Ravindran is currently Dean of Studies at SPA, and has a particular interest in the peri-urban field. Ashok Lall is Dean of Studies at TVB School of Habitat Studies in Delhi. He studied at the Architectural Association in London and was a juror for the *Holcim Awards* in 2008. Ravindran is one of the leading Indian urbanists and is the head of the Urban Design programme at SPA. He teaches urban morphology and strategies for humanizing cities, integrated into his urban design studio. His practice includes the design of cultural buildings, memorials, urban conservation and greenfield cities. www.spa.ac.in, www.ashoklallarchitects.com

Richard Register, `Ecocity Builders' activist and researcher (Oakland, California, USA). Richard Register is an author and theorist in ecological city planning. He is the founder of the non-profit Ecocity Builders organization and convened the first International Eco-City Conference in 1990. His latest book is entitled: `Eco-Cities – Rebuilding Cities in Balance with Nature' (2006). He works with his colleague Kirstin Miller in the Californian Bay area. www.ecocitybuilders.org and www.ecocityprojects.net

Roger-Bruno Richard, architect and educator (Montreal, Canada).
Professor Richard teaches *Design & Systems* in the School of Architecture at the University of Montreal. He is specialized in industrialized building systems and manufactured housing prototypes, simplifying production to make adaptable prefabricated housing types affordable to a vast majority of people. www.umontreal.ca

Saffa Riffat, engineer and researcher (Nottingham, UK).
Professor Riffat holds the Chair in Sustainable Energy Technology and is director of the Institute of Sustainable Energy Technology at the University of Nottingham. He has a wide range of experience of renewable energy, sustainable buildings, heat transfer, heat pumps, ventilation systems and air quality. He holds a PhD from the University of Oxford for his research contribution in the field of heat pumps and ventilation technology and is named as the inventor on 20 patents. www.nottingham.ac.uk

Susan Roaf, scientist and university researcher (Edinburgh, UK).
Architect and author Susan Roaf is Professor of Architectural Engineering at Heriot Watt University in Edinburgh and Visiting Professor at the Open University and Arizona State University. Having spent ten years in Iran and Iraq, she completed academic studies on the wind catchers of Yazd, nomadic architecture, and ancient water systems. She has written books on landscaping in arid lands, eco-house design, benchmarks for sustainable buildings and adapting buildings and cities for climate change. Her research work focuses on thermal comfort, photovoltaics, passive building design, eco-housing and the education of architects. She co-chaired the 2006 International Solar Cities Congress in Oxford and the 2008 Oxford Conference. She has served on a range of national and international committees and think tanks, and is currently engaged in research in the fields of thermal comfort, micro-grid communities and the adaptation of buildings and cities for climate change. From 2000 until 2006, she held the Chair in Sustainable Architecture at Oxford Brookes University. www.hw.ac.uk

Richard Rogers and colleagues, architect and urban designer (London, UK).
Lord Richard Rogers is one of the most eminent architects of the late 20th-century. His BBC lecture series 'Cities for a Small Planet' (1997) was followed by the book publication 'Cities for a Small Country' (2000, co-authored with Anne Power), which became standard reading for architects and urban designers. Sir Richard Rogers was born in Florence, Italy, in 1933, and studied at the Architectural Association in London. He is a prize-winning architect, and was the chair of the *Urban Task Force* for the revitalization of English cities and towns. His study `London as it could be' (1986) was a visionary blueprint for a sustainable city. He proposes radical solutions to overcome suburban sprawl, the over-use of energy and environmental damage. He has been active in the English labour party for many years. In 2008, his practice changed its name to Rogers Stirk Harbour + Partners. www.richardrogers.co.uk

Hans Rosenlund, researcher at Lund University (Stockholm, Sweden).
Dr. Rosenlund is a former Associate Professor in the Department of Architecture and Built Environment, Lund University, and works as an architect in Sweden. His research is in the area of climatic design of buildings, and the relationship of building to urban design. www.cecdesign.se

Saskia Sassen, urban theorist and university researcher (New York City, USA).
Dr. Saskia Sassen shares the passion for ground-breaking research in urban theories with her partner, Professor Richard Sennett. She is the Lynd Professor of Sociology and a member of the *Committee on Global Thought* at Columbia University. Her recent books include: 'A Sociology of Globalization' (2007), and the 3rd fully updated 'Cities in a World Economy' (2006). She wrote a lead essay in the 2006 Venice Biennale of Architecture catalogue and has recently completed, for UNESCO, in conjunction with a network of researchers and activists in over 30 countries, a five year project on sustainable human settlement, published as one of the volumes of the Encyclopedia of Life Support Systems (2008). 'The Global City' book came out in a new fully updated edition in 2001. Her books have been translated into sixteen languages. She serves on several editorial boards and is an advisor to several international bodies. She is a member of the Council on Foreign Relations, a member of the National Academy of Sciences panel on cities, and she has chaired the Information Technology and International Cooperation Committee of the Social Science Research Council (USA). She has also written for newspapers, such as *The Guardian, The New York Times, International Herald Tribune, Newsweek International, and The Financial Times*. www.columbia.edu, www.eolss.net

David Satterthwaite, urban poverty researcher, author and editor (London, UK).
Dr. Satterthwaite is a senior fellow at the International Institute for Environment and Development (IIED), where he researches on urban poverty reduction strategies. He is the editor of *Environment and Urbanization.* www.iied.org

Willy A. Schmid, university research and planner at ETH Zurich (Zurich, Switzerland).
Until 2008, Professor Willy Schmid is the former director of the Institute for Spatial and Landscape Planning, at the ETH Zurich, where he taught and researched sustainable urban planning for over 30 years. www.nsl.ethz.ch

Thomas Schroepfer and **Christian Werthmann**, eco-planners and researchers at GSD (Harvard University/Cambridge, USA).
Associate Professor Schroepfer teaches in the architecture design studios and courses on materials and construction at the Graduate School of Design. His doctoral dissertation examined the impact of globalization on contemporary design dynamics, theoretical discourse and building practices. This ongoing research has also been the topic of his publications. He is a registered architect in Germany and has been associated with several architectural practices in Berlin, among them Studio Daniel Libeskind and the Hochtief Group construction company. His recent book is on *Material Culture* (2010).
Associate Professor Werthmann teaches in the landscape architecture design studio at the GSD, where he is Director of the Master Programme. He received his Masters degree in Germany, before moving to the United States in 1997, and worked for the landscape architects Latz and Partners. In the US, he became an associate at Peter Walker and Partners. Werthmann's current research includes green roofs, rain gardens and constructed wetlands in heavily urbanized areas. His recent book: *Green Roof: A Case Study* (2007). He founded

the *GSD Green Roof Initiative* that installed an experimental green roof on the GSD building in 2006. As co-founders of the interdisciplinary research group *TransUrban*, Werthmann and Schroepfer examine built experiments in sustainable urbanism. www.gsd.harvard.edu

Andreas Schüler, solar researcher (Lausanne, Switzerland).
Dr. Schüler studied physics in Freiburg, at the University of Michigan at Ann Arbor, and at the University of Basel. His R&D experience includes a wide variety of fields such as plasma- and sol-gel thin-film deposition processes, optical and electronic properties of nanostructured materials, laser spin polarized noble gases in medical imaging (functional MRI), and advanced ray-tracing simulations for solar thermal technology. He is a lecturer at the EPFL Lausanne, where he is a research group leader in the Solar Energy and Building Physics Laboratory (LESO-PB). His research group focuses on nanotechnology for solar energy conversion. Targeted applications include nanostructured coatings for solar architectural glazing, selective solar absorbers, thermochromic solar collectors and quantum dot solar concentrators for photovoltaics. Schüler participates actively in the organization of conferences on solar energy and nanostructured materials. www.epfl.ch

Matthias Schuler, architect and 'Transsolar' founder (Stuttgart / Harvard, USA).
Professor Schuler teaches at Harvard University, where he holds the Chair in Environmental Technologies and is one of the managing directors of 'Transsolar Energietechnik' in Stuttgart, Germany. Educated as a mechanical engineer, he worked at University Stuttgart in international research projects about low energy commercial buildings. In 1992, based on this experience, he founded the company *Transsolar*, as a climate engineering consulting company that introduces, by an integral approach in early building design steps, new energy saving and comfort optimizing strategies. Nowadays, with offices in Stuttgart, Munich and New York, Matthias Schuler works as a consultant on national and international projects with architects like Jean Nouvel, Kazuyo Sejima, Frank Gehry, Steven Holl, and Ben van Berkel. He is assisted by Dr. Wolfgang Kessling and other experts. www.transsolar.com

Niels B. Schulz, university researcher and team leader (London, UK).
Dr. Schulz is a research fellow of the 'Urban Energy Systems Project' at the Energy Futures Lab, Imperial College, London, where he works with Dr Nigel Brandon, director of the Lab. He is a research scholar at the International Institute of Applied Systems Analysis (IIASA) in Laxenburg, Austria. Before joining the Energy Futures Lab, he worked for two years as a postdoctoral fellow at the United Nations University, Institute of Advanced Studies (UNU-IAS) in Yokohama, Japan, in the ecosystem programme, addressing environmental challenges of cities in the Asian-Pacific region. In particular, he developed indicators of sustainable production and consumption on the urban scale. Schulz holds a PhD in ecology from Vienna University, where his research examined changes in energy use and resource consumption during the industrialization of England. Past research has included integrated measures for land-use and land-cover change, such as human appropriation of net primary production, ecological footprint analysis, and other measures of society's material and energy metabolism. www.iiasa.ac.at and www.imperial.ac.uk/energyfutureslab

Andrew Scott, educator and architect at MIT (Boston, USA).

Andrew Scott is associate professor of architecture at the Massachusetts Institute of Technology, and coordinator of sustainable urban housing project in China, which develops methods for testing the performance of a micro-climatically sensitive urban structure plan for new communities, as an alternative to energy-inefficient and limited technologies of contemporary building types. His research is focused around the understanding of 'sustainability' to the built form, most significantly through the formal ideas and technological systems of bio-climatic design. Scott studied architecture at the University of Manchester (UK), and worked for Foster and Partners (1986-93). He has won a number of prizes, including the 'Building Integrated Photovoltaics' competition (1996), sponsored by the AIA Research and US Department of Energy, for a project named Intelligent Pavilion. In 2000, he won the commission to design and build the low-energy and environmentally responsible Thompson Island Education Center in Boston Harbor. He published 'Dimensions of Sustainability' in 1998, which has a focus on design strategies that architects and engineers make at various stages of the design process. www.mit.edu

Werner Sobek, engineer, architect and educator (Stuttgart, Germany / Chicago, USA)

Professor Sobek is the president of the DGNB, *Deutsche Gesellschaft fuer nachhaltiges Bauen* (German Society for Sustainable Construction), founder of WS Green Technologies in Stuttgart and a professor at the IIT in Chicago. www.wernersobek.com www.dgnb.de

Veronica Soebarto, researcher and educator (Adelaide, Australia).

Associate Professor Soebarto has a particular interest in the research of Urban Heat Island effect, which she explores in collaboration with Associate Professor Terry Williamson at the University of Adelaide. www.adelaide.edu.au

Paolo Soleri, architect and planner of *Arcosanti* (at Cordes Junction, Arizona, USA).

Born in Turin, Italy in 1919, Soleri received a PhD in architecture from the Torino Polytechnico in 1946. In the following year he went to the US to continue his studies, with Frank Lloyd Wright at Taliesin West in Arizona. His major project is Arcosanti, an experimental prototype town in the desert of Arizona (70 miles north of Phoenix) for 5,000 people, under construction since 1970. Soleri proposes cities for walking, not designed around automobiles; compact and three-dimensional, not flat and scattered over large distances. He advocates urban design that maximizes the interaction and accessibility associated with an urban environment, and minimizes the use of energy, materials and land, thus reducing waste and environmental pollution. Over the last twenty years, Prof. Jeff Stein, director of the architecture programme at the Boston Architectural College, has been working with Soleri on the Arcosanti project. www.arcosanti.org

Michael Sorkin, urban designer and researcher (New York City, USA).

Currently a professor of architecture and director of the Graduate Urban Design programme at City College (CUNY), New York. Sorkin has architectural training from Havard and MIT. His publications include: 'Local Code' and 'Giving Ground'. He is the president of Terreform, a non-profit organization involved in urban research, which recently started to advocate the 'Greening of Cities'. www.sorkinstudio.com

Nicholas Stern, government advisor (London, the UK); and **Ross Garnault**, government advisor (Canberra, Australia).

Both top economists, Lord Nicholas Stern and Professor Ross Garnault have been advising their governments on the economic impact of climate change. Professor Stern published, in 2007, *The Economics of Climate Change: The Stern Review* (www.sternreview.org.uk). The Stern Review is regarded as the most comprehensive review ever carried out on the economics of climate change. It was first published in October 2006 and was led by Lord Stern, then Head of the Government Economic Service and former World Bank Chief Economist. He stepped down as Head of the Government Economic Service in March 2007 to take up the IG Patel Professorship at the London School of Economics and Political Science (LSE). Nicholas Stern became Lord Stern of Brentford in December 2007 when he was appointed to the House of Lords as a non-party political peer.

In September 2008, *The Garnault Climate Change Review: Final Report* (the Australian version of the Stern Report) was published by the Australian Department of Climate Change (www.climatechange.gov.au). Both reports clearly show that inaction and delay in the transformation towards a 'post-carbon society' is likely to be much more costly for economies and the environment if action is postponed. Lord Stern has recently pointed out that 'the economical impact of global warming has been grossly underestimated, and scientists must warn that inaction will spell disaster' (2009).

www.hm-treasury.gov.uk/stern_review_report.htm   and   www.sternreview.org.uk   and www.climatechange.gov.au

David T. Suzuki, environmental activist, broadcaster and author (Toronto, Canada).

The David Suzuki Foundation (DSF) was co-founded by David Suzuki in 1990, and is based in Toronto. Mr. Suzuki is the author of over 40 books (including 17 for children), including: 'Tree- a life story', 'Inventing the Future', 'Genethics' and 'The Sacred Balance'. He is an environmental activist, ecologist and sociologist, with a particular focus on climate change. Dr. Suzuki is particularly interested in the relationship between humans and nature, how cities disconnect people from the natural world, the potential for eco-friendly cities and the science of various ecological phenomena. He is renowned for his radio and television programmes that explain the complexities of the natural sciences in a compelling, easily understood way. He received a PhD in Zoology from the University of Chicago, and is now Emeritus Professor of The University of British Columbia, Sustainable Development Research Institute. Dr. Suzuki has written 47 books, including 17 for children. He is recognized as a leader in sustainable ecology. He is the recipient of UNESCO's Kalinga Prize for Science, the United Nations Environment Program Medal and the Global 500. At the Foundation, he is assisted by Peter Robinson, Jose Etcheverry, and others.

www.davidsuzuki.org

Steven V. Szokolay, scientist, architect and energy expert (Brisbane, Australia).
Associate Professor Szokolay has conducted intensive study into passive design strategies
for various climates. His publication 'Climatic Data and its use in Design' contains climatic
data for sun, wind, rainfall and temperature for various areas throughout Australia. His
focus is on passive solar design and environmental sustainability in the built environment.
Dr. Szokolay published, in 2004 the standard book 'Introduction to Architectural Science.
The Basics of Sustainable Design'. He retired in 2005 from the University of Queensland.

Kaarin Taipale, architect and researcher (Helsinki, Finland)
Dr. Taipale worked with the City of Helsinki and with ICLEI, before she became a Senior
Researcher at the *Centre for Knowledge and Innovation* at Aalto University School of
Economics in Helsinki, where she coordinates the UN-initiated *Marrakech Task Force on
Sustainable Buildings and Construction.* www.kaarintaipale.net

Pattaranan Mook Takkanon and **Pasinee Sunakorn**, university researchers and
building technology lecturers (Bangkok, Thailand).
Dr. Takkanon and Associate Professor Sunakorn lecture in the MBIT Programme and research
compact cities, green urban design and assessment methods of sustainability, in the Faculty
of Architecture at Kasetsart University, Bangkok. They have a special focus on strategies for
hot and humid regions, by using 'Cool Wall' systems and plants to shade buildings, in which
they collaborate with Dr. Joseph Khedari and others. They note: "Sustainability has become
mainstream in design field. Its concepts have been applied to greening architecture and cities.
Green urbanism is becoming a global norm. Its principles are applicable and transferable
globally. However, exemplary cities in many regions, such as in Europe, America, Australia
and Asia, show the differences in context. When implementing the principles of green urbanism, the local context must always be taken into account." (2009) www.ku.ac.th

Arjan van Timmeren, architect (Delft/Amsterdam Haarlem, The Netherlands).
Architect van Timmeren has worked in several internationally-known architectural and engineering
offices and is currently a partner in 'Atelier 2T' (Haarlem, NL). He is an associate professor at the
Delft University of Technology, Faculty of Architecture, in the 'Climate Design and Sustainability' and
'Green Building Innovation' divisions, specialized in self-sufficiency in relation to urban scale optimi-
zation. His publications include: 'Smart Building in a Changing Climate' (eds. Dobbelsteen, Dorst,
Timmeren, 2009), and 'Integrated Solutions for a Sustainable Urban Metabolism. Climate Integrated
Design' (2009). He has received international awards for his work and is a member of international
scientific advisory committees and panels. www.atelier2t.com and http://bk.faculteiten.tudelft.nl

Henning Thomsen, researcher in sustainable cities (Copenhagen, Denmark).
Thomsen was the head of the 'Sustainable Cities' division at the Danish Architecture Centre
(DAC) in Copenhagen (2007-09). He is a member of the Danish green think tank CONCITO,
and the World Future Council Expert Commission on cities and climate change. He is now an
associate at Jan Gehl Architects. The 'Sustainable Cities' division is now managed by Anne Esbjoern

Hess and Fredrik Gyllenhoff. www.sustainablecities.dk

Klaus Töpfer, policy-maker, former Director-General of the UN in Nairobi (lives in Germany) . Professor Töpfer is the former United Nations Undersecretary-General and Executive Director of the United Nations Environment Programme (UNEP). He is widely recognized as having spearheaded environmental policy as Minister of Environment in Germany. He introduced ground-breaking environmental regulations, including the law on life-cycle economy, subsidies for solar energy, and the 'green dot' packaging recycling system. He is the Chair of the Global Assurance Group for the Energy Efficiency in Buildings (EEB) project, an initiative of the World Business Council for Sustainable Development (WBCSD). The three-year EEB project developed a roadmap to focus the global building industry on designing, financing, building and operating commercial and residential structures that are completely energy self-sufficient. Dr. Töpfer studied economics and completed a PhD in political science in 1968. Before his political career, he was a professor at the University of Hannover, where he directed the Institute of Regional Research and Development (1978-79). Töpfer was Minister of the Environment, Nature, Conservation and Nuclear Safety from 1987 to 1994 in the German federal parliament; and Minister of Regional Planning, Building and Urban Development from 1994 to 1998. He is the recipient of several honours, including the Order of Merit and the Grand Cross of the Federal Republic of Germany (1986). In 2002 he was awarded the Bruno Schubert Environment Prize and the German Environment Prize. He became Executive Director of UNEP and Director-General of the United Nations Office in Nairobi in 1998. He was also appointed Acting Executive Director of the United Nations Centre for Human Settlements (UN-Habitat) from 1998 to 2000, a position held today by Dr. **Anna Tibaijuka** (the first African woman elected by the UN General Assembly as Under-Secretary-General of a UN programme). Töpfer stepped down from his position at UNEP in April 2006. Other urban researchers at UN-Habitat include Prof. Toshiyasu Noda and Dr. Daniel Biau. www.nachhaltigkeitsrat.de, www.dsw-online.de

Brent Toderian, Director of Planning, at the City of Vancouver (Vancouver, BC, Canada).
In 2006, Brent Toderian was appointed the city of Vancouver's Director of City Planning. Since then, he has developed the city-wide 'Eco-Density' initiative, which uses densification strategically to reduce the city's ecological footprint, while making Vancouver more sustainable, livable and affordable. Vancouver has emerged as one of the leading examples in what can be achieved if we stop suburbs growing and adopt a positive approach to urban compacting. The City of Vancouver has made environmental sustainability a primary goal in all planning decisions and launched the 'Eco-Density Charter'. 'This evolving urbanism offers bold opportunities around sustainability and architectural risk-taking, enabling mid-density, compact, transport-oriented developments.' (Toderian, 2008) Mr Colin Grant is a strategic advisor and member of the *Vancouver Mayor's Sustainability Council.* www.vancouver-ecodensity.ca

Martin Treberspurg, architect and urban designer (Vienna, Austria).
Professor Treberspurg heads the Institute for Sustainable Constructions at the University of Natural Resources and Applied Life Sciences (BOKU) in Vienna. His architectural practice Treberspurg & Partner Architekten in Vienna is one of the urban design leaders of the 'SolarCity'

project in Linz, Austria. He is the vice-head of the Department of Building Physics of the Austrian Chamber of Architects and Engineers, and has been a lecturer in solar architecture since 1993 at the Technical University of Vienna. His main focus is on energy saving constructions and residential architecture (Passiv-Haus). He is the author of 'Neues Bauen mit der Sonne' and other books concerning solar architecture. www.boku.ac.at, www.treberspurg.com

Brenda Vale and **Robert Vale**, architects, urban designer and pioneer researchers in sustainable housing (Wellington, New Zealand).

Both are eco-architects, writers, researchers and leading experts in the field of sustainable housing in New Zealand. English-born Professor Brenda and Dr. Robert Vale, at Victoria University in Wellington, are pioneers in sustainable design. After studying architecture together at the University of Cambridge, in 1975 the Vales published 'The Autonomous House', a technical guide for developing housing solutions that are energy self-sufficient, powered by the sun, relatively easy to maintain, with thick walls for thermal mass and a vernacular appearance consistent with its context. The book has been translated into five languages and is widely recognized as a basic text in the field of green building. Their houses, built in the 1980s, are completely off-grid, except for the telephone line and a connection to the electrical supply. The latter supplies power from the grid when the occupants are using more electricity than is being produced by the solar panels, and exports at times of surplus generation. Their book 'Green Architecture: Design for an Energy Conscious Future' (1991) was an important milestone in sustainability. The Vales emigrated to Waiheke Island near Auckland, New Zealand, in 1996, taking positions at the University of Auckland. Commissioned by the Australian government, they have developed a unique building rating system called NABERS, which measures the ongoing environmental impact of existing buildings. www.creative.auckland.ac.nz

Mathis Wackernagel and **William Rees**, researchers on the 'Ecological Footprint' (Oakland, California, USA; Vancouver, Canada).

The term 'ecological footprint' refers to the area necessary to sustain a person's lifestyle. Mathis Wackernagel, who developed this term, is a Swiss-born sustainability advocate who advises governments on sustainability issues on several continents. Wackernagel previously served as director of the Sustainability Program for Global Footprint Network, at Redefining Progress in Oakland, California, and directed the Centre for Sustainability Studies in Mexico. These organisations focus on developing and promoting metrics for measuring sustainability. After earning a degree in mechanical engineering from the Swiss Federal Institute of Technology (ETH), Wackernagel completed his doctorate in community and regional planning at the University of British Columbia (UBC) in Vancouver, Canada. There, as his doctoral dissertation, with Professor William (Bill) Rees, he co-created the 'Ecological Footprint' concept. Professor Rees teaches in the School of Community and Regional Planning at the University of British Columbia. Their co-authored book 'Ecological Footprint Analysis' (1996) has been translated into ten languages. Wackernagel's recent book is entitled: 'Ecological Footprint: Reducing Human Impact on the Earth'. Today, many researchers are interested in the further development of the 'Ecological Footprint' concept, Assistant Professor Ryan E. Smith at the University of Utah being one of them. www.footprintnetwork.org, www.scarp.ubc.ca

Charles Waldheim, researcher at the GSD, Harvard University (Cambridge, USA). Professor Waldheim was director of the landscape architecture programme at the University of Toronto,. Since 2009, he has been head of the Department of Landscape Architecture at GSD, Harvard University, where his research focuses on contemporary urbanism and landscape. In the 1990s, he coined the term 'landscape urbanism' to describe emerging design practices in the context of urbanism. He has taught at the University of Pennsylvania, the University of Michigan, the Swiss Federal Institute (ETH), and other universities. He has been named recipient of the Rome Prize from the American Academy in Rome, and is a research fellow at the Canadian Centre for Architecture (CCA). He served as a member of the Toronto Waterfront Redevelopment Corporation Design Review Panel and is on the editorial board of *Canadian Architect* journal. His consulting practice, *Urban Agency*, advises on issues related to contemporary urbanism. www.gsd.harvard.edu

Rusong WANG, President, Ecological Society of China (Beijing, P. R. China). Mr Wang is head of the Center for Ecological and Environmental Sciences at the Chinese Academy of Science and has been involved in ecological city theory. He is one of the founders of the Ecological Society of China, an ecologist, and a champion of solutions in waste treatment and pollution abatement for the health delivery systems in China. He is one of the founders of SCOPE (Scientific Committee on Problems in the Environment). He expounds a theory based on remapping cities for reshaping them for minimum energy demand and maximum eco-diversity. He is also a member of the Peoples Congress of China. Ecological Society of China. www.rcees.ac.cn/dse/en/team

Youwei WANG, Green Building Council China (Beijing, P. R. China). Mr Wang is the chairman of China's Green Building Council and works closely with the Chinese Ministry of Housing and Urban-Rural Development (MHURD), where he has been leading the development of China's Green Building Evaluation Standards. Mr Wang is also the deputy director of the Expert Committee of the China Construction Industry Association. He collaborates with Mr **Xun LI**, who is Secretary-General of the Chinese Society for Urban Studies. Mr Li graduated as urban planner from Tongji University in Shanghai. www.chinagreenbuildings.blogspot.com

Nyuk Hien WONG, university researcher and author (Singapore). Dr. Wong is an associate professor in the Department of Building, at the National University of Singapore, where he is the principal investigator for a number of research projects to study the Urban Heat Island (UHI) effect in Asian cities, exploring the various mitigation measures, such as the effective utilization of urban greenery and cool roof materials. He has been working on Singapore's 'Zero-Energy Building' and is a member of advisory boards to various government agencies. He has been involved in an international research project commissioned by the Planning Department of Hong Kong, to develop an air-ventilation assessment system and which is now in use. His latest book is 'Tropical Urban Heat Islands: Climate, Buildings and Greenery' (2008). www.nus.edu.sg

Kam Sing WONG, architect and urban designer in Hong Kong (HK, China). Mr Wong's topic of research is in high-density urban and residential areas for Hong Kong and Mainland China. He is chairman of the Professional Green Building Council (PGBC) and vice-president of the Hong Kong Institute of Architects. He was the founding chairman of the HKIA Committee on Environment & Sustainable Development. In architectural practise, he is the director of Sustainable Design at Ronald Lu & Partners (Hong Kong), with projects ranging from masterplanning and urban design, to a wide spectrum of building projects that apply the principles of sustainable design in the high density urban context of Hong Kong and Mainland China. www.rlphk.com

Tony WONG, designer of urban water management principles (Melbourne, Australia). Malaysian-born Dr. Wong is a principal of the global design firm AECOM (formerly EDAW), and has a particular focus on sustainable urban water management. He was one of the industry leaders who developed concepts of water-sensitive urban design (WSUD), stormwater quality improvement, and water conservation. The integration of these concepts into the design of urban landscapes and sustainable communities is one of his special areas of research. His recent book: 'A Guide to Water-Sensitive Urban Design'. In 2008, he was appointed a honorary professor at Monash University in Melbourne. www.aecom.com, www.watersensitivefutures.org

The World Bank Eco² Cities Team, *Eco² Cities* Program of the World Bank (Washington, USA). In 2009, with the 'Eco² Cities Program', the World Bank has developed an analytical and operational framework that can be adapted by cities in all regions. The objective of the Eco² Cities Program is to help cities in developing countries achieve greater ecological and economic sustainability. *Eco²* means: Ecological Cities as Economic Cities. At the Word Bank, the following people have been involved in this initiative: Keshav Varma, Urban Sector Director, East Asia Pacific Region; Zoubida Allaoua, Director, Finance, Economics & Urban Department, Sustainable Development Network; Ede Jorge Ijjasz-Vasquez, Sector Manager, China & Mongolia Sustainable Development Unit, East Asia & Pacific Region; Hiroaki Suzuki, Sector Leader, East Asia & Pacific, and Team Leader of Eco² Cities Program; Patricia McCarney, Director; Arish Dastur, Urban Specialist, Co-Team Leader of Eco² Cities Program, East Asia and Pacific Region; Abha Joshi-Ghani, Sector Manager, Urban Development, Sustainable Development Network. www.worldbank.org/eco2

Siegfried Zhiqiang WU, urban designer and university researcher (Shanghai, P.R. China). Professor Wu is the former dean of the College of Architecture and Planning (CAUP) at Tongji University, Shanghai; and director of the Academy of Urban Strategy & Management. He is one of the Chief Planners of Shanghai EXPO 2010, where he proposed the 'H-city' (Harmony City) scheme as a guideline for the design at all levels, to illustrate the EXPO's 'Better City, Better Life' theme. He researches urban development strategies for Shanghai, developes environmental assessment systems for the Chinese building industry and in eco-city planning research. Professor Wu received his Masters from Tongji University and a PhD (1996) from the Technical University of Berlin. He has been project manager for a range of projects, such as: Shangyang development strategy plan and Yili City masterplan. He has been involved in more than 30 urban design projects. Wu is also a permanent member of the UNESCO-UIA World Architectural Education Council; and is a former president of the Asia Planning Schools Association (APSA), from 2003-2007. www.tongji.edu.cn/english, www.tongji-caup.org, www.gpean.org

Simos Yannas and **Koen Steemers**, researchers, engineers and organizers of the PLEA conferences (London/Cambridge, UK).
Steemers is Professor of Sustainable Design in the Department of Architecture at Cambridge University, where he was director of the Martin Centre for Architectural and Urban Studies, and where he works with Prof. Marcial Echenique and others. Steemers is president of PLEA International (2005-2010). Yannas is programme director of the Sustainable Environmental Design course at the Architectural Association School of Architecture in London. Both have been instrumental in organizing the PLEA conferences. Their research explores the relationship between architectural form, materiality and environmental performance, and how this relationship should evolve. Steemers is an architect and environmental design consultant. His work deals with the architectural potential of environmental issues. His research activities are focused on the environmental performance of buildings and cities, with a particular interest in human perception and behaviour, which are the topics of funded research projects. Simos Yannas is an architect who studied at the EPF in Lausanne, the NTU Athens, and the AA Graduate School. PLEA is a non-profit organization engaged in a worldwide discourse on sustainable architecture and urban design through annual international conferences, workshops and publications. It has a membership of several thousand professionals, academics and students from over 40 countries. *PLEA* stands for 'Passive and Low Energy Architecture'. It has a commitment to the development, documentation and diffusion of the principles of bio-climatic design. PLEA serves as an open, international, interdisciplinary forum to promote high quality research, practice and education in environmentally sustainable design. www.plea-arch.net, www.aaschool.ac.uk, www.cam.ac.uk, and www.carl.co.uk

Ken Yeang, eco-architect, urban designer and author (London and Kuala Lumpur).
Dr Ken Yeang is principal of the London-based, globally-operating architectural firm Llewelyn, Davies, Yeang (Eco Planning and Eco Systems), a multidisciplinary firm of urban designers and architects (in Malaysia: Hamazah & Yeang). He is regarded as one of the world's leading architects in ecological and passive low-energy design. He has delivered over 100 projects and his theory of 'bio-climatic' towers has had an impact around the world, fusing high-tech with organic principles. Born in Penang, Malaysia, in 1948, Yeang was educated there, as well as at the Architectural Association in London, and in the US, receiving a PhD from Cambridge University in 1974. His ongoing R&D interests have led to the publication of a number of books on the topic of ecological planning and high-rise design ('The Skyscraper: Bio-climatically Considered', 1996; 'Eco-Masterplanning', 2009). His designs include vertical landscaping of towers and sophisticated façade technology (intelligent building systems), combined with expressive external louvers to reduce solar heat gain. His concentration on energy conservation and environmental impact of architecture in the early 1990s was a radical departure from mainstream architecture's view of the profession, which was at that time more concerned with pure aesthetics.
www.ldavies.com, wwwtrhamzahyeang.com   *(see interview in this Appendix)*

Jiang YI, building technology expert and university educator (Beijing, P. R. China).
A professor at Tsinghua University in Beijing, Yi Jiang is a member of the Chinese Academy of Engineers and acts as Vice Dean in the School of Architecture. He holds the Chair

of the Department of Building Science and Technology and he is a senior consultant to the Beijing government for energy-efficiency in construction. www.arch.tsinghua.edu.cn

Jechul YOO, officer at United Nations Environment Programme (Bangkok, Thailand).
Mr. Yoo works as a senior programme officer in the Climate Change Adaptation Unit of the Division of Environmental Policy Implementation, in the United Nations Environment Programme (UNEP). Yoo is currently dedicated to developing a UNEP-wide climate change adaptation programme. He was seconded to UNEP from the Korean Ministry of Environment in 2006. His primary area of expertise is on urban environment issues, with a focus on the Asian region, including nature conservation, industrial and solid waste management, extended producers' responsibility for recycling and urban planning. At UNEP he collaborates with Jaime Webbe, Abdul Haddad, and others; the UNEP Asia-Pacific office is based in Bangkok. **Achim Steiner** is director of UNEP. Architects Dr. Peter Graham (based in Sydney), and Dr. Wynn C. N. Cam (based in Singapore), are both involved with UNEP as coordinators of the Sustainable Building Initiative. Dr. Noeleen Heyzer is, since 2007, Excecutive Sectretary of ESCAP, based in Singapore. www.unep.org/climatechange, www.unepsbci.org

Kongjian YU, university researcher and landscape architect (Beijing, P. R. China).
Professor Yu received his PhD from Harvard GSD in 1995. He has been Professor of Urban Planning at Beijing University since 1997, where he is Dean of the Graduate School of Landscape Architecture (GSLA). He is the founder of *Turenscape*, which is an internationally awarded firm with more than 400 professionals, and one of the first private landscape architecture firms in China. Dr. Yu is a five-time winner of the ASLA Award (The American Society of Landscape Architects) for ecologically and culturally sensitive projects. He serves as consulting expert for the Ministry of Housing, Rural and Urban Construction of China, for the cities of Beijing and Suzhou. He has published widely, including more than 200 papers and 16 books. His most recent book is *The Art Of Survival - Recovering Landscape Architecture (2008)*. He currently acts as chief editor of *Landscape Architecture China* journal. www.turenscape.com, www.arch.tsinghua.edu.cn

Muhammad Yunus, economist and founder of a micro-credit bank (Dhaka, Bangladesh).
Dr. Yunus is founder of the Grameen Bank, which successfully developed a micro-credit system in rural Bangladesh. The Grameen Bank was awarded the Nobel Peace Prize 2006 for their efforts to create economic and socially just development from below. After completing a PhD in the US, he returned to Bangladesh to become head of the Economics Department at Chittagong University in 1972. The famine that devastated Bangladesh in 1974 changed his life forever. He began to examine the inadequacies of economic theory and determined that the problem was a lack of credit to the poor. The idea of micro-credit was developed, and flourished. Today the bank has 6.6 million borrowers, 97 per cent of whom are women, and provides services in more than 70,000 villages in Bangladesh. Its model of micro-financing has inspired similar efforts around the world. Dr. Yunus was named by *Business Week* as one of the '30 greatest entrepreneurs of all time' (2007). He is author of the book 'The poor people's banker'. The Grameen Bank is now the largest rural bank in Bangladesh. www.muhammadyunus.org, www.grameen-info.org

A – Z Glossary of Terms

- **Active Systems** generally refers to mechanical heating, ventilation and air-conditioning (HVAC) systems (as opposed to passive systems).

- **Adobe** are large molded, sun-dried blocks of mud forming a thick wall, used for thermal mass to keep interiors cool; common in hot and arid regions, such as in Mexico or Arizona.

- **Agenda 21** is the non-binding agreement ratified by world nations at the 1992 United Nations Conference on Environment and Development (UNCED). It sets out conditions and recommendations for moving towards global sustainability involving various stakeholders from the community, business and government sectors.

- **Albedo** is the amount of heat (solar radiation) from the sun that Earth or a surface reflects back into space. Snow and ice covered surfaces have high albedo, reflecting back most of the warmth they receive, while low-albedo oceans, land

Glossary and Key Web Sites

and plants absorb most of the heat that falls on them. As polar ice melts, the planet's overall albedo is lowered, and it soaks up more solar heat.

- **Anthropogenic** means resulting from human activities (e.g. global warming is understood to be anthropogenic, human-induced, resulting from human activities); man made.

- **Aquifer Storage and Recovery (ASR)** is a technique whereby stormwater or treated wastewater can be stored below ground for later extraction and reuse. This technique is particularly useful in urban areas which are underlain with suitable aquifers, as the cost of land for above-ground storage is usually too high. Aquifers are underground layer of water-bearing permeable rock, gravel, or sand from which groundwater can be usefully extracted.

- **Autonomous** means that a building or district is operating independently of any inputs except those available in its immediate environment.

- **BASIX Assessment Tool**, as introduced by the NSW Government in Australia, is the Building Sustainability Index. BASIX ensures homes are designed to use less potable water and are responsible for fewer greenhouse gas emissions by setting energy and water reduction targets. Strategies used include the use of rainwater tanks, water-saving fixtures, improved insulation, passive solar orientation, natural lighting and native plants for gardens.

- **Balance of Plant** means the optimization of a technical plant's equipment aimed at maximizing energy, water efficiency, as well as minimizing pollution and waste.

- **Battery Electric Vehicles (BEV)** are vehicles that completely rely on electricity storage batteries as a power source and are driven by electric motors. They usually use a plug-in charging system with power from the grid. PHEVs are plug-in hybrid electric vehicles.

- **Bio-Climatic** in architecture, means to respond to the climate with minimal reliance on non-renewable energy for achieving comfort. Climate-responsive means a design approach that seeks to achieve year round comfort using exclusively passive means, thereby significantly reducing energy consumption.

- **Biodiversity** is the variety and essential interdependence of all life forms within a given ecosystem or community (the different plants, animals, and micro-organisms, the genes they contain, and the eco-systems they form). It is generally considered that the more species an eco-system has, the healthier and better.

- **Biofuel** is a liquid or gaseous fuel derived from fermented (raw, biological) organic matter, such as farm waste or crops like sugar cane and corn; some times called biogas. Typical and most common biofuels are bioethanol and biodiesel, used in automobiles.

- **Biogas** is a type of biofuel that is produced by the breakdown of organic matter via fermentation.

- **Biomass** is a renewable energy source derived from wood or biogas, comprised of living or recently dead biological material (plant or animal matter) that can be converted into bioenergy and fuel.

- **Biosphere** describes the entire global ecological system and the relationship of its inhabitants.

- **BREEAM**, or Building Research Establishment Environmental Assessment Method, is a voluntary rating tool for green buildings, established 1990 in the UK. www.breeam.org

- **Brownfield Site** defines land or premises which has previously been used or developed and is currently not fully in use, lying vacant, underutilized, or is abandoned. In some cases it may be partially occupied or utilized; or it may be vacant, derelict or contaminated. Typical brownfields are docklands, heavy industry plants, or military areas which have ceased to be used. The opposite of brownfields are greenfields, previously undeveloped open space.

- **Building-Integrated Photovoltaics (BIPV)** describes photovoltaic systems which are integrated into the building's structure or facade cladding. This normally replaces parts of the building envelope, such as roof, skylights or facades.

- **Bus Rapid Transit (BRT)** is an efficient bus system resulting from improvements in infrastructure, vehicles and schedules. See also: MRT.

- **CABE, the Commission for Architecture and the Built Environment** is an advisory body in the UK, which developed out of Lord Richard Rogers 'Urban Design Task Force' in 1999, developing recommendations to the UK Government, to improve urban spaces. See: www.cabe.org.uk

- **Carbon** is a chemical element essential to all forms of life on Earth, and which bonds with oxygen to form carbon dioxide, a potent greenhouse gas. Carbon dioxide (CO_2) is a colourless, odorless gas produced by animal respiration, the decay of plant or animal remains, and a by-product of the burning of fossil fuels. Of the six principal greenhouse gases that contribute to climate change, CO_2 is the one most directly affected by human activity.

- **Carbon Credits** are unit amounts of CO_2 emissions that can be bought and sold in carbon emission trading schemes. Carbon tax is a tax on emissions resulting from burning fossil fuels due to contributions to the greenhouse effect; it's a charge imposed on the consumption of carbon in any form to encourage greener energy practices.

- **Carbon Cycle** describes the natural process of worldwide passage of carbon between four 'reservoirs': the oceans, the atmosphere, the ground, and the bodies of all plants and animals. When one reservoir gives up too much carbon and overloads another, a delicate balance is upset, with uncertain results.

- **Carbon Footprint** is the amount of total CO_2 emissions produced annually by all activities, for instance by a person's daily life, a company, building, or city. There is still some dispute over the best way to accurately calculate and measure the carbon footprint of a city, district or building.

- **Carbon Neutral** means to reduce the net amount of CO_2 emissions for which a city, building or company is responsible to zero. In practical terms, it is impossible to attain total carbon neutrality; it means a city or organisation reduces its carbon emissions as much as it possibly can, and then offsets the reminder (which moves part of the responsibility to the offsetting projects).

- **Carrying Capacity** refers to the upper limits of an urban development beyond which the quality of human life, health, welfare, safety or community character and identity might be unsustainably altered. It's the level (upper limits) of land use or human activity that can be permanently accommodated without causing irreversible change in the quality of air, water, land, or plant and animal habitats.

- **Catchment Area** is the term used to describe the area which is drained by a river.

- **Centralized Energy Generation Model** describes the traditional system (introduced by Westinghouse), where energy is generated in large-scale centralized power plants (usually outside the city) and distributed to the end user via the long-distance power grid. The opposite model is distributed energy generation, using small-scale power generation technologies (typically in the range of 3 kW to 10,000 kW), where power generation is achieved on or off-grid.

- **Combined Heat-and-Power (CHP)** is an energy conversion process that uses a heat engine or power station to simultaneously generate electricity and usable heat (frequently waste heat, which would otherwise be lost). Primary energy sources include a variety of fuels (natural gas, biomass and fossil fuels) and renewable energy sources. Also called co-generation, it is the simultaneous production of two forms of useful power from a single fuel source in a single process; e.g. the re-use of waste heat to provide space heating. If the waste heat is also used to produce chilled water for cooling through the use of an absorption chiller, it is called tri-generation.

- **Compactness: the A/V Ratio** is the ratio of the surface area of a building to the enclosed (heated/cooled) volume. Typical A/V ratio values vary from 0.4 for compact multi-storey buildings to 1.1 for inefficient, detached bungalows in suburbs. The A/V ratio is an important factor in the calculation of energy consumption. The more compact the urban form (with smaller facade surfaces, therefore less solar gain in summer or heat loss in winter), the more energy-efficient.

- **Composting** is a waste management option involving the controlled biological decomposition of organic materials (biomass) into a relatively stable humus-like product that can be stored and applied to the (agricultural) land without adversely affecting the environment.

- **Concentrating Solar Power (CSP)** uses lenses or mirrors and tracking systems to concentrate a large area of sunlight into a small beam. The heat produced by this small beam of light is then used to generate electricity.

- **Cost-Benefit Analysis** describes a method of evaluating projects or investments by comparing the present value of expected benefits to costs. It's a useful technique for making transparent the benefits of up-front investments in sustainable design features or technologies (payback times).

- **Courtyard** an outdoor patio space, open to the sky and enclosed by walls or buildings, commonly found in Mediterranean, Latin American, or Asian cultures and used for natural cross-ventilation.

- **Cradle-to-Grave** measures the environmental impact of a product from the extraction of its raw materials until the product is disposed (i.e. to landfill). This does include the transport to the construction site. Opposite: *Cradle-to-Cradle*.

- **Density and Floor Space Ratio (FSR)** is a measure of the built environment in either the number of habitable rooms per hectare, or the number of dwellings per hectare. It determines the spatial property, ensuring that over-crowding or over-development is not an issue. Density describes the average number of people, households (families), or housing units (dwellings per hectare) on one unit of land; for instance, density can be expressed as dwelling units per hectare (or acre). FSR is the primary way of controlling the size of buildings, with the maximum FSR requirements varying in different zones and areas. On the other hand, if the density is too low, sustainability cannot be achieved. Floor Space Ratio (FSR), or Floor Area Ration (FAR), is the total floor area of all buildings or structures on a lot divided by the total area of the lot. (1 ha is 10,000 sqm; 100 ha is 1 sqkm).

- **Deforestation** is the conversion of what once was a forest or woodland area of natural vegetation to non-forest land. Deforestation can lead to many negative environmental effects, including global warming, loss of biodiversity and soil erosion. Rainforests are responsible for global weather patterns. Urban design of the future should reduce urban sprawl and therefore limit the amount of deforestation. Any tree loss due to the built environment should be replaced with new trees, enabling the absorption of CO_2 and sustainability of the future. Clearing forests by setting fires pumps CO_2 into the air. Opposite: Afforestation means the planting of new forests on lands which historically have not contained forests.

- **Desalination** is the process by which salt and other minerals are removed from saline water (such as sea water) to produce freshwater suitable for human consumption or irrigation. Brackish water is water that has higher salinity than fresh water, but lower salinity than seawater.

- **Desertification** means the removal or loss of plant cover, which turns fertile soil into desert. Overgrazing, deforestation, drought, and extensive burning are among the causes of desertification.

- **Design, Build, Own and Operate (DBOO)** is a form of public-private partnership (PPP), to achieve cost efficiencies. Frequently a government service or private business venture which is funded and operated through a partnership of government and one or more private sector companies.

- **Eco-City** enhances the well-being of its citizens and of society through integrated urban planning and management that fully harnesses the benefits of ecological systems and renewable energies – aiming for zero-emissions and zero-waste. An Eco-City or Eco-District protects and nurtures these assets for future generations.

- **Ecosystem** describes the species and natural communities of a specific location interacting with one another and with the physical environment. The terms 'Ecology' and 'Ecosystem' were coined by the German biologist Ernst Haeckel in 1866.

- **Ecological Footprint (EF)** is a measure of environmental impact, defined as an index of the area of productive land and aquatic ecosystems required to produce the resources used and to assimilate the wastes produced by a defined population at a specified material standard of living.
  See: www.ecologicalfootprint.com

- **Embodied Energy** is the total energy required directly and indirectly to produce (manufacture or construct) a product: in the production processes, transportation, and maintenance of that product/material ready for use at a point in time). It is the sum total of the energy necessary for the entire life-cycle of a product. Environmental Product Declarations (EPD) give information on the entire lifecycle of a product.

- **Emission Caps** Emissions are the release of substances, such as greenhouse gases, into the atmosphere. Emission caps are legal limits on how much greenhouse gas a business, city or nation can emit. Emission trading is a market-based approach to achieving environmental objectives that allows those reducing greenhouse gas emissions below what is required, to use and trade the excess reductions. ETS means Emissions Trading Scheme. Cap-and-Trade means an emissions trading scheme that places firm limits on total emissions in future years.

- **Energy-Efficiency/Energy-Effectiveness** is the ability to use less energy to provide the same level of output. Energy-efficiency in buildings means employing strategies to minimize the use of energy imported from utility companies. Examples include: insulation, high-performance glazing, fluorescent lighting. Efficient energy use is achieved by using a more efficient/effective technology in processes and helps to control emissions of greenhouse gases.

- **Energy-Efficient Building Retrofit Programme** unites many of the world's largest energy service companies, financial institutions and cities in an effort to reduce energy consumption in the existing built environment. This includes municipal, educational, private, commercial and public housing sectors. By 'retrofitting' (upgrading) existing buildings to incorporate more energy-effective products, technologies and systems, energy consumption can be significantly reduced through improving (retro-fitting) a building's fabric and installations. Energy-effectiveness is hereby the ratio between useful output and the energy needed to achieve it.

- **Energy Service Companies (ESCOs)** are firms that offer turnkey performance-based services, using energy performance contracting for the implementation of cost savings measures in buildings.

- **Environmental Impact Analysis (EIA)** is a comprehensive procedure which involves different dimensions of a planning problem such as social, administrative and physical, to identify potential damaging effects or positive influences that a proposed development project may have on the environment. EIA is the process of assessing the physical and social impacts of projects, to identify options in order to minimize environmental damage, for example selecting sites for development with minimal environmental impact.

- **Epidemiology** is the study of factors affecting the health and illness of populations.

- **Evaporative Cooling** is a physical process where liquid is evaporated, typically water, into surrounding air, and cools an object or liquid in contact with it.

- **Exergy** is the maximum work potential of a material; the quality and unused part of the energy potential (e.g. the use of waste heat, or waste water).

- **Expansion Areas** comprise vacant, undeveloped, or under-utilized (brownfield) land, lying within a defined settlement area (a land use term).

- **Extended Producer Responsibility** means that the producer or manufacturer bears responsibility for the disposal and recycling of the goods sold.

- **Feedback Loop** describes the process following the initial generation of the feedback to the subsequent modification of the event; adding to global warming, it further increases the rate of climate change itself. Once sufficient feedback is received, changes and improvements are made for further feedback to occur. This continuous process is known as a feedback loop, which plays a major role in understanding global warming.

- **Feed-in Tariff (FiT)** is a policy which guides the reimbursement of private producers of renewable energy above the usual market price. It is a long-term electricity tariff paid by a utility for electricity that it must purchase, and which is fed back into the grid from a renewable energy source. The price for this electricity is guaranteed by the government.

- **Fossil-Fuels** are non-renewable (finite) resources, including coal, oil, and natural gas, which were generated over millions of years from the organic remains of prehistoric plants and animal remains, which when burnt, release CO_2/greenhouse gases in the atmosphere. Long before these combustible geological deposits run out, they will become uneconomic to extract. Transforming the primary energy into the net energy used by consumers at the end of the energy chain (e.g. as electricity or district heat) leads to losses inherent in the conversion and transmission process. Opposite of fossil-fuels are renewable (infinite), clean energy sources.

- **Framework** is a concept used to solve complex issues. A design framework requires a logical environment to frame elements precisely.

- **Geothermal Energy**, also known as ground-source energy, is a natural resource of heat energy contained within the Earth's crust, emitted in form of hot water or steam. The heat is transferred from the planet's molten core to water and rocks and lies fairly close to the surface, where it can be tapped to produce energy. It can be extracted and used either indirectly to generate electricity, or directly for heating applications. This includes use in heavy and light industry, domestic heating, plant growing, and has many other applications.

- **Global Radiation** is the quantity of solar energy incident on the Earth's surface, related to a horizontal surface. It consists of direct and diffuse, non-aligned radiation, depending on the solar altitude angle (which is dependent on latitude and time of year) and on atmospheric disturbances (clouds, particles). For instance, in Germany the annual total global radiation is around 1000 kWh/sqm pa. In Australia, it is around 2000 kWh/sqm pa.

- **Grassroots Strategies** are small-scale initiatives characterized by their bottom-up approach, low budgets and mobile (mostly temporary) characters, like small enterprises or artist workshops, frequently nurtured by subsidies or free rent. A grassroots strategy is a bottom-up approach of individuals sharing common interests; it's an active and deliberate support by ordinary people in an area. Opposite to top-down approaches.

- **Greenhouse Gas (GHG)** is any gas that, once emitted in the atmosphere, contributes to the warming of the Earth (e.g. CO_2, ozone or methane). The greenhouse effect is the process by which greenhouse gases allow incoming solar radiation to pass through the Earth's atmosphere but prevent part of the outgoing heat from escaping, thus increasing temperatures.

- **Greenfield Site** is the opposite of brownfields. 'Virgin lands', sites that are not yet developed for intensive or urban use, such as meadows, parks and forests. Greenfield sites have not experienced any previous development.

- **Greenpeace** is an independent global campaigning organization that acts to change attitudes and behaviour, to protect and conserve the environment. See: www.greenpeace.org

- **Green Roof** is a vegetated roof which has the potential to assist in mitigating poor urban air quality and heat island effects, provide building thermal and acoustic insulation, collect rainwater and increase occupant amenity and biodiversity. Usually extensive planting is used for green roofs. A 'living roof' is an area of green space that provides a habitat for birds and wildlife, and increases biodiversity. See: www.greenroofs.org

- **Green Urbanism** is a conceptual model for zero-emission and zero-waste urban design, which arose in the 1990s, promoting compact energy-efficient urban development, seeking to transform and re-engineer existing city districts and regenerate the post-industrial city centre. *Green Urbanism* promotes the development of socially and environmentally sustainable city districts.

- **Greywater Systems** are systems that focus on the reuse of water generated from domestic processes such as dish washing, laundry and bathing for either indoor use or in irrigation.

- **Grid** is a network of transmission lines joining a number of powerstations to the main sites of electricity use. Base-load is the minimum daily level of power.

- **Heat Storage Capacity** is the value which designates the ability of a building component to store thermal energy. It is the product of the specific heat capacity, the material density, and the thickness of the specific component. The amount of heat gained by a space from all sources (including from people, incoming and reflected radiation, internal loads from machines, computers, lights, etc) represents the amount of heat that must be removed from the space to maintain the desired indoor conditions; this is called cooling load.

- **Infill** is the act of building on a vacant lot within an otherwise developed neighbourhood. Infill development occurs in the established areas of a city.

- **International Council on Local Environmental Initiatives (ICLEI)**, now: Loccal Governments for Sustainability; an association of over 1,100 local governments from 68 countries, who are committed to sustainable development. See: www.iclei.org

- **International Energy Agency (IEA)**, an intergovernmental organization which acts as energy policy advisor to 28 member states, established in 1974. See: www.iea.org

- **Infrastructure** is typically recognized to be of two types: hard and soft. Hard infrastructure is the physical assets used to produce, consume and provide access to the factors of production, such as ports, warehouses, bridges, roads, railways, airports, electricity grid, utilities and telecommunication systems. Soft infrastructure is social overhead capital such as education, health, social and recreational support and environmental aspects. In recent years, soft economic infrastructure has been introduced as 'smart infrastructure', such as institutional and cultural capital, and the use of technology to enable large pools of highly skilled human resources to operate within a global community.

- **Intelligent Transport Systems** utilise real-time information and communication technology to improve links between the road, public and private sector vehicles and users, to better manage traffic, enhance access to public transport services and avoid congestion.

- **Integrated Design** is a multi-disciplinary approach that brings together all the stakeholders in the building process at an early stage to maximize building comfort and usability, while minimizing resource use.

- **Intensification, Densification (Urban Infill), and Expansion** are different development terms describing urban strategies for under-developed land.

- **Intergovernmental Panel on Climate Change (IPCC)** is the United Nation's independent international group of scientists, established in 1988, with headquarters in Switzerland. The IPCC is an official leading advisory body to the world's governments, issuing periodic assessments on global climate change and its effects. In 2007, based on the continuous research work on climate change, the IPCC was awarded the Nobel Peace Prize, alongside Al Gore. Dr. Rajendra Pachauri is currently the Chair of the IPCC; he is a chief scientist based at TERI in New Delhi. See: www.ipcc.ch

- **Kyoto Protocol**: Following the 1992 Earth Summit in Rio de Janeiro, the UN produced 'The United Nations Framework Convention on Climate Change' (UNFCCC). In this ground-breaking treaty, industrialized signatories agreed to reduce their emission levels to below 1990 levels. The Kyoto Protocol – a codicil to the UNFCCC – is an international agreement which was signed in Japan in 1997 and commits most industrialized countries to reducing their emissions by 6 to 8 per cent below 1990 levels by 2012. It is signed by 175 nations; however, some of the world's largest contributors of CO_2 emissions (for instance, the US and China) have not ratified the Kyoto Protocol and are not bound by these targets. It will expire by 2012 and will be replaced by a new global agreement. See: www.kyotoprotocol.com

- **Land-Use Change** is a change in the use or management of land by humans, which may lead to a change in land cover. Landuse and land cover changes may have an impact on the albedo, evapotranspiration, sources and sinks of greenhouse gases, or other properties of the climate system.

- **Life-Cycle Assessment (LCA)** is a technique for measuring and assessing the environmental aspects and potential impacts associated with a product or process, by compiling an inventory of inputs and outputs and analyzing the results of the inventory. All inputs include (i.e. raw materials, water, energy) and outputs (i.e. the end product, waste, emissions) of manufacture, transport, use, maintenance and disposal of the product.

- **Low-Impact Materials** are building materials that use less resources and produce less pollution compared to conventional building materials over their life-cycle.

- **Masterplan** is a detailed plan carried out under supervision of an architect or urban designer. This frequently used tool is officially an exception not anchored in spatial planning legislation. The construction is based on consensus and shared interest, and involves different interest groups (stakeholders).

- **Mass Rapid Transit (MRT) System** is a rapid public transit system that is fast, efficient, affordable and comfortable (on rail above or underground; or via bus, such as in Curitiba); it is the backbone of urban mobility, spanning an entire city or region.

- **Mega-Cities** are metropolitan areas with a total population exceeding 10 million people. Mega-Cities include rapid growth, new forms of spatial density of population, formal and informal economics, as well as crime, poverty and high levels of social fragmentation. Recently, with the urbanization in Asia, the number of Mega-Cities has significantly increased.

- **Metropolitan Governance** determines the guidelines and policies within which the city must remain. In terms of urban planning, restrictions can apply due to government policies and frameworks for urban management.

- **Metropolitan Growth Centre** describes an overlay designation that defines significant clusters of higher-density, mixed-use development, typically located at important intersections and/or gateways, serving as metropolitan transport hubs (Transport-Oriented Development, TOD).

- **Mitigation and Adaption** Mitigation means first steps taken to fight the effects of climate change, by reducing CO_2 emissions. The second response to global warming is adaptation. As the environment changes, governments, businesses and designers have to be prepared to adapt to a set of new challenges and be ready to take opportunities that arise.

- **Millennium Development Goals (MDG)** were formulated by the United Nations and adopted in 2000. The eight MDGs aim to halve extreme poverty by 2015. The MDGs are much wider than the issue of global warming. www.un.org/millenniumgoals

- **Mixed-Use (MU)** describes a development that combines residential, retail, commercial, and/or office uses, clustered together: either layered vertically in a single building, or in a horizontal arrangement, in adjacent buildings.

- **Natural Ventilation** is caused by natural convection; it is non-mechanical air flow through open-able windows, doors, louvers and other openings due to differences in thermal and pressure gradients.

- **Neighbourhood** Since ancient times, neighbourhoods have been the basic unit of human settlements; they have a defined centre and edges (bounded by major streets), are walkable and mixed-use. By definition, a neighbourhood has a population large enough to support a walk-to elementary school.

- **Net-Zero Buildings (NZB)** are buildings that draw no net-energy from the grid on an annual basis. This is achieved through a combination of energy efficiency and on-site (off-grid) generation. All new buildings in the EU will have to be Net-Zero Buildings from 2018 onwards.

- **New Towns** are a town planning concept to deal with urban growth, where each new town designed and built from scratch, to be completely self-sustainable (well-known new towns are Milton Keynes or Almere).

- **New Urbanism** is an urban design movement, which arose in the USA in the early 1980s, promoting walkable, mixed-use neighbourhoods and transit-oriented development, seeking to end suburban sprawl and promote community. Characteristics include narrow streets, wide sidewalks and higher densities. See: www.newurbanism.org and www.dpz.com

- **Non-Governmental Organization (NGO)** is a term that refers to a legally constituted organization with no participation of any government. See: www.ngo.org

- **One-Planet Living** is a programme developed by UK-based initiative *BioRegional*. It involves ten guiding principles to healthy living and preserving the Earth's scarce natural resources. These include: zero-carbon, zero-waste, sustainable transport, use of local and sustainable materials, local and sustainable food, sustainable water, natural habitats and wildlife, culture and heritage, equity and fair trading, and overall health and happiness. Each city dweller has a certain global area and a certain amount of resources at his/her disposal, calculated proportionally. See: www.oneplanetliving.org

- **Organization of the Petroleum Exporting Countries (OPEC)** is an intergovernmental organization, created in 1960, consisting of 12 member countries. See: www.opec.org

- **Open Space System (OSS)** defines a linked network of (usually public) open spaces that can include parks, recreation facilities, green-way and trail corridors.

- **Orientation** means a building's on-site placement in regard to the direction of prevailing winds and solar position, and its resulting sun exposure.

- **Passive (Solar) Heat Gain** involves the increase in temperature in a space, object or structure resulting from solar radiation. The amount of heat gain increases with the strength of the sun and any intervening material that transmits or resists the projected radiation (e.g. sun shading or glazing).

- **Passive Design** is an integrated building design approach that takes advantage of the local climate to provide some or all of the heating, cooling, ventilation and lighting needs of the occupants ('harnessing nature' approach). For instance, thermal energy is collected and stored by natural means, exploiting the building's orientation, layout and form and the choice of materials in relation to solar radiation, that reduces the building's energy requirements. A typical passive design strategy is night purging: the flushing-out of internal spaces with lower night temperature air levels, thus naturally cooling down built-up heat from daily internal loads and solar gains to avoid overheating. Passive solar design is one of the simplest and established forms of adaptation to climates with intense heat or humidity. It includes site orientation, sun shading, cross-ventilation, evaporative cooling and other strategies to reduce operational energy needs.

- **Passivhaus Standard** (Germany), similar to the Minergie Standard (CH), is concerned with high insulation and reduced energy consumption, below 15 kWh/sqm pa. See: www.passiv.de and the Swiss standard: www.minergie.ch

- **Pedestrian-Scaled Development** is designed so that a person can comfortably walk from one location to another, providing visually interesting details and good public space; usually not more than 500 metres walking distances.

- **Photovoltaic Cells (PV)** are solar panels with the capability of transforming the sun's radiation into electricity (converting ligt into direct current). PV devices capture photons of light from solar insolation and convert it into electrical energy stored as direct current (DC). Conversion is direct, with the generated power fed directly into existing power supplies. The effective energy storage of the gained power is still a challenge.

- **Plot Ratio** is calculated as the ratio of the total floor area to the net site area. It is a building control and planning value deployed for controlling the density of a development, especially in urban settings.

- **Polluter Pays Principle (PPP)** is the policy that countries should in some way compensate others for the effects of pollution they generate.

- **Post-Occupancy Evaluation (POE)** is the systematic data gathering and analysis, comparing the actual building performance with stated performance criteria (usually undertaken by facility managers), after the building has been completed and occupied for at least one year. POE seeks to measure and evaluate technical performance, fitness for purpose and user satisfaction.

- **Parts Per Million (ppm):** Most scientists agree that the sustainable level of GHG concentration in the Earth's atmosphere is around 280 ppm.

- **Prefabrication** describes building components (usually modular) fabricated or manufactured prior to delivery and on-site assembly. Prefabrication enables 'design-for-disassembly' for the reuse or recycling of components and materials of a building at the end of its use life. Mainly for timber, steel and concrete elements with reversible joining details. See: www.fabprefab.com

- **Primary Energy Input (PEI)**, also known as grey or embodied energy, is the energy required for manufacturing and use of a product, measured in MJ (joule). It includes all the energy quantities necessary for production, transport, intermediate states, and storage; it is an indicator of the environmental impact of the product.

- **Primary Growth Areas** consist of vacant land within metropolitan growth plans designated for future urban uses, such as residential, institutional, educational, commercial and industrial. Opposite: Limited and No-Growth Areas.

- **Rating Tools** can be used as an assessment of measures for building performance. An example of this are LEED, BREEAM, CASBE, Green Mark, GreenStar or DGNB, where building capabilities are rated according to specific criteria, giving a better understanding of its overall performance.

- **Recycling** means a cyclic process of respecting the ecological integrity of all products and materials, by extending their use or form, so that their useful material cycle is not terminated to landfill or incineration. Closed-loop recycling means a recycling system in which a particular mass of material is re-manufactured into the same product. The 'cradle-to-cradle' approach ensures that materials and products are considered and accounted for throughout their life-cycle.

- **Renewable Energy Sources** are any source of energy that can be used without depleting natural reserves. It includes: wind, geo-thermal, water/hydro/wave/tidal, biofuels, biomass, solar and solar water heating. Renewable energy is energy generated from natural resources which are infinite, inexhaustible (unlike fossil fuels) and can be naturally replenished (and are not derived from burning hydrocarbons). By using regenerating natural resources and converting them into needed energy, we ensure that an energy is produced with minimal waste and harm to the Earth. Renewable (alternative) energy technologies include wind turbines, solar panels and hydro-electric dams.

- **Run-off** is the flow of water, from rain, snow melt, or other sources, over the surface of the land, without being absorbed into the soil (e.g. stormwater run-off).

- **Rural-Urban Migration / Rural-Urban Disparities** is the increase in population in urban areas due to migration. This urbanization results in the physical growth of urban areas, usually more dense cities, and an out-of-balance relationship between city and countryside.

- **Shrinking Cities and Economic Decline** occurs when economic investment moves elsewhere, whether that be in the region or a country. This also includes when governmental policy creates a cycle of disinvestment, which causes urban decay, and a process by which the city falls into a state of disrepair. Warning signs include population loss, housing stock deterioration, decay of public space, and increase in crime. The size of some cities has declined despite a growth in world population, and shrinking city districts have often occurred side-by-side with expanding ones. Shrinking cities have been studied in Eastern Europe, former East Germany. Two well-known case studies for shrinkage are: Detroit in the US; Leipzig in Germany.

- **Smart Grid Networks** are networks supported by digital technology capable of exerting 'smart control' over all aspects of the electric power sector, including: generation, transmission, distribution, customer service and power dispatch at all voltage levels. Smart grids deliver power in an efficient manner and can better integrate power from renewable sources.

- **Soft Port** is the opposite of **Hard Port.** Soft port describes a leisure oriented maritime programme, like marinas and cruise ships, generally city friendly. Hard port is an industrial port, e.g., for containers or coal loading.

- **Solar Cooling Systems** use the process of absorption (sometimes adsorption), where heat is evaporated and the condensation of vapors provides a cooling effect (e.g. with chilled water). Solar cooling provides a much more sustainable method of cooling with a pollution-free process.

- **Solar Energy** is solar radiation exploited for hot water production and electricity generation, by: flat plate collectors, photovoltaic cells or solar thermal electric plants. Solar radiation is short wave radiation emitted by the sun, which has a distinctive range of wavelengths (spectrum).

- **Solar Gains (Q)** are measured in kWh/pa. It describes heat that contributes to heating up the interior of a building and to reducing the heating requirement, due to the incidence of solar energy on transparent and opaque building components. The location of the building, its orientation, the inclination and size of the building components, and the amount of radiation absorbed by the facade material, all influence this energy input. Solar gains take place at all building components, but they are very much higher with transparent components than with other components. High solar gains (e.g. from the strong western sun) can lead to overheating in the building.

- **Solar Hot Water** is water which is heated by the use of solar energy using a renewable energy source: the sun. Solar hot water systems (SWH) are now compulsory for all developments in many countries.

- **Sprawl** defines patterns of low-density growth; see: *Urban Sprawl*.

- **Strategy** is a carefully devised plan of action to achieve a goal, and the art of developing and carrying out such a plan (it's more than a `tactic'). Central is the lack of total control. By action, other parties are inspired, are seduced, challenged, or forced to act.

- **Sustainable**: A definition of sustainable is derived from the Latin verb 'sustinere', which describes relations that can be maintained for a very long time, or indefinitely. The idea of 'sustainable urban development' originated probably at the 1992 UCED-Conference and *Earth Summit* in Rio de Janeiro, and is based on the concept of balanced environmental planning instruments and methods.

- **Sustainable Urban Development** is development that considers environmental, economic and social impacts and has the ability to maintain activities, without this activity using up crippling levels of resources and creating a future debt that is not offset by equal levels of future benefits. It is suggested that cities should have a defined commitment to sustainable urban development, with the aim to reduce poverty and balance social, economic and environmental needs of present and future generations (UN, 1992). Sustainable urban planning is defined as planning that optimizes the use of the built environment, transportation system, energy, water and land, while aiming to minimize the negative impact of the community on the natural environment.

- **Thermal Expansion**, in connection with sea level, refers to the increase in volume (and decrease in density) that results from warming water. A warming of the ocean leads to an expansion of the ocean volume and hence an increase in sea level.

- **Thermal Mass** defines the availability of a material to act as a storage medium for heat; measured as a function of a material's specific heat and its density. Materials suitable for thermal mass (for instance, as trompe wall) are heavy materials with the ability to store large amounts of heat energy, such as concrete, masonry, brick or rammed earth walls.

- **Transit-Oriented Development (TOD)** is a form of development that emphasizes forms of public transportation other than the automobile – such as walking, cycling, and mass transit – as part of its urban design. Transit-oriented neighbourhood development locates activity centres composed of office space, housing and retail, as multi-storey compact mixed-use development, around a transit stop. These activity centres offer a variety of housing options, such as apartments, townhouses and duplexes, often above ground-floor commercial uses.

- **Typology** is the classification system according to general building type, which, in architecture and urban design, could include the range of common identity, plan geometry, spatial pattern, functional programmes, etc.

- **UNESCO, the United Nations Educational, Scientific and Cultural Organization** has currently 193 member states. See. www.unesco.org

- **UNFCCC, the United Nations Framework Convention on Climate Change** is an international treaty founded on the Kyoto Protocol; the UN Climate Secretariat is based in Bonn, Germany. See: www.unfccc.int

- **UN-Habitat, the United Nations Human Settlements Programme** is based in Nairobi, Kenya. UN-Habitat promotes socially and environmentally sustainable cities and towns. See: www.unhabitat.org

- **Urban Design** is the interdisciplinary outcome of applying the art of planning (involving various disciplines, such as landscape architecture, etc), which is concerned with the 3-dimensional form of the city, its public space networks, masses, open spaces, and distribution of activities. Good urban design considers the full complexity of the city and its buildings in relation to their context, layers of history and local typology. The resulting urban form encompasses the pattern and density of land use and the nature of transportation within cities and towns.

- **Urban Envelope** means an overlay designation encompassing all lands located within a defined development boundary.

- **Urban Growth Boundary** is a legally binding development boundary, in form of a line drawn around a city that prohibits development outside that boundary. An Urban Growth Boundary is introduced to slow or prevent sprawl, to accommodate growth for a designated period of time. It is used to guide infrastructure development.

- **Urban Heat Island (UHI) Effect** is found in metropolitan areas that are significantly warmer than their surrounding areas (urban micro-climate, in a confined local area). It is a man-made feature: a dome of elevated temperatures over an urban area (like a street, sidewalk, parking lot or building), which traps heat, caused by waste heat from energy-using processes in a city (for instance, the air-condition units in Hong Kong city centre). The differences in temperature are usually greater at night and in winter months. It is caused primarily by urban development, which alters the original land surfaces and their potential for absorbing heat. Also caused by waste heat from air-conditioning units, generated by the use of energy. As the population of an area grows, the land alteration becomes greater, thus increasing average temperatures in the region.

- **Urbanization** is the increase of the proportion of a population living in urban centres (cities and towns), caused by a net movement of people from rural to urban areas, accompanied with manufacturing and commerce replacing agriculture, and associated patterns of land use. Urbanization is driven by economic growth and a concentration of new investment in particular urban areas. Urbaization is different from Urban Growth (see below).

- **Urban Growth** is fuelled by the natural increase of a city as well as by net in-migration. Urban growth is usually the dominant factor behind an urban centre's growing population.

- **Urban Farming (Urban Agriculture)** is the practice of cultivating, processing and distributing food in or around a town or city. Urban agriculture contributes to food security and safety by increasing the amount of available food to people living in cities, and allows fresh vegetables, fruit and meat products to be available to the urban consumer. Urban farming ensures that the city's community consumes natural produce at nearby urban residences and minimizes the need for transportation of these products. `Local food' is usually food that travelled less than 200 km.

- **Urban Sprawl** is a low-density pattern of residential urban growth; the spreading of a city and its suburbs to the surrounding urban fringe, pushing the city boundaries outward. Sprawling neighbourhoods tend to live in single-family homes away from urban centres, are highly car-dependant, have low population densities, involve single-use zoning with rigid separation between uses, have low-density land use and lack public transportation options. Sprawl is often characterized by placeless commercial strip development along main street and otherwise large expanses of low-density or single use development, where the major form of transportation is the automobile. Urban planners try to adapt pedestrian-friendly neighbourhood qualities to these regions, as well as attempting to create higher density and more compact, mixed-use communities in close proximity to work and retail. Sprawl negatively impacts on land

and water quantity and quality, and can often be linked to a decline in social capital. For instance, the lack of land-use diversity (typical for suburbs) results in and increases automobile dependency. A growth boundary is usually necessary to curb sprawl and similar scattered development that leaves large tracts of undeveloped land between developments.

- **U-Value of Materials**, also known as the overall heat transfer coefficient, measures how well a building element (e.g. a window frame) will conduct heat. It measures the rate of heat transfer (flow) through a building element over a given area, under standardized conditions. U-value is the reciprical of R-Value. For instance, the U-Value of glazing, or of a window frame, is measured in W/sqmK. It is a specific thermal performance characteristic value that designates the heat flow through the element or material, taking into account the number of panes of glass, the nature of coatings, material thickness, quality of the seals, and the filling in any cavities between the glass panes.

- **View Corridor** is a visual channel, or axis, defined by a privileged, or established, viewing position and the object to be viewed.

- **Waste-to-Energy Strategy (WtE)** is the process of creating energy in the form of electricity or heat from the incineration of a waste source. There are several methods by which waste (or sludge) can be converted to energy, such as bio-chemical conversion, chemical processes and thermal processes. WtE is a form of energy recovery that mostly produces electricity directly through combustion or composts, or produces a combustible fuel commodity, such as methane, methanol, ethanol or synthetic fuels.

- **World Health Organization (WHO)** is the United Nations public health arm and specialized sub-agency that acts as coordinating authority on international public health issues. See: www.who.int

- **Worldwatch** is an international institute that analyzes interdisciplinary environmental data on how to build a sustainable society. See: www.worldwatch.org

- **WWF International** (Worldwide Fund for Nature), founded in 1961, was formerly known as the World Wildlife Fund. It is a global organization: the world's largest conservation organization, with the goal to build a future where people live in harmony with nature. WWF International is based in Switzerland. See: www.worldwildlife.org, and: www.wwf.org

- **Zero-Energy Buildings / Zero-Energy Districts** are buildings or city districts, which were constructed environmentally responsible and produce at least as much energy as they consume.

Terminology sources for the glossary include: www.eea.europa.eu and www.gbca.org.au

Some Key Web Sites and Online Sources on *Sustainable Urban Development*

American Collegiate Schools of Architecture (ACSA) www.acsa-arch.org
American Institute of Architects (AIA) and Landscape www.aia.org www.asla.org
Australian Institute of Architects (AIA) www.architecture.com.au
Archinect Online Community www.archinect.com
Architects for Peace www.architectsforpeace.org
Architecture 2030 (Ed Mazria) www.architecture2030.org
Architecture Week - Environment www.architectureweek.com/environment.html
Arup Engineers www.arup.com
Australian Conservation Foundation (ACF) www.acfonline.org.au
Australian Department of Climate Change www.climatechange.gov.au

BBC World News www.bbcworld.com
Building Green www.buildinggreen.com
Bureau of Meteorology (BoM climate data) www.bom.gov.au
Business Council for Sustainable Energies www.bcse.org.au
Breathing Earth www.breathingearth.net
Car-free and Cool Cities (USA) www.carfree.com, www.coolcities.com
Chinese Urbanization www.dynamiccity.org
Climate Change www.climateprogress.org
Commission for Architecture (CABE, UK) www.cabe.org.uk
Council for Research and Innovation in Building and Construction (CIB) www.cibworld.nl

Eco-City Builders (Oakland, California) www.ecocitybuilders.org
Ecological Footprint www.footprintnetwork.org
European Environment Agency (EEA) www.eea.europa.eu
European Cities (EU) www.eurocities.org
European Green Cities Network (EGCN) www.europeangreencities.com
Freiburg Solar City (Germany) www.solarregion.freiburg.de
Future Technology Network www.futurismnews.com
Green Building Council of Australia www.gbca.org.au
Green Building Resource Harvard www.greencampus.harvard.edu/theresource
Go Green Creative www.gogreencreative.com.au
Green Roofs www.greenroofs.org
Holcim Corporation www.holcimfoundation.org
Intergovernmental Panel for Climate Change (UN: IPCC) www.ipcc.ch
International Initiative for a Sustainable Built Environment (iiSBE) www.iisbe.org
Inhabitat Sustainable Future www.inhabitat.com
Institute of Ecosystems Studies www.ecostudies.org
Jaime Lerner (Curitiba) www.jaimelerner.com
Laneways Sydney www.lanewaysbygeorge.com.au

Climate Manifest of German Architects www.klima-manifest.de
MVRDV architects www.mvrdv.nl
Nachhaltigkeit (CH) www.nachhaltigkeit.org
National Renewable Energy Laboratory (USA) www.nrel.gov
Netzwerk Nachhaltigkeit (D) www.netzwerkzeug.de
Online Newspapers around the World (listing) www.world-newspapers.com
One Planet Living (London) www.oneplanetliving.org

Passive Low Energy Architecture (PLEA) www.plea-arch.net
Renewable Energy Business www.energy.sourceguides.com
Rocky Mountains Institute (RMI) www.rmi.org
Rudi Resource for Urban Design www.rudi.net
Space Laboratory for Architectural Research and Design www.slab.com.au
Stern Review www.sternreview.org.uk
On Stuff www.storyofstuff.com
Super Colossal Blog (Trimble, Sydney) www.supercolossal.ch
Sustainable Cities (Denmark) www.sustainablecities.dk
Sustainable Cities Research Institute (UK) www.sustainable-cities.org.uk
Sustainable Sydney Strategy www.sydney2030.com.au
Sustainable Development www.sustainabledevelopment.org
TED www.ted.com/talks
Tools for Sustainability, Cal Poly Pomona site www.toolsforsustainability.com
Transmaterial (Brownell) www.transstudio.com
The United Nations (UN) and UN Environment Program (UNEP) www.un.org www.unep.org
UNESCO www.unesco.org
UN-Habitat www.unhabitat.org
Urban Age (Burdett, LSE) www.urban-age.net
Urban Poverty issues www.squattercity.blogspot.com
Urban Land Institute (ULI) www.uli.org
Urban Ecology Center (USA) www.urbanecologycenter.org
US-Green Building Council www.usgbc.org

Volunteers, Tree People www.treepeople.org
The Worldbank www.worldbank.org/wbi/urban
Whole Building Design Guide (Washington) www.wbdg.org/design/sustainable.php
World Business Council for Sustainable Development www.wbcsd.org
Worldwatch Institute www.worldwatch.org
Worldwide Metropolitan Governance www.citymayors.com
Ken Yeang, LDY architects (London/Kuala Lumpur) www.ldavies.com
ZEDfactory (Dunster, London) www.zedfactory.com

* The above selection
of useful web sites was
active at the point of
listing, in Jan. 2010

1

2

The *City Futures + Urban Regeneration* Studios and Exhibitions

The UNESCO Chair for Sustainable Urban Development in the Asia-Pacific as a team comprises Professor Steffen Lehmann and colleagues of the *Chair of Architectural and Urban Design*. Together with the s_Lab Space Laboratory for Architectural Research and Design, the Chair has been responsible for a series of energy-efficient buildings, urban design concepts and research publications in the area of sustainable cities.

3

4

| 1 Professor Thomas Herzog and Professor Erich Schneider-Wesseling with the author, Berlin, March 2008 | 2 Professor Jan Gehl and Henning Thomsen with Prof. Steffen Lehmann, Copenhagen, December 2009 | 3 The Lord Mayor, John Tate, and Minister for the Hunter, MP Jodi McKay, with Prof. Steffen Lehmann | 4 Steffen Lehmann with the Lord Mayor of Sydney, Clover Moore, MP, at the exhibition opening, September 2009 |

Over the last years, we enjoyed a brilliant team of visitors and consultants in the studio, who ensured the discussions crossed disciplines and remained relevant. Invited architects, engineers, planners, landscape architects, urban theorists and other experts came regularly to critique the students' elegant masterplans and contributed generously with ideas.

| 1 SL in Singapore, with Mr Tay Kim Poh (CEO of HDB) and Mr Peter Head (Arup), October 2009 | 2 and 4 Visitors to the studio: Teaching with John Denton (DCM), and Karl Fender (FKA), March 2009 | 3 Speakers, April 2009: Professors Richard Leplastrier, Lindsay Johnston, Adrian Carter, Helge Solberg and SL |

1

2

3

1 Year 4 student group in front of the *City Centre Studio* in Auckland Street, February 2007

2 Conjoint Prof. Richard Leplastrier visiting the City Campus studio, April 2007

3 'Port Ciy' student group exploring the site from above, by helicopter, March 2007

1

2

3

4

1 Guest in the Port City studio: Mark Haycox, from VicUrban, Melbourne, May 2007

2 Architect John Wardle talking to the students in the City Campus studio, Feb. 2007

3 On a walking tour through the city centre with Lawrence Nield, September 2008

4 Landscape architect Adrian McGregor, visiting tutor in the Port City studio, April 2007

CITY CAMPUS

Studio coordinator and tutor: Professor Steffen Lehmann, 2007 and 2008 (both one semester long studios). The City Campus studio received generous support from the Deputy Vice-Chancellor (Research) office, Professor Barney Glover, and from GHD Engineers. The following guests have been involved in tutoring or lecturing in the studios (in alphabetical sequence):

- Stuart Campbell (tutor)
- Michael Chapman (tutor)
- Jason Elsley (tutor)
- Susan Young (tutor)
- Stephen Cameron
- John Denton, DCM
- Andrew Killen
- Bill Dowzer, BVN
- John Drake
- Conj. Prof. Peter Droege
- Edward Duc
- Kimberley Everett
- Gary Fielding

Studio Credits:
The Participants in the *City Futures + Urban Regeneration Studios*

- Assoc. Prof. Kenn Fisher
- James Grose, BVN
- Prof. Lindsay Johnston
- Chris Landorf
- Conj. Prof. Richard Leplastrier
- Stephen Manton
- Neil Masterton, ARM
- Rachel Neeson
- Noelle Nelson
- Kevin O'Brien, Merrima
- Phillip Pollard
- Gerard Reinmuth, Terroir
- David Rose, Suters
- Carol Seymour
- Adrian McGregor
- Conj. Prof. Brian Suters
- Conj. Prof. Peter Stutchbury
- Rodney Uren, Hassell
- John Wardle

Participating students in the City Campus studio 2007:
David Arnott, Jamie Bonnefin, Leanne Borg, Andrew Brook, Elizabeth Brown, Chen Sinhui, Nicholas Cini, Dean Cotter, James Craft, Lachlan Craggs, Katherine Daunt, Michael Dawes, Sarah Donnelly, David Grejsen, David Hamilton, Phillip Hendrie, Evan Howard, Karolin Hunger, Tim Hulme, Vibeke Johansen, In Kim, Dean Macmillan, Aaron Maybury, Tafara Mbara, Gabriel McLean, Poulad Naghoni Bakhtiari, Christopher Norris, Bronwyn Nymeyer, Leo Payne, Joshua Rhodes, Jason Roberts, Lilly Simkin, Michael Smith, Adrian Strudwick-Barker, Lane Tucker, Wee Yee.

Participating students in the City Campus studio 2008:
Josephine Bastian, Luke Farrugia, Justin Spaull, Hoon Har Oon, Jesse Lockhart- Krause, Emmanuel Materu, Mohd Fadhlan Mahbob, Tabizi Tahir, Luke Keating, Emilie Westergren, Barbara Busina, Romi McPherson, Allison Wilson, Simon Frost, Andrew Dowe, Jake Sainsbury, Kine Husas, Corinne Anton, Aaron Maybury, Steve Gartsky, Muthu Srinivasan, Chi Ying Liew, David Buehler-Craig, Iness Czarnecki, Lachlan Seegers, Ksenia Totoeva, Shahril Ramzi, Raeana Henderson, Emily Formentini, Joel Fitzgerald, Yen Benjamin Yeo, Wui K.Yap, Andrew Shaper, Adrian Walsh, Meagan Kerr, Jamie Bonnefin, Shellee Venaglia, Azfar Badarus Salleh, Andrew Cavill, Sepehr Sami, Joel Hoddinott, Aaron Hughes, Katherine Tracey, Sarah Jozefiak, Mitch McGuire, Munirah Abdul Mokhti, Teck Tee, Jongmoon Kim, Botlhe Scotch.

PORT CITY

Studio coordinator and tutor: Professor Steffen Lehmann, 2007-2008 (one year long final year studio). The Port City studio received generous support from the Newcastle Port Corporation. The following experts and guests have been involved in tutoring or lecturing in the studio (in alphabetical sequence):

- Wilton Ainsworth, Port Corp.
- Keith Brewis, Grimshaw
- Rachel Neeson
- Marc Garcia, Barcelona
- Dr. Ranulph Glanville
- Mark Haycox, Vic Urban
- Prof. Tom Heneghan
- Prof. Lindsay Johnson
- Richard Kirk
- Conj. Prof. Richard Leplastrier
- Assistant Prof. Ulf Meyer
- Adrian McGregor (visiting tutor)
- Paul Minifie
- Shane Powers, City of Melbourne
- Igor Peraza, Barcelona

- Dr. Ron Robinson
- David Stafford
- Conj. Prof. Brian Suters
- Conj. Prof. Peter Stutchbury
- Shane Thompson, BVN
- John Wardle
- Chris Tucker (technical tutor)
- Gary Webb, Port Corp.

Participating students in the Port City studio, 2007-2008:
Masterplan team 1: Joyce Lim, Judith Bujack, Walid El Chiekh
Masterplan team 2: Cherry Williamson, Patrick Maitland, Michael Whitley, Ruby Pauwels
Masterplan team 3: Bede Campbell
Masterplan team 4: Cassie Stronach, Robert Mann.

THE GREEN CORRIDOR

Studio coordinator and tutor: Professor Steffen Lehmann, 2009 (one semester long studios). The Green Corridor studio received generous support from the Hunter Development Corporation. The following experts and guests have been involved in tutoring or lecturing in the studio (in alphabetical sequence):

- Michael Chapman (tutor)
- Karen Lambert (tutor)
- Jason Wedesweiler (tutor)
- Troy Zwart (tutor)
- Assoc. Prof. Adrian Carter, Aalborg
- John Denton, DCM
- John Drake
- Edward Duc
- Karl Fender, Fender Katsalidis
- Brent Knowles, City of Newcastle
- Conj. Prof. Richard Leplastrier
- John de Manincor, draw
- Michael McPherson, Suters
- Ian Moore
- Lawrence Nield, BVN
- David Rose, Suters
- Assoc. Prof. Helge Solberg, NTNU
- Evan Steverson, HVRF
- Conj. Prof. Brian Suters
- John Webber
- Susan Young

Participating students in the Green Corridor studio 2009:
Leah Adamthwaite, Lee Bateman, Kylie Burgess, Daniel Bush, Toni Butterworth, Jeremy Capodicasa, Cassandra Halpin-Smyth, Peter Golema, Emma Guthrey, Matthew Woodward, Simon Hayward, Jonathan James, Kenneth Lau, Daniel Leith, Sarah Maguire, Luke Mahaffey, Fadhlan Mohd Mahbob, George Mather, Laura Milner, Toni Norton, Robin Palmer, Darin Phare, Mohd Shahril Ramzi, Zane Alcorn, Claire Sibert, Andrew Wilson, Camilla Tierney, Alyssa Turner, Benjamin White, Poh Kung Tang, Anita Christou, Rudyanto, Wen J. Kenneth Fung, Muhammad Rahim, Siew Serene Chong, Yaw-Pong Chong, Taiyo Namba, Benjamin Walters, Kabelo Raphane, Prue Parsons, Ming Calvin Chua.

TAREE WATERFRONT MASTERPLAN

The publication presents the 1st Prize in the masterplan competition. The urban design competition for the Taree Pitt Street Waterfront Masterplan ran from February to May 2007, and was organized by Greater Taree City Council (GTCC), New South Wales. Six design teams were selected to compete in the final stage. Following the competition, the winning consortium was commissioned in 2007 with the further development of a Concept Plan and Development Control Plan (DCP), based on the successful masterplan scheme. The DCP was formally adopted by GTCC in August 2008. Project manager is Sinclair Knight Merz.

The members of the winning consortium and planning team (2007-09):
Sustainable Urban Design: s_Lab, Professor Steffen Lehmann
Suters Architects, Newcastle (David Rose, Michael McPherson, Maarten Hollebrandse)
Landscape Architects: Adrian McGregor, McGregor Partners, Sydney
Sustainable Communities: Ove Arup, Sydney
Traffic Planning: Connell Wagner, Sydney. Regional Planning, DCP: Asquith DeWitt, Sydney.

Support received for the UNESCO Chair's Design Studios

Over the last five years, we have been able to intensively explore ideas and innovative concepts in the design studios, dealing with zero-carbon architecture and urban design. The generous support of our partners and major institutions for the ongoing work of my `City Futures + Urban Regeneration Studios' and seminars is acknowledged, such as from:

The New South Wales State Government, the City of Sydney, Hunter Development Corporation, Newcastle City Council, Suters Architects, Arup Engineers, GHD Engineers, Newcastle Port Corporation, Hunter Valley Research Foundation, Bayer Material Science, and the s_Lab Space Laboratory for Architectural Research and Design. I also wish to thank UNESCO, the United Nations Educational, Scientific and Cultural Organisation (Dr. Hassmik Tortian and Brigitte Colin), and the DAAD, the German Academic Exchange Service (Dr. Christian Bode and Dr. Ursula Toyka-Fuong), for the ongoing support of my work and research activities.

I am grateful that I was able to work on this book with a group of people whom I know and respect. My colleagues, assisting tutors and students, who participated in the various design studios, gave a considerable amount of their time to make this publication happen. To all of them a big thank you, particularly to the students involved in my `City Futures + Urban Regeneration Studios' and seminars (between 2006 and 2009) for their enthusiasm and talent. I hope you will find the book a worthy reflection on your outstanding contributions.

No author is an island, and I would like to thank those who gave me valuable advice: Professor Peter Herrle (Berlin), Dr. Christian Bode (Bonn), Cheong Koon Hean (Singapore), Professor Miki and Madhavi Desai (Ahmedabad), Melinda Dodson (Canberra), Professor Peter Droege (Sydney), Professor Roger Fay (Tasmania), Government Architect Philip Follent (Brisbane), Professor Mads Gaardboe (Adelaide), Professor Gert Groening (Berlin), Professor Herbert Girardet (London), Professor Barney Glover (Darwin), Emeritus Professor Thomas Herzog (Munich), Professor Richard Horden (Munich/London), Emeritus Professor Lindsay Johnston (Sydney), Professor Arvind Krishan (New Delhi), Emeritus Professor Norbert Lechner (Auburn), Dr. Andres Lepik (New York), Jaime Lerner (Curitiba), Professor Ken Maher (Sydney), Conjoint Professor Richard Leplastrier (Sydney), Professor Zhenyu Li (Shanghai), Professor William Logan (Geelong), Professor David Lung (Hong Kong), Professor Ian McDougall (Melbourne), Professor Anne Graham (Newcastle), Dr. Sunand Prasad

Acknowledgements

(London), Professor K.T. Ravindran (New Delhi), Gavan Ranger (Brisbane), David Rose (Newcastle), Associate Professor Thomas Schroepfer (Cambridge), Conjoint Professor Brian Suters (Newcastle/ Sydney), Emeritus Professor Jennifer Taylor (Brisbane), Emeritus Professor Gerold Wech (Luenen), Associate Professor Y. C. Wong (Singapore) and Dr. Ken Yeang (London/Kuala Lumpur).

It was a great pleasure to work with some of the best Australian architects in my studios, and their input and wise advice was a real buzz for the students: John Wardle, Ian Moore, Shane Thompsen, Richard Kirk, John Denton, Karl Fender, Rachel Neeson, Adrian McGregor, Paul Minifie, Lawrence Nield, and James Grose, just to name a few. Thank you for your generosity.My thanks to the publisher, Edward Milford, Michael Fell and the team at Earthscan (London) for their patience; and to Stephen Thompson: his intelligent proof-reading made this a better book. Fresh graphic design was (again) supplied by Cida de Aragon, thank you. Diagrams were illustrated by Linda Wright and Wenli Dong. Students helped in compiling images and preparing the huge amount of data. I am especially grateful to: Anita Christou, Bede Campbell, Joshua Rhodes, Matt Woodward, and Michael Whitley.

I wish to thank my colleagues at the universities in Adelaide, Newcastle, Berlin, Munich and Singapore, and my colleagues at UNESCO, for generously supporting my work over the last years. Many more people have contributed to the development of this book and its concepts. My thank you goes to all of you for your ongoing and valuable support.

Steffen Lehmann

Professor Dr. Steffen Lehmann is a German architect and urban designer, active as university educator and curator. He has been involved in architectural design research, teaching and consultancy since the late 1980s. He has lectured in 25 countries and is an advisor to governments, city councils and industry in Europe, Asia and Australia.

Professor Lehmann holds the UNESCO Chair in Sustainable Urban Development for Asia and the Pacific. Since August 2010, he is Professor of Sustainable Design and Director of the sd+b research centre at the University of South Australia in Adelaide, exploring zero waste, material flows and low carbon design. He has held the Professorial Chair in the School of Architecture and Built Environment at the University of Newcastle and at the Queensland University of Technology, where he was Head of Architecture Program. He is Founding Director of the s_Lab Space Laboratory for Architectural Research and Design (Sydney-Berlin).

The s_Lab is an international interdisciplinary research and design cluster. Steffen founded the ideas-driven and research-based s_Lab in 1993, to combine practice with research in pursuit of a sustainable design ethic and interdisciplinary collaborations. Today, Sydney and Berlin-based, the s_Lab is active in urban and architectural research, operating as an international research network engaged in the creation of the next generation of cities and adaptive buildings. The firm's work has been widely published and has received awards internationally.

About the Author

International perspective

Steffen's work has a global perspective and he has practised architecture in four countries. Since 1990, he has presented his work and research at more than 350 conferences and symposia, in 25 countries, in over 100 different cities. He has lectured extensively from Europe to Asia, the Middle-East to the US and Brazil. He has researched, built and taught on informal urban design, urban renewal and energy-efficient cities since the late 1980s. He is primarily interested in the holistic relationship between architectural/urban form and the resulting environmental performance, and how we can re-conceptualize cities in response to climate change and newly emerging programmatic requirements for urban developments and public space. He is currently advising several municipalities in the Asia-Pacific Region on new approaches to sustainable urban design and urban growth. His current work includes urban design of Australia's first zero-carbon emissions masterplan.

Education

Steffen holds two post-graduate degrees. After graduating in Germany and from the Architectural Association School of Architecture in London (1990), he worked one year with James Stirling in London, and for three years with Arata Isozaki in Tokyo, before starting his own ideas-driven practice in Berlin in 1993. In February 2003 he completed his doctoral thesis on `Modernism and Regionalism' at the Technical University Berlin. Before being appointed a Professor in December 2002, he ran his own practice for more than ten years, where he designed numerous award-winning buildings.

Practice and research in sustainable design

Steffen Lehmann is a registered architect in Germany, with over 20 years successful professional experience in designing and building significant large-scale multi-disciplinary projects. The scale of his built projects range from selected signature houses to housing, to careful conversions of historically preserved buildings to high-rise towers and urban design masterplanning. He has a particular interest in sustainable strategies for urban waterfront regeneration and the revitalization of post-industrial cities. During the 1990s, he was instrumental in the urban renewal and re-development of Berlin's city centre and has built small and large-scale buildings in Berlin's Potsdamer Platz, Hackescher Markt and Pariser Platz (for instance, the French Embassy, in partnership with Christian de Portzamparc, 1997-2002).

Four main research fields

Steffen has been awarded significant scholarships, prizes and research grants. He integrates design studio teaching as a way of research in his research fields. There is a recognition that relevant research needs to address some of the 'big questions' faced by society today, relating to global and demographical change, sustainable resources and societal needs. With the aim of encouraging a closer cooperation between university researchers and private sector industry, Steffen's main – and intertwined – priority research areas are:

• **Architectural and Urban Theory and History**: Identity and regionalism. How to maintain regional diversity and meaning in architecture in times of rapid urbanization and globalization, especially in the Asia-Pacific? Cultural diffusion through globalization. Architecture's social dimension. Architectural and urban design for city campuses and coastal urban developments, with particular interest in urban waterfronts and subtropical design. Steffen has been the leading designer on waterfront developments in Berlin, Hamburg, Sydney, Brisbane and other cities.

• **Design of Urban Public Spaces**: Urban space networks to transform and revitalise our centres. The changing role of the public domain, and the impact of IT on public space. The effect of urbanization – understanding urban areas as sites where we can work with occupants to co-design, reflecting the urgent social needs and possibilities of 21st-century design. Identity in urban design, and the impact of the network society on urban form.

• **Interdisciplinarity and Collaborative Design Practice**: Collaboration between different disciplines, for instance, art and architecture. Strategies for informal, site-specific interventions in public space. Design as an 'agent for social change'. The transformation of European and Asian urban areas, and forms in which different disciplines observe and influence the contemporary city.

• **Green City Futures**: Sustainability of architectural and urban design. Energy, waste, water and materials in the city of the future. Capacity building using sustainability knowledge in the developing world. Long-term strategic research alliances with countries in Asia and along the Pacific Rim. New sustainable design technologies: Research in emerging models of energy-efficient, zero-carbon cities and buildings, with a focus on the urban scale and high density housing. The im-pact of migration. Compacting urban form; density versus sprawl. Contemporary material technologies. The conceptual model of `Green Urbanism'. The need for complexity and diversity in urban design. Growth and shrinkage of cities. Renewing urban infrastructure.

International teaching

Steffen Lehmann's expertise is in architectural and urban history and theory, with a focus on sustainable healthy cities, the conceptual model of `Green Urbanism', and the design of energy-efficient buildings and districts. Since 1990, he has been lecturing and coordinating advanced design studios in these areas. In 2002 he was appointed a Full Professor and Chair. In recognition of the international significance of his work, he has been invited as Visiting Professor to coordinate design studios at leading universities in six countries. He has taught as Visiting Professor at the Art Academy Berlin-Weissensee, the National University of Singapore, Tongji University Shanghai, TU-Berlin, among other leading universities.

In 2009, Steffen was appointed the DAAD-Visiting Professor at the Technical University Munich. He has lectured at top universities, such as in Oxford, New York, Harvard, Melbourne and Milan, among numerous others. He has been a leader in research projects and is frequently appointed as jury member of design competitions. In 2008, he received the Vice-Chancellor's Award for Teaching Excellence, the university's highest award for teaching.

UN-work and global initiatives

In 2008, Steffen was appointed to the *UNESCO Chair in Sustainable Urban Development for Asia and the Pacific*. This is the first UNESCO Chair in the area of sustainability and sustainable cities, established in the Asia-Pacific Region, and Steffen is now consulting for the governments (on a pro-bono basis) of China, India, Vietnam and Jordan, on sustainable urbanization models, to harmonize extreme conditions of urban development and rapid growth in the face of climate change. He is a member of different think tanks and the expert panel `Cities and Climate Change' for the Australian Academy of Science and ATSE. As UNESCO Chair, he is raising awareness and educates on the choice of construction materials, energy use and green urbanism.

Publications and exhibitions

Steffen is a member of numerous international scientific committees and is a guest editor in academic journals. He is the General Editor of the US-based, academic *Journal of Green Building* (2006 – to date). He has published over 180 academic papers, twelve books, and has contributed to over 20 edited books. His writings have been translated into several languages. He has organized interdisciplinary exhibitions as Chief Curator and has coordinated various research projects, among which are the `Back to the City' (2008) and `Laneways - Hidden Networks' (2009) exhibitions. See: www.backtothecity.com.au and www.lanewaysbygeorge. com.au He has designed installations reflecting contemporary urban conditions for Berlin, Cologne, Sydney, and Brisbane. This research resulted in a series of collaborative design+build studios and four book publications documenting these outcomes.

A full list of publications, lectures, and exhibitions can be found at: **www.slab.com.au**

Recent presentations at international conferences, symposia and universities

The author is regularly invited to present his research in Green Urbanism at leading universities, symposia and important conferences. Between 2000 and 2010, he presented his concepts over 350 times at conferences, in 25 different countries, in over 100 different cities, at over 80 universities, including:

2003 – 2005
Technical University Berlin, Faculty of Architecture, Germany
Academy of Fine Arts, Berlin-Weissensee, Germany
'Urban Drift - Beta 01' Conference, Berlin, Germany
University of Applied Sciences Biberach, School of Architecture, Germany
Technical University Braunschweig, School of Architecture, Germany
John Moores University Liverpool, UK
University of South Florida, School of Architecture and Urban Design, Tampa, USA
University of Florida, School of Architecture, Gainsville, USA
Florida International University, Miami, USA
California Poly State University, St. Luis Obispo, USA
Queensland University of Technology, Brisbane, Australia
American University of Sharja, School of Architecture, UAE
Stilwerk, Berlin, 'Meeting Global Challenges', Germany
BBC Radio, London, UK; and ZDF (German TV), Mainz, Germany
John Moores University, Department of Architecture, Liverpool, UK
Brisbane City Council, Brisbane, Australia
City University, Hong Kong, China
Tongji University, College of Architecture & Planning, Shanghai, China
TU-Delft, School of Architecture, Delft, Netherlands
University of Queensland, Brisbane, Australia
Queensland College of Art, Griffith University, Brisbane, Australia
Queensland University of Technology, Brisbane, Australia
'1:1 Seductions' Symposium, Brisbane, Australia
RAIA 'Tusculum Wednesday Night Talk Series', Sydney, Australia
University of New South Wales, Faculty of Built Environment, Sydney, Australia
Department of Housing, Queensland Government, Brisbane, Australia
Uni Tech, Lae and PNG Institute of Architects, Port Moresby, PNG
'New Partnerships' AILA Landscape Architecture Conference, Brisbane, Australia
The University of Newcastle, School of Architecture & Built Environment, Newcastle, Australia
RAIA Annual Dinner, Newcastle, Australia
State Library of Queensland Forum, Brisbane, Australia
'Architecture and Identity' Conference, TU-Berlin and Volkswagen Stiftung, Berlin, Germany
Mackenzie University, Faculdade de Arquitetura e Urbanismo, Sao Paulo, Brazil
'Architecture and Regionalism' Symposium, Savannah College of Art and Design, Georgia, USA
'Indigenous Environment Forum', Queensland University of Technology, Brisbane, Australia
Gold Coast City Council, Gold Coast, Australia
'Science, Technology and Research' Conference, University of Duisburg-Essen, Germany
Technical University Berlin, Faculty of Architecture, Germany
Curtin University of Technology, Department of Architecture, Perth, Australia

2006 – 2007
'Claiming Ground' Conference, Hobart, Tasmania, Australia
'The Art of Politics-The Politics of Art' Conference, Griffith University, Brisbane, Australia
'Small Bridges Conference', Conference, Powerhouse Museum, Sydney, Australia
City University New York, College of Architecture, New York, USA
'Social and Environmental Sustainability' Conference, The Hanoi Architectural University, Hanoi, Vietnam
'Subtropical Urbanism' Forum, Queensland Government, Department of Housing, Brisbane, Australia
Newcastle City Council and Newcastle Alliance, Australia
National University of Singapore (NUS), Department of Architecture, Singapore
'Other Modernisms' Symposium, Goethe-Institute, Max Mueller Bhavan, Mumbai, India
Rizvi College of Architecture, Mumbai, India
'Partnering' ACSA Symposium for Continuous Education, Salt Lake City, Utah, USA
'Science, Technology, Research' Conference, NTUA National Technical University Athens, Greece
'ICTC 7th International Cities & Communities Conference', Newcastle, Australia

'Urban Renewal' Conference, Urban Development Institute of Australia (UDIA), Australia
'World Conference of Historical Cities', Ballarat, Victoria, Australia
'Changing Trends in Architectural Education' International Conference, Rabat, Morocco
'Third Forum on Architectural Education' Istanbul Technical University (ITU), Turkey
University of Newcastle-Upon-Tyne, Faculty of Built Environment, UK
National Trust Heritage Festival; and Engineers Australia, Newcastle, Australia
'Sustainable Architectural Design and Urban Planning' Conference, Hanoi, Vietnam
City Forum of NSW Architects Registration Board, Newcastle, Australia
'GREX International Green Build & Renewable Energy' Conference, Sydney, Australia
'ENHR Housing & Sustainable Urban Areas' Conference, TU-Delft, Rotterdam, Netherlands
'Lunchtime Forum', Monash University, Faculty of Art & Design, Melbourne, Australia
'Innovations' Symposium, the University of Sydney, Australia
'Building across Borders' CIB Conference, Pokolbin, Australia
'Liquid Cities: Berlin-Sydney' International Symposium, the University of Western Sydney, Australia
City of Adelaide and Norwood Payneham, St Peters City Councils, Adelaide, Australia
University of South Australia (UniSA), School of Architecture & Interior Design, Adelaide, Australia
'Regional Architecture and Identity' Conference, Tunis, Tunisia
Singapore Polytechnic, School of the Built Environment, Architecture Division, Singapore
Anna University, School of Architecture and Planning, Chennai (Madras), India
CEPT University, School of Architecture & Urban Design, Ahmedabad, India
Delhi University, School of Planning and Architecture (SPA), New Delhi, India
'Architectural Heritage and Globalisation' International Conference, National Trusts, New Delhi, India
Technical University Munich, Faculty of Architecture, Munich, Germany

2008 – 2009
'Generative Art' International Conference, Politecnico di Milano, Milan, Italy
'Art in the Urban Context' Symposium, Newcastle Regional Art Gallery, Newcastle, Australia
'Regeneration of PortCity' Urban History and Planning History Conference, Caloundra, Australia
'Green Urbanism' International Conference 'Eurosolar: Sun and Sense' Berlin, Germany
'Seeking the City' 96th Annual ACSA Meeting & Conference, Houston, Texas, USA
'Instant Cities' CSAAR International Conference, Sharjah, UAE
'Eco-City World Summit 2008', UC Berkeley, San Francisco, USA
The City of Sydney, Public Art Advisory Panel, Sydney, Australia
'The Oxford Conference 2008', Brookes University Oxford, UK
Hunter Valley Research Foundation (HVRF), Newcastle, Australia
'Community, Health, and Arts' Conference, University of Melbourne, Australia
'What is Green Architecture?' Symposium, Goethe Institute New York and MOMA, New York, USA
University of Minnesota, College of Design, Department of Architecture, Minneapolis, USA
'Sustainable Urbanism', Boston Architecture College (BAC), Boston, USA
'Principles of Green Design', GSD, Harvard University, Cambridge, USA
'PLEA 2008' International Conference, Dublin, Ireland
'Shifting Context: Transferring Knowledge', Metropolis World Congress, Sydney, Australia
'WUF IV - World Urban Forum 4', Nanjing, China
JUCCCE China Energy Forum in Beijing, China
Department of Planning, New South Wales Government, Urban Design Taskforce, Australia
ANZAScA Conference, the University of Newcastle, Australia
World Future Energy Summit, International Conference, Abu Dhabi, UAE
'Green Urbanism', Chulalongkorn University; Kasetsart University, Department of Architecture, Bangkok, Thailand
'Ile Durable – Sustainable Mauritius', Ministry of Renewable Energy, The Republic of Mauritius, Africa
'Climate Futures', University of Adelaide, School of Architecture & Urban Design, Adelaide, Australia
'Diversity and Growth', American Institute of Architects (AIA) Convention, San Francisco, USA
Conference Australian Property Institute; and 'Envirohunter' Conference, Newcastle, Australia
'Green Energy and Sustainability for Arid Regions' International Conference, Amman, Jordan
'SASBE'09 Smart and Sustainable', International Conference, TU-Delft, Netherlands
'Climate Change and the Urban Environment', the Australian Academy of Science (AAS/ATSE), Melbourne
'New Urban Centres and Networks' Zhenru Urban Forum & Tongji University, Shanghai, China
National University of Singapore, School of Design and Environment, Department of Architecture, Singapore
'Sustainable Energy Technologies SET'09' International Conference, Aachen, Germany
Technical University Munich, Faculty of Architecture, Munich, Germany
'Urban Expo China', Shijiazhuang City, Hebei, China
'Re-Compacting the City', Technical University Berlin, Germany
iNTA-SEGA 2009 International Conference, Kasetsart University, Bangkok, Thailand
'Cities and Climate Change' Expert Panel at COP15 UN Climate Summit, Copenhagen, Denmark

Other book publications by the same author (1995–2010)

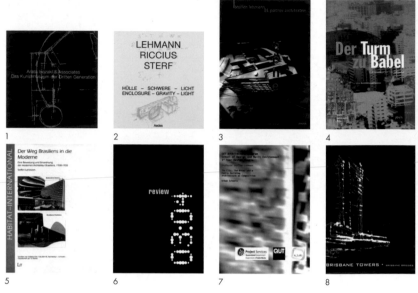

1 Steffen Lehmann: *Arata Isozaki: The next Generation Art Museum,* with Daniel Libeskind; Aedes Catalogue, Berlin

2 Steffen Lehmann: 2 Aedes Catalogues. *Huelle - Schwere - Licht,* with K. Feireiss (ed), S. Sterf, T. Riccius; *Steffen Lehmann - Works and Projects 1990-95,* Aedes Catalogue, Berlin

3 Steffen Lehmann: *S_Lab: Breite x Hoehe x Tiefe. Works 1990-1995,* co-authored with Michael Moenninger; Junius Verlag, Hamburg

4 Steffen Lehmann: *Der Turm zu Babel. Architektur fuer das dritte Jahrtausend,* co-authored with Heinrich Klotz and Wolf Prix; Jovis Publishers, Berlin

5 Steffen Lehmann: *Der Weg Brasiliens in die Moderne,* LIT-Verlag, Berlin/Muenster

6 *Steffen Lehmann (ed): 03:04 Projects Review;* QUT Press, Brisbane

7 Steffen Lehmann: *The City, The River and a Public Building;* QUT Press, Brisbane

8 Steffen Lehmann: *Brisbane Towers - Brisbane Bridges. High-rise and Infrastructure for the Sub-tropical City,* QUT Press, Brisbane

9   10   11   12

13   14   15   16

9 Steffen Lehmann (ed): *Absolutely Public. Crossover: Art and Architecture*; Images
  Publishing, Melbourne

10 Steffen Lehmann (eds): *Rethinking: Space - Time - Architecture. A Dialogue between
   Art and Architecture*; co-edited with Caroline Raspe, Jovis Publishers, Berlin

11 Steffen Lehmann (ed): *Back to the City. Strategies for Informal Urban Interventions*;
   Hatje Cantz Publishers, Berlin/Stuttgart

12 Steffen Lehmann (ed): *Journal of Green Building*, General-Editor of quarterly journal;
   College Publishing, USA (since 2006 – ongoing)

13 Steffen Lehmann (eds): Cida de Aragon - *Temporary and Permanent. 3 Works*, co-edited
   with Angela Philp; Infinite Press, Sydney

14 Steffen Lehmann (ed): *Flow. Projects Review*; Infinite Press, Sydney

15 Steffen Lehmann: *The Principles of Green Urbanism*; Earthscan Publishers, London

16 Steffen Lehmann (forthcoming): *Intersecting Nexus: Teaching - Research - Practice*;
   Jovis Publishers, Berlin

Index

M

S

Illustration and photo credits

Every effort has been made to correctly identify the original source material and copyright holders of photos contained in this book. We are greatful to Linda Kelly for help in securing the permissions for photographs. A series of images have been sourced from *Flickr Image Commons* and the *Creative Commons Image Sharing Gallery*. Thank you. All image sources are listed directly in the image captions or in the following list below. The photo was taken by the author, if there is no source given. Where the attempt has been unsuccessful, the publisher and the author apologize for any unintentional omission, and would be pleased in such cases, to place an acknowledgement in future editions of this book. The publisher and author would like to thank the following for their kind permission to reproduce their photographs, illustrations and diagrams.

Page numbers of illustrations and photos are given below

Cover:	Design by Cida de Aragon. Photo: Nelson Kon, Sao Paulo
Diagrams:	UNESCO Chair; Illustrations by Steffen Lehmann and Linda Wright
Model photos:	Various faculty members and students of the School of Architecture and Built Environment, design studios Prof. Steffen Lehmann

List of Illustrations and Photo Credits

9	Diagram: Courtesy Herbert Girardet, WFC, London
30-31	Aerial photo: Suters, Newcastle NSW www.sutersarchitects.com.au
28-59	Photos of commissioned city series: Roger Hanley, Newcastle; and Steffen Lehmann , Adelaide
60-61	Cida de Aragon, Newcastle NSW
70	Photo: Courtesy Le Corbusier Foundation, Paris
71	Photos: Courtesy Frank Lloyd Wright Foundation, USA
72-73	Diagram: Steffen Lehmann, UNESCO Chair www.slab.com.au
81	Diagram: Courtesy Eco-CityProjects.Net/Ecocitybuilders (K. Miller)
105	Diagram: Courtesy Philip O'Neil, Sydney
106	Sketch: Courtesy Rudosfsky, MOMA
124	Photo: Courtesy OJK Architects, San Jose
127	Seoul photos: Image Sharing Commons
133, 136, 375	Bus photos: E. Penalosa, Bogota / Image Sharing Commons
138, 377	Photo: Courtesy Jaime Lerner, Curitiba: www.jaimelerner.com
147	Map: Courtesy IPCC, CH
152	Diagram: Courtesy Christian de Portzamparc, Paris
152	Diagram: Courtesy Peter Rand, 2004

249	Photo: Courtesy Arata Isozaki, Tokyo
249, 304	Photo: Courtesy Bill Dunster, ZEDFactory, Surrey
262, 288	Diagram: Courtesy Herbert Girardet, WFC, London
265	Photo: Courtesy Zero Waste SA, Adelaide
266	Photo: Courtesy Bart Princen, 2009
274	Diagram: Courtesy Knab/Strunz/E.ON, Berlin, 2010
278	Photo: Courtesy Linde, 2009
278	Photo: Courtesy spiegel.de
279	Diagram: Courtesy Siemes AG, 2009
288-289	Diagrams: Courtesy Grimshaw Architects (K. Brewis), 2009
291	Photo and Diagram: Courtesy Delfin Lend Lease, 2007
293	Diagram: Courtesy R. Brown, Melbourne, 2009
294	Images: Courtesy Holcim and M. Tirana, 2008
296	Images: Courtesy Atelier Data & MOOV, Lisbon, 2009
297	Photo: Courtesy P. Newman, Perth
300, 391	Images: Courtesy HOK Architects, 2009
303	Images: Courtesy City of Hanover (Moenninghof), 2009
306	Images: Courtesy City of Stockholm (E. Freudenthal), 2009
307, 373	Diagram: Courtesy Paul Kohlenbach, Solem Consult, 2010
308	Images: Cobe Architects & Sleth, Copenhagen, 2009
308, 483	Image: Courtesy Ken Yeang, London/Kuala Lumpur, 2009
309, 379	Photo and image: Courtesy Rolf Disch, Freiburg; btga, Wuppertal
312	Diagram: Courtesy Neutlings Riedjik, Amsterdam, 1999
314	Photos: Courtesy J. Tetro; T. Ott (M. Haegger), Darmstadt, 2010
322	Diagram: CCAA Sydney, 2007
326	Diagram: Courtesy NSW Dept. of Primary Industries, Sydney
326, 342	Drawing and photo: Courtesy Waugh & Thistleton, London, 2009
327	Photo: Courtesy Detail, Munich
327, 341	Photo: Courtesy Scheitlin & Syfrig (Renggli AG), Luzern
331-333	Photos: Courtesy Frank Lattke, TU-Munich; FGH; Lignotrend
336, 340	Photos: Courtesy Hermann Kaufmann, TU-Munich
337	Photo: Courtesy MGF Architects (C. Richters)
338	Photos: Courtesy J. Musch, Trondheim
339	Photos: Courtesy Hubert Riess; KLH Austria
340	Photo: Courtesy B. Klomfar
343	Photos: Courtesy Kaden & Klingbeil, 2009
345	Photo: Courtesy O. L. Kaufmann/A. Ruef; MOMA, 2008
349	Diagram world map: Courtesy spiegel.de
359	Images: Courtesy Arup, London, 2007
360	Photo: Courtesy Toyo Ito, Tokyo, 1993
361	Image: Courtesy GMP, Hamburg, 2002

362	Image: Courtesy Le Corbusier Foundation, Paris
363	Photo: Courtesy Peter Davidson, 2009
364	Sketch: Courtesy Franco Purini, Milano
365	Photo: Courtesy SAANA, Tokyo, 2001
365	Images: Courtesy MVRDV Amsterdam, 2008
366	Image: Courtesy William Mitchell, MIT, 2008
370	Image: Courtesy L. Blundell, 2009
372	Diagram: Courtesy A. van Dobbelsteen, Delft, 2009
374	Photo: Courtesy Atelier 5, Zurich
377	Diagram: Courtesy Douglas Farr, Chicago, 2008
378	Photo: Courtesy Hannover Congress Centre, Hannover
378	Photo: Courtesy ATS, Melbourne, 2009
380	Photos: Courtesy Renzo Piano Building Workshop, Genua
380	Diagram: Courtesy Schroepfer/Werthmann/Hee, 2006
381	Photos: Courtesy Image Sharing Commons
382	Images: Courtesy manufacturers
383	Diagram: Courtesy Ichinose, Tokyo, 2008
385	Photo: Courtesy Troppo Architects, 2008
386-387	Photos: Courtesy M. Hegger, HHS/ee, TU-Darmstadt, 2007
388	Photo: Courtesy R. Adams, City of Melbourne
388	Photo: Courtesy City of Barcelona
391	Photos: Courtesy IBA Emscher Park, Duisburg
392	Image: Micro Compact Home prototype 'm-ch', a registered patent of the Micro Compact Home Ltd, London; Richard Horden, TUM, 2005
393	Photo: Courtesy PTW Architects, Sydney
396-397	Aerial photo: Matt Woodward; courtesy Google Earth
400, 509, 506, 587	Photos: Courtesy Historical Archive, Newcastle Region Library
510	Photos: Courtesy P. Elenbaas, Amsterdam/NAI, Rotterdam
514-515	Dixson Library, State Library of NSW, Sydney: Melvin Vaniman Panorama, DLPg 36. Digital: a113018.`Panorama of Newcastle from the Dyke' (1904)
577, 582	Aerial photos: Courtesy Greater Taree City Council, NSW
589	Diagram: Courtesy M.Gandelsonas, New York, 1991
620, 673	Diagrams: Courtesy Chr. de Portzamparc; P. Rand; A. Bertaud
624	Aerial photo: Courtesy Ed Burtynsky, 2006
627	Photo: Courtesy Stephan Canham, Hamburg
628	Diagram: WSP Environment & Energy, London, 2009 (P. Kapoor)
630	Diagram: Courtesy Joe Ravetz, Manchester, 2000
632	Diagram: BgAP Group/ N. Al Sayyad, Berkeley, 2006
646-647	Photos: Courtesy D. Francis Kere; Mette Lange
670	Diagrams: BP Statistical Review/China Cleantec Report, 2009